EXPERIENTIAL RETAILING

EXPERIENTIAL RETAILING

Concepts and Strategies That Sell

YOUN-KYUNG KIM
University of Tennessee

PAULINE SULLIVAN
Florida State University

JUDITH CARDONA FORNEY
University of North Texas

Fairchild Publications, Inc.
New York

Director of Sales and Acquisitions: Dana Meltzer-Berkowitz

Executive Editor: Olga T. Kontzias

Acquisitions Editor: Joseph Miranda

Assistant Acquisitions Editor: Jaclyn Bergeron

Senior Development Editor: Jennifer Crane

Development Editor: Michelle Levy

Art Director: Adam B. Bohannon

Production Manager: Ginger Hillman

Production Editors: Beth Cohen and Jessica Rozler

Assistant Editor: Justine Brennan

Copy Editor: Vivian Gomez

Interior Design: Renato Stanisic

Page Composition: Matrix Publishing Services

Cover Design: Adam B. Bohannon

Copyright © 2007

Fairchild Publications, Inc.

Library of Congress Catalog Card Number: 266935009

ISBN: 978-1-56367-399-3

GST R 133004424

Printed in the United States of America

TP12

CONTENTS

EXTENDED CONTENTS

PREFACE

The purpose of this book is to generate excitement about and understanding of new consumer and retail trends that are changing consumer expectations and business strategies. More than ever before, consumers are seeking hedonic (emotional) as well as utilitarian (functional) benefits in their shopping and consumption experiences. Both the expansion and extension of branding and the merging of retail, hospitality, and entertainment industries have generated new business venues whose competitive advantage is achieved by creating total consumer experiences.

Throughout the last ten years, increased consumer incomes, referred to as the "wealth effect," have changed buying behavior. Consumers are no longer focusing on product or service consumption, but rather seeking experiences. Increasingly, consumers no longer simply buy commodities; instead, their consumption habits express who they are and the relationships that are important to them. In the marketplace, multiple businesses (e.g., retail merchandising, hospitality, andentertainment) are merging to deliver products and services to the same consumer segment. This is illustrated by many retail stores, such as restaurants and soft-goods retailers, for which both food and soft goods (e.g., gifts, apparel) have become an integral part of the product mix as well as by hotels that have ventured into merchandising products that enhance the guest experience (e.g., bedding, home furnishings, fashion, and food). Evidence of these crossover businesses also can be found in shopping malls and tourist attractions where fashion, food, and fun have become key components in creating optimal consumer experiences. Additionally, brand extension offers companies opportunities to move into new product categories that expand the range of sensory experiences available to consumers.

Experiential Retailing: Concepts and Strategies That Sell offers to students the insight into what drives consumer behavior; it also offers to professionals strong and effective strategies to make retail ventures more profitable and enduring in both domestic and international markets.

Retailers need to position themselves with strategies that respond to consumer and retail trends.

This book has several unique features. First, it uses an interdisciplinary approach to understanding consumer demand trends. Second, it builds on a concept that explores how retailers can add value to their customers' lives. Third, it supports the concepts it presents with a rich assortment of visual, descriptive, and electronic examples. Finally, it outlines opportunities for retailers and entrepreneurs to reformat their current retail mix.

We organized this book to provide an understanding of current consumer behavior in the context of a total consumer experience. In addition, suggestions and strategies are offered that supply consumers with the experiences they desire. The concept of a total consumer experience is considered within the context of experiential retailing.

We suggest a model to guide the conceptualization of experiential retailing that meets consumer demand in a dynamic and competitive environment. In building a total consumer experience, we argue the importance of symbolism, ritual, sensory involvement, and consumer efficiency to increase the value of consumption. In terms of managing the retail environment, we suggest strategies such as entertainment retailing, thematic retailing, lifestyle retailing, value retailing, branding, brand extension, and strategic alliance. We created the Experiential Retailing Model as the framework for the textbook chapters (See Figure 1.11). Part 1 (Chapters 1 through 3) introduces the concept of experiential retailing, its conceptual framework, and its historical background. Part 2 (Chapters 4 through 7) describes the total consumer experience. Part 3 (Chapters 8 through 15) outlines different experiential retailing practices and provides a comprehensive view of experiential retailing from a global perspective.

This textbook engages students in the learning process with its innovative approach. In addition to providing students with a strong foundation upon which they can build knowledge, it prompts them to move through the cognitive domain and evaluate and apply what they learn to real-life examples. The text provides many examples that place theory into practice, helping students understand the value of a theoretical model as a way of framing their thinking. It also emphasizes the need for students to conduct a wide environmental scan so they can develop a comprehensive understanding of consumer behavior in the marketplace. Because the examples of experiential retailing are drawn from many areas of business, and encompass a broad geographical reach, social psychology, economics, demographics, and more, this textbook exemplifies an interdisciplinary approach to problem solving.

There is a critical need to develop a nontraditional, innovative course that integrates several related multidisciplinary fields. However, research expertise and information sources in this area are lacking. Therefore, this book draws on historical literature while also addressing an urgent need to embrace new retailing concepts. The experience of consuming goes beyond owning products and patronizing services; consumers genuinely want to add value to their lives. These experiences can be incorporated into the marketing and retailing mix. This textbook may be of particular interest to instructors who integrate concepts from several areas and require students to think critically, creatively, and analytically. It could equally support a seminar or lecture/discussion course.

The pedagogy of this textbook is grounded in the educational philosophy of experimentalism, where it is assumed that the world is an ever-changing place in which change is accepted. From this philosophical viewpoint, the learner continuously seeks new ways to expand and improve society—that is, to meet consumer needs and desires through experiential retailing and to build sustainable, ethnically diverse businesses. Experimentalism encourages students to take active roles in the learning process through problem solving and inquiry that is stimulated through projects, discussions, and experiences.

ACKNOWLEDGMENTS

We would like to express our appreciation to a number of students for contributing additional information, updating statistics on demographic and socioeconomic information, and handling mechanical components such as formatting text, obtaining images, and editing the manuscript. Graduate students (listed in alphabetical order) include Kelly Atkins, Peria Gober, Hye-Young Kim, Archana Kumar, Min-Young Lee, Donetta Poisson, and Cynthia Yeldell at the University of Tennessee; Thao-Vi Thi Dotter and Shelly Wiltz at the University of North Texas; and Vivian Fong at Florida State University. Undergraduate students include Jeffrey Johnson at University of Tennessee, Stacie Kniatt at University of North Texas, and Katherine Lease at Florida State University.

We also greatly appreciate the guidance and support from the staff at Fairchild Publications. Jennifer Crane and Michelle Levy were especially patient and helpful. We are also grateful to Adam Bohannon for his skill and expertise with the visuals. Fairchild Books also found reviewers who provided valuable feedback and constructive criticism: Debi Forse, Holland College; Naomi Gross, Fashion Institute of Technology; and Melody Le Hew, Kansas State University. Thanks also to Beth Cohen, Production Editor.

Youn-Kyung Kim—I would like to acknowledge Dr. Nancy Fair, the head of the Retail, Hospitality, and Tourism Management Department at the University of Tennessee, for providing the financial support necessary to complete the book. I also thank my colleagues in my department for their continuous support, insights, and encouragement. Most important, I want to thank my husband, Jin-Kee Hyun, and my daughter, Jessica Hyun, for their patience, sacrifice, persistent support, and encouragement.

Pauline Sullivan—First and foremost I thank Mike Rucker for his unfailing good humor, support, and encouragement throughout the long hours spent writing and rewriting. I am grateful to have two of the best colleagues who one could have asked for in bringing this book to fruition. I thank my family and friends, especially my sister Nina and her husband and Wanda and J. P. Brown, for cheering me on toward completing this project. My appreciation goes to the outstanding library staff at Florida State's London Program for their assistance in uploading pictures. I express my gratitude to Florida State University, the College of Human Sciences, and the Department of Textiles and Consumer Sciences for their support in completing this book. Last, but not least, I thank my mentors for their example, guidance, and the lessons they taught me, which contributed to my being able to write this book.

Judith Cardona Forney—I would like to acknowledge the faculty and staff in the School of Merchandising and Hospitality Management at the University of North Texas for their continuous encouragement, support, and help during the time I was writing this book. Collectively, they have embraced the concept of experiential retailing and supported its inclusion in courses, programs, and an annual school-wide symposium. I want to extend my thanks to Christy Crutsinger, Bharath and Raji Josiam, Jerry Dickenson, Joronda Crow, Elizabeth Jordan, Thao-Vi Thi Dotter, Sua Jeon, and K. N. Vinod, as well as Amber Geisler, Shawn McClure, and Timothy Ng, students in the SMHM Asia Study Abroad Program, for generously sharing their photos and describing the many experiences associated with the photos. I want to thank my coauthors for their insights, creativity, and collaborative efforts throughout the process. Finally, and most important, I want to express heartfelt thanks and appreciation to my husband, Scott Forney, and my son, Will Forney, for their constant support and encouragement. As enthusiastic experience seekers, they were my inspiration for this book.

PART

INTRODUCTION

CHAPTER 1

Stew Leonard's: The Disneyland of Dairy Stores

Shopping for toothpaste and laundry detergent can be a real drag. But imagine that you've just rounded the bend at the end of the supermarket aisle, casually walking past a stall of shopping carts, to encounter a flock of human-sized ducks. No, it's not a flashback from your college days; it's just a typical day at Stew Leonard's.

The three-unit chain of fresh food supermarkets and bakeries operates locations in Connecticut and New York and has been dubbed the "Disneyland of Dairy Stores" by three prominent national publications, including the *New York Times*. To anyone who has visited Stew Leonard's, it is no secret that they work very hard to create a country fair atmosphere at each store. On a typical day, customers can find employees dressed as chickens, ducks, or "WOW the Cow" roaming the aisles, actual animals, including goats, cows, chickens, sheep, and geese penned in front of the stores, and children visiting the animals free of charge while their parents shop. And yet, there's even more zaniness to be found.

The Leonard's family business dates back to 1924, when Charles Leo Leonard began bottling milk in an old barn and delivering it to his customers by horse and wagon. His son, Stew Leonard, took over the business later along with his brother and added many modern implements. When the building of a state highway in 1969 forced the company to move its operations, Stew Leonard Sr. opened the store that now stands on the Norwalk, Connecticut, site.

Because of the distinctive position they hold in the communities where they operate, Stew Leonard's receives hundreds of requests for contributions and donations for an assortment of causes. In keeping with the philosophy of Stew Leonard Sr. ("Give a little to a lot!"), the company proudly donates to a variety of worthy causes from its "Wishing Well." This includes The American Cancer Society, Courage To Speak Foundation, Crohn's and Colitis Foundation, MADD, and many, many others. The company also regularly donates bread and pastries to more than a hundred local churches, charities, and soup kitchens.

To say that the company is doing something right would understate its success. Each week more than 100,000 shoppers visit. Yet while most supermarkets offer between 15,000 and 20,000 products, Stew Leonard's offers only about 1,000 and the stores generally offer only one brand of its products. But in this case, the "less is more" strategy works. Customers come from as far as 50 miles away to shop at the stores, and the Guinness Book of World Records lists Stew Leonard's as the store with the fastest moving inventory. The annual average sales per square foot is $3,470 (a typical supermarket will do well to average $500 per square foot). From its Danbury and Norwalk stores, the company has generated sales of almost $150 million. No wonder they named the cow mascot "WOW"!

Source: Sacks, Bryan. 2000. Stew Leonard's: The Disneyland of Dairy Stores, www.specialtyretail.net/issues/july00/lifesytle_tenant.htm. Permission from *Dealmaker*s.

INTRODUCTION

It is Saturday and there is no milk, coffee, bread, or fruit in the house. You cannot bear the thought of yet another Saturday morning spent shopping in a boring, repetitive grocery store and wandering through a vast number of aisles where the packages all look the same. Just as you are resigned to embark on your Saturday shopping trip, the telephone rings. Your best friend from high school is in town. She wants to drive to Norwalk and go to Stew Leonard's to get some groceries for her parents. You think a half hour drive to the grocery store is odd when there is one a half mile from her house. However, you have not visited with your friend in months and look forward to spending time with her. She drives over to pick you up and off you go with her to Stew Leonard's (See Figure 1.1).

When you get to the parking lot, you begin to discover that this store offers a unique grocery shopping experience. An attendant hands you a cart, and you walk past the outdoor tent that serves lobster and corn, past the ice-cream stand, and into a market that beckons you with the aroma of fresh bread. Next, you smell popcorn and coffee and see the milk packaging plant at the right side of the store. This leads you into the dairy, past the mechanical chicken that lays eggs upon request, through the meat department, and past the fish, cheese, and endless supplies of product samples. Finally, you arrive at the dancing lettuces. This successful retailer provides the consumer with something that is greater than the product performance and the emotional experience, creating a total consumer experience.

EXPERIENTIAL RETAILING

Experiential retailing creates a total consumer experience that satisfies the consumers' emotional or expressive desires as well as their rational or functional needs. We define experiential retailing as "a strategy that transforms products and services into a total consumption experience, including aspects that are both utilitarian and hedonic." Therefore, the sum of the product or service purchased is greater than either the performance or the emotional experience.

1.1 Stew Leonard's has been dubbed the Disneyland of dairy stores. Each store has a county fair atmosphere.

Consumers are expecting more from retailers than ever before. They have begun to demand full service where they once may have merely expected products and transactions. Many retailers, such as the Forum Shops at Caesar's Palace in Las Vegas, are incorporating the customer experience as a component of their customer offerings. Stores are "routinely practicing one-upmanship in inducing more store visits by making shopping fun and entertaining" (Poulsson and Kale 2004, 268). Retailers can expect to encounter both opportunities and risks as they attempt to use customer service and experiential retailing to differentiate themselves from the competition (Reynolds 2003). While the overall payoff can be substantial, the initial investment in such endeavors is also substantial.

Pine and Gilmore (1999) suggested that there is a linear progression through which undifferentiated commodities can be transformed to differentiated premium products with staged experiences that are relevant to the consumer. Consider the example of the teddy bear, the stuffed animal named after Theodore Roosevelt and considered a childhood commodity in the United States. Although teddy bears are available at all price ranges, created by many different manufacturers, and produced in the United States and abroad, they all have the same basic physical composition. Consider a consumer's response to an undifferentiated teddy bear.

Now let us consider a consumer's experience at a Build-A-Bear Workshop. One of the largest teddy bear retailers in the United States, Build-A-Bear Workshop sells its products through malls, direct mail, and on the Internet. The interactive store environment encourages participation and creativity as evidenced by the company's slogan "Where best friends are made." At Build-A-Bear, customers engage in bear building by selecting personalized components to create their bears—sounds, stuffing, stitches, names, clothes, and accessories (See Figure 1.2). A similar

1.2 Consumer involvement at Build-A-Bear transforms the consumption of a generic teddy bear into a differentiated premium experience.

process is available online at www.build-abear.com. This consumer involvement transforms the consumption of a generic teddy bear into a differentiated premium experience. The premium experience yields profits for the retailer.

We see additional anecdotal evidence of experiential retailing in restaurants. Examples include the Hard Rock Cafe, Rainforest Cafe, and Planet Hollywood. Consider the case of Hard Rock Cafe. When you visit the website (www.hardrock.com) or restaurant, notice there are many products for sale. The corporate organization that combines the spirit of rock music, memorabilia, classic American food, and a commitment to humanitarian causes considers itself a global phenomenon with a presence in 41 countries. Hard Rock Cafe seeks to fulfill consumers' tangible needs (food) and emotional needs (high-energy atmosphere) through experiential retailing to create additional benefits that add utility and value to the shopping experience. It transforms a traditional exchange of goods for money to an exchange of time for the experience of shopping. For example, Hard Rock Cafe Barbie, illustrated in Figure 1.3, enhances the consumption experience by visual appeal through dress. This food retailer achieves its goals through a combination of entertainment, unified themes, branding, technology, and signature merchandise. Hard Rock Cafe Barbie appeals to young customers as well as parents and enhances the consumption experience.

These examples demonstrate that experiential retailing contributes to the value added to the purchase and to differentiation in the market place. Moreover, these strategies contribute to repeat patronage. For example, the Algerian Coffee Store Ltd. was established in 1887 and still operates at its original Soho, London, location, as well as on the Web. The Algerian Coffee Store Ltd. displays and sells a broad assortment of coffee and related products (See Figure 1.4). In this retail store, the tempting aroma of fresh coffee beans stimulates a consumer's sense of smell and encourages consumers to try the coffees. Thus, customers have an incentive to allocate their scarce resources of time and money to a unique consumption experience in a traditional retail setting. Customers who have a positive, unique experience will return.

HIERARCHY OF CONSUMER NEEDS

Individuals consume, in part, because they must. In this instance, the need to consume is related to a real or perceived lack of something that consumers deem necessary. Needs may be considered either simple and obvious or complex and abstract. Buying a one-pound can of ground coffee during the weekly visit to the grocery store is a simple and obvious way of meeting a need to drink coffee to wake

1.3 Products like Hard Rock Cafe Barbie help restaurants create a unique experience for customers.

1.4 At the Algerian Coffee Store, the tempting aroma of fresh coffee beans stimulates the consumer's sense of smell.

up in the morning. Stopping at Starbucks on the way to work each morning to buy a double mocha latte is a complex, ritualistic way of satisfying a craving that goes beyond getting a caffeine jolt. Consumption in postmodern societies is interlaced with expressive manifestations that are reflective of different tastes and preferences. Consumers with incomes that allow them to live beyond subsistence level are free to choose what they consume.

Different tastes and preferences are molded in part by variations in individual need structures. Consumer needs are explained in part by Abraham Maslow's hierarchy of needs (Maslow 1968). Maslow's hierarchy can be categorized into deficiency needs and growth needs (Eggen and Kauchak 1999) (See Figure 1.5).

Deficiency needs direct people to meet unfulfilled needs. Deficiency needs include the *physiological* need for survival, including shelter, warmth, food, and water; the *safety* need that removes physical and emotional threats; the *belonging* need that encompasses love and acceptance from family and peers; and the need for *self-esteem* that brings recognition and approval. It is unlikely that people will seek to meet growth needs until deficiency needs are met (Eggen and Kauchak 1999).

Growth needs are never really met since they expand and grow as people attain them. Growth needs include the need for *self-fulfillment* and *self-actualization*. The *self-fulfillment* need is associated with the intellectual achievement that comes from knowing and understanding the appreciation of order, truth, and beauty. The *self-actualization* need is at the top level of growth needs, where one seeks to become all that one can be (Maslow 1968 and 1970). In short, consumers who seek growth needs look for experiences that broaden their knowledge, give them an aesthetically pleasing experience, and help them become self-actualized. Barnes and Noble Bookseller is a retailer that builds on the growth needs of consumers. It has moved from selling books to selling a book experience. Large, comfortable chairs, a sophisticated Barnes and Noble Cafe, poetry readings, organized book clubs, and a children's area complete with a stage and larger-than-life storybook characters give customers a sense of personal growth and

1.5 Abraham Maslow's hierarchy helps to explain how needs drive consumption.

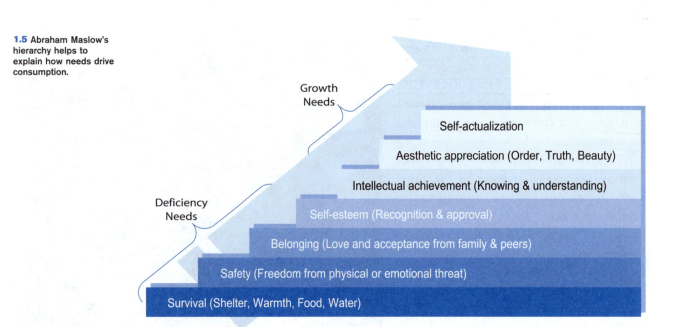

aesthetic pleasure. Meeting consumers' growth needs offers retailers enormous opportunities to develop strategies that lead to total consumer experiences. Growth needs dominate consumer motivations over deficiency needs in most postindustrial societies.

MARKET ENVIRONMENT FOR EXPERIENTIAL RETAILING

An understanding of retail history requires an understanding of supply side conditions as well as consumer demand (Savitt 1989). The model in Figure 1.6 describes the system that influences the development of consumer demand–driven experiential retailing. The system includes cultural, technological, economic, political, social, and physical environments. A retailer's ability to meet consumer demand by providing the right product or service at the appropriate time requires an understanding and evaluation of these systems.

Culture

Culture reflects learned values, mores, and symbols that affect behavior and consumption. One of Geert Hofstede's (1980) dimensions of culture compares individualism with collectivism. This dimension describes whether or not a society emphasizes the individual, community, or social group. Traditionally, postindustrial countries such as the United States and countries in Western Europe are known for focusing on individuals. However, recent changes in the consumer behavior of these countries have led to the development of brand communities. A **brand community** is formed among admirers of a brand, and it is marked by "a shared consciousness, rituals and traditions, and a sense of moral responsibility" (Muniz and O'Guinn 2001, 413). Like other communities, it is marked by a shared consciousness, rituals and traditions, and a sense of moral responsibility" (Muñiz and O'Guinn 2001, 412–413). Marketers can strengthen brand communities by facilitating shared customer experiences (McAlexander, Schouten, and Koenig 2002). Consumers may use brands to express their individual and social identities. Thus, brand meaning extends beyond the actual product to communicate additional social meaning.

Kokon To Zai, an avant-garde clothing boutique, began as a music store in London's Soho district in the 1990s. Sasha B., the store's owner, designs the store's private label line, KTZ. Most items sold in the store are exclusive, thus limiting the

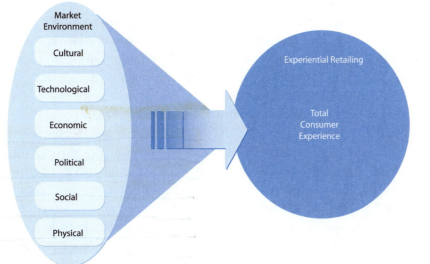

1.6 Market environment drives experiential retailing

1.7a–c Kokon To Zai, an avant-garde clothing boutique

possibility of customers seeing other people in their same outfits. Kokon To Zai is at the forefront of London's club fashion scene, inspiring many stylists. The store sells creative and up-and-coming designs by Marjan Pejoski. Marjan Pejoski created the "swan" dress worn by singer/actress Björk at the 2001 Academy Awards ceremony (Davies 2005). This is an example of how a designer brand is used to communicate individuality and social meaning. Since Kokon To Zai continues to sell music, art, and fashion, a visit to the store is a cultural experience (See Figures 1.7a–c).

Brooks (2000) described the material world as one that creates "intellectual capital" and "the culture industry." Consider the brand Ben & Jerry's. It represents both individual and social expression of consumers. A consumer justifies the price of a pint of Ben & Jerry's Wavy Gravy ice cream because part of the proceeds goes to Camp Win-a-Rainbow—a summer camp that gives scholarships to children. The popularity of this brand supports Pine and Gilmore's (1999) description of the experience economy. **The experience economy** is where a product engages and connects with customers in a personal and special way. Consumers no longer buy commodities; they express who they are and identify the relationships that are important to them through consumption.

Technology

Technology is a process that transforms inputs into outputs through the application of skill and energy (Rousseau 1979). Retail information and communication technologies allow firms to manage inventories better, keep less inventory on hand, and monitor consumer demand

(Keegan, O'Callaghan, and Wilcox 2001). Electronic data interchange creates real-time exchanges where, when the merchandise inventory begins to run low, a replacement is ordered from the supplier. These innovations are driving different industry sectors to go from traditional supplier-buyer relationships to strategic partnerships in which information is shared. Technology also allows manufacturers and merchants to individualize product offerings. For example, Levi Strauss provides a Personal Pair jeans service by manufacturing custom-fit jeans to customers' individual measurements. Pine and Gilmore (1999) described **mass customization** as a way for merchants not only to serve customers efficiently but also provide them with good value.

In terms of shopping, consumers value technology. Online shoppers use technology to research prices at the closest retail stores, product specifications, instructions for use, warranty information, and sales. In-store shoppers desire knowledgeable, helpful sales associates as well as access to sales representatives in person or by telephone, and cashiers who are available to complete merchandise transactions. As such, retail technology is an integral component for satisfying customer information needs.

The pervasive presence of information technology has caused consumers to desire experiences (Schmitt 1999). The speed of information transfer has not only increased, but the information itself has transformed as well, through the use of sight, sound, smell, and taste. Schmitt (1999) commented on futurist Michael Dertouzos's prediction that "we will see products like the 'bodynet' a web of integrated devices—functioning as cellphone, computer, television, camera, and more—that will be confined to an invisible envelope around our bodies. This device—or a similar one—will allow people and companies to connect and to share an experiential universe with one another at any time" (54).

Economics

Economics describe a study of the allocation of scarce resources among an array of uses (Nicholson 1987). Economics affect retailing through market conditions and firm-level operations. Gross Domestic Product, or national earnings, in the United States increased from 7.3 trillion dollars in 1995 to 9.1 trillion dollars in 2002 (Organization for Economic Cooperation and Development 2003) with per capita annual income at $34,100 (World Bank 2003).

In 2004, the services-producing sector led real growth in the U.S. economy (Smith and Lum 2005). This reflects the strength in the information, professional and business services, trade, real estate, rental, and leasing industries. Overall, there was broad economic growth with expansion in all 15 industry groups and acceleration in growth rates of almost all groups. Further, there was a 4.9 percent growth in 2004 in the services-producing industries, which was higher than the 4.6 percent real average annual growth during the period from 1996 to 2000 (Smith and Lum 2005).

These numbers mean that most consumers in the United States have more money available than is required to sustain their basic needs. Affluence affords consumers the ability to choose among products, services, and retail outlets. Affluent consumers have the financial ability to buy products that reflect their values and lifestyles. Affluent consumers often seek lifestyle brands such as Ralph Lauren for classic luxury clothing and Pottery Barn for cozy and stylish home furniture and accessories. Sara Cross introduced the *CoolNotCruel* apparel line, which merged upscale fashion with environmental responsibility (DeBlanc-Knowles 2003). The Sierra Club, an organization that supports the environment, is developing a new line of eco-friendly apparel (Vobril 2003). By purchasing these lines of products, fashion-conscious, eco-friendly customers can support their values through consumption.

Government

Government influences consumer behavior by controlling the availability of goods and services. A government might restrict the hours a store operates or when certain products can be sold. The blue laws enacted by communities to regulate retail hours are an example. In some geographic locations, blue laws allow stores to be open for business six days a week, but require them to remain closed one day a week. This law allows workers a chance to observe the Sabbath. This law is implemented in different ways. Paramus, New Jersey, requires the stores in its town to close on Sunday. New York allows stores to operate for six days, but they can choose the day of the week they are closed. Government policy related to free trade is another example of an environmental factor that influences consumer demand. Member nations of the World Trade Organization, which are governments, can lessen some barriers to market entry and increase the accessibility of global products available to consumers. Globalization and decreasing trade restrictions from free trade agreements provide consumers with a wider range of available products. This wider selection of products reduces consumer boredom by allowing them to experiment with and sample different products and taste new foods. Despite the abundance of products available in U.S. stores, the *New York Times* reported in Christmas 2002 that consumers were bored with the sameness of retail offerings. Consumers complained specifically about the similarity of products and the sameness of the look. Experiential retail strategies can help differentiate retail offerings and further enhance the consumer experience.

Society

Society refers to a set of relationships among people, organizations, and institutions (Hamilton 1987). Organizations and institutions serve as reference groups for consumers. In turn, these reference groups influence the consumption decisions individuals make (Childers and Rao 1992). Schwer and Daneshvary (1995) found that consumers' Western clothing purchases were related to their involvement with a rodeo society and that frequency of Western clothing usage was related to involvement with a reference group. Take, for example, the Rodeo Shop in Eaton, Ohio, and its rugged style that adds to the authenticity of the consumer's shopping experience. The sales staff dresses in Western wear to create a sense of authenticity. This store could just as easily be located in Texas as in Ohio. This kind of authentic western wear is getting popular in different regions of the United States (See Figures 1.8a and b). Thus, group identification is not limited by physical proximity.

Michael J. Weiss's book *The Clustered World* (2000) discussed the current trend of fragmentation in the United States. He described formerly homogeneous groups of consumers that are now categorized by lifestyle behavior and how these consumer clusters apply globally. He suggested that yuppie (young, upwardly mobile, professional) clusters are cultural bridges to globalization because they are educated cosmopolitans who are receptive to foreign goods and ideas in their respective countries. There is a shift from the influence of traditional consumer reference groups (i.e., family and friends) to postmodern lifestyle clusters.

Personalization is a retail trend that attempts to meet a consumer's lifestyle

1.8a–b The authentic Western wear is getting popular in different regions of the United States.

preference. Consumers want the marketing information they receive and the products and services they consume to be personalized according to the way they live (*MarketWatch* 2005). Restaurants that allow you to customize drinks are gaining popularity. Consider Starbucks Coffee, which boasts 32 coffees on the coffee menu board and hundreds of combinations that can be tailored to each consumer's individual preferences (www.starbucks.com). Likewise, Jones Soda offers customized labels and Senseo coffee offers customizable single-serve machines (*MarketWatch* 2005).

Consumers also make consumption decisions based on their desire for more intense experiences. They participate in extreme sports, take busy weekend breaks, and try intensely flavored food and drink, such as sour soft drinks and peppery liqueurs (*MarketWatch* 2005). These behaviors are primarily exhibited by young consumers since they tend to be the most tolerant of risk and change.

Physical Environment

The physical environment refers to the natural or built environment (Hamilton 1987). In terms of retailing, the physical environment dictates where consumers can shop as well as what they can buy. In the Makola market in Ghana, for example, a lack of refrigeration and perhaps electric infrastructure limits the shelf-life of food products for sale. Contrast the Makola market with a hypothetical situation where Wal-Mart superstores are located along highway and interstate exits in Ghana and the available physical infrastructure facilitates the shipments of goods to retail outlets.

The built environment is one component of the physical environment. It influences how products reach the marketplace. For instance, to ship flowers from all over the world to a local florist, a complex distribution system is required. Aalsmeer, the world's largest flower auction, is located 10 miles south of Amsterdam. The Aalsmeer complex covers approximately 250 acres, with the auction building alone taking up 160 acres. Flowers are sent to Aalsmeer from growers located all over the world. The flowers are put onto flower pallets and shipped via refrigerated airplanes to Amsterdam where the pallets are taken off the plane and loaded onto trucks for the short drive to Aalsmeer. Finally, the pallets are unloaded and checked into the automated auction system. When buyers press the button for the bid, the clock stops, the bid is accepted unless it is below market value, and the flowers are shipped out to customers worldwide. Usually, the next destination is a wholesaler who sells the flowers to retail firms. The time required to send flowers around the world from growers to Aalsmeer to final customers is about 48 hours (Moore 2006). The Aalsmeer flower auction is an example of how a physical infrastructure to move products to market quickly supports experiential retailing.

Retailers can develop new ways of differentiation by varying or increasing the product assortment and offering it when and where the consumer wants to shop. Consumers have enough money to choose among suppliers, while suppliers have dwindling numbers of new consumers. Moreover, population growth in post-industrial countries such as the United States is forcing manufacturers and retailers to differentiate themselves from their competitors. As a result, the amount of store square footage per person increased in the United States during the last half of the twentieth century and created a situation of retail saturation or being over-stored. Thus, the retail sector is highly competitive and differentiation is essential to beating the competition. In summary, as dynamic systems (see Figure 1.6) drive experiential retailing, retailers need to continually monitor these systems for changes that bring about a need for innovation.

CONSUMER DESIRE FOR EXPERIENCES

Retail environments are pushing consumers to appreciate the hedonic aspects of consumption. For example, as consumers have become more affluent, their shopping patterns and purchasing behaviors have changed. People are spending more money on CDs, videos, video games, movies, restaurants, gambling, and theme parks. People are looking for products and services that evoke fun and reflect their individuality and lifestyles. People seek entertainment and emotional stimulation throughout the shopping process, not just through the act of purchasing the goods.

The symbolic role in consumption is also important because people do not buy goods as objective entities (i.e., what the goods are), but as subjective symbols (i.e., what the goods mean) (Hirschman and Holbrook 1982; Levy 1959). Symbolic consumption is especially salient for procuring brands, licensed products, signature merchandise, and souvenir merchandise (Holbrook and Hirschman 1982). Symbolic consumption may suggest increasing revenues for retailers due to the willingness of consumers to pay extra for the special meaning and pleasure associated with purchasing a product or service (Longo 1995). Coca-Cola and Disney capitalized on each other's symbolic brand heritage when Mickey Mouse appeared on packs of Coke (Campbell 1999).

The Bluewater mall, located south of London in Kent, is one example of a retail development for post-modern consumers (See Figure 1.9). The mall positions itself as Europe's most innovative and exciting shopping and leisure destination. The Bluewater mall tries to convince customers that they not only exchange cash for goods, but also participate in a collective experience (Meades 2003). The mall is a two-story triangular building with three distinctive themed shopping zones: the Rose Gallery, Guildhall, and Thames Walk. Each shopping zone sells distinctive merchandise, such as fashion labels or street clothing, and has its own entertainment and eating areas. The exterior of the Bluewater mall is modern with a strong emphasis placed on the aesthetics of design. The grounds have seating areas around a pond designed to provide breaks from shopping. A relaxing break area keeps consumers in the shopping area longer, which stimulates higher spending per person. Bluewater illustrates how retailers merge utilitarian and hedonic aspects that appeal to consumers who have a need for a total consumer experience.

A study on restaurants by Josiam, Mattson, and Sullivan (2003) supports the observation that consumers want an experience in addition to the functional product. They examined two similar eating establishments: one a restaurant and the other a diner with a historic designation. The diner with the historic designation was referred to as a *historaunt* because it was both a historic attraction and restaurant. Good food was important to both groups' patronage; however, the customers at the historaunt, in contrast to those at the restaurant, were motivated by preferences for history, culture, and sightseeing. In 2004, Andersson and Mossberg assessed the multidimensional experience

1.9 The Bluewater mall positions itself as Europe's most innovative and exciting shopping and leisure destination.

of restaurants and determined that customers are predominantly seeking to meet social needs when they dine at restaurants in the evening, which implies that customers patronize lunchtime restaurants mainly to fulfill physiological needs. Restaurant retailers can use these ideas to determine what steps they can take to satisfy customers who desire different dining experiences at different times of the day.

Creating an experience for consumers is more important than ever. Rauen (2006) quotes Pine and Gilmore, authors of *The Experience Economy:* "Food is not enough. Getting people there is not enough. What consumers want is a memorable event that engages them. It's about what happens inside the space as well as the décor" (99). Why is the consumer desire for experiences changing? Rauen (2006) reiterates several points Pine and Gilmore (1999) made in *The Experience Economy.* The first reason is the additional supply of time and money to more affluent consumers who desire enjoyable activities. The second reason is that consumers have become more knowledgeable about design and have begun to expect high style. Finally, the abundance of competitors in the market has pushed retailers of products and services to distinguish themselves from one another.

STRATEGIES FOR EXPERIENTIAL RETAILERS

Experiential retailing exists not only in a single organization, but also in multi-unit businesses, shopping centers, and tourist attractions. At the store level, the customer experience drives design. Consider the award-winning example of La Maison Simons located at Carrefour Laval in Quebec, Canada. In 2003, it received the best overall entry and first in the department store category in *Chain Store Age's* annual Retail Store of the Year design competi-

tion. The design for this 79,000-square-foot store was driven by the desire to create a unique space that consumers would enjoy exploring (*Chain Store Age* 2003). La Maison Simons attempts to create a visual experience for customers before they ever enter the store. In addition, store layout supports high customer service standards and optimizes customer sight lines so that store areas are appealing to the consumer (See Figure 1.10).

To remain competitive and appeal to consumers in today's experiential retailing market, many retailers have discovered they must include entertainment or unique themes in their retail mix (Barbieri 2005). Retailers that are thriving now and will continue to thrive in the future are the ones that provide enjoyable shopping, recreational activities, and educational opportunities for consumers.

Current consumer trends indicate that the mall of the future will be designed like a community, not just a place to shop (Hazlett 2003). Corresponding to this trend, a growing number of lifestyle and town centers are being built. Thus, it becomes more important for developers to plan centers that have interesting shopping and experiential environments. The Mall of America is an example of an entertainment-based shopping center that combines the experience of Camp Snoopy with a retail environment that includes traditional retail stores such as Abercrombie and Fitch, Brooks Brothers, Victoria's Secret, and Ann Taylor. Other examples of entertainment-based shopping centers include Mega Park at Les Galeries de la Capitale in Quebec City, Canada; River Fair Family Fun Park at River Falls Mall in Clarksville, Indiana; and Easton Town Center in Columbus, Ohio.

In September 2005, Warner Bros. Consumer Products closed a deal with Taubman Centers to launch children's play areas with a Looney Tunes theme in some of the 22 malls that it owns nationwide. Taubman Centers began building the play areas at the Northlake Mall in Charlotte, North Carolina. By including themes in the play areas, they create sponsorship opportunities for not only the mall but also the retailers. In addition to the themed play areas, Taubman Centers began creating a series of themed interactive experiences at its malls (Barbieri 2005, 53). In 2004, themed interactive experiences were created by the Walt Disney Company movie *The Chronicles of Narnia: The Lion, the Witch and the Wardrobe*, which was run by 11 Taubman malls during the pre-holiday season. The set included scenes from the movie, such as life-size snow globes, a magic wardrobe that leads to Narnia and simulates snowfall, and lifelike figures from the story. This themed interactive experience was designed to be an immersive experience that brought the film to life and created a "magical holiday destination" (Barbieri 2005).

Entertainment- or theme-based retailing attracts tourists and is growing throughout the world. Examples in the United States include Riverwalk in New Orleans, Pier 39 in San Francisco, Faneuil Hall Marketplace in Boston, and the South Street Seaport in New York. Examples in other countries include Disney Paris in Paris, France; the Space Center in Bremen, Germany; and the Garden Walk in Tokyo, Japan. For tourists, shopping and dining are the most popular activities. Retail sectors that attract tourists have exceptional opportunities for experiential retailing (Kim 2001).

Although many value retailers have focused on utilitarian benefits such as low price, convenience, and wide assortments of products, they also provide hedonic benefits for customers who want to receive emotional advantages from bargain hunting and exploring. Famous designers have capitalized on this consumer trend by developing less expensive product lines that reach more price-conscious consumers. They have also partnered with mid- or low-end stores to make luxury items available to the masses.

Retailers seek to enhance the consumer experience via brand extension. Brand extension introduces a company's brands into new product categories. A number of apparel designers, such as Calvin Klein, Donna Karan, Liz Claiborne, and Giorgio Armani, have extended their brands into home furnishings. This extension takes advantage of the growing home furnishings industry, which has resulted mainly from

1.10 Departments in La Maison Simon store are separated by walls and different ceiling heights. Pedestrian traffic is facilitated by store layout.

more affluent consumers and the cocooning effect. People are spending more time at home and more money on making the home a place that satisfies their needs and desires.

Retailers also implement strategic alliances to create a total consumer experience and drive product sales. These alliances are created by combining two or more brands in one product (or service) or a set of products (or services). The idea behind this strategy is to create synergy and power with several brands by increasing customer awareness and loyalty, which yields more traffic than a single brand-name operation. In summer 2006, Nike used the center atrium space in their Oxford Circus store to display floor-length hanging flags. The flags promoted Nike's and Apple's joint production of a chip that could be worn in running sneakers and linked to their iPods to record workout information. The strategic partnership between Nike and Apple illustrates how brands can come together to provide lifestyle appeal to consumers. Both brands provide innovative products for consumers who like to try new things. Other examples of strategic alliance include Starbucks in Kroger and Target stores, Delta Airlines partnering with American Express through the SkyMiles credit card, and Nike's partnering with collegiate licensed apparel.

THE NEXT STEP FOR RETAIL STRATEGIES

Retailers in the new millennium face complex changes in consumer demand and a dynamic competitive environment. In North America and many Western European countries retailing has reached a level of maturity in which retailers are confronted with an overcapacity of retail space. Consumers, on the contrary, demand consumption experiences that bring emotional rewards. An examination of traditional models that focus on product assortments in retail outlets can provide limited insight into why consumers may be bored with their shopping experiences.

To meet consumer demand, we suggest a model to guide experiential retailing (See Figure 1.11). This model can assist in explaining how and why there is a need for experiential retailing and how to develop strategies to meet consumer demand. This model includes demand-side variables that support a total consumer experience and supply-side variables that encourage experiential retailing.

The first part of the book further explains the evolution of consumption (Chapter 2), and how utilitarian and hedonic functions are integrated to explain a total consumer experience (Chapter 3). The second part describes the consumer desire for a total consumer experience that considers the importance of symbolic consumption (Chapter 4), ritual consumption (Chapter 5), sensory consumption (Chapter 6), and consumer efficiency (Chapter 7). The last part explains how retailers can enhance the consumption experience through strategies such as entertainment retailing (Chapter 8), thematic retailing (Chapter 9), lifestyle retailing (Chapter 10), value retailing (Chapter 11), branding (Chapter 12), brand extension (Chapter 13), strategic alliance (Chapter 14), and a discussion about how experiential retailing applies to global retailing (Chapter 15).

CHAPTER SUMMARY

Consumers expect to receive both utilitarian and hedonic benefits: a total consumer experience. Experiential retail strategies transform products and services into a total consumption experience that fulfill utilitarian (rational or functional) and hedonic (emotional or expressive) needs. When consumers receive utilitarian or functional benefits along with hedonic or

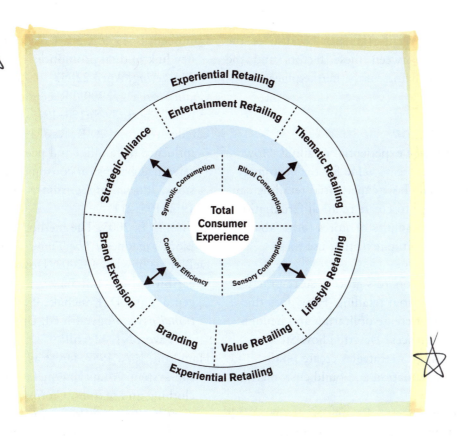

1.11 This experiential retailing model shows consumer-side and supply-side variables that create a total consumer experience.

emotional benefits, the consumption experience is more satisfactory.

This chapter identifies environmental factors that influence the evolution of consumer demand and contribute to experiential retailing. Elements in the market environment include culture, technology, economics, government, society, and physical environment. They affect what consumers value and how they learn about products, shop, access goods, and pay for goods. These elements have created an environment in which informed consumers have the ability to choose among similar products, services, or both.

Traditional models focus on product assortments in retail outlets and provide limited insight into why consumers may be bored with their shopping experiences. Retailers need to meet the needs of their target customers and establish an emotional connection with them. Retailers can accomplish this by bundling products, services, and experiences that are best suited to their target markets and differentiated from those of their competitors. Anecdotal examples illustrate how product assortment, sales staff knowledge, and experiential dimensions of shopping create a differentiated consumer experience that cannot be substituted.

In this text we propose a model to guide experiential retailing (see Figure 1.11). This model can assist in explaining why there is a boom in experiential retailing and how to develop strategies to meet consumer demand. This model includes demand-side factors (which support a total consumer experience) and supply-side factors (which encourage experiential retailing). Demand-side factors are symbolic consumption, ritual consumption, sensory consumption, and consumer efficiency. Supply-side factors are entertainment retailing, thematic retailing, lifestyle retailing, value retailing, branding, brand extension, and strategic alliance. Retailers need to consider both demand-side and supply-side factors when planning retail strategies because of the synergy between these factors and the dynamic nature of the marketplace.

Discussion Questions

1. Describe experiential retailing. How does it create value for the customer?

2. Explain how experiential retailing can be used to create retail differentiation. Give examples of stores (other than those in the text) that use these strategies.

3. Stew Leonard's grocery store practices experiential retailing. How does this retailer create utilitarian and hedonic experiences? Describe how Stew Leonard's strategies create retail differentiation and build customer loyalty.

4. Consumers seek experiences that fulfill their needs, as described in Abraham Maslow's hierarchy. Provide some examples of retailers that fulfill the needs of self-actualizing consumers. What strategies are they using?

5. Identify and describe socioeconomic changes that contribute to a demand for experiential retailing.

6. Explain how Marjan Pejoski's designs sold at Kokon To Zai illustrate cultural influences in the consumer experience. Why is this store unique?

7. Look at the model for the total consumer experience. Give examples of retail strategies listed and describe the benefits they add to a total consumer experience.

REFERENCES

Barbieri, K. 2005. The mall is dropping the ball. *Amusement Business* 118(1):52–53.

Brooks, D. 2000. *Bobos in paradise: The new upper class and how they got there.* New York: Simon & Schuster.

Campbell, L. 1999. Coca-Cola and Disney link in dual promotion. *Marketing*, April 22, 5.

Chain Store Age. 2003. Reception honors retail's best. 79(5):190–191.

Childers, T., and A. R. Rao. 1992. The influence of familial and peer-based reference groups on consumer decisions. *Journal of Consumer Research* 19(2):198–211.

Davies, L. L. 2005. The method behind Bjork's madness, *The Times.* April 2, 6.

DeBlanc-Knowles, J. 2003. Down to earthwear. *E,* 14(3):58.

Eggen, P., and D. Kauchak. 1999. *Educational psychology,* 4th ed. Upper Saddle River, NJ: Merrill.

Hamilton, J. A. 1987. Dress as a cultural sub-system: A unifying metatheory for clothing and textiles. *Clothing and Textiles Research Journal* 6(1):1–7.

Hard Rock Cafe corporate mission. Retrieved August 30, 2006 from *www.hardrock.com/corporate/mission/*

Hazlett, C. 2003. The future. *Retail Traffic* 32(5):64.

Hirschman, E. C., and M. B. Holbrook. 1982. Hedonic consumption: Emerging concepts, methods and propositions. *Journal of Marketing* 46(3):92–101.

Hofstede, G. 1980. *Culture's consequences: International differences in work-related values.* California: Sage Publication.

Holbrook, M. B., and E. C. Hirschman. 1982. Experiential aspects of consumption: Consumer fantasies, feelings, and fun. *Journal of Consumer Research* 9(2):132–140.

Josiam, B. M., M. Mattson, and P. Sullivan. 2003. The histourant: Heritage tourism at Mickey's dining car. *Tourism Management* 25:453–461.

Keegan, J., E. O'Callaghan, and M. Wilcox. 2001. Facilitators and inhibitors of supply chain innovation-prospects for supply chain management in the Irish grocery sector, *Irish Marketing* 14(2):26–39.

Kim, Y-K. 2001. Experiential retailing: An interdisciplinary approach to success in domestic and international retailing. *Journal of Retailing and Consumer Services* 8(5):287–289.

Levy, S. 1959. Symbols for sale. *Harvard Business Review* 37 (July–August): 117–119.

Longo, D. 1995. Retail rides character-building brandwagon. *Discount Store News* 34(12):36, 54.

MarketWatch: Personal Care. 2005. Revealed: The top 10 consumer megatrends dictating the shape of things to come. February 2005, 4(2):10–12.

Maslow, A. 1968. *Toward a psychology of being*, 2nd ed. New York: Van Nostrand.

———.1970. *Motivation and personality*, 2nd ed. New York: Harper and Row.

McAlexander, J. H., J. W. Schouten, and H. F. Koenig. 2002. Building brand community. *Journal of Marketing* 66(1):38–54.

Meades, J. 2003. Bluewater is yob-free, almost cosy. The questionable means may be justified by the end. *The Times Magazine (London)*, 20.

Moore, M. 2006. A rose is a rose. What's the price? *The Washington Post.* October 4, A17.

Muñiz, A. M., and T. C. O'Guinn. 2001. Brand community. *Journal of Consumer Research* 27(4):412–32.

Nicholson, W. 1987. *Intermediate Microeconomics*. New York: The Dryden Press.

Organization for Economic Co-operation and Development. 2003. Retrieved September 1, 2006 from www.oecd.org.

Pine II, B. J., and J. H. Gilmore. 1999. *The experience economy*. Boston: Harvard Business School Press.

Poulsson, S., and S. Kale. 2004. The experience economy and commercial experiences. *Marketing Review* 4(3):267–277.

Rauen, S. 2006. Shoemaker, can't stop this feeling. *Hospitality Design* 28(3):99–102.

Reynolds, J. 2003. Editorial. *European Retail Digest*, 38:1–2.

Rousseau, D. M. 1979. Assessment of technology in organizations: Closed versus open systems approaches. *The Academy of Management Review* 4(4):531–542.

Sacks, B. 2000. Stew Leonard's: The Disneyland of Dairy Stores. Retrieved August 30, 2006 from www.specialty retail.net/issues/july00/lifestyle_ tenant.htm.

Savitt, R. 1989. Looking back to see ahead: Writing the history of American retailing. *Journal of Retailing* 65(3):326–356.

Schmitt, B. 1999. Experiential marketing. *Journal of Marketing Management* 15(1–3):53–67.

Schwer, R. K., and R. Daneshvary. 1995. Symbolic products attributes and emulatory consumption: The case of rodeo fan attendance and the wearing of Western clothing. *Journal of Applied Business Research* 11(3):74–82.

Smith, G. M., and S. Lum. 2005. Annual industry accounts. *Survey of Current Business*, Retrieved July 25, 2006, from *www.bea.gov/bea/ARTICLES/2005/ 12December/1205_indyAccts.pdf*

Vobril, M. 2003. Buying to save; Sierra Club debuts its eco-friendly line. *Newsday* (New York). August 13, B03.

Weiss, M. J. 2000. *The clustered world*. New York: Little, Brown and Company.

World Bank. 2003. *Focus on the United States of America*. Retrieved July 25, 2006, from www.worldbank.org/html/ schools/regions/nam/unitstat.htm

CHAPTER 2

EVOLUTION OF CONSUMPTION

U.S. Designers Launch Campaign to Try to Stimulate Retail Sales

Soon after the September 11 terrorist attacks in 2001, New York Mayor Rudolph Giuliani exhorted people to take in a Broadway show, go out to dinner, or do a little shopping to help get the city back to normal. Fashion companies such as Nicole Miller, Tahari, and Lafayette 148 launched the "Proudly Made in New York" ad campaign, a new label sewn in garments for apparel makers that manufacture in New York City.

These efforts were aimed locally to help rebuild New York City. With the economy slipping fast and the number of layoffs increasing steadily, the promotion of shopping as a civic duty is becoming a nationwide idea.

Earlier this month at a rally, San Francisco Mayor Willie Brown launched a campaign dubbed "America: Open for Business," which distributed to local businesses thousands of posters featuring an American flag with shopping-bag handles.

The Council of Fashion Designers of America (CFDA) campaign is expected to wrap its message around American patriotism, suggesting that the best way for consumers to demonstrate their patriotism is to go shopping, especially on the day after Thanksgiving. That day, called black Friday in the retail trade, marks the traditional start of the holiday shopfest. In a Deloitte survey conducted after President Bush told Americans to resume their normal lives and routines, 73 percent of the respondents said they "view shopping as their patriotic duty." But Mr. Steidann says the fashion industry's shopping campaign "may have a small effect to the degree that advertising has the ability to get people to spend."

Meanwhile, Adbusters, a controversial anticonsumerism group in Vancouver, British Columbia, is taking the opposite stance, as it once again promotes its ninth annual "Buy Nothing Day" on the day after Thanksgiving, to promote "consumer awareness and simple living." Adbusters executive director Kalle Lasn said that this year, its shopping boycott is "now more relevant than ever. American overconsumption is part of the reason why the Islamic world hates us so much."

Source: Agins, Teri. 2001. U.S. Designers Launch Campaign to Try to Stimulate Retail Sales. *Wall Street Journal* (Eastern edition). October 22, B.7. Reprinted with permission.

INTRODUCTION

Consumption makes up around 60 percent of the U.S. gross domestic product, with a similar situation existing in other developed countries (Bryant and Macri 2005). Although the things people consume and the manners in which they consume have changed dramatically since World War II, some concepts regarding consumerism remain remarkably similar. While production for the war drove the U.S. economy from 1939 to 1946, the need to produce still drives consumption. Mihaly Csikszentmihalyi (2000) stated: "economic forecasts are based on increasing demands: unless people buy more houses, more cars, more sporting equipment and clothes, the economy will falter" (271). Thus, it is important to understand what drives the U.S. household's consumption level.

Consumption level is reflected in the amount and quality of goods and services that a consumer expects to have throughout a lifetime (Davis 1941). If the consumption level is diminished for any reason, such as unemployment or divorce, the consumer strives to regain it. Physical, economic, and spiritual consumptions make up the consumer's quality of life. Creation of new consumption experiences is the result of electing what is relevant in existing goods or services and devaluing the irrelevant. Csikszentmihalyi (2000) defined the **consumption** process: "Consuming consists of energy expended to improve the quality of life by means of increasing entropy. In other words, consuming entails an exchange of psychic energy (usually in its symbolic form, i.e., money) for objects or services that satisfy some human need. These objects are relatively high in potential energy to begin with, but through the process of consuming they are broken down into useless things with low potential energy" (267). Csikszentmihalyi recognized the paradox of entropy, a decaying of ordered systems and objects, in corporate selling, but argued that we benefit from it in the long run.

A culture of consumption exists (Rassuli and Hollander 1986). Culture works in three ways: groups of people consume at a level substantially above that of crude, survival-level subsistence; people obtain goods and services for consumption through exchange rather than through self-production; and society views consumption as an acceptable and appropriate activity. People, in fact, tend to judge others and perhaps themselves in terms of consumption level and its appropriateness for their perceived lifestyles.

Increasing affluence, demographic changes, technological innovations, and changing tastes and lifestyles have contributed to current consumer behaviors. Consumers are spending more money on discretionary goods than they do on basic needs (Moran and McCully 2001). The consumer market is transitioning from modern consumption associated with production-era values to postindustrial consumption in postmodern societies.

CONSUMPTION AND RETAIL DURING WORLD WAR II

World War II began in winter 1939 in Europe and the United States entered it in 1941. World War II impacted consumption and retail in various ways. Product scarcity was created by the war and consumers saved and conserved to support the war effort. Although retailers were challenged by the shortage of consumption and limited controls on production, pricing, and distribution, their support for war efforts was evident in the retail strategies they implemented.

Consumption

During World War II, consumers around the world faced daily challenges due to limited supply and rationed quantities of goods, while new black markets for products developed. C. A. Lejeune (1942) stated: "For English housewives in the third winter of war, intelligent catering and contriving with food is a major problem. There is no real shortage, and nobody is hungry, but meals tend to have a horrid sameness. Extras can be found, but they have to be strenuously looked for. Most housewives go out early in the morning, hurry from store to store, supplementing the ration with a slice of breakfast sausage here, a can of soup there, a cake from the shop where they still use butter and eggs. Everything has to be planned, and everything has to be carried home" (SM18).

The situation in the United States was similar to the one depicted above. Enacted product rationing covered 75 percent of food purchases as of April 1, 1943 (Morris 1943). This rationing provided each family with an allotment of stamps used to purchase specific products. Examples of product rationing are numerous. U.S. residents were limited to three pairs of shoes annually (Shalett 1943). In England, a dress required 11 ration coupons or stamps, no matter its cost (*New York Times* 1941).

Ration plans set quotas for annual household consumption to help war efforts with needed goods. In addition to ration plans, the government worked with industries to develop new strategies to serve both the war effort and consumer needs. For example, wool was needed for the war effort and industry responded by developing blended fabrics for civilian consumers. In terms of shopping, "Mr. and Mrs. America will have to get acquainted with their neighbors, trade at their neighborhood stores, attend their neighborhood movies, accept a greatly curtailed variety of goods and disperse with the customary desire for a change of scenery" (*New York Times* 1942d, 20). Thus, clothing frills were eliminated and travel was curtailed.

In addition to rationing, the United States enacted the emergency Price Control Act of 1942, which established maximum prices for commodities (*New York Times* 1942a). The Price Control Act made it illegal to sell specified commodities and services for more than the regulated price. The act covered a range of products, including tobacco; aspirin; toothbrushes; facial tissue; ice cream; canned juices and fruit; meat; household furniture; appliances; and women's, girls', men's, boys', and infants' clothing. An article in the *New York Times* described how Mrs. Jenkins clipped a list of food prices from the newspaper and placed it in her ration-book holder in preparation for grocery shopping (McBride 1943). She shopped early for meat because product selection decreased as the day progressed. Poster campaigns during World War II officially sanctioned and promoted the U.S. core value of frugality by supporting thriftiness with goods and services, recycling materials, growing food, obeying price and ration controls, and buying war bonds (Witkowski 2003).

Aspects of the war economy created new jobs, which allowed the United States to recover from the Great Depression of the 1930s and helped some family incomes to grow. The income growth rates were faster for African Americans and households with lower economic levels than the rest of the population as a whole. Even with a 25 percent inflation rate during 1940 to 1943, consumption of goods and services rose 10 percent between the first quarter of 1940 and 1943 (Witkowski 2003). Support for World War II contributed to a temporarily controlled economy with challenging consumption and price limits on consumers. As a result of living through these tough times, consumers from this historic period are known for their frugality and patriotism (Crispell 1993).

Retail

Retailers that operated during World War II were challenged by controls on production, distribution, and consumption. In addition, there were price controls, limited product supplies in some categories, limited labor supply, changes in personnel, added taxes, wage freezes, and inventory management challenges (*New York Times* 1943a). Retailers could only replenish their inventory levels in proportion to the amount of ration stamps or coupons they collected (*New York Times* 1941), which, in turn, limited the amount of goods retailers could sell and negatively influenced their profit potential.

Earl C. Sams, president of JCPenney Company in 1943, responded to this situational challenge with the following statement: "My observations and experience is that as a group, merchants have met all these added tasks with a spirit of determination and with a desire to cooperate fully in every demand and every effort necessary for the winning of this war" (*New York Times* 1943a, A35). Mr. Sams recognized the influential role of retail in economic development and the support of war efforts. Mr. Sams also stated: "Retailers know the importance and value of their work and that if the armies of workers are to supply the tools for the fighting forces, retailing deserves recognition as 'first aid' to the maintenance of national morale. It is unthinkable that those charged with the conduct of our war effort could regard retailing as a non-essential industry, or treat it as an unwelcome stepchild of the American way of life. To do so would invite a serious disruption of civilian life. Such a disruption would be disastrous in the task that lies ahead" (*New York Times* 1943a, A35). Although consumer prices were held constant during World War II and product costs went up, U.S. stores supported war efforts by promoting savings bond and stamp sales (*New York Times* 1942c). In addition, retailers taught consumers about the value of conserving goods and how to do so (*New York Times* 1942b).

While supporting war efforts, the retail trade evolved through innovative merchandising and sales strategies. In response to the needs of increased numbers of working females, Wanamaker opened a new Manhattan store for business women with fashionable merchandise from accessories to fur coats (*New York Times* 1943b). Shades of yellow, gray, and green were used in the store's color scheme, and the store's fixtures and furniture were manufactured out of materials that were nonessential to war efforts. Specific department merchandising features were used: "Concessions to the busy girl are wide shopping lanes and deep counters planned for easy selection" (*New York Times* 1943b, 20).

Two other important merchandising innovations were refined during this time. Retailers developed labor saving measures such as self-service shopping and new packaging strategies. Self-service sales provided consumers with additional information so they could select the type of merchandise they desired (*New York Times* 1943c). The self-service strategy was used in a variety of retail formats, including grocery stores. In addition, new packaging allowed retailers to decrease selling costs through the use of informative labels and increased product visibility (*New York Times* 1944).

The U.S. manufacturing era peaked during the World War II period, and service industries emerged as an influential economic force (Rosen 1998). As a result, economic emphasis on production of tangible goods transitioned to provision of intangible services. The retail sector made an important contribution to the economic transformation from an industrial economy with production emphasis to a postindustrial one focused on providing services.

World War II drove retail firms to develop new and efficient merchandising, sales, and operational strategies that would continue to serve the industry well in the future.

CONSUMPTION AND RETAIL OF THE POSTWAR

World War II and full employment policies helped transform the U.S. economy, consolidate the standard of living, and contribute to the emergence of new consumer groups (Medeiros 2000). While the U.S. real gross domestic product dropped almost 20 percent between 1944 and 1947, 1948 began a period of two decades of growth referred to as the American Golden Age. This period was characterized by increased income and employment.

The U.S. Census Bureau reported that between 1947 and 1958 median household incomes grew from $3,000 to $5,400 without adjusting for inflation and from $4,000 to $5,400 with adjustments for inflation (*New York Times* 1961). During this time, family income increased more than twice as fast as the cost of living. The average family budget was spent on food (35 percent), clothing (13 percent), rent (11 percent), fuel (3 percent), home furnishings (6 percent), and miscellaneous items such as automobiles and recreation (32 percent). At this time, the product consumer price index did not include goods like televisions and frozen foods. However, subsequent revisions of the consumer index reflected changes in buying patterns, as well as the relative importance of different goods and services. The index reflected a modest but adequate living standard for a family of four (*New York Times* 1952). Average annual household incomes continued to rise during the 1960s. Incomes grew 60 percent in New York City between 1959 and 1970 (Burks 1972). However, half of income gain went to increased living costs.

Rosen (1998) suggested that high growth rates, low inflation, favorable agricultural and industrial product trade, along with union bargaining power helped workers' wage rates increase. Military and government spending and related job creation also contributed to the postwar economic boom. Some of this economic growth was fueled by increased automobile use and the availability of consumer credit. Further, consumers were able to spend their money on things they wanted, and products were readily available.

After World War II, the number of white-collar and service workers increased, while the number of blue-collar jobs fell (Medeiros 2000). In 1950, 54 percent of the labor force was employed in the service sector (Rosen 1998). Today, service sector jobs provide 85 percent of U.S. employment (Porter 2005). Rosen (1998) argued that the current techno-service economy reflects industrialization's most recent development stage and drives change. Economic changes after World War II made material goods less expensive. Cheaper product costs and increased income provided consumers with more spending potential, but challenged businesses to compete for consumers' shopping dollars.

In response to this rising competition, marketing strategies to target consumer segments that were previously ignored by businesses have become a necessity (Scott and Leonhardt 2005). One example is the cruise ship industry. Once somewhat exclusive and a symbol of the good life, cruise lines now sell packages that appeal to a variety of consumer groups. Disney sells family-oriented cruises with entertainment and activities that appeal to multiple age groups. BMW and Mercedes-Benz now sell their cars at lower prices, while Wal-Mart and Kmart sell designer lines such as George and Martha Stewart, respectively. Status and fashion have

TABLE 2.1 TWENTIETH-CENTURY CONSUMER ATTITUDES AND GIFT LISTS

TIME PERIOD	CONSUMER ATTITUDES	PRODUCTS DESIRED			
		MEN	*WOMEN*	*BOYS*	*GIRLS*
1920–1940	Euphoria to Depression	Phonograph, radio, leather razor strap, spats, cufflinks, watch chain, silk shirts, tie clip, waterproof watch, pipe tobacco, electric shaver, 16-mm. movie camera, Stetson hat, folding camera.	Silver-plate tableware and serving items, crystal, fine wristwatch, automatic waffle iron, Waring blender, steam iron, silk stockings, feminine lingerie, Chanel No. 5, Frigidaire.	Pogo stick, yo-yo, Red Ryder BB gun, toy soldiers, cowboy outfit, chemistry set, trampoline, Superman comics, Monopoly, Charley McCarthy "dummy", croquet set.	Kangru-Springshus (springs that could be fastened to shoes), middies (sailor blouses), jacks, Little Princess Elizabeth doll in coronation robes, Anne Shirley doll from popular Anne of Green Gables book series, foot-propelled car.
1940–1960	Escalating confidence	Long-playing records, pink shirt, slide projector, black-and-white television set, pocket-sized transistor radio, Polaroid land camera, reel-to-reel tape recorder.	Percolator, pressure cooker, nylon stockings, Tupperware, Betty Crocker's Picture Cook Book, mink coat, Pop-It jewelry, automatic dishwasher.	Slinky, Scrabble, Davy Crockett coonskin cap, Legos, *Mad* magazine, Frisbee, Silly Putty, Mr. Potato Head, electric guitar, Matchbox cars, Lincoln Logs.	Roller skates, Tiddlywinks, Howdy Doody theme toys, Betsy McCall doll, Tiny Tears doll, Play-Doh, Etch-A-Sketch, Hula Hoop, Cootie, trip to Disneyland (founded 1955), View Master.
1960–1980	Economic whiplash	Solid-state stereo, color and portable television sets, eight-track tape player, quartz watch, CB radio, pocket calculator, home computer, videocassette recorder.	Teflon cookware, microwave oven, Crock Pot, electric toothbrush, Shalimar perfume, lava lamp, Cuisinart food processor, Kodak Instamatic camera, Jacuzzi Whirlpool bath, Saturday Night Fever soundtrack and dance steps.	G.I. Joe, Batmobile, telescope, Man from U.N.C.L.E. and James Bond merchandise, Pong video game, 10-speed bicycle, Sony Walkman, *Star Trek* and *Star Wars* paraphernalia, Hot Wheels cars, Nike shoes.	Barbie and accessories, Beatles merchandise, Twister game, Cheerful Tearful doll, spirograph, trolls, pet rocks, mood rings, Sesame Street toys, Princess telephone, Underoos superhero underwear (first available 1978), Chatty Cathy doll.
1980–2000	Conspicuous consumption	Camcorder, Palm Pilot, portable CD or DVD player, Sony Watchman, stone-washed jeans, cordless drill, laptop computers, Rolex.	Filofax, health club membership, in-line skates, exercise bike, running shoes, Trivial Pursuit, pashmina, cordless telephone, Pictionary, diamonds.	Nintendo and Sony Playstation video games, Teenage Mutant Ninja Turtles, Power Rangers, Thomas the Tank Engine paraphernalia, Smurfs, Super Soakers, Pokémon, X-Men action figures, skateboard, snowboard, mountain or racing bike, Pac-Man video game, Dungeons and Dragons, *Harry Potter* paraphernalia.	Barney merchandise, Care Bears, Tickle-Me Elmo, Cabbage Patch dolls, Furby, Tamagatchi and Digimon, Beanie Babies, kickboard scooter, tennis racket, Li'l Miss Makeup doll, Milky Gel Roller pens.

Source: Crossen, C. 2000. The Evolution of Gift Giving: Last 100 Years Show Growth of Luxury, Greed—Gifts Go From Practical to Plush as Tastes, Budgets Change, Wool Mufflers to Pashmina. *Wall Street Journal*, Nov. 22, B1.

become commodities for all income levels. Gift-giving has also become more common and thus has received increasing attention from marketers. Marketers have promoted different gift attributes and categories when they target different consumer groups based on gender and age group. Table 2.1 shows how consumers' demand for gifts has changed over time.

A 41-year analysis by Moran and McCully (2001) of postwar consumer spending identified several consumer trends. Consumer spending grew slightly faster than demand, with an average annual increase of 3.6 percent. Spending on consumer services, such as medical care, financial services, recreation, and education, increased 18 percent. Consumers spent almost half their budgets on nondurable goods in 1959, but that statistic decreased to 30 percent by 2000. More specifically, between 1959 and 2000, the proportion of household spending (in current dollars) decreased from 25.4 percent to 14.1 percent on food, from 8.3 percent to 4.9 percent on clothing and shoes, and from 4.8 percent to 2.7 percent on energy (Moran and McCully 2001). The decreased share of food can be explained by the reduction in the number of meals prepared at home versus the number of meals purchased outside the home. The other decreases can be explained by declining relative prices. Important factors that influenced consumer spending during the 1959 to 2000 time period include increasing affluence, demographic changes such as an aging U.S. population, technological innovations, and changing tastes and lifestyles (Moran and McCully 2001).

Today, consumers spend more on discretionary goods than on necessities. These expenditures on discretionary goods include home furnishings, motor vehicles, recreation (at home and away from it), brokerage fees and investment counseling, intercity travel, and electricity. Recreational spending includes cable television and Internet connections.

MODERN AND POSTMODERN CONSUMPTION

Consumers have an infinite number of products available for purchase, and there are many choices within these product categories. Modern society, as well as postmodern society, seemingly reflects bits and pieces of the past while also creating the

new. There has been discussion regarding what is modernism versus postmodernism. One illustration is how the trend of new urbanism town centers is interpreted. New urbanism includes planned communities that are designed to replicate communities of previous generations, thus they are somewhat postmodern because of nostalgia. The public spaces in the new urban communities are privately owned and maintained. Southwood in Tallahassee, Florida, is a planned new urban community designed to meet modern consumers' living needs with homes, town houses or condominiums, recreation areas and activities, and a town center complete with shopping venues. Thus, new urbanism communities are functional and logical responses to demand, illustrating how marketing meets modern consumption needs. Consumers not only purchase products in these communities, but also buy into the lifestyle of the development.

Modern Consumption

Modernist society is rational and ordered as illustrated by the following statement by J. J. Kacen (2000): "Consumption has always been gendered. Consumer society developed within a culture that distinguished between men and women, and masculine and feminine, on almost every issue imaginable; consumption was no exception" (347).

Veronique Aubert-Gamet and Bernard Cova (1999) reported that modern consumption emphasized the use-value or functional value of services. They discussed the current proliferation of non-places where a person can be alone in a crowd or anonymous. In modern non-places, such as airports, cars, hotels, and supermarkets, individuals do not have the appropriate conditions for interaction or dialogue with others. As a result, people feel alone and not part of a larger community. An understanding of a non-place can be gleaned from the following excerpt from Aubert-Gamet and Cova (1999): "Thus, in the modern world, the ideal norm has become that of a home where everything that concerns the upkeep of the family takes place between four walls: the washing machine replaces the wash-house, the tumble drier replaces the washing lines between houses, the television replaces the cinema, the fax replaces the mail, the telephone replaces the local square" (40).

Postmodern Consumption

Postmodern is chaotic and the opposite of modern (Dolfsma 2004). **Postmodernism,** according to Mestrovic (1997), describes a fashionable intellectual movement centering on "nostalgia, the blurring between fiction and reality, and other anti-modern tendencies" (39). Goulding (2003) discussed the philosophical foundation of postmodernism as follows: "At its heart, postmodernism's philosophical roots lie in the poststructuralist rejection and denial of the possibility of absolute truths and a questioning of Western metaphysics with its perceived aim of defining, naming, and knowing the world" (152–153).

In a sense, postmodernism is a reaction to logical values associated with modernism. Kacen (2000) stated, "In a postmodern society, gender identities, like personal identities, are individual creations." Thus gender identity is "a malleable cultural product," as well as "an instrument of self-expression." Kacen (2000) provided insights into postmodern marketing of gender: "If under modernity, marketers and advertisers sold products that provided prepackaged, preconstructed, gendered consumer identities, and consumers, through consumption of these products, maintained their identities by accepting these gendered prescriptions; then under postmodernity, the role of marketers and advertisers is to provide consumers with the raw materials with which consumers can construct unique identities. Masculinity and femininity become semiotic signs and artistic resources, component parts with which consumers can construct other possible selves. Deconstructed into its discrete meanings and images, gender is merely another possible element to add to the identity mix" (349).

Postmodern society has become synonymous with a consumer society where fashion is consumed (Firat and Venkatesh 1993). Retailers seemingly serve customers by providing them with the ability to buy according to their wants rather than their needs. Postmodernism should be used to create experiences and meaningful pictures for consumers (Goulding 2003). Langman (1991) stated:

> In postmodern consumption, individuals create a sense of who they are through purchases and acquisitions. As a commodity, social interaction is appropriated by the market and realized in consumption. Self-productions as commodified dramaturgy are the simulacra of social life, "hyper-real" expressions of alienated selfhood and fragmented social life. Self-presentations are increasingly shaped by popular imagery, at time becoming parodies of media celebrities—life imitates mass produced art. But since most people work in organizations, its expressions are more likely seen in the private worlds of amusement.

Current postmodernity requires a new look at consumer behavior. Postmodern behavior, a break from modernity whereby traditional or classical elements are reintroduced, emphasizes the value of the social link or the linking value (Aubert-Gamet and Cova 1999). The community is considered to be immensely important in the postmodern era and satisfies the consumer's need for social exchange (Aubert-Gamet and Cova 1999). Malls become stages where commoditization and consumption occur. Shoppers take in signals and purchase goods that are used in the construction of their identities (Langman 1991).

FRAGMENTATION

Fragmentation is based upon two interrelated assumptions: markets are broken down into smaller and smaller segments, and more products are created to serve the increasing number of market segments (Goulding 2003). Consumers are seemingly conditioned for fragmented experiences from activities such as television watching. Consumers' lives are further fragmented by daily activities such as work, travel, and home activities. Consumers may present different images according to situation and time. Each situation becomes a stage where consumers can create their roles and act out their identities and status. Consider a line from William Shakespeare's play *As You Like It*: "All the world's a stage and all the men and women merely players. They have their exits and their entrances, and one man in his time plays many parts." This idea of a stage can apply to contemporary consumer behavior.

Postmodern consumers seem to dismantle Shakespeare's stage and reconstruct it as a mall. On the postmodern stage, props (e.g., clothing) or mannerisms (e.g., speaking) vary according to the consumer's role (e.g., friend or parent). Each consumer has his or her own stage. The market has many possible segments, from aspiring divas to authors, to reincarnations of actors. As such, retailers operating in a postmodern market have an abundance of consumer segments and consumer lifestyles to satisfy.

Alan Tomlinson (1990) claimed that "our personal identity is created out of elements created by others and marketed aggressively and seductively" (13). Modern consumerism or the consumer culture, he argues, reflects cultural transformation, including shifts in values and confusion regarding class, regional, generational, and gender identities. Affluence, free time, individualism, a middle-aged population, middle-class society, and cultural separation have influenced the shift in the consumer market from a hierarchal structure to fragmentation. These fragmentations allow for increased lifestyle choices and need fulfillment.

Consumption Communities

An era of mobility has contributed to the development of **consumption communities** where people seek the sense of social belonging associated with neighborhoods (Friedman, Abeele, and De Vos 1993). Cova (1997, 306) suggested that consumers satisfy their want for community in two ways: "rejection of virtual satisfaction through the purchasing and above all the repeated purchasing of the 'new', which lost all its meaning with the crumbling of the modern myth of progress" and "seeking for direct satisfaction through emotion shared with others, not through consuming with them, but through being with them."

The sense of community that surrounds rock bands such as Phish and the Grateful Dead is an example of a consumption community. These bands have been known to attract loyal fans who followed them from concert to concert and place to place, creating a simulated family experience. These bands not only sold music, but also branded commodities, such as T-shirts, for their fans. Ben & Jerry's developed ice cream flavors named after Phish (Phish Food) and Jerry Garcia (Cherry Garcia), the late, revered lead musician of the Grateful Dead.

Another example of a U.S. consumption community is Bruegger's Bagels, which originated in Burlington, Vermont. Of particular interest is its location on

TABLE 2.2 POSTMODERN BRANDING TECHNIQUES

TECHNIQUE	STRATEGY	EXAMPLES
Ironic, reflexive brand persona	The point of the ad is to sell to forge distance between the brand and its competitor's hard sell commercialism.	• Nike's Just Do It • Levi's 501 Blues
Coattailing on cultural epicenters	Weave the brand into cultural epicenters, the center of new expressive culture. Forges a credible ongoing relationship within such a community to create an impression for the mass audience that the brand is a vested member of the community and that its stature within that community is deserved.	• Tommy Hilfiger, Nike, Fubu, and African American communities
Life world emplacement	Show the brand's value emanates from disinterested everyday life situations far removed from commercial sponsorship. Consumers look for evidence that suggests that a brand has earned its identity.	• Levi's 501 (1980s) used cinema verite to create the perception that the sponsor was offering the audience a transparent lens into everyday life. • Harley Davidson used product design, staged events, and sponsorship to create the notion that Harley's heart remains in the 1950s.
Stealth branding	Companies seek out the allegiance of tastemakers who will use their influence to diffuse the idea that the firm's brand has cultural value.	• Products placed in popular television programs or films or used by hired celebrities or anyone deemed to have social influence, ranging from barflies to sociable people with lots of friends.

Source: Holt. 2002. Why do brands cause trouble? A dialectical theory of consumer culture and branding. *Journal of Consumer Research* 29(1):70–91.

Capital Circle Northeast. In this location, there exists a community of morning coffee drinkers who meet regularly. The only criterion for joining this community is that you eat or drink something from Bruegger's. Some community members buy Bruegger's mugs that identify them. On December 27, 2005, this Bruegger's community had its first wedding. Two early morning swimmers were introduced, found they had much in common, and fell in love. They hosted their 6:30 A.M. wedding at Bruegger's, after an early morning swim. Bruegger's coffee and bagel sandwiches were served at the reception, which was attended by more than 100 people. The newly married Browns gave their guests Bruegger's coffee mugs as mementos of their wedding. The newlyweds continue to have coffee at Bruegger's regularly.

Brands allow consumers to experience and express the social world (Holt 2002). Consumers seek cultural guidance from companies. Postmodern marketing positions the brand as a cultural resource and a useful ingredient in creating the self and expressing the lifestyle that a consumer chooses. Table 2.2 shows techniques and strategies for branding in a postmodern market. Branded cultural resources should be perceived as authentic. The brands need to be created and offered by companies that are intrinsically motivated by their inherent value, rather than an economic agenda.

Niketown at Oxford Circus in London exemplifies postmodern retailing. Nike's retail operation has successfully linked its products to lifestyles. The center of the store displays a multi-floor collage of pictures of people participating in sports activities. Niketown's collage depicts the cultural and inherent value of its products. These pictures illustrate an image of sports and Nike products that evolve throughout consumers' lifetimes, but remain part of their identities.

Brands should also be incorporated in cultural epicenters or communities focused around an aspect of popular culture, such as stores that sell knitting yarns. Knitting is a retro hobby in these stressful times (Schatz 2003). Celebrity knitters include Julia Roberts and author Suss Cousins. CDs, videos, books, and magazines such as *Hollywood Knits* teach consumers how to knit. Stores such as New York's Yarn Company create a place for knitters and wannabe knitters. The store targets customers in their twenties and thirties. Supplies are sold and knitting classes are offered so consumers can buy and experience the products, which fosters a knitting community where knitters can meet and speak with like-minded people.

To meet consumer need for community, managers can create marketplaces or common places through the use of servicescape. Servicescape, or the physical environment, influences consumer behavior by "encouraging and nurturing particular forms of social interaction among customers" (Aubert-Gamet and Cova 1999, 37). Barker (1968) suggested that repeated social behavior patterns can be associated with a particular setting, and when a particular person encounters a typical setting, his or her social behavior can be predicted. Thus, community encounters are associated with particular service settings. Consequently, companies need to create servicescapes that provide community encounters where consumers can meet through the use of nooks and corners within the business (Aubert-Gamet and Cova 1999). In addition, servicescapes could include events or incidents such as art exhibits or live musical performances that bring people together (Aubert-Gamet and Cova 1999).

DIMENSIONS OF CONSUMPTION

Consumers evaluate consumption dimensions or individual attributes that describe their relative importance in the consumer decision-making process when considering a purchase. Important dimensions of consumption are social personalities, possession attachment, leisure, luxury, technology, and energy.

Social Personalities

Social personalities are associated with the types of personality people project in public. The chameleon personality, acquired in childhood and reinforced in adulthood, exists in all sectors of our society (Rosen 1998) and has four components: chameleonism or core traits, narcissism, hedonism, and perfectionism. The chameleon wants to please and blends into the larger group. Sometimes the chameleon is obsessed with others' opinions. The narcissist may create a fictional character to fool others. The hedonist finds pleasurable consumption acceptable, but not self-denial and frugality. The perfectionist wants to satisfy his or her needs and fulfill his or her genetic potential. Thus appearance, manners, power, and status are important to the perfectionist (Rosen 1998). Retailers have developed strategies such as lifestyle marketing and branding in response to these types of social personalities.

Possession Attachment

As goods take on symbolic meanings, possession attachment develops. Kleine and Baker (2004) defined possession attachment as a "multi-faceted property of the relationship between a specific individual or group of individuals and a specific, material object that an individual has psychologically appropriated, decommodified, and singularized through person-object interaction" (1). Possession attachment has nine characteristics: specific material goods oriented, not centered, on product categories or brands; psychologically appropriate goods; extension of self; decommodification and singularization of goods; personal history between people and possessions; strong; multifaceted; emotionally complex; and evolution of meaning as the self changes (Kleine and Baker 2004). Attachment has three forms: place, brands, and experience.

Retailers can use these ideas about possession attachment when developing marketing offers to consumers. Cold Stone Creamery uses the ideas to turn a childhood commodity, ice cream, into a consumption experience, an ice-cream creation. Shoppers select their ice-cream flavor and extras such as candies, fruits, or marshmallows, and watch entertaining servers mix the ingredients on a frozen granite stone. Cold Stone Creamery allows consumers to participate in the production of the ice-cream creation and develop possession attachment because of their relationship with what they eat. They've participated in designing the finished product. Each one is unique and will never again be created.

Leisure

The commercialization of leisure time is linked to the importance of shopping to tourists. For many tourists, shopping is the largest significant expenditure on holiday vacations or trips (Oh, Cheng, Lehto, and O'Leary 2004). This leisure time contributes to situations where tourists' shopping behaviors are different from their rational and ordinary behaviors. Tourists are in a unique environment where the stimulation is out of the ordinary; so in a sense they consume the place. This hedonic or emotional consumption is facilitated by uniqueness, attractive shops, a range of goods sold, and the ambience of stores. Souvenir buying is one outcome of the consumer's consumption of a tourist location. Tourists buy souvenirs in all product categories. Oh, et al (2004) studied shopping during tourism trips and found 50.2 percent of tourist shoppers visited book and music stores; 39.3 percent visited antiques

shops; 27.2 percent visited gourmet food stores; 48.4 percent visited local arts and crafts shops; and 53.9 percent visited clothes, shoes, and jewelry shops. Littrell, Paige, and Song (2004) found older consumers aged 50 and up participated in value shopping, particularly at malls, as part of their tourism activities.

A current trend in the United States is development projects that merge leisure, historic venues, and retail. These projects are designed to meet the wants of the populations they serve and are customized according to the region. For example, Midwestern consumers are tired of the same shopping environments; they want something fresh and new (Field 2005). New retail concepts and destination retail formats are introduced to Kansas City residents in the Legends shopping center. Retail offerings include Cavender's Western apparel and experience store, Jimmy Buffet's Cheeseburger in Paradise, Off Broadway Shoe Warehouse, and a themed restaurant concept T-Rex Cafe (new from Rainforest Cafe founder Steve Schussler).

Luxury

Personal wealth and household incomes increased during the last half of the twentieth century and the beginning of the new millennium. People with annual household incomes of more than $100,000 increased to 15 percent in 2004 from 4 percent in 1989 (U.S. Census Bureau 2004). The increasing number of affluent consumers pushes the luxury market to grow.

Luxury is perceived differently among varied groups. Encino, a California-based online research firm, surveyed a nationally representative sample of 876 adults to assess how consumers' definitions of luxury vary by gender, ethnicity, and age. Significant differences were found among these groups. For instance, Caucasian consumers (53 percent) were more likely to define luxury as something prestigious or

TABLE 2.3 DEFINITION OF LUXURY

	MEN	WOMEN	18–34	35–54	55+	BLACK	HISPANIC	WHITE
Glamorous/classic/elegant	67%	73%	72%	66%	74%	69%	64%	72%
Comforting/relaxing/pampering	55%	54%	52%	56%	54%	38%	51%	58%
Status symbol/exclusive/prestigious	51%	51%	39%	50%	57%	43%	41%	53%
Wasteful/unnecessary/extravagant	27%	19%	19%	28%	19%	32%	14%	23%
Trendy/fashionable/in	21%	23%	26%	19%	24%	30%	33%	18%
Flashy/gaudy/elitist	28%	12%	37%	22%	10%	**	31%	16%
Practical/quality/enduring	14%	18%	**	15%	20%	**	**	18%

**Sample size too small
Note: Columns do not total 100 percent because more than one answer was allowed.
Source: Gardyn, R. 2002. Oh, the good life. *American Demographics* 24(10):30–35.

exclusive than were African Americans (43 percent) or Hispanics (41 percent). On the contrary, Hispanics (33 percent) and African Americans (30 percent) were almost twice as likely as Caucasians (18 percent) to define luxury as trendy or fashionable. Definition of luxury also varied by consumer age. Among older consumers (people ages 55 or older), 74 percent associated luxury with elegance. Luxury was also defined as flashy or elitist by 37 percent of the Gen X/Y group (people ages 18 to 34) and 22 percent of baby boomers (people ages 35 to 54), compared with only 10 percent for the older consumers (Gardyn 2002). Surprisingly, baby boomers (28 percent) were more likely to think of luxury as being wasteful or unnecessary than either Gen X/Y or older consumers (19 percent). Detailed information is shown in Table 2.3.

A consumer's motivation for luxury spending is associated with personality and state of mind, as well as with demographic characteristics. SRI Consulting Business Intelligence (SRIC-BI), a firm based in Menlo Park, California, identified three distinct mindsets that drive the majority of luxury spending. As shown in Table 2.4, the three groups view luxury as functional, a reward, or indulgence. The Legends shopping center (www.legendsshopping.com) in Kansas City houses retailers and services that are a combination of functional, reward, and indulgence. Legends shopping center has the specialty food retailer Harry and David, which offers customers the opportunity to send out personalized gift boxes to friends and family. Customers who take a break from shopping at Legends can eat, as well as shop, at the T-Rex Cafe, which is an interactive prehistoric experience.

Technology and Energy

Since World War II, retail assortment and formats have evolved thanks to technological innovation. Technology facilitates supply management and distribution, as well as shopping experiences. Consumers can shop 24 hours a day, 7 days a week at brick-and-mortar stores, on televisions, at kiosks, by mail, and online. Technology allows retailers to customize offerings for specific target groups. QVC, an electronic retailer, developed divisions for the Gen X and the active 18- to 24-year-old markets (Gruen 1994).

TABLE 2.4 LUXURY CONSUMER GROUPS

LUXURY CONSUMER GROUP	DESCRIPTION
Luxury is functional	This group tends to buy luxury products for their superior functionality and quality. Consumers in this segment, the largest of the three, tend to be older and wealthier and are willing to spend more money to buy things that will last and have enduring value. These consumers buy a wide array of luxury goods, from luxury automobiles to artwork and vacations. They conduct extensive pre-purchase research and make logical decisions rather than emotional or impulsive decisions. Messages that highlight product quality and are information-intensive are powerful with this group.
Luxury is a reward	These consumers tend to be younger than the first group but older than the third group. They often use luxury goods as status symbols or to say *I've made it*. The desire to be successful and to demonstrate their success to others motivates these consumers to purchase conspicuous luxury items, such as luxury automobiles and homes in exclusive communities. Luxury brands that have widespread recognition are popular with this segment. Yet, this segment is also concerned that owning luxury goods might make them appear lavish or hedonistic, especially in these economic times. They want to purchase smart luxury that demonstrates their importance, while not leaving them open to criticism. Marketing messages that communicate acceptable exclusivity resonate with this group.
Luxury is indulgence	This group is the smallest of the three and tends to include younger consumers and slightly more males than the other two groups. To these consumers, the purpose of owning luxury is to be extremely lavish and self-indulgent. This group is willing to pay a premium for goods that express their individuality and make others take notice. These consumers are not overly concerned with product quality or longevity or with the possibility that others might criticize their purchases. Rather, they enjoy luxury for the way it makes them feel—if a product makes them feel good, they will likely make the purchase. These consumers have a more emotional approach to luxury spending and are more likely than the other two groups to make impulse purchases. They respond well to messages that highlight the unique and emotional qualities of a product.

Source: Gardyn, R. 2002. Oh, the good life. *American Demographics* 24(10):30–35.

As a result of new technology and its use, modern consumer societies are energy intensive. Electricity has become the dominant energy form. However, other energy sources and their costs influence shopping behavior. Gable and Mathis (1983) analyzed data from the 1979 gasoline crisis and found that high prices and shortages negatively affected retail sales. Between August 2004 and 2005, consumers paid 26 percent more for increased gas prices (Johnson 2005). During the summer of 2005, gasoline prices increased 17 percent. Increased gasoline prices are expected to impact lower-income consumers and retailers serving them more than other consumer and retail groups. Low-income shoppers are expected to reduce the number of times they visit stores. Mass merchants such as Target lost more than 2 percent of total sales, which was blamed on gasoline price increases (Ostroff 2005).

DIVERSITY AND POSTWAR CONSUMPTION AND RETAIL

Sociodemographic changes after World War II impacted consumption and created a diverse and fragmented retail market. Diversity in ethnicity, generation, gender, and sexual orientation contributes to the vast assortment of consumer experiences in the United States. World War II changed the flavor of grocery shopping: "Soldiers returning from wartime contact with European cooking customs brought home new food tastes" (*New York Times* 1953, 13). Travel and exposure to other cultures contribute to what was available in U.S. stores: "The postwar rise in American tourist travel also has meant many persons have been introduced to new taste experiences" (*New York Times* 1953, 13).

Increasing population diversity creates additional retail sales opportunities that can be addressed through retail marketing strategies, product development, and delivery formats. To determine consumer target market opportunities, a variety of demographic segmentation techniques exist. The popular segmentation parameters include ethnicity, age, and gender. Sexual orientation has emerged as another dimension that influences consumer behavior. In this section, the four major parameters of ethnicity, generation, gender, and sexual orientation are discussed.

Ethnicity

Hispanics and Asians began immigrating to the United States in larger numbers after World War II and experienced faster growth in size and buying power than other ethnic groups. It is well noted that the three main ethnic minority groups in the United States—African Americans, Hispanic Americans, and Asian Americans—exhibit different consumption patterns from Caucasians; differences exist among the three groups as well.

AFRICAN AMERICANS

Prior to desegregation in the United States, African Americans encountered injustice regarding goods and appearances. In response to bigotry, there were a series of boycotts of white-owned stores in the early 1960s by many in the African American community. The boycotts put pressure on merchants to eliminate racially unequal treatment. Slogans such as "Don't Buy Segregation" (Morris 2002) were used in protests. African American protesters wanted more employment opportunities, better wages, and more respectful treatment for shoppers.

Sabir and Brown (2005) reported that African American households experienced a decline in earnings during times of eco-

nomic recession, but they have made up for it during economic recoveries since the 1980s. Furthermore, during the late 1990s, African Americans and Caucasians realized substantial increases in family incomes. During this period, employment rates rose dramatically for African Americans. In 2000, reduced unemployment, along with increased wages, contributed to higher African American family incomes. Although family income ratios between African Americans and Caucasians have increased throughout the past decade from 0.54 in 1990 to 0.58 in 2000, there is still a visible racial gap in family income (Sabir and Brown 2005). This gap may be due to the fact that "African Americans are less likely to be married and are more likely to have families headed by females than are whites" (Sabir and Brown 2005, 30). This wealth gap between African American and Caucasian family incomes has become larger since the 2001 recession (Sabir and Brown 2005).

The growing African American market is important to retailers. In 2002, this market represented almost 37 million consumers, or 12.7 percent of the total U.S. population of 288.4 million. This market is expected to increase to 13.3 percent of the population by 2010 and 13.8 percent by 2020. According to the 2000 U.S. Census, the average African American consumer is approximately five years younger when compared with the population mean of 35.5 years of age (Ahmed 2003).

The Selig Center for Economic Growth reported that in 2004, African American buying power rose to $723 billion from $585 billion in 2000. The report projected that African Americans could have $965 billion in buying power by 2009, up 203 percent from 1990 (Holmes 2005). The growing consumption power of the African American demographic makes it a viable marketing target for businesses.

The African American market is not homogenous and can be segmented, as with any other market. Advertising content and products should be selected accordingly. African American women head one third of all family households, which makes them an important group to target (Ahmed 2003). They also influence the purchase of expensive items such as cars and houses (Yin 2003).

The current generation of African Americans has achieved middle-class status in larger numbers and aspires to a higher standard of living. Appeals for success, achievement, and aspirations of becoming more affluent resonate within this group (Ahmed 2003). The rising education level among African Americans means they are likely to be demanding consumers.

Though price conscious, African Americans are motivated by product quality and choice. African Americans tend to be fashion-conscious and choose to spend money on clothing and accessories. African Americans also show a strong preference for branded goods, shop more frequently, shop more with friends, and enjoy shopping, even when they do not purchase anything (Freifeld 2005, *License!* 2006). The Selig Center for Economic Growth found that African Americans spend more than the average U.S. consumer on telephone services, shoes, personal care products, and children's apparel but less on health care, reading materials, entertainment, and household textiles (Holmes 2005).

Many marketers believe marketing targeted at African Americans remains most effective with the use of African American celebrities, event sponsorship, grassroots marketing, and community involvement as integral parts of the campaign (*License!* 2006). Retailers also need to provide quality brand-name products that appeal more to female customers. Brands developed for African American women include *Black Radiance* and *Shades for You*.

HISPANIC AMERICANS

The Hispanic population is increasing much faster than the general U.S. population, with Hispanic births accounting for half of all U.S. births (Moran 2005). The Hispanic population increased from 21 million in 1990 to 40 million in 2003. Hispanics have surpassed African Americans as the nation's largest minority group. The number of Hispanics will continue to grow, reaching nearly 73 million, or 20 percent of the U.S. population, by 2030 (U.S. Census Bureau 2004).

The Hispanic market is young; 35 percent is 18 years or younger (Moran 2005). They are geographically concentrated, with about half of all Hispanics living in six U.S. cities—Chicago, Houston, San Antonio, Miami, New York, and Los Angeles. Currently, about 46 percent of Hispanics has a high school diploma or some college education. As their educational levels increase, so does their demand for consumer goods, as well as their purchasing power. From 1996 to 2001, the average Hispanic household income rose 20 percent, from $27,977 to $33,565, while annual household income of the U.S. population grew 6 percent from $39,869 to $42,228 (*Brand Strategy* 2004).

The Hispanic market is fragmented and complex. While Mexicans represent a large number of U.S. Hispanics, increasing numbers come from Central and South America and Caribbean countries such as Cuba and Jamaica (*Brand Strategy* 2004).

Language is an important characteristic of Hispanic consumers. About 96 percent of Hispanics uses some Spanish at home and 86 percent uses it either at work or at school (Humphreys 2004). Hispanics feel more included when retailers employ bilingual associates and when they provide advertisements and store signage in Spanish (Humphreys 2004). As a result, they are more likely to patronize retailers who make these cultural adaptations. In addition, many Hispanics equate the ability of store employees to speak Spanish with friendliness (Humphreys 2004).

An important factor for retailers to keep in mind while marketing to Hispanics and any other ethnic groups is their level of acculturation. The most acculturated Hispanics might show characteristics similar to American consumers. Donthu and Cherian (1994) found that Hispanics with a strong attachment to their traditions and culture were more likely to seek Hispanic vendors, were more loyal to brands preferred by family and friends, were influenced by targeted media, preferred to shop as a family, and tended to be more concerned about monetary costs than Hispanics with greater levels of acculturation. Eastlick and Lotz (2000) found that first-generation Hispanic Americans were more attracted to retailers whose merchandise reflects the Hispanic culture and showed greater preferences for the use of Spanish-language media than other generational groups. To this Hispanic consumer group, retailers could provide culturally oriented merchandise, Spanish-speaking customer service personnel, and bilingual and culturally oriented advertising. Retailers could also focus on providing value by offering competitive pricing, coupons, promotions, and liberal return policies (Eastlick and Lotz 2000).

Retail initiatives that target Hispanic consumers are becoming more popular every year. Retailers should recognize Hispanic cultural celebrations, such as the 15th birthday (quinceañera) celebration for Hispanic girls (the equivalent of the U.S. sweet sixteen). Brands are also important to Hispanic consumers, which can be seen in the conspicuous consumption of brand logo merchandise. Home Depot recently established a partnership with four national Hispanic organizations, which was aimed at recruiting more Spanish-speaking employees (*Associated Press* 2005) as a means of targeting Hispanic consumers. Wal-Mart also caters to the Hispanic market with their extended produce assortment, including peppers, Mexican cheeses, and meats preferred by Latinos (e.g., Chorizo Sausage and Milanesa Beef).

ASIAN AMERICANS

As of the 2000 U.S. Census, there were approximately 10.2 million Asian Americans in the United States. This number is expected to increase 33 percent (mostly through immigration) by 2010, resulting in more than 14 million Asian Americans. This will make the Asian American population more than 5 percent of the total U.S. population (Ahmed 2005). This market segment has annual purchasing power of $254 billion; the average Asian American consumer is 30.1 years old, which is younger than the general U.S. population. The average household size is 3.8 people, larger than the overall U.S. family mean of 3.2 people (Gitlin 2002).

Although the Asian American population is one third the size of the Hispanic population, their buying potential of $397 billion is more than half that of Hispanics ($686.3 billion) and is projected to reach $579 billion by 2010. It is predicted that between 1990 and 2010, the gain in Asian American buying potential (near 400 percent) will be substantially greater than the gains projected for Caucasians (164 percent) and African Americans (222 percent) (Reyes 2006).

Though many Asian Americans are immigrants, this consumer group has the highest annual household income and educational attainment among the three major ethnic groups in the United States (*Best's Review* 2005). Despite the relatively small size of this ethnic population, many companies, particularly financial services and insurance, consider this market a very attractive consumer segment because of their younger age, larger household size, and the higher proportion of married households with children (Ahmed 2005). In addition, higher levels of education and higher household incomes make them the prime targets for these types of services. Further, there are unusually high rates of entrepreneurial activity found in the Asian American market segment. Overall, Asian American consumers share core values such as safety, education, and reverence for elders and they value brand names and are brand-loyal and cost-conscious (Kaufman-Scarborough 2000).

Similar to the Hispanic market segment, the Asian American market is fragmented, since it is made up of people from a variety of countries. About 89 percent of the Asian American market is made up of consumers from six countries—China, the Philippines, India, Vietnam, Korea, and Japan (Gitlin 2002). The diversity within the Asian American population includes different countries of origin, different languages, and different cultures. Also, acculturation rate and the length of time a family has lived in the United States influence whether or not Asian Americans want English-language messages.

Asian Americans tend to be geographically concentrated in major metropolitan markets in several states such as California, New York, Hawaii, Washington, D.C., Texas, Illinois, and Georgia. Therefore, they could be targeted along geographic lines. However, in an attempt to address each of these Asian subgroups, companies need to invest in strategies that have a high likelihood of succeeding at the local level. For example, using selective print or cable TV channels could target a specific ethnic group. In many cases, companies are reaching out to the specific ethnic groups by using language in the native tongue for media (Ahmed 2005). In recognition of the importance of the Asian American buying potential, Wal-Mart developed television, print, and radio advertisements in several languages to appeal to this market (Troy 2005). Consumers' testimonials about shopping at Wal-Mart were aired in Cantonese, Mandarin, Vietnamese, and English.

Marketers are beginning to use multicultural marketing agencies that specialize in understanding the Asian market. The number of such agencies rose from 3 in 1989 to more than 50 (Reyes 2006). One of the first marketing firms in the 1980s that began targeting Asian consumers in the telecommunications, auto, retail, and finance industries was InterTrend. Some InterTrend clients include Northwest Airlines, JC Penney, State Farm Insurance, Western Union, Toyota, and Verizon. These companies were pioneers in targeting Asian immigrants with in-language advertising, sales promotions, and outreach during Asian holidays such as the Vietnam Tet Festival and the Chinese New Year.

However, Asian Americans still receive a small percentage of the marketing resources allocated for multicultural marketing in the United States. Most marketers in 2004 aimed at Hispanics ($3.9 billion) and African Americans ($1.7 billion) and dedicated only $100 million to Asian Americans (Reyes 2006). It seems that many U.S. companies have left the Asian consumer market largely untapped (Reyes 2006). Marketers need more research to better understand the shopping behaviors of the Asian consumer.

Generation

Consumers can be classified by generation, developmental stage, and marketing segment. In the United States, consumers are classified as generations of baby boomers,

Generation X, Generation Y, and Generation Z; the developmental stages of teens and emerging adults; and the market segments of twixters, echo boomers, tweens, and tinies. The manner in which consumers are categorized may influence the approach a retailer takes to create meaningful experiences and offer desired products and services.

BABY BOOMERS

Baby boomers—people born between 1946 and 1964—are the largest consumer segment at 78 million. They represent 27.5 percent of the U.S. population (U.S. Census Bureau 2006). They were part of a philosophical and cultural awakening that created a more open-minded generation. As the most significant proportion of the population, they represent 42 percent of all U.S. households and control half of the wealth in the United States (Matorin 2003). More than $2 trillion in income and in excess of 50 percent of discretionary spending power is accounted for by the more-than-50-years-of-age market (Consumer Trends Institute 2003).

Generations who lived before World War II were the keepers of family traditions and passed down practical knowledge about living frugally. They had personal memories of living without and in need. Today's baby boomers, as well as younger generations, are rapidly losing touch with this cultural memory of hardship. Instead, they are consumers who express their wants, desires, and dreams in their consumption behavior.

Although they are growing older, the impact of baby boomers on consumer spending can hardly be overstated. Baby boomers have changed the notion of middle age. As baby boomers refuse to age, they are trying to look, act, and feel younger. For example, many female boomers attempt to make their faces wrinkle-free with the help of Botox, while many male boomers seek out the benefits of Viagra. Additionally, baby boomers spend a great proportion of money on hair coloring, health club memberships, and personalized vitamins (Francese 2003). This is reflected in a noticeable trend in the media market where baby boomers are shown looking, acting, and feeling younger. They are active in sports, exercise, and healthy living. They volunteer at inner-city schools, serve on corporate boards, build houses for Habitat for Humanity, electronically trade stocks from their home offices, or take art history courses at local colleges (Consumer Trends Institute 2003). In the 2002 New York City Marathon, 40 percent of the runners were between 40 and 54 years old (Nayyer 2002). As a large number of boomers continues to age, boomers will need more assistance with their finances, retirement planning, and asset management.

GENERATION X

Generation X refers to consumers born between 1965 and 1976. They treat time as a premium commodity and often outsource the tasks of daily life (*The Gen X Budget* 2002). Much of their budget is designated to personal services. Retailers offering housecleaning services and convenience foods can capitalize on this time-starved consumer segment.

The three things that typically represent the good life to Gen X are home, a happy marriage, and children. Their necessities include cell phones, PDAs, and other time-saving gadgets that make their lives easier. This group, formerly self-sufficient latchkey kids, tend to sneer at attempts to get them to make purchases. They know how to consume, buy, and say no. While Gen X men are more involved in home decisions than boomer men, women are still the primary decision makers when it comes to purchases for the home. Overall Gen X consumers are less brand-loyal than boomers, shopping at both high-end stores and discount shops and seeking quality products and effective customer service. They are well-informed consumers; they pre-shop online and then shop at brick-and-mortar stores (DeBaugh 2003).

Online retailers such as www.bluefly.com cater to the changing needs of Gen X consumers who want high-end merchandise at below-retail cost. Bluefly.com offers designer brand items such as Prada handbags and Manolo Blahnik shoes. Customers of this online retailer can expect to pay around 35 percent less for these items than they would at department stores.

Gen X consumers think for themselves, are determined, and reject dogma associated with institutions and traditions (Morton 2003). They are likely to make judgments about people based on character instead of ethnicity or gender. They determine their own morality and question authority. Most Gen Xers do not want to be grouped, labeled, or categorized. They romanticize the 1950s American lifestyle and buy homes at a faster rate than boomers since they have dual income earnings (Scally 1999). For this generation, purchasing a home is a sign of their individuality, not of their material success. They want their homes to reflect their personalities and style and are interested in home-improvement and repair projects.

GENERATION Y, EMERGING ADULTS, AND TWIXTERS

Generation Y, emerging adults, and twixters refer to young adults who are generally ages 18 to 25 (Ritchie 1995). This segment is the oldest group of Generation Y and were born between 1977 and 1993, grew up in a digital revolution, and are technologically savvy. A unique and profitable opportunity exists to target these younger consumers as they achieve increasing disposable income and begin setting up households both as singles and as parts of young families.

Emerging adulthood represents a developmental stage. These young adults exhibit a higher degree of demographic diversity and instability (Arnett 2000). In the marketplace, their substantial buying power generates new consumption patterns that exert a major influence on their consumption behavior in later life (Olshavsky and Granbois 1979). These young adults use experimentation and exploration to extend their individual sense of identity. Among ethnic young adults, emerging adulthood is even more critical because it is a period where ethnic identity is established and expanded. As an essential component of the ethnic young adult's social identity, ethnic identity becomes a central element in developing self-concept and self-image (Phinney and Rosenthal 1992).

Twixters is the marketing term for the social phenomenon of the intermediate transitional life stage between adolescence and adulthood. The product of U.S. affluence and social liberation, twixters are also referred to as *youthhood, adultescence, kidults, boomerang kids,* and *thresholders.* These young adults have not settled into jobs, careers, or familial responsibilities. In many cases they still live with their parents, a percentage that has almost doubled from 11 percent in 1970 to 20 percent in 2005 (Grossman 2005). Twixters tend to hop from job to job and have greater interest in their careers and immediate gratification. They are getting married later with marriage postponed to the late twenties or into the thirties. In lieu of marriage, they develop especially strong friendship networks. The TV show *Friends* depicts the life of twixters. They are the optimum electronics consumers and seek exotic vacations and couture fashions. Twixters represent a new life stage that society has not yet adjusted to through cultural change (Grossman 2005).

GENERATION Y, TEENS, AND ECHO BOOMERS

Generation Y, teens, and Echo Boomers are ages 13 to 17. They are the most consumer-savvy segment ever in the United States. They have significant influence over their parents' purchasing decisions (Meyers 2004). This group represents more than one third of the 71 million children born to baby boomers in the United States (Kids age segmentation 2002).

The Internet is a prime entertainment and information site for teens who have global interests. In comparing media usage, Yahoo! UK and Ireland found that teens spent an average of 16.7 hours a week on the net compared with 13.6 hours viewing TV and 7.7 hours using the phone. The main reasons teens go online is to access entertainment (56 percent) and for music (47 percent) (Bashford 2004).

In 2003, teens spent about $10 billion on personal care and cosmetics. Teens are savvy consumers and more sophisticated than what many marketers expect (Serviss 2004). The designer of the new cosmetic line Candy Care, which targets teens, stated: "It's important to offer something that is different, fun, and also promotes good health and grooming habits" (Serviss 2004, 26). One of the most effective tools for Cover Girl cosmetics is the Internet, where they offer basic information about makeup application and skin care and interactive tools (Serviss 2004). Even upscale companies are targeting the teen market. Chanel created the new fragrance Chance for 14- to 24-year-old consumers—the youngest age group it has ever targeted. Its media campaign included MTV; TV advertising for programs such as *Buffy the Vampire Slayer, Friends,* and *Dream Team*; magazines *Elle Girl, Bliss, 19,* and *B*; and cinema packages (*Marketing* 2003).

In the United States, Hispanic youths ages 12 to 19 represent 14 percent of the total Hispanic population and 13.6 percent of all U.S. teens. By 2005, they made up the single largest ethnic minority youth population in the United States (Stapinski 1999). Through fashion, music, dance, and media, Hispanic teens are changing the cultural landscape of mainstream America. Marketers who can translate Latino youth culture to a mass audience could be very successful. "It's hard to capture the essence of Hispanic teens in one product in terms of clothing and music," explained Angelo Figueroa, editor of the fast-growing *People en Español.* "Hispanic teens are culturally all very, very different, unlike African American teens in the U.S. who are basically listening to the same kind of music. You have to walk this fine line to make sure it appeals equally to all these groups" (Stapinski 1999, 68).

Capturing and positioning Hispanic soul in fashion can lead to success in the marketplace. The forecast for U.S. fashions is a Tommy Hilfiger–like fashion explosion that draws from Latino trends. Latin-influenced fashions are being adopted by mainstream teens. Garments such as the boxy, lightweight, short-sleeved *Guayabera* shirts, originally worn by older Cuban men, became hip dress for teens everywhere. Some Latino teens immediately identify with baseball shirts sporting the number 77, which is the former area code for Puerto Rico. Straw hats, Che Guevara T-shirts, and embroidered feminine clothes were picked up by U.S. apparel retailers such as Urban Outfitters and Bebe (Stapinski 1999). Cosmetics are especially important among urban Latina teens and women. Cosmetics have gained general popularity. Compared with all teen girls, Hispanic girls spend 60 percent more on makeup, 50 percent more on acne products, and more than twice as much on hair products (Stapinski 1999).

GENERATION Z AND TWEENS

Generation Z and tweens are pre- and early adolescents ages 8 to 14, which in the

2000 U.S. census represented a population of 29 million (Kennedy 2004). Generation Z is a classification for consumers who were born after 1993. This generation group is smaller than Generation Y but larger than Generation X. Gen Zs are characterized by an unprecedented access to information, an exceedingly diverse ethnic makeup, and "a more varied family background than has been experienced in recent history" (Wellner 2000, 63). This generation will be considered Generation 1-to-1 because of their access to mass customization in every aspect of their lives from school classrooms to custom-fit shoes (Wellner 2000). They are discerning consumers but seem to notice brands that harness the power of celebrity (Kennedy 2004).

Tweens is a marketing term where the defined age spread often varies by product category. If only youngsters ages 8 to 12 are included, this population is still a formidable 20.9 million. This age segment may be the youngest true consumer group (See Table 2.5). Tweens are more self-aware and exhibit more independence from their parents (Mummert 2004). Thus, the tween market is a crucial, and possibly last, chance for retailers to build loyalty before these young consumers rebel against choices imposed on them by their parents (Duff 2002).

Tweens are noted for their spending enthusiasm (Romano 2004). A wide range of industries cater to this age group, including media, fashion, personal hygiene, and magazine and book publishers. Tweens have enormous buying power when their personal purchasing power of $38 billion is added to the nearly $126 billion that their parents spend on them. Tweens seek products and services that help them define themselves. They tend to

TABLE 2.5 EARLY STAGES OF CONSUMER DEVELOPMENT LEADING TO TWEENS AS CONSUMERS

AGE OF CHILD IN MONTHS	STAGE OF CONSUMER DEVELOPMENT	CONSUMER BEHAVIOR
2	Observation	• Form impressions of brandscape through smell, touch, taste, sight, and sound. • Use olfactory senses to construct first images of environment.
24	Requesting	• Ask for products when in their presence. • Request items such as cereal by name.
42	Selection	• Retrieve products from store shelves as the result of more experience and better motor skills.
66	I want to do it myself	• Attempt to purchase products on their own with parents' help and encouragement.
96–100 (tweens)	Independent	• Buy products independent of parents. • Start to reason like adults. • Exhibit cognitive maturity by understanding the perspective of others. • Tend to be naive and trusting. • Understand merchants own the goods. • Understand they must exchange money for goods. • Understand advertisers are promoting products so they will buy them.

Source: All the small world's a stage. 2001. *Brandweek*. April 16, 24.

TABLE 2.6 ANNUAL FAMILY EXPENDITURES ON FOOD, CLOTHING, PERSONAL-CARE ITEMS, ENTERTAINMENT, AND READING MATERIALS FOR 8- TO 14-YEAR-OLDS BY PERCENT OF TOTAL FOR EACH AGE GROUP, 2001 ($ VALUES IN MILLIONS)

AGE GROUP	FOOD		CLOTHING		PERSONAL-CARE ITEMS, ENTERTAINMENT AND READING MATERIALS		TOTAL	
	AMOUNT	% OF TOTAL	AMOUNT	% OF TOTAL	AMOUNT	% OF TOTAL	AMOUNT	% OF TOTAL
8–11	$33.605	27	$9.916	8	$23.661	19	$67.183	53
12–14	$26.728	21	$12.248	10	$19.660	16	$58.636	47
Total	$60.333	48	$22.164	18	$43.321	35	$125.818	100

Note: Food expenses include food and nonalcoholic beverages purchased at grocery, convenience, and specialty stores, including purchases with food stamps, dining at restaurants, and household expenditures on school meals. Clothing expenditures include children's apparel, such as shirts, pants, dresses, and suits, footwear, and clothing services, such as dry cleaning, alterations and repair, and storage.
Source: U.S. Department of Agriculture. Expenditures on Children by Families. 2001 Annual Report: Packaged Facts, a publishing division of MarketResearch.com.

have brand preferences and like books and music. Girls, however, tend to be attracted more to apparel, beauty products, and magazines while boys want electronics and games and are just starting to be interested in apparel (Mummert 2004). Table 2.6 summarizes annual family expenditures for food, clothing, personal care items, entertainment, and reading materials. Almost 50 percent of total spending in households with tweens is spent on food purchases (Kennedy 2004). This suggests an important opportunity for food companies to target this age group.

Important influences on the tween market are movies, TV, and rock stars. Publishers are taking note with an explosion among tweens for reading. Book series such as *A Series of Unfortunate Events* by Lemony Snicket published by Harper-Collins Children's Books target this age group. HarperEntertainment's *New Adventures of Mary-Kate and Ashley Olsen Series* shipped about 6 million books in 2002. The Mary-Kate and Ashley brand produced in excess of $1 billion for other tween-targeted consumer products (Maughan 2002). Wal-Mart carries Mary-

Kate and Ashley branded junior apparel and a 165-product line of cosmetics, hair care products, and hair care appliances marketed as Real Beauty for Real Girls (*DSN Retailing Today* 2002). Kmart offers a fashion-oriented (not character-oriented) Disney brand for tweens that was unveiled at its Austin Place, New York City, store (Duff 2002). Disney Channel is associated with a Lizzie McGuire book series. The popularity of Scholastic's *Harry Potter* series by J. K. Rowling and its spin-offs into movies, video games, action toys, Legos, and apparel is just one example of how a book creates multiple consumer experiences across product categories. Moreover, the popularity of the *Harry Potter* series has created crossover reading among this age group. The Internet is a major medium that publishers are using to attract tweens' attention. Tyndale Kids (www.cool2read.com) allows tweens to share messages and learn how to be active in their communities. Disney uses online marketing such as e-cards and contests to attract tween consumers (Maughan 2002).

Tweens are a complex age group due to the somewhat radical differences

between genders in their preferences for entertainment and consumer products. Although tweens like reality TV such as Discovery Kid's *Trading Spaces: Boys vs. Girls* and ABC Family *Knock First*, animé (See Figure 2.1), *Pokémon*, and *Dragon Ball Z* are popular with boys (Romano 2004). Icons are important as decorative elements, and tweens particularly look to Japanese animé such as *Yu-Gi-Oh!* (Hisey 2001). Nickelodeon has a spin-off cable channel, The N, which is aimed at tweens and teens. Entertainment companies such as Disney Channel Entertainment are addressing these differences through programming that creates aspirations and shows that appeal to 9- to 11-year-olds but use older stars such as Lizzie McGuire and Raven (Romano 2004).

A major change for tweens compared with past generations is their fascination with electronics. It is not uncommon to see a tween with a cell phone, portable CD player, electronic game like Nintendo's Game Boy, or even a PDA. Carrying these electronic accessories has created an entirely new market for wearable accessories and has influenced traditional products such as backpacks and belts (Hisey 2001). Sixty-two percent of tweens use the Internet, and they use e-mail and cell phones. Tweens use the Web to research products and services that interest them and their families. Their acuity with technology influences household spending as they take part in household purchasing decisions, including selecting restaurants, movies, cars, and their parents' clothing styles (Mummert 2004, Romano 2004). IKEA, a big-box home furnishings retailer, appeals to children in this age group as a way to reach parents. The IKEA catalog focuses on living with children and living with parents. IKEA's most important consumer touchpoint is how it has designed its stores to create a whole family experience through playroom facilities, family-friendly restaurants, and show-rooms that present home furnishings in multipurpose settings (Meyers 2004).

Merchandising is a critical aspect of capturing and retaining tween loyalty. Buyers need to stay current on tween preferences and be ready to constantly update silhouettes, colors, and patterns (Duff 2002). In-house cross-merchandising is used by Pleasant Company (American Girl) through online interactive content, in-store promotions, point-of-sale marketing, and targeted consumer catalogs (Maughan 2002). The American Girl brand is an experiential brand that directly targets each stage of a girl's development from preschool where the focus is on baby dolls and fantasy play through the tween years where girls are developing self-expression and individuality (See Figure 2.2). "American Girl is one of the nation's top direct marketers, children's publishers, and experiential retailers. American Girl's mission is to celebrate girls. Our age-appropriate, beautifully made books and playthings foster girls' individuality, intellectual curiosity, and imagination" (www.americangirl.com/corp/index.hl). American Girl Place is its proprietary retail store that offers girls the opportunity to shop and experience the American Girl product. Girls can click on the brand's website to locate American Girl special events such as fashion shows, sign up for a gift registry, interact with online activities, and get updates on the *American Girl* magazine and movies.

Tweens are targeted for their food preferences. Schwan Food repositioned its Tony's Pizza brand to target tweens. Their research indicated that pizza is the favorite food choice of 53 percent of this group and as a consumer segment they influence 45 percent of frozen pizza purchases. In 2003, Tony's Pizza launched a $10 million campaign using visuals, not text, to connect tweens to the brand. Since tweens are passionate poster collectors, Tony's Pizza

2.2 The American Girl brand is an experiential brand that directly targets each stage of a girl's development.

used a highly stylized illustration-style format for its poster. Their ads ran in kids' magazines such as *SI for Kids*, *Disney*, and *Nickelodeon* (Reyes 2003). In a study of eating habits and technology usage of 400 young consumers ages 10 to 13 in 43 states, Wharf Research and the Center for Culinary Development found that the majority (81 percent) of these young consumers ate out at restaurants with family or friends at least once a week. The study also found that 60 percent of the tweens ate while using their computers, which suggests the computer experience might be expanded to include a new subsegment of snack food that is computer-friendly (Krummert 2002).

Fast-food companies target young markets by promotional appeals that offer unique premiums and experiences that they cannot get anywhere else. Although McDonald's is the top fast-food designation for young children, Burger King is quickly taking this position among tweens by building a Honbatz cartoon-like icon that targets tweens. The icon is directed at a global tween audience, including the United States and four international markets, one in Europe, one in Asia, and two in Latin America. Honbatz are 2-D characters. The characters were created after 18 months of qualitative research that revealed tweens like being between childhood and teens, and they enjoy playing as well as seeking the individualism associated with teenagers. The Honbatz characters help older children ages 6 to 10 explore their emerging personalities through characters such as the rebel, the student, and the practical joker. Burger King and Nickelodeon are connecting with tweens emotionally by creating stories that appeal to them, offering related merchandise in restaurants and sustaining a year-round Honbatz dedicated website (www.honbatz.com). The Honbatz icon is engaging because it invites tweens to think they have discovered the characters (Stewart 2005).

INFANTS AND TINIES

Infants and Tinies have become important consumer segments in the United States. **Tinies** is a marketing term for newborns and toddlers who are targeted for branded consumer products. Affluence among U.S. consumers is creating lavish environments for newborns and toddlers where parents create fashionable images for their children through branded consumer products. Retailers, manufacturers, and media have identified a growing market for upscale products targeting these youngest age groups. Hot trends for babies include Bugaboo's limited-edition $2,000 leather-lined strollers that are fashionably exciting with their use of colorful designer creations. Diaper bags have become fashion statements. Fleurville launched a $400 all-leather diaper bag called the Luxe in fall 2005 and a baby home collection that includes a high chair that is more than $1,000, high-end branded apparel such as $240 cashmere cardigans by Juicy Couture, $110 to $150 denim jeans and jackets by Seven, and $58 rock and roll T-shirts from Trunk. Tapping into the growing market of upscale kids' products, Condé Nast launched *Cookie* in Fall 2005 to cater to the almost 22 million U.S. households that have incomes greater than $75,000 and children under the age of 10 (Thompson 2005).

Gender

During World War II, women entered the workforce in larger numbers to support the war effort. Since that time, the number of working women has grown (Moran and McCully 2001). Between 1979 and 1998, women's earnings (adjusted for inflation) grew about 14 percent while men's incomes decreased about 7 percent (Bowler 1999). In 1998, women earned about 76 percent of what men earned, with an average female earning $456 per week. Women's earnings as a percentage of men's hardly changed in the eight years since 1998; females were reported to earn 76.5 cents for every dollar made by males in 2006 (Mcaleavy 2006). The situation in Canada is similar, with women earning 71 percent of what men do (Greenaway 2006). These earnings vary according to education, ethnicity, and age. During this same time period, education levels grew, especially for females. In addition, the divorce rate in the United States has risen since World War II, resulting in more single employed women. All of these changes have influenced consumer behavior. There were 2.6 million single females ages 25 to 44 years old with annual incomes of $30,000 to $59,000 in 2004, up from 1.8 million women in that category in 1990 (Barack 2004). According to the 2000 U.S. Census, there were 13 million unmarried women heading U.S. households, and many of these single, upscale professionals purchase cars and homes, invest for retirement, take solo vacations, date via the Internet, cook gourmet meals, and shop for designer products (Barack 2004).

For both genders, price is the most important criteria when selecting a place to shop, followed by other common criteria such as merchandise quality, treatment by staff in the store, and low-pressure selling (Klein 1998). However, there are significant differences in how men and women consume products and services. A majority of women describes shopping as relaxing and entertaining, but men do not (Klein 1998). However, as the number of working women has increased in the United States shopping and other household tasks have become particularly challenging. Time-pressured working women shop for convenience (Schiffman and Kanuk 1997). Men are known to be utilitarian shoppers because they like to keep shopping simple, value convenience, and prefer knowledgeable store personnel.

There are also differences regarding the way men and women respond to advertising. Women are influenced by verbal, harmonious, complex, and category-oriented advertisements, while men are influenced by comparative, simple, and attribute-oriented advertisements. J.Crew opened a store with different entrances for men and women in their West Palm Beach Store (Sturrock 2006). Clothes were displayed differently in the men's and women's departments. Clothes for women were displayed to project emotional needs and benefits, whereas displays for men recognized they usually shop once a season and stock up on needed products.

The genders also have different retail outlet preferences and product category shopping preferences. In the case of online shopping, women are less adaptive to new technologies, and hence female shoppers have been slow to adopt the Internet. Women tend to browse products online but purchase them in the actual stores, whereas men prefer to purchase online. Females are more likely to purchase on eBay, but males are more willing to pay higher product prices (Black 2005). Men and women shop for different types of items online. Men are more likely to buy consumer electronics, sporting goods, software, computers and peripherals, cars and accessories, and video games than women. Meanwhile, bed linens and home fashions, personal care items and cosmetics, toys, gift certificates, jewelry and watches, and pet food and supplies account for the majority of female spending (Greenspan 2003). However, the gender differences in the case of online shopping are quickly disappearing as retailers begin to develop website content that appeals more to women.

Since men and women appear to be different in their shopping orientations, retailers could modify their formats to meet the needs of each target market. Retailers could provide a more relaxing and pleasant shopping environment for women but a more get in and get out format to cater to their male customers. This may explain, in part, the success of some retail store merchandisers who have turned their attention to creating an entertaining physical shopping environment targeting female shoppers. For women to stay longer in their stores, retailers could provide amenities such as child care areas, cafés, and various forms of in-store entertainment. Given that women typically continue to be the family buying agent, such enhancements to the shopping experience might be expected to strengthen patronage intentions as well as increase sales volume.

Online retailers can convert the time women spend browsing into sales. They could make their websites more interactive, provide leisure atmospherics, and provide simple and user-friendly tools for navigation (Alreck and Settle 2002). On the contrary, retailers can provide more convenient amenities to satisfy male consumers. While milk and bread products are typically located in the back of grocery stores to draw customers through the entire store, Kroger has chosen to place a small cooler of milk and juice near the front of the store. This satisfies the needs of the hurried shopper and keeps that customer from going to the local convenience store because he or she can get in and out very quickly.

Marketers must watch for changes in gender preferences over time. For example, men and women are expected to have different tastes in color. The assumption is that women prefer brighter tones and men prefer darker, richer neutrals, and blues. However, men can now be found buying and wearing bright yellow fleece jackets or pink Polo oxfords. An example of blurred traditional gender boundaries exists in spa services. Some white-collar males are getting in touch with their feminine sides through antiaging facials, massages, con-

touring body therapies, executive manicure and pedicure services, sports-related water therapies, body buffs, scalp treatments, and hair growth programs. Men desire the latest spa therapies as a means of relaxation, but they also want the experience to be easy to plan and convenient (Mintron 2004).

Sexual Orientation

The gay, lesbian, bisexual, and transgender (GLBT) consumer market segment is growing. Gay people, in particular, make up approximately 15 million people in the United States (Thau 2006). Overall, their average annual household income—$42,698 for gay men and $36,072 for lesbians—was higher than the U.S. median household income of $34,076 (Nayyer 2003). However, exact information about GLBT consumers is challenging to obtain since not all are accounted for in the U.S. Census. The aggregate buying power of this U.S. market segment is thought to be $640 billion (Said 2006).

GLBT consumers are "affluent, highly-educated, sophisticated, brand aware, product loyal, and trendsetting," as well as "technologically savvy" (Cherkassky 2004). This consumer segment is twice as likely as the average consumer to catalog shop, and spends five times as much money as the average mail-order buyer (Gardyn 2001). In 2001, 88 percent of GLBT individuals were white and 48 percent were between the ages of 18 and 34 (Gardyn 2001). The areas of the country with the largest gay populations are San Francisco, New York, West Hollywood, Los Angeles, Washington, D.C., Chicago, and Dallas (Gardyn 2001).

Gay and lesbian consumers patronize companies that are supportive of their physical and emotional needs (Barr 2004). Marketing to the GLBT population traditionally used venue-based promotions, neighborhood specific outdoor advertising, occasional TV commercials, and direct mail (Gardyn 2001). Openly gay neighborhoods, such as San Francisco's Castro Street, are identifiable; however, it is not easy to reach the GLBT consumer market that lives in mixed neighborhoods. The Internet and virtual communities can be used to assist retailers in more efficiently reaching the GLBT market. Retailers now attempt to target the GLBT market segment. In 2004, Cartier, the luxury jewelry store, placed an advertisement in magazines, such as *Vanity Fair*, of two women holding hands (Barr 2004). Singer Melissa Etheridge and actress Tammy Lynn Michaels were the women featured in the advertisement wearing Cartier's white gold Menotte bracelet. *Out*, a gay men's fashion magazine, has staged in-store fashion shows at Macy's. Crate and Barrel has a registry for gay couples. Recently, Wal-Mart has moved to draw gay shoppers who are a significant part of its customer base. Wal-Mart does this by partnering with the National Gay and Lesbian Chamber of Commerce and by setting an antidiscrimination policy that covers sexual orientation (Geewax 2006).

Acceptance of alternative sexual preferences has contributed to the consumer trend of metrosexual males. These young men are attractive urbanites, either straight or gay, and care about how they look (Simpson 2006). They place a great priority on personal grooming and elegance. The cable television reality show *Queer Eye for the Straight Guy* appealed to metrosexuals. This show was popular with versions developed for and aired in the United Kingdom and Australia. In the television show, five homosexual men helped straight men with their wardrobes, cuisine, beauty, and coolness. *Queer Eye* casts created lifestyle makeovers for average straight men. It is predicted that metrosexual style and consumption in areas of self-enhancement products, such as deodorant, hair styling products, and moisturizers, should continue as a trend for a while (Simpson 2006).

CHAPTER SUMMARY

Since World War II, retail markets have evolved from a limited number of goods and shopping formats to shopping experiences through multiple channels. The period after World War II witnessed increasing affluence, demographic changes, technological innovation, and changing preferences and lifestyles that influenced consumer demand and retail formats. Consumers have more discretionary income than prior to World War II and now seek hedonic or emotional benefits in addition to the utilitarian or functional product or service benefits. Consumer purchases reflect lifestyles, and products may be selected because of their symbolic value.

Economic and geographic mobility combined with advances in technology have created new opportunities for retailers. The traditional retailer role was to collect a bundle of assortments and services for targeted customers. Now the retail bundle of benefits includes emotional experiences. Overall, there has been a shift in the marketplace from an emphasis on autonomy, novelty, and uniqueness to an environment where consumption is used to create meaning and identity. Researchers and retailers have studied the relative importance of dimensions of consumption (i.e., social personalities, possession attachment, consumption communities, leisure, luxury, technology, and energy) influencing consumer behavior to satisfy target market needs.

This chapter also discussed modern and postmodern consumption to better explain changes in consumer behavior throughout time. The consumer market has transitioned from modern consumption associated with production and product procuring to postmodern consumption associated with consumers seeking experience and emotional connections.

The United States has changed from a homogeneous group of consumers to a fragmented and diverse market characterized by different ethnicities, generations, genders, and sexual orientations. The diversity in the U.S. market indicates that retail offerings should reflect the needs of various consumer segments. This is especially important considering that ethnic consumer segments are growing much faster than Caucasians. Also, the growing number of gay, lesbian, bisexual, and transgender (GLBT) consumers cannot be ignored, given their purchasing power and consumption behavior, which is different from those of the average consumer.

These changes support a need for retailers to understand the total consumer experience and what drives consumption, as well as strategies that can be used to address consumers' desires. Retailers need to understand that identity and community can be developed around product or service purchases. Shopping is a primary leisure-time activity. It contributes much to national economic well-being and reflects individual and social needs. In today's fast-changing marketplace, retailers must deliver true experiences that meet consumers' demands.

Discussion Questions

1. Describe how consumers shopped and the challenges they faced during World War II.
2. Contrast the role that retail played in World War II with the role it played after the September 11, 2001 terrorist attacks in New York.
3. Describe how consumer spending has evolved since World War II.
4. What are the major influences contributing to changes in consumer behavior since World War II?
5. Describe how ethnic diversity influences the apparel market.
6. How has the increase in populations of different groups of consumers influenced the retail sector? Give examples of retailers that now target each consumer group.
7. Describe the evolution of postmodernism and its influence on retail offers.
8. What are consumption communities, and why are they relevant to consumers? Give current popular examples of consumption communities.
9. Explain what drives luxury consumption. How is it affected by changes in the economic situation?
10. Explain how changes in the retail market since World War II contribute to the need for total consumer experience.

REFERENCES

Agins, Teri. 2001. U.S. Designers Launch Campaign to Try to Stimulate Retail Sales, *Wall Street Journal* (Eastern edition). October 22, B7.

Ahmed, N. 2003. Marketing strategies should reflect changing needs of African-Americans, *National Underwriter* 107(36):8.

Ahmed, N. R. 2005. A Small but Attractive Target Market. *National Underwriter/Life and Health Financial Services* 109(44):14–38.

Alreck, P., and R. Settle. 2002. Gender effects on Internet, catalogue and store shopping. *Journal of Database Marketing* 9(2):150–162.

Arnett, J. J. 2000. Emerging adulthood: A theory of development from the late teens through the twenties. *American Psychologist* 55(5):469–480.

Associated Press. 2005. "Home Depot wants Spanish-speaking workers" available at www.msnbc.msn.com

Aubert-Gamet, Veronique, and Bernard Cova. 1999. Servicescapes: From Modern Non-Places to Postmodern Common Places. *Journal of Business Research* 44(1):37–45.

Barack, L. 2004. Ads, mags and the single girl. *Folio* 33(4):42–47.

Barker, R. G. 1968. *Ecological Psychology: Concepts and Methods for Studying the Environment of Human Behavior*. Stanford, CA: Stanford University Press.

Barr, V. 2004. Coming out to shop. *Display and Design Ideas*, retrieved from LexisNexis July 27, 2006.

Bashford, S. 2004. Tap into the teen market. *Revolution*. April, 92–94.

Best's Review. 2005. Asian Americans: Facts and Figures. 106(4):24–25.

Black, G. S. 2005. Is eBay for everyone? An assessment of consumer demographics, S.A.M. *Advanced Management Journal* 70(1):50–60.

Bowler, M. 1999. Women's earnings: An overview. *Monthly Labor Review* 122(12):13–21.

Brand Strategy. 2004. Marketing to Hispanics in the US. October, 48.

Bryant, W. D. A., and J. Macri. 2005. Does sentiment explain consumption? *Journal of Economics and Finance* 29(1):97–111.

Burkes, E. C. 1972. Median family income here up 60 percent in 60s, *New York Times*. July 19, 41.

Chanel debuts in teen market with chance perfume. (2003). *Marketing*. April 10, 4.

Cherkassky, I. 2004. A valuable consumer niche. *Target Marketing* 27(12):55–56.

Consumer Trends Institute. 2003. Baby boomers. Retrieved July 27, 2006 from http://trendsinstitute.com/baby.h

Cova, Bernard. 1997. Community and consumption towards a definition of the "linking value" of product or serv-

ices. *European Journal of Marketing* 31(3,4):297–316.

Crispell, D. 1993. Where generations divide, a guide. *American Demographics* 15(5):9,10.

Csikszentmihalyi, M. 2000. The costs and benefits of consuming. *Journal of Consumer Research* 27:267–272.

Davis, J. S. 1941. Consumption level; Consumption standard; Plane of living, Standard of living. *The Journal of Marketing* 6:164–166.

DeBaugh, M. 2003. Like a Gold Mine: The New Generation of Customers. *ABA Bank Marketing* 35(10):52.

Dolfsma, W. 2004. Paradoxes of modernist consumption-reading fashions. *Review of Social Economy* 67(3):351–364.

Donthu, N., and J. Cherian. 1994. Impact of strength of ethnic identification on Hispanic shopping behavior. *Journal of Retailing* 70(4):383–393.

DSN Retailing Today. 2002. *What's hot: Tween makeup.* 41(8):19.

Duff, M. (2002). Big three refocus lines to meet tweens' growing influence. *DSN Retailing Today* 41(6):19.

Eastlick, M. A. and S. Lotz. 2000. Objective and multidimensional acculturation measures: implications for retailing to Hispanic consumers. *Journal of Retailing and Consumer Services* 7(3):149–160.

Field, K. 2005. Building Across America. *Chain Store Age* 81(5):104–107.

Firat, A. F., and A. Venkatesh. 1993. Postmodernity: The age of marketing. *International Review of Research in Marketing* 10:227–249.

Francese, P. 2003. Top trends for 2003. *American Demographics* 24(11):48–51.

Freifeld, Lorri. 2005. Who Is Your Customer? *License!* 8(5):42.

Friedman, M., P. V. Abeele, and K. De Vos. 1993. Boorstin's consumption community concept: A tale of two countries. *Journal of Consumer Policy Dordrecht*: 1993. 16(1):35–59.

Gable, M., and S. A. Mathis. 1983. Retail sales and the gasoline crisis: An empirical analysis. *Journal of Retailing* 59(4):93–106.

Gardyn, R. 2002. Oh, the good life. *American Demographics* 24(10): 30–35.

———. 2001. A Market Kept in the Closet. *American Demographics* 23(11):36–44.

Geewax, Marilyn. 2006. Wal-Mart moves to draw gay shoppers. *St. Paul Pioneer Press*. www.twincities.com/mld/twincities/business/15347941.html

The Gen X budget. 2002. *American Demographics* 24(7):S5.

Gitlin, S. 2002. Meet the Lee family. *Retail Merchandise* 42(1):42–45.

Goulding, C. 2003. Issues in representing the postmodern consumer. 6(3): 152–160.

Greenaway, N. 2006. Women still make only 71 percent of what men do, report says: A woman's world? While female athletes are soaring to new heights, in the workplace women are standing still—on the wrong side of the wage gap. *The Gazette*. March 8, A1.

Greenspan, R. 2003. Europe, U.S. on the different side of the gender divide, Retrieved on March 12, 2006 from www.clickz.com/stats/sectors/demographics/article.php/3095681.

Grossman, L. 2005. Grow up? Not so fast. *Time,* January 24, 43–3.

Gruen, N. J. 1994. The technological revolution in retailing-from mall to cyberspace. *Journal of Property Management* 59(6):20–23.

Hisey, P. 2001. Tween sophistication. *Retail Merchandiser* 41(3):36–37.

Holt, D. B. 2002. Why do brands cause trouble? A dialectical theory of consumer culture and branding. *Journal of Consumer Research* 29(1):70–91.

Holmes, Tamara E. 2005. No Parallels Between Buying Power and Wealth. *Black Enterprise* 35(11):50.

Humphreys, J. M. 2004. The multicultural economy 2004: America's minority buying power. *Georgia Business and Economic Conditions* 64(3):1–27.

Johnson, K. 2005. As Gasoline Prices Soar, Drivers Seek More Ways to Save at Pump. *New York Times*. August 13, A1.

Kacen, J. 2000. Girrrl power and boyyy nature: The past, present, and paradisal future of consumer gender identity. *Marketing Intelligence and Planning* 18(6/7):345–356.

Kaufman-Scarborough, C. 2000. Asian-American consumers as a unique market segment: fact or fallacy? *The Journal of Consumer Marketing* 17(3):249.

Kennedy, D. G. 2004. Coming of age in consumerdom. *American Demographics,* 26(3):14.

Kids age segmentation. 2002. *Home Textiles Today* 6.

Klein, M. 1998. He shops, she shops. *American Demographics* 20(3):34–36.

Kleine, S. S., and S. M. Baker. 2004. An integrative review of material possession attachment. *Academy of Marketing Science Review* 2004:1.

Krummert, B. 2002. Tweens now crave ethnic foods. *Restaurant Hospitality* 86(2):22.

Langman, M. 1991. Alienation and everyday life: Goffman Meets Marx at the shopping mall. *The International Journal of Sociology and Social Policy* 11(6–8):107–125.

Lejeune, C. A. 1942. John Bull learns to do without. *New York Times*. March 1, SM18.

License! 2006. Consumer View: African-American. 8(12):16.

Littrell, M. A., R. C. Paige and K. Song. 2004. Senior travelers: Tourism activities and shopping behaviors. *Journal of Vacation Marketing* 10(4):348–361.

Matorin, J. 2003. Generation 'G': Baby boomer grandparents a growing market offering glittering opportunity. *Nation's Restaurant News* 37(33):26.

Maughan, S. 2002. Betwixt and be 'tween.' *Publishers Weekly* 249(45):32–35.

McBride, E. S. 1943. Early to market: the housewife finds it pays to check food prices. *New York Times*. May 16, X10.

Mcaleavy, T. M. 2006. Gender wage inequality persists, study says. *Houston Chronicle*. February 20, Business 5.

Medeiros, C. A. 2000. Hig wage economy, sloanism and fordism: The American experience during the golden age. *Contributions to Political Economy* 19(1):33–40.

Mestrovic, S. 1997. *Postmotional Society*. London: Sage Publications.

Meyers, T. 2004. Kids gaining voice in how home looks. *Advertising Age* 75(13):S4.

Mintron, M. 2004. Metrosexual: Dare We Say It? *Club Industry* 1.

Moran, M. 2005. Consumer Series II: Cultural Diversity, The Gourmet Retailer, retrieved from LexisNexis September 5, 2006.

Moran, L. R., and C. P. McCully. 2001. Trends in consumer spending, 1959–2000, *Survey of Current Business* 81(3):15–21.

Morris, J. D. 1943. Policing of the food front up to the housewife in the end *New York Times*. February 28, E10.

Morris, V. G. 2002. The price they paid [electronic resource]: desegregation in an African American community. New York: Teachers College Press.

Morton, L. P. 2003. *Targeting Generation X, Public Relations Quarterly* 48(4):43–45.

Mummert, J. 2004. The 'between' market. *Target Marketing* 27(1):49–50.

Nayyar, S. 2002. Forever young. *American Demographics* 24(9):6.

———. 2003. The missed market. *American Demographics* 23(11):6.

New York Times. 1941. Coupon Values Illustrated. June 1, 2.

New York Times. 1942a. Text of General Maximum Price Regulation Decreed by OPA to Control Inflation. April 29, 15–16.

New York Times. 1942b. Stores to Promote Merchandise Care. May 4, 35.

New York Times. 1942c. Praises Retailers for Price Control. June 6.

New York Times. 1942d. Rationing of Tea and Coffee Likely This year, but Not of Clothing. June 9, 1, 20.

New York Times 1943a. Confident Retailers Will Meet Problems. June 3, A35.

New York Times. 1943b. Liberty St. Shop for Wanamaker. September 8, 20.

New York Times. 1943c. BIDS Stores Weigh Self Service Plan. September 17, 37.

New York Times. 1944. Sees Packaging Aid to Impulse Sales. June 30, 25, 28.

New York Times 1952. Budget for Four Calculated. May 20, 19.

New York Times. 1953. News of Food: Use of Spices and Herbs Rising Sharply in U.S. Trade Figures Show. October 4, 13.

New York Times. 1961. U.S. Family Incomes Increase in 12 Years. January 6, 12.

Oh, J. Y. J., C. K. Cheng, X. Y. Lehto and J. T. O'Leary. 2004. Predictors of tourists' shopping behavior: Examination of socio-demographic characteristics and trip typologies. *Journal of Vacation Marketing* 10(4):308–320.

Olshavsky, Richard W. and Donald H. Granbois. 1979. Consumer decision making—Factor or fiction? *Journal of Consumer Research* 6(2):93–100.

Ostroff, J. 2005. Sales impact from fuel costs to be moderate, Kiplinger Business Forecasts, 2005 (0826): retrieved from LexisNexis August 30, 2005.

Phinney, J. S., and D. Rosenthal. 1992. Ethnic identity in adolescences. In G. R. Adams, T. P. Gullotta, and R. Montemayer, eds., *Adolescent identity formation* (145–172). Newbury Park, CA: Sage.

Porter, E. 2005. True or False: Outsourcing Is a Crisis. *New York Times*. June 19, Section 3, Column 4:4.

Rassuli, K. M., and S. C. Hollander. 1986. Desire—Induced, innate, insatiable? *Journal of Macromarketing*. Fall, 4–24.

Reyes, S. 2003. Tony's takes new tack targeting pizza to tweens. *Brandweek* 44(2):5.

Reyes, Sonia. 2006. The 'Invisible' market. Brandweek 47(5):22–26.

Ritchie, K. 1995. *Marketing to Generation X*. New York: Lexington Books.

Romano, A. 2004. Tween and mean. *Broadcasting and Cable* 134(16):17.

Rosen, Bernard Carl. 1998. *Winners and Losers of the Industrial Revolution*. Westport, CT: Praeger.

Sabir, Nadirah, and Carolyn M. Brown. 2005. Earnings gain, wealth loss. *Black Enterprise* 35(6):30.

Said, C. 2006. Marketing comes out of the closet; advertisers woo gays and lesbians in ways they never did before. *San Francisco Chronicle*. June 25, F1.

Scally, R. 1999. Gen X grows up: They're in their 30s now. *Discount Store News* 38(20):40–41.

Schary, P. B. 1971. Consumption and the problem of time. *Journal of Marketing,* 35(2):50–55.

Schatz, E. 2003. Cranky consumer: Cranky consumer learns to knit, *Wall Street Journal*. January 23, D2.

Schiffman, L. and L. Kanuk. 1997. *Consumer Behavior,* 6th ed. Upper Saddle River, NJ: Prentice-Hall.

Scott, J. and D. Leonhardt. 2005. Class in America: Shadowy Lines That Still Divide. *New York Times*. May 15, Section 1, Column 1: 1.

Serviss, N. 2004. Attracting the teen market. *Global Cosmetic Industry* 172(3):24–27.

Shalett, S. M. 1943. Shoe ration put at 3 pairs a year, sales are frozen. *New York Times*. February 8, 1.

Simpson, Mark. 2006. This trend is not dead, but dead common—just look at Gavin Henson. *The Times*. April 7, 4

Stapinski, H. 1999. Generacion Latino. *American Demographics* 21(7):62–68.

Stewart, L. 2005. Burger King beefs up its global tween icon. *Kidscreen*. June, 65.

Sturrock, S. 2006. Never undersell women. *Toronto Star*. May 27, M8.

Thau, Barbara. 2006. Courting the gay consumer. *Home Furnishing News*. February 27, 12.

Thompson, S. 2005. Million-dollar baby. *Advertising Age*. May 30, 1.

Tomlinson, Alan. 1990. *Consumption, Identity, and Style: Marketing Meanings and the Packaging of Pleasure*. London: Routledge.

Troy, M. 2005. Wal-Mart unveils Asian ad campaign. *DSN Retailing Today* 44(7):5–7.

U.S. Census Bureau. 2004. Race and Ethnicity. Retrieved August 10, 2006 from http://factfinder.census.gov

U.S. Census Bureau. 2006. www.census.gov.

Wellner, A. S. 2000. Generation Z. *American Demographics* 22(9):60–64.

Wilensky, D. 1995. Retailers make over H&BC to lure ethnic shoppers. *Discount Store News* 34(1):41.

Witkowski, T. H. 2003. World War II poster campaigns: Preaching frugality. *Journal of Advertising* 32(1):69–82.

Yin, S. 2003. Color blind. *American Demographics* 25(7):22.

UTILITARIAN AND HEDONIC CONSUMPTION

CHAPTER 3

Mass Retailing Enters Post-Wal-Mart World

When stores opened the day after Thanksgiving in 2004, it became clear that retailers across the country had finally learned to compete in a Wal-Mart world. Stores opened early, they stacked merchandise high, and they priced it low. Prestigious department store Saks Fifth Avenue had an early post-Thanksgiving sale where customers who shopped between 8 A.M. and 11 A.M. that Friday received an additional 40 percent discount off their purchases. What Wal-Mart has taught American shoppers over the last two decades is that, regardless of income, or where or how they live, consumers should not overpay for anything. They should expect low(er) prices and good values every day—and they have begun to do so. Simultaneously with other stores' early Black Friday sales, Wal-Mart opened its doors with fewer deep discounts on fewer hot items. As a result, many shoppers were disappointed with Wal-Mart, so they went up the strip or down the street to look for a better deal at one of many retailers that have learned how to compete with Wal-Mart. Retailers of all types, sizes, and price points have learned from Wal-Mart how to operate more efficiently, to move merchandise more effectively, to use technology to achieve both, and, ultimately, to price more competitively. Big-box Costco, small-box dollar stores, and "cheap chic" fashion retailers H&M and Zara are some examples that come to mind. H&M and Zara are two fashion retailers that have dazzling supply chains that enable them to ship fresh merchandise to stores daily and to put hot fashion trends on the racks only weeks after they are seen on fashion runways. Another example is eBay, the largest consumer marketplace in the world, where shoppers wheel and deal to their heart's content for everything from technology and sneakers to bathroom fixtures and vintage cars. What's the right price every day? At eBay, the shopper decides.

Another factor that is moving us into a post-Wal-Mart world is the consumers' desire for a better shopping experience—easier, more shopable, and more enjoyable. While many consumers still prefer to shop where they can get a lot done under one roof, they are increasingly wanting an easier shopping experience—easier to get in and out, easier to find what they want, and even an edited mix of products. This raises a problem for 200,000-square-foot supercenters. It's not that consumers don't still shop at supercenters; it's that they are beginning to shop there less often. They are compensating with a quick fill-up at such smaller, easier-to-shop places as specialty stores, dollar stores, chain drug stores—where they can park right in front, find what they want (even if it means fewer choices), and get in and out more quickly. Fewer choices? This sounds like heresy in a world where shoppers always seem to demand more options instead of less. The reality is, however, that as life has become more complicated and connected 24/7, "shopping life" is where consumers demand more ease and more control. Not only ease of access but also ease in every aisle. A post-Wal-Mart world is all about ease. In addition, it's about having pleasant experiences.

In the latest edition of *How America Shops,* 45 percent of shoppers—women and men—said they would spend "a few dollars more on household products and groceries in a pleasant environment." Is it any wonder, then, that Whole Foods is one of the hottest retailers in the country? Shopping at this store is a wraparound experience; a better emotional reward for a chore well done. It is clearly not the lowest price every day. This doesn't mean shoppers don't know what the lowest price is—they do. Sometimes they demand it (as in the day after Thanksgiving, when they will not be deterred). Sometimes they will pay more (for an enjoyable experience or a special service). The key in this post-Wal-Mart world is to know when they will demand low prices and when they won't.

Source: *Chain Drug Review*. 2005. Mass retailing enters post-Wal-Mart world 27(2, May):28.

INTRODUCTION

In today's market, power has shifted from the marketer or retailer to the consumer. Consumers express their desires and expectations through their purchase of products and services and the retail outlets they visit. However, these consumers are not satisfied by just purchasing products or services; they desire a more holistic experience. The consumption experience, rather than the product or service per se, has become a major emphasis for consumer spending (Holbrook 1999). Pine and Gilmore (1999) illustrated evolving consumption patterns involved in throwing a birthday party as follows:

Consider that common event everyone experiences growing up: the birthday party. Most baby boomers can remember back to childhood birthday parties when Mom would bake a cake from scratch. Which meant what, exactly? That she actually touched such commodities as butter, sugar, eggs, flour, milk, and cocoa. And how much did these ingredients cost back then? A dime or two, maybe three. Such commodities became less and less relevant to the needs of consumers when companies such as General Mills with its Betty Crocker brand and Proctor and Gamble with Duncan Hines packaged most of the necessary ingredients into cake mixes and canned frostings. And how much did these goods cost as they increasingly flew off the supermarket shelves in the 1960s and 1970s? Not much, perhaps a dollar or two at most, but still quite a bit more than the cost of the basic commodities. The higher cost was recompense for the increased value of the goods in terms of flavor and texture consistency, ease of mixing, and overall time savings. In the 1980s, many parents stopped baking cakes at all. Mom or Dad simply called the supermarket or local bakery and ordered a cake, specifying the exact type of cake and frosting, when it would be picked up, and the specific words and designs desired on top. At $10 to $20, this custom service cost ten times the goods needed to make the cake at home and still involved less than a dollar's worth of ingredients. Many parents thought this a great bargain, however, enabling them to focus their time and energy planning and throwing the actual party. What are families doing at the dawn of the twenty-first century? They outsource the entire party to companies such as Chuck E. Cheese, the Discovery Zone, Club Disney, and Creativities. These companies stage a birthday experience for family and friends for costs between $100 and $250 (20–21).

Consumption experiences extend from the acquisition of products to the consumption of services (i.e., its use or appreciation) (Hirschman 1984, Holbrook 1994) and to use and enjoyment of the environment in which the products or services are consumed (Griffin, Babin, and Modianos 2000; Kim 2002). Hence, consumption experiences are now considered in a more holistic way that encompasses these elements (objects, environment, emotional needs, and functional purpose).

CURRENT CONSUMER AND RETAIL TRENDS

Consumers attribute different degrees of importance to utilitarian versus hedonic experience. They may desire more utilitarian than hedonic shopping experience or vice versa depending on the consumption situation and the type of product or service they buy. A good example of utilitarian versus hedonic shopping experiences can be found in the grocery store sector. At Wal-Mart Supercenter, consumers can buy food, groceries, and discounted general merchandise all in one place. Wal-Mart stores take a utilitarian approach, saving customers time and money with a wide selection of merchandise and services under one roof with no frills. On the opposite end of the spectrum, North Carolina–based grocer The Fresh Market offers consumers a hedonic shopping experience. The store focuses on customer serv-

ice and allows shoppers to customize their purchases by picking and choosing the amount of each product they want. There are no prepackaged meats or other items and products are attractively displayed loosely and unpackaged. In this market, consumers receive emotional satisfaction by validating their sense of personal freedom and using some creative, individual expression.

Although consumers exhibit different preferences for utilitarian versus hedonic shopping experiences, both aspects are important to meet the needs of today's consumers. Indeed, retailers need to understand why and in what way consumers buy and consume certain products or services. This need can be explored through current consumer and retail trends.

Consumer Trends

Consumers wish to receive both utilitarian and hedonic benefits from their product or service consumption and from their shopping experience. The need for both utilitarian and hedonic consumption can be explained by several consumer trends such as baby boom effects, polarized demographics, and rising educational levels.

BABY BOOM EFFECTS

In 2000, an estimated 26.5 percent of baby boomer households had more than $150,000 in wealth (*Datamonitor* 2002). Historically, the Census Bureau data confirm that households headed by 45- to 54-year-olds have the highest median income of any age group. In 2000, households headed by boomers ages 35 to 54 had an average after-tax income of $53,352. The actual purchasing power of this generation is impressive. According to U.S. Department of Labor Statistics (2005), baby boomers accounted for 56 to 58 percent of purchases in most consumer product and service categories in 2003. As a matter of fact, affluent baby boomers have fueled the growth of upscale department stores such as Nordstrom, Neiman Marcus, Bloomingdale's, and Saks Fifth Avenue.

Baby boomers are approaching retirement age. They are trying to make up for lost time and the things they may have missed by directing their energy and money toward consuming experiences and away from the continued acquisition of material things. Boomers often express an attitude of been there, done that toward buying more things. They are shifting their consuming focus on things to a desire for experiences and personal development in the form of vacations, dining, entertainment, and shopping (Danziger 2004).

Catering to aging baby boomers means providing goods and services that make them feel better as they age. Companies in health care and pharmaceutical industries have made it onto *BusinessWeek's* Hot Growth list of America's 100 fastest-growing small companies because of this lucrative target market (Weintraub, Carey, Mullaney, and Jespersen 2006). Companies such as NutriSystem, Inc. are tailoring their businesses to meet the needs of boomers who are waging a war against the aging process. They launched an over-60 program with a menu featuring more protein and fiber and an exercise program tailored to people with stiff joints. Another example is Palomar Medical Technologies Inc., which sells machines that remove unwanted wrinkles, varicose veins, and unwanted hair.

Retailers are offering goods and services to diminish the effects of the aging process because the healthier boomers stay, the more they can focus on life's joys, such as entertaining. An example of a company that is succeeding in providing improved home entertainment options for consumers is Lifetime Brands Inc. It sells and licenses housewares products such as KitchenAid and Farberware. Jeffrey Siegel, CEO of the company, believes his upscale products appeal to less price-sensitive customers such as baby boomers (Weintraub et al. 2006).

POLARIZED DEMOGRAPHICS

The children of baby boomers typically fall into the millennial generation (also called Generation Y) and make up about 28 percent of the U.S. population (Halliday 2003). These two largest segments of the population, boomers and millennials, have created two huge generational waves—one group near the oldest age category and the other near the youngest (Morton 2003).

As a result, the overall consumer economy is polarizing. There is significant growth at the luxury end of retail targeting the affluent, empty-nest baby boomers. Conversely, there is a strong demand for low-priced goods by the millennials as they begin careers, set up homes, and have families, while facing the challenge of stretching small paychecks. These polarized demographics direct the consumer economic action toward opposite ends of the spending spectrum (Danziger 2004).

Another reason for the current and forthcoming polarization of consumer society is the separation of U.S. households into two major income groups: higher-income and lower-income households. The upper 20 percent of households in the United States consume more goods and services than the bottom 60 percent of all households combined. People in the upper 20 percent, with their additional discretionary income, demand high-quality goods and additional services. They also demand more experience-based leisure activities such as entertainment, dining out, and social activities, including interacting with one another and feeling as if they are part of a community (Marks 2002).

These polarized economic and demographic trends will undoubtedly influence retailing. Due to significant growth opportunities at both the luxury and economy ends of the retailing spectrum, the future of retailing faces a paradox. Affluent consumers who can afford to pay full price for their luxury goods and services reach down market to take advantage of bargain-priced offerings targeted at those with less household income. At the same time, the millennials, with limited budgets and growing families, desire to buy high-priced luxury items that they aspire to own (Danziger 2004).

These polarized trends also influence the consumer concepts of wants versus needs. People who are driven by wants exhibit consumption patterns associated with products or experiences that give them more emotional rewards. Consumers who are driven by basic needs tend to be involved in buying products and experiences that meet their practical goals. This situation is visible in the coexistence of retailers on the two extreme retail market ends. Just as upscale department stores targeting high-income consumers (e.g., Neiman Marcus and Nordstrom) are growing, so are discount stores targeting middle-and low-income consumers (e.g., Wal-Mart and Target).

RISING EDUCATION LEVELS

The average education level of U.S. consumers is on the rise, and a continuation of this trend is expected. Figure 3.1 illustrates that people in the United States are becoming more educated. The most current data shows that the proportion of young adults with bachelor's degrees increased by 5 percentage points during the period of 1993 to 2003 (Danziger 2004).

Consumers with higher levels of education have greater needs and expectations of companies, brands, and services that are very different from those of less educated consumers. For example, consumers with higher levels of education are thought to be more concerned about their privacy online than consumers with less education (Sheehan 2002). Communities with highly educated populations have more gourmet coffee shops, such as Starbucks, than do less-educated communities. In contrast,

3.1 People in the United States are becoming more educated.

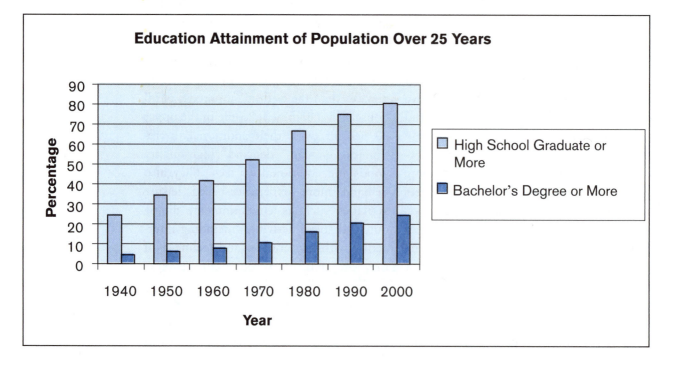

communities with fewer college graduates have more fast-food restaurants than do areas where more residents have college degrees (Spielberg 2005). To target more sophisticated, educated customers, retailers can hire mature, knowledgeable salespeople to create a more desirable environment for this consumer segment (Danziger 2004).

Retail Trends

Consumption patterns can also be influenced by what is happening in the retail market. Two major retail trends that facilitate consumers' consumption experience are retail competitiveness and the emergence of new economy.

RETAIL COMPETITIVENESS

The emergence of new types of retail formats provides consumers with many more shopping alternatives than ever before. In addition to the existing traditional retail formats such as department stores, specialty stores, discount stores, and catalogs, consumers are bombarded with alternative retail formats such as TV shopping and Internet e-commerce sites. On a macro level, consumers can choose among many different types of shopping centers such as regional malls (i.e., 50 to 70 percent anchored by department stores and attracting consumers from 10 to 30 miles), factory outlet malls, and lifestyle shopping centers. Lately, a shakeout on the Internet has caused an evolution from single-channel e-tailing to multichannel retailing that delivers products and services online, from a catalog, or in a retail store (Xing and Grant 2006).

Many brick-and-mortar retailers are responding to the threat of Internet-based shopping by providing entertaining and fun retail environments that virtual retailers cannot match. One of the retailers that creates a unique customer experience is Land Rover. Land Rover does not stop at the normal car sales and dealership experience; they offer a rugged rocky course for test driving the vehicles at the Land Rover Centers. This course is designed to enable the consumer to try out the vehicle on rough terrain without having to drive to outlying rural areas.

Due to consumers' growing desire for experiences, the hedonic aspect of shopping has become an important component of successful in-home retailing. With catalogs and television shopping as well as e-tailing on the Internet, consumers enjoy pictures of a wide variety of merchandise presented in a visually pleasing environment. Over the Internet, additional entertainment may be provided with interactive games, online puzzles, chatting with others who share common interests, downloading music, and opportunities to watch movies or live rock band concerts.

In addition to the increase in the number of retail formats, the sluggish growth of the U.S. population has intensified further competition among retailers. In this competitive retail environment, consumers have more retailers from which to choose. Going shopping is no longer a question of what product they need and where they are likely to find it; rather, consumers are primarily concerned with the kind of shopping experience they desire (Danziger 2004). Thus, it is no longer enough for a retailer to try to satisfy consumer demand for experiences by conventional operations that entice customers with broad assortments, low prices, quality merchandise, and customer service such as answering a question and wrapping a package. These operations are easily duplicated by the competition. The ability to gain a differential retail advantage depends on understanding what experiences consumers expect and desire and then developing strategies to give them more of those experiences.

EMERGENCE OF NEW ECONOMY

Traditional marketing that was developed in response to the industrial age with an emphasis on product features and benefits is losing significance. Instead, a new version of marketing is emerging that focuses on customer experiences in a more holistic way (Schmitt 1999). Bernard Schmitt (1999) coined the term experiential marketing as a response to the information, branding, and communication revolution we face today. He attested in his book *Experiential Marketing*: "Today, customers take functional features and benefits, product quality, and a positive brand image as a given. What they want are products, communications, and marketing campaigns that dazzle their senses, touch their hearts, and stimulate their minds. They want products, communications, and marketing campaigns to deliver an experience" (Schmitt 1999, 22).

Similarly, Pine and Gilmore (1999) acknowledged the emergence of what they call the experience economy. They pointed out that the nature and progression of economic value goes from commodities to goods, to services, and finally to experiences (See Figure 3.2). In this progression of economic value, the characteristics and attributes of the offering advance from fungible and natural (commodities) to tangible and standardized (goods), to intangible and customized (services), and then to memorable and personal (experiences). In an emerging experience economy, a retailer can become an experience stager as a source of memorable experiences, rather than a source of goods. Pine and Gilmore (1999) underlined this point in their statement: "An experience occurs whenever a company intentionally uses services as the stage and goods as props to engage an individual" (11). There are several examples of experiential retailers on the current retail stage. The Mall of America in Bloomington, Minnesota, has become an experience stager with a number of activities and events to be enjoyed by consumers (See Figure 3.3). The Forum Shops at Caesars, located adjacent to Caesars Palace on the Las Vegas strip, have transformed a traditional shopping experience into an amazing shopping mall that simulates ancient Roman streets complete with fountains, statues, and Romanesque facades. Other retailers such as Bass Pro Shops Outdoor World and Recreational Equipment, Inc. (REI) sell goods as tools for use in creating experiences and make their retail spaces an experience in itself.

3.2 The progression of economic value goes from commodities to goods, to services, to experiences.

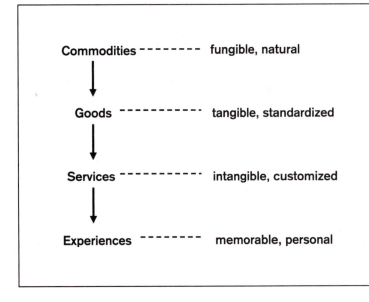

Commodities - - - - - - - fungible, natural

Goods - - - - - - - - - tangible, standardized

Services - - - - - - - - intangible, customized

Experiences - - - - - - memorable, personal

TWO STREAMS OF CONSUMPTION EXPERIENCE

Two essential modes of consumption are thinking and sensing. These modes include almost all acts that are involved in the consumption experience and have the stimulation of thoughts and sensations as their outcome. Thus, consumption may be viewed as a process that provides the individual with cognitive and sensory experiences (Hirschman 1984). Cognitive consumption seeks tangible benefits from

performing utilitarian functions. It involves satisfying basic physiological needs (e.g., clothing, food, and shelter) and assures the security of satisfactory purchase performance. Sensory consumption is associated with the intangible benefits pertaining to emotional and hedonic aspects of experiences (Hirschman and Holbrook 1982).

By nature, people are motivated to enjoy themselves, yet they are often bombarded with conflicting feelings of guilt and must rationalize or justify their actions or purchases (Okada 2005). People consume hedonic products when they are able to justify the consumption because hedonic products are viewed as more discretionary in nature rather than utilitarian goods, which are viewed as more necessary. Nike's launch of LeBron James's signature shoes at the Niketown store in Portland, Oregon, an example. This store sold out of the $110 shoes in 18 minutes while lines of customers still waited outside. Shortly thereafter, the signature shoes appeared on eBay for prices close to $200. This is an example of one type of customer who paid for the hedo-

nic purchase in time (waiting outside the store) and another type of customer who paid for the utilitarian purchase in money (purchased on eBay). Some customers may use the shoes for utilitarian reasons such as playing basketball and others may only enjoy the shoes as a collectible (Okada 2005).

Every consumption event involves an interaction between a subject and an object, where the subject of interest is a consumer or customer and the object of interest is some good, service, person, place, thing, event, or idea (Holbrook 1999). Both streams of consumption experiences—utilitarian consumption experience and hedonic consumption experience—can be viewed as subject-object interactions.

Product Focus

Traditionally, the subject-object interaction was confined to analysis as a consumer-product interaction (Addis and Holbrook 2001). Two streams of consumption—utilitarian consumption and hedonic consumption—focus on features embedded in the product alone and help identify archetypical product categories. In other words, consumer products are viewed as offering benefits that serve to satisfy desires for cognitive experiences, sensory experiences, or both. Products that offer practical functionality (e.g., toothpaste, soft drinks, computers) have been categorized as utilitarian products, products that satisfy emotional wants (e.g., music, fine jewelry, spas) have been categorized as hedonic products, and products that offer both utilitarian and hedonic aspects (e.g., cars, blue jeans) have been called balanced products (Okada 2005).

UTILITARIAN PRODUCTS

The traditional view of utilitarian consumption was derived from the rational model of economy that assumes the consumer is a logical thinker or problem solver. This perspective views consumers as mainly interested in what they can gain from the physical characteristics or technical performance (e.g., durability, quality, convenience) of the product (Addis and Holbrook 2001).

Similarly, traditional economics views products as objects for which the consumer desires to maximize utility, where utility is typically measured as some function of the product's tangible attributes (Hirschman and Holbrook 1982). In this sense, utilitarian products provide tangible benefits based on relatively objective features (e.g., durability, price per ounce, gallons per mile).

Utilitarian products are perceived as necessities driven by basic needs. It should be noted, however, that utilitarian goods these days are not always necessities. Typical purchases by most consumers in the Western hemisphere are made long after the basic necessities for human survival (e.g., nourishment, protection) have been met. Therefore, in these situations, utilitarian consumption, like hedonic consumption, is discretionary, and the difference between the two types of consumption may be a matter of degree or perception (Okada 2005).

HEDONIC PRODUCTS

The hedonic perspective recognizes that subjectivity increases as consumption is seen as an interaction between a product and a consumer (Addis and Holbrook 2001). Products are viewed not as objective entities but rather as subjective entities where emotions play a major role (Hirschman and Holbrook 1982). In consuming hedonic products, the relative weight of the consumer's subjective response is greater than the weight of the objective features of the product. Thus, a subject-object interaction occurs when a consumer responds to highly intangible, affective, hedonic aspects of product consumption (Addis and Holbrook 2001).

This hedonic paradigm recognizes the importance of often-neglected subjects such as the role of emotions in behavior, symbolic product meanings, consumers as feelers as well as thinkers and doers, demand for fun and pleasure in consumption, and personal expression. Satisfactory hedonic consumption hinges on an appreciation of the product for its own sake and the resulting feeling of pleasure it evokes, not on the utilitarian function that it may or may not perform (Hirschman and Holbrook 1982).

According to the hedonic consumption paradigm, perception of hedonic attributes represents multisensory experiences (Hirschman and Holbrook 1982). Indeed, many products project important nonverbal cues that must be seen, heard, tasted, felt, or smelled to be appreciated properly. Hedonic product-related experiences include eating in fine restaurants, playing golf, and consuming luxury products, entertainment, plays, movies, and television shows. In such experiences, several sensory channels operate simultaneously (Holbrook and Hirschman 1982). As a matter of fact, in consuming hedonic products, "individuals not only respond to multisensory impressions from external stimuli . . . but also react by generating multisensory images within themselves. For example, smelling a perfume may cause the consumer not only to perceive and encode its scent but also to generate internal imagery containing sights, sounds, and tactile impressions" (Hirschman and Holbrook 1982, 92). These consumption experiences with hedonic products tend to evoke strong emotions of fantasies, feelings, and fun (Holbrook and Hirschman 1982). The following statement illustrates this aspect of hedonic consumption:

> Closing the door of a Rolls Royce produces a more elegant sound than closing the door of a Volkswagen Beetle. Handling certain luxury fountain pens gives a more sophisticated tactile impression than with a ballpoint pen. Discovering the decoration of a suite in a palace hotel causes the guest to feel a luxurious atmosphere, very different from the sensation created by the view of most hotel rooms. The first mouthful of a dish in a French gourmet restaurant offers an impression of refinement, very different from that produced by the taste of most foods. The first olfaction, when entering couture boutiques, creates a feeling of luxury, very different from that created by a record shop (Lageat, Czellar, and Laurent 2003, 97).

The characteristics of hedonic products may influence pricing and promotion decisions. For instance, products and brands highly valued for their hedonic dimension rather than their utilitarian dimension have attributes that yield greater emotional rewards and thus allow a premium price (Dhar and Wertenbroch 2000) or

engage in sales promotions (Chandon, Wansink, and Laurent 2000). Advertising campaigns for hedonic products can stress emotional positioning strategies. For example, marketers of OnStar, the in-vehicle safety and security system, are using commercials that play on the consumer's emotions through real-world advertising. In this campaign, the commercials use actual recordings of OnStar subscribers' voices during both minor and critical requests for assistance. This type of commercial enables the listener to witness the emotional connection between the subscriber and the OnStar adviser. Through the use of similar advertising campaigns, companies can build upon the hedonic aspects of the product offerings and reduce the consumer focus on price.

BALANCED PRODUCTS

Utilitarian and hedonic products are not necessarily at opposite ends of a one-dimensional scale. Some products can have the similar weightings of objective features and subjective responses. In other words, some products can carry both hedonic and utilitarian attributes. The consumption experience derived from using these products can be relatively balanced according to the respective weights of the contributions by the objective product-based and subjective consumer-related components (Addis and Holbrook 2001). As illustrated in Figure 3.4, this representation distinguishes balanced products from utilitarian and hedonic products.

Crowley, Spangenberg-Halton, and Hughes (1992), in their study of consumer attitudes toward 24 product categories, were able to separate product categories representing utilitarian products (e.g., cooking oil or dish-washing detergent), hedonic products (e.g., ice cream or expensive restaurants), and those with an equal balance of both kinds of properties (e.g., cars or blue jeans). Clearly, these distinctions

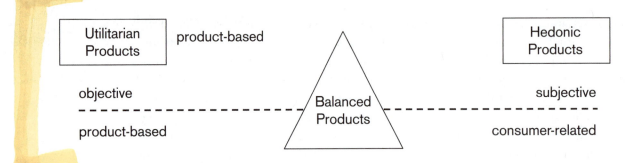

3.4 This representation distinguishes among utilitarian, hedonic, and balanced products.

correspond to utilitarian products, hedonic products, and balanced products, respectively. As an example of a product that can offer both utilitarian and hedonic attributes, the appeal of Rolex watches lies not only in the functional aspect of a time-keeping device, but also in the image of sophistication and affluence.

PRODUCT CATEGORIZATION

The concept of **product categorization** is valued and important because it helps develop and communicate the position of a brand in relation to other products. There have been a number of approaches to measure product categorization. These approaches encompass techniques that assess the presence or absence of attributes among products and those that measure a product's relationship to a category (Adams and Auken 1995).

Vaughn (1980) introduced the Foote, Cone, and Belding (FCB) grid as a technique to assess product-category relationship. According to FCB, product categories can be classified into four categories based on whether they are think or feel products and on whether they are high or low in

involvement that is associated with personal relevance a product or a brand has for a consumer. Ratchford (1987) mapped a number of products on the FCB grid, as illustrated in Figure 3.5. A high involvement product is one that has important personal consequences to a consumer or will help achieve important personal goals. A low involvement product is not significantly linked to important personal consequences or goals. Think products are associated primarily with rational meanings or functional consequences from using the product. Examples of think products that have high involvement include big-ticket items such as cars, appliances, and insurance (See Figure 3.6a); low-involvement products include paper towels, household cleaners, and gasoline (See Figure 3.6b). In contrast, feel products are associated with nonverbal images and emotional factors, such as psychosocial consequences and values. Examples of feel products that have high involvement include perfumes, jewelry, and fashion clothing (See Figure 3.6c); low involvement products include beer, cigarettes, and candies (See Figure 3.6d). When you apply the

3.5 Products can be placed into categories based on whether they are think or feel products and whether they demand high or low involvement.

	"THINK"	"FEEL"
HIGH INVOLVEMENT	"Informative" TV, Washer/Dryer, Life Insurance, Headache Remedy	"Affective" Sports Car, Expensive Watch, Perfume, Ground Coffee
LOW INVOLVEMENT	"Habit-Formation" Liquid Bleach, Paper Towels, Regular Shampoo, Insecticide	"Self-Satisfaction" Fast Food Restaurant, Cigarette, Imported Beer, Pizza

FCB grid to utilitarian and hedonic products, low involvement-think products can be considered highly utilitarian products and high involvement-feel products can be considered highly hedonic products. The other two categories, high involvement-think products and low involvement-feel products, may belong to the balanced product category.

In her book *Why People Buy Things They Don't Need*, Danziger (2004) categorized products based on two lines or continuums used to define discretionary spending. The vertical continuum extends from necessities (e.g., food, clothing, and shelter) to the most extravagant purchases (i.e., things that you do not need). The horizontal continuum spans the range from physical, material comforts to emotional gratification resulting from buying something that is not needed but wanted. Within the matrix defined by these two continua reside the four different categories of discretionary purchases: utilitarian

3.6a This car is depicted as a high-involvement think product.

3.6b Products purchased at grocery stores are perceived as low-involvement think products.

3.6c Designer perfume is an example of a high-involvement feel product.

3.6d Consumers buy candies as low-involvement feel products.

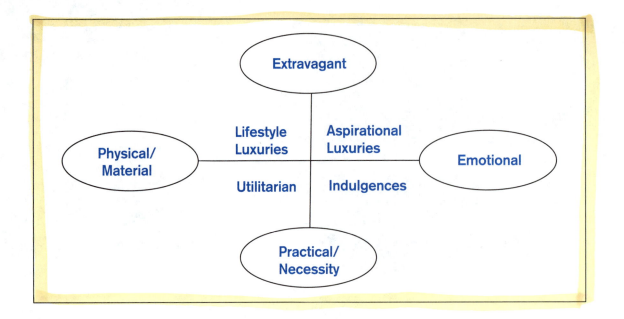

3.7 Danzinger's discretionary product matrix helps describe what might be a necessity and what might be a frivolous expense.

purchases, indulgences, lifestyle luxuries, and aspirational luxuries (See Figure 3.7). This discretionary product matrix helps describe what might be included as a necessity and what might be a frivolous expense. The categories may differ at each life stage as the person evolves and changes.

1. *Utilitarian purchases.* These products are ones that consumers do not necessarily need but are perceived as making their lives better in measurable, physical ways. The focus is on practicality or functionality. These products, such as blenders, rotisserie ovens, bread machines, food processors, microwave ovens, and water purifiers, enable individuals to perform functions better or save time.

2. *Indulgences.* These are life's little luxuries that allow people to indulge without feeling guilty. Primarily, they bring emotional satisfaction to the consumer because they are frivolous or somewhat extravagant, but not so expensive that the consumer feels remorse. Examples include candles, cosmetics, costume jewelry, contemporary collectibles and figurines, gourmet chocolates, fresh flowers, perfume, entertainment products, games, videos, books, and crafts and hobbies.

3. *Lifestyle luxuries.* These luxuries fulfill more than the needs of the consumer but they have a practical aspect to their purchase as well. While they offer utility and usefulness to fulfill a practical need, lifestyle luxuries also offer the prestige, image, and superior quality conferred by the brand. Practical luxuries include automobiles (e.g., Mercedes-Benz, BMW), designer clothes (e.g., Gucci, Chanel), decorative furniture, fine china, expensive watches (e.g., Rolex), gourmet appliances (e.g., Jenn-Air), and fine dining items (e.g., Riedel, Waterford, and Wedgwood).

4. *Aspirational luxuries.* These products make a statement about buyers—who they are, what their aspirations are, their value systems, their interests, and their passions. The products in this category primarily satisfy consumers' emotional needs. As with lifestyle luxuries, aspirational luxuries are usually tied to a brand. However, unlike lifestyle luxuries, aspirational luxuries are purchased largely for the pure joy that owning them brings, such as

original art, antiques and vintage collectibles, boats, and fine jewelry.

Danziger's four product types also can be categorized along a utilitarian versus hedonic product continuum. Utilitarian purchases could be placed on the continuum close to utilitarian products and the other three product types—indulgences, lifestyle luxuries, and aspirational luxuries—could be placed at different points along the continuum toward hedonic products.

Consumption Experience

Viewing consumption with a product focus has been criticized. The overall phenomenon of the consumption experience is viewed as the outcome of a multifaceted interaction involving the consumer, the product, the distribution channel, the organization, and the environment (Chandon, Wansink, and Laurent 2000; Wakefield and Baker 1998). Consumption must be interpreted as a holistic experience. This holistic perspective suggests that product usage is not separate and isolated from the rest of the consumer's world. Rather, it is embedded in that world. The product is closely related to a person's feelings, other products, relationships with other individuals, and the surrounding society. Also, an increasing number of people are buying and consuming goods such as food and clothing as integral elements of other experiences, rather than seeing it as an activity in its own right (Mitchell 1998). This suggests that the act of consuming, rather than the item being consumed, satisfies the consumer's needs (Danziger 2004). In linking this concept to mall shopping, the mall becomes a product. Consumption of the product can be linked directly to the shopping experience through the mall itself, its atmosphere, the entertainment it offers, and its range of goods and services (Langrehr 1991).

This multifaceted interaction is manifested in both consumption motivations and consumption experiences. As early as 1972, Tauber identified a number of shopping motives based on the premise that shoppers are motivated by various psychosocial needs other than those strictly related to instrumental goals such as acquiring products. These motives can be classified into personal motives (i.e., role playing, diversion, self-gratification, learning about new trends, physical activity, and sensory stimulation) and social motives (i.e., social experiences, communication with others, peer group attractions, status and authority, and pleasure of bargaining).

Westbrook and Black (1985) suggested that shopping arises for one of three fundamental reasons: to acquire a product, to acquire a desired product and to provide satisfaction with nonproduct-related needs, and to primarily attain goals not related to product acquisition. These fundamental shopping motives are captured in seven dimensions of shopping motivation that are outlined in Table 3.1: anticipated utility, role enactment, negotiation, choice optimization, affiliation, power/authority, and stimulation. While these motivations can be described as containing both hedonic and utilitarian elements, some are more utilitarian in nature (e.g., negotiation and choice optimization), while others are more hedonic in nature (e.g., affiliation, power/authority, and stimulation).

Rohm and Swaminathan (2004) developed a typology based on motivations for shopping online. They identified four motivations: online convenience, physical store orientation (i.e., immediate possession and social interaction), information use in planning and shopping, and variety seeking in the online shopping context. These online shopping motivations also reflect either utilitarian experience (e.g., online convenience, information use) or

TABLE 3.1 WESTBROOK AND BLACK'S SHOPPING MOTIVATIONS

SHOPPING MOTIVATION	DESCRIPTION
Anticipated utility	Denotes shopping motivation linked to the expectations of benefits or hedonic states that will be provided by the product(s) to be acquired through the shopping activity
Role enactment	Describes the motivation to identify with and assume culturally prescribed roles regarding the conduct of shopping activity
Negotiation	Describes the motivation to seek economic advantage through bargaining interactions with sellers
Choice optimization	Identifies motivation to search for and secure precisely the right product to fit one's demands
Affiliation	Describes the motivation to affiliate directly (e.g., through social interactions and communications) or indirectly (e.g., by identifying with particular reference groups) with other individuals involved in marketplace institutions, principally other shoppers and retail merchants
Power/authority	Refers to motivations which concern the attainment of elevated social position
Stimulation	Denotes motivation to seek novel and interesting stimuli from the retail environment encountered during the shopping activity

Source: Westbrook, R. A., and W. C. Black. 1985. A motivation-based shopper typology. *Journal of Retailing* 61(1): 78–103.

hedonic experience (e.g., social interaction, variety seeking).

A general view of the holistic consumption experience further recognizes that a basic duality of rewards for much human behavior is captured by both a utilitarian outcome resulting from accomplishing any prespecified goal and a hedonic outcome related to enjoyment resulting from the fun and play arising from the experience (Hirschman and Holbrook 1982). Babin, Darden, and Griffin (1994) conducted a series of focus group interviews to assess consumer respondents' perceptions of both utilitarian and hedonic values after they completed their shopping. The researchers found that utilitarian shopping value resulted from shopping done out of necessity and procuring a product in a deliberate and efficient manner, while hedonic shopping value was drawn from fun and playfulness. Babin et al. attested that these two dimensions maintain a basic underlying presence across consumption phenomena.

Many retailers have already developed strategies to create relationships based on the holistic experience consumers expect to receive in the retail setting. For example, Tiffany and Co. creates a unique shopping experience with distinctive storefronts, superb service, and purchases that have come in the traditional Tiffany Blue Box since 1837. A shopping trip to Tiffany and Co. is as much about the experience as it is about the purchase.

To summarize, just as a product can provide a relatively more utilitarian or hedonic experience, the consumption experience in general can be relatively more utilitarian, hedonic, or balanced according to the respective weights of the contributions by the objective and subjective components.

UTILITARIAN CONSUMPTION EXPERIENCE

Utilitarian consumer behavior has traditionally portrayed consumers as rational and goal-oriented (Howard and Sheth 1969). In this view, consumers try to maximize total utility by purchasing products in an efficient and timely manner to achieve their goals with a minimum of sacrifice and irritation (Childers, Carr, Peck, and Carson 2001). In other words, consumers seek to maximize the tangible benefits from their consumption activity and minimize the costs such as money, time, and energy needed to participate in the activity.

The utilitarian consumption experience manifests itself in many shopping studies. The utilitarian aspect of the shopping experience has often been related closely with whether or not a particular consumption goal was accomplished (Babin et al. 1994). It is related to necessity, rather than to recreation. Its success is evaluated based on work performance or accomplishment, as reflected by a respondent's discussion in Babin et al.'s (1994) study: "To me, shopping is like a mission, and if I find what I'm looking for, I'm satisfied—mission accomplished!" (646). In addition, several consumer behavior studies extended from the shopping as work theme to the dark side of shopping, accounting for distressed consumer experiences. This is expressed by a respondent in Babin et al.'s study who said, "I like to get in and out with a minimum amount of time wasted . . . I get irritated when I can't find what is needed . . . and I have to go to another store to find it" (646).

Among all the utilitarian components, convenience has been repeatedly identified as a distinct motive for consumer choice in virtual as well as real settings (Eastlick and Feinberg 1999, Rohm and Swaminathan 2004). Convenience can be related to time or effort savings or, in cases of online shopping, a consumer may be able to search, compare, access information, and place orders online at home or at the office any time of day. If retailers want to provide utilitarian experiences to target customers, they need to offer multiple, tangible attributes such as value, assortment, customer service, convenience, and confidentiality (i.e., security, privacy). These attributes will positively enhance the consumers'

experience. Consumers can therefore purchase what they want, the way they want it, at the right time, and preferably at a competitive price.

HEDONIC CONSUMPTION EXPERIENCE

Viewing consumption as utilitarian experience fails to recognize numerous intangible and emotional states that arise during consumption. In this view, the consumption as a whole must be considered as a Gestalt—not just a sum of several parts but as a holistic experience. This holistic consumption often includes many entities that are shared with individuals who are in similar social and economic circumstances. For example, an individual may choose to consume certain products or services to express his or her social identity. This is effectively demonstrated by Solomon's (2002) proposition that people, products, and settings are combined to express a certain consumption style.

It has been noted that in this consumer-driven market, satisfying consumer needs has less to do with meeting physical needs and more to do with gratifying wants or desires based upon emotional needs. As consumers are turning focus away from the object that is consumed to the experience, they are choosing products, services, and shopping places associated with their lifestyles or with their self-image. This is reflected in Maslow's hierarchy of needs that moves through the human experience from physiological and security needs to needs for self-esteem and ultimately self-actualization. The latter needs (self-esteem and self-actualization) dominate consumer motivations above basic physiological needs in most postindustrial societies. This supports the growing importance of hedonic consumption experience.

Consumer researchers have made headway in elucidating the hedonic aspects of shopping. Arnold and Reynolds (2003) identified several hedonic shopping motiva-

TABLE 3.2 HEDONIC SHOPPING MOTIVATIONS

HEDONIC SHOPPING MOTIVATION	DESCRIPTION
Adventure shopping	Refers to shopping for stimulation, adventure, and the feeling of being in a different universe of exciting sights, smells, and sounds. This shopping motivation stresses the need for stimulation and self-expression through play and creativity among human organisms.
Social shopping	Refers to the enjoyment of shopping with friends and family, socializing while shopping, and bonding with others while shopping. This shopping motivation is derived from the basic premise that people are altruistic, cohesive, and seek acceptance and affection in interpersonal relationships.
Gratification shopping	Involves shopping for stress relief, shopping to alleviate a negative mood (e.g., to forget problems), and shopping as a special treat to oneself. The basic premise is that humans are motivated to act in such a way as to reduce tension, thereby maintaining inner equilibrium and returning the self to a state of homeostasis.
Idea shopping	Refers to shopping to keep up with the latest trends and fashions, and to keep abreast with the new products and innovations that are available. Idea shopping is rooted in the human need for structure, order, and knowledge, as well as the need for external guidelines and information in an attempt to make sense of oneself.
Role shopping	Reflects the enjoyment that shoppers obtain from shopping for others. This activity has an influence on the shoppers' feelings and moods, and creates excitement and intrinsic joy for shoppers when they find the perfect gift for someone. Role shopping is linked to an individual's motivation to play the perceived roles at any given time, which enhance the individual's ego and self-concept through the addition of satisfying roles and acting out the role's responsibilities.
Value shopping	Refers to shopping for sales, looking for discounts or low prices, and hunting for bargains. Value shopping makes a consumer feel almost as if shopping is a challenge to be conquered or a game to be won. This shopping motivation views the human as a competitive achiever, seeking success and admiration, and striving to develop his potential to enhance self-esteem.

Source: Arnold, M., and K. Reynolds. 2003. Hedonic shopping motivations. *Journal of Retailing* 79(2):77–95.

tions. As illustrated in Table 3.2, they are labeled as adventure shopping, social shopping, gratification shopping, idea shopping, role shopping, and value shopping. In Babin et al.'s (1994) study, respondents expressed a sense of escapism while shopping, often describing the shopping trip as an adventure. These consumers seemed to enjoy shopping per se, rather than shopping for product acquisition. This hedonic concept can be linked to Langrehr's (1991) statement: "People buy so they can shop, not shop so they can buy" (428). Consumers also receive hedonic value through the enjoyment of bargaining that provides increased excitement, as expressed by a respondent in Babin et al.'s study: "I like to hunt through the stuff for bargains. When you find something really cheap it's great because it makes me feel like I'm stealing something" (647). Cox, Cox, and Anderson (2005) identified several potential sources of shopping pleasure. These sources consisted of mingling with other shoppers, bargain hunting, browsing, sensory stimulation (e.g., store decorations and displays, pleasant smells), being pampered by retail salespeople, and kinesthetic experience (i.e., an opportunity to move about or walk for exercise).

The distinction between utilitarian and hedonic experiences becomes blurred when the definition of a utilitarian consumption experience that contains task completion is revisited. Hedonic responses gleaned from shopping activities may sometimes be the intended goal as opposed to product acquisition as a goal; thus, shopping with a goal can be distinguished from shopping as a goal. However, since enjoying the experience is the desired end, a utilitarian experience might be reflected as well as hedonic experience. For instance, the consumer may feel that his or her task is accomplished by improving his or her mood. This example is illustrated by one respondent's statement in Babin et al.'s (1994) study: "Christmas gift buying is work, but even work can be a pleasant experience. Just seeing a larger experience softens the job context of Christmas shopping" (647).

Hedonic consumption experiences can bring several contributions to retailers. When companies stage many different kinds of consumption experiences, they can more easily differentiate their offerings from competitors and charge a premium price based on the distinctive value that is provided, not the current market price (Pine and Gilmore 1999). Furthermore, the presence of pleasurable retail attributes and surroundings that excite consumers translate into a desire to continue shopping (Wakefield and Baker 1998) and increase the likelihood of cross-shopping and subsequent shopping trips (Shim and Eastlick 1998). Additionally, advertising can focus on the hedonic aspects of the store environment by positioning the shopping experience as an adventure or a chance to visit with friends.

BALANCED CONSUMPTION EXPERIENCE

Utilitarian and hedonic experiences are not opposite or mutually exclusive experiences. For example, some consumption situations include both utilitarian and hedonic experiences. At the first store visited on a shopping trip, a consumer might find a product at an exceptionally low price. This example includes both hedonic and utilitarian experiences or a **balanced consumption experience**. The utilitarian consumption experience is present because

the product acquisition is completed easily; the hedonic consumption experience comes from the bargain-related excitement. Gift shopping and shopping in flea markets can also bring both experiences: the utilitarian experience from finding several necessary products in one place and the hedonic experience from finding a wide range of unique and exclusive products in an exciting and sensory stimulating environment.

Browsing has also been acknowledged as providing a balanced consumer experience. Consumers can examine a retailer's merchandise for recreational or informational purposes without a current intent to buy. This can be considered as a leisure activity and as an external search behavior. Through browsing, consumers can obtain information concerning a particular product class or the marketplace in general. Further, the search aspect of browsing may be pleasurable in itself because it satisfies the browser's curiosity motives and adds to feelings of self-esteem through the acquisition of product-specific or marketplace expertise (Bloch, Ridgway, and Sherrell 1989).

Total Consumption Experience

The behavior of consumers is the endlessly complex result of a multifaceted interaction between organism and environment (Holbrook and Hirschman 1982). In this dynamic process, neither utilitarian nor hedonic components can be safely ignored. Understanding of consumer experience will be limited if the consumer is single-mindedly perceived as a rational thinker or problem solver or if the focus is only on the emotional aspects of consumption.

Both utilitarian and hedonic experiences—whether they are derived from consuming products or the total experience, including products, people, places, and the environment—contribute, in differing degrees, to the overall experience of consumption. However, consumers may differ in their overall capacity or desire to obtain hedonic and utilitarian experiences. Some may desire to consume a balanced mixture of utilitarian and hedonic experiences, while others desire to obtain a higher level of one type of experience over the other (Hirschman 1984).

The relative weights of two experiences can differ by gender and situation. Consumer behavior research indicates that women tend to shop more out of a desire for a hedonic experience than their male counterparts do. Women who enjoy going to the mall outnumber men who enjoy going to the mall. Further, 60 percent of all shopping addicts are women (Slyke, Comunale, and Belanger 2002). However, since shopping is still an activity in which the female plays a dominant role for family purchasing, she may feel it is less of a hedonic experience when completing a task. Also, the female shopper who ordinarily enjoys shopping may feel stressed when she has to purchase specific items for specific recipients as a holiday or birthday gift.

Based on this reasoning, a **total consumption experience** results from both utilitarian experiences and hedonic experiences derived from multiple attributes of objects (e.g., products, ideas, people) and the environment in which consumption occurs. Therefore, the experience can vary substantially in how strongly a consumer receives a utilitarian experience and how strongly a consumer receives a hedonic experience. A consumer's total experience can be explained as the summed set of the utilitarian and hedonic experiences. The challenge to retailers is to shape consumption into a total experience. Offering varying degrees of utilitarian and hedonic experiences to target consumers will assist retailers in meeting a consumer's desire for a satisfactory total consumption experience.

RETAIL PRACTICES

Different retail formats such as brick-and-mortar stores, catalogs, and the Internet provide different types and different degrees of utilitarian and hedonic experiences. Consumers have gained hedonic experiences more from brick-and-mortar stores than from catalogs or the Internet. Although the Internet is more associated with a utilitarian benefit of convenience derived from being able to shop anywhere, anytime, it begins to incorporate hedonic components in line with the current consumer trend—seeking entertainment and emotional rewards. In the following pages, each retail format is discussed in terms of the utilitarian and hedonic benefits it provides to consumers.

Brick-and-Mortar Retailers

Despite a growing assortment of non-store outlets (including catalogs, party-concept selling, QVC, personal shopping services, and the Internet), consumers still do the vast majority of their shopping at traditional brick-and-mortar stores (Cox et al. 2005). Even in a product category like apparel, where catalog and Internet outlets have made some of their greatest inroads, consumers still make most of their purchases at traditional brick-and-mortar stores. In this regard, the following section describes how brick-and-mortar retailers can meet consumers' need for both utilitarian and hedonic experiences. The **brick-and-mortar retailers** described are department stores, specialty stores, category killers, and discount stores at a micro level, and shopping centers at a macro level.

DEPARTMENT STORES

Department stores were developed in the late 1800s and were the first retailers to introduce fixed pricing and guaranteed product quality. In their beginnings, department stores provided basic products that could not be produced at home, but actual social interaction among consumers was limited. These stores were more attractive places to shop than the old country stores and often had amenities such as carpeting and marble fixtures. After World War II, retailing grew due to the pent-up demand for goods and services (May 1989) and social interaction outside the home became an important component of shopping.

Now, department store retailing appears to be in a mature sector of the retail industry and as a result, it is difficult to grow department store business. One reason for the decline of department store shopping is the failure of department stores to provide convenience to consumers. Department stores, in general, do not offer an in and out experience. In addition, department stores are not providing excellent service, return policies, or an exciting shopping experience (Roy 2005). An article in *Women's Wear Daily* (2005) reported that department stores must "create more compelling shopping experiences, be less reliant on malls, where traffic has been diminishing, and focus on off-mall sites, get quicker deliveries, higher product turnover, and increased merchandise exclusivity, broaden the offerings to food and other categories that department store retailers abandoned in the past two decades and replenish talent, which is getting scarce, for fresh approaches" (10).

Several department stores, such as Nordstrom, JCPenney, and Neiman Marcus, have recently improved service technology, merchandise quality, and their assortment of trendy merchandise to create a more satisfying customer shopping experience (*Women's Wear Daily* 2005). Further, high-end department stores such as Neiman Marcus are performing best because the luxury market is doing very well (Roy 2005). Customers enjoy buying luxury or designer brands because it makes them feel special. Other emotions associated with purchasing top-of-the-line merchandise are feelings of success, confidence, happiness, stylishness, and sophistication (Seckler 2004). With the number of baby boomers continuing to grow over the next decade or so, the boomers are expected to continue to drive this increasing desire for affluence (Betts, Novack, and Toyama 2004).

Department stores can more effectively satisfy the utilitarian needs of consumers by providing the right products and offering shopping trips that require the least amount of time and effort. Then, they can strive to meet the hedonic needs of consumers by creating positive emotional feelings through atmosphere, social interaction, and pleasant experiences. Using these strategic offerings can help department store retailers improve competitive positioning. This is especially important considering the glorious history as well as the current lackluster situation for department stores.

SPECIALTY STORES

Specialty retailers focus primarily on the interests of narrow market segments through a limited range of styles. Concentration on limited product categories results in cohesiveness between the merchandise and the retail presentation. Specialty stores such as Gap, Chico's, Express, and American Eagle Outfitters are popular because of their more trendy, exciting shopping experiences and because customers often want more than low prices. Specialty store offerings create an emotional, enjoyable experience that can be hedonic as well as utilitarian for the customer. Specialty stores such as Victoria's Secret are doing better than department stores because they are utilizing convenience, personalization, and customization (Roy 2005, Tsao 2004). Further, specialty retailers are better at merchandising, creating a unique environment, and presenting more stylish products than discounters or department stores (Tsao 2004).

American Eagle Outfitters created a unique experience in their stores during a recent holiday season by allowing customers to personalize their newly purchased AEO jeans. In this experience, customers used bleach, knives, paint, and more to embellish the jeans they intended to purchase and were assisted in the process by trained sales associates. This embellishment process created a buzz within the stores and provided a unique experience for customers purchasing the jeans and for customers observing the process. The promotion turned a potentially utilitarian purchase into a unique hedonic experience.

Housewares and home furnishings stores such as IKEA and Williams-Sonoma are succeeding because they are meeting the needs of the consumers who are cocooning or creating a sanctuary within their homes. IKEA offers planning tools through computer terminals that plan layouts for kitchen and office designs (Szuchman 2005). In addition, IKEA has the design planner tools online under customer service. The virtual kitchen planning tool allows customers to drag and drop different kitchen components into the layout. Consumers can view the kitchen in 3-D and save it on their personal computers. This planning also supplies customers with a printed shopping list when they visit the local IKEA store. This process allows customers to feel confident in their new kitchen plans before spending any money (www.ikea.com). Several home retailers meet the needs of customers who no longer want to do-it-themselves by adding design services (Szuchman 2005). The availability of additional personalized services are

making small businesses stand out from several big-box retailers although Lowe's and Home Depot do offer kitchen design experts for a minimal fee.

Many specialty stores are now choosing to locate in open-air centers that have a unique appeal for certain consumers. These open-air centers often have personalized architecture that requires specialty stores to meet certain strict design standards (Fenley 2003). The unique architecture adds to the customer experience of pedestrian shopping in the main street shopping area.

CATEGORY KILLERS

Category killers, single-focus mega stores that could kill local competitors in a particular retailing category, include stores such as Home Depot, Linens 'n Things, CompUSA, and Toys "R" Us. Category killers accomplished an upward growth in the late 1980s due to convenience, value orientation, and the depth and breadth of merchandise offerings. Consumers reported liking the category killers because their stand-alone locations offered better visibility and exposure, and more efficient shopping with direct access to the parking lot, in addition to abundant surface parking (O'Connor 1999).

Many category killers create desirable experiences for customers by offering classes or meetings in the store. For example, Michael's arts and crafts stores offer weekly in-store craft classes and events designed to create a unique hedonic experience for the customer. Similarly, Barnes and Noble regularly schedules book group meetings, story times, and events. The book groups are made up of members who have regular meetings at the store to talk about a specific work. The July 16, 2005 launch of J. K. Rowling's *Harry Potter and the Half-Blood Prince* is an example of a series of events surrounding the launch of a consumer product. The U.K. publisher,

Bloomsbury, sponsored a contest to enable 70 youngsters to meet Ms. Rowling after a weekend-long celebration at Scotland's Edinburgh Castle. In addition, Scholastic Inc., the U.S. publisher, held a "Why I love reading *Harry Potter*" contest in which there were 10 winners (Trachtenberg 2005). In addition to these larger events, local bookstores and retailers hosted book parties at midnight of the 16th to launch the sale of the sixth book in the best-selling *Harry Potter* series. These parties included customers of every age dressed in character costumes. The purchase of the newest J. K. Rowling book was surrounded with experience opportunities for children, young and old.

However, category killers have entered the mature stage of their lifecycle, reaching a point where the main competition is among themselves (Barta, Martin, Frye, and Woods 1999). Category killers compete against one another and against shopping malls in a given product category because they share customers located within a reasonable driving distance. Recently, sales growth at some category killers (e.g., Toys "R" Us) has slowed, and several others (e.g., Incredible Universe computer and electronics stores, Just for Feet shoe stores) have closed. In addition, category killers are especially susceptible to competition from Internet sales for products such as books, toys, and CDs (Warson 2000). As the growth of category killers is expected to become stagnant, delivering a total consumer experience by analyzing consumer perspectives regarding product category purchase decisions and the shopping experience is a crucial step toward positioning for the future.

DISCOUNT STORES

Discount stores driven by low prices rather than fashion and service include Wal-Mart, Kmart, and Target. Though Wal-Mart is the world's largest retailer, it is being challenged from department stores such as Sears, JCPenney, and Kohl's with low price promotions that match Wal-Mart prices. It is also challenged by dollar stores such as Dollar General with smaller store layouts that are easier to access (Bowers, Williamson, and Young 2004). In response to this stiff competition, Wal-Mart introduced a prototype supercenter in Northwest Arkansas that boasts more merchandising initiatives. With more fun and excitement in the electronics department, a more accessible photo department, and a drive-through pharmacy to compete for customer patronage, this prototype store is targeting consumers who desire a more unique, convenient experience in addition to the traditional Wal-Mart everyday low prices (Troy 2005).

Discounted stores, in general, provide utilitarian benefits such as convenience, low prices, and a wide assortment of goods. However, they also provide hedonic benefits such as treasure hunting experiences and the opportunity to become smart shoppers by purchasing expensive brand-name merchandise with low prices. Chains such as many discount stores employ top designers for private-label goods. Target's Mossimo brand has contributed to the great share of the sale increase. Wal-Mart's successful George brand of clothing has taken off internationally (*Economist* 2005).

SHOPPING CENTERS

From their inception around 1950, enclosed malls have offered patrons the advantage of climatic comfort and freedom from the noise and traffic that characterizes other shopping venues. In addition to providing a wide range of products, early mall developers included benches, artwork, and piped-in music to make the shopping experience more pleasurable. Since the 1970s, shopping malls have added entertainment tenants and

TABLE 3.3 A TYPOLOGY OF CONSUMER VALUE: MALL SHOPPING VERSUS INTERNET SHOPPING

HOLBROOK'S CONSUMER VALUE TYPOLOGY			SHOPPING VALUE	MALL SHOPPING	INTERNET SHOPPING
Extrinsic	Active	Efficiency	Convenience	One-stop shopping, comparison shopping, multipurpose shopping (e.g., vision care office, banking service, hair salon)	24-hour accessibility at any place, ease of ordering and payment, simple navigational capabilities, search engines, direct access to a multitude of products/services, access to specialized goods and services, links to related sites
			Resources (time, effort, and money)	Transportation to the mall, traffic, parking, time spent in mall, energy spent on pushy salespeople, finding product wanted, and waiting on check-out lines	Internet connection fee, navigating to find a specific item or address, loading information, transaction, shipping, delivery, computer viruses, broken links, slow transmission
	Reactive	Excellence	Product performance	Quality, selection, price	Quality, selection, price
			Customer service	Real-time human contact, safe and secure shopping environment	Virtual contact via e-mail, instructional support, quick product advice, customization of product/service offerings
Intrinsic	Active	Play	Sensory stimulation/ entertainment	Appeal to the five senses (sight, sound, smell, touch, and taste), instant gratification, family entertainment centers, cinema, games, eateries, special events or exhibits, walking for exercise, window shopping	Appeal to two senses (sight and sound), Web surfing, online puzzles, interactive games (e.g., chess), lottery
			Social interaction	People-watching, socializing with friends, talking with other shoppers, escaping from the routine	Chatting with others who have common interests, Internet phone, electronic dating
	Reactive	Aesthetics	Ambience	Architecture, interiors, visual display	Virtual display, multimedia presentation

Source: Kim, Y-K. 2002. Consumer value: An application to mall and Internet shopping. *International Journal of Retail and Distribution Management,* 30(12):595–602.

ambiance such as unique architecture and special events as strategies to compete with non-store retailers, including catalogs and the Internet.

As such, shopping centers provide both utilitarian and hedonic benefits. Kim (2002) compared the mall with the Internet on multiple dimensions of consumer value ranging from economic or functional value to hedonic or experiential value, based on Holbrook's (1999) consumer value typology (See Table 3.3). Holbrook's typology was based on the extrinsic value that is instrumental in accomplishing some further purpose versus intrinsic value that characterizes an experience appreciated for its own sake, apart from any other consequences that may result thereof; and active value that entails some physical or mental manipulation of an object or experience versus reactive value that occurs when the individual simply apprehends, appreciates, or responds to an object. The typology consists of four components: efficiency (extrinsic/active), excellence (extrinsic/reactive), play (intrinsic/active), and aesthetics (intrinsic/reactive) in the context of shopping malls and the Internet. Among these components, efficiency and excellence are associated with the utilitarian aspect of shopping; play and aesthetics are associated with the hedonic aspect of shopping. The following pages give a brief discussion on the two types of consumer experiences—utilitarian and hedonic—that can be obtained in shopping centers, followed by an elaboration of shopping center types and their contributions to the total consumer experience.

Utilitarian Experience Shopping centers usually consist of a mix of anchor stores and specialty stores. Anchor stores (i.e., mass merchandisers and department stores) help draw customers to a shopping center. Non-anchor specialty stores that have high consumer drawing power can also serve as super performers for a shopping center. These formats meet the needs of consumers who are shopping out of necessity and are attempting to obtain products in a deliberate and efficient manner. In fact, consumers may be drawn to a particular shopping center because it hosts a store that appeals to them. To capitalize on this, retail merchants frequently locate their stores in close proximity to direct competitors, reasoning that the consumer's desire for convenient comparison shopping is an important motive for patronizing a shopping center.

Many shopping malls are clustering stores together in response to customers' needs for convenience. Clustering means congregating similar stores in the same area so shoppers can walk from one store to another and shop in close proximity (Warson 2000). This type of store placement encourages customers to cross-shop between stores within the mall. Cross-shopping occurs when a single consumer patronizes multiple types of retail stores in a single trip. This shopping phenomenon can offer one-stop for all needs shopping for more cost- and time-efficient functional shoppers.

Hedonic Experience The mall itself offers experiences that are consumable. Mall management has built upon this offering by instituting many special events such as home improvement expos, walking clubs, art exhibits, health screening, auto shows, and live music. Many people enjoy the pleasant, park-like atmosphere of shopping malls. Some shoppers may be interested in seeing new items and learning about new trends while others may go shopping when they feel a need for exercise or to enjoy leisure time (Hirschman and Holbrook 1982, Tauber 1972). Malls have also become important places for social experiences outside the home (e.g., meeting friends or watching people).

To further encourage cross-shopping, shopping malls are reshaping the tenant mix (e.g., adding family entertainment centers) and reconsidering the destination attractions (e.g., movie theaters or restaurants instead of traditional department stores) within the mall. Shopping malls are using multiscreen cinemas as anchor businesses because they draw as much traffic as anchors and offer an entertainment component to the center.

An important part of a shopper's hedonic consumption activity in the mall is the mall environment. Retailers appeal to the multiple senses of sight, sound, scent, touch, and taste (in the case of food). Fantasies can be played out in a mall as a shopper walks through the mall, sits in a mall atrium or is waited on by a responsive retail associate (Langrehr 1991). To enhance a shopper's experience, many shopping malls have revamped their look to gain competitive advantage. Mall interiors have evolved from comfortable yet mediocre spaces, to architecturally rich spaces with lavish materials and sophisticated design elements, such as multilevel atriums and curved escalators.

Expansion of Shopping Center Types

According to the International Council of Shopping Centers (ICSC), shopping center types are numerous, ranging from neighborhood shopping centers, to the festival shopping centers, to regional shopping centers (International Council of Shopping Centers 2004). A few types of shopping centers, such as factory outlet stores, lifestyle shopping centers, and mixed-use developments, have recently been successful by providing satisfactory total consumer experiences.

Factory outlet centers are shopping developments that offer discount prices, a varied mix of tenants, a wide product selection, and a one-stop shopping venue. They are made up of brand-name manufacturers of electronics, apparel, shoes, and other merchandise that use the outlet as an additional vehicle to sell their merchandise. Factory outlet shoppers who obtain satisfaction from the purchase of brand-name merchandise gain an emotional hedonic experience from the purchase itself (Reynolds, Ganesh, and Luckett 2002). On the contrary, the price savings obtained from shopping at a factory outlet could satisfy some of the utilitarian benefits of efficiently using one's money. Though the outlet malls tout bargain prices, the price difference between merchandise purchased in traditional malls and in factory outlet malls is shrinking; thus, the price advantage seems to be evaporating.

Lifestyle shopping centers were created as a result of the phenomena that consumers, more than ever before, are choosing products, services, and shopping locations because they are associated with a certain lifestyle. Traditionally, lifestyle retailing has been applied at the product and store levels. Retail examples of companies that use lifestyle segmentation include Gap, IKEA, Pottery Barn, Laura Ashley, and Benetton. These brands and stores use lifestyle along with demographics in their positioning strategies. Retailers merchandise their stores to fit a particular target market's style of life (*Women's Wear Daily* 2005).

The concept of lifestyle retailing has also been extended to the shopping center level. Lifestyle shopping centers can offer a specific tenant mix and market position that represents a special type of customer experience and retail environment. ICSC research has shown that customers spend more money at lifestyle centers than at regional malls, though they spend less time at lifestyle centers (Fenley 2003). By identifying strategies such as image, product/service mix, and target marketing tactics that match the customer profile, retailers in lifestyle shopping centers can satisfy both the utilitarian (functional) and hedonic (emotional) needs of their customers.

In the twenty-first century, two major trends have characterized the metropolitan United States; the resurgence of downtown areas and renewed interest in transit use and investment (Hemakom 2002). As a result, new urbanism, which advocates the concentrated live-work-play environment, contributes to the development of *mixed-use centers* (Bartlett 2003). While the popularity of mixed-use developments as outlets for retail has fluctuated in the past, there is an undeniable resurgence in the demand to combine retail offerings with upscale residences in close proximity to entertainment, retail, and work environments. Hence, mixed-use developments generally focus on pedestrian-friendly environments, main street ambience, lifestyle-oriented merchandising, and convenient access (*Chain Store Age* 2000). This environment meets the consumer demand for more convenient, efficient shopping, more leisure activities such as entertainment and dining out, and more social activities such as interacting with one another and feeling as if they are part of a community. These types of centers, with this appropriate mix of retailers and unique shopping environment, certainly meet consumer need for both utilitarian and hedonic experiences.

Catalogs

Catalogs, which were originally developed in the late nineteenth century to counteract the transportation problems of rural consumers, have seen continuous growth since the 1970s due to their convenience, low prices, uniqueness, and variety of merchandise. Functional motivations are of primary importance to consumers who shop by catalog. In Eastlick and Feinberg's (1999) study of catalog shoppers, perceived value and order services were the strongest functional motives followed by convenience. Sisal Rugs Direct offers up to three rug samples at no cost to the consumer. The sample allows consumers to see the color and touch the texture of the rug and to match it with other furnishings within their homes. Having the samples creates a utilitarian experience for consumers because they can decide if the product is suitable before they purchase. It can also create a hedonic experience because consumers can experience the rug before purchasing it. Sisal Rugs Direct also offers a service called Create a Rug online. Through this service, consumers can design their own rugs by choosing weaves, colors, bindings, and sizes that meet their individual needs and tastes (www.sisalrugs.com).

In a study by Mathwick, Malhotra, and Rigdon (2002), catalog shopping appeared to be based on more experiential value sources than Internet shopping. The researchers state: "Not only does it offer efficiency and affordability, catalog shop-

ping appears to entertain and delivers visual appeal that is either missing from, or, was not noticed in the on-line context" (Mathwick et al. 2002, 51). Based on this study, catalog shopping appears to deliver more aesthetic value than online shopping.

Catalogs also seem to satisfy a desire to browse, which is similar to brick-and-mortar stores but different from the Internet. For example, Pottery Barn catalogs offer living room, dining room, bedroom, and bathroom decorating ideas for the customer. Whether the customer chooses to purchase Pottery Barn products is up to the individual, but consumers can use the catalog to get decorating ideas.

The Internet

The Internet also provides both the utilitarian and hedonic aspects of a shopping experience. While comparatively more has been written about the utilitarian aspects of the Internet, the emergence of the Web as a hedonic medium has only recently gained momentum. Consumers have been using the Internet for a limited number of entertainment applications (e.g., downloading music), but a greater variety of entertainment opportunities have more recently become available. Consumers can now use the Web to watch streaming media, play games, and participate in virtual communities, while also experiencing aesthetic appeals such as music, color, layout, and animation. Pleasure-oriented consumers typically enjoy surfing the Web just for the sake of the interaction itself and not for the accomplishment of tasks (Childers et al. 2001).

The importance of both utilitarian and hedonic aspects of online shopping has been evidenced in several research projects. Some Web visitors were identified as entertainment seekers, looking for features such as animation, sound clips, online puzzles, and games, and others as directed buyers, seeking a particular item to buy online

(Breitenbach and Doren 1998). In addition, Internet shopping motivations of respondents in a study by Korgaonkar and Wolin (1999) included social escapism motivation, socialization motivation, and economic motivation. Kim (2002) also identified several attributes of the Internet and the mall based on multiple dimensions of consumer value (See Table 3.3).

UTILITARIAN EXPERIENCES

Compared with brick-and-mortar stores, the Internet is viewed as providing more utilitarian benefits. The utilitarian aspects of the consumption experience through the Internet include easy-to-use navigation, interactive decision aids, customer-generated information, and personalized service.

Easy-to-Use Navigation One of the important characteristics of a website that makes a customer comfortable is the ease with which it can be navigated. Consistent navigation links to each page of the website, useful navigational tools such as search engines, and an index to the website help consumers locate merchandise and related information within the site. Most companies design their websites to provide these navigation functions, and many software firms and entertainment companies provide product samples in the form of package demonstrations. For example, www.amazon.com offers book reviews and detailed product descriptions. Also, www.cdnow.com offers a tool with which a consumer can search for compact discs based on the artist name, album title, song title, or record label.

Interactive Decision Aids Interactivity in e-commerce website design is an important feature that attracts and keeps online customers (Fiore, Jin, and Kim 2005). The

two-way online communication between customers and companies not only facilitates relationships, but also enhances customers' abilities to learn how to reduce search costs and increase shopping efficiency simultaneously (Liu, Arnett, Capella, and Taylor 2001). The virtually infinite shelf space available in online stores allows retailers to offer an extremely large number of alternatives within a product category. From a consumer's perspective, having access to a very large number of products is highly desirable. At the same time, however, consumers may simply be unable to process the vast amounts of information surrounding these alternatives. A potential solution to this dilemma is to provide consumers with sophisticated interactive decision aids designed to help them effectively manage potential information overload (Häubl and Trifts 2000). Decision aids can be used to sort products by type, brand name, price, size, and popularity or relevance. These features make it easier for consumers to narrow down their search to identify products that meet their individual preferences.

An example of such decision aids is the Mix and Match feature or the My Virtual Model feature. In apparel retail research by Fiore and Jin (2003), customers select products, develop the body forms, and evaluate a product's level of coordination or appearance on the body form. These features enable the customer to receive more information about products through direct contact with the product, which creates enjoyment, involvement, and a sense of control. The image interactivity of these two features enable customers to make better evaluations in the decision-making process. Further, these features provide a sense of control because more product-body interaction information, needed in the decision-making process, is available (Fiore and Jin 2003).

Customer-Generated Information The Internet has freed customers from their traditionally passive role as receivers of marketing communications, giving them greater control over the information search and knowledge-acquisition process. As a result, customers have become active participants in both information exchange and learning (Ind and Riondino 2001). Apart from firm-driven education, customers often educate other customers through online resources such as e-mail, message boards, and reputation scoring. The communication aspects of the Internet provide customers with the ability to share their experiences, opinions, and knowledge with others on specific topics (Kaiyanam and McIntyre 2002). For instance, a registered user of Amazon (www.amazon.com) can write and disseminate a review of a book or share product testimonials. These features enable consumers to read and compare opinions before purchasing the product themselves. This opportunity to rely on the expertise of many other consumers to gauge the quality of products or services is made more effective by the Internet environment.

Personalized Service Personalized customer service has become the key differentiating factor that can potentially determine the success or failure of a company (Lennon and Harris 2002). Kleindl (2001) noted seven best practice components of online customer service: furnishing product, security, and shipping information; providing link(s) to inventory to determine if products are available; sending automatic order confirmations; avoiding fees that are not charged by brick-and-mortar retailers; responding to customers quickly; providing alternative means of contact (toll-free numbers, e-mail, fax, postal address); and using live individuals to support automated functions.

To provide immediate and accurate answers, some innovative firms, including 1-800-Flowers (www.1-800-flowers.com), Stew Leonard's (www.stewleonards.com), and Delia's (www.delias.com), offer live interaction with a tutorial staff member. Some of these sites feature real-time chat sessions; others feature voice-over Web capabilities.

HEDONIC EXPERIENCES

Although Internet shopping is increasingly becoming more popular, a major disadvantage is that it cannot enable customers to experience the actual products. When online consumers are unable to touch, feel, or taste the merchandise, they can sometimes be deterred from making a purchase. Advances in technology, however, are making it possible for online retailers to bring some of the hedonic experiences customers get at brick-and-mortar stores to the Internet. These experiences attempt to allow customers to interact with products in the same way they would at brick-and-mortar stores. Kim and Kim (2007), based on Pine and Gilmore's (1999) experiential framework, classified online customer experience into four categories: entertainment, education, estheticism, and escape. In the following pages, three major hedonic aspects of the Internet—entertainment, social interaction, and aesthetics—are discussed.

Entertainment As noted earlier, entertainment has become a critical component in creating positive hedonic consumer experiences, which is made possible because of advances in technology and computer graphics. Among a number of entertainment tools, Massively Multiplayer Online Role-Playing Games (MMORPG) provide one of the latest Internet-only gaming experiences and represent a highly compelling online experience. While players experience a virtual world through their own player character in these games, the lines between reality and fiction become blurred with a loss of player self-consciousness. This compelling experience during play triggers flow, the state that intensely involves individuals in an activity to such an extent that nothing else seems to matter (Csikszentmihalyi 1990). Creating flow in Internet games may have numerous positive consequences, including a strong word-of-mouth network, which is a key driver of customer traffic to e-commerce sites (Coupey 2001). Also, the creation of flow experiences can mitigate a consumer's price sensitivity and positively influence subsequent attitudes and behaviors (Novak, Hoffman, and Yung 2000).

With the rapid growth of the Internet gaming industry, e-marketers have turned to interactive games as venues for disseminating advertising and promotional messages. One good example is Ford's online game for the Ford Escape, which features a lunar racetrack that allows visitors to challenge friends via e-mail to a virtual race. In 2002, the launch of Nike's Secret Tournament featuring a global virtual football match was also a phenomenal event. More than a half million football lovers flocked to the online site to train their own dream team and engage in an online tournament (Lee 2003).

Despite the common belief that entertainment on the Internet must provide highly interactive and participatory components, some Internet users remain in the role of pure observers or as part of an audience, simply seeking fun and enjoyable performances to view or listen to. This group of users represents so-called *streamies*, who listen to and watch Internet-based (i.e., streamed) audio and video broadcasts (Rose and Lenski 2005). Arbitron/Edison Media Research estimated that the U.S. Internet broadcast audience is 30 million viewers weekly, accounting for approximately 13 percent of all Americans (Rose and Lenski 2005). This number may continue to grow as more and more users want and like less clicking and more watching experiences on the Internet.

Barnes and Noble's website (www.barnesandnoble.com) operates BNTV and BandN Radio, which enables book shoppers to review a book of poetry or listen to a daily interview series with authors, all from the comfort of their own homes. Travelocity's site (www.travelocity.com) offers 6,000 hours of short clips with voice-overs of travel destinations and 360-degree panoramic videos inside cruise ships. Victoria's Secret (www.victoriassecret.com) broadcasts its exclusive fashion shows on the Internet and TV simultaneously to drive more customer traffic to the website. As such, e-marketing is gradually adding a new degree of entertainment through viewable TV-like experiences.

Today, broadband has the potential to offer better quality and diversity of online entertainment than previous dial-up connections based on its powerful Internet access attributes, such as greater speed, instant access, and the capacity for local area networks (Firth and Mellor 2005). Roughly half of all U.S. households are projected to have broadband connections between 2007 and 2009 (Rose and Lenski 2005) and as the availability of broadband connections expands, sophisticated streaming media presentations will act as competitive advantages differentiating an e-commerce firm from its competitors.

Social Interaction Stemming from work by E. M. Tauber (1972), the concept of social interaction has been positioned as a source of shopping motivation. Consumers motivated by social interaction may choose to shop within a conventional retail store format as opposed to the online context (Rohm and Swaminathan 2004);

however, the Internet has transcended its initial role as an economic or functional entity to become a community center for social and recreational activity through virtual communities.

The notion of community has been at the heart of the Internet since its inception. For many years, scientists have used the Internet to share data, collaborate on research, and exchange messages (Armstrong 1996). Now virtual communities are being used by online retailers to allow customers to interact while making their purchases. Virtual communities are cyberspaces where individuals who have common goals or interests may interact (Balasubramanian and Mahajan 2001, Lechner and Hummel 2002).

Internet relay chat (IRC) in virtual communities, formed primarily for social purposes, is at the heart of online hedonic experiences. IRC is a multiuser, multichannel chatting network that allows people over the Internet to talk with one another in real time without physical or visual contact (Peris et al. 2002). Because online chat rooms are still based predominantly on text, most cues used in traditional face-to-face community settings, such as nonverbal expressions and social characteristics, are filtered out. This filtered out environment is often described as a virtual pub or coffee shop that boosts freedom to express oneself (Bagozzi and Dholkia 2002). Although it is argued that lack of a real presence in online chats results in weaker relationship ties in terms of intensity and depth (Parks and Roberts 1998), chat relationships can be as real as face-to-face relationships and are not only deep and compelling but also rich and pleasant (Peris et al. 2002). In addition, digital video cameras are now affordable enough for many users to incorporate live action into a chat. Recognizing the importance of social interaction, Martha Stewart's website offers regular chat sessions with styl-ish living experts, including Martha Stewart herself, and publishes those transcripts for future reference. Members are also encouraged to share constructive how-to ideas with one another through eight different bulletin boards (e.g., cooking, gardening, crafts) (www.marthastewart.com).

Another type of virtual community—communities of transaction—facilitate the buying and selling of products and services and deliver information related to those transactions. They are not communities in the traditional social sense. Participants are encouraged to interact with one another to engage in a specific transaction. Other participants in the community can give input on products and consumers can speak to other consumers directly. Visitors to communities of transaction may want to buy a used car or a vintage wine, and they may want to consult with other consumers in the community before doing so (Armstrong 1996).

Aesthetics In off-line settings, retail atmosphere elements such as color, music, scent, lighting, and interior design affect retail patronage behavior. Likewise, online aesthetic factors such as attractive color combinations play an important role in generating positive feelings that affect consumer purchasing behavior. E-retailers have recently begun to focus on the need to consider aesthetics and emotions in Web design. Childers et al. (2001) coined the term *webmospherics* to represent the virtual environment counterpart to the physical surroundings associated with the retail atmosphere. Included in the webmospherics are structural design attributes (e.g., frames, pop-up windows, search engine configuration, hypertext links), multimedia dimensions (e.g., graphics, text, audio, color, streaming video), and site layout dimensions (e.g., organization and grouping of merchandise). Each webmospheric dimension represents an important set of design choices that when combined make up an online shopping environment that can either enhance or detract from the customer's aesthetic immersion (Pine and Gilmore 1999).

Image interactivity features on the Web can provide more of the visual sensory information (e.g., seeing how outfits look together or checking the side and back views of the product on the body) than can be found when shopping for the actual product at brick-and-mortar stores. Thus, online enjoyment may come from the actual process involved in developing ensembles alone or on the body form. Through online shopping, consumers can evaluate the product in relationship to products they already own or on a body form that is similar to their body type (Fiore et al. 2005).

Companies are developing several concepts to make Internet shopping more of a sensory experience. One idea is a virtual experience called next generation shopping carts. These three-dimensional audio carts let shoppers hear other shoppers scrambling for a sale in the next aisle. Shoppers can rush over and join them. The wheels of the cart squeak as the shopper goes down the aisle and the shopper can even choose to hear the sounds of a crying baby to complete the shopping experience (Van Name and Catchings 1998).

Another important aspect of online aesthetics can be explained by the extent to which cyberspace can create telepresence (i.e., the extent to which customers feel their presence in the virtual shopping environment). When customers feel an intense telepresence, they can be transported to a virtual storefront, where they can browse and shop as if they were in a real store. In an effort to activate a customer's sense of telepresence, some websites provide a virtual reality (VR) interface that allows the customer to experience a 3-D representa-tion of a store. For example, Herman Miller (www.hermanmiller.com), a furniture retailer, provides a free downloadable application that lets customers browse furniture in 3-D room layouts.

To date, website design has been focused on elements such as colors, text messages, images, logos, and sounds since Internet technologies have been able to capture only the visual and aural senses. In the near future, it may be possible to integrate scent and haptic stimuli into the online shopping environment as the applications of virtual reality technologies advance and expand. If so, these stimuli will bring new dimensions into the online atmosphere, elevating the aesthetic ambiance of the website and resulting in higher quality of online customer experiences.

CHAPTER SUMMARY

This chapter discusses two streams of consumption experience—utilitarian and hedonic consumption experiences. Shoppers who are rational and goal-oriented engage in utilitarian consumer behavior as they seek to purchase products or services efficiently and in a timely manner, with a minimum of sacrifice and irritation. Shoppers who want to interact with a product and view the product's subjective entities where emotions play a major role engage in hedonic consumer behavior. Hedonic shoppers recognize the role of fun and pleasure and personal expression in consumption.

Consumers are turning away from a focus on the object consumed to the consumption experience. The self-esteem and self-actualization needs dominate consumer motivations over physiological needs in most postindustrial societies. The consumption experience, rather than the product, has become a major emphasis of those responsible for a substantial portion of consumer expenditures. The reasons for this phenomenon can be reviewed from both consumer trends and retail trends. Consumer trends include increasing numbers of baby boomers, the polarized demographics driven by the two huge generational waves—baby boomers and millennials—and the widening gap between high-income earners and low-income earners, and rising educational levels. Retail trends include competitiveness due to the increased number of shopping venues and the emergence of new experience economy.

The utilitarian and hedonic consumption experiences have evolved from a product focus to a holistic consumption experience that involves products, people, places, and the environment. Retailers' success seems to be dependent on whether they are keeping up with the consumer shopping expectations of receiving a total consumption experience. A consumer's total experience can be explained as the summed set of the utilitarian and the hedonic experiences.

Utilitarian and hedonic consumption principles can be viewed within the context of many retail practices. Retailers, whether they are online retailers, catalog outlets, or brick-and-mortar retailers, can provide both utilitarian and hedonic experiences to their customers. For example, brick-and-mortar stores can satisfy the utilitarian needs of consumers by providing the right products and offering shopping trips that require the least amount of time and effort. Brick-and-mortar retailers can also provide hedonic benefits to consumers through atmosphere, social interaction, and pleasant experiences. Non-store retailers, such as the Internet, catalogs, and personalized sales, also provide shoppers with utilitarian and hedonic benefits. The Internet provides utilitarian benefits such as ease of navigation, interactive decision aids, customer-generated information, and personalized service. Hedonic benefits include entertainment (e.g., interactive games), social interaction (e.g., virtual communities), and aesthetics (e.g., webmospherics, image interactivity). Indeed, all types of retailers, when developing their retail mix, must consider the consumer's desire to receive a total consumption experience.

Discussion Questions

1. Market power has shifted from marketer and retailer to whom? Explain and describe how this shift has occurred.

2. What are the current consumer trends that are impacting retailing? How have they contributed to a need for experiential retailing?

3. Explain Pine and Gilmore's (1999) *Experience Economy*. What are some examples of brick-and-mortar retailers that are creating experiences for the customer?

4. How is utilitarian consumption different from hedonic consumption in the context of catalog shopping? Identify retail examples.

5. Into what categories does the FCB grid divide products? Explain the grid.

6. Arnold and Reynolds (2003) identify six hedonic shopping motivations. List and explain at least four of the six and explain how experiential retail practices can satisfy them.

7. How can a consumption experience be balanced?

8. Describe two types of brick-and-mortar stores and comment on the effectiveness of the experiences they currently create for the customer.

9. How do shopping centers offer a utilitarian experience? A hedonic experience?

10. In your shopping experience, does catalog shopping or online shopping offer a better experience? Support your opinion with examples.

11. Why is it important for the Internet to provide utilitarian components to the online shopping experience?

12. In this chapter, the hedonic aspect of Internet shopping contains three components: entertainment, social interaction, and aesthetics. How does each of these affect a customer's shopping experience?

REFERENCES

Adams, A. J., and S. Auken. 1995. Observations: A new approach to measuring product category membership. *Journal of Advertising Research* 35(5):73–79.

Addis, M., and M. Holbrook. 2001. On the conceptual link between mass customization and experiential consumption: An explosion of subjectivity. *Journal of Consumer Behaviour* 1(1):50–66.

Armstrong, A. 1996. The real value of online communities. *Harvard Business Review* 74(3):134–141.

Arnold, M., and K. Reynolds. 2003. Hedonic shopping motivations. *Journal of Retailing* 79(2):77–95.

Babin, B. J., W. R. Darden, and M. Griffin. 1994. Work and/or fun: Measuring hedonic and utilitarian shopping value. *Journal of Consumer Research* 20(4):644–656.

Bagozzi, R., and U. Dholakia. 2002. Intentional social action in virtual communities. *Journal of Interactive Marketing* 16(2):2–21.

Balasubramanian, S., and V. Mahajan. (2001). The economic leverage of the virtual community. *International Journal of Electronic Commerce* 5(3):103–138.

Barta, S., J. Martin, J. Frye, and M. Woods. 1999. Trends in retail trade. *Oklahoma State University, Oklahoma Cooperative Extension Web Site, Facts Sheets.* http://pods.dasnr.okstate.edu/docushare/dsweb/Get/Document-2492/F-565web.pdf. (accessed February 27, 2003).

Bartlett, R. 2003. Testing the "Popsicle Test": Retailing of retail shopping in new traditional neighborhood development. *Urban Studies* 40(8):1471–1485.

Betts, K., K. Novack, and M. Toyama. 2004. Luxury fever. *Time* 164:50–54.

Bloch, P. H., N. M. Ridgway, and D. L. Sherrell. 1989. Extending the concept of shopping: An investigation of browsing activity. *Journal of the Academy of Marketing Science* 17(1):13–21.

Bowers, K., R. Williamson, and V. Young. 2004. Discounters challenged from the top, bottom. *Women's Wear Daily* 188(118):45.

Breitenbach, C., and V. Doren. (1998). Value added marketing in the digital domain: Enhancing the utility of the Internet. *Journal of Consumer Marketing* 15(6):558–575.

Chain Drug Review. 2005. Mass Retailing Enters Post-Wal-Mart World. 27(8):28.

Chain Store Age. 2000. Mixed-Use Projects Serve. 78(1):144–148.

Chandon, P., B. Wansink, and G. Laurent. 2000. A benefit congruency framework of sales promotion effectiveness. *Journal of Marketing* 64(4):65–71.

Childers, T. L., C. L. Carr, J. Peck, and S. Carson. 2001. Hedonic and utilitarian motivations for online retail shopping behavior. *Journal of Retailing* 77(4):417–424.

Coupey, E. 2001. *Marketing and the Internet*. Upper Saddle River, NJ: Prentice-Hall, Inc.

Cox, A., D. Cox, and R. Anderson. 2005. Reassessing the pleasures of store shopping. *Journal of Business Research* 58(3):250–259.

Crowley, A., E. Spangenberg-Halton, and K. Hughes. 1992. Measuring the hedonic and utilitarian dimensions of attitudes toward product categories. *Marketing Letters* 3(3):239–249.

Csikszentmihalyi, M. 1990. *Flow: The psychology of optimal experience.* New York: HarperPerennial.

Danziger, P. N. (2004). *Why people buy things they don't need*. Chicago, IL: Dearborn Trade Publishing.

Datamonitor. (2002). U.S. niche baby boomers 2002: Capturing ethnic and low-income consumers. www.mindbranch.com/products/R313-4452.html (accessed August 3, 2006).

Dhar, R., and K. Wertenbroch. 2000. Consumer choice between hedonic and utilitarian goods. *Journal of Marketing Research* 37(1):60–71.

Eastlick, M., and R. Feinberg. 1999. Shopping motives for mail catalog shopping. *Journal of Business Research* 45(3):281–290.

Fenley, G. 2003. Reinventing the mall. *Display and Design Ideas* 15(4):20–23.

Firth, L., and D. Mellor. 2005. Broadband: Benefits and problems. *Telecommunications Policy* 29(2/3):223–236.

Fiore, Ann M., and Hyun-Jeong Jin. 2003. Influence of image interactivity on approach responses towards on online retailer. *Internet Research: Electronic Networking Applications and Policy* 13:38–48.

Fiore, Ann M., Hyun-Jeong Jin, and Jihyun Kim. 2005. For fun and profit: Hedonic value from image interactivity and responses toward an online store. *Psychology & Marketing* 22(8):669–694.

Griffin, M., B. Babin, and D. Modianos. 2000. Shopping values of Russian consumers: The impact of habituation in a developing economy. *Journal of Retailing* 76(1):33–52.

Halliday, Jean. 2003. Automakers focus more on young buyers *Automotive News* 77(6035):1M.

Häubl, G., and V. Trifts. 2000. Consumer decision making in online shopping environments: The effects of interactive decision aids. *Marketing Science* 19(1):4–21.

Hemakom, R. 2002. New directions. *Journal of Housing and Community Development* 59(September/October): 32–40.

Hirschman, E. C. 1984. Experience seeking: A subjectivist perspective of consumption. *Journal of Business Research* 12:115–136.

Hirschman, E. C., and M. B. Holbrook. 1982. Hedonic consumption: Emerging concepts, methods and propositions. *Journal of Marketing* 46(3):92–101.

Holbrook, M. 1994. The nature of customer value: An axiology of services in the consumption experience. In R.T. Rust and R. L. Oliver, eds., *Service Quality: New Directions in Theory and Practice* (21–71). Newbury Park, CA: Sage.

———. 1999. Introduction to consumer value. In Morris Holbrook, ed., *Consumer Value: A Framework for Analysis and Research* (1–28). New York: Routledge.

Holbrook, M. B., and E. C. Hirschman. 1982. Experiential aspects of consumption: Consumer fantasies, feelings, and fun. *Journal of Consumer Research* 9(2):132–140.

Howard, J. A., and J. N. Sheth. 1969. *The theory of buyer behavior.* New York: John Wiley and Sons.

Ind, N., and M. Riondino. 2001. Branding on the Web: A real revolution. *Journal of Brand Management* 9(1):8–19.

International Council of Shopping Centers. 2004. Shopping center definitions. www.icsc.org/srch/lib/SCDefinitions.pdf (accessed January 25, 2006).

Kaiyanam, K., and S. McIntyre. 2002. The e-marketing mix: A contribution to the e-tailing wars. *Journal of the Academy of Marketing Science* 30(4):483–495.

Karat, C., J. Karat, J. Vergo, C. Pinhanez, D. Riecken, and T. Cofino. 2002. That's entertainment! Designing streaming, multimedia web experiences. *International Journal of Human-Computer Interaction* 14(3/4):369–384.

Kim, Y-K. 2002. Consumer value: An application to mall and Internet shopping. *International Journal of Retail and Distribution Management* 30(12):595–602.

Kim, H., and Kim, Y-K. 2007. Enriching the customer experience: Implications for e-marketers. *Journal of Value Chain Management*. In press.

Kleindl, B. 2001. *Strategic electronic marketing: Managing e-business*. Cincinnati, OH: SouthWestern Publishing Co.

Korgaonkar, P., and L. Wolin. 1999. A multivariate analysis of web usage. *Journal of Advertising research* 39(2):53–68.

Lageat, T., S. Czellar, and G. Laurent. 2003. Engineering hedonic attributes to generate perceptions of luxury: Consumer perception of an everyday sound. *Marketing Letters* 14(2):97–109.

Langrehr, F. W. 1991. Retail shopping mall semiotics and hedonic consumption. In R. Holman & M. Solomon, eds., *Advances in Consumer Research, Vol. 18* (428–433). Provo, UT: Association for Consumer Research.

Lechner, U., and J. Hummel. 2002. Business models and system architectures of virtual communities: From a sociological phenomenon to peer-to-peer architectures. *International Journal of Electronic Commerce* 6(3):41–53.

Lee, V. 2003. Advergaming your way to online brand building successes. *Media Asia*. September 5, 15.

Lennon, R., and J. Harris. 2002. Customer service on the Web: A cross-industry investigation. *Journal of Targeting, Measurement and Analysis for Marketing* 10(4):325–338.

Liu, C., P. Arnett, L. Capella, and R. Taylor. 2001. Key dimensions of web design quality as related to consumer response. *Journal of Computer Information Systems* 42(1):70–77.

Marks, D. 2002. Values change, markets follow. *Shopping Center World* 31(5):142–146.

Mathwick, C., N. K. Malhotra, and E. Rigdon 2002. The effect of dynamic retail experiences on experiential perceptions of value: An Internet and catalog comparison. *Journal of Retailing*, 78(1):51–60.

May, E. 1989. A retail odyssey. *Journal of Retailing* 65(3):356–367.

Mitchell, A. 1998. What's the big idea of experience marketing? *Marketing Week* 21(19):28–29.

Morton, Linda P. 2003. Targeting Generation X. *Public Relations Quarterly* 48(4):43–45.

Novak, T., D. Hoffman, and Y. Yung. 2000. Measuring the customer experience in online environments: A structural modeling approach. *Marketing Science* 19(1):22–42.

O'Connor, P. C. 1999. Which retail properties are getting market share? *The Appraisal Journal* 67(1): 37–40.

Okada, M. 2005. Justification effects on consumer choice of hedonic and utilitarian goods. *Journal of Marketing Research* 42(1):43–53.

Parks, M., and L. Roberts. 1998. Making MOOs: the development of personal relationships on line and a comparison to their off-line counterparts. *Journal of Social and Personal Relationships* 15:517–537.

Peris, R., M. Gimeno, D. Pinazo, G. Ortet, V. Carrero, M. Sanchiz, and I. Ibáñez. 2002. Online chat rooms: Virtual spaces of interaction for socially oriented people. *CyberPsychology and Behavior* 5(1):43–51.

Pine, J. B., and J. H. Gilmore. 1999. *The experience economy: Work is theater and every business is a stage.* Boston, MA: Harvard Business School Press.

Ratchford, B. 1987. New insights about the FCB grid. *Journal of Advertising Research* 27(4):24–38.

Reynolds, K., J. Ganesh, and M. Luckett. 2002. Traditional malls vs. factory outlets: comparing shopper typologies and implications for retail strategy. *Journal of Business Research* 55:687–696.

Rohm, A., and V. Swaminathan. 2004. A typology of online shoppers based on shopping motivations. *Journal of Business Research* 57(7):748–757.

Rose, B., and J. Lenski. 2005. Internet and multimedia 2005: The on-demand media Consumer. *Arbitron/Edison Media Research.* www.edisonresearch.com/home/archives//Internet percent202005 percent20Summary percent20Final.pdf (accessed August 3, 2005).

Roy, S. 2005. On sale this season: Retailers. *Display and Design Ideas* 17(6):6.

Schmitt, Bernard. 1999. *Experiential marketing.* New York: The Free Press.

Seckler, V. 2004. Fashionistas: Crossing shopping's great divide. *Women's Wear Daily* 188(51):24–25.

Sheehan, K. B. 2002. Toward a typology of Internet users and online privacy concerns. *Information Society* 18(1):21–32.

Shim, S., and M. Eastlick. 1998. The hierarchical influence of personal values on mall shopping attitude and behavior. *Journal of Retailing* 74(1):139–160.

Slyke, C. V., C. L. Comunale, and F. Belanger. 2002. Gender differences in perceptions of Web-based shopping. *Communications of the ACM* 45(8):82–86.

Solomon, M. 2002. *Consumer behavior,* 5th ed. Upper Saddle River, NJ: Prentice-Hall.

Szuchman, P. 2005. Can this kitchen be saved? *The Wall Street Journal Eastern Edition* 245(84):W1.

Tauber, E. M. 1972. Why do people shop? *Journal of Marketing* 36(4):46–49.

Trachtenberg, J. 2005. Selling Harry: 1 castle, 70 kids, 2,000 business ads. *Wall Street Journal* 245(109):B1.

Troy, M. 2005. Merchandising mindset on display in Wal-Mart prototype. *Retailing Today* 44(11):19.

Tsao, A. 2004. Retail's little guys come back. *Business Week Online.* November 23, www.Businessweekonline.com (accessed July 8, 2005).

U.S. Department of Labor Statistics. 2005. Consumer Expenditures in 2003. www.bls.gov/cex/csxann03.pdf (accessed July 14, 2006).

Van Name, Mark, and Bill Catchings. 1998. E-Commerce expose reveals secret plans. *PC Week* 15(42):36.

Vaughn, R. 1980. How advertising works: A planning model. *Journal of Advertising Research* 20(5):27–33.

Wakefield, K., and J. Baker. 1998. Excitement at the mall: Determinants and effects on shopping response. *Journal of Retailing* 74(4):515–539.

Warson, A. 2000. The Re-malling of America. *National Real Estate Investor* 42(10):96–101.

Weintraub, Arlene, John Carey, Timothy Mullaney, and Fredrick F. Jespersen. 2006. Hot Growth. *Business Week* 3987(June 5):48–52.

Westbrook, R. A., and W. C. Black. 1985. A motivation-based shopper typology. *Journal of Retailing* 61(1):78–103.

Women's Wear Daily. 2005. Still Roaring. 189(129):10–12.

Xing, Y. and D. B. Grant. 2006. Developing a framework for measuring physical distribution service quality of multichannel and "pure player" Internet retailers. *International Journal of Retail and Distribution Management* 34(4/5):278–289.

PART

SYMBOLIC CONSUMPTION

Image is the Key to Differentiation

When it comes to advertising, Target is in a class of its own. Over the course of the last decade, in particular, Target has used its marketing muscle to transform its trademark bull's-eye into a universally recognized symbol, and, in turn, establish its retail format as a unique destination in the eyes of the discount consumer. By conveying this high-end, pop-art image through such media as glossy magazines, prime-time television commercials, billboards, and circulars, Target has shown the rest of the world there's something refreshingly different about this big-box retailer. In short, its image comes off as hipper, edgier, and more fun than the discount retailer down the street.

Most important, though, this trendy image has not come at the expense of a value message. Take, for example, Target's campaign in apparel. According to Carol Henderson, partner and creative director at McKee Wallwork Henderson, the company has succeeded in impressing upon consumers that spending $8 on a basic white T-shirt in its stores, rather than $18 at Gap stores, is not only smart, but also cool. "I'd love to think it was all planned," Henderson said. "But I think they just wanted to make Target a cool place to shop." To create its differentiated bargain shopping experience, Target takes its cue from successful specialty retailers, such as Pottery Barn, Restoration Hardware, and Gap, who are outside the discount world.

Target borrows from these retailers to create compelling merchandising displays for its growing list of exclusive brands, such as Michael Graves, Mossimo, and Freestyle by Danskin. Its expect more, pay less strategy resonates with consumers. "Value always wins," president of Target.direct Dale Nitschke told an audience of analysts and media at a recent Forrester Research conference. "Consumers demand more and are not willing to pay a premium price for it," he added. That said, reinforcing price perception without sacrificing quality, trend-right merchandise underlines Target's strategy. Each initiative the retailer undertakes—from the flashy Times Square billboard to the outfitting of a Tribeca town house—aims to ensure the ongoing ascendance of the Target brand.

The Kmart brand also takes a backseat to those it carries in its stores. It has traditionally been "Martha Stewart at Kmart." Target's message is the opposite, "Target has Mossimo," said Henderson. Yet that's not to suggest Target fails to support the national brands lining its shelves. Its recent postmodern style Color My World Campaign, a continuation of last year's award-winning Pop Art program, features a monochromatic sampling of national brands. One ad, for example, includes a trio of crimson-clad models, Big Red chewing gum, Iams dog chow, Pringles potato chips, and Coca Cola against a red backdrop. The campaign won Target Best in Show for the eighth year running at Retail Advertising Council's award ceremony in February 2001.

Programs such as Lullaby Club and Club Wedd also succeed in winning over consumers, forming an emotional relationship with them as they plan for family life. Target's community outreach may also have a long-term influence on buying. "There are lots of consumers who want to do business with socially conscious retailers," said Whalin. "Target stores give back more than $1.5 million per week to its local communities through grants and special programs. Its philanthropic efforts make mom shop there not because she has to, but because she wants to," said Henderson. "There's a difference between trademarks and love marks," she added. "Target customers feel like they are part of a club."

Source: Prior, M. 2002. Image is the key to differentiation. *DSN Retailing Today* 41(7):54–55. Reprinted with permission.

INTRODUCTION

Consumers symbolically create themselves, in part, through everyday consumption. Whether it is through products purchased, activities pursued, or philosophies and beliefs accepted, consumption behavior reveals stories about who one is and with whom one identifies (Wattanasuwan 2005). A consumer may purchase an expensive item such as a Lexus automobile because the Lexus brand symbolizes prestige. A shopper may identify with a particular retailer such as Target and shop there because of the symbolic association with the cool, hip image that Target portrays through advertisements, store environment, and products. Choosing to purchase organic groceries may symbolize concern for one's health. Driving a Honda automobile may symbolize one's desire for quality and dependability. Wearing a Rolex watch may symbolize desired status.

Consumption is central to everyday lives. It is an element of social position, and it is used to create and sustain the self. Consumers tend to consume products and services that hold individualized symbolic meanings (Wattanasuwan 2005). Consumers subjectively evaluate goods or services as they pursue their self-identities through consumption and seek to satisfy their identity needs that are analogous with Maslow's hierarchy. Belk (1988) iden-tified possessions as contributing to and reflecting individual identity. Because of the importance of possessions to the consumer's constructed self-identity, their loss is considered a "lessening of self" (Belk 1988, 142).

Bauman (2001) suggested that socially produced individualization liberates a person from official and inherited roles or statuses. Personal identities are transformed so that new tasks can be undertaken. Nike takes advantage of socially constructed individualism in its advertisements. Its products are designed for athletes and sports excellence. Nike marketing suggests that if you purchase Nike products, you can be a winner too.

SYMBOLIC INTERACTION

Symbolic interaction seeks to understand the nature of the socially constructed world through theory and methodology (*International Encyclopedia of the Social and Behavioral Sciences* 2001). A theory of symbolic interaction proposes that human events are understood through the continuous adjustment of behavior in response to the way others act (Becker and McCall 1990). Thus, meaning is gleaned from observing the way others act in response to previous actions. Symbolic interaction sees society as a process of ongoing activities and interactions affecting interpersonal relationships (Manis and Meltzer 1978). According to Blumer (1978), "the term symbolic interaction refers, of course, to the peculiar and distinctive character of interaction as it takes place between human beings. The peculiarity consists of the fact that human beings interpret or 'define' each other's actions instead of merely reacting to each other's actions" (97).

Social interaction theory assumes that social roles, belief systems, and other forms of social structure objectify and externalize meaning (Lewis and Smith 1980). Thus, symbols are effective when people find meanings in them. Blumer (1978) stated "human interaction is mediated by the use of symbols, by interpretation, or by ascertaining the meaning of one another's actions. This mediation is equivalent to inserting a process of interpretation between stimulus and response in the case of human behavior" (97). Glasser (1990) suggested people experience selfhood through magazines such as *GQ*, *Vogue*, and *Self* that model how people should fashion their appearance.

Whether it is a distinctive package, an elaborately staged television commercial, or perhaps a model on the cover of a magazine, we try to make sense of a marketing stimulus by interpreting the meaning associated with an image. Much of the meaning is influenced by what we make of the symbolism we perceive. Wal-Mart uses its iconic smiley face to appeal to their customers, who it views as the U.S. population (O'Loughlin 2005a). Wal-Mart built its customer foundation around alluring and unbeatable opening price-points. The yellow smiley face acts as a symbol that stimulates consumers to shop at Wal-Mart. It is important for retailers to understand how the symbolic meanings they project are interpreted by their customers.

Social behavior is not only a response to others' behavior, but also incorporates their behavior (Manis and Meltzer 1978).

Individuals use symbols as cues to take on the roles of those around them. Malls design symbolic landscapes that alter shoppers' moods and dispositions, creating the illusion that something other than consumption is occurring (Gross 1993). The shopping center gives symbolic expression to cultural values of consumption and creates social order, in addition to providing material goods for consumption. Consumers learn how to interpret and react to the signs around them. Meaning is created as consumers interact with these signs. They understand the meaning of the mall and react accordingly.

Purchasing behavior influenced by symbolic interactionism exists when consumers buy a product or service because of what it represents based upon societal symbols (Leigh and Gabel 1992). A series of advertisements that have received prestigious awards illustrate the association between symbolic interaction and consumption. An ad by Grey and Trace in Barcelona for a Pilot G-Tec Extrafine pen won a London International Advertising Award. It plays on the maxim "There is a fine line between love and hate." Another London International Advertising Award was given to Ogilvy and Mather for Unilever's Dove. The message for the consumer is that Dove's oversized soap bar is aligned with "outstanding." In this case, the consumer can purchase Dove soap and be associated with outstanding beauty.

Consumers find symbolic value in high-priced products (e.g., boats, luxury cars), products associated with performance risk (e.g., sporting equipment), complex products (e.g., iPods, digital cameras), specialty products (e.g., gourmet food, jewelry), and products associated with one's ego (e.g., perfume, aftershave) (Leigh and Gabel 1992). A favorable symbolic image that is consistent and congruent should be incorporated in all aspects of the marketing mix. A retail outlet's symbolic image should match that of its products and recognize that symbolic interaction is influenced by both products and services.

SYMBOLIC CONSUMPTION AND CULTURE

All consumption is symbolic because it has cultural meaning, even though that meaning may not be shared (Slater 1997). Wattanasuwan (2005) suggested that "contemporary society is first and foremost a consumer culture—where our social life operates in the sphere of consumption" (179). Thus, consumption is culturally specific and manifested through unique cultural patterns. This perspective is viewed from cognitive symbolism, cultural meaning of goods, consumer culture theory, and cultural subgroups.

Cognitive Symbolism

In his book *Culture: Reinventing the Social Science*, Martin (1996) discussed three ways that consumers might think about culture: the ideal, documentary, and a way of life. The ideal represents perfect and universal values. Hamilton (2003) described the General Foods ideal 1949 consumer as "coming from an upper-middle-class background, capable of appreciating Wall Street metaphors for the exchange of affection" (43). The idealized customer is portrayed in Birds Eye advertisements in *Life* January 1949 edition as "a well-off woman, wearing pearls, high heels, and an elegant satin outfit" (43) and "relaxing comfortably on a pillow, reading a novel" (43). The advertisement positions Birds Eye frozen spinach as "grander than the grandest spinach" and "work-free-est," which means it is already prepared for cooking (Hamilton 2003). Documentary records human thoughts, language forms, conventions, and experiences in relation to their value to the ideal

or societal traditions. The British Broadcasting Companies series *Are You Being Served* is a satirical documentary about a fictional past-its-prime department store and its employees. The show first aired in 1972 and chronicled day-to-day activities in the fictional Grace Brothers department store. "Way of life" refers to the structure of a social group's feelings. ING DIRECT, a U.S. online and telephone banking brand, has a café and offers free Internet access to its customers (Hein 2005). This service brand creates a physical space to facilitate a sense of belonging for ING customers. These three modes of thinking about culture are interrelated and contribute to distinctive cultural patterns.

Cultural Meaning of Goods

Consumers purchase material goods because they perceive them to have meaning. These goods acquire symbolic meaning when they take on a significance that is unique to the purchaser. That is, symbolism is embedded in objects and contributes to meaningful consumption expressed through objects. For example, a common color line for newborn clothing is blue for boys and pink for girls. Because babies often appear to be gender neutral, parents may choose to visually express whether they have a new son or daughter using color as the visual cue and gender symbol.

Objects can symbolize security, and express self-concept, connection, and differentiation (Wallendorf and Arnould 1988). Objects can be used to create personal storehouses of meaning. When this happens, the symbolic value that is attached to an object takes on new significance. When a symbolic object is lost, it can generate a loss of status. For example, a consumer might create status by taking annual vacations to exotic places. When economic factors eliminate that consumption option, there may be a loss of status since the consumer is no longer defined by this significant experience. Consumers do not consume only to satisfy needs, but rather use goods in self-creation (Wattanasuwan 2005).

Cultural meanings of goods are dynamic (McCracken 1988). As these meanings are communicated to others and through different cultures, their significance may change. Different types of goods vary in meaning and they fill different niches throughout a consumer's lifetime (Oropesa 1995). Young adults enjoy owning and showing off possessions, while older consumers find satisfaction in financial products. Some goods remind consumers of the time a particular object was purchased or became part of their lives. Often, consumers base purchase decisions for products and services on symbolic connections to past experiences. If a new mother needs to choose a specific laundry detergent to launder her baby's clothes, she may select the same detergent her own mother used when she was a baby. The emotional association the product creates for the new mother helps reassure her that she is using the best possible product for the health and safety of her own baby. Otnes and Scott (1996) stated, "Cultural meaning has shifted from the culturally constituted world to the consumer good" (33). Retailers need to understand the meanings that each consumer segment attaches to symbols.

The use and purchase of symbolic products allows consumers to achieve elevated status through consumption. The product's social meaning contributes to an individual's self identity. Thus, a distinction is created between the use value and exchange value of products. An example of symbolism in a product comes from the home furnishings industry. Emerson et Cie has an upholstery choice called Gandhi-26 that is used on the Rattan Lounge Chair and Ottoman. The name of the upholstery evokes a symbolic meaning—Gandhi was a famous Indian politician internationally respected for his keen intellect and dedication to nonviolent protest to create social change; when the consumer sits in this chair, he or she associates the chair with Gandhi's attributes.

Brands with clear and consistent images result in well-defined and strong world-wide images (Bhat and Reddy 1998). For example, brand orientation helps a fashion retailer's competitive position relative to merchandise, trading format, customer service, and customer communication advantage (Bridson and Evans 2004). Even shopping bags communicate store and shopper equity (Luthro 2003). Shopping bags provide an opportunity for displaying advertising and art, and serve both symbolic and utilitarian purposes; they can even be souvenirs. For example, carrying a signature bag means that the carrier is part of a distinct class of retail shoppers. A shopping bag from Coach says you can afford to shop there; carrying the shopping bag is equal to wearing a symbol of the store brand. The little, medium, or large brown bag from Bloomingdale's is like the much desired blue box from Tiffany and Co.

Consumer Culture Theory

Consumer culture is derived from the symbolic and material resources that support meaningful ways of life. It explains the way in which markets mediate the social arrangement between lived culture and its social resources. **Consumer Culture Theory** (CCT) offers a framework for understanding this social arrangement. CCT addresses the dynamic links among consumer behavior, the marketplace, and cultural meanings by examining the contextual, symbolic, and experiential aspects of the consumption cycle as it moves through the processes of acquisition, consumption and possession, and disposition processes (Arnould and Thompson 2005). CCT examines consumption across a variety of social spaces such as retail settings and tourist sites. It offers a consumer-centric perspective of the marketplace that conceptualizes consumers' cultural and social motivations for retail patronage, purchase behaviors, and retail purchase decisions.

Arnould and Thompson (2005) explained consumer behavior from this consumer culture perspective and identified cultural process as transmitted, learned, shared, transformed, communicated, and cumulative. In a trend comparison of families from 1960 and 2000, Oswald (2003) concluded that the trends, innovations, conflicts, and aspirations of society at large are observable in the contemporary family unit. In 1960, women learned social cues from television stars such as Donna Reed and Harriet Nelson. "Women gladly cooked and cleaned, dressed in pearls and high heels, no less, while awaiting the arrival home of the all-knowing husband" (Oswald 2003, 315). Oswald (2003) further stated that men were idealized as "the man in the gray flannel suit" (315). Children lived with their parents. They wore tailored clothing similar to what their parents wore, not clothing that reflected their own tastes or trends. Families shopped in department stores. Social roles were gender specific; mothers were characterized as stay-at-home moms and fathers were characterized as white-collar corporate employees. Family life and consumption were dependent upon the corporation, as many families relocated for corporate America. Furthermore, "eating out was for special occasions and ordering take-out was unusual. Betty Crocker was required reading for new wives. Meat and potatoes were the standard. No one expected the range of ethnic dishes available today" (Oswald 2003, 316).

The marketing symbols that induce consumer desire for market-produced commodities are a fundamental aspect of consumer culture. CCT accounts for how retailers and consumers engage in the co-creation of culturally constituted endeavors. Retailers produce a collection of resources (e.g., brands, personnel, pricing strategies, and advertising) that are packaged into retail environments. Consumers use their own cultural resources (i.e., economic, social, and ideological assets) along with retailer-provided resources to create the experiences they desire. Consumers secure the outcomes they want through patronage, purchase, and consumption (Arnould 2005). In this process, consumers continuously transfer cultural resources that build consumer-retailer relationships and transfer culturally specific meanings (Creighton 1998).

Arnould (2005) identified four categories of cultural resources that retailers offer consumers (See Table 4.1): economic, utopian, ludic, and temporal. These retailer cultural resources help consumers connect to their own cultural resources that they use to organize their personal and social life external to the retail store. As such, consumer experiences depend upon the co-activation of the retailers' and consumers' operant resources. The operant resources that consumers bring to the marketplace are embedded in the subgroups to which they belong, such as ethnicity, social class, religion, gender, and family.

Cultural Subgroups

Culture can be associated with a generational cohort or group. A consumer cohort might consist of individuals born during the same time period or be based on occupation and employment. Each cohort group, such as the hippies of the 1960s, has identifiable lifestyle characteristics,

TABLE 4.1. CO-PRODUCTIVE ROLES OF CULTURAL AND OPERANT RESOURCES FROM CONSUMER TO RETAILER USED TO CREATE CONSUMER EXPERIENCES

CULTURAL AND OPERANT RESOURCES USED TO CREATE CONSUMER EXPERIENCES

CONSUMER		RETAILER	
CULTURAL	**OPERANT**	**CULTURAL**	**OPERANT**
Value for money	Frugality Thriftiness	Economic	Auctions Discounts Everyday low pricing Longer payment terms Low interest rates Sales promotions Value pricing Savings promotions
Pursuit of a utopian world of selves	Arranging consumer place in imaginary, perfect reality Weaving the ideals for the perfect world into everyday lives and selfhood	Utopian	Festival malls Tourist destinations Religious theme parks Hypermarkets Retrobrands Retail retroscapes Eco-retailers
Pursuit of play	Ongoing search Imaginative role playing Fan behaviors Beat-the-market games Treasure hunts Transcendent experiences	Ludic	Independent toy stores ESPNZone Thrift stores
Preferred timestyles	Time allocation Nostalgia	Temporal	Time-saving utilities Alternative timestyles Servicescapes

Source: Arnould, E. J. 2005. Animating the big middle. *Journal of Retailing* 81(2):89–96.

including consumption of particular goods or services.

Consumer cohorts may travel through life together and experience similar external events during their late adolescent or early adulthood years (Schewe and Meredith 2004). Shared experiences and defining moments shape values of consumer cohorts. These values become embedded and can remain with individuals over a lifetime. Schewe and Meredith (2004) segmented global markets by generational cohorts that are composed of depression cohort (born between 1912 and 1921), second World War cohort (born between 1922 and 1927), postwar cohort (born between 1928 and 1945), leading-edge baby boomer (born between 1946 and 1954), trailing-edge baby boomer (born between 1955 and 1965), Generation X cohort (born between 1965 and 1976), and N Generation cohort (born after 1976). These cohorts were compared in their values as shown in Table 4.2.

Rosenbaum (2005) found that objects and artifacts suggest similar meanings among members of specific ethnic groups. In Rosenbaum's study, Jewish consumers emotionally responded to delicatessen pictures and associated them with memories and nostalgia. Generational differences exist in hot spots to visit, jewelry consumption, reading materials, and media consumption.

Hip-hop has become a dominant subculture after being viewed as a niche music market that had an association with gangster rappers (Devany 2004). The amount of

TABLE 4.2 SEVEN AMERICAN COHORTS

COHORT PROFILE	COHORT DESCRIPTION
Depression cohort (born from 1912–1921; came of age during the Great Depression; ages 83–92 in 2004)	This group's coming-of-age experience consisted of economic strife, elevated unemployment rates and having to take menial jobs to survive. Financial security–what they most lacked when coming of age–rules their thinking.
Second World War cohort (born from 1922–1927; came of age during the Second World War; ages 78–82 in 2004)	Sacrifice for the common good was widely accepted among members of this cohort, as evidenced by women working in factories for the war effort and men going off to fight. Overall, this cohort was focused on defeating a common enemy and their members are more team-oriented and patriotic than those of other generational cohorts.
Postwar cohort (born from 1928–1945; came of age after WWII; ages 59–76 in 2004)	These individuals experienced a time of remarkable economic growth and social tranquility, a time of family togetherness, the Korean conflict, McCarthyism, school dress codes, and moving to the suburbs. Overall, this cohort participated in the rise of the middle class, sought a sense of security and stability, and expected prosperous times to continue indefinitely.
Leading-edge baby boomer cohort (born from 1946–1954; came of age during the turmoil of the 1960s; ages 50–58 in 2004)	This group remembers the assassinations of John and Robert Kennedy and Martin Luther King Jr. It was the loss of JFK that largely shaped this cohort's values. They became adults during the Vietnam War and watched as the first man walked on the moon. Leading-edge boomers were dichotomous: They championed causes (Greenpeace, civil rights, women's rights), yet were simultaneously hedonistic and self-indulgent (pot, free love, sensuality).
Trailing-edge baby boomer cohort (born from 1955–1965; came of age during the first sustained economic downturn since the Depression; ages 39–49 in 2004)	This group witnessed the fall of Vietnam, Watergate, and Nixon's resignation. The oil embargo, the raging inflation rate, and the more than 30 percent decline in the S&P Index led these individuals to be less optimistic about their financial future than the leading-edge boomers.
Generation X cohort (born from 1965–1976; came of age during a time of instability and uncertainty; ages 28–38 in 2004)	These are the latchkey children of divorce who have received the most negative publicity. This cohort has delayed marriage and children, and they do not take these commitments lightly. More than other groups, this cohort accepts cultural diversity and puts quality of personal life ahead of work life. They are free agents, not team players. Despite a rocky start into adulthood, this group shows a spirit of entrepreneurship unmatched by any other cohort.
N Generation cohort (born from 1977–?; came of age during the Information Revolution; ages 27 and under in 2004)	The youngest cohort is called the N Generation or N-Gen because the advent of the Internet is a defining event for them, and because they will be the engine of growth over the next two decades. While still a work in progress, their core value structure seems to be quite different from that of Gen-X. They are more idealistic and social-cause oriented, without the cynical "What's in it for me?" free-agent mindset of many Gen-Xers.

Source: Schewe, C. D., and G. Meredith. 2004. Segmenting global markets by generational cohorts: Determining motivations by age. *Journal of Consumer Behaviour* 4(1):51–62.

money associated with hip-hop's bling culture is attractive to retailers. There is interest in what this cultural subgroup wears, eats, and drives. The hip-hop market is an estimated group of 45.3 million people who spend $12.6 billion on related media and merchandise (Devany 2004). This market segment is between the ages of 12 and 34 and 80 percent white with $1 trillion overall spending power. Eminem is a cultural icon for consumers in the urban hip-hop cultural subgroup. Eminem, the rapper,

now is a brand associated with a radio station, clothing line, and movie properties. These Eminem brand-related product extensions reportedly are related to the rapper's artistic growth. They are a genuine attempt to meet fans' needs (Conniff 2004).

SEMIOTICS

Semiotics explains the meaning of verbal and nonverbal language by examining the correspondence among signs, symbols, and their roles in the assignment of meaning (Mick 1986). Language is a compilation of signs and symbols that are embedded in cultural space and time. To many consumers worldwide, the English language symbolizes modernism and internationalism (Alden, Steenkamp, and Batra 1999). Sherry and Camargo (1987) found that among the Japanese the use of English on packaging was associated with social mobility, modernization, and an internationalized outlook.

Semiotics addresses three basic components: an object, a sign, and an interpretant. These components are embedded in every marketing message. The object is the product that is the focus of the message (e.g., McDonald's food). The sign is the sensory imagery that represents the intended meanings of the object (McDonald's golden arches). The interpretant is the meaning derived from the object (American hamburgers and American-style food).

4.1 The mega concert at Woodstock, New York, became a defining event for the hippie counterculture. Here, a hippie couple enjoys guitar music.

Signs

Signs are unique representations of specific objects. They can resemble objects, be connected to objects, and be conventionally tied to objects (Berger 1984). As existing social structures, cultural norms, and traditions disappear, consumers are reinterpreting and incorporating signs into their own culture (Uusitalo 1998). Signs are represented as icons, indexes, and symbols.

ICON

An **icon** is a sign that resembles the product in some way. Bell Telephone represents itself through the image of a bell.

Many hippies were guided by a vision of improving social conditions and enjoyed guitar music in the 1960s (See Figure 4.1). They expressed this vision through collective art, music, and propaganda. The mega concert at Woodstock, New York, became a defining activity for the hippie counterculture. Through his participation as concert emcee, Wavy Gravy became a cultural icon. A stand-up comic, a social activist, and an author, he was the inspiration for Ben & Jerry's vanilla-based ice cream with caramel and cashew Brazil nuts, chocolate hazelnut fudge swirls, and roasted almonds (See Figure 4.2). In this example, a multi-flavored ice cream was used to translate the iconic image of Wavy Gravy's many talents (caramel, cashews, and Brazilian nuts) and activism (chocolate hazelnut fudge swirls). Royalties derived from Wavy Gravy ice cream sales help fund scholarships for children ages 7 to 14 who could not afford to attend Camp Winnarainbow, a circus and performing arts camp in rural California founded by Wavy in 1983 (Johnson 1997). Wavy's activities and merchandise fund his charitable works, including the Seva Foundation that focuses on curing blindness in the Third World. Wavy's logo, merchandise, and website illustrate how icons are associated with products to express and transform cultural ideas (McCracken 1988).

INDEX

An **index** is a sign that is connected to a product because they share similar property. Nike's swoosh conveys the shared property of activity. Ben & Jerry's positioned its brand as representing caring capitalism, environmentally friendly manufacturing, and a home-grown company (Murray 2006). However, these relationships make sense only to a person who is a member of a particular culture, as the connections are often culturally bound and meanings do not automatically transfer from one cultural context to another.

SYMBOL

A **symbol** is a sign that is related to a product through either conventional or agreed-upon associations. Symbols can include words, gestures (Berger 1984), colors and images. However, the consumer has to learn what the symbol means. For example, the Levi's symbol is two horses pulling apart a pair of Levi's jeans. It appears on the leather waist patch and symbolizes the strength and functionality of the jeans. In ancient China, the color red was thought to drive away evil sprits; it now symbolizes luck or happiness in many contemporary Asian cultures. Among the Vietnamese, kumquat trees symbolize fertility or childbearing; thus, the more fruit on the tree, the more children in a home (Konigsmark 2001). The swastika is a widely used design element used in decorative arts in many Asian cultures; its use, however, is not allowed in Germany where the image symbolizes Nazism. A semiotic analysis of Gloria Vanderbilt's swan, Munsingwear's penguin, Izod Lacoste's alligator, and Ralph Lauren's polo pony revealed that the animal icons were interpreted by consumers as representing human dominance over the natural world and the symbols were identified as subtle status markers (Morgado 1993).

4.2 Cultural icon Wavy Gravy was the inspiration for a Ben & Jerry's ice cream flavor.

SHIFTS IN SYMBOLIC CONSUMPTION

The symbolic value of shopping is likely to be prominent in societies where there are inequalities in wealth and power (Shipman 2004). Achieving new status represents beating the odds and can be communicated to others through the acquisition of new goods and services or conspicuous spending. An example is a consumer who communicates his wealth to others by purchasing bottled water by La Mer, a prestige skin-care line for the face (Harris 2006). Consumers who are moderately affluent can buy water by Nuxe Eau Demaquillante's—a floral-water for $20 ($ Canadian) or Evian's Brumisateur, a 150-ml mineral-water spray for $10.75 ($ Canadian). Symbolism extends the product's value beyond a purely functional purpose. Branded products with an image bring premium-priced symbolic content within the reach of mass market consumers, while generic goods face pricing constraints that produce lack of differentiation. Symbolic consumption evolves from conspicuous consumption so that "in a cultural sense, we are what we wear, hear, see, and otherwise sense or experience" (Shipman 2004, 278).

Symbolic consumption has shifted from conspicuous waste to taste (Shipman 2004). In the past, status existed in consuming a greater number of goods such as owning two or more cars when you only needed one. The trend in symbolic consumption has shifted to spending money on goods and services that reflect your taste. Examples are getting a good education at a nationally recognized university and achieving quality of life by indulging in a luxury spa experience. Another trend in consumption is possession without ownership, which provides implication for conservation and tourism. Possession without ownership existed in China before economic reforms. During that time, the state provided their citizens places to live and study (Arredy 2006, A1). China's growing middle class is creating a consumer culture in which consumers "live life for the moment" and spend at the expense of savings (Arredy 2006). China's new middle class purchases merit goods such as U.S.-branded products, including computers, Tommy Hilfiger clothes, Buick cars, Heinz steak sauce, and oranges packaged by Sunkist (Arredy 2006).

The meanings associated with consumer goods are shifting from culturally derived understandings to meanings derived from consumption (Otnes and Scott 1996). In fact, commercialization is reinventing the symbolic ways that consumers think about culture. "Once, people wanted products that were new and improved; now, they want products that are original, natural, and utilitarian. People want to live in converted barns or warehouses with bamboo, hardwood, tile, or anything but carpet on the floor and with an industrial-size cooking range in the kitchen; food should be organic, coffee should be fresh-roasted, medicine should be holistic, and cars should be four-wheel-

drive so that they can travel over natural terrain" (Tomkins 2005, 12).

Consumption is increasingly sign- and style-oriented (du Gay 1993). Wattanasuwan (2005) observed consumption is used "symbolically not only to create and sustain the self but also to locate us in society" (179). As such, consumption reflects status. The U.S. brands mentioned previously represent a middle-class level of status in China. An interesting part of Wattanasuwan's statement is that he views consumption as self-sustaining. When shoppers order on the Internet, the retailer has software that can build a database of shopper information and use direct personalized marketing to sell additional products. This allows retailers to establish relationships with customers and build loyalty. This practice illustrates how consumption behaviors "simultaneously enchain us to the illusive sense of self and the endless realm of consumption" (Wattanasuwan 2005, 183). In this situation, consumers produce future consumption. This influences interest in customer relationship management (CRM), a practice that uses customer information to capture additional share of one individual's purchases over a lifetime. Companies using CRM symbolically call customers guests and refer to sales people as associates.

Consider caring capitalism in all its forms, such as cause-related marketing, which has emerged from antiestablishment values from the 1960s and environmentalism of the 1990s. Cause-related marketing can be a positive part of a firm's activities and important to society (Lachowetz, Clark, Irwin, and Cornwell 2002). An examination of meanings in a Wal-Mart advertising flyer might find family, community, and national norms communicated, in addition to a promise of price advantages on merchandise (Arnold, Kozinets, and Handelman 2001). Wal-Mart creates an identity of a subtly utopian, nostalgic hometown, where U.S. citizens can balance economic and moral desires, and it seeks to legitimize itself as a neighborly, small-town shopkeeper serving its customers. Another example of cause-related marketing is the Kohl's Cares for Kids campaign developed by Kohl's national chain of specialty department stores. The store donates 100 percent of net profits from special items sold in its Massachusetts stores to the Children's Hospital Boston. Kohl's also funds the Children's Hospital's Blood Mobile and sponsors the Children's Miles for Miracles Walk to raise money for the hospital (Kohl's Corporation 2006).

GLOBAL CONSUMPTION SYMBOLS

Brands, product categories, and consumption activities are shared as consumption symbols in global consumer cultures and give meaning to consumer segments (Alden et al. 1999). Symbol sharing offers retailers the opportunity to expand brand equity into competitive global markets. Food, fashion, music, entertainment, housing, home furnishing products, personal products, and travel are consumer product categories that increasingly are produced and consumed as global products and brands.

The global consumer is characterized by purchases of certain brands that symbolically reinforce membership in a specific global segment, such as teenager, business, and elite. Brands that appeal to specific human universals are able to transfer cultural meanings at different levels. These brands become symbols of a global culture and are recognized because of that association.

As more companies view the entire world as their market, brand builders look to firms that have created global brands. These global brands use positioning tactics that relate the personality, look, and feel of the brand in strategic advertisements,

which for the most part are the same from one country to another (Aaker and Joachimsthaler 1999). Advertisers target and promote global consumer cultures by appealing to human universals that are characterized by particular brands. Sony targeted young people around the world with the advertising pitch My First Sony. Philips used the catchphrase Let's Make Things Better in advertisements that feature people from different countries. Benetton emphasized the unity of humankind through its slogan The United Colors of Benetton (Alden et al. 1999).

ORGANIZATIONAL SYMBOLISM

Organizational symbolism communicates aspects of a company to consumers. Companies use symbolism to reveal or make understandable feelings, images, and values that exist within the organization (Dandridge, Mitroff, and Joyce 1980). Companies communicate organizational symbolism through logos, trademarks, myths, legends, ceremonies, day-to-day activities, and political activities.

Organizational meaning is created through interactions and interpretation by organizational members and their leaders (Karathanos 1998). Crafted corporate meaning employs specific types of symbolism to create and institutionalize it. An example of an institutionalized symbol is Wal-Mart. Their culture is communicated to employees through on-the-job training and Sam Walton's Guiding Principles appear in Wal-Mart flyers (Arnold and Fernie 2000). Company flyers show family activities with employees' children as models. Store signage and checkout displays use national flags and colors. Wal-Mart's greeters welcome shoppers into their stores. These signs communicate Wal-Mart's organizational values and allow consumers to find meaning through interactions with the company.

Retail organizations are supported by marketing systems, design, and advertising that help turn commodities into consumer fantasies (du Gay 1993). It is increasingly important to capture customers' hearts, as well as their minds (du Gay 1993). Retail image conceptualizes and reinforces consumers' associations with a particular store (Kunkel and Berry 1968). These are based on a consumer's experiences with the store. Positive experience leads to customer loyalty while negative experience leads to avoidance behavior.

The retail environment is full of sensory stimuli and leisure experience (du Gay 1993). They are found in mall food courts where food is served and tables allow shoppers to stop and socialize. Similarly, a shopping trip to Target gives consumers an opportunity to visit and catch up over a cup of coffee. Thus, the mall or store represents a cultural site with socially constructed meaning.

Logos and Trademarks

A company **logo** is a material symbol that communicates a concrete representation of the organization (Dandridge et al. 1980). Hudson's Bay, a Canadian retailer, developed a corporate identity program with a new company logo that united the organization's different retail divisions. Hudson's Bay operates more than 500 Canadian stores, including The Bay, a full-line department store chain; Zellers, a mass merchant; Home Outfitters, a kitchen, bed, and bath superstore chain; and Hbc.com, an e-tailer.

Logos are adopted by companies for different reasons. A logo may appeal to those with a concern for the environment (Regalado 2004). Virgin Megastores sell small, green logo pins that make a symbolic statement for the neutralization of the 34 pounds of CO_2 emitted in the production of 10 CDs. The cost of the pin at $3.99 symbolizes the cost of CO_2 neutralization. Another logo symbolizing eco-friendly behavior is Future Forests Ltd.'s carbon neutral seal of approval that was designed to offset the impact of carbon production in the music industry. Rock bands such as the Rolling Stones and Foo Fighters have received the carbon neutral seal of approval.

A **trademark** can be a word, symbol, or design that distinguishes a company's goods from all others. Burberry's distinctive plaid is a registered trademark. The recognizable red, white, black, and camel check plaid began as a lining for trench coats in 1924. In 1997, Burberry revived the distinctive plaid to broaden its appeal through new products such as Burberry's check baseball cap. Today, Burberry's beige signature plaid represents a luxury good and accounts for up to 20 percent of total company sales in the firm's 180 stores in Asia, the United States, and Europe (Loeb 2004).

Myths and Legends

Myths and **legends** tell a story through verbal symbols. They may motivate rituals or actions (Dandridge et al. 1980).

Stanley Marcus is an example of a retail legend whose personality was synonymous with Neiman Marcus. He was eight when he started to work at the store owned by Mr. Marcus, his father, and the Marcuses, his aunt and uncle, in downtown Dallas. By the age of 10 he visited New York markets and fashion showrooms with his father and learned about design and buying. Stanley Marcus went to Harvard at the age of 16 and went back to Dallas to try his hand at a career in retail at the urging of his father. He remained at Neiman Marcus for the next 50 years and tried new strategies that earned him a reputation for thinking outside the box. These strategies included store extravaganzas and the Neiman Marcus Christmas catalog (Pugh 2002).

Ceremonies

There is symbolic value in **ceremonies** including retail extravaganzas. Through Macy's Thanksgiving Day Parades, and appearances in movies, such as the classic *Miracle on 34th Street*, Macy's has a national reputation with brand identity that is associated with their name (O'Loughlin 2005b). Thus, national expansion of Macy's stores is a natural progression and allows them to reach a larger market, save on costs, and increase profits (See Figure 4.3). Another example of symbolic value related to products is the Cosmetic Executive Women's (UK) first official Beauty Awards in 2006 that celebrated product innovation and excellence in the beauty industry (Evison 2006). This ceremony had members testing and voting on the best beauty products available in the marketplace.

Ceremonies associated with children's achievements, social development, and coming of age are occasions to celebrate and give gifts. These celebrations include baptisms, First Communions, confirmations, Bar and Bat Mitzvahs, special graduations, and *quinceañeras* for Hispanic girls. Heebner (2002) reported that 79.4 percent of jewelry stores sell items for baptisms, First Communions, and confirmations; 43.8 percent sell special graduation-themed items; 36.3 percent sell items for Bar and Bat Mitzvahs; and 7.5 percent sell items for other ceremonies, such as the *quinceañera*. Stores can position jewelry as a lasting memory of the event.

Selfridges, a U.K. retailer, uses extravaganza as a means of creating customer interest in its store. The Selfridges flagship store staged a Bollywood extravaganza (refers to India's Hollywood and a genre of romance movies with dancing) when it

introduced 18 Indian fashion designers to London (Bidwell 2003). The Selfridges brand is about presenting its customers with new ideas. This store seeks to be more than just a transaction. Selfridges understands that things sold in their store also can be purchased elsewhere, so they strive

4.3 The Macy's Thanksgiving Day Parade helps the company establish a national reputation.

to create energy and a vibe to make their store a place where people like to be. Their approach to retail is expressed as editing Selfridges's content and animating and bringing their space to life.

Day-to-Day and Political Activities

Firms also use their **day-to-day activities** or **political activities** to communicate organizational values and stories (Dandridge et al. 1980). The Whole Foods Market, based in Austin, Texas, sells organic food and packages customer goods in recycled bags. These practices communicate health and environmental concerns to the customer. The Whole Foods Market, the largest natural food and fastest growing grocery retailer in the United States, has expanded from a single-store operation in 1980 to 143 stores with 23,000 employees and sales of $2.8 billion in 2002 (Boorstin 2003). The store's founder, John Mackey, believes that consumers work their way up Maslow's hierarchy of needs from food and safety to self-actualization. His unique personality characteristics that include part "Texan don't-tread-on-me libertarianism" and part "hippie," influence his desire to create "truth, love, and beauty" in his stores. To this end, the Whole Foods Market uses consumer pamphlets to discuss meat safety and a sustainable seafood industry and store signs to draw attention to free-range (naturally pastured) and organic products. The Whole Foods Market has a website that contains information about organic foods and sustainable agriculture. Thus, the Whole Foods Market illustrates how a retailer communicates its company values to consumers through its actions. Consumers are made aware of a retail store's image through its product assortment, communications, day-to-day activities, and political statements regarding the agriculture policy.

SOCIAL SYSTEMS IN CONSUMPTION

Individuals define themselves and develop self-concepts through social roles. Association with an identifiable status is contingent upon possession of goods that communicate signs of belonging (McCracken 1988). Relevant information about the product or the person's wealth is communicated to members of a social system. Retailers are interested in how people live their lives and make choices as they supply consumers with the items and experiences. Ahles (2002) wrote, "Along with its stone walls, covered bridges, and town greens, an enduring symbol of New England and its Yankee ways is the general stores" (CT 1). Country stores no longer play a vital role in the local retail sector, but they perform an important function in the community. The country store provides people with a place to meet. The country store illustrates the symbolic and cultural role retail plays in society.

Technology and consumer mobility have altered consumers' social system of reference. Consumers can associate themselves with a physical location, an online blog, or an Internet community that is concerned with specific products or brands. Shoppers' preferences for shopping online or in stores is influenced by age, gender, education, and income. Websites offer opportunities for custom-designed items and serve as informational sources. Overall, young people spend almost 11 hours a week online. However, about 20 percent of people ages 12 to 17 spend 20 hours or more online weekly (Taylor 2005). Teenagers and preteens use technology for text messaging, game downloads, listening to music, and watching television (Wilson, 2005). In addition to Internet use, Generation Y also uses non-voice wireless services. Generation Y text messages frequently and desires real-time information. Vanity Shops, a 175-store junior apparel chain from Grand Forks, Fargo, North Dakota, experimented with full-text, non-register-ringing promotions messaging to reach its core target audience of teen girls. Its messaging program was supported by special window signs, in-store posters, e-mail messages, and website information. The promotion asked shoppers to connect with the individual members of an alternative band by texting in one of four designated numbers. The prize was a free secret, all via their cell phones. The chain also supported the initiative with an e-mail blast to its shoppers and information on its website. The promotion's goal was to build a customer base of telephone numbers (Wilson 2005). Personalized product offerings and discount coupons can be sent to shoppers via text messaging. Amazon is a good example of an online retailer selling personalized products. The company has invested in technology allowing HD-DVD formatting on its U.S. site. This technology allows discs to be made upon demand and transforms companies from carrying inventory to owning the content (Birchall 2006).

The Diderot Effects and Diderot Unities of Symbolic Consumption

Diderot Effects and Unities were named after Denis Diderot, a French Enlightenment philosopher (McCracken 1988). The concepts of Diderot Effect and Diderot Unities relate to symbolic consumption. They help maintain consumption that is consistent with an individual's experience and self-concept. The **Diderot Effect** either constrains a consumer to maintain current consumption patterns or to change consumption behavior to something different. The Diderot Effect occurs when consumers purchase an assortment of goods and services that are consistent with their lifestyles. It also limits consumers' choices to products that are associated with a particular lifestyle. This allows the consumer to avoid incongruence or mixed messages in their consumption decisions. The act of joining a golf club could be considered a Diderot Effect because it requires a specific set of goods to participate. These goods are symbolic of the membership in that specific group. The Diderot Effect is rather obvious among many graduating college seniors. As they prepare for job interviews and new positions, their wardrobe shifts from informal clothes worn to class to those appropriate for the workforce. A suit and related items are purchased first, followed by complementary products such as briefcases. Thus, through purchases that support the consumer's self-concept and new role, the consumer embraces symbolic consumption.

The Diderot Effect also applies to situations where the consumer makes a departure purchase. A departure purchase occurs when consumers make purchases that are not part of their usual patterns of consumption. Departure purchases can occur with role changes, such as marriage or divorce, or mobility, such as job change. After a departure purchase, the new purchase requires complementary assortments of goods, or **Diderot Unities**.

Davis and Gregory (2003) studied possible triggers for the creation of a new Diderot Unity among university working women. Participants read description of lifestyle cohorts and then placed themselves in a group that best described them. They were then asked to write a script about how they made an initial departure purchase and two follow-up purchases that represented a new Diderot Unity. Analysis of the scripts resulted in two groups of consumers. The first group was emotive themes and had feelings of adrenaline rush, satisfaction, and pleasure at getting it right and a sense of serendipitous discovery. The second group was cognitive or reasoned themes with an emphasis on ensemble/completion, life cycle/transition, self gift/reward, and role-play props. Their results suggested that Diderot Unities support desired and aspirational lifestyles.

Bloomingdale's uses customer relationship management (CRM) to communicate with customers about topics and merchandise that is of interest to them. Bloomingdale's uses this information to inform customers of in-store events, personal appearances, promotions, new product launches, or other events relevant to that particular customer's preferences. This use of CRM informs consumers of product groups, or Diderot Unities, that are associated with their lifestyles.

CHAPTER SUMMARY

Symbolic consumption helps consumers develop their self-concept and social identity. Products that we buy (e.g., low-calorie beverages, natural cosmetics, leather jackets, or Victorian homes), activities that we do (e.g., volunteering, fly-fishing, or traveling), and philosophies or beliefs that we pursue (e.g., astrology, religion, or politics) tell stories about who we are and with whom we identify.

Symbols add meaning to a consumer's experiential world. Consumer goods have cultural meaning when they take on a significance that is unique to the purchase. These cultural meanings are communicated to others who understand their symbolism. The meanings associated with consumer goods are dynamic and may vary according to culture and a consumer's lifetime. The meaning of consumer goods is communicated through logos or trademarks, myths and legends, ceremonies, and day-to-day and political activities. These are marketing tools for the experiential retailer. Therefore, it is important for retailers to understand their meaning in relationship to the consumer and others in their social group.

Consumer Culture Theory (CCT) is a framework for understanding cultural meanings and the social dynamics that shape the experiences and consumer identity in a variety of social spaces such as retail settings and tourist sites. This framework conceptualizes consumers' cultural and social motivations for retail patronage, purchase behaviors, and retail purchase decisions. CCT's framework also considers the dynamic links among consumer behavior, the marketplace, and cultural meanings. It examines the contextual, symbolic, and experiential aspects of the consumption cycle as it moves through the processes of acquisition, consumption and possession, and disposition processes.

Semiotics is a tool that helps explain the meaning of verbal and nonverbal language by examining the correspondence among signs, symbols, and their roles in the assignment of meaning. Semiotics examines three basic components of symbolism: the object, sign or symbol, and interpretant. Signs include icons (e.g., Windows software using the window as an icon), index (e.g., Nike's swoosh conveying motion and activity), and symbol (e.g., two horses pulling apart a pair of Levi's jeans that appear in advertising, which symbolize strength and durability). Since purchases have symbolic meaning, they need to exist in harmony with other signs associated with use. Thus, the Diderot Effect constrains a consumer to maintain current consumption patterns or to change consumption behavior to something different. Diderot Unities guide consumption so that it is consistent with the desired symbolic meaning.

The retail organization creates consumer culture with symbolic meaning by providing an appropriate mix of goods and services. Experiential retailers create an environment where something more than mere consumption of a product occurs.

They provide consumers with an experience that is incorporated into their constructed social identities.

Discussion Questions

1. Discuss the symbolic value of Target's logo as compared with its competitors.

2. Explain how the concept of symbolic interaction is applied in retail shopping outlets. Name stores and give retail store and service examples.

3. Provide three current examples of symbolic consumption. Why do you think this has become so important among consumers?

4. Compare and contrast Generations X and Y in their symbolic consumption behavior.

5. Discuss the reasons for the increasing popularity of Whole Foods Market. What is its symbolic meaning?

6. What are some examples of symbolic services? Symbolic goods?

7. How does symbolic consumption of goods differ from symbolic consumption of services?

8. What are the three basic components of every marketing message from a semiotic perspective?

9. How does symbolic consumption relate to social behavior?

10. Describe ways that symbolic consumption adds to the total consumer experience.

References

Aaker, D. A., and E. Joachimsthaler. 1999. The lure of global branding. *Harvard Business Review*. November–December, 137–144.

Ahles, D. 2002. A way of life hangs on. *New York Times*. October 13, CT1, 4.

Alden, D. L., J. E. Steenkamp, and R. Batra. 1999. Brand positioning through advertising in Asia, North America, and Europe: The role of global consumer culture. *Journal of Marketing* 63:75–87.

Arndorfer, J. B. 2004. Stretching into an icon. *Advertising Age* 75(22/23):62.

Arnold, S. J., and J. Fernie. 2000. Wal-Mart in Europe: Prospects for the UK. *International Marketing Review* 17(4/5):416.

Arnold, S., R. Kozinets, and J. Handelman. 2001. Hometown ideology and retailer legitimating: The institutional semiotics of Wal-Mart flyers—Part 1 of 5. *Journal of Retailing* 77(2):243.

Arnould, E. J. 2005. Animating the big middle. *Journal of Retailing* 81(2):89–96.

Arnould, E. J., and C. J. Thompson. 2005. Consumer culture theory (CCT): Twenty years of research. *Journal of Consumer Research* 31(4):868–882.

Arredy, J. T. 2006. Spent force: As families splurge, Chinese savings start to take a hit; long-awaited cultural shift may not ease trade gap with U.S. in short term; Mr. Su gets a new townhouse. *Wall Street Journal*. May 2, A1.

Bauman, Z. 2001. *Identity in the Globalizing World*, in *Identity, Culture, and Globalization*. Ben-Rafael, E. and Sternberg, Y., eds. Leiden: Brill.

Becker, H. S., and McCall, M. M., eds. 1990. *Symbolic Interaction and Cultural Studies*. Chicago: University of Chicago Press.

Belk, R. W. 1988. Possessions and the extended self. *Journal of Consumer Research* 15(2):139–168.

Berger, A. A. 1984. *Signs in contemporary culture: an introduction to semiotics*. New York: Longman.

Bhat, S., and Reddy, S. (1998). *Journal of Consumer Marketing*, 15(1):32–43.

Bidwell, James. 2003. There's more to Bidwell than window dressing. *Brand Strategy*. October, 14–15.

Birchall, J. 2006. Amazon puts a bet on both DVD formats Retailing. *Financial Times*. April 25, 22.

Blumer, J. 1978. *Society as symbolic interaction, in Symbolic Interaction: a Reader in Social Psychology*. Manis, J. G., and B. N. Meltzerr, eds. Boston: Allyn and Bacon.

Boorstin, J. 2003. No Preservatives, No Unions, Lots of Dough. *Fortune* 148 (5):127–128, 130.

Bridson, K and J. Evans. 2004. The secret to a fashion advantage is brand orientation. *International Journal of Retail & Distribution Management* 32(8/9):403.

Conniff, T. 2004. Eminem's back a vision. *Billboard*. November 20, 3, 91.

Creighton, M. 1998. Preindustrial dreaming in postindustrial Japan: Department stores and the commoditization of community traditions. *Japan Forum* 10:127–150.

Dandridge, T. C., I. Mitroff, and W. F. Joyce. 1980. Organizational symbolism: A topic to expand organizational analysis. *The Academy of Management Review* 5(1):77–82.

Davis, T. and Gregory, G. 2003. Creating Diderot unities-quest for possible selves? *Journal of Consumer Marketing* 20(1):44–54.

Devany, P. 2004. Hip-hop's "bling" culture is wooing corporate America, *Marketing Week*. January 24, 38.

du Gay, P. 1993. 'Numbers and souls': Retailing and the de-differentiation of economy and culture. *The British Journal of Sociology* 44(4):563–587.

Evison, J. 2006. Recognizing greatness. *Global Cosmetic Industry* 174(6):24.

Glasser, B. 1990. *Fit for postmodern selfhood, in Symbolic Interaction and Cultural Studies*, H. S. Becker and M. M. McCall, eds. Chicago: University of Chicago Press.

Gross, J. 1993. The magic of the mall: An analysis of form, function, and meaning in the contemporary built environment. *Annals of the Association of American Geographers* 83(10):18–47.

Hamilton, S. 2003. The economies and conveniences of modern-day living: Frozen foods and mass marketing, 1945–1965. *Business History Review* 77(1):33–61.

Harris, M. 2006. Pricey cosmetic waters all the rage: One energy drink for the face retails at $75 a bottle at Holt Renfrew—$3 for every five ml. *The Vancouver Sun*. May 4, A12.

Heebner, J. 2002. Carats for Kids: The Children's Jewelry Market, *JCK-Jewelers Circular Keystone*. September 1, 67.

Hein, K. 2005. Marketers' brand new world has free coffee, cabs, coifs. *Brandweek* 46(40):16.

International Encyclopedia of the Social and Behavioral Sciences, Vol 26. 2001. Amsterdam: Elsevier. 15347–15350.

Jackson, K. 1996. All the world's a mall: Reflections on the social and economic consequences of the American shopping center. *The American Historical Review* 101(4):1111–1121.

Johnson, D. 1997. Grateful Gravy—Tie-dyed-in-the-wool icon is glad hippie image boosts his efforts to help others. *The Boston Herald*. June 5, Lifestyle Section, 41.

Karathanos, P. 1998. Crafting corporate meaning. *Management Decision* 36(2):123.

Kohl's Corporation. 2006. Kohl's cares for kids. Retrieved August 29, 2006, from www.kohlscorporation.com/CommunityRelations/Community01.htm.

Konigsmark, A. R. 2001. Asian Americans celebrate the year of the snake.

San Jose Mercury News. January 24, Sec. B, 1.

Kunkel, J. H and L. L. Berry. 1968. A behavioral conception of retail image. *Journal of Marketing* 32:21–27.

Lachowetz, T., J. Clark, R. Irwin, and T. B. Cornwell. 2002. Cause-related sponsorship: A survey of consumer/spectator beliefs, attitudes, behavioral intentions, and corporate image impressions. *American Marketing Association Conference Proceedings* 13:14.

Leigh, J. H., and T. G. Gabel. 1992. Symbolic interactionism: Its effects on consumer behavior and implications for marketing strategy. *The Journal of Services Marketing* 6(3):5–16.

Lewis, J. D., and R. L. Smith. 1980. *American Sociology and Pragmatism.* Chicago: The University of Chicago Press.

Loeb, W. F. 2004. Burberry is a unique brand. *Stores* 86(8):100.

Luthro, A.M. 2003. Necessary Baggage. *Retail Merchandiser* 43(11):30.

Manis, J. G. and B. N. Meltzer. 1978. *Symbolic Interaction.* Boston: Allyn and Bacon, Inc.

Martin, A. S. 1996. Makers, buyers, and users: Consumerism as a material culture framework. *The William and Mary Quarterly* 53(1):5–12.

McCracken, G. 1988. *Culture and Consumption.* Bloomington: Indiana Press.

McKechnie, S., and C. Tynan. 2006. Social meanings in Christmas consumption: An exploratory study of UK celebrants' consumption rituals. *Journal of Consumer Behaviour* 5(20):130–134.

Mick, D. G. 1986. Consumer research and semiotics: Exploring the morphology of signs, symbols, and significance. *Journal of Consumer Research* 13(2):196–213.

Morgado, M. A. 1993. Animal trademark emblems on fashion apparel: A semiotic interpretation. *Clothing and Textiles Research Journal* 11(2):31–38.

Murray, B. 2006. Ben & Jerry's Homemade Inc. *Hoover's Company Records* 12763.

O'Loughlin, S. 2005a. New CMO Says Wal-mart will reach more customers. *Brandweek* 46(18):5.

O'Loughlin, S. 2005b. From 34th St. to Main Street, *Brandweek* 46(4):16–17.

Oropesa, R. S. 1995. Consumer possession, consumer passions and subjective meanings. *Sociological Forum* 2 (10):215–244.

Oswald, L. 2003. Branding the American Family: A Strategic Study of the Culture, Composition, and Consumer Behavior of Families in the New Millennium. *Journal of Popular Culture* 37(2):309–335.

Otnes, C., and L. M. Scott. 1996. Something old, something new. *Journal of Advertising* 25(1):33–50.

Prior, M. 2002. Image is the key to differentiation. *DSN Retailing Today* 41(7):54–55.

Pugh, C. 2002. Retail legend dies at 96; Stanley Marcus led Neiman chain to fame. *The Houston Chronicle.* January 23, A1.

Regalado, R. 2004. New Lifestyle Option for the Eco-Minded: 'Carbon-Neutral.' *Wall Street Journal.* May 14, B1.

Rosenbaum, M. S. 2005. The symbolic servicescape: Your kind is welcomed here. *Journal of Consumer Behaviour* 4(4):257–267.

Schewe, C. D., and G. Meredith. 2004. Segmenting global markets by generational cohorts: Determining motivations by age. *Journal of Consumer Behaviour* 4(1):51–62.

Sherry, J. F. Jr., and E. G. Camargo. 1987. "May your life be marvelous:

English language labeling and the semiotics of Japanese promotion." *Journal of Consumer Research* 14:174–188.

Shipman, A. 2004. Lauding the leisure class: symbolic content and conspicuous consumption. *Review of Social Economy* 62(3):277–289.

Slater, D. 1997. *Consumption, Culture, and Modern Identity*. Cambridge: Polity Press.

Taylor, P. 2005. Teenagers more tech-savvy than ever before, says study young consumers. *Financial Times*. December 7, 4.

Tomkins, R. 2005. A fake world where even authenticity comes in cans. *Financial Times*. February 8, 12.

Uusitalo, L. 1998. Consumption and postmodernity: social structuration and the construction of the self. *The Active Consumer*. Bianchi, M., ed., London: Routledge.

Wallendorf, M., and E. J. Arnould. 1988. My favorite things: a cross-cultural inquiry into object attachment, possessiveness, and social linkage. *Journal of Consumer Research* 14(4):531–546.

Wattanasuwan, K. 2005. The Self and Symbolic Consumption. *Journal of American Academy of Business* 6(1): 179–184.

Wilson, M. 2005. R U there? *Chain Store Age* 81(12):91.

RITUAL CONSUMPTION

CHAPTER 5

As Families Get Busier, Americans Get Creative with Holiday Rituals

You would think this holiday season that Americans, who seem to agree on little else these days, would fall into step to celebrate traditional meals and rituals on the appointed dates, in accordance with custom. You would be wrong. What Americans will actually be doing is bending, folding, spindling, and mutilating holiday traditions with abandon to suit rushed lifestyles, 24/7 jobs, and diverse families. It's all part of a cultural shift that reflects big changes in families and their work.

Sandy Cover-Houchen, for example, has given up on Thanksgiving dinner and instead will hold a holiday breakfast at her house tomorrow. Her family includes five children ages 12 through 21 from her and her husband's previous marriages, so having dinner with grandparents requires splitting up, she explains. "I kind of stress out over this," says Mrs. Cover-Houchen, who operates her own retail store. "I so much want the traditional family where you all sit down with 18 people at the table and you serve turkey dinner. But it doesn't quite happen that way for us. So we decided this year we'd beat the clock and try to do ours early."

Other families are tossing out the calendar altogether. One far-flung Colorado family held a Christmas gathering in mid-January to accommodate the schedule of one member, a consultant who had to toil nonstop the week before New Year's to close year-end books for a client.

"The tree was a bit dry, but everything else was fine," one sister says. While she admits to feeling "kind of strange and slightly out of place" skipping the calendar Christmas, "when you have your own celebration it's wonderful, because you did it for your own reason. It's like a shared joke."

A cultural change is at work, says Bradd Shore, director of the Emory University Center for Myths and Ritual in American Life in Atlanta. "Traditional rituals like holidays usually require common time and common space, but the contemporary world makes this very difficult," he says. Beyond our rushed pace and round-the-clock schedules, technology, cell phones, voice-mail, and e-mail have liberated us from the need to be in the same place at the same time to communicate. Individuals gain flexibility, but "the traditional notion of face-to-face holiday gatherings" gets pushed into the past.

Source: Shellenbarger, S. 2000. As families get busier, Americans get creative with holiday rituals. *Wall Street Journal* (Eastern edition). November 22, B1.

INTRODUCTION

With nearly half (44 percent) of employers in the United States requiring employees to work on either Christmas or New Year's day, families are changing celebrations and traditions to meet the demands of changing lifestyles (Shellenbarger 2000). Rituals that are retained, rediscovered, or reinvented allow consumers to escape from the mundane of everyday life. Artifacts (e.g., products) are required for participation in most rituals; thus, the role of consumer products in creating ritual experiences supports an important and growing consumer market for associated products.

5.1 Ordinary objects, such as this Mustang, can be viewed as extraordinary or sacred objects.

5.2 The Route 66 Museum can be part of a ritualized experience when it is associated with sacred objects such as 1960s muscle cars.

Rituals are customary, formalized, ceremonial acts or rites that are embedded in culture. They can be either sacred or profane (ordinary). Many rituals are prescribed, such as observing dietary laws (Kashruth) among Orthodox Jews. Rituals prepare individuals and groups to participate in transcendental (supernatural) experiences and to interact with an object that has associated abstract feelings. These events and objects elicit respect, reverence, and sometimes fear. They are set apart from everyday life and viewed as extraordinary or sacred (Belk, Wallendorf, and Sherry 1989).

Ordinary objects can become elements of rituals. A ritual can be as simple as swirling and emptying hot water in a teapot before making tea. Flags, collections, automobiles (See Figure 5.1), motorcycles, food, the home, and personal beauty products take on new meanings when consumers create rituals for their care, maintenance, and use.

Experiences can assume ritualized aspects. Travel experiences, visits to museums, themed amusement parks, and national parks become ritualized when consumers link them to important occasions or memories. For example, an owner of a 1960s muscle car might stop at the Route 66 Museum on every annual trip on this historic highway (See Figure 5.2).

Places are ritualized when consumers give them meaning beyond their physical presence. For example, visiting Elvis Presley's Graceland each year on his birthday is an example of a ritual associated with an enshrined place.

Holidays are ritualized. Halloween, a secular holiday, requires costumes and candy to participate (See Figure 5.3). It has created a whole new category of interior and exterior decorative accessories for the home. Easter, a religious holiday, uses dyed eggs to symbolize new life (See Figure 5.4). Ritualized objects can be recre-

ated in new formats. For example, Pottery Barn offered pastel colored wooden eggs that could be opened and filled with candy.

Celebrations are yet another type of ritual. When they observe specific life events, such as birthdays and anniversaries, they become important markers in one's life.

5.3 One Halloween ritual involves dressing up in costumes, such as action figures.

5.4 Dyeing eggs is an Easter ritual for many families.

5.5 Blowing out candles on a birthday cake is a birthday ritual.

5.6 Events such as the local Parker County Peach Festival in Weatherford, Texas, can become an annual ritual.

Blowing out candles that equal the number of years of age is a ritual for many families (See Figure 5.5).

Events such as sports, festivals, performances, and musical tours can be ritualized. Attending the annual Peach Festival (See Figure 5.6) may be a family ritual where peaches are purchased and taken home to make special seasonal desserts.

Personalities such as athletes, actors, music stars, and politicians are assigned ritualistic characteristics by their fans and supporters. Wearing a numbered jersey of a favorite sports team member can be a ritual. Marilyn Monroe, the actress, and Elvis Presley, the singer, have become larger-than-life icons (symbols) who are ritualized by incorporating their movies, music, and physical images in daily life (See Figure 5.7)

Understanding ritual consumption is prompted by recognizing its cultural relevance. Cultural meaning comes from the experiences that are fundamental aspects of culture (Goodenough 1999). This chapter explores rituals in the context of culture. It explains cultural values, orientations, and patterns, as well as subcultures and cultural diffusion. Sacred and profane consumption is described as it relates to rituals, pilgrimage, quintessence, gift-giving, collecting, inheritance, and external sanctions.

CULTURE

Culture is " . . . the collective programming of the mind [that] distinguishes the members of one group or category of people from another" (Hofstede 2001, 9). It reflects commonly held values, beliefs, and behaviors that are held by a large group of people. Culture is influenced by how individuals interact with their natural, human constructed, and human behavioral environments (See Figure 5.8).

The **natural environment** includes natural resources (e.g., water, land, vegetation, and animals), climate (e.g., humid equatorial, dry, humid temperate, humid cold, cold polar, and highland), space and time, and geography. Cultures that benefit from abundant natural resources develop differently from those where resources are scarce, limited, or unduly affected by climate and geography.

The **human constructed environment** includes production, consumption, and sociocultural systems at a macro (e.g., societal) level. Advanced technology cultures have sociocultural systems that have evolved to high levels of production and consumption. In these cultures, consumption is promoted among its members to support continuous production.

The human behavior environment includes relationships, roles, affiliations, and attitudes, which is culture at the micro (e.g., subgroup, organization, market segment) and individual (e.g., consumer) levels.

5.7 Personalities, such as Marilyn Monroe and Elvis Presley, can be ritualized as larger-than-life icons.

5.8 Environmental influences on culture

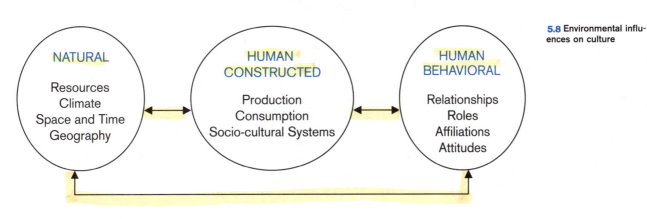

TABLE 5.1. CULTURAL VARIATIONS IN TIME ORIENTATION

TIME ORIENTATION	PERCEPTIONS	CONTEXT OF PERCEPTIONS
Linear-separable	Time includes the past, present, and future that stretches to infinity.	Time can be separated into discrete units along this line.
Circular-traditional	Time is relative to repeated patterns such as cycles of the sun, moon, and seasons.	Time does not stretch into a future so the future is expected to be like the past. The focus is on the present.
Procedural-traditional	Time is viewed as irrelevant.	Behavior is driven by activity rather than by time.

Source: Graham, R. J. 1981. The role of perception of time in consumer research. *Journal of Consumer Research* 7(4):335–342.

Cultural Time

Time, a component of the natural environment, plays an important role in rituals and celebrations. Time defines how people anticipate, live through, and reflect upon their experiences. Cultural perceptions of time differ (McGrath and Rotchford 1984); cultural time can be classified as either linear, circular, or procedural (See Table 5.1) (Graham 1981).

Seasonal time follows changes in the natural environment. For example, autumn is a time of meaningful gatherings among many cultures. Oktoberfest, which originated as a fall festival, is celebrated in Germany. Sukkot is a ritual celebration among Jews where an outdoor hut is built out of vegetation and decorated with fruits, foliage, and other seasonal bounty. The Chinese celebrate the harvest moon with lanterns and moon cake. Thanksgiving is celebrated in the United States, Canada, Argentina, and Brazil.

Marketers often assume that all consumers think about time linearly (Cote and Tansuhaj 1989); however, this can have detrimental effects on how products are presented. In the United States, a popular piece of jewelry for women is a necklace with three stones or pearls (See Figure 5.9), where one stone or pearl symbolizes the past, one the present, and one the future. For this necklace to be relevant for a consumer, she must be able to separate her experiences into linear time as well as place value on past, present, and future events. A marketing strategy to promote a necklace such as this might include experience-based scenarios where each stone represents marriage, the birth of a child, and future grandchildren, respectively. This strategy, however, is not appropriate in places where time is viewed circularly or

5.9 This three-pearl pendant can represent linear cultural time by symbolizing past, present, and future events in a consumer's life.

TABLE 5.2. SUMMARY OF JEWISH FEASTS AND FESTIVALS

HOLIDAY OR FESTIVAL		PURIM	PESACH	SHAVUOT	ROSH HASHANA	YOM KIPPUR	SUKKOT	HANUKKAH
CELEBRATION		FEAST OF LOTS	FESTIVAL OF FREEDOM	FEAST OF PENTECOST	NEW YEAR	DAY OF ATONEMENT	FEAST OF TABERNACLES	FESTIVAL OF REDEDICATION FESTIVAL OF LIGHTS
JEWISH CALENDAR	YEAR							
5765	2005	March 25	April 24	June 13	September 16	September 25	September 30	December 26
5766	2006	March 14	April 14	June 2	October 4	October 13	October 18	December 16
5767	2007	March 4	April 3	May 23	September 23	October 2	October 7	December 5
5768	2008	March 21	April 20	June 9	September 13	September 22	September 27	December 22

procedurally, as it is in many Asian cultures.

Celebrations and holidays are affected by how people calculate time, whether it is determined by solar or lunar years. Western cultures use the Gregorian calendar, which is based on a solar year. It divides time into a 12-month year containing 365 days, with every fourth year or leap year having an extra day in February. Holidays, such as Christmas on December 25, always fall on a set date each year, based on the solar calendar. In contrast, a considerable number of celebrations have movable dates because they are based on a lunar calendar, which is the case for Jewish (See Table 5.2) and Islamic (See Table 5.3) holidays and celebrations.

New Year's celebrations are an example of contrasting time elements. Retailers need to include experiences and products in their merchandising mix that respond to celebrations of culturally diverse consumers. The New Year is one of the most important celebrations for Chinese, Taiwanese, Korean, Vietnamese, Tibetan, Hmong, and Jewish cultures. In Asian cultures, the New Year falls in January or February based on a lunar calendar, not on the first day of January on the Gregorian calendar as celebrated in Western cultures. The heart of Asian New Year celebrations is in the home, where family rituals take on profound meaning. Families can spend up to a month preparing for the rituals that mark a new beginning for wealth and good

TABLE 5.3. SUMMARY OF ISLAMIC HOLIDAYS

ISLAMIC HOLIDAYS		MUHARRAM	MAWLID AL-NABI	RAMADAN	EID AL-FITR	EID AL-ADHA
ISLAMIC YEAR	YEAR	NEW YEAR	MUHAMMAD'S BIRTHDAY	FASTING BEGINS	RAMADAN ENDS	FESTIVAL OF SACRIFICE
1426	2005	February 10	April 21	October 5	November 4	January 10
1427	2006	January 31	April 11	September 24	October 24	December 31
1428	2007	January 20	March 31	September 13	October 13	December 20
1429	2008	January 10	March 20	September 2	October 2	December 9

fortune. Cleaning house is thought to bring a fresh start because it is an opportunity to sweep away the previous year's bad luck. Reuniting with family permeates celebrations, whether that reunion is through family gatherings or by phone. Retail shops are flooded with the color red, from holiday candies wrapped in red cellophane to red envelopes used to give money. Plants and flowers are preferred gifts since they signify good luck. In addition, some foods are associated with luck, money, long life, and fertility. During the Vietnamese Tet (New Year), candies made of coconut, winter melon, and banana are eaten in the hopes of ensuring a sweet and happy year (Konigsmark 2001).

Cultural Values

People's view of the world is shaped by the primary culture and the basic and essential cultural values it contains (Hall 1983). There are four common characteristics of all cultural values. First, cultural values are learned. Children undergo socialization through the contact they have with their parents and other significant others. They learn the values of their own culture. Second, cultural values guide behavior by defining acceptable standards in daily life such as eating habits, appropriate clothing, and safety. Third, cultural values are both permanent and dynamic. Values are passed from generation to generation, which retains permanence; at the same time, cultural values continuously change as society changes. Fourth, cultural values are held widely within a society that differentiates one culture from another (Assael 1987).

Cultural values direct attitudes, behaviors, relationships, assessments, and justifications of the self and others. Because cultural values determine what is desirable, they provide insights for developing acceptable consumer-market-product relationships. However, cultural values are not all held by individuals to the same degree. These variations are consumer value orientations and are important considerations for retailers when segmenting markets.

Value Orientations

Value orientations, which are commonly held values, underlie consumer behavior. These culturally implicit orientations shape the importance that consumers attach to broad product categories. In addition, value orientations influence consumers' consumption motivation and brand comprehension as well as their use of criteria to make choices, and they can inhibit purchases of specific products.

F. Kluckhohn and F. Strodtbeck (1961) identified four basic value orientations in American society that can be applied to consumer behavior: relationship to nature, time dimension, personal activity, and relationship to others.

The value orientations associated with relationship to nature includes simply taking events as they come and making the best of them, being prudent and planning for change and avoiding many hazards, or being masters of their environments. The value orientations associated with time orientation include individuals determining whether to emphasize tradition and the past, live for today, or invest in the future. The value alternatives associated with personal activity include an emphasis on being nonmaterialistic and enjoying life (being), learning and self-fulfillment (being-in-becoming), or stressing the results of one's activity (doing). Finally, the value alternatives associated with relationships with others include a focus on family and a patriarchal orientation (filial), a collective and democratic orientation (collateral), or an emphasis on individualism.

Understanding personal value orientations as they relate to consumer behavior offers important insights into why consumers make certain choices. Vinson,

TABLE 5.4. CONSUMER'S VALUE-ATTITUDE SYSTEM

VALUE-ATTITUDE	INCIDENCE	DESCRIPTION OF SYSTEM
Global values	Dozens	Established beliefs about preferred states of being or types of behavior.
Domain-specific values	Hundreds	General beliefs about economic, social, political, religious and other behaviors.
Evaluative Beliefs	Thousands	Broader beliefs about product and brand attributes.

Source: Vinson, D. E., Scott, J.E., & Lamont, L.M. (1977). The role of personal values in marketing and consumer behavior. *Journal of Marketing* 41, 44–50.

Scott, and Lamont (1977) identify three interdependent consumer value-attitude systems: global, values, domain specific values, and evaluative beliefs (See Table 5.4). Global values are central to a relatively small number of continuing beliefs that influence consumer behavior, evaluation, and choice. These values are abstract and provide a general description of a consumer's value system. Domain-specific values come from the experiences consumers have in specific situations. Vinson et al. suggested these values are activated in situations where there is an economic transaction or enough social values that develop when interacting with peers. A consumer could have hundreds of domain-specific values. Evaluative beliefs are descriptive judgments about classes of products and specific brands. Thousands of arrangements of evaluative beliefs exist due to the wide number of choices consumers make daily in the marketplace. These beliefs coexist with global values and domain-specific values.

Cultural Patterns

Cultural patterns are shared intrinsic and extrinsic characteristics within a particular cultural group. Intrinsic patterns are vital aspects of cultural heritage that when removed will cause the loss of cultural heritage. They include religious beliefs and practices, ethical values, musical tastes, folk and recreational patterns, literature, historical language, and a sense of a common past. Extrinsic patterns are the products of a cultural group's historical adjustment to its local environment. These patterns are external to ethnic cultural heritage. Extrinsic traits include dress, manners, patterns of emotional expression, and patterns of pronouncing language.

In the United Kingdom, Indian food is one of the top five foods for take-out, restaurant meals, and supermarket meals. In 2003, people spent £613 million on Indian food, which represented the highest market share of ethnic food retail sales (Mintel Intelligence Group 2003). H. White and K. Kokotsaki (2004) explored traditional and take-out Indian foods in the United Kingdom to determine if its consumption differed by ethnicity and personal values embedded in culture. They found that hedonistic values of health and enjoyment were important regardless of ethnic background, English or Indian (See Figure 5.10). For the English, social life, adventure, and savings were important, which reflects motive for social, hedonic, and economic benefits. The Indian consumers were motivated by culture, continuity, and religion, which are all intrinsic cultural traits. Marketers and restaurateurs need to consider underlying cultural patterns related to foods when they extend ethnic food products to new markets.

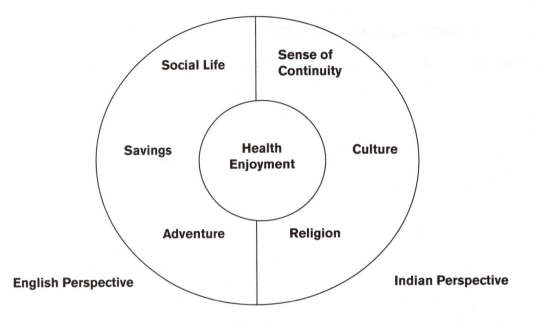

Social Life

Sense of Continuity

Savings

Health Enjoyment

Culture

Adventure

Religion

English Perspective

Indian Perspective

UNIVERSALS

People share similar characteristics, regardless of cultural and social backgrounds. Universals are exhibited across cultures and include social, political, technological, economic, and ideological cultural phenomenon. Understanding universal aspects of culture offers retailers inspirations for adapting aspects of the human behaviors, cultural traditions, and social lives found in other cultures to the creating of unique consumer experiences. By differentiating from the indigenous or local, retailers can look to other cultures to generate new products (e.g., foods, accessories, music, and gifts) and create novel experiences. Retailers seeking entry into new international markets might start with a universal concept (e.g., gift-giving, kin relationships, diet, or woodworking) that is associated with their product category and expand it to local offerings.

A comprehensive tool for understanding and investigating universal behaviors is the Human Relations Area File (HRAF) Collection of Ethnography (www.yale.edu/hraf). This cross-cultural electronic database has universal application. It can be used for cross-cultural, regional, and culture-specific examinations of all aspects of cultural and social life. Its purpose is to promote and facilitate worldwide and comparative study of human behavior, society, and culture. The HRAF collection of ethnography contains more than 700 subject codes that are categorized by subject terms, such as food consumption, clothing, arts, commercialized entertainment, and religious practices (See Table 5.5). Understanding these groupings offers insights into aspects of human behavior that have universal applications, such as gift-giving, celebrations, and rituals. While the specific way each of these universals occurs within a culture varies, they have a place in each culture. Innovations in retailing can come from applying different cultural processes for universal behaviors.

TRADITIONS

Traditions are created when customs are scheduled in relationship to one another. Over time, these traditions become habitual cultural patterns that are transmitted across generations and societies (Kroeber 1948).

For traditions to be maintained and transmitted, they must have human

TABLE 5.5. SUBJECTS USED TO INDEX DOCUMENT TEXTS IN THE HRAF DATABASE

SUBJECT CODES	SUBJECT TERMS	SUBJECT CODES	SUBJECT TERMS
100–199		500–599	
100	Orientation	500	Water and air transport
110	Information sources	510	Living standards and routines
120	Research methods	520	Recreation
130	Geography	530	Arts
140	Human biology	540	Commercialized entertainment
150	Behavior procedures and personality	550	Individuation and mobility
160	Demography	560	Social stratification
170	History and cultural change	570	Interpersonal relations
180	Total culture	580	Marriage
190	Language	590	Family
200–299		600–699	
200	Communication	600	Kinship
210	Records	610	Kin groups
220	Food quest	620	Community
230	Animal husbandry	630	Territorial organization
240	Agriculture	640	Government institutions
250	Food processing	650	Government activities
260	Food consumption	660	Political behavior
270	Drink and drugs	670	Law
280	Leather, textiles, and paper	680	Offenses and sanctions
290	Clothing	690	Justice
300–399		700–799	
300	Adornment	700	Armed forces
310	Exploitative activities	710	Military technology
320	Processing of basic materials	720	War
330	Building and construction	730	Social problems
340	Structures	740	Health and welfare
350	Equipment and maintenance of buildings	750	Sickness
360	Settlements	760	Death
370	Energy and power	770	Religious beliefs
380	Chemical industries	780	Religious practices
390	Capital goods industries	790	Ecclesiastical organizations
400–499		800–899	
400	Machines	800	Numbers and measures
410	Tools and appliances	810	Sciences and humanities
420	Property	820	Ideas about nature and people
430	Exchange and transfers	830	Sex
440	Marketing	840	Reproduction
450	Finance	850	Infancy and childhood
460	Labor	860	Socialization
470	Business and industry organization	870	Education
480	Travel and transportation	880	Adolescence, adulthood, old age
490	Land transport	890	Gender roles and issues
		900–910	
		900	Texts
		910	Archaeological measures, techniques, and analysis

Reprinted with permission from Terms and codes in the *Outline of Cultural Materials,* 6th edition, 2006. (George P. Murdock, et al., editors). Copyright Human Relations Area Files, Inc.

involvement. Consumers work to maintain the conditions necessary to retain a tradition much like they would stockpile products (Goodenough 1999). Individuals learn cultural traditions through enculturation (process of learning cultural traditions, practices, and values) by families and social institutions (e.g., social organizations, churches, schools). A tradition may decline and fade away when consumers make alternative choices that are not part of the cultural tradition.

Creating cultural traditions can have an enormous effect on product demand. For example, traditional foods play an important role in holiday rituals. The distinctive odors associated with food can elicit connective emotional reactions (Foster 2003). A traditional holiday dish in the United States is green-bean casserole, a recipe developed in 1955 at Campbell Soup Company by Dorcas Reilly. This simple dish has become a marketing powerhouse for food marketers Campbell and Reckitt Benckiser. More than 30 million consumers make this green-bean casserole every holiday season. Holiday consumption of green-bean casserole accounts for almost $20 million or 20 percent of Campbell's $100 million annual sales for its brand of cream of mushroom soup. Moreover, holiday sales represent $56 million or 80 percent of Reckitt Benckiser's $70 million annual sales for its brand of French's French Fried Onions. For many Americans, having green-bean casserole at Thanksgiving is as important as having turkey. Recipe development is an important tool for food companies. By creating new combinations of ingredients, recipes become key revenue sources as the recipe grows to become a family favorite for generations to come (Thompson 2005).

Changing food patterns in France are a classic example of the demise of a cultural tradition. Historically, French people have consumed large quantities of bread, an important staple of French culinary arts. A French tradition was to eat croissants every morning that were picked up daily at the local baker's shop. Because of the market entrance and promotion of Kellogg's breakfast cereal as a breakfast alternative, the French Institute of Taste blamed the United States and Kellogg's for the demise of the communal family breakfasts of croissants (Goode 1998). In 1995, the per capita consumption of artisan breads in France declined to about one sixth of the two pounds per person consumed at the turn of the twentieth century. French consumers' demand for traditional breads declined as the result of mass-produced bread sold at supermarkets, and there were concerns regarding the contribution of bread to obesity and young consumers' preferences for manufactured cereals and cakes. More than 1,000 artisan bakers had to shut down their businesses in 1994 because of reduced demand. The president and prime minister of France enacted emergency measures that included a law regulating ingredients. They determined five stages required to make authentic bread, and began stamping artisan bread with its own *Appellation d'Origine Contrôlée* (AOC or AC) seal, which indicates top quality. Further initiatives were aimed at improving the bread served to children in school cafeterias and steering children toward superior bread (Drozdiak 1995).

SUBCULTURES

Subcultures are groups of people or consumer segments whose similar values and customs make them distinctly different from society as a whole. The distinctiveness of a subculture may be evident as extrinsic patterns (e.g., spoken language, dress and appearance, or other tangible artifacts) and shared cultural values. As cultural values become stronger, more standardized, and more restricted, there is greater subgroup influence on its members. Consumer behavior within a subculture is related to its distinctiveness, homogeneity, and exclusion. Although subcultures can be defined by a variety of characteristics (e.g., ethnicity, religion, age, consumption, occupation), this section focuses on ritual consumption related to ethnic, bicultural or multicultural, and consumption subcultures.

Ethnic Subcultures

Ethnicity can be defined from an objective or a subjective perspective. An objective view of ethnicity defines an **ethnic subculture** by its cultural traits, national origin, race, religion, wealth, social status, political power, segregated neighborhoods, or some combination of these attributes that set it apart from other groups (Gordon 1964, Keefe and Padilla 1987). A subjective perspective assigns a psychological phenomenon of ethnic identity that is more complex than ethnic or national origin (Hraba 1979; Laroche, Kim, and Tomiuk 1998).

Retailers need to consider the cultural aspects of the ethnic markets that they enter (Gore 1998). Ethnic individuals differ by their prior social and cultural experience (Forehand and Deshpandé 2001). The first step is to determine which ethnic individuals are shopping in retail stores; then identify the distinctiveness, similarity, and exclusiveness of that ethnic group; and finally, find out the strength of ethnic identity among the customers.

ETHNIC IDENTITY

Ethnic identity is a subjective description of the self (Hirschman 1991, Minor 1992).

It transmits self-identity regarding one's strength of affiliation with a particular group (Chung and Fischer 1999) and the attitudes and behaviors associated with that group (Phinney and Rosenthal 1992) in relationship to the dominant society (Phinney 1990). Ethnic identity expresses the continuing connection between one's sense of self and ethnicity (Forehand and Deshpandé 2001), belonging and commitment (Ting-Toomey 1981; Phinney, Horencyk, Liebkind, and Vedder 2001), shared values (White and Burke 1987), and shared cultural patterns, including language, behavior, and historical knowledge of the group (Rogler, Conney, and Ortiz 1980). Language, friendship networks, religious affiliation, participation in clubs and organizations, endogamy (marriage is required within a specific ethnic group), food preferences, and traditional celebrations are the most widely accepted indicators of ethnic identity (Rosenthal and Feldman 1992).

Ethnic identity can be thought of as a two-dimensional model (See Figure 5.11) that includes strong and weak relationships with the ethnic and dominant cultures (Berry, Trimble, and Olmedo 1986; Phinney 1990). Consumers who have strong identification with the majority group, as well as strong ethnic identification, may exhibit acculturated, integrated, and bicultural identities. If they have weak

5.11 Strong and weak orientations of identification with one's own ethnic group and the majority group

Identification with Majority Group	Identification with Ethnic Group	
	Strong	Weak
Strong	Acculturated Integrated Bicultural	Assimilated
Weak	Ethnically identified Ethnically embedded Separted Dissociated	Marginal

ethnic identification, then they are considered assimilated. Ethnic consumers who have weak identification with the majority group and strong identification with their ethnic group exhibit identities that are ethnically identified, imbedded, separated, and dissociated from the majority culture. Marginal ethnic consumers have weak identifications with both the majority and ethnic groups. Ethnic individuals may possess a strong or weak ethnic identity with their original culture as well as with the majority culture (Phinney 1990).

Strong ethnic identities in the United States are associated with African Americans (Williams and Qualls 1989), Asian Americans (Ellis et al. 1985), and Hispanics (Deshpandé, Hoyer, and Donthu 1986; Saenz and Aguirre 1991). Among Hispanics, shopping is a family activity; however, among African Americans, shopping often occurs with friends as a social outing and a social escape (Facenda 2004). The potency of ethnic identification shapes how much attention consumers give to ethnic information and the probability that they will purchase ethnic products (Deshpandé et al.; Hirschman 1991). Buying ethnic products is more likely when the social context includes people with a similar ethnicity than when multiple ethnic groups are represented in the social context (Stayman and Deshpandé 1989).

In some situations, where ethnic identity is more visible, minority individuals are more sensitive to their ethnic membership and have greater ethnic self-awareness. Ethnic self-awareness occurs when individuals process ethnic information and categorize themselves as ethnic. Generally, individuals with strong ethnic identification are more likely to have greater ethnic self-awareness compared with those who have weak ethnic identification (Forehand and Deshpandé 2001).

Increased ethnic awareness in the 1960s revived many little-known Christmas customs. For example Santa Lucia is a Swedish festival that was rarely celebrated by ethnic Swedes in the United States up to that time. Santa Lucia was a martyred Christian maiden who brought food to Christians in the catacombs. She was murdered and mutilated by the Romans. In 1962, Linsborg, Kansas, a predominantly Swedish American town, boosted Christmas business when it began to publicly observe the festival of Santa Lucia. Holiday shoppers were served cookies and coffee by local girls who were dressed in white robes and crowns fashioned from candle-lit evergreen wreaths. Midwestern tourists were enticed to shop in Linsborg and experience the food, art sales, musicians, and folk dances that became part of the Christmas season there. The Linsborg Christmas experience highlights the desire of some consumers to escape the commercialism and sameness of U.S. shopping malls, which have become synonymous with Christmas shopping (USA Today 1997).

When there is a high degree of ethnic identity, then the impact of culture on consumption may be strong. The Jewish celebration of Hanukkah always falls in December. The strength of identity among Jewish consumers has provided retailers with the opportunity to extend the Christmas holiday shopping time to include Hanukkah. Retailers now offer items such as Hanukkah cards, mementos, gift wrap, food, and decorations.

Some retailers are making ethnic marketing their core business. Asian consumers are attracted to the California retailer Ranch 99, where they can purchase rice cookers and Asian foods as well as mainstreamed consumer-packaged products. Because of its size, Wal-Mart is positioned to deliver optimal shopping experiences that are relevant to its ethnic customers. It reaches out to its multicultural clientele with its selection of merchandise, which incorporates brand preferences, size, and allocation, and with multilingual packaging and signage. National drugstore chains are improving their efforts to meet consumer needs in multicultural environments. Walgreens offers a product mix that is tailored to a store's neighborhood. It prints prescription directions in 10 languages besides English. Rite Aid features bilingual shelf sound installations where consumers can hear about a product in a variety of languages. Bilingual signage is used by Lowe's and Home Depot in Hispanic communities (Facenda 2004).

SITUATIONAL ETHNICITY

The phenomenon of **situational ethnicity** occurs when an ethnic individual demonstrates higher visibility of ethnic membership in some situations but not in others. This generally happens during interactions with people who share similar ethnic characteristics. R. W. Belk (1974) described a situation as "something outside the basic tendencies and characteristics of the individual, but beyond the characteristics of the stimulus object to be acted upon" (156–157). R. W. Belk (1975) also identified five dimensions of situational characteristics: physical surroundings, social surroundings, temporal perspective, task definition, and previous behaviors (e.g., antecedent states) (See Table 5.6). Furthermore, he (1975) indicated that "these features have a demonstrable and systematic effect on current behavior" (159).

D. M. Stayman and R. Deshpande (1989) examined situational ethnicity and consumer behavior where situational ethnicity is defined as how one feels ethnically in and about specific situations. They suggested the most pertinent to situational ethnicity, previous behaviors, and social situations. Given these influences, they developed a model for examining situational ethnicity and consumption (See Figure 5.12). In testing this model, they

examined Mexican, Chinese, and Caucasian consumers in food consumption situations, since food is ethnically cued, and in two social situations (with business associates and with their parents). Stayman and Deshpande found consistent support for situational differences in ethnic group perceptions of appropriate food for consumption. For example, ethnic groups preferred ethnic food in ethnically consistent situations (e.g., with their parents). Conversely, ethnic groups preferred to avoid ethnic food in ethnically inconsistent situations (e.g., with their business associates).

Bicultural or Multicultural Subcultures

Changing demographic trends are creating bicultural consumers (Maheswaran and Shavitt 2000). Bicultural individuals switch between cultural meaning systems based on the cultural cues (e.g., symbols and extrinsic and intrinsic patterns) that are embedded in their environment. **Bicultural or multicultural subcultures** retain a strong ethnic identity while simultaneously developing a strong sense of belonging to a new or dominant culture (Laroche, Kim, and Tomimuk 1998). Their "relationship with the traditional or ethnic culture and the relationships with the new or dominant culture must be considered, and these two relationships may be independent" (Phinney 1990, 501).

Bicultural individuals are characterized by two dimensions of cultural change: maintaining or losing traditional culture, and gaining new cultural traits (Dohrenwend and Smith 1962). To successfully integrate bicultural consumers is to accept the differences between their cultures and integrate their cultural meaning systems as they switch back and forth in response to environmental cues. This temporary access of independent or interdependent cultural

TABLE 5.6. SITUATIONAL DIMENSIONS THAT INFLUENCE ETHNIC CONSUMER BEHAVIOR

SITUATIONAL DIMENSIONS	DEFINED	EXAMPLES
Physical surroundings	Readily apparent features of a situation.	Geographic location Institutional location Décor Sounds Aromas Lighting Weather Visible configurations of merchandise Material surrounding the stimulus object
Social surroundings	The involvement and interaction with others in a situation.	Presence or absence of others Characteristics of others present Apparent roles of others present Interpersonal interactions
Temporal perspective	Specific units in which the situation may be described.	Time of day Day of week Season Past/future Time constraints
Task definition	Intent or requirement to select, shop for, or obtain information about a general or specific purchase.	Information search Product purchase Different buyer/user roles
Antecedent states	Momentary moods and conditions that are an immediate precursor to the current situation. They are differentiated from states that the individual brings to the situation versus the states that are a result of the situation.	Anxiety Pleasantness Hostility Excitation Cash on hand Fatigue Illness

Source: Belk, R. W. 1975. Situational variables and consumer behavior. *Journal of Consumer Research* 2(3):157–164.

meaning systems is referred to as alternation (i.e., independent cultural meaning) (LaFramboise, Coleman, and Gerton 1993) and frame switching (i.e., interdependent cultural meaning) (Hong, Morris, Chiu, and Benet-Martinez 2000). Alternating bicultural consumers disengage from their cultural meaning systems by grouping their responses to independent cultural cues in the environment.

Many Asian Americans are bicultural consumers. They respond to Western cul-

5.12 Model of situational ethnicity and consumption

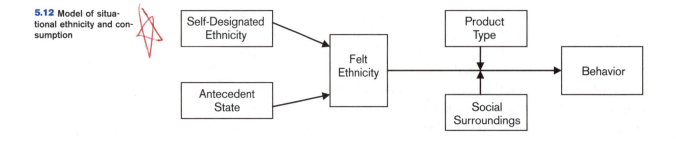

tural symbols much in the same way Western consumers do; however, they also respond to East Asian cultural symbols much in the same way East Asian consumers do (Lau-Gesk 2003). In examining various types of advertising appeals that promoted values unique to consumers with interdependent and independent cultural outlooks, L. G. Lau-Gesk (2003) found that bicultural consumers who were interdependent across the two cultural orientations favored persuasion appeals that activated both cultural perspectives. Conversely, bicultural consumers who had independent views of the two cultural orientations preferred persuasion appeals that activated only one cultural perspective.

Retailers need to understand the cultural outlook of their bicultural customers as they develop persuasive buying appeals. Creating retail environments that contain too many mixed cultural cues can create a dissatisfying shopping experience for the independent bicultural consumer, but a stimulating one for the interdependent bicultural consumer.

V. L. Facenda (2004) identified several retail initiatives that can have an immediate impact on both ethnic and bicultural consumers. These include displaying a welcome sign in the community-dominant language, installing multilingual signage, and hiring store associates who are fluent in the consumers' dominant language. Expanded strategies would include using multilingual communications throughout the retail store, offering multilingual credit applications, expanding key ethnic product selections, participating in ethnic community-based events, and using in-language television ads and circulars. Language is a critical marketing issue for retailers; they must determine when it is best to promote in English, a foreign language, or both. However, it is important to understand that ethnic and bicul-

tural consumers will value companies that adapt their marketing strategies to specific ethnic perspectives and not just translate information into another language.

Consumption Subcultures

Consumption subcultures are defined by the multitude of activities and interpersonal relationships that consumers undertake to give their lives meaning. These subcultures can create powerful consumption categories that define how consumers choose to spend their money and time. Consumption subcultures are not predefined by ascribed characteristics such as ethnicity, gender, age, lifestyle, or social class. Rather, consumption subcultures are unique, self-selected subgroups that are centered on shared commitments to a particular brand, or product class, or consumption pursuit. Consumption subcultures may develop from everyday activities that direct consumers' consumption and social activities, which subsequently influence product choice, retail patronage, social interaction, and media use (Schouten and McAlexander 1995).

The Red Hat Society is a consumption subculture. They consider themselves a *dis-organization* since there are no rules or bylaws. The purpose of the Red Hat Society is to have fun by providing a social experience where female members, ages 50 and older, attend just to have a good time. The only requirement is that they wear red hats and purple clothing to all events (See Figure 5.13). If prospective members under the age of 50 want to participate, they wear pink hats and lavender clothes. This consumption subculture created a consumer demand for red hats and purple clothing, which has expanded into products such as T-shirts, costume jewelry, signs, boas, scarves, shoes, clothing, and greeting cards. There are Red Hat Society conventions,

5.13 Members of the Red Hat Society riding on a float in the Krum Texas Christmas Parade.

5.14 Motorcycle enthusiasts have included wearing leather in their wedding ritual.

cruises, and other travel events. A visit to the Red Hat Society website (www.redhat-society.com) offers links to shop the store, apply for the RHS credit card, review RHS travel information, and view publications.

Consumption subcultures are characterized by identifiable, hierarchical social structures; distinctive sets of shared beliefs and values; and unique jargons, rituals, and modes of symbolic expression (Schouten and Alexander 1995). Through its exclusive membership in the international Harley Owners Group (HOG) that is based on ownership of a Harley motorcycle, the Harley-Davidson brand has created a consumption subculture. Harley motorcycles command premium prices; thus, the economic factor further limits membership in this consumption subculture. HOG members receive publications and information about local, national, and international sponsored events and rallies.

Harley-Davidson's distinctive motorcycles and associated merchandise have produced loyal Harley consumers. The Harley-Davidson brand is built on core values of personal freedom, patriotism, American heritage, and machismo. Personal freedom is associated with liberation (i.e., freedom *from*) and symbolized by the Harley eagle with outspread wings, while personal freedom associated with license (i.e., freedom *to*) is symbolized by the Harley-as-horse metaphor. Americanism is an important core value represented by patriotism and U.S. heritage, which is represented by the motorcycle itself (American made) and the profuse use of American flags as symbols on bikes, clothes, patches, pins, and in rallies. The company emphasizes tradition through the names it assigns to each of its motorcycles such as Heritage, Classic, and Evolution. Machismo, the third core value, is evident in the Harley-Davidson interpretation of the biker image. It incorporates a designer flair for the upscale consumers who are attracted to the Harley-Davidson bikes. Black leather clothing (See Figure 5.14) and personal and bike accessories are prominent and impart a sense of power, fearsomeness, and invulnerability to the rider (Schouten and McAlexander 1995).

CULTURAL DIFFUSION

The growth of diverse consumer populations within the United States, as well as

TABLE 5.7. CULTURE CONTINUATION THROUGH SIX CULTURAL PROCESSES

CULTURAL PROCESSES	METHOD
Transmitted	Generation-to-generation
Learned	Socialization
Shared	Common meanings Shared symbols
Transformed	Continuous change
Communicated	Common spoken language Symbolic language
Cumulative	Accumulate and transmit ideas and skills

in other countries throughout the world, has generated multiple consumer cultures with shared consumption values. Cultural characteristics continue because they are transmitted from one generation to the next through processes where the culture is learned, shared, transformed, communicated, and accumulated over time (See Table 5.7).

Cultural change occurs when there is contact between cultures (Peñaloza 1989) and individuals learn new technologies, share new experiences, and accept new patterns of behavior. While these changes are evolutionary, the speed at which the changes occur is accelerated or hindered by a group's access to new phenomenon. This change is called cultural diffusion.

Cultural diffusion occurs when diverse societies come in contact, either directly or indirectly. A society is made up of groups of people who interact regularly with one another. When different societies come into contact, new cultural elements can either be accepted or rejected depending on whether the elements fit into the total patterning of the receiving culture. If the new element is accepted, it may be modified as it is being adopted. Through recurring activities associated with living and working together, people acquire cultural guide-lines for speaking, doing, interpreting, and evaluating (Goodenough 1999).

When group interactions encompass a wide range of activities with similar cultural understandings, the society becomes culturally uniform (Goodenough 1999). The strong sense of national identity and a low level of racial and ethnic diversity in Japan make it a homogeneous society. Japanese people strongly believe in the widely accepted role of the traditional or *continuing family*. It relates to the premise that even if family members do not live together in the same dwelling, they should always live close enough that it is possible to bring over a cup of soup. This sense of family closeness is respected and practiced by most people in Japan. Conversely, when groups interact across a wide range of activities, but their cultural understandings differ, then this represents a culturally diffuse society (Goodenough 1999).

Cultural diffusion is evident in new taste patterns in foods. A trend among chefs is to create "higher levels of culinary détente, turning out globally inspired dishes that speak of harmony, possibility, and pizzazz. From this deliciously ambiguous pot come new approaches to fusion cooking that blend an international array of flavors. Hints of Asia, the Middle East and the

Mediterranean, Latin America, the islands, and beyond increasingly lend intrigue to menus, stirring excitement in familiar and exotic fare alike" (Yee 2004, 30).

Acculturation

Acculturation is one form of cultural diffusion that occurs when "groups of individuals having different cultures come into continuous first-hand contact, with subsequent changes in the original cultural patterns of either or both groups" (Redfield, Linton, and Herskovits 1936, 149).

When consumers with significantly different cultures live in close contact with one another, they learn cultural traits outside their own culture. Immigration from one country to another is one way that this happens. Likewise, when people relocate within a country to access new resources such as jobs, homes, and schools they expose themselves to different cultures. Acculturation can take place at the level of the individual and group concurrently (Berry 1980). In practice, although change may occur in both groups, there is generally more substantial change in the group that has immigrated or relocated (Ogden, Ogden, and Schau 2004). A traditional viewpoint of acculturation is that it represents a bipolar continuum, where one end represents an unacculturated group while the opposing end represents the assimilated extreme (Ogden et al. 2004).

Consumer Acculturation

Consumer acculturation is specific to the consumption process (Ogden et al. 2004) and focuses on cultural adaptation in the marketplace (Peñaloza 1989). Through acculturation, consumers learn consumption values, knowledge, and behavior by modeling, reinforcement, and social interaction (Moschis and Churchill 1978). It describes how consumers in one culture acquire the skills and knowledge relevant to consumer behavior in another culture (Peñaloza 1989). Consumer acculturation includes learning to buy and consume goods as well as learning the meanings assigned to the consumption of goods. It emphasizes the cultural bases of consumption behaviors and consumer learning processes and how they are affected by the interactions of two or more cultures.

Consumer acculturation occurs through assimilation, integration, separation, and a hybrid form that creates a new cultural outlook. Through assimilation, consumers assume the cultural or behavioral features of the more dominant society as they reduce conflict and adapt to their environments. Integration supports a positive relationship between a dominant culture and a minority culture. Consumers in the minority culture retain their cultural identities while seeking to become a part of the dominant acculturating group. This form is sometimes referred to as the salad bowl, where the cultural differences are appreciated and valued by the dominant host society. The society then becomes a collective group of various cultures. Separation is an adaptive process aimed at decreasing conflict. In this case, consumers would move away from the dominant host society. Rejection occurs when consumers rebuff both the host culture and the original culture. Hybrid acculturation reinvents culture so that it is unlike either the original or host culture. The Chicano culture in the United States is a hybrid. Chicanos are U.S.–born citizens of Mexican descent; their cultural values, orientations, and patterns differ from those found in Mexico, as well as the *dominant culture* in the United States (Peñaloza 1989). "Chicano" is a relatively recent ethnic identity established during the 1960s in the United States. It grew from organized efforts against discrimination and was associated with political activism. Not all U.S. born Americans of Mexican descent accept the Chicano identity (Healy 1995).

L. N. Peñaloza (1994) and M. C. Gilly (1999) (with L. N. Peñaloza) suggested consumer acculturation is related negatively to ethnic affiliation because people who affiliate with their ethnic communities are less likely to adapt to and adopt mainstream values and behaviors. M. Laroche, C. Kim, and M. A. Tomiuk (1998) concluded that the primary difference between acculturation and ethnic identity is that acculturation focuses on acquiring the host culture while ethnic identify focuses on maintaining or retaining of the culture of origin.

Understanding consumer acculturation is an important component of retail segmentation strategies (Facenda 2004). This understanding needs to include knowledge of the intrinsic and extrinsic traits that characterize specific cultural groups. Many times U.S. retailers classify ethnic consumers by the amount of time they have spent in the United States or by generalized categories such as surname. However, this does not give a true picture of an ethnic consumer's buying habits. Retailers need to assess the levels of consumer acculturation as well.

Consumer acculturation occurs at both individual and group levels of consumption behavior. At the individual level, norms, rules, expectations, and knowledge are transformed through life experiences. Ethnic identity is influenced through transitions such as marriage and child bearing, geographical migration, and political and religious conversion. At the group level, the emphasis is on interpersonal relationships and information exchange that affect individual consumer learning (Burnkrant and Cousineau 1975). At the individual level, consumption motives are related to

how an individual learns to interpret consumption cues of others and use goods as a means of self-expression (Peñaloza 1989).

Immigrant populations have sources of information from both their cultures of origin and the cultures of the places into which they have moved. Their learning process is influenced by both of these information sources as well as by a number of personal traits. Collectively, demographic characteristics, cultural consumption values, language preferences, generation or age, intensity of affiliation, and environmental factors influence consumer acculturation.

According to Facenda (2004), about half of the Hispanic population in the United States is foreign born. This is an important statistic since foreign-born consumers bring with them brand experiences from their home countries. Recent immigrants have a high tendency to continue using their native language, staying true to their traditional cultures, and eating their native cuisine. Also, with increasing age it becomes more difficult for immigrants to learn a new language, although immigrants with higher socioeconomic levels and education are more likely to be bilingual (Facenda 2004). L. N. Peñaloza (1994) suggested an empirical model (See Figure 5.15) for examining the consumer acculturation for Mexican immigrants to the United States.

Ethnic identity may vary due to the level of acculturation and assimilation (Ogden et al. 2004, Peñaloza and Gilly 1999). J. Xu, S. Shim, S. Lotz, and D. Almeida (2004) examined the influence of ethnic identity on culture-specific food and entertainment consumption of Asian American young adults. Young adults with strong ethnic identities were more likely to consume ethnic food in all meal situations and participate in ethnic entertainment activities (e.g., movies, music, and cultural

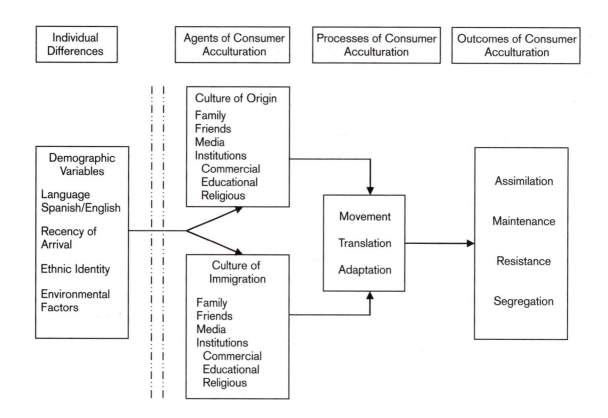

| Individual Differences | Agents of Consumer Acculturation | Processes of Consumer Acculturation | Outcomes of Consumer Acculturation |

Culture of Origin
Family
Friends
Media
Institutions
  Commercial
  Educational
  Religious

Demographic Variables

Language
Spanish/English

Recency of
Arrival

Ethnic Identity

Environmental
Factors

Culture of Immigration

Family
Friends
Media
Institutions
  Commercial
  Educational
  Religious

Movement

Translation

Adaptation

Assimilation

Maintenance

Resistance

Segregation

5.15 Model of consumer acculturation of Mexican immigrants to the United States

performances). Moreover, Xu et al. found that the culture-specific consumption behavior of Asian American young adults was greater when they were among ethnic minority friends versus Caucasian friends, regardless of the strength of their ethnic identity. This is an example of situational ethnicity. The study also provides insights into the importance of the transitional period of young adulthood in developing culture-specific consumption behavior.

Product Acculturation

A product considered at one time to be an ethnic-specific product can cross a cultural bridge and become mainstream. Food is an excellent example of this phenomenon. The tortilla, a Mexican staple food, is an ethnic food that has become mainstream in the United States. Estimated sales of tortillas in 2004 were more than $5.3 billion, up 20 percent in just two years (Robinson-Jacobs 2005). The fastest growing market

in the United States is the Hispanic market. The economic implications are significant in Texas where there are 150 tortilla makers, including the two largest in the nation: Mission Foods (Grupo Maseca's Gruma Corporation of Mexico) and Tia Rosa (Bimbo Bakeries USA) (Robinson-Jacobs 2005).

Active lifestyles have contributed to the growth of tortilla consumption in the United States. U.S. consumers have developed grab-and-go eating patterns, where they want something that is quick, easy to eat, and relatively healthy. In the mid-1990s, delis began using tortillas to repackage traditional sandwiches and salads as wraps. Soon chefs and sandwich makers began using unconventional flavored tortillas (e.g., spinach, sun-dried tomato, habanero) for wraps. These new versions of wrapped sandwiches can command a higher price than the burrito, which is the traditional Mexican wrap. By 2002 tortillas gained popularity because of low-carb diets that became the craze and led dieters to shun white bread. Tortillas have developed international appeal with U.S. companies specifically targeting European markets to expand the tortilla business (Robinson-Jacobs 2005).

SACRED AND PROFANE CONSUMPTION

Consumption is distinguished by social groups based on what is considered a sacred (i.e., set apart) and transcendent experience and what is considered profane (i.e., ordinary and part of everyday life). In examining consumption behavior in naturalistic settings and through in-depth interviews, R. W. Belk, M. Wallendorf, and J. F. Sherry Jr. (1989) found that consumers made distinctions between sacred and profane behaviors and their use of space, time, and objects. Belk et al. provided a comprehensive summary of 12 properties of sacredness that they drew from the works of earlier theorists (Beane and Doty 1975, Durkheim 1975, Eliade 1958, Mol 1976, Pickering 1984) and related these experiences to consumption experiences (See Table 5.8).

Belk et al. (1989) further examined domains of sacred consumption. They suggested that sacred status does not occur indiscriminately across culture; rather, consumers make a distinction between the sacred and profane across all their of experiences. Belk et al. aligned six major categories of probable sacred consumer domains with probable sacred religious domains (See Table 5.9). The six domains of place, time, tangible things, intangibles, people, and experiences were used to build a definition of sacredness related to consumption.

An example of a sacred domain is the Harley-Davidson experience for the Harley owner. The Harley motto "Live to ride, ride to live" suggests that riding and owning a Harley is a transforming experience. "The Harley consumption experience has a spirituality derived in part from a sense of riding as a transcendental departure from the mundane" (Schouten and McAlexander 1995, 50). Often, Harley bikes are housed in special places that are treated as shrines. Special attention is paid to their constant care, with elaborate rituals in cleaning and maintaining the bike. There is a brotherhood among Harley bikers that signifies a community of shared belief, purpose, and experience (Schouten and McAlexander 1995). The special Harley experience extends to owning Harley artifacts such as clothing and accessories for adults and children and can include sacred items such as wedding rings and wedding dresses.

In examining consumption principles associated with advertising, Hirschman (1991) identified three types for U.S. consumers: secular consumption, sacred consumption, and mediating consumption. Images of the secular consumption focus on technology, urbanism, personal achievement, and mastery over nature. Sacred consumption focuses on familial bonding, friendship, ecological concern, and nurturance. Mediating consumption incorporates both secular and sacred aspects of consumption.

Retailers who want to meet consumers' needs for status enhancement or competitive achievement might position products with an appeal to a secular lifestyle. When they want to meet consumers' cognitive association with culturally viewed sacred phenomenon, they need to emphasize naturalness, wholesomeness, kinship, and friendship. In situations where undesirable attributes are associated with a product, adding a sacred element to the imagery through words and visual objects can

TABLE 5.8. TWELVE PROPERTIES OF SACRED CONSUMPTION

PROPERTIES OF SACRED CONSUMPTION

PROPERTY	DEFINED	PURPOSE
Hierophany	Experiences the manifestation of an object as sacred.	Convey unique sacredness that is not revealed to everyone.
Kratophany	Elicits ambivalence through a propensity for strong approach and strong avoidance.	Create care in how people approach an overwhelming power.
Opposition to profane	Distinguishes the sacred as distinct by keeping it separate from contact with ordinary, daily life.	Provide social control that separates the sacred from the profane.
Contamination	Extends the sacredness to other objects, places, and persons through contact.	Attain aspects of the sacred through exposure to the sacred.
Sacrifice	Communicates with the sacred through offerings.	Prepare the individual to connect, commit, and defer to the sacred.
Commitment	Focuses on emotional attachment to the sacred.	Create commitment to the sacred.
Objectification	Assigns meaning to a transcending experience.	Use objects to provide tangible evidence of the sacred.
Ritual	Prescribes rules of behavior in the presence of sacred objects.	Prepare individual to approach the sacred.
Myth	Documents historical status of the sacred through narratives, iterative tales, and speculations.	Use repetition to define the place of individuals in the world and the status of the sacred.
Mystery	Confers a dignity that elevates the sacred above the ordinary.	Identify profound experiential phenomenon that cannot be explained cognitively.
Communitas	Produces camaraderie with shared equivalent status among individuals.	Create a social structure that releases individuals from their ordinary status.
Ecstasy and flow	Creates ecstasy through extraordinary experiences of joy outside one's self.	Identify ecstasy as phenomenon of individual momentary sacred experience different from ordinary experience of pleasure.
	Creates flow by centering attention and control of the self and environment.	Associate flow with a peak experience that makes it its own reward.

Adapted with permission from Belk, R. W., M. Wallendorf, and J. F. Sherry. 1989. The sacred and the profane in consumer behavior: Theodicy on the odyssey. *Journal of Consumer Research* 16:1–38.

compensate for the unnatural attributes. "Nature and family are strong iconic images for sacredness in the American consumption ideology, and . . . they can be effectively used to position the product" (Hirschman 1991, 41).

The sacred status of consumer products can be attained through seven processes (See Table 5.10). These sacrilization processes include: ritual, pilgrimage, quintessence, collecting, inheritance, gift-giving, and external sanction.

Ritual

Rituals symbolically transform an ordinary object into a sacred one. Through the process of singularization (i.e., making something unique and individual), an object is assigned attributes or changed so that it has unique sacred characteristics. Thus, the object is changed so it is no longer a standard product that can be purchased by anyone (i.e., it is decommodized). Furthermore, consumers transform objects by changing or customizing objects

TABLE 5.9. SIX DOMAINS OF SACRED CONSUMPTION

DOMAINS OF SACRED CONSUMPTION

DOMAINS	MANIFESTATION	CONCEPT ASSOCIATED WITH SACRED PROPERTY
Place	• Nature • Events • Dwellings	• Ecstasy and flow is obtained through beauty, majesty, power. • Contamination through sacred activities that occurred in that place. • Mystery and transcendental aspect of private spaces in the home; a sense of otherworldliness in the space (i.e., the department store).
Times	• Recoverable • Episodically • Infinite • Replacement of sacred place	• Rituals and celebrations recover a previous time such as Christmas, initiations, graduations, weddings, funerals, and birthdays. • Myths posit that sacred time is infinite and without meaning. • Sacred times during the year serve in lieu of a sacred place.
Tangibles	• Icons • Clothing • Furnishings • Artifacts • Possessions	• Objectification of the sacred through symbolic link to a tangible item. • Myths, rituals, and signs make tangible things sacred. • Kratophany is associated with sacred tangible objects.
Intangibles	• Magic formula • Dances • Crests • Names • Songs • Rituals	• Kratophany is assigned through strong ambivalent reactions that are generated by attracted to and fear of intangible sacred powers.
Persons and other beings	• Religious people • The body • Pets	• Were chosen for position by nonrational, hierophanous vision. • Body care rituals, clothing, body decoration • Sacralized animal within the family.
Experiences	• Travel • Sightseeing • Eating • Holiday rituals • Spectator sports	• Nostalgic places convey a sacred time. • Festive, liminal time provides experiences. • Food is a sacred experience as it takes on meaning beyond nourishment. • Pre- post-, and during game rituals create sacred time.

Adapted with permission from Belk, R. W., M. Wallendorf, and J. F. Sherry. 1989. The sacred and the profane in consumer behavior: Theodicy on the odyssey. *Journal of Consumer Research* 16:1–38.

to impart their own identities (Belk et al. 1989).

While rituals are culturally patterned activities that create unique and important experiences to a cultural group, ceremonies are a series of interdependent rituals that are executed at a particular time. "Much ritual in contemporary consumer culture has been secularized—in effect reduced to ceremony or habit—but some ritual may be reclaimed or singularized, and consciously returned to the realm of sacred" (Belk et al. 1989, 14). Rituals become functional routine ceremonies when they are performed without deliberate thought (Bossard and Boll 1950).

Rituals provide families with a sense of identity, comfort, and security (Foster 2003). When these rituals are transmitted from one generation to the next, they become tradition. Ritual performers often require specialized accoutrements and dress. Simon Jaffee created a "Plagues Bag" to help Jewish families act out the events of the Passover story at the ritual seder meal, where the story of the Jews' exodus from Egypt is retold and reenacted. The Plagues Bag, which sells for $10, includes items such as a plastic frog, false boils, rubber dice, and jigsaw puzzles that promote interactive learning for children. In response to concern that it might trivi-

TABLE 5.10. PROCESSES OF SACRALIZATION

PROCESS OF SACRALIZATION	DESCRIPTION
Ritual	Objects are transformed symbolically to the realm of sacred. This can occur in public or private and be done by an individual or collectively in a group. The process may include transforming the object through personalization.
Pilgrimage	Travel away from home to a consumption site where an intense experience of sacredness occurs.
Quintessence	Ordinary objects are treated as extraordinary. Often associated with branded products where the sacredness goes beyond the object. It includes a search for authenticity.
Gift-giving	Gift-giving obtains special meaning through selection of the gift. Gifts communicate bonds between people and they are sanctified by their links to other sacred elements of life. Gifts attain sacred status as expression of deeply held cultural values.
Collecting	Collections are unique by their completeness. Once objects are added to a collection, they take on meaning beyond their individual existence because they help complete the collection. Objects become sacralized when they are rescued from those who do not know their value or worth. Collections often start as gifts and can become expressions of the self. Collections are sacralized by systematic labeling, arranging, and displaying objects.
Inheritance	Family heirlooms become sacred due to their age and sentimental associations with past history. Heirlooms help explain the origin of the inheritor as well as who they are and where they are going.
External sanction	Objects are sacralized by the endorsement of an external authority, such as a museum.

Adapted with permission from Belk, R. W., M. Wallendorf, and J. F. Sherry. 1989. The sacred and the profane in consumer behavior: Theodicy on the odyssey. *Journal of Consumer Research* 16:1–38.

alize the importance of the Passover story, Mr. Jaffee stated, "I suppose with more traditional segments of the community, there could be a feeling that the seder is something not to be touched. But my own feeling and that of many educators is that the important thing is to make the seder relevant to young people, to conjure up images and memories" (Keller 1996, 13). Rituals can be broadly classified as rites of passage, rites of intensification, or a combination of both.

RITES OF PASSAGE

Rites of passage mark important life transitions. Many of these transitions are universally recognized, such as the occasion of birth, naming, puberty or coming of age, marriage, and death. Because most of these rites require special dress and accoutrements for participation, retailers can offer products that commemorate these important life transitions.

Celebrating rites of passage varies across cultures. In the United States newborns and their parents are showered with gifts prior to a child's birth. Among Koreans, the 100th day of life was considered a traditional time of celebration that is now celebrated on the first birthday. The child is dressed in traditional garb and a party is celebrated in his or her honor (See Figure 5.16). Many ethnic couples retain traditional wedding rituals that are part of their cultural heritage. Figure 5.17 illustrates a Hindu wedding in the United States, while Figure 5.18 shows the same couple on their honeymoon.

Birthday experiences have become a large industry in the United States. About 12 percent ($3.5 billion) of toy sales is from birthday party purchases (Keates and Gubernick 2002). Parents who work full-time and overloaded schedules for parents and children have created a culture where outsourcing the birthday party has become

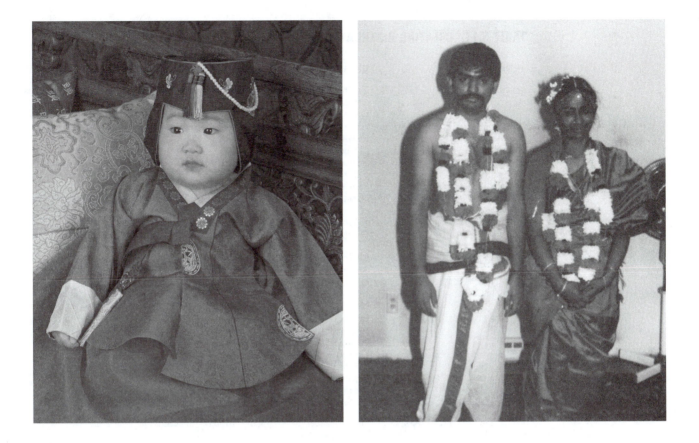

an acceptable and often preferred way to mark the annual birthday rite. Birthdays have become coordinated themed events, often with branded characters. A number of Internet sites offer parents all they need (invitations, party favors, napkins, plates, and cups) to host the themed party of their choice (Better 2001). Birthdaypartyideas.com is an example of a website that offers ideas and solutions for birthday parties. Retail chains and franchises have become important birthday purveyors that offer complete packages (See Table 5.11).

The *quinceañera* celebration is an important rite of passage for Hispanic girls. *Quinceañera* means 15th birthday and is the equivalent of the American sweet sixteen. The *quinceañera* can be traced to the Aztecs where a 15-year-old girl's spiritual and physical coming-of-age was a ritual celebration. The coming-of-age ceremony transitioned into a private religious

ritual that, for Catholics, includes holding a Roman Catholic Mass.

The *quinceañera* is an important celebration that preserves Latino culture (Chozick 2004). Initially, the religious ritual was followed by a family reception but

5.16 Korean child in traditional dress for her first birthday

5.17 A Hindu couple of the Tamil Brahmin Lyengar sect at their wedding that took place in Washington, D.C.

5.18 The same Hindu couple on their honeymoon

TABLE 5.11. CREATING BIRTHDAY EXPERIENCES FOR KIDS

VENUE	EXPERIENCE	COST
American Girl Place	One hour at the café Invitation Silver-charm goody bag	$30 per person $55 deluxe per person
Build-A-Bear Workshop	Party leader Stuffed animals for guests Stuffed animals + pillow for host child	$10–$25 for bears only
Imagine It! Children's Museum of Atlanta	Party room for 90 minutes Museum admission Food Invitations Goody bags	$375.00 for 10 children
Chuck E Cheese	Reserved table for 90 minutes Single topping pizza, soft drinks Cake 16 game tokens Birthday song/show from Chuck E. Birthday child receives a collector's cup, a bag of cotton candy, a 14-inch helium balloon, and a crown	Price varies by location
Universal Studios	Park admission 2 hours in decorated room Meet/greet with character actor	$895 for 16 people

Source: Lundegaard, L. 2004. The cranky consumer: Making kids' birthdays an event. *The Wall Street Journal*, Aug. 12, D2.

the reception has transitioned into a secular event where sometimes several hundreds of guests attend. The highlight of the *quinceañera* is the daughter dancing a waltz with her father (or father figure) and performing a dance with her court in front of the guests (Chozick 2004, Miranda 2004).

The *quinceañera* has become a commercialized and secular celebration among the growing number of Latino families in the United States (Miranda 2004) and can even cost more than a wedding (Chozick 2004). Families, whether they are affluent or of modest means, often plan and save for years for a daughter's *quinceañera* (Chozick 2004, Miranda 2004). The celebration can cost about $10,000 for gowns, DJ, banquet hall, limousines, and food. More elaborate and extravagant affairs can exceed $30,000 (Chozick 2004, Miranda 2004).

Driving a *quinceañera*'s increasing cost is the commercialization of the experience. In 2000, Walt Disney Company began offering customized *quinceañera* events starting at $7,500. After weddings, *quinceañeras* are Disney's fastest growing event category. Royal Caribbean Cruises, Ltd. works with travel agencies to book *quinceañera* cruises that cost between $900 and $1,600 per person.

Preparations for the *quinceañera* include buying a special gown and selecting 6 to 10 *damas* (single female friends) who are dressed specially for the celebration (See Figure 5.19). Retailers now offer *quinceañera* dresses that range from designer to budget gowns. David's Bridal, the nation's largest bridal retailer, offers *quinceañera* gowns in 41 of its 240 stores. Wal-Mart Stores Inc. sells specially designed *quinceañera* dresses for $24 to $30 at 200 of its 3,200 U.S. retail outlets.

There is a *quinceañera* Barbie from Mattel, Inc. and Spanish-language *quinceañera* cards from Hallmark Cards, Inc. JC Penney Company markets itself as a one-stop retailer where everything for the *quinceañera* can be purchased, including personalized portraits.

In the Jewish community, a spiritual rite of passage is known as the *Bar Mitzvah* for boys and *Bat Mitzvah* for girls. The Bar Mitzvah is an ancient event that marks the coming of age for Jewish males (See Figure 5.20). The Bar Mitzvah occurs at ages 12 or 13 after an extended study of Jewish history, traditions, and the Hebrew language. The Bat Mitzvah provides girls with a rite of passage similar to boys. Generally, children begin preparing for the Bar Mitzvah or Bat Mitzvah about one year ahead of time by spending several hours a week studying and doing charity work. By 1960, Bar Mitzvahs evolved into themed celebration parties that include a hall, caterer, music, decorations, and the necessary dress and accessories (Bernstein 2004, Nathan 2005).

The secularization of the Bar Mitzvah illustrates cultural diffusion from a subculture into mainstream society. Children approaching age 13 are requesting and having parties similar to Bar Mitzvahs that they attend, even though they themselves are not Jewish. E. Bernstein (2004) reported on one girl whose parents threw her a $12,000 faux Bat Mitzvah at a Manhattan hotel with 150 guests. Since 2000, companies that cater Bar Mitzvahs and Bat Mitzvahs are reporting that they are also catering Bar Mitzvah and Bat Mitzvah lookalikes to non-Jewish clients (Bernstein 2004).

RITES OF INTENSIFICATION

Rites of intensification mark events and transitions within a society as a whole. Often these rites are seasonal and mark changes in weather and activities. Retail-

ers use seasonal transitions to promote certain types of clothing, foods, and household products. Spring cleaning is a ritual in many households and it is promoted through special sales of cleaning products, new furnishings, and home accessories. Upscale retailers such as Restoration Hardware have taken household cleaning

5.19 A 15-year-old girl, her mother, and her *damas*, all in special dress, on her *quinceañera*

5.20 The Bar Mitzvah is a rite of passage for 13-year-old Jewish boys.

to the next level with coordinated accessories and cleaning products.

New Year's celebrations are associated with setting new goals. Some common goals are to develop healthier lifestyles and lose weight. Retailers often promote this intensified effort for healthy living through healthy foods and activewear. Creating experiences in the retail store that promote healthy living can draw in customers and create sales. Experiences might include cooking demonstrations in the housewares department and a physical fitness trainer to give tips in the activewear department.

Rites of intensification also mark historical transitions. *Cinco de Mayo*, the fifth of May, commemorates the 1862 victory of Mexico over the French army at the Battle of Puebla. It is primarily a regional holiday celebrated in the Mexican state's capital city of Puebla and throughout the state of Puebla, with some recognition in other parts of Mexico. *Cinco de Mayo* celebrations have become more visible in the United States, especially in cities with a significant Mexican population. Retailers are targeting *Cinco de Mayo* celebrations to sell products and services that include Mexican foods and beverages. Bars and restaurants offer Mexican dinner specials and promotions such as discounted Mexican beers. Associated products are opportunities for retailers to offer related toys, party accessories, and small gifts.

Kwanzaa (taken from *matunda ya kwanza*, which means "first fruits" in Swahili) is an African American and pan-African holiday celebrated from December 26 through January 1. It builds on the five basic endeavors associated with continental African first fruits celebrations: ingathering, reverence, commemoration, recommitment, and celebration. Kwanzaa was founded in 1966 in response to the Black Freedom Movement in the United States. Created by Dr. Maulana Karenga,

a professor in the Department of Black Studies at California State University– Long Beach, Kwanzaa was designed to create and strengthen a sense of community, identity, purpose, and direction of a people and a world community. Kwanzaa serves to reaffirm and restore a sense of roots in African culture and the bonds among African Americans as a people and to introduce and reinforce the traditional values of *Nguzo Saba* (the Seven Principles): *Umoja* (unity), *Kujichagulia* (self-determination), *Ujima* (collective work and responsibility), *Ujamaa* (cooperative economics), *Nia* (purpose), *Kuumba* (creativity), and *Imani* (faith).

Kwanzaa uses seven traditional symbols and two supplemental symbols to represent African cultural values. *Mazao* (the crops) symbolize African harvest celebrations and productive and collective work. *Mkeka* (the mat) symbolizes a foundation built on tradition and history. *Kinara* (the candle holder) symbolizes the roots of the parent cultural heritage of continental Africa. *Muhindi* (the corn) symbolizes children and their future. *Mishumaa Saba* (the seven candles) symbolize the values of *Nguzo Saba* that can help African people be free and recreate their lives according to their own needs. *Kikombe cha Umoja* (the unity cup) symbolizes the basic principles and practice of unity. *Zawadi* (the gifts) symbolize parents' love and labor and their children's commitments. *Bendera* (the flag) is a supplemental symbol that represents the colors of the Organization Us. Black stands for people, red for their struggle, and green for hope for the future that comes from struggle. *Nguzo Saba Poster* is the other supplemental symbol that represents a poster of the Seven Principles. Gifts are generally given to children and always include a book and a heritage symbol. Books emphasize the value placed on learning while the heritage symbol reiterates and emphasizes the African commitment to cultural heritage (www. officialkwanzaawebsite.org).

KwanzaaFest (formerly The Kwanzaa Holiday Expo) held in New York City was first celebrated in 1981. As the oldest African American cultural expo in the United States, it has become the nation's largest celebration of African-centered producers of products, culture, and services offered by African Americans, African, and African Caribbean communities. "KwanzaaFest is a vibrant cultural 'edu-tainment' experience and bustling Afrocentric mall. Thousands of consumers are drawn to KwanzaaFest over and over again. They not only come to purchase holiday gifts but [also] to enjoy cultural activities, live concerts, fashion shows, food, children's activities, educational forums, and meet other progressive and exciting people who have the interest of the community in mind" (Brathwaite 2004, 24).

Pilgrimage

A pilgrimage occurs when a consumer travels to a "consumption site where an experience of intense sacredness occurs" (Belk et al. 1989, 15). The pilgrimage might be to a national park (e.g., The Grand Canyon or Yellowstone) where the consumers make the trip sacred by their experience with nature. Pilgrimages are made to historic places (e.g., the Statue of Liberty), homes of sacralized people (e.g., George Washington and Mount Vernon), and sites of catastrophic human events (e.g., Gettysburg, Pearl Harbor). Secular pilgrimages also occur at places that convey nostalgia (e.g., Walt Disney World). Consumers might make pilgrimages to regional malls and themed shopping centers.

Quintessential

Objects that are treated as extraordinary, even though they may seem ordinary, are quintessential. Products made by hand can be sacralized as **quintessential** objects. Buying sweet-grass baskets from street peddlers in Charleston, South Carolina offers tourists a sacred object to commemorate the travel experience. Similarly, native Hawaiians at the Dole Pineapple Plantation on the Island of O'ahu sit outside and create baskets made of pineapple leaves for tourists to buy. A visit to the gift shop at the Arizona-Sonora Desert Museum in Tucson, Arizona, reveals a wide assortment of handmade baskets by Native Americans of the Tohono O'odham nation. By purchasing items such as these, consumers can create sacred collections of ordinary things (i.e., baskets).

Consumers' desire for authenticity makes some places quintessentially sacred. Often, this need is part of a tourist's motivation to go to certain destinations (Belk et al. 1989). For example, cultural tourists can be highly motivated to travel to either seek shallow experiences or seek to have deep experiences with culture. Cultural tourism is defined by its central purpose and the depth of experience desired by the tourist.

There are five types of cultural tourists: purposeful, sightseeing, casual, incidental, and serendipitous (McKercher 2002, McKercher and du Cross 2003). B. McKercher (2002) defined these five types of cultural tourists and determined that the centrality of the experience is related to what makes a particular destination important. The main travel motivation for the purposeful cultural tourist (high centrality/deep experience) is to gain a deep cultural experience by learning about other cultures or heritage. The sightseeing cultural tourist (high centrality/shallow experience) is more entertainment-oriented when learning about other cultures or heritage. The casual cultural tourist (modest centrality/ shallow experience) participates in cultural tourism activities but this is not central to the decision to visit a destination. The incidental cultural tourist (low centrality/shallow experience) participates in cultural tourism activities but travel is not motivated by cultural reasons. The serendipitous cultural tourist (low centrality/deep experience) does not use culture as a basis for the travel decision; however, while there, this tourist has deep cultural experiences.

B. Gordon (1986) identified four types of sacred souvenir icons: pictorial images, pieces-of-the-rock, symbolic shorthand, markers, and local products (See Table 5.12). Retailers can capitalize on consumer experiences by offering products that visually and tangibly represent the place and experience. Harley-Davidson has captured a unique retail market that includes pictorial images and markers. Harley-Davidson dealerships sell Harley-Davidson T-shirts that are imprinted with brand symbols. The T-shirts have a unique characteristic in that the name and location of the dealership is imprinted on the T-shirt as well. The only way to get a T-shirt from a specific location is through that dealership. Thus, T-shirts have become a way to mark where Harley riders have traveled.

Offering products at different price points and levels of taste and appropriateness is important. When the Fort Worth Texas Stockyards needed a tourist souvenir to commemorate its daily historic cattle drive of long-horn steers (See Figure 5.21), it sought something that was authentic to the time (nineteenth century) and place. The need for an affordable souvenir (less than $5.00) led them to decide on shot glasses imprinted with the stockyard's name. This souvenir created a problem for the hundreds of fourth-grade students who visited the historic area as part of their Texas history classes because it is an inappropriate souvenir for children.

TABLE 5.12. FIVE TYPES OF SACRED SOUVENIR ICONS

SOUVENIR ICONS	EXAMPLES OF SOUVENIR ICONS
Pictorial images	Photographs Postcards Videos and DVDs Picture books
Pieces-of-the-rock	Seashells Pinecones Sand/dirt Driftwood
Symbolic shorthand	Miniature Eiffel Tower Collectible historic buildings such as Cat's Meow
Markers	Harley-Davidson T-shirts imprinted with local dealership name Matchbooks, coasters, menus Ticket stubs Souvenir pins and patches
Local products	Wool sweaters from New Zealand Caithness paperweights from Scotland Gouda cheese from The Netherlands Peanuts from Georgia Pineapples from Hawaii Leather jacket from Milan, Italy

Source: Gordon, B. 1986. The souvenir: Messenger of the extraordinary. *Journal of Popular Culture* 33(1):84–197.

5.21 The historic long-horn cattle drive at the Fort Worth Texas Stock-yards draws tourists who are interested in the life and culture of nineteenth-century Texas.

Retailers can enhance tourists' experiences by providing objects that reflect their interests. Authentic products produced in traditional ways with indigenous materials would appeal to purposeful and serendipitous cultural tourists. These are the tourists who will purchase jade at a market in Taiwan, herringbone wool plaid in Scotland, and a Kachina Doll in Santa Fe, New Mexico. Sightseeing cultural tourists would be more likely to buy photos, books, and audiovisual products that portray their experience. Casual cultural tourists are probably not compelled to purchase objects to remind them of their travel experience. Products with more universal appeal, such as jewelry, T-shirts, food products, and general merchandise may be better suited to their needs. The incidental tourist might purchase sourdough bread, Ghirardelli chocolate, or California wine while visiting San Francisco because these items have practical and possibly immediate use, but odds are slim that they would spend money on items that provide lasting memories of the visit.

Collecting

Collecting can be a hobby, a financial investment, an expression of self-identity, or even an occupation. Generally, collections take on sacred qualities because they are unique assemblages of objects that are different from everyday items. Size, completeness, time to assemble, and energy expended to find items are often the defining elements of a collection. An item is profane when it is sold but becomes sacred when it is used to complete a collection. Searching for objects and displaying collections can become a ritual of hunting and enshrining. A collection takes on greater meaning than the individual items because it constitutes a greater whole. Many times, collections begin with a gift. In expanding a collection through personal acquisitions, the individual invests the self in the collection. Systematic labeling, arranging, and displaying of collections elevates collections to sacred status (Belk et al. 1989).

Developing collectible objects can extend demand in a product category. The U.S. Post Office promotes stamp collecting through expanded merchandise such as stamp collecting books, tote bags, gift cards, bags, toys, picture frames, and pins. Toy manufacturers entice tweens to buy collectibles such as Yu-Gi-Oh! and Pokémon trading cards and action characters such as Bionicle. With scheduled releases of new cards and action figures, there is a steady consumer demand to add to the existing collections. Royal Copenhagen expanded its annual Christmas plate offering to include an annual Christmas bell and tree ornament that are created with the same blue color and decorated with the same image picture as on the plate.

Inheritance

Inherited objects gain sacred status as heirlooms (Shammas, Salmon, and Dahlin 1987). If the heirloom is a handmade object worn close to the body, such as clothing and jewelry, it has greater contamination and symbolism and thus is more sacred. Personal objects can symbolize a person's physical body. Heirlooms that were originally ordinary objects can become sacred by the meanings associated with the person who previously owned them (Belk et al. 1989). This phenomenon occurs when items from noted personalities (e.g., Jacqueline Kennedy Onassis) are auctioned or sold outright.

When an inherited object is from the native land of the original owner who passed it down, then the object becomes sacred because it is part of one's heritage. The tag line for Shannon's fall 2006 duty-free catalog was "come back to Ireland." It featured pages of merchandise where customers could "celebrate [their] Irish heritage," gain "Celtic inspiration," "Bless this Irish house," and discover "the magic of Irish whisky." Customers have the option of customizing some orders with one of 119 personalized family crests. They can also have their first names written in Celtic lettering and receive information on the origin, meaning, and saint's day associated with their names. These objects more than likely will become sacred because they represent personal heritage.

Passing down objects from one generation to the next nurtures and maintains family ties. Bequests help preserve sacred significance and can form same-sex lineal connections such as father to son to grandson. When heirs are not appreciative, the inherited objects lose their sacredness (Belk et al. 1989).

Retailers can promote intergenerational sacred experiences that offer opportunities and mementos of those experiences. Positioning products as having significance to future generations can increase consumer interest in purchasing. A big holiday gift for 2005 was a chocolate fountain that costs about $100. It created a continuous flow of liquid chocolate for dipping foods. While the advertising theme suggested creating a fun activity for family and friends, it is unlikely that an object such as this would be preserved for a bequest. However, holiday gifts such as collectable Christmas ornaments, personal items such as a pocket watch or jewelry, and brands such as Waterford can be positioned as sacred objects for future generations. Furniture retailers can emphasize the heirloom quality of their furniture, promoting it as an investment that can be passed on to family members.

External Sanctions

When an object receives external approval or sanction from a museum or an antique expert, the object can assume sacred qualities. The popularity of the PBS television program *Antiques Roadshow* demonstrates the importance given to external sanctions. The program features people who bring in objects for expert evaluations. They want to know how much their heirlooms; collections; gifts; and assorted finds at flea markets, antique malls, and garage sales are worth.

Gift-Giving

Gift-giving is a universal cultural phenomenon. Among the many reasons why gifts are given are social expectations (e.g., a house warming gift), rituals and celebrations (e.g., birthdays), and expressions of loving and caring feelings. In the advertising campaign for its new Iridesse concept, Tiffany & Co. promoted pearls as a way to express loving and caring feelings with the messages of "Find yourself in pearls" and "Diamonds may be a girl's best friend, but pearls are truly her soul mate" (Frazier 2005).

The economic impact of gift-giving can be measured by the rise in retail sales during the traditional holiday seasons. In the United States, Christmas, Valentine's Day, Mother's Day, and Father's Day have gift-giving traditions. Easter has become one of the biggest gift-giving holidays for the video industry (Desiardins 2005). In England, gift-giving for Easter is gaining on Christmas. Traditional gifts of eggs are being replaced by more expensive items. The average 9- to 12-year-old in England receives a gift worth £20 to £22 and about £20 to £22 in cash. Children who are 5 to 6 years old receive gifts worth £12 to £15 and about the same amount in cash (Grimshaw 2005).

The status of a giver can be conveyed through a gift. Mauna Loa, a U.S. snack-food brand that markets nuts, used gift-giving traditions associated with the Chinese New Year to promote Mauna Loa nuts. Mauna Loa's competitors, Planters and Ferrero Rocher, positioned their nuts as the perfect gift. By promoting its nuts as a precious gift, Mauna Loa elevated the status of the giver by projecting that "giving and receiving a Mauna Loa gift is a meaningful gesture as it is a premium brand" (*Media Asia* 2005).

The symbolic significance of gift-giving that is associated with color, style, and design can create a devastating effect for the gift-giver if they are not understood. In Asian countries, red is associated with wealth and happiness, while white and black are colors connected with death and funerals. The Mandarin word for clock is very similar to the word for death, so clocks are not good gift choices for Chinese consumers. Linen handkerchiefs symbolize sadness among Koreans. Among all Asian cultures, cutlery represents severance of a relationship. In Europe, roses are considered very personal and chrysanthemums are funeral flowers. The role of religion in culture is an important consideration when selecting gifts. Leather goods are generally not appropriate gifts to Hindus since the cow is a sacred animal to them. Muslims and Mormons do not drink alcohol, so it is not an appropriate gift for them (Foster 1998).

Rituals and codes of etiquette define how gifts are given. In Asian countries, it is customary for the recipient to not open a gift in front of the giver. In Europe, flowers need to be given in odd numbers and presented unwrapped. In Muslim countries it is considered taboo to present a gift with the left hand because it is considered unclean. In Korea, great respect is denoted by using the right hand to extend the gift while using the left hand to support the right arm at the elbow (Foster 1998).

SACRED AND PROFANE GIFTS

Gift-giving is differentiated from commodity purchases in that gifts have special meaning and usually represent a relationship between individuals (Belk et al. 1989). The distinction between sacred and profane is evident in B. Malinowski's (1922) bipolar continuum, which placed gifts where there is no thought of return at one end and pure trade at the opposing end.

"Gift-giving is a ritual that may be used not only to sacralize . . . but also to maintain the sacredness of personal goods" (Belk et al. 1989, 27). Gifts can take on sacred meaning by their association with sacred places. For example, souvenirs are mementos of sacred experiences. Gift shops offer mass-produced gifts that are associated with the sacred place or event. Imprinting the name of the place or event on the object further enhances its sacredness (Belk et al. 1989).

Gifts can also be metonyms, which means they are so closely linked to an experience that they symbolize it (Lakoff and Johnson 1980). A turquoise necklace purchased from a Native American woman sitting on a blanket on the town square in Santa Fe, New Mexico, becomes a metonym for the Santa Fe experience.

Gifts attain a sacred status as a manifestation of intensely held cultural values. They can express the values of a social group and be self-expressive for an individual. Gifts can celebrate relationships, although the sacredness of a gift is not greater than the person it represents. Handcrafted gifts honor individual labor and denote friendships. "Gifts are kratophanous in their ability to separate us from the material world and simultaneously bind us to it" (Belk et al. 1989, 18).

Some gifts are considered profane; they do not relay cultural values that give enduring meaning to the gift. These obligatory gifts may be easily discarded because they have no inherent value or sacredness to the recipient. At holiday time, many retailers display gifts of this sort. Although they may create a sale, they generally do not offer value to the gift recipient and can create disposable gifts. Effective advertising that helps the gift-giver assign value to gift-giving might not only increase sales but also increase the average sale price. Many times, the gift-giver does not know what to buy as a gift. This is an opportunity for the retailer to create gift ideas. Gifts are more valuable when they are associated with other types of sacred objects, such as collections, heirlooms, or

a souvenir that provides links with a sacred site (Belk et al. 1989). Retailers who create experiences that make the selection and purchasing of gifts more meaningful and bring the giver status may be able to create a niche that has potential for high revenues.

Gift buying and giving can generate anxiety for gift-givers and recipients because the gift communicates symbolic significance on numerous levels (Sherry, McGrath, and Levy 1993). The type of relationship the giver has or desires with the recipient can be symbolized by the type of gift selected. In other words, the image and functionality of the gift signifies both the giver's impression of the image and personality of the receiver. In addition, the gift can be a reflection of the persona and thoughtfulness of the giver.

RITUAL GIFT-GIVING

Life events, which are very important in Japan, are acknowledged through ritual gift-giving where the presentation and meaning of the gift goes beyond the gift itself. A strict code of etiquette defines gift-giving. It has created an environment where gift-giving is an accepted practice that occurs daily.

The Japanese accept gift-giving as *giri*, a social duty and obligation. If a gift is given, it is certain that a gift will be received in return. If a person wants a gift, he or she must give a gift first. When a gift is received, it is expected that a bigger and better gift will be given to the original giver. Retail stores are staffed with experts to help customers purchase just the right gift. In many stores, clerks roam the stores and take customer purchases and credit card or cash payments and return the purchase elaborately gift wrapped (Olmsted 2006).

The gift-giving market in Japan revolves around seasonal gifts, such as the gifts given at midyear (*chugen*) and at year-end *(seibo)*. During these seasonal times, there is an increase in department store gift sales. Many gifts are perishable food products, including fruit, fish, coffee or tea, jam, and oils (See Figure 5.22). In addition, elaborate packaging and wrapping of gifts has become part of the gift-giving process (*Focus Japan* 2004).

SELF-GIFTING

Self-gifting has become a common practice for many consumers. Self-gifts offer "personally symbolic self-communication through special indulgences that tend to be premeditated and highly context-bound" (Mick and DeMoss 1990, 328). The planned self-gift purchase often occurs within the context of celebration, congratulations, or consolation. D. Mick and M. DeMoss (1990) propose that reward and therapy are the two primary reasons for self-gifts. They identified six themes for self-gifts to be self esteem, identity, deserving, perfect thing, escape, and discovery. They found the most prevalent circumstances for self-gifts were rewards for personal accomplishments, therapy for disappointments, holiday celebrations, and having extra money to spend. Appeals to a consumer's sense of reward or deserving is exemplified by the McDonald's slogan "You deserve a break today," while General Foods suggests you "Celebrate the moments of your life" by drinking its international coffees.

Self-gifts provide a window through which consumer behavior can be viewed in some of its most "adaptive, dramatic, and personally significant forms" (Mick and DeMoss 1990, 331). Through advertising, marketing, store display, pricing, and sales associates, retailers can appeal to consumers' desires for self-gifts. Retailers cannot afford to underestimate, ignore, or misinterpret the importance of this consumer behavior (Mick, DeMoss, and Faber 1992). Predetermination of the brand, the

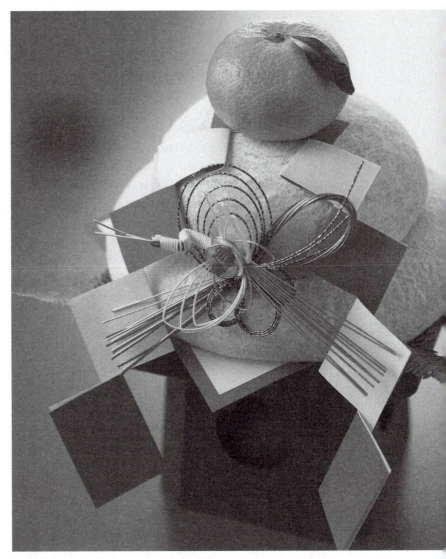

brand's price, and the sales associate's empathy for the buyer's personal needs are all factors that affect the self-gifting process in retail settings (Mick and DeMoss 1990, Mick et al. 1992). Through better communication with consumers, retail sales associates can identify the reason for the purchase and make appropriate suggestions that meet the needs of the consumer and increase sales for the store. This results in satisfaction on the part of the consumer and profit for the retailer.

Self-communication is an essential part of self-gifts. The consumer is both the giver and the gift recipient, so the self-gift can be especially symbolic. This communication

5.22 The visual presentation of gifts in Japan can be as important as the gift itself.

with oneself often results in self-contracts whereby the self-gift is earned. For example, people might offer themselves an ice-cream cone on Saturday if they manage to stay on their diets until then. This envisioned self-gift might act as an incentive for consumers to stay on their diets just so they can earn the ice-cream cone at the end of the week. D. Mick and M. DeMoss (1990) indicated that consumers justify this consumption indulgence as a fulfillment of the self-contract.

The self-gift can be described as a message between selves. The ideal self congratulates the real self, resulting in self-dialogue. This exchange is similar to interpersonal gift-giving in its reciprocity. Further, by setting and achieving goals and rewarding oneself with gifts, self-gifting can be motivational. Further, this process may encourage setting higher goals for one's self (Mick and DeMoss 1990). Mick and DeMoss (1990) found that consumers thought of a self-gift as a reward before they purchased it. Because the gifts were premeditated, they were seldom second-guessed, regretted, or associated with feelings of buyer's remorse. This is important for retailers to note, since the likelihood of returns would be greatly reduced and there is an opportunity to add on to sales when consumers are buying self-gifts.

Mick and DeMoss (1990) found self-gifts were special and not ordinary acquisitions. The relative infrequency of self-gifts point to the special aspect of self-gifts. Self-gifts are often used to elevate the self-esteem and to develop and sustain better self-concepts. Self-gifts can make consumers feel "stable, spoiled, confident, youthful, successful, fulfilled, enthusiastic, beautiful, secure, independent, or in control" (Mick and DeMoss 1990, 328).

Often, self-gifts are purchased to memorialize feelings or events so that they can be rekindled with the later use and observation of the gift (Mick et al. 1992).

The consumer is willing and often intends to spend more than normal on self-gifts. Retailers could capitalize on the fact that self-gift situations seem to "reduce concerns about spending" (Mick et al. 1992, 137). If retailers hired and trained salespeople to use active listening skills, a consumer's needs could be met and the retailer could benefit from the increased sales.

Self-gifts have a negative aspect. When consumption is equated with well-being, then self-gifts could be considered an egocentric consumer behavior (Mick and DeMoss 1990). Self-gifting might seem to imply that psychological wellness can be achieved through consumption behaviors, yet this is not entirely true. In addition, overindulging on self-gifts can lead to financial devastation and compound an individual's problems.

Retailers may be able to boost store sales by attracting consumers to purchase self-gifts as long as their store image, atmosphere, and sales associates are focused on these consumer behaviors. Sales associates could receive additional sales training to build an understanding of selling to consumers who are purchasing gifts for themselves. This would enable the business to generate sales for frequently recurring events of self-gifting.

Retaining Sacredness

Retaining sacredness requires effort. Sacredness is associated with objects, people, places, and experiences; however, through habituation, forgetting, or intrusion of the profane, the sacred may become profane. Belk et al. (1989) identifies four ways in which sacredness in consumption can be retained: separation of the sacred from the profane; performing sustaining rituals; continuation through inheritance; and association with material corruption (e.g., tangibilized contamination).

Separating sacred from profane continues the sacredness of an object, place, or experience. Collections are placed apart from everyday objects because they are for viewing, not using, which would make them sacred.

Sustaining rituals is done to preserve sacredness and to prevent rationalization and habituation. Rationalization transforms a sacred object to profane by using rational logic, which reduces its mystery and mythical or enchanting power, or by ignoring, discarding, or not giving it reverence. Habituation refers to continuous exposure to and use of a sacred object so that it moves toward the profane. As an object loses its sacredness, it may be placed in a more profane location in the home. "While newness may initially sacralize an object as being quintessential, irreverence creeps in with time. Later, someone again sees the object's potential for sacredness and saves it from obscurity" (Belk et al. 1989, 27).

In the United States, the National Trust for Historic Preservation engages in preservation and rituals associated with how tourists can view historic properties. Many times souvenirs are offered that can only be purchased at that one location, thus sacralizing the object and the place.

Souvenirs convey status related to sacred places a consumer has visited. Objects accumulated from these travels often are displayed prominently in the home for enjoyment and authentication of the experience. Losing a sacred object that commemorates a sacred experience can be terrible to the owner (Belk et al. 1989).

CHAPTER SUMMARY

Rituals that are retained, rediscovered, or reinvented can give consumers transcending experiences that allow them to escape from everyday life. They are embedded in culture and an important part of consumer culture. Rituals, which are customary, formalized, ceremonial acts or rites, can be simple or complex, sacred or profane. Secular examples that are ritualized include objects such as flags, experiences such as travel and themed amusement parks, and celebrations such as birthdays and *quinceañeras*; events such as sports; and personalities such as actors and politicians. Sacred rituals are associated with religious celebrations such as Christmas and weddings. Interaction or involvement with these objects, experiences, celebrations, events, and personalities offer transcending experiences that can be ritualized in a consumer's everyday life. What is important is that rituals elicit respect, reverence, and sometimes fear from the consumer as they are set apart from everyday life (secular) and viewed as extraordinary or sacred. This adds value to the consumer experience.

Rituals are influenced by culture or how individuals interact with their natural, human-constructed, and human-behavioral environments. The natural environment includes natural resources, climate, space and time, and geography. The human-constructed environment includes production, consumption, and sociocultural systems at a macro level. The human-behavior environment includes relationships, roles, affiliations, and attitudes, which is culture at the micro (e.g., market segment) and individual (e.g., consumer) levels.

Cultural values are beliefs that there is some general state of existence that is personally and socially important to seek. Consumers' view of the world is influenced by their primary culture and the basic and essential cultural values contained in it. Cultural values have four characteristics in common: they are learned, they guide behavior by defining acceptable standards in daily life, they are both permanent and dynamic, and they are widely held within a culture. Cultural values are what differentiate one culture from another.

Value orientations are the commonly held values that are underlying determinants of consumer behavior. Consumers' attachment to broad product categories is influenced by these culturally implicit orientations. The basic U.S. value orientations that are applicable to consumer behavior are: relationship to nature, time dimension, personal activity, and relationship to others. These value orientations are dynamic and, as such, need to be constantly monitored by retailers for change.

Cultural patterns are shared characteristics within a cultural group that are exhibited as either intrinsic or extrinsic traits. Extrinsic patterns are historical products of the group's adjustment to its local environment. They are external to ethnic cultural heritage. Intrinsic patterns are vital aspects of cultural heritage that once removed will cause the demise of that cultural heritage. Cultural patterns are traditions or customs that become habitual or customary over time. These patterns are transmitted across generations and societies and incorporated into consumer culture.

Subcultures are groups of people or consumer segments whose homogeneous values and customs make them distinctly different from society as a whole. Their distinctiveness may be through extrinsic patterns and shared cultural values. As cultural values become stronger, more standardized, and more restricted, there is greater subgroup influence on its members. Consumer behavior within a subculture is related to its distinctiveness, homogeneity, and exclusion. Ethnic, bicultural, and consumption subcultures differ in their consumption habits based on the cultural values that influence their behavior. In some cases, as with situational ethnicity, consumption varies by the context in which the consumption occurs.

Cultural diffusion occurs when diverse societies come in contact, either directly or indirectly. When they come into contact, new cultural elements can either be accepted or rejected depending on whether the elements fit into the total patterning of the receiving culture. If the new element is accepted, it may undergo considerable modification as it is being adopted. Acculturation, consumer acculturation, and product acculturation are all examples of cultural diffusion.

Social groups distinguish their consumption of space, time, and objects based on what is considered sacred (i.e., set apart) and a transcendent experience and what is considered profane (i.e., ordinary and part of everyday life). Sacred status does not occur indiscriminately across culture; rather, consumers make a distinction between sacred and profane in their collective domains of experience. R. W. Belk et al. (1989) aligned six major categories of probable sacred consumer domains with probable sacred religious domains: places, times, tangible things, intangibles, people, and experiences to build a definition of sacredness related to consumption. Sacred and profane consumption are associated with ritual, including rites of passage and rites of intensification, pilgrimage, quintessence, gift-giving, collecting, inheritance, and external sanction.

Discussion Questions

1. Explore a culture that differs from your own by exploring into a distinctly sacred ritual that is commonly practiced. What are the events and/or objects that are reverently consumed for this particular event?

2. What is a common U.S. viewpoint of time? Discuss its cultural distinction and the rituals or symbols that are characteristic to this viewpoint.

3. Cultural values are both permanent and dynamic. Name three values you have adopted through your

upbringing. Provide an example of how your values influenced the direction of a particular purchase that you needed to make.

4. What are some theme restaurants that successfully address the American cultural orientation to foods?

5. Ethnic identity often shapes shopping behavior. Discuss how some retailers are satisfying the cultural needs of particular ethnic groups via their shopping activities.

6. The Red Hat Society and the Harley-Davidson brand Harley Owners Group (HOG) are examples of consumption subcultures. What other subcultures have been created by meaningful commercial activity or commonly held attitudes?

7. Fusion in ethnic foods is a popular trend in modern cuisine. Describe a restaurant chain that has been successful in the re-styling of a particular cultural cuisine.

8. Hello Kitty is a popular Japanese brand icon that has been integrated into the U.S. consumer culture. Discuss the particular market segments to which this brand appeals and the marketing strategy used to reach them.

9. As a quintessential tourist attraction, what type(s) of cultural tourists does the city of Las Vegas attract? Explain.

10. Kitsch is discussed as being mass-produced and in bad taste. What are possible motivations behind the consumption of kitsch products?

11. The gift of fruitcake is a common sacred U.S. offering during the Christmas season. What are other gift offerings that are characteristic to a cultural holiday or event?

12. Self-gifts have a negative aspect. What are possible detrimental effects of self-gifting? How can retailers turn this into positive behaviors?

13. Choose one of the HRAF categories, and create a list of associated products that comes from that culture.

REFERENCES

Assael, H. 1987. *Consumer behavior and marketing action*, 3rd ed. Boston: Kent Publishing.

Beane, W. C., and W. C. Doty. 1975. *Myths, rites, and symbols: A Mircea Eliade Reader*, vol. 1. New York: Harper Colophon.

Belk, R. W. 1974. An exploratory assessment of situational effects in buyer behavior. *Journal of Marketing Research* 1(2):156–163.

———. 1975. Situational variables and consumer behavior. *Journal of Consumer Research* 2(3):157–164.

———. 1996. The perfect gift. In C. Otnes and R. F. Beltramini, eds., *Gift-Giving* (30–34). Bowling Green, OH: Bowling Green University Press.

Belk, R. W., M. Wallendorf, and J. F. Sherry Jr. 1989. The sacred and the profane in consumer behavior: Theodicy on the odyssey. *Journal of Consumer Research* 16(91):1–38.

Bernstein, E. 2004. You don't have to be Jewish to want a Bar Mitzvah; more kids on cusp of 13 get faux post-rite parties; picking Hawaiian theme. The *Wall Street Journal*. January 14, A1.

Berry, J. W. 1980. Acculturation as varieties of adaptation. In Padilla, A., ed. *Acculturation Theory, Models and Some New Findings* (9–25). Boulder, CO: Westview Press.

Berry, J., Trimble, J., and E. Olmedo. 1986. Assessment of acculturation. In W. Lonner and J. Berry, eds. *Field Methods in Cross-cultural Research* (291–324). Newberry Park, CA: Sage.

Better, N. M. 2001. Catalog critic: The out-of-the-box birthday. *The Wall Street Journal*. June 29, W15.

Bossard, J. H. S., and E. S. Boll. 1950. *Ritual in family living: A contemporary study*. Philadelphia: University of Pennsylvania Press.

Brathwaite, K. 2004. KwanzaaFest to feature FashionArt=Kuumba. *New York Amsterdam News* 95(50):42.

Burnkrant, R. E., and A. Cousineau. 1975. Informational and normative social influence on buyer behavior. *Journal of Consumer Research* 2(3):206–215.

Chozick, A. 2004. Fairy-tale fifteenths; the 'Quince' marks a big rite for Latin teens and marketers; coming of age at Disneyland. *The Wall Street Journal*, Eastern ed. October 15, B1.

Chung, E., and E. Fischer. 1999. It's who you know: Intercultural differences in ethnic product consumption. *Journal of Consumer Marketing* 16(5):482–501.

Cote, J. A., and P. S. Tansuhaj. 1989. Culture bound assumptions in behavior intention models. In T. K. Srull, ed. *Advances in Consumer Research*, vol. 16 (105–109). Provo, UT: Association for Consumer Research.

Deshpandé, R., W. D. Hoyer, and N. Donthu. 1986. The intensity of ethnic affiliation: A study of the sociology of Hispanic consumption. *Journal of Consumer Research* 13(2):214–220.

Desiardins, D. 2005. Kids and religious-themed titles to get Easter push. *DSN Retailing Today* 44(2):17.

Dohrenwend, B., and R. J. Smith. 1962. Toward a theory of acculturation. *Southwestern Journal of Anthropology* 18:30–39.

Drozdiak, W. 1995. Let them eat bread, please! French bakers fret over staple's decline in popularity. *The Dallas Morning News*. September 29, A44.

Durkheim, E. 1975. *Durkheim on religion: A selection of readings with bibliographies and introductory remarks*. J. Redding and W. S. F. Pickering, trans. London: Routledge and Kegan Paul.

Eliade, M. 1958. *Patterns in comparative religion*. London: Sheed and Ward.

Ellis, S., J. McCullough, M. Wallendorf, and C. T. Tan. 1985. Cultural values and behavior: Chineseness within geographic boundaries. In E. Hirschman and M. Holbrook, eds. *Advances in Consumer Research,* vol. 12 (126–128). Provo, UT: Association for Consumer Research.

Facenda, V. L. 2004. Know your multicultural shopper. *Retail Merchandiser* 44(4):17–21.

Forehand, M. R., and R. Deshpandé. 2001. What we see makes us who we are: Priming ethnic self-awareness and advertising response. *Journal of Marketing Research* 38:336–348.

Foster, D. 1998. The gift that keeps on grating. *Brandweek* 39(8):21.

———. 2003. The healthy feast. *Natural Health* 33(9):74–83.

Frazier, M. 2005. Tiffany thinks outside blue box to peddle pearls. *Advertising Age*. May 12, 12.

Goode, S. 1998. Corn flakes aren't going down well in France. *Insight on the News*. December 14, 4.

Goodenough, W. H. 1997. Phylogenetically related cultural traditions. *Cross-Cultural Research* 31:16–26.

———. 1999. Outline of a framework for a theory of cultural evolution. *Cross-Cultural Research* 33(1): 84–197.

Gordon, B. 1986. The souvenir: Messenger of the extraordinary. *Journal of Popular Culture* 20(3):135–146.

Gordon, M. M. 1964. *Assimilation in American life*. New York: Oxford University Press.

Gore, J. P. 1998. Ethnic marketing may become the norm. *Banking Marketing* 30(9):12–15.

Graham, R. J. 1981. The role of perception of time in consumer research. *Journal of Consumer Research* 7(4):335–342.

Gregotti, V. 1969. Kitsch and architecture. In G. Dorfles, ed. *Kitsch: The world of bad taste* (255–276). New York: Universal Books.

Grimshaw, C. 2005. Easter presents surge in value. *Marketing (UK)* 1.

Hall, E. T. 1983. *The dance of life.* Garden City, NY: Anchor Press/ Doubleday.

Healey, J. F. 1995. *Race, ethnicity, gender, and class: The sociology of group conflict and change.* Thousand Oaks, CA: Pine Forge Press.

Hirschman, E. C. 1991. Point of view: Sacred, secular, and mediating consumption imagery in television commercials. *Journal of Advertising Research* 30(6):38–44.

Hofstede, G. H. 2001. *Culture's Consequences: Comparing Values, Behaviors, Institutions, and Organizations Across Nations,* 2nd ed. Thousand Oaks, CA: Sage Publications.

Hong, Y-Y., M. Morris, C-Y. Chiu, and V. Benet-Martinez. 2000. Multicultural minds: A dynamic constructivist approach to culture and cognition. *American Psychologist* 55:709–720.

Hraba, J. 1979. *American Ethnicity.* Itasca, IL: F. E. Peacock Publishers, Inc.

Immigrants' holiday rituals changing. 1997. *USA Today Magazine* 126(2631):4–5.

Keates, N., and L. Gubernick. 2002. Family: The hot new birthday gift: Nothing—Fed-up parents decide to throw 'gift-free' parties for kids: A value lesson for junior? The *Wall Street Journal*, Eastern edition. August 16, W1.

Keefe, S., and A. Padilla. 1987. *Chicano Ethnicity.* Albuquerque: University of New Mexico Press.

Keller, S. 1996. Taming the Passover plagues for easy consumption. *The New York Times*, East Coast. March 24, 13.

Kluckhohn, F., and F. Strodtbeck. 1961. *Variations in value orientations.* Evanston, IL: Row, Peterson.

Konigsmark, A. R., 2001. Asian-Americans celebrate the year of the snake. *San Jose Mercury News.* January 24, B1.

Kroeber, A. L. 1948. *Anthropology: Race, Language, Culture, Psychology, Prehistory.* New York: Harcourt, Brace & World, Inc.

LaFromboise, T., H. Coleman, and J. Gerton. 1993. Psychological impact of biculturalism: Evidence and theory. *Psychological Bulletin* 114:395–412.

Lakoff, G., and M. Johnson. 1980. *Metaphors We Live By.* Chicago: The University of Chicago Press.

Laroche, M., C. Kim, and M. A. Tomiuk. M. A. 1998. Italian ethnic identify and its relative impact on the consumption of convenience and traditional foods. *Journal of Consumer Marketing* 15(2):121–151.

Lau-Gesk, L. G. 2003. Activating culture through persuasion appeals: An examination of the bicultural consumer. *Journal of Consumer Psychology* 13(3):301–315.

Lundegaard, L. 2004. The cranky consumer: Making kids' birthdays an event. The *Wall Street Journal.* August 17, D2.

Maheswaran, D., and S. Shavitt. 2000. Issues and new directions in global consumer psychology. *Journal of Consumer Psychology* 9(1):59–66.

Malinowski, B. 1922. *Argonauts of the Western Pacific.* London: George Routledge and Sons.

Mauna Loa sells premium brand for festive giving. 2005. *Media Asia* 10.

McGrath, J. E., and N. J. Rotchford. 1983. Time and behavior in organizations. *Research in Organizational Behavior* 5:57–101.

McKercher, B. 2002. Towards a classification of cultural tourists. *International Journal of Tourism Research* 4:29–38.

McKercher, B., and H. du Cross. 2003. Testing the cultural tourism typology. *Journal of Tourism Research* 5(1):45–58.

Mick, D., and M. DeMoss. 1990. Self-gifts: Phenomenological insights from four contexts. *Journal of Consumer Research, Inc.* 17:322–332.

Mick, D., M. DeMoss, and R. Faber. 1992. A projective study of motivations and meanings of self-gifts: Implications for retail management. *Journal of Retailing* 68:122–144.

Minor, M. 1992. Comparing the Hispanic and non-Hispanic markets: How different are they? *Journal of Services Marketing* 6(2):29–32.

Mintel Intelligence Group. 2003. *Indian foods*. London: Mintel.

Miranda, C. A. 2004. Fifteen candles. *Time* 164(3):83.

Mol, H. 1976. *Identity and the sacred: A sketch for a new socio-scientific theory of religion*. New York: Free Press.

Moschis, G. P., and G. A. Churchill Jr. 1978. Consumer socialization: A theoretical and empirical analysis. *Journal of Marketing Research* 15:599–609.

Murdock, G. P., et al., eds. 2006. Terms and codes in the Outline of Cultural Materials, 6th ed. Copyright Human Relations Area Files, Inc.

Nathan, B. 2005. The rite stuff? *The New York Jewish Week*, Manhattan edition 217(45):26.

Ogden, D. T., J. R. Ogden, and H. J. Schau. 2004. Exploring the impact of culture and acculturation on consumer purchase decisions: Toward a micro-cultural perspective. *Academy of Marketing Science Review* 2004(3): 1–21.

Olmsted, L. 2006. One-stop shopping in Japan. *American Way*. February 15, 34–38. Packaged Facts, a publishing division of MarketResearch.com.

Peñaloza, L. N. 1989. Immigrant consumer acculturation. In T. K. Srull, ed. *Advances in Consumer Research*, vol. 16 (110–118). Provo, UT: Association for Consumer Research.

Peñaloza, L. N. 1994. *Atravesando fronteras*/border crossings: A critical ethnographic study of the consumer acculturation of Mexican immigrants. *Journal of ConsumerResearch* 21(6):32–53.

Peñaloza , L. N., and M. C. Gilly. 1999. Marketer acculturation: The changer and the changed. *Journal of Marketing* 63(3):84–104.

Phinney, J. S. 1990. Ethnic identity in adolescents and adults: Review of research. *Psychological Bulletin* 108(3):499–514.

———. 1990. Stages of ethnic identity development in minority group adolescents. *Journal of Early Adolescence* 9:34–49.

Phinney, J. S., G. Horenczyk, K. Liebkind, and P. Vedder. 2001. Ethnic identity, immigration, and well-being: An interactional perspective. *Journal of Social Issues* 57(3):493–510.

Phinney, J. S., and D. Rosenthal. 1992. Ethnic identity in adolescences. In G. R. Adams, T. P. Gullotta, and R. Montemayer, eds. *Adolescent identity formation* (145–172). Newbury Park, CA: Sage.

Pickering, W. S. F. 1984. *Durkheim's sociology of religion: Themes and theories*. London: Routledge and Kegan Paul.

Presents of mind—New kinds of gifts and gift-giving. 2004. *Focus Japan* 25(1):6.

Redfield, R., R. Linton, and M. J. Herskovits. 1936. Memorandum for the study of acculturation. *American Anthropologist* 38(1):149–152.

Robinson-Jacobs, K. 2005. Tortillas, the new white bread? *The Dallas Morning News.* November 27, D1,6.

Rosenthal D. A., and S. S. Feldman. 1992. The nature and stability of ethnic identity in Chinese youth: Effects of length of residence in two cultural contexts. *Journal of Cross-Cultural Psychology* 23(2):214–227.

Saenz, R., and B. E. Aguirre. 1991. The dynamics of Mexican ethnic identity. *Ethnic Groups* 9:17–32.

Schouten, J. W., and J. H. McAlexander. 1995. Subcultures of consumption: An ethnography of the new bikers. *Journal of Consumer Research* 22(6):43–61.

Shammas, C., M. Salmon, and M. Dahlin. 1987. *Inheritance in America: From Colonial times to the present.* New Brunswick, NJ: Rutgers University Press.

Shellenbarger, S. 2000. As families get busier, Americans get creative with holiday rituals. *The Wall Street Journal,* Eastern edition. November 22, B1.

Sherry, J. F., M. A. McGrath, and S. L. Levy. 1993. The dark side of the gift. *Journal of Business Research* 28(3):225–244.

Stayman, D. M., and R. Deshpande. 1989. Situational ethnicity and consumer behavior. *Journal of Consumer Research* 16:361–371.

Thompson, S. 2005. How to make one dish that serves up millions. *Advertising Age.* May 23, 9.

Ting-Toomey, S., ed. 1994. *The Challenge of Facework: Cross-Cultural and Interpersonal Issues.* Albany, NY: State University of New York Press.

Vinson, D. E., J. E. Scott, and L. M. Lamont, 1977. The role of personal values in marketing and consumer behavior. *Journal of Marketing* 41:44–50.

White, C., and P. Burke. 1987. Ethnic role identity among white and black college students: An interactionist approach. *Sociological Perspectives* 30:310–331.

White, H., and K. Kokotasaki. 2004. Indian food in the UK: Personal values and changing patterns of consumption. *International Journal of Consumer Studies* 28(3):284–294.

Williams, J. D., and W. J. Qualls. 1989. Middle-class black consumers and intensity of ethnic identification. *Psychology and Marketing* 6(4):263–286.

Xu, J., S. Shim, S. Lotz, and D. Almeida. 2004. Ethnic identify, socialization factors, and culture-specific consumption behavior. *Psychology and Marketing* 21(2):93–112.

Yee, L. 2004. Deliciously mixed messages. *Restaurants and Institutions* 114(3):30–32.

SENSORY CONSUMPTION

Places and Spaces: In the Mood

How can you create memorable experiences and tap the right inspiration for a successful meeting? The answer, according to current hotel trends, is to involve your attendees on every level, starting with the five senses—sight, sound, smell, touch, and taste.

"Most hotels today are visually beautiful," says Stephen Rosenstock, senior vice president of brand standards for Omni Hotels, based in Dallas, Texas. "However," he adds, "beauty only takes you so far." Consulting Scent Air and Muzak, Omni implemented a brandwide sensory campaign featuring a lemongrass scent and music program for the lobby of each of its 38 properties. "We feel incorporating sensory elements into our facilities will harmoniously 'balance' our guests, providing them with memorable experiences." The experience can also be customized: Some meetings that take place at the 730-room Omni Orlando at ChampionsGate opt for a chocolate-themed break, where a waft of chocolate and the soundtrack from *Charlie and the Chocolate Factory* subtly greet attendees as they approach a break display that's been filled with gourmet sweets, oversized rainbow lollipops, and various chocolate drinks.

As part of W's "Sensory Set-Up" themed meetings, Jolene Di Salvo, senior director of field marketing for W, says, "We include aromatherapy within the meetings, like scent sticks, as well as creative catering, such as fruit-infused water; mood music like wave or nature sounds; candles; and inspiring notes and games." Since 1998, "Sensory Set-Up" has helped attendees cultivate new ways to visualize, which, according to Di Salvo, "ultimately foster unforgettable experiences." Recently, W Worldwide added "Recess," a program that's designed to create unique and effective teambuilding and networking opportunities by "entertaining, inspiring, and reviving" guests. At the 423-room W San Francisco, Darrin Zeer, a San Diego–based relaxation expert, recently led a yoga "Recess" for 36 clients where he took all the business elements and furniture out of a conference room. "It felt like a living room," says Zeer. "We had blankets and pillows, and the W gave out yoga mats as well as herbal teas, bottled waters, fresh fruit, and body butter for the face and body. Floating clouds were displayed on a video screen, complemented by soothing music."

Part of the sensory trend is getting visual inspiration from galleries that are now frequently sited at hotels; these also serve as a cultural element and space for meetings and events. At the 511-room Omni San Diego, for example, the L Street Fine Art opened in September 2006, with 7,000 [square-feet] of pre-function and meeting space. "The gallery," says Patsy Bock, area director of sales and marketing for Omni San Diego, "is all about creating experiences. This type of environment taps into the visual sense, which stimulates motivation and inspiration." Bock has planned the "Art of an Exceptional Meeting" for groups, and cocktail receptions that she calls "Bringing the Masters Together."

Then there's setting the mood. Beginning in August 2006, Maryland's newly revamped 269-room Doubletree Hotel and Executive Meeting Center Bethesda (formerly Holiday Inn Select) plans to light [more than] 300 candles in the lobby area. "Dusk at the Doubletree" will incorporate "Sweet Music by Doubletree" with scents. "The hotel is also incorporating a Zen-like philosophy," says Michael McMahon, general manager. Taking a holistic approach, McMahon says, "the hotel will have scent pods in each guest room, where guests can select what scent they want. We will also implement a new system of air quality in the meeting rooms, which casinos use, where it will change the air out frequently, getting rid of carbon dioxide, which makes people sleepy."

At the 350-room Hyatt Regency Tamaya Resort & Spa, which is on Native American land near Albuquerque, New Mexico, the pueblo style serves as a bridge between the past and the future. According to Jerry Westenhaver, general manager: "We capture all the senses and take the guests back in time. You will hear Native American flute sounds, see historic pottery and rugs, walk through pueblo-styled courtyards, and smell the scents of cedar and herbs. Everything we do has a cultural experience around it." Larry Hollingsworth, planner for the 2005 annual conference for the Southwest Association of Student Financial Aid Administration, says his group of 400 was wowed: "We took a chance with its Native American welcome blessing. I wasn't sure how attendees were going to react to it, but everyone loved it." The elaborate experience—featuring incense, flute music, and an introduction by the GM followed by a blessing from a tribal elder—was captivating and exciting. Says Hollingsworth, "There was something different that I encountered while being there. It was the sensory elements of sound and sight adding to the experience, making it most memorable."

Source: Torrisi, A. I. 2006. Places and spaces. *Successful Meetings* 55(6):89–91.

INTRODUCTION

Sensory consumption is being driven by conspicuous consumption and the desire for scarce things. Mass production has created a marketplace where almost any product can be purchased at some price point, although there may be sacrifices in materials and quality (Goldman 2000). Moreover, homogenized retail environments where stores seem similar in environments, products, and brands—and the *MacDonaldization* of products and services on a global scope—have led to boring, predictable consumer experiences (Finkelstein 2003, Ritzer 1998).

Consumers are looking for experiences that stimulate, elicit psychological excitement, and produce sensory pleasure. One of the attractions of visiting entertainment venues (Chuck E Cheese, GattiTown, and Dave & Busters), theme parks (Universal Studios, Disneyland, and Six Flags), malls, and many restaurants and hotels is the range of sensory stimuli they offer. Adding a retail mix to the experience can further expand consumption. For example, Universal Studios added an extensive retail mix to its park, where the retail builds on the themed rides and restaurants (See Figure 6.1).

Lighting, color, music, ambient noise, odor, temperature, touch, and crowding are all environmental stimuli that can meet the shoppers' psychological needs that include sensory stimulation, social interaction, security, and comfort (Ng 2003). Sensory involvement is triggered by the modalities of sight, sound, feel, taste, and smell. Sensory cues create emotional reactions by stimulating consumers' feelings during interactions with goods, services, and the environment in which they are experienced. Store environments are important in creating pleasant consumer emotional reactions and attracting and retaining customers. Talbot's creates a pleasant shopping experience that starts

when the customer enters the store through its bright red doors, walks across the polished wooden floors, views clothes through soft ambient lighting, and listens to subtle background music (See Figure 6.2). Retailers need to incorporate sensory stimuli that generate pleasant shopping experiences.

SENSORY INVOLVEMENT

Sensory involvement is an integral part of how consumers experience everything. Consumers use sensory cues as guides in consumption (Underhill 1999). For retailers, success relies on finding ways to promote consumer-product interactions. In the context of shopping, sensory cues are essential because "virtually all unplanned purchases—and many planned ones, too—come as a result of the shopper seeing, touching, smelling, or tasting something that promises pleasure, if not total fulfillment" (Underhill 1999, 161–62).

Shoppers generally want to spend time examining products where they have a high level of involvement. Examining by touch and trial are important strategies in getting consumers involved with a product (See Figure 6.3). Furthermore, sensory involvement directs how consumers move through a store. When a product is new, consumers want to see, smell, touch, hear, and taste it, so they can deem it appropriate before buying it. Retailers who offer consumers trial opportunities (e.g., free samples, single-use sizes, discounted prices, limited time use, or no-time commitment use) and encourage sensory involvement, help consumers gain confidence in their decisions to buy

6.1 Universal Studios in Orlando, Florida, offers multisensory experiences to its visitors through sight, sound, scent, touch, and taste.

6.2 Talbots creates a pleasant shopping environment through sensory involvement.

(or not buy) the product. This is why it is important that retailers offer multiple opportunities for consumer sensory exploration (Underhill 1999).

Multisensory Experiences

Multisensory experiences combine sight, sound, scent, touch, and taste stimuli to promote consumer involvement in the environment (Allen 2000). When the shopping experience appeals to multiple senses, there is a synergy of sensory feelings that can be leveraged to increase consumption (*In-Store Magazine* 2005). The Thomson travel group created a multisensory experience that included sight, sound, and scent stimuli. The sensory experience started when customers entered the store. Citrus grove and sea spray scents were pumped into the store entrance areas. When Thomson launched a brochure on travel to Egypt, they offered a full sensory, 3-D experience using virtual technology. This strategy was aimed at growing sales by educating consumers. Headsets allowed consumers to experience the trip through surround vision, sounds, and smells. Odors were linked to visual content and emitted through a time-release apparatus. Moving through the experience, the virtual tourists smelled herbs and spices in the market, coconut suntan oil by the hotel swimming pool, a refreshing sea breeze, and the musty odors of a pharaoh's tomb. The experience created a positive effect on customer behavior, which created sales (*In-Store Magazine* 2005).

Many retailers fail to comprehend the importance of sensory involvement in the creation of pleasant shopping experiences. This is not the case for Calmia, a holistic lifestyle store and retail brand in the United Kingdom that offers customers opportunities for multisensory exploration. The goal of Calmia is to promote well-being and simple rituals that help con-

sumers achieve a relaxed, stress-free life. Tranquility and natural beauty are the primary environmental elements found in the store. Visual stimuli come from a tropical Indonesian garden and pools of water that have petals and flowers floating in them. Eastern music provides auditory cues while the use of essential oils provides the olfactory stimulus needed to create a calming and balancing ambiance. Taste is stimulated through green tea and herbal elixir bars. The Calmia brand includes a day spa, a collection of yoga and relaxation clothing, yoga accessories, music and incense for yoga and meditation, natural skin and body care, herbal tonics and green teas, candles, books, and fragrances for the home (www.calmia.com).

Multisensory experiences with branded products can build strong brand-consumer relationships. However, fewer than 5 percent of branded products is considered excellent in creating sensory involvement (Lindstrom 2005). Intense product experiences promote differentiation among branded products and create opportunities for intense customer relationships that translate into brand loyalty. Quick-serve

6.3 Examining products by touch and trial use are important strategies in getting consumers involved with a product.

experiences that the consumer receives. Taste, smell, and sight are ways that restaurateurs can engage consumers in sensory consumption (See Figure 6.4). Another way that retailers can increase brand loyalty is by using touchpoints that generate sensory consumption.

Touchpoints

Touchpoints refer to how consumers interact with a brand and communicate about that brand. Touchpoints create emotional associations and reinforce beliefs about a brand. According to Davis (2002), when brand beliefs are consistent, consumers "experience high levels of loyalty, great word-of-mouth, higher price points, and greater overall customer satisfaction" (16).

Consumer-brand relationships are represented by different touchpoints in the consumer's pre-purchase, purchase, and post-purchase experiences (Davis 2002) (See Table 6.1). These touchpoints help consumers remember, savor, and communicate to others a product's experience. Nokia is an example of how the brand was

6.4 This Burger King restaurant in London engages its customers in sensory consumption through sight, smell, and taste.

restaurants have gained global appeal through their low price points, efficient service, and standard fare. In many markets intense competition means brand differentiation relies on the multisensory

TABLE 6.1. EXPANDING CONSUMER-BRAND RELATIONSHIPS TO SENSORY TOUCHPOINTS

CONSUMER EXPERIENCE	BRAND-CONSUMER RELATIONSHIPS	TOUCHPOINTS	
		TRADITIONAL	SENSORY
Pre-purchase	Influences whether the brand is included in the consumer's final purchase consideration set.	Advertising Sales reps Word-of-mouth Internet	Sight Sound Feel Taste Smell
Purchase	Moves the consumer from consideration of a brand to purchasing a brand.	Direct field sales Physical stores Financing	Atmospherics Memory Emotion
Post-purchase	Influences after sale brand experience.	Customer service Customer satisfaction Surveys Loyalty programs	Sight Sound Feel Taste Smell Memory Emotion

Source: Davis, S. 2002. Great brand building is just a touch away. *Brandweek* 43(24):16,20.

extended to include sensory touchpoints (See Figure 6.5). According to Lindstrom (2005), a leading expert in branding:

> almost every industry has the potential to employ sensory branding—converting every possible touchpoint into a branded experience. Even the neglected details will become powerful tools. Like the simple ring of a Nokia cellphone. The Nokia tune has created an awareness similar to the Intel Inside tune, with more than 100 million consumers listening to the tune seven hours a year. There is only one difference between Intel and Nokia. Intel paid millions of dollars to create this sound awareness—Nokia paid nothing (136).

Retailers who identify ways to use sensory cues as touchpoints may strengthen consumers' brand affinity and communication about the brand. For example, in the pre-purchase experience, multiple sensory touchpoints are associated with purchasing a Starbucks coffee. The sound of coffee beans being ground, the smell of the brewing coffee, and the sight of the coffee being poured offer sensory experiences that allow consumers to interact with the brand.

P. Underhill (1999) posed the question, "When does a shopper actually possess something?" (168). He suggested that consumers possess an object at the moment their senses become involved. This involvement is an emotional and spiritual process that generally begins with the sense of sight, shortly followed by the sense of touch. Once the object is in a consumer's hand, on the body, or in the mouth, the consumer has started the process of taking in the object. At this point, paying for the object becomes a technical process; it's important to note, however, that the paying experience is often unpleasant. Underhill further suggests that "the quicker an

6.5 Nokia is an example of how a brand uses the ring of its cell phone as a sensory touchpoint.

object is placed in the shopper's hand, or the easier it is for the shopper to try it or sip it or drive it around the block, the more easily it will change ownership, from the seller to the buyer. That's shopping" (168).

ATMOSPHERICS

Atmospherics encompass all of the "physical and non-physical elements of a store that can be controlled in order to enhance (or restrain) the behaviors of its occupants, both customers and employees. These elements present a multitude of possibilities, including ambient cues such as color, smell, music, lighting, and textures, as well as architectural and artifactual elements" (Eroglu and Machleit 1993, 34).

The physical environment "subsumes spoken word, attitudes, gestures, smells, flavors, and non-verbal messages" (Ward, Davies, and Kooijman 2003, 290) by communicating certain characteristics about the space to the consumer. Hot Topic is a retail store geared toward a unique segment of the youth market, which is immersed in pop music culture. Its store, or physical, environment appeals to this particular aesthetic (See Figure 6.6), as both emotions and behaviors are stimulated.

The retail store is a complex environment that contains multiple atmospheric cues that can be categorized as exterior, general interior, layout and design, point-of-purchase and decoration, and human variables (Turley and Milliman 2000) (See Table 6.2). Retailers need to offer sensory stimulation in each of these areas that match the image of the store and the consumers who are targeted.

In examining the strategic planning process for linking retail strategy, atmospheric design, and shopping behavior, L. W. Turley and J. C. Chebat (2002) identified general retail strategies, atmospheric design, and shopping behavior outcomes as important considerations of a plan (See Figure 6.7). Turley and Chebat (2000)

6.6 The store environment of Hot Topic has sensory appeal for a unique segment of the youth market that is immersed in pop music culture.

TABLE 6.2. CATEGORIES OF ATMOSPHERIC CUES

CATEGORIES OF ATMOSPHERIC CUES	CUES
Exterior	Building size Building shape Marquee Exterior windows Parking availability Surrounding area
General interior	Lighting Music Interior colors Ambient smells Temperature General cleanliness
Layout and design	Merchandise groupings Traffic flow Aisle placements Department locations Racks and fixtures Placement of cash registers
Point-of-purchase and decorations	Point-of-purchase displays Signs and cards Product displays Interactive displays Kiosks
Human variables	Employee characteristics Employee uniforms Retail crowding Density

Source: Turley, L. W., and R. E. Milliman. 2000. Atmospheric effects on shopping behavior: A review of the experimental evidence. *Journal of Business Research* 49(2):193–211.

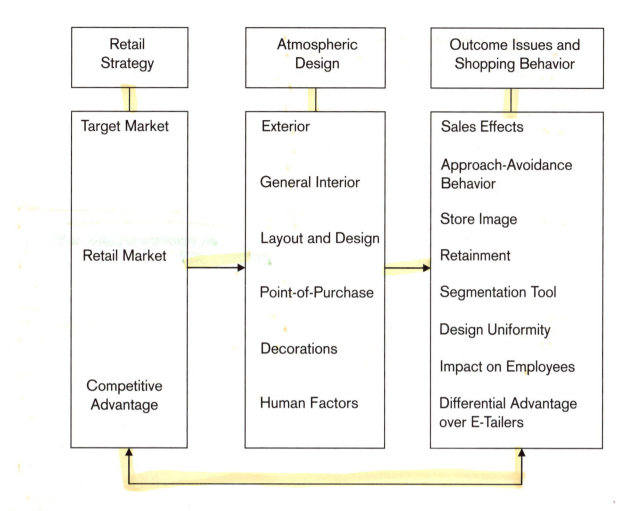

Retail Strategy	Atmospheric Design	Outcome Issues and Shopping Behavior
Target Market	Exterior	Sales Effects
	General Interior	Approach-Avoidance Behavior
	Layout and Design	Store Image
Retail Market	Point-of-Purchase	Retainment
		Segmentation Tool
	Decorations	Design Uniformity
		Impact on Employees
Competitive Advantage	Human Factors	Differential Advantage over E-Tailers

6.7 A retail strategy for using atmospheric design to influence shopping behavior

concluded that it is important "for retail managers to have specific atmospheric goals for the atmosphere in mind before creating a store design since the retail environment is capable of creating a wide range of behaviors from consumers" (125). Two important areas of consumer behavior related to atmospherics, consumer approach-avoidance behavior and pleasantness and arousal during shopping, are presented in greater detail in the following discussion.

Approach–Avoidance Behavior

Environmental stimuli create approach–avoidance behavior. A. Mehrabian and J. A. Russell (1974) suggested that the Stimulus-Organism-Response (S-O-R) paradigm could be applied to how individuals react to environments. S-O-R

is an important retail concept to manage, and it requires precise identification of the retailer's target market. Retailers can draw targeted customers into their stores by triggering approach behaviors while simultaneously creating an environment that leads to avoidance behavior by those consumers who were not identified as the intended target. Retailers can manipulate environmental cues that create specific and immediate behavioral responses where consumers want to stay, browse, and purchase. Furthermore, retailers can create delayed behavioral responses where consumers come back and purchase again because they enjoyed the store during a previous experience. The first behavioral situation responds to a short-term strategy while the second situation is a long-term strategy (Ward et al. 2003).

Environmental approach-avoidance behavior occurs in four ways. First, store patronage intent is determined by a basic desire to physically approach or avoid an environment. Second, the desire or interest to approach the store is reinforced by looking around and exploring, or avoiding to move through or interact with the environment. This behavior relates to in-store search and exposure to a broad or narrow assortment of retail offerings. Third, there is a desire or interest to engage in communication with others in the store versus a tendency to avoid interaction with others. Communication approach or avoidance is directed most often to sales associates and staff. Fourth, consumers who exhibit approach behavior are satisfied more with their shopping performance. Conversely, consumers who practice avoidance are hindered in their shopping performance and satisfaction. Avoidance consumers miss shopping opportunities, which translates into fewer shopping experiences, fewer choices, and lower shopping satisfaction. Approach–avoidance behaviors relate to the frequency of repeat shopping as well as to reinforcements of time and money spent in the store (Donovan and Rossiter 1982).

A classic example of approach–avoidance consumer behavior is illustrated by a specialty retailer in Marin, California, who opened a store that sold brass beds. When customers approached the brass beds and instinctively reached out to touch them, they experienced the unpleasant physical sensation of electrical shocks. The customers had built up static electric charges as they walked on the store's carpeting. When customers came in contact with the brass bed (i.e., the conducting metal), the charges were dissipated as electrical shocks. Sales quickly declined as customers rethought the idea of owning a brass bed. What had started as a pleasurable experience to purchase a new bed turned into a painful tactile experience that customers did not want to repeat daily at home. The static electric shock problem was resolved by installing flooring that did not conduct static electricity.

Pleasantness and Arousal

In addition to S-O-R, Mehrabian and Russell (1974) proposed that environmental stimuli and approach–avoidance behavior are linked through three states of emotion: pleasure (P), arousal (A), and dominance (D), which they referred to as PAD. The manner in which these emotional states of PAD are combined determines whether a consumer approaches or avoids an environment such as a retail store (Ward et al. 2003).

Perceptions of pleasantness and arousal are important in consumer evaluations of physical and nonphysical store elements. R. J. Donovan, J. R. Rossiter, G. Marcoolyn, and A. Nesdale (1994) confirmed that when consumers experience pleasantness in a store environment, the experience can have a significant positive influence on their purchasing behavior. They concluded that by adding upbeat music, using bright colors, and implementing other elements that create arousal, retailers can create a store that is perceived by shoppers as more pleasant.

The relationship between consumer behavior and retail atmospherics can influence a consumer's decision to shop at a particular place. In a survey of 1,000 shoppers in one of the largest city center shopping malls in Europe, P. J. McGoldrick and C. P. Pieros (1998) found higher levels of pleasure and arousal among consumers with stronger shopping motives. They also found that expectations influenced the levels of novelty, complexity, and spaciousness that consumers experienced. If their experience matched their expectations, then the consumers perceived the environment as more novel, complex, and spacious. Moreover, when the consumers' expectations were confirmed positively, they experienced higher levels of pleasure. However, when expectations were negated, consumers were more likely to experience lower pleasure and ultimately dislike the shopping mall.

FENG SHUI

Consumer involvement with the physical environment can be linked to the ancient practice of feng shui. Feng shui is a 3,000-year-old art of placement that seeks balance between the five elements that flow through life (water, earth, fire, wood, and metals), yin and yang (acceptance of opposites or polarities), and chi (energy flow and the essence of life) (Mingfang and Zhou 2005, Rasmusson 1998). Originating in China, feng shui spread to Japan, Malaysia, Singapore, the Philippines, Vietnam, Laos, Thailand, and Korea (Hobson 1994). Contemporary practices of feng shui illustrate the influence of the intermingling of Chinese traditional belief systems rooted in Confucianism and Taoism, and Western ideologies and cultures that are reflected in consumption, consumerism, and brand buying of consumers (Eckhardt and Houston 2002).

In interior environments feng shui becomes a system for arranging physical space so it is in harmony and balance with nature. For example, a building's location is an important consideration in feng shui. A site that is on a corner, has a rounded design, and has no roads directly aimed at the building is good feng shui (See Figure 6.8). The use of auspicious colors (i.e., red, gold) is another application of feng shui.

Retail and hospitality companies have found feng shui to be a potent urban force in Asian countries. Asian businesses often contract with a feng shui consultant or geomancer (i.e., a person who interprets the meanings of figures, lines, or geographic features) for advice on site locations and aspects of building design. Hobson (1994) identified five aspects of feng shui used in hotel properties: location, exterior physical design, interior physical design, marketing, and employees (See Table 6.3). The use of feng shui is validated by major developers such as Donald Trump who uses its principles in his multi-billion-dollar projects (Whong 2005). In the United States, consultants certified in feng shui are hired to create home environments for their clients that reflect individual energies and balances between life elements (Rasmusson 1998).

6.8 Its corner site, rounded design, and lack of any roads aimed directly at the building make this Express retail store a good example of feng shui.

TABLE 6.3. APPLICATION OF FENG SHUI TO HOTELS

CATEGORY	APPLICATION OF FENG SHUI TO HOTELS
Location	• Have no roads aimed directly at the building. • Use a corner site and a round design. • Use auspicious design symbols (e.g., scorpions for restaurants) as framework for creating building design.
Exterior physical design	• Use a tall glass wall when there is a harbor location. • Place an open hole in center of building when there is an ocean view.
Interior physical design	• Offset hotel room doors. • Use care when positioning furniture. • Use mirrors to reflect undesirable and evil spirits. • Use auspicious colors (i.e., red, yellow, gold) • Build main doors at an angle. • Use care in locating fountains and determining best spout heights.
Marketing	• Refer to the feng shui properties of the business. • Use feng shui symbols and references.
Employees	• Develop management sensitivity towards employees affected by feng shui beliefs. • Use care in the design of offices and workspaces. • Employ a geomancer to ensure improved feng shui.

Source: Hobson, J. S. P. 1994. Feng shui: Its impacts on the Asian hospitality industry. *International Journal of Contemporary Hospitality Management* 6(6):21–26.

ATTITUDES

Consumer response is the result of a three-part experience that includes cognition (awareness and thought), affect (emotion and feeling), and conation (actions and behaviors). Attitudes influence how consumers approach, process, evaluate, and remember experiences, and they encompass the motivational, emotional, perceptual, and cognitive processes that occur in a specific environment or situation. Attitudes are enduring and difficult to change, and they reflect how favorable or unfavorable a person feels toward a specific object, an experience, or a concept. Moreover, attitudes can be used to predict the likelihood that a person will perform a behavior under consideration (Ajzen and Fishbien 1980). Managing a total consumer experience requires attention to the functional and affective attributes of that experience (Haeckel, Carbone, and Berry 2003).

Functional attributes are associated with cognition (i.e., awareness and thought). Functional attributes reveal consumer attitudes toward benefits offered by goods and services when solving problems. Cognitive attitudes can measure utilitarian or instrumental (i.e., functional) attributes. These attitudes are a collection of beliefs and knowledge about a product, service, situation, or experience. Beliefs create a framework for understanding and evaluating specific attributes of an object or the object as a whole. Beliefs exist, even though they may not be correct or true. Objects generally contain multiple attributes. Although consumers may consider each attribute specifically, this is often an unconscious process unless there is high involvement with the object (Hawkins, Best, and Coney 2003).

Affective attributes are produced through the evaluation of an object. They reflect the emotional benefit to consumers and are expressed as feelings or emotional reactions. Affective attitudes measure hedonic or consummatory attributes (Haeckel et al. 2003; Pham, Cohen, Pracejus, and Hughes 2001). Affective attitudes may or may not be based on cognitive information. Moreover, feelings can precede and impact cognition. Beliefs are associated with affective reactions or evaluations; however, they differ by individual and context. Affective attitudes and emotional reactions tend to be similar when the beliefs are tied to cultural values (Hawkins, Best, and Coney 2003).

COGNITIVE EXPERIENCE

A consumer's cognitive experience is the result of deliberate reasoning and evaluations derived from cognition. Cognition includes all the thoughts, beliefs, and knowledge held by an individual as well as the activities that are associated with perception, memory, learning, and information processing. Cognitive experiences differ by consumer knowledge, need for cognition, cognitive effort, cognitive structures, environmental influences, and developmental stages. Consumer knowledge is distinguished by familiarity and expertise.

Familiarity is the most inclusive aspect of consumer knowledge, and it comes from the consumer's overall product-related experiences. Information search, shopping episodes, shopping interactions (e.g., product and people), decision making, and product use produce familiarity. Expertise is the knowledge that supports successful performance of product-related tasks (Alba and Hutchinson 1987).

The need for cognition differs among consumers based on their cognitive motivation and situational involvement. This dichotomy is referred to as the theory of need for cognition (Cacioppo, Petty, Kao, and Rodriguez 1986). Individuals who desire cognitive engagement like to think and solve problems. For these individuals, there is an inherent motivation to use cognitive effort. Barnes and Noble Booksellers is a retailer that would be attractive to consumers with a high need for cognition (See Figure 6.9). In contrast, cognitive misers are individuals who find thinking to be unfulfilling.

Consumer involvement is linked to cognitive effort. In situations of high involvement, consumers are more likely to seek activities that require thinking compared with situations where there is low involvement (Celsi and Olson 1988, Greenwald and Levitt 1984). In examining the need for cognition related to intrinsic motivation to process print advertisements, J. W. Peltier and J. A. Schibrowsky (1994) found that individuals with a high need for cognition spent more time processing print ads and had greater brand and brand claim recall compared with individuals with low need for cognition. Also, individuals with high involvement with a product ad had superior recall of character and product. Need for cognition may also be connected to mood and risk-taking. C-H. Lin, H. R. Yen, and S-C. Chuang (2006) found mood had a greater influence on risk-taking decisions by individuals with low need for cognition.

The need for cognition is reduced by the act of repeating tasks. Brand knowledge is an example of how thinking can be reduced. By knowing brands, consumers

6.9 Consumers who exhibit a high need for cognition would be attracted to retailers such as Barnes and Noble Booksellers.

can make quick decisions regarding product purchase and use. As consumers repeatedly think and make decisions, they are able to do so with greater speed and efficiency of involvement. Consumer "performance time decreases as a power function of amount of practice—without any loss in the quality of performance" (Alba and Hutchinson 1987, 412). Consumers may not want to increase cognitive effort in situations where the effort exceeds the perceived benefit. Greater cognitive effort is required when new products are introduced and in first-time experiences.

In 2005, Albertson's grocery stores launched an automated shopping experience using product bar-code scanning. After signing up for automated shopping, consumers were given a code to activate a scanning wand that read the bar code of each item placed in the shopping cart. Grocery carts were outfitted with plastic holders to carry the scanners while shopping. For products without bar codes, such as produce, consumers weighed each item at a weigh station and affixed a printed bar code label on each produce item. Upon completing their shopping, consumers moved through a self-serve checkout lane to finalize their purchase. Purchase required inserting the scanning wand into a reader that generated an itemized list on a touch screen. Consumers then used the touch screen to redeem coupons and complete payment. What was intended to speed up the shopping experience took more time as the consumer had to think more when shopping and had difficulty in getting scanners to read bar codes. The scanning wand was phased out. However, the self-service checkout stations remained when consumers found it took less effort to scan their purchases across a bar-code reader at the final point of sale.

Environmental influences such as family, peers, and mass media affect the type, amount, and quality of knowledge and cognitive processes that children acquire (John and Whitney 1986). J. M. Mandler (1979) suggested children use categorical structures and schematic memory structures to organize information and past experiences. Categorical structures describe how objects relate to one another by membership in a specific class (i.e., quick-serve restaurants, video games, and apparel). Schematic structures (i.e., detailed plans) describe what expectations are held about an object and the process one goes through to obtain that object. Compared with younger children, older children tend to have better categorical and schematic structures due to a more developed capacity to learn greater amounts of information (John and Whitney 1986).

Developmental stages influence consumer cognitive development. For children, these developmental stages influence how they make sense of and categorize their consumer experiences and the information they gather over time. There are differences in brain development among the age categories that define tweens, teens, young adults, and adults. Younger consumers often make dissimilar choices when compared with older consumers. M. Richards (2005) suggested marketers might reconsider similar brand presentations across younger age groups. Instead, consumer segments need to be defined by smaller age groups. Teens differ from other young consumers in terms of risk-taking, use of multiple stimuli when making purchase decisions, variability of responses based on situation and location, and the likelihood that emotions will trigger a response.

Neuromarketing is a new tool that is being used to understand cognitive development and attitudes. It applies the use of magnetic resonance imaging (MRI) to understand the cognitive activity of consumers and to map how stimuli activate certain areas of the brain. MRI scanning has distinguished physical differences in the growth and pruning of neurons in the brain as children mature into adolescence and then into early and older adulthood. W. D. Kilgore and D. A. Yugelun-Todd (2005) used functional MRI to examine how children's and adolescents' brains respond to visually presented food images. They found age-related changes linked to adolescent maturation where brain functioning went from lower-order sensory processing to higher-order stimuli processing related to anticipated rewards, self-monitoring, and inhibited behavior. Companies such as Daimler Chysler and Ford Motor Company are using MRI scans as a tool to gain better information regarding consumer responses toward product attributes and advertisements (Wilkinson 2005).

AFFECTIVE EXPERIENCE

Affect refers to feeling, emotion, preference, and attitude, and it can be a combination of affect, cognition, and conation (Fishbein and Ajzen 1975). Affect is a mental state of personal feeling that is knowingly experienced along with emotion and mood. It comes from the individual's assessment of the meaning, causes, and personal implications of a particular incentive (Westbrook 1987). Consumption experiences are influenced by affective assessments that produce experiential feelings and emotional responses. However, compared with cognition, affect is recognized as being more important in the decision-making process (Sherman, Mathur, and Smith 1997).

Affective response is a powerful motivator that influences consumer information processing and choice (Zajonc 1980). Different affective responses are created from how a consumer thinks about an experience (Weiner, Russel, and Lerman 1979). Affective response is generally classified by a fundamental emotion (Izard 1977) (See Table 6.4). Anger, disgust, and contempt result from negative affective experiences that assign the cause to a spe-

TABLE 6.4. A TAXONOMY OF AFFECTIVE EXPERIENCE

AFFECT	NATURE OF SUBJECTIVE EXPERIENCE	REACTION
Interest	Engaged, attentive, caught-up, curious, fascinated; when intense, a feeling of excitement and animation	Positive
Joy	Sense of confidence and significance, feeling loved and lovable, a good relationship to the object of joy	Positive
Anger	Hostility, desire to attack the source of anger, physical power, impulsiveness	Negative
Disgust	Feelings of revulsion; impulses to escape from or remove the object of disgust from proximity to oneself	Negative
Contempt	Superiority to other people, groups, or things; hostility (mild); prejudice; coldness and distance	Negative
Distress	Sadness, discouragement, downheartedness, loneliness and isolation, feeling miserable, sense of loss	Negative
Fear	Apprehension to terror, depending on intensity; sense of imminent danger; feeling unsafe; slowed thought; tension	Negative
Shame	Suddenly heightened self-consciousness, self-awareness; feeling of incompetence, indignity, defeat; in mild form, shyness	Negative
Guilt	Gnawing feelings of being in the wrong, not right with others or the self	Negative
Surprise	Fleeting sense of interruption of ongoing thought, brief uncertainty, amazement and startle	Neutral

Source: Izard, C. E. 1977. *Human emotion*. New York: Plenum Press.

TABLE 6.5. LAWS OF EMOTION

LAW	EMOTIONAL RESPONSE
Situational Meaning	Classifies and explains emotional intensity and cognitive outcomes.
Concern	Occurs in an important event that is linked to goals, motives, or concerns.
Apparent Reality	Is evoked by unconditional affective stimuli, sensory stimuli, and unsuccessful action in situations that may be real, not real, or not taken seriously.
Change, Habituation, and Comparative Feeling	Addresses actual or expected positive or negative situational change associated with emotions. Greater situational change creates more intense emotions. Repeated exposure (habituation) results in less intense pleasure or hardship. The viewpoint used to judge the situation creates the comparative feeling that generates emotional intensity.
Conservation of Emotional Momentum	Implies emotional situations retain their intensity indefinitely unless repetitive situational exposure results in extinction or habituation. Habituation, not time, explains diminishing emotions.
Closure	Explains the absolute nature of emotional response. Feeling and controlling behavior tend to be unconditional and closed to assessments of their relative impact and to the requirements of other goals.
Care for Consequences	Evokes secondary responses that consider probable consequences and may modify a succeeding emotional response.
Lightest Load and Greatest Gain	Suggests when it is possible to view a situation in another way, negative emotions are generally minimized to maximize emotional gain.

Source: Frijda, N. H. 1988. The laws of emotion. *American Psychologist* 43(5):349–358.

cific motivation. Guilt and shame blame the individual. Fear and sadness are attributed to the situation. Interest and joy are the outcomes from getting an incentive and the behavior involved with that incentive. Surprise is a greater affective response to involvement with a positive or negative incentive (Westbrook 1987).

As retailers shift their strategies to target consumers on an emotional level, they need to arouse the various senses and encourage consumers to make purchase decisions based on how they feel (*In-Store Magazine* 2005). An individual's readiness to interact is conveyed by the complex, expressive response patterns that are emotions (Frijda 1988, Frijda and Mesquite 1994).

Specific emotional responses are suggested by how a situation is interpreted (Neidenthal, Tangney, and Gavanski 1994). Awareness of a situation and an experience can generate negative and posi-

tive feelings (Frijda 1988). Negative emotion results from either failing to meet personal or social values or a situation that was painful, destructive, or difficult to endure (Frijda 1988, Harris 2003). Positive emotion results from situations that satisfy desire. Although different emotional responses are influenced by different situations, they are highly predictable (Frijda 1988). Emotions also convey consistent messages (Averill 1998) that go across incidences, individuals, situations, and cultures (Consedine, Strongman, and Magai 2003).

N. H. Frijda (1988) identified eight laws of emotion that are driven by situational meaning (See Table 6.5). These laws explain the emotional responses that individuals experience in different situations. One law of emotion that is of great importance to retailers is the law of change, habituation, and comparative feeling. Consumers who are exposed to greater change in situations have more intense emotional experiences. When consumers have repeated exposure to the same situation (i.e., habituation) their pleasure becomes less intense. Retailers who continue to present the same store environment to their customers may over time find their customers have less intense feelings about their experience in the store. Continuously changing and updating the store creates the excitement needed to generate customer emotions. This phenomenon impacts store design, which needs to be flexible enough to support and encourage change.

Consumer emotional response can be generated from the situational meanings that are assigned to a retailer. The Body Shop, which has 1,900 stores in more than 50 countries, offers high quality skin and body care (See Figure 6.10). This company has created situation meaning through its unique corporate mission that supports social and environmental change, ecologically sustainable products, environmental protection, and human and civil rights, and has banned animal testing in the cosmetics and toiletries industry (www.thebodyshopinternational.com). Customers who support these social and environmental causes are emotionally drawn to The Body Shop. The emotional appeal of The Body Shop became a successful marketing strategy for growing this company (Hartman and Beck-Dudley 1999). In 2006, L'Oreal purchased The Body Shop to expand its vast distribution networks and gain new market share. A challenge for these companies was to "convince consumers that integration of distribution, purchasing, or production would not compromise the companies' [The Body Shop] social mission" (Harrison 2006, p. 30). Retailers who can link their business to important consumer concerns through the use of sensory motivations can create an apparent reality that builds on customers' emotions.

6.10 The Body Shop creates situational emotional responses from consumers by making known its corporate mission that supports social change, ecologically sustainable products, environmental protection, and human and civil rights, and for the banning of animal testing in the cosmetics industry.

SENSORY MEMORY

There are two different types of **sensory memory stores**; memory is a long-term sensory store, while sensation is formed by short sensory stores that last 200 milliseconds or less (Kaernback 2004). Memory is also differentiated by whether it is a sensory or categorical code that is memorized (Cowan 1988) although sensory memory and categorical memory show similar dynamics and interactions (Kaernback 2004).

The emotional meaning of a stimulus seems to influence consumers' particular awareness of memory (D'Argembeau and Van der Linden 2004). Emotional stimuli generally are recalled and recognized more clearly than neutral stimuli. Emotional words and pictures are generally remembered better when compared with neutral words and pictures. Likewise, emotionally charged situations are remembered better than neutral situations (Dewhurst and Parry 2000, Ochsner 2000).

Stimulating the memory of an object or experience may use many types of information, such as any semantic (i.e., language) characteristics of the object, the time and place it was acquired, the way in which the item was presented, thoughts and emotions associated with the item, and attributes of the item such as size and color (Johnson, Hashtroudi, and Linsay 1993). Sometimes **mnemonics,** the use of rhymes, key word, first letter, link/chain, figure alphabet (Malhotra 1991), music, imagery, and storytelling (Scruggs and Brigham 1991, Yalch 1991) can be used as a means for improving memory.

The interrelated features of a stimulus include attributes such as color, shape, spatial location, and time (i.e., temporal) (D'Argembeau and Van der Linden 2004). T. J. Perfect, A. R. Mayes, J. J. Downes, and R. Van Eijk (1996) demonstrated that individuals use two or more pieces of interrelated (i.e., contextual) information when they are asked to remember something. These contextual pieces might be time or appearance. The greater probability that individuals will respond by remembering an emotional item over a neutral item indicates that emotions are more useful for recalling interrelated information that is associated with a specific object (D'Argembeau and Van der Linden 2004).

6.11 Consumers assign meaning to a stimulus through its contextual details that become part of memory and produce emotional response. Coke is a global brand that stimulates a sensory memory of the Coke brand through the contextual details of the color of the word (i.e., white) and the color of the frame (i.e., red background).

Contextual details can influence the memory of the affective intrinsic and extrinsic affective meanings of stimuli (D'Argembeau and Van der Linden 2004). Intrinsic context is the aspect of a stimulus that is processed when that stimulus is recognized and understood in a specific setting. Color and case (i.e., uppercase versus lowercase font) of written words are two examples. S. Doerksen and A. P. Shimamura (2001) found the color of the word and the color of the frame that bordered the word were remembered significantly better for emotional words compared with neutral words. Coke is a global brand that stimulates sensory memory of the Coke brand through the use of the color of the word (i.e., white) and the color of the frame (i.e., red background border) (See Figure 6.11). This process can produce emotional connections to the Coke brand. Extrinsic context includes external characteristics of a situation that are not actual parts of the situation (Godden and Baddeley 1980). Although some stimuli are automatically converted (Hasher and Zacks 1979), contextual features may differ in how they are processed into memory. For example, the location and space used by a stimulus is automatically programmed into memory (Andrade and Meudell 1993) while color is not (Light and Berger 1974).

The distinctiveness of the conditions in which something occurs contributes to remembering. This distinctiveness refers to the "differences among items that presumably uniquely specify some items or the salience of items that make them stand out from among the background items" (Rajaram 1998, 72). Emotional words are remembered more than neutral words possibly because the distinctiveness of emotional words creates a link between a particular item and its use (D'Argembeau and Van der Linden 2004, Dewhurst and Parry 2000).

SENSORY CHANNELS

Sensory channels that are associated with atmospheres include sight, sound, scent, and touch. The sense of sight includes the visual dimensions of color, brightness, size, and shapes. The sense of sound takes in aural dimensions of volume and pitch. The sense of scent takes in olfactory dimensions of scent and freshness. The sense of touch takes in tactile dimensions of softness, smoothness, and temperature. While an atmosphere can be seen, heard, smelled, and felt, it cannot be tasted (Kotler 1973–1974). The fifth sense, taste, is associated with four dimensions associated with distinct receptors on the tongue: sweet, sour, salt, and bitter. The sense of taste is experienced primarily through foods, beverages, personal care products, and some cosmetics. All five senses can be incorporated in a multisensory consumption experience.

Companies that are known for products in a particular sensory channel may find opportunities to expand into new sensory channels. For example, The Body Shop and L'Oreal, two beauty companies that are focused primarily on scent, are using their combined product development departments to develop products for the food sector that will primarily focus on taste. These companies plan to expand The Body Shop brand into the growing organic and fair-trade food market. The brand lends itself to beverages, chocolates, and fruit-based products (*Marketing Week* March 23, 2006).

Sight

Sight stimuli in retail atmospheres are created through visual displays, store layout, and store design. Color, brightness, size, and shapes are integrated into all of these components. Color, images, copy (i.e., words, letters), patterns, designs, luminousness, brightness, and size are visual

stimuli. Visual cues are important aspects of merchandising, and they create interest in retail settings.

Lighting can intensify environmental sensory experiences. Neon lights are a classic example of how colors, brightness, size, shapes, designs, luminousness, imagery, and copy can create visual appeal and stimulate the sense of sight (See Figures 6.12 and 6.13). Obviously, these images trigger affective responses, made more memorable by the visuals and the situations in which they are experienced.

6.12 Words can create visual appeal.

6.13 Neon lights are a classic example of how colors, brightness, sizes, shapes, designs, and imagery create visual appeal and stimulate the sense of sight.

Lighting is being incorporated into apparel to heighten the sight sensory channel. In fall 2006, Lands' End introduced its exclusive Cool Blue lighting technology for outerwear and gear. Cool Blue features electroluminescent lamps composed of millions of separate luminous dots that create effective lighting for low-visibility situations. The lights can be easily switched on and off and use a rechargeable battery.

Color coveys a message or mood and can have a dramatic effect on consumer experiences and sales. How consumers interact with color is changing with social and demographic trends as gender, age and ethnicity contribute to shifting color preferences of consumers. Color is a perceptual tool that can "enhance a consumer's search for, purchase, and consumption of products" (Kaufman-Scarborough 2000, 464).

Color preferences are associated with gender differences. Traditionally, among U.S. consumers, women prefer brighter tones and subtle shading and patterns, while men prefer darker, richer neutrals and blues and avoid brighter, more complex and warm hues. Part of this difference in preference may be because females see color better than males, and males are 16 times more likely to be color-blind (Paul 2000).

A 2002 American Demographic BuzzBack survey found greater convergence between men and women in their color choices than was expected. For example, men and women selected blue, silver, and black cars over white, yellow, red, or green cars. Consumers under the age of 30 had even less differences in color preferences. This change in color preference is evident in the wide range of colors that are used in sports uniforms and a lessening of strict color assignments based on gender roles, such as purple and pink being worn only by females (Paul 2002).

Consumers' color preferences change with age as vision changes. Older consumers see objects as less bright, with a yellow cast, and they have trouble seeing very dark hues. Because white and other bright tones are preferred by older consumers, Lexus produces 60 percent of its cars in a light color to meet the color preferences of its targeted customer segment (Paul 2002).

Cultural trends and ethnic influences are impacting consumers more now than in past generations. Greater cultural and ethnic exposure among younger consumers has made them more receptive to a greater range of colors. For example, Generation X and Y children were exposed to a broader color palette than previous generations (Paul 2002). Crayola brand crayons grew from offering 8 colors in 1903 to 120 colors in 1998 (www.crayola.com). Table 6.6 summarizes crayon colors across the past century. Part of this color change is attributed to the greater color sophistication of tweens and teens where their preferences include nontraditional color combinations and the use of glitter, translucence, pearlescence, and metallics as color effects (Paul 2002).

Color appeals to children. It plays a prominent role in the introduction of new food products to children. Children see unexpected colors in food as fun. ConAgra Foods' Parkay brand introduced pink- and blue-colored spread in late 2001 and Hershey's offered green-colored chocolate syrup to tie in with the release of *The Hulk* (Howell 2003). Because children constitute an important consumer group in food retailing, understanding children's attitudes toward sensory cues related to food is particularly important (Howell 2001).

Ketchup is a good an example of the impact color has had on children's product demand. Young consumers consume 55 percent of all ketchup (Reyes 2001b). In 2000, H. J. Heinz Company launched the E-Z Squirt bottle in traditional red

TABLE 6.6. CRAYOLA CRAYON CHRONOLOGY

YEAR(S)	# OF COLORS	COLORS	COLORS ADDED	COLORS RETIRED
1903	8	Black, Blue, Brown, Green, Orange, Red, Violet, Yellow		
1949–1957	48	Apricot, Bittersweet, Black, Blue, Blue Green, Blue Violet, Brick Red, Brown, Burnt Sienna, Carnation Pink, Cornflower, Flesh**, Gold, Gray, Green, Green Blue, Green Yellow, Lemon Yellow, Magenta, Mahogany, Maize, Maroon, Melon, Olive Green, Orange, Orange Red, Orange Yellow, Orchid, Perwinkle, Pine Green, Prussian Blue*, Red, Red Orange, Red Violet, Salmon, Sea Green, Silver, Spring Green, Tan, Thistle, Turquoise Blue, Violet (Purple), Violet Blue, Violet Red, White, Yellow, Yellow Green, Yellow Orange		
1958–1971	64	All previously listed colors, plus 16 colors added in 1958.	Aquamarine, Blue Gray, Burnt Orange, Cadet Blue, Copper, Forest Green, Goldenrod, Indian Red***, Lavender, Mulberry, Navy Blue, Plum, Raw Sienna, Raw Umber, Sepia, Sky Blue	
1972–1989	72	All colors previously listed, plus 8 fluorescent colors added in 1972.	Chartreuse, Hot Magenta, Ultra Blue, Ultra Green, Ultra Orange, Ultra Pink, Ultra Red, Ultra Yellow	
1990–1992	80	All colors previously listed as well as 8 additional fluorescent colors. The fluorescent colors from 1972 were renamed to the following in 1990: Atomic Tangerine, Blizzard Blue, Hot Magenta, Laser Lemon, Outrageous Orange, Screamin' Green, Shocking Pink, Wild Watermelon.	The following colors replaced the 8 retired colors: Cerulean, Vivid Tangerine, Jungle Green, Fuchsia, Dandelion, Teal Blue, Royal Purple, Wild Strawberry	Green Blue, Orange Red, Orange Yellow, Violet Blue, Maize, Lemon Yellow, Blue Gray, Raw Umber. These retired colors were enshrined in the Crayola Hall of Fame on August 7, 1990.
1993	96	All previously listed colors, plus 16 new colors named by consumers.	Asparagus, Cerise, Denim, Granny Smith Apple, Macaroni and Cheese, Mauvelous, Pacific Blue, Purple Mountain's Majesty, Razzmatazz, Robin's Egg Blue, Shamrock, Tickle Me Pink, Timber Wolf, Tropical, Rain Forest, Tumbleweed, Wisteria	
1998	120	All previously listed colors, plus 24 new colors added. In addition, Binney & Smith produces several assortments of specialty crayons.	Almond, Antique Brass, Banana Mania, Beaver, Blue Bell, Pink Sherbet, Canary, Caribbean Green, Cotton Candy, Blush, Desert Sand, Eggplant, Fern, Fuzzy Wuzzy Brown, Manatee, Mountain Meadow, Outer Space, Piggy Pink, Pink Flamingo, Purple Heart, Shadow, Sunset Orange, Torch Red, Vivid Violet	

(continued)

TABLE 6.6. CRAYOLA CRAYON CHRONOLOGY (*continued*)

YEAR(S)	# OF COLORS	COLORS	COLORS ADDED	COLORS RETIRED
2000	120	All previously listed colors with the following exceptions: Thistle was removed from the 120-count assortment to make room for Indigo; Torch Red was renamed Scarlet.		
2003	120	All previously listed colors plus 4 new colors (4 colors were retired). To mark Crayola's 100th birthday, consumers name new colors and vote four out of the box.	Inch worm, Jazzberry Jam, Mango Tango, Wild Blue Yonder	Blizzard Blue, Magic Mint, Mulberry, Teal Blue

* Prussian Blue: Name changed to Midnight Blue in 1958 in response to teachers' requests.
** Flesh: Name voluntarily changed to Peach in 1962, partially as a result of the U.S. Civil Rights Movement
*** Indian Red: Renamed as Chestnut in 1999 in response to educators who felt some children wrongly perceived the crayon color was intended to represent the skin color of Native Americans. The name originated from a reddish-brown pigment found near India commonly used in fine artist oil paint.
Note: Crayola Crayon Chronology is based on information compiled from company records and internal sources.
Source: http://www.crayola.com/colorcensus/history/chronology.cfm

ketchup. The bottle size and shape solved the problem of children not being able to handle bulky ketchup bottles. It also offered the product packaging design that revolutionized condiment colors. Casey Keller, an R&D researcher for H. J. Heinz, used this new bottle to launch the innovative green-colored ketchup called Blastin' Green that was targeted to children (Reyes 2001b). In one year, 10 million bottles of Blastin' Green were sold and the brand share grew to 51.2 percent. A year later, after asking children what color they would like to see next, Heinz introduced Funky Purple as the newest crazy condiment color (Howell 2001a). Mystery Color was the third crazy ketchup introduced. Packaged in a white, opaque, 19-ounce squeezable bottle with a special rainbow-colored shrink-sleeve, Mystery Color was smaller in size than the other two colors. Consumers did not know if they had Passion Pink, Awesome Orange, or Totally Teal until they opened the bottle and squirted it out. The bottle shape and thin nozzle made it easy to squirt designs with ketchup. Only one million Mystery Color bottles were produced, which added to the excitement (*Packaging Digest* 2002). The three colors were retired when Stellar Blue was introduced. This ketchup line was a phenomenal success, in part because it was not understood by parents and loved by children (Howell 2003). In its first year, ketchup consumption increased by 12.6 percent (Reyes 2001b). By the second year, the new colored condiments generated $23 million in sales (Paul 2002). More than 25 million bottles were sold in the first three years after their introduction (Howell 2003). Because adults wanted to continue using red ketchup in the traditional bottle and their children wanted the funky-colored ketchup, families started buying multiple ketchup bottles (Reyes 2001a).

So how does ketchup generate a consumer experience? The new ketchup bottle liberated children so they could serve themselves their own ketchup and not depend on adults. Ketchup provided an expressive outlet for making colorful ketchup designs on food. Retailers welcomed the excitement generated by a new product category. S. Reyes (2001b) reported one Midwest store owner found consumers would "line up in the condiment aisle, waiting for the stock clerk to arrive with boxes of Blastin' Green, which they'd immediately rip open before it even went onshelf. . . . Consumers just couldn't get their hands on the stuff fast enough" (Reyes 2001b, M8).

Sound

Sound stimuli in retail atmospheres are created through noise and music that vary in volume and pitch. Consumers have physiological, psychological, cognitive, and behavioral responses to aural (i.e., the sense of hearing) stimuli. M. Lindstrom (2005b) found that for 44 percent of consumers surveyed in a brand-sense study, the sound of a car was more important than its design. Mercedes-Benz has 12 engineers that focus only on the sound associated with opening and closing doors. "Check out the competing Acura TSX and you'll notice the perfect sound of an opening and closing door—the feeling seems right. No wonder—the sound is artificially generated and even the vibrations in the door [are] generated by electric impulses" (136).

Sound generates environmental ambiance, and it can communicate a precise message to one or millions of consumers at the same time. Some consumer experiences have strong associations with specific sounds. For example, the sound of water moving or falling can be pleasant and calming (e.g., fountains), or noisy and invigorating (e.g., water parks) (See Figure 6.14).

Often the importance of sound in creating consumer experiences is overlooked or not fully understood by retailers and marketers. Furthermore, most retailers do not identify a consistent sound with their brand, store, or advertising (*In-Store Magazine* 2005). Most retail soundscapes are not designed to provide acoustically beneficial sound. Often the sound in a retail

6.14 The sound of water falling in an indoor water park can generate invigorating feelings.

environment is noise, a consistent dull stimulus that is characterized by its loudness (Kaernback 2004).

Sound is linked to perceptions of time. This is an important concept for retailers since dwell time, the amount of time consumers spend in a retail environment, is linked to sound. P. F. Yalch and E. R. Spangenberg (2000) used music to demonstrate the dwell time concept. They found when familiar music was played consumers had increased arousal and shorter shopping times, even though they reported having longer shopping times. When unfamiliar music was played they had longer shopping times. P. Fraisse (1984) suggested that shoppers who listen to familiar music are more aware of the beginning and ending of the song. By noticing changes in the music they are more aware of a time period. R. E. Ornstein (1969) proposed that time intervals seem longer when an individual can remember more about that period. In this case, consumers who listen to familiar songs may be able to remember more about the song and what they were doing during the song.

Music expresses emotion, induces relaxation, and creates feelings of affiliation with others (Coloma and Kleiner

TABLE 6.7. THE EFFECTS OF MUSIC ON EMOTIONAL RESPONSE

TYPE OF MUSIC	EMOTIONAL RESPONSE
Faster tempos	Happy Animated
Slower tempos	Tranquil Sentimental
Higher keys and/or major mode	Happy
Lower and/or minor keys	Less happy
Consonant harmonies	Playful Happy
Dissonant harmonies	Ominous Sad

Source: Coloma, D., and B. H. Kleiner. 2005. How can music be used in business? *Management Research News* 28(11/12):115–120.

6.15 Creating events that have sensory appeal, such as jazz concerts on the town square, create excitement and draw consumers to a shopping area.

2005). Music impacts emotions through the elements of volume, tempo, pitch, and texture and by the specific song that is played (Coloma and Kleiner 2005, Yalch and Spangenberg 2000). For example, music that is played in faster tempos generates happy and animated emotional responses while dissonant harmonies pro-

duce ominous and sad emotional responses (See Table 6.7).

Retailers can use music as an effective tool to extend brands, create a pleasant shopping experience, and extend the length of time that customers shop in the store (Korolishin 2004). Retailers who offer pleasant soundscapes can generate greater sales (*In-Store Magazine* 2005). Retailers can create events around music to generate excitement and can pull in customers (See Figure 6.15).

Music is an important aural stimulus that influences shopping pace and involvement. Consumers tend to shop quickly with louder and faster music, and they tend to browse with calmer music (Bainbridge 1998). S. A. Eroglu, K. A. Machleit, and J-C. Chebat (2005) found music tempo along with retail density (i.e., the number of people and objects within a limited space) had interactive effects on shoppers' cognitive and behavioral responses to the retail environment. Shoppers who experienced slow music and high density or fast music and low density had the highest hedonic (i.e., pleasurable) and utilitarian (i.e., functional) evaluations of the retail environment. Browsing and purchasing snacks were more likely to occur when there was slower music playing. Furthermore, shoppers who had fast music playing during a shopping experience indicated they would probably avoid shopping in that retail environment in the future. P. Fraisse (1984) found individuals reported more pleasure when listening to unfamiliar music. In addition, pleasure, but not arousal, positively affected product evaluations during a fixed time period. D. Coloma and B. H. Kleiner (2005) suggested that although familiar music can attract attention and create positive responses, it may result in an undesired effect. Music that was pleasurable at one point in time can become less enjoyable if there is too much exposure. This scenario is often created during the Christmas holiday season when the same music is played repeatedly in multiple retail outlets.

Scent

Scent stimuli in retail atmospheres are created through purposefully delivered aromas and odors. The associated smells generate powerful memory cues that function better for evoking emotion than for remembering facts. Emotional memories are triggered more by scents than by visual cues (i.e., seeing a picture) or auditory cues (i.e., hearing a voice) (LeTourneau 2000). Unlike the other senses, which require some degree of conscious response (i.e., the consumer can choose to touch, see, hear, and taste), smell is instinctive and involuntary. Moreover, odors can create moods, influence the transference of hedonic states, and become part of long-term memory (Ellen and Bone 1998).

A consumer shift has created an increased demand for scented product lines. For example, in 1995, Limited Brands Inc. generated 70 percent of its sales through its apparel stores (Victoria's Secret, Express, Limited Too, Structure, and Limited). Ten years later, 70 percent of its sales come from skin-care products, cosmetics, and lingerie. These product categories are more stable than the apparel fashion category, which has faster turnover. Bath and Body Works, a Limited Brands store, has contributed to this growth in sales. Victoria's Secret, which is known for its lingerie, has entered the personal products market as well with scents, lotions, and related beauty products (Merrick 2005) (See Figure 6.16).

SMELL RECEPTION AND PROCESSING

Humans are capable of distinguishing between 2,000 and 4,000 different aromas. They do this through the 6 to 10 million receptor cells that are located in the olfactory membrane tissues (i.e., epithelium)

6.16 Consumer interest in purchasing scented products has generated high growth for retailers such as Bath and Body Works.

(Strugnell and Jones 1999). The complex relationship between smell molecules and receptor cells creates a sense of smell (Ward et al. 2003).

Odors can be difficult to recognize and label (Ellen and Bone 1998). F. R. Schab (1991) concludes that a consumer can identify only about 40 to 50 percent of odors that are included in an ordinary set of odors. In addition, surrounding cues influence a consumer's accuracy in detecting and recognizing odors (Davis 1981). For example, lavender-scented products usually are packaged with a lavender color, lemon scents with yellow colors, and vanilla with white. Consumers would probably find it inconsistent and hard to discern odors if lavender scents were packaged in brown, lemon in blue, and vanilla in yellow.

Odors provide consumers with vital biological cues. Olfactory preferences of children are learned slowly over time through recurring exposure to odors. However, negative reactions to odors by parents and peers teach a child that an odor is unpleasant. It is not until about age five that children are able to reliably differentiate between pleasant odors (Guinard 2002).

Infant product manufacturers such as Baby Boom, Fisher-Price, Playskool, and Imagiix are expanding scented toys into the arena of aromatherapy by using scents such as chamomile, lavender, vanilla, and orange bloom. SmartScents, a line of developmental toys produced by Baby Boom Consumer Products, was the idea of Dr. Alan Hirsch, director of the Smell and Taste Treatment and Research Foundation of Chicago. According to Hirsch, "using scent in toys makes the ultimate sense because the maximum speed and capacity for learning occurs in the first 18 months of a child's life" (Prior 2002, 13). Furthermore, Hirsch believes a child is more awake when there is a scent, which enhances learning ability. Hirsch and his team claim "babies respond easily to floral scents because they are a part of nature, increasing the speed of learning in children by 17 percent by activating a part of the brain that is normally inactive" (Prior 2002, 13). Scent adds value to the product, especially if it makes the child come back repeatedly to play with the toy. Scented toys are part of the aromatherapy trend that has mainstreamed the use of scents in the home (Prior 2002).

Electronic high-tech noses or sniffers that can accurately determine scents are now available. These sniffers, composed of polymers that act as spongy sensors, absorb scent vapors that are then matched to computer-generated scent models. Applications for these scent sniffing machines include medical diagnosis, sewage treatment, and personal care products. Perfume makers in the United Kingdom, where smells can be patented, are using scent sniffers to identify fraudulent products by differentiating real fragrances from fakes. Also, scent sniffers have wide application in food and beverage production. One area of use is in food grading, such as grading fish at docks, or determin-ing premium quality oranges for juice, or grapes for wine (Pope 1995).

AMBIENT SCENTS AND AROMAS IN THE RETAILING MIX

Ambient scent is the odor that is in an environment; however, it does not emanate from a particular object in that environment. In retail environments, ambient scents have gained increasing notice as retailers seek new ways to influence consumers' perceptions of their stores and products (Spangenberg, Crowley, and Henderson 1996). In a study of the effects of ambient scent in a simulated retail environment, E. R. Spangenberg et al. (1996) found that consumer evaluations and behaviors in a scented store environment differed from those in an unscented store environment. They concluded that retailers might benefit from scenting the retail environment with neutral or pleasing scents.

Spangenberg et al. (1996) made three suggestions when choosing a scent for retail environments. First, the scent needs to be distinctive. "Just as managers attempt to create distinctive environments that differ from their competitors by using store layout, color, and so on, they also should consider scent as a mechanism for differentiating their store environment from others" (Spangenberg et al. 1996, 77). Second, scents used in retail environments need to be congruent with the products that are offered. Many stores carry a wide assortment of products; thus, scents that are appropriate for one category of products may not be congruent with other categories. Scents should not be associated with any single product category and retailers should avoid using strong scents associated with cleaning products, such as pine or lemon. Third, costs are important considerations when choosing scents. Costs include the scenting product (i.e., scenting oils can be very expensive) as well as the cost of diffusing the scent in the store (Spangenberg et al. 1996).

Aromas are distinctive and usually pleasant or savory smells. An effective aroma stimulates a specific association. The durian fruit of southeastern Asia is known for its unique size, appearance, and particularly strong odor (See Figure 6.17). This is an example of an odor that is perceived as either appealing or distasteful. A classic concept in retail formats such as bakeries, grocery stores and restaurants is the use of aromas to pull people in. General aromas can produce a welcoming atmosphere and a sense of well-being. What is difficult is translating the use of aromas into increased sales (Bainbridge 1998).

Aromas are part of the buying experience. For example, "new car smell" is an aroma that consumers associate with purchasing a new car. This smell is sprayed into the cabin of the car and lasts about six weeks. Rolls Royce has spent considerable time and money to recreate a new car smell that it has benchmarked against its classic 1965 model (Lindstrom 2005b). In a brand-sense study, M. Lindstrom (2005b) found that 86 percent of consumers in the United States and 69 percent of consumers in Europe felt the new car smell was appealing.

In their review of olfactory research and the study of environmental stimuli within retail settings, P. Ward et al. (2003) generated a developmental discussion on ambient smell and the potential for novel ambient aromas that distinguish a retailer's marketing mix. Their conclusions have implications for the inclusion of olfactory stimuli in retailing settings. First, ambient scent is part of a larger and more complex set of stimuli that creates an impression of a store in the consumer's mind. Retailers need an improved under-

standing of the congruence between olfactory cues and other sensory stimuli (i.e., visual stimuli) and how this is perceived by consumers. Also, this understanding needs to extend to the totality of the retail experience. Second, Ward et al. (2003) determined that "smell can be perceived through pre-attentive processing; and this may lead to a situation where consumers respond to a smell without realizing . . . the use of smell can achieve a (positive) response without distracting from attention to other stimuli—for example, visual information drawn from merchandising displays" (299). Ward et al. (2003) suggested retailers consider developing a corporate scent that is congruent, liked, and significant to strengthen retail brand image and positive behavioral outcomes.

SCENT MEMORY AND EMOTIONS

Scent can produce a powerful and evocative memory, which provides retailers the opportunity to develop a strong consumer–retailer bond. When the consumer is outside the store, the scent can make the

6.17 Consumers perceive odors as either appealing or distasteful. The durian fruit of southeastern Asia is known for its unique size, appearance, and particularly pungent odor, which consumers either completely accept or reject.

consumer recall the retailer (Ward et al. 2003). Singapore Airlines introduced Stefan Floridian Waters, an aroma designed specifically for this company, in the late 1990s as a strategy to create a strong brand memory. It was used in the perfume worn by flight attendants, the hot towels provided before takeoff, and it permeated the cabin during flight. Travelers reported instantaneous recognition of this scent when they travel on Singapore Airlines (Lindstrom 2005a).

Scent memory triggers emotions. Retailers might create corporate scents that are associated with emotional memories generated in their stores. Where such emotions are pleasant, this also helps further the consumer–retailer bond (Ward et al. 2003, 299). Associations with the retail brand are linked to the strength of scent memory and emotion. When retailers have a sound understanding of consumers' scent recall and the associations they make with that scent, then they would profit from cre-

ating a novel corporate scent that is an integral element in their store design and identity (Ward et al. 2003).

Similar recommendations to use scent memory might also be made for retail advertisements. P. S. Ellen and P. F. Bone (1998) examined the role of olfactory cues that are used as a novelty, versus providing a sample, in promoting products. They found that when a scratch-and-sniff patch was consistent with a product advertisement, neither the attitude toward the ad nor the attitude toward the brand was affected. However, when the scent was a poor fit, attitudes were lower. They concluded that attitudes associated with olfactory cues appeared to be "a function of the mood evoked by the scented advertisement and of the scent's perceived pleasantness in the advertising context" (Ellen and Bone 1998, 29).

Touch

Touch stimuli include dimensions of tactility (also called haptics), such as softness, smoothness, and temperature, that have functional and emotional elements. Materials that are used to create an environment influence consumer reactions to that environment. Tactile sensations differ among natural, metal and synthetic, or man-made materials. Retailers can create warmth that pulls in customers by using wood instead of metal on surfaces consumers touch, such as on shelves or door handles (*In-Store Magazine* 2005). Stocking merchandise in open bins and on shelves offers consumers greater interaction with tactile stimuli (See Figure 6.18).

Temperature is an atmospheric element that often goes unnoticed unless it is too hot or too cold. The Gaylord Texan Resort and Convention Center in Grapevine, Texas, created a new family holiday tradition with its Lone Star Christmas that included temperature as a sensory stimulus.

6.18 Stocking merchandise in open bins offers consumers opportunities for tactile stimulation.

This extravaganza offered a multisensory experience with the sounds of holiday music, carriage rides, unique outdoor holiday designs, holiday-inspired menus, and special one-of-a-kind merchandise in its retail stores. The biggest attraction was "ICE!," which is also offered at Gaylord Opryland Resort and Convention Center in Nashville, Tennessee, and Gaylord Palms Resort and Convention Center in Kissimmee, Florida. "ICE!" was a 14,000-square-foot structure filled with 2 million pounds of ice kept at 9 degrees. Artisans from Harbin, China, hand-carved the blocks of ice into lifesize monuments and sculptures. Guests were provided with oversize parkas to wear when they walked through "ICE!" While in the exhibition, guests experienced an ice fantasy world, exciting slides, dramatic lighting, and soaring music (www.gaylordhotels.com/gaylordtexan/press/Aug_10_05.cfm). "ICE!" is an example of using touch stimuli to create a unique consumer experience.

The White Rose Faraday Packaging Partnership in the United Kingdom is exploring how the sense of touch and consumers' tactile interactions with product packaging can produce emotional responses that make consumers repeat buyers. Their research is measuring consumer physical and emotional responses to a variety of surfaces to link specific physical surfaces and emotions. Based on their findings, they expect to develop packaging materials that engage consumers' emotions through tactile stimuli (*Packaging Magazine* 2003).

A new frontier in tactile stimulation is pain. While most American businesses have focused on comfort, pleasure, and eliminating discomfort, they have dismissed pain, potentially the ultimate subjective experience, as a profit center (Goldman 2000). D. Goldman (2000) provided the example of Americans "paying good money to spend a week working on a replica of the Endeavor, the sailing ship Captain James Cook sailed to the South Pacific in 1768. In return, they experience such authentic sea-going moments as climbing to vertiginous heights in lashing winds, and heaving their dinner over the bow during the night watch" (60). The hardship associated with this experience has status because it is a rare commodity among those who can afford the affluence of comfort and pleasure. The example of consumers volunteering to work on the Endeavor and calling it a vacation, while the eighteenth century ship crews were forced into service, illustrates a new dichotomy of how experiences are redefined to gain new sensual pleasure (Goldman 2000). Experience vacations, such as the 64-day trek up Mount Everest offered by Alpine Ascents International for $65,000, have become more popular as people seek experiences that stretch the senses (Stracher 2005).

Taste

Taste stimuli are influenced by personal preference, exposure to different taste combinations, and cultural practices. They provide consumers with pleasure through the flavorful combinations of sweet, sour, salt, and bitter (See Figure 6.19). The strong sour taste of kimchi, a traditional pickled cabbage, is preferred among Koreans, but its taste may be too potent for some consumers in many other cultures. With migration to new environments and the introduction of new foods in traditional cuisines, consumer tastes and the authenticity of cuisine are changing. Pizza is a good example. Pizza in the United States reflects a vastly different taste palate from what would be found in Italy, its traditional home. Pizza Hut's Stuffed Crust pizza, Thin 'N Crispy pizza, and Meat Lover's pizza are unique to the cultural

6.19 Consumers gain sensual pleasure through the flavorful combinations of sweet, sour, salty, and bitter tastes. Mango Lassi is a popular sweet and sour beverage in India. It consists of mangos blended with yogurt, sugar, and lemon juice. This drink was prepared at Indique Heights, an Indian restaurant in Chevy Chase, Maryland.

tastes found in the United States. A Pizza Hut restaurant in New Zealand may look similar, but its pizza will have a different flavor due to the types of meat and cheese that are used.

Children and adults differ in their taste stimuli. At birth, infants have five times as many taste buds as adults, which creates an active gustatory (taste) system. However, children have difficulty in discerning between taste and texture and sweet and tart, while adults can sense the differences between perceptions of appearance, taste, and texture (Guinard 2002). Food companies are stretching their flavor offerings to appeal to children such as cheeses flavored with grape, pepperoni, tomato ketchup, and chocolate (Gerdes 2006).

Greater consumer involvement with taste stimuli is influencing the types of products retailers offer. For example, higher consumer demand for organic foods is fueled in part because consumers perceive it as tasting better than nonorganic

foods (Kuhn 2005). Product displays can be created to appeal to consumers' sense of taste. Phillips Newman, an off-license chain in the United Kingdom, does not display wines in the typical format of region. Rather, wines are organized and displayed in six unique taste zones: bright, smooth, and round for white wines and fruity, mellow, and chunky for red wines (*In-Store Magazine* 2005).

Implicit in the industrialization of food is the standardization of food production. While standardization improves quality and safety, it has homogenized food tastes and removed the consumer from many original food tastes (Finkelstein 2003). G. Ritzer (1998) proposed the concept of McDonalization of food as an argument to examine and explain the increasing prevalence of nonhuman technologies impacting effectiveness, calculability, dependability, and power in society and the world in general. J. Finkelstein (2003) used McDonalization to explain how Australian consumers are experiencing boredom with food due to standardizations of taste. When McDonald's entered the Australian market, it offered consumers a food product that was safe and standardized in taste, portion, and appearance across dining experiences. However, over time, these stable attributes have created a boring product for consumers. This standardization of food has transferred to limited-service and full-service restaurants as well. Commercial kitchens have become centers to assemble ingredients rather than centers of food preparation (Finkelstein 2003). Any food item can be delivered to a restaurant preprepared, cooked, baked, and portion controlled. All that is needed is for the food to be assembled, plated, garnished, and served. This industrial approach to food preparation has led to boring foods. Through the use of preprepared food, restaurants are offering similar tastes to their customers.

SENSORY CHANNELS AND THE INTERNET

The Internet poses a sensory challenge to retailers since it does not allow for consumer experiences with tactile, olfactory, and taste stimuli. The limitation of sensory experiences to visual and auditory cues is a significant deterrent to online purchases, especially for person-to-person communication and product involvement. The online store, however, does possess other experiences such as flexibility across time and space, which can make the context of the online shopping experience significantly different from the conventional physical retail store (Eroglu, Machleit, and Davis 2001). "In the online shopping context, the entire store environment is all but reduced to a computer screen. The traditional store designer's ability to appeal to all senses of the shopper through an infinitely complex combination of ambient, structural, social, and aesthetic elements has now been constrained to a predominantly visual appeal via a screen" (Eroglu et al. 2001, 179).

E-tailers face the problem of understanding a person's mood while that person is shopping online. When retailers are able to sense a customer's mood during shopping, they are better able to develop trust, determine the best way to offer personalized service, and build customer loyalty (Barlow, Siddiqui, and Mannion 2004).

Tactile cues are important considerations in many consumer purchases, but they are not viable stimuli in online shopping environments. Citrin, Stem, Spangenberg, and Clark (2003) examined the need for tactile input on the likelihood of purchasing products using the Internet. They found that loss of tactile input negatively impacted the purchase of products, especially for those consumers who required more tactile cues when evaluating prod-

ucts. This situation was particularly evident for female consumers who demonstrated a higher need for tactile input when compared with male consumers. A. V. Citrin et al. suggested that for products that are highly experiential, retailers need to offer product trials or retain some form of brick-and-mortar presence to capture those consumers who require multisensory inputs when evaluating products. They also suggested "the challenge for Internet retailers of experiential products is to shift consumer's focus from certain experiential cues (such as tactility) to more shopping cues (such as product reliability)" (920). Research in tactility is moving technology toward the creation of commercially viable sensing controls of touch and gesture through three-dimensional imagery (Salisbury 1999). "Thus, technology may provide the means to bridge the gap that is created in reaching out and virtually *touching* the consumer, thereby promoting successful retailing to consumers via the Internet" (Citrin et al. 2003, 921).

CHAPTER SUMMARY

Sensory consumption is being driven by conspicuous consumption and the desire for scarce things. Environmental stimuli such as lighting, color, music, ambient noise, odor, temperature, touch, and crowding create sensory stimulation.

Sensory involvement is an integral part of how consumers experience everything and it is triggered by the modalities of sight, sound, scent, touch, and taste. These sensory channels create emotional reactions through consumers' feelings about their interactions with goods, services, and the environment in which they are experienced. Sensory involvement directs how consumers move through a physical space such as a store, and select and use products.

Multisensory experiences combine sight, smell, sound, touch, and taste stimuli to promote consumer involvement in the environment. When multisensory experiences occur with branded products, they can build strong brand-consumer relationships. Intense product experiences promote differentiation among branded products and create opportunities for intense customer relationships that translate into brand loyalty.

Touchpoints refer to how consumers interact with a brand, communicate information, generate sensory consumption, create emotional associations, and reinforce beliefs about a brand. Consumer-brand relationships are represented by different touchpoints in the consumer's pre-purchase, purchase, and post-purchase experiences.

Atmospherics include controlled physical and nonphysical environmental attributes that can enhance or restrain customer and employee behaviors. Both emotions and behaviors are stimulated through the physical environment. Atmospheric cues can be categorized as exterior, general interior, layout and design, point-of-purchase and decoration, and human variables. Atmospheric design is an important consideration of a retail strategic plan.

Consumer approach–avoidance behavior and pleasantness and arousal during shopping are linked to store atmospherics. The Stimulus-Organism-Response (S-O-R) approach describes how individuals react to environments. Retailers can target customers and draw them into their stores through approach behavior so that consumers want to stay, browse, and purchase. Furthermore, retailers can create delayed behavioral responses where consumers come back and purchase again because they enjoyed the store during a previous experience. Retailers can also create an unwelcoming environment that consumers avoid. The intervention between environmental stimuli and approach–avoidance behavior is linked to three states of emotion: pleasure, arousal, and dominance (i.e., PAD). How these emotional states are combined determines whether a consumer approaches or avoids a retail store.

Consumer involvement with the physical environment can be linked to the ancient practice of feng shui, which seeks balance between the five elements that flow through life, yin and yang, and chi. In interior environments, feng shui becomes a system for arranging physical space so it is in harmony and balance with nature.

Consumer attitudes are the result of a three-part experience that includes cognition (awareness and thought), affect (emotion and feeling), and conation (actions and behaviors). Attitudes influence how consumers approach, process, evaluate, and remember experiences, and they encompass the motivational, emotional, perceptual, and cognitive processes that occur in a specific environment or situation. Cognition is associated with the functional elements associated with consumer attitudes toward the benefits offered by goods and services when solving problems. Cognitive attitudes measure utilitarian or instrumental attributes (i.e., functional). Affective elements are produced through the evaluation of an object. They reflect an emotional benefit to consumers and are expressed as feelings or emotional reactions. Affective attitudes measure elements associated with hedonic consumption.

Sensory channels of sight, sound, scent, and touch are associated with atmospheres. The sense of sight includes the visual dimensions of color, brightness, size, and shapes. The sense of sound takes in aural dimensions of volume and pitch. These aural stimuli have physiological, psychological, cognitive, and behavioral effects on consumers with sound linked to perceptions of time. The sensory channel of scent includes olfactory dimensions of scent and freshness. Aromas and odors are olfactory stimuli that create powerful memory cues. They function better for generating emotion than for remembering facts.

The sense of touch takes in tactile dimensions of softness, smoothness, and temperature. Tactile stimuli have both functional and emotional dimensions. A new frontier in tactile stimulation is pain.

While an atmosphere can be seen, heard, smelled, and felt, it cannot be tasted. The fifth sense—taste—has four dimensions associated with distinct receptors on the tongue: sweet, sour, salt, and bitter. The sense of taste is experienced primarily through foods, beverages, personal care products, and some cosmetics, by association with fruits and flavorings like vanilla. Standardized food production has homogenized food tastes and reduced the sensory pleasure associated with taste. It is possible to incorporate all five senses in a multisensory consumption experience.

The Internet poses a challenge to retailers since it does not allow for consumer experiences with the sensory channels of scent, touch, and taste. The limitation of sensory experiences to sight and sound is a significant deterrent to online purchases, especially for person-to-person communication and product involvement through smell, touch, and taste.

Discussion Questions

1. Although online retail sites have limited sensory involvement, what sites have been successful in retaining your interests? What sensory channels do these sites activate and how?
2. Discount warehouse chains such as Sam's Club and Costco do not provide a sensory-stimulating environment; however, they are successful in tapping into other consumer needs. What are these needs? Explain how they are met.
3. Choose one of the following themed restaurant chains and discuss its sensory appeal: Cracker Barrel Old Country Store, Rainforest Cafe, Hard Rock Cafe, or Planet Hollywood.
4. Discuss the advantages and disadvantages of self-service checkout lanes, and include the level of cognitive motivation and situational involvement necessary to make it successful.
5. What brands have successfully triggered your interests through the use of distinctive emotional wording? Explain.
6. Have you experienced a transition in attitude toward a particular color, as you have gotten older? Explain this transition and its causes.
7. How are organic foods marketed to support the perception of having a better taste than nonorganic foods?
8. Explain the product composition of baby foods in terms of differing taste stimuli of age groups.

REFERENCES

Alba, J. W., and J. W. Hutchinson. 1987. Dimensions of consumer expertise. *Journal of Consumer Research* 13:411–454.

Allen, P. 2000. Has the Web come to its senses yet? *Brandweek* 41(36): 32–33.

Ajzen, I., and M. Fishbein. 1980. *Attitudes and predicting social behavior.* Englewood Cliffs, NJ: Prentice-Hall.

Andrade, J., and P. Meudell. 1993. Is spatial information encoded automatically in memory? *The Quarterly Journal of Experimental Psychology* 46A:365–375.

Averill, J. R. 1998. What are emotions, really? A review of "Ideas and realities of emotion" by B. Parkinson. *Cognition and Emotion* 12:849–855.

Bainbridge, J. 1998. Scenting opportunities. *Marketing* 36–37.

Barlow, A. K. F., N. Q. Siddiqui, and M. Mannion. 2004. Developments in information and communication technologies for retail marketing channels. *International Journal of Retail and Distribution Management* 32(3):157–163.

Belk, R. W. 1975. Situational variables and consumer behavior. *Journal of Consumer Research* 2(3):157–165.

Bloch, P. H., N. M. Ridgway, and A. Dawson. 1994. The shopping mall as consumer habitat. *Journal of Retailing* 70:23–42.

Body Shop, L'Oreal plot food range. 2006. *Marketing Week*. March 23, 3.

Brucks, M. 1986. A typology of consumer knowledge content. In R. J. Lutz, ed., *Advances in Consumer Research* 13:58–63.

Cacioppo, J. T., R. E. Petty, C. F. Kao, and R. Rodriguez. 1986. Central and peripheral routes to persusasion: An individual difference perspective. *Journal of Personality and Social Psychology* 51:1032–1043.

Celsi, R. L., and J. C. Olson. 1988. The role of involvement in attention and comprehension processes. *Journal of Consumer Research* 15(2):210–224.

Centaur Media. 2005. Retail focus: Sensual selling. *In-Store Magazine* 33.

Citrin, A. V., D. E. Stem, E. R. Spangenberg, and M. J. Clark. 2003. Consumer need for tactile input an internet retailing challenge. *Journal of Business Research* 56:915–922.

Coloma, D., and B. H. Kleiner. 2005. How can music be used in business? *Management Research News* 28(11/12):115–120.

Consedine, N. S., K. T. Strongman, and C. Magai. 2003. Emotions and behaviour: Data from a cross-cultural recognition study. *Cognition and Emotion* 17:881–902.

Cowan, N. 1988. Evolving conceptions of memory storage, selective attention, and their mutual constraints within the human information-processing system. *Psychological Bulletin* 104(2):163–191.

D'Argembeau, A., and M. van der Linden. 2004. Influence of affective meaning on memory for contextual information. *Emotion* 4(2):173–188.

Davis, R. G. 1981. The role of nonolfactory context cues in odor identification. *Perception and Psychophysics* 30(1):83–89.

Davis, S. 2002. Great brand building is just a touch away. *Brandweek* 43(24):16,20.

Dewhurst, S. A., and L. A. Parry. 2000. Emotionality, distinctiveness, and recollective experience. *European Journal of Cognitive Psychology* 12:541–551.

Doerksen, S., and A. P. Simamura. 2001. Source memory enhancement for emotional words. *Emotion* 1:5–11.

Donovan, R. J., and J. R. Rossiter. 1982. Store atmosphere: An environmental psychology approach. *Journal of Retailing* 58(Spring):34–57.

Donovan, R. J., J. R. Rossiter, G. Marcoolyn, and A. Nesdale. 1994. Store atmosphere and purchasing behavior. *Journal of Retailing* 70(3):283–294.

Eckhardt, G. M., and M. J. Houston. 2002. Cultural paradoxes reflected in brand meaning: McDonalds in Shanghai, China. *Journal of International Marketing* 10(2):68–82.

Ellen, P. S., and P. F. Bone. 1998. Does it matter if it smells? Olfactory stimuli as advertising executional cues. *Journal of Advertising* 274:29–39.

Eroglu, S. A., and K. A. Machleit. 1993. Atmospheric factors in the retail environment: Sights, sounds and smells. *Advances in Consumer Research* 20:34.

Eroglu, S. A., K. A. Machleit, and J-C. Chebat. 2005. The interaction of retail density and music tempo: Effects on shopper responses. *Psychology and Marketing* 22(7):577–589.

Eroglu, S. A., K. A. Machleit, and L. M. Davis. 2001. Atmospheric qualities of online retailing: A conceptual model and implications. *Journal of Business Research* 54:177–184.

Faraday gets all touchy feely. 2003. *Packaging Magazine*. January 9, 18.

Finkelstein, J. 2003. The taste of boredom. *American Behavioral Scientist* 47(2):187–200.

Fishbein, M. A., and I. Azjen. 1975. *Belief, attitude, intention and behavior: An introduction to theory and research*. Reading, MA: Addiso-Wesley.

Fraisse, P. 1984. Perception and estimation of time. *Annual Review of Psychology* 35:1–36.

Frijda, N. H. 1988. The laws of emotion. *American Psychologist* 43(5):349–358.

———. 1992. The empirical status of the laws of emotion. *Cognition and Emotion* 6:467–477.

Frijda, N. H., and B. Mesquite. 1994. The social roles and functions of emotions. In S. Kitayama and H. Marcus, eds. *Emotion and Culture: Empirical Studies of Mutual Influence*. Washington, DC: American Psychological Association.

Gardiner, J. M., C. Ramponi, and A. Richardson-Klavehn. 1998. Experiences of remembering, knowing, and guessing. *Consciousness and Cognition* 7:1–16.

Gerdes, S. 2006. Dairy DETECTIVE: What's new in cheese for the children's market. *Dairy Foods* 107(3):58.

Godden, D., and A. Baddeley. 1980. When does context influence recognition memory? *British Journal of Psychology* 71:99–104.

Goldman, D. 2000. Pain? It's a pleasure. *American Demographics*. January, 60–61.

Greenwald, A. S., and C. Levitt. 1984. Audience involvement in advertising: Four levels. *Journal of Consumer Research* 11(June):581–592.

Guinard, J-X. 2002. A kid's perception. *Prepared Foods*. September, 28–30.

Gulas, C. S., and P. H. Bloch. 1995. Right under our noses: Ambient scent and consumer responses. *Journal of Business Psychology* 10(1):87–98.

Haeckel, S. H., L. P. Carbone, and L. Berry. 2003. How to lead the customer experience. *Marketing Management* 18–23.

Harris, N. 2003. Reassessing the dimensionality of the moral emotions. *British Journal of Psychology* 94:457–473.

Harrison, J. 2006. Mission-oriented firms change hands. *Mergers and Acquisitions* 41(5):30.

Hartman, C. L., and C. L. Beck-Dudley. 1999. Marketing strategies and the search for virtue: A case analysis of The Body Shop, International. *Journal of Business Ethics* 20(3):249–263.

Hasher, L., and R. T. Zacks. 1979. Automatic and effortful processes in memory. *Journal of Experimental Psychology: General* 108:356–388.

Hawkins, D. I., R. J. Best, and K. A. Coney. 2003. *Consumer Behavior: Building Marketing Strategy*, 9th ed. Boston, MA: BPI/Irwin.

Heinz kicks off bold, new ketchup packaging . . . and adds a ketchup mystery bottle for kids. 2002. *Packaging Digest* 39(4):4.

Hobson, J. S. P. 1994. *Feng Shui:* Its impacts on the Asian Hospitality Industry. *International Journal of Contemporary Hospitality Management* 6(6):21–26.

Holbrook, M. B., and E. C. Hirschman. 1982. The experiential aspects of consumption: Consumer fantasies, feelings and fun. *Journal of Consumer Research* 9(September):132–140.

Holloway, M. 1999. The ascent of scent. *Scientific American* 281(5):42–43.

Howell, D. 2001. Colored ketchup? Who would've anticipated it? *DSN Retailing Today* 40(16):29.

Howell, D. 2003. Wacky colors, unconventional flavors appeal to the savvy younger set. *DSN Retailing Today* 42(10):42. Retrieved July 1, 2006 from http://www.calmia.com

Izard, C. E. 1977. *Human emotion.* New York: Plenum Press.

John, D. R., and J. C. Whitney Jr. 1986. The development of consumer knowledge in children: A cognitive structure approach. *Journal of Consumer Research* 12:406–417.

Johnson, M. K., S. Hashtroudi, and D. S. Lindsay. 1993. Source monitoring. *Psychological Bulletin* 114:2–28.

Jones, G. V. 1983. Identifying basic categories. *Psychological Bulletin* 94(November):423–428.

Kaernbach, C. 2004. The memory of noise. *Experimental Psychology* 51(4):240–248.

Kaufman-Scarborough, C. 2000. Seeing through the eyes of the color-deficient shopper: Consumer issues for public policy. *Journal of Consumer Policy* 23(4):461–492.

Kilgore, W. D., and D. A. Yugelun-Todd. 2005. Developmental changes in the functional brain responses of adolescents to images of high and low calorie foods. *Developmental Psychology* 47(4):377–397.

Korolishin, J. 2004. Converting browsers to buyers with in-store music. *Stores* 86(1):28.

Kotler, P. 1973–1974. Atmospherics as a marketing tool. *Journal of Retailing* 49(4):48–64.

Kuhn, K. 2005. Consumers like the taste of organic food. *Caterer and Hotelkeeper* 195(4390):10.

LeTourneau, M. 2000. Smell no evil. *Psychology Today* 33(5):24.

Light, L. L., and D. E. Berger. 1974. Memory for modality: Within-modality discrimination is not automatic. *Journal of Experimental Psychology* 103:854–860.

Lin, C-H., H. R. Yen, and S-C. Chuang. 2006. The effects of emotion and need for cognition on consumer choice involving risk. *Marketing Letters* 17:47–60.

Lindstrom, M. 2005a. Don't follow Coke's neglect of sensory branding. *Media.* March 25, 20.

———. 2005b. Follow your nose to marketing evolution. *Advertising Age.* May 23, 136.

Malhotra, N. K. 1991. Mnemonics in marketing: A pedagogical tool. *Journal of Academy Marketing Science* 19:141–149.

Mandler, J. M. 1979. Categorical and schematic organization in memory. In Puff, C. R., ed. *Memory Organization and Structure* (259–299). New York: Academic Press.

McGoldrick, P. J., and C. P. Pieros. 1998. Atmospherics, pleasure and arousal: The influence of response moderators. *Journal of Marketing Management* 14:173–197.

Mehrabian, A. and J. A. Russell. 1974. The basic emotional impact of environments. *Perceptual and Motor Skills* 38:283–252.

Merrick, A. 2005. Inside out: For Limited Brands, clothes become the accessories; specialty retailer stresses lingerie, beauty products; seeing P&G as role model; Victoria's Secret Hair Care. *Wall Street Journal*, Eastern edition. March 8, A1.

Mesquite, B. and N. H. Frijda. 1992. Cultural variations in emotions: A review. *Psychological Bulletin* 112:179–204.

Mingfang L. and Z. Haiwei. 2005. Knowing the business environment: The use of non-market-based strategies in Chinese local firms. *Ivey Business Journal Online, Nov/Dec.* 1.

Neidenthal, P. M., J. P. Tangney, and I. Gavanski. 1994. "If only I weren't" versus "If only I hadn't": Distinguishing shame and guilt in counterfactual thinking. *Journal of Personality and Social Psychology* 67(4):585–595.

Ng, C. F. 2003. Satisfying shoppers' psychological needs: From public market to cyber mall. *Journal of Environmental Psychology* 23(4):427–437.

Ochsner, K. N. 2000. Are affective events richly recollected or simply familiar? The experience and process of recognizing feelings past. *Journal of Experimental Psychology: General* 129:242–261.

Ornstein, R. E. 1969. *On the Experience of Time*. New York: Penguin.

Paul, P. 2002. Color by numbers. *American Demographics* 24(2):30–35.

Peltier, J. W., and J. A. Schibrowsky. 1994. Need for cognition, advertisement viewing time and memory for advertising stimuli. *Advances in Consumer Research* 21:244–250.

Perfect, T. J., A. R. Mayes, J. J. Downes, and R. Van Eijk. 1996. Does context discriminate recollection from familiarity in recognition memory? *The Quarterly Journal of Experiential Psychology* 49A:797–813.

Pham, M. T., J. B. Cohen, J. W. Pracejus, and E. D. Hughes, 2001. Affect monitoring and the primacy of feelings in judgment. *Journal of Consumer Research* 28:167–188.

Pope, K. 1995. Technology improves on the nose as scientists try to mimic smell. *Wall Street Journal*. March 1, B1.

Prior, M. 2002. Aromatherapy-enhanced toys help enliven early learning. *DSN Retailing Today*. March 11, 13.

Rajaram, S. 1998. The effects of conceptual salience and perceptual distinctiveness on conscious recollection. *Psychonomic Bulletin and Review* 5:71–78.

Rasmusson, E. 1998. Designing your success. *Sales and Marketing Management* 150(12):112–113.

Reyes, S. 2001a. Heinz picks purple as new E-Z squirt color. *Brandweek.* October 15, 7.

Reyes, S. 2001b. Unleashing the big red rocket. *Brandweek* 42(38):M6.

Richards, M. 2005. The brain's growing pain. *Brand Strategy*. June, 50–51.

Ritzer, G. 1998. *The MacDonalization thesis*. London: Sage.

Salisbury, J. K. 1999. Making graphics physically tangible. *Communication ACM* 42(8):75–80.

Schab, F. R. 1991. Odor memory: Taking stock. *Psychological Bulletin* 109(2):242–251.

Scruggs, T. E., and F. J. Brigham. 1991. Utility of musical mnemonics. *Perceptual and Motor Skills* 72:881–882.

Sherman, E., A. Mathur, and R. B. Smith. 1997. Store environment and consumer purchase behavior: Mediating role of consumer emotions. *Psychology and Marketing* 14(4): 361–378.

Spangenberg, E. R., A. E. Crowley, and P. W. Henderson. 1996. Improving the store environment: Do olfactory cues affect evaluations and behaviors? *Journal of Marketing* 60:67–80.

Stracher, C. 2005. Taste: Getting away from it all. *Wall Street Journal*, Eastern edition. March 4, W13.

Strugnell, C., and L. Jones. 1999. Customer perceptions and opinions of fragrances in household products. *Nutrition and Food Science* 99:21–24.

Torrisi, A. I. 2006. Places and spaces. *Successful Meetings* 55(6):89–91.

Turley, L. W., and J-C. Chebat. 2002. Linking retail strategy, atmospheric design and shopping behaviour. *Journal of Marketing Management* 18:125–144.

Turley, L. W., and R. E. Milliman. 2000. Atmospheric effects on shopping behavior: A review of the experimental evidence. *Journal of Business Research* 49(2):193–211.

Tversky, B., and K. Hemenway. 1984. Objects, parts, and categories. *Journal of Experimental Psychology, General* 113(June):169–193.

Underhill, P. 1999. *Why we buy: The science of shopping*. New York: Simon and Schuster.

Ward, P., B. J. Davies, and D. Kooijman. 2003. Ambient smell and the retail environment: Relating olfaction research to consumer behavior. *Journal of Business and Management* 9(3):289–302.

Weiner, B., D. Russel, and D. Lerman. 1979. The cognition-emotion process in achievement-related contexts. *Journal of Personality and Social Psychology* 37(July):1211–1120.

Westbrook, R. A. 1987. Product/consumption-based affective responses and postpurchase processes. *Journal of Marketing Research* 25:258–270.

Wilkinson, A. 2005. Neuromarketing: brain scam or valuable tool? *Marketing Week* 22.

Whong, V. L. 2005. Feng-Shui: Chinese good luck using it for the clear road to success. *Asian Pages*. Retrieved August 29, 2006 from http://www.highbeam.com/Doc.aspx?DocId=1P1:115605617&tab=LIB

Yalch, R. F. 1991. Memory in a jingle: Music as a mnemonic device in communicating advertising slogans. *Journal of Applied Psychology* 76: 268–275.

Yalch, R. F., and E. R. Spangenberg. 2000. The effects of music in a retail setting on real and perceived shopping times. *Journal of Business Research* 49:139–147.

Zajonc, R. B. 1980. Feeling and thinking: Preferences need no inferences. *American Psychologist* 35(February): 151–175.

CONSUMER EFFICIENCY

Will that be cash, credit, or finger?

In need of toothpaste and ice, Laura Wadsworth dashed into a supermarket . . . in Mount Pleasant, South Carolina. She didn't bring her wallet. Wadsworth paid by touching her index finger to a scanner. Ten seconds later, she was out the door. A week before, Denise Day, a self-described "gas-station junkie," grabbed a vanilla cappuccino and gum at a 7-Eleven in Denver. She paid in seconds by waving her Chase Blink contactless card in front of a reader, which lit up and beeped to tell her the transaction was done. "It's definitely saved me a bit of time," Day says. "I think it's pretty cool."

These new technologies, being rolled out at convenience stores, supermarkets, and gas stations, could some day make it passé to carry bulky wallets. Without the need to dig for cash and checks at the register, the quick stop-and-go payments promise speedier transactions for consumers—and perhaps fatter profits for retailers. They're yet another step in society's evolution from paper to electronic payments. In 2003, electronic payments such as credit and debit cards overtook cash and checks as the most common way to pay for purchases, the American Bankers Association reported. The appeal is that there's no need to run them through a machine. And no signing for purchases less than $25. By the end of 2006, banks will issue 25 million contactless debit and credit cards, according to the Nilson Report, which tracks the card industry. That's one for about every nine adults in the USA.

The pay-by-finger system is already being used in hundreds of U.S. supermarkets, including Albertsons and Piggly Wiggly. It relies on fingerprinting, a biometrics technology that identifies people by physical traits. Your finger is scanned and linked to your payment information. At the register, you touch your finger to the reader, enter your phone number, and select bank account or credit card. No cash or checks or credit cards to carry. Ann Edwards of Coon Rapids, Minn., was one of the first to sign up for the pay-by-finger method at a Cub Foods supermarket last spring. Now, she uses it about once a week, because she thinks it's "safe, easy, and convenient." "A lot of it is how you were approached about it," Edwards says. "They were very positive about it, so I felt like I could get on their bandwagon, too."

Pay By Touch, a provider of the finger-touch technology, says it's signed up hundreds of stores in large grocery chains. It doesn't disclose customer enrollment rates. But at a typical Piggly Wiggly, an average of 30 to 40 percent of customers enroll, and they tend to shop more often and spend more each time, says Rita Postell of Piggly Wiggly Carolina Co., which has put the technology in all 83 company-owned stores. A competitor, BioPay, has signed up 2.1 million consumers at 1,600 retail locations for its pay-by-finger technology and paycheck-cashing services combined. Pay-by-finger transactions are twice as fast as a cash

CHAPTER 7

payment, three times as fast as a credit card, and four times as fast as a check, BioPay estimates. Convenience comes at a price, though. If your credit card or Social Security number is stolen, you can replace it. Not so with your fingerprint.

Source: Chu, Kathy. 2005. Will that be cash, credit, or finger? *USA Today*. Retrieved August 31, 2006, from www.usatoday.com/tech/news/techinnovations/2005-12-01-cash-credit-finger_x.htm.

INTRODUCTION

With ever-increasing demands on their time and energy, consumers continuously look for ways to manage their schedules more efficiently. Consumers are choosing retailers based upon who can most satisfactorily provide the goods and services needed with the greatest ease and convenience. It is important for consumers to not only get good quality goods for low prices, but also to have some additional value for the time and energy they invest in the consumption experience. The **biometric technology** used at Piggy Wiggly stores is continuing to gain acceptance among retailers and consumers (See Figure 7.1). Some retailers have described biometric payment systems as the wave of the future. An official with BioPay, a biometric services provider that is owned by Pay By Touch, said BioPay was first used as a payment option in 2003 and more than 2,000 retailers, grocery stores, and restaurants now use it. The company has more than 2 million consumers signed up to use the biometric payment option (*Community Banker* 2005). U-Scan is another technology used at many grocery stores that provides a self-service checkout option where consumers scan their own items and pay without having to come in contact with store employees. The main function of these new technologies—biometric and U-Scan payment options—is to reduce costs for retailers and to save time for consumers.

Several changes in the current U.S. consumer market have significantly altered consumers' expectations and demands during their shopping experiences. These changes include the expanding number of dual-income, single, and single-parent households; the aging of consumer population; an ever-growing modern-day concern over time poverty; and the evolution of technology. Consumers are increasingly demanding time savings as well as pleasure from their shopping experiences. They tend to shop with more knowledge and awareness of their product and service options, but also with less time and often less money. This trend can be observed in the continuing decline in shopping frequency and higher average transaction size per shopping trip. For example, the average U. S. consumer made 69 trips to the grocery store in 2004, down from 92 in 1995 (Wellman 2005).

7.1 Biometric devices like this one save time because money is automatically deducted from the consumer's account. This payment method is faster than credit cards or cash.

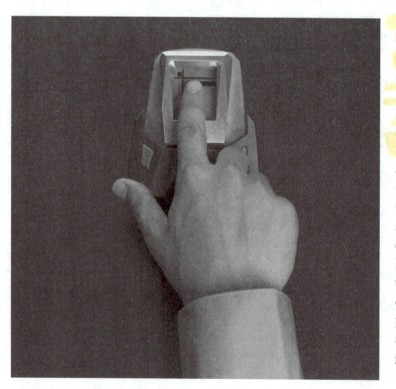

Today's consumers are considered efficient shoppers because they select retailers they perceive provide shopping environments where shopping can be done most easily and satisfactorily. To many consumers, shopping satisfaction comes not only from quality and price but also, and oftentimes more important, a return on the investment of the time, effort, and money they spend on their shopping experiences (Kim and Kang 1997; Mathwick, Malhotra, and Rigdon 2002). More specifically, consumers spend their money, time, and energy trying to maximize the satisfaction they receive from their shopping experiences.

THE CONCEPT OF CONSUMER EFFICIENCY

The general concept of **consumer efficiency** is deeply rooted in the discipline of economics, with emphasis placed on the principle of maximizing efficiency or obtaining the greatest useful output for a particular level of input (Sproles 1980). From a consumer's point of view, consumer efficiency refers to the degree to which a consumer obtains the greatest possible utility or satisfaction from a consumption activity, given a fixed set of resources allocated to that activity (Sproles 1980). A. Downs (1961) elaborated upon the notion that consumers seek to minimize the costs of shopping (e.g., money, time, and energy) relative to the benefits or outputs (e.g., goods, information, and pleasure) they expect to receive from their shopping activities. Therefore, the quality of the shopping experience depends on the way in which consumers are able to trade off time, money, and energy to increase efficiency. In a similar concept, L. P. Bucklin (1966) labeled the consumer as a "profit-maximizing entity" (22).

Consumer efficiency is linked to consumer value, which is derived from summing up the various perceived benefits and costs, and taking into account differently weighted factors. In the marketing literature, the concept of value is generally discussed in the context of exchange or a return for something (Kotler 1999, Richins 1994). P. Kotler's 1972 pioneering work on broadening the concept of marketing regards the process of exchange as an essential part of marketing activity: "The core concept of marketing is the transaction. A transaction is the exchange of values between two parties. The things-of-value need not be limited to goods, services, and money; they include other resources such as time, energy, and feelings" (Kotler 1972, 48).

V. A. Zeithaml (1988) describes four distinct definitions for value: "low price, whatever I want in a product, the quality I get for the price I pay, [and] what I get for what I give" (13). The last two definitions of value can be conceived as a trade-off between the two components of shopping efficiency: what is received (i.e., get or benefit) and what is given (i.e., give or cost). The notion of a trade-off between benefits received and costs incurred is associated with various components. These trade-offs lead to interchangeable concepts of consumer efficiency. John F. Gaski (1986) identified interchangeable terms of benefits versus costs: output versus input; satisfaction versus expenditure; utility versus total spending; and return versus investment.

An increasing number of consumers buys larger commodity purchases of products from warehouse stores or discount clubs such as Sam's Club or Costco. Warehouse stores offer discounted items from product categories such as household goods, apparel, food, and more. The ability to buy larger quantities saves the consumer time, which would otherwise be spent shopping in a traditional store format on more frequent occasions. Also, the unit cost per item in large quantities can be lower than the cost of items in smaller packages that are purchased on weekly trips to the grocery store. This enables consumers to improve efficiency by getting more (larger quantities of products) from what is given (lower prices and less time spent shopping).

TRANSITION OF CONSUMER EFFICIENCY

Traditionally, the concept of consumer efficiency is discussed in the context of product consumption. The product focus is now extended to service consumption. This product-focused and service-focused consumer efficiency has evolved to include a holistic perspective of the consumption activity.

Product Consumption

In a simple way, benefits were historically characterized as the basic reason consumers used products (Haley 1968). From a broader perspective, the general notion of consumption was viewed as a process in which its benefits were derived from a product acquisition experience (Hirschman and Holbrook 1982). Products were viewed as objects for which the consumer

desired to maximize utility, and the utility typically was measured as some function of the product's tangible attributes such as price, quality, durability, and taste, compared with costs expended (Carsky, Dickinson, and Smith 1995; Hirschman and Holbrook 1982). Typically, a consumer purchase involves an amount of money exchanged for a product. For the exchange to occur, consumers must value the product more than they value the money. When consumers attach a greater value to the object of purchase than is represented by the price, or the amount of money that must be given up during the whole process of getting it, then they will make the exchange.

Focusing on the benefits that may be derived from product use, J. N. Sheth, B. I. Newman, and B. L. Gross (1991) categorized five consumption values: functional, social, emotional, epistemic, and conditional (See Table 7.1). However, consumption involves a constellation of goods and desirable benefits. If consumers are engaged in a constructive process by which they obtain desirable benefits, a variety of holistic benefits are involved as consumers use the products (Lai 1995). To this end, A. W. Lai (1995) proposed a typology of product benefits that a consumer may

TABLE 7.1 CONSUMPTION VALUES

VALUE	THE PERCEIVED UTILITY IS ACQUIRED FROM . . .
Functional	a product's capacity for functional, utilitarian, or physical performance
Social	a product's association with one or more specific social groups (i.e., positively or negatively stereotyped demographic, socioeconomic, and cultural-ethnic groups)
Emotional	a product's capacity to arouse feelings or affective states
Epistemic	a product's capacity to arouse curiosity, provide novelty, and/or satisfy a desire for knowledge
Conditional	a product as the result of the specific situation or set of physical or social circumstances facing the choice maker

Source: Sheth, J. N., B. I. Newman, B. L. Gross. 1991. When we buy what we buy: A theory of consumption values. *Journal of Business Research* 22:159–170.

TABLE 7.2 TYPOLOGY OF PRODUCT CONSUMPTION BENEFITS

TYPOLOGY	DEFINITION
Functional benefits	The benefit acquired from a product's capacity for functional, utilitarian, or physical performance. Functional benefits are derived from the tangible and concrete attributes that a consumer may directly experience when using or consuming the product.
Social benefits	The perceptual benefit acquired from a product's association with social class, social status, or a specific social group. Highly visible products (e.g., clothing, jewelry, and automobiles) often carry social benefits.
Affective benefits	The perceptual benefit acquired from a product's capacity to arouse feelings or affective states. Affective benefits are often associated with cultural-ethnic meanings (e.g., Christmas trees, Thanksgiving turkeys) or personal, idiosyncratic meanings, tastes and memories (e.g., foods that arouse feelings of comfort through their association with childhood experiences, or cars with which consumers are said to have love affairs).
Epistemic benefits	The benefit acquired from a product's capacity to satisfy curiosity, provide novelty, and/or meet a desire for knowledge. Exploratory, novelty-seeking, and variety seeking consumption behaviors and a consumer's propensity to adopt new products are examples of epistemic value pursuit.
Aesthetic benefits	The benefit acquired from a product's capacity to present a sense of beauty or to enhance personal expression. Aesthetic benefit usually is subjective and idiosyncratic. Style demands, product-appearance demands, art purchases, and fashion-following are examples of consumers' pursuing aesthetic benefits.
Hedonic benefits	The benefit acquired from a product's capacity to meet a need of enjoyment, fun, pleasure, or distraction from work or anxiety. In addition to looking for rational or "serious" benefits, consumers may want to relax or be distracted. Taking a vacation trip; going to bars; watching sports, movies, or TV programs; or even buying funny trinkets to make fun of friends are some examples.
Situational benefits	The benefit acquired from a product's capacity to meet situational needs in specific circumstances. A product acquires situational value in the presence of antecedent physical or social contingencies that enhance its functional, social, or other benefits. Situational benefit is measured on the profile of a particular consumption situation.
Holistic benefits	The perceptual benefit acquired from the complementarity, coherence, compatibility, and consistency in a product constellation as a whole. Holistic benefits are frequently required and perceived in clothes, furniture, and food consumption. Holistic product benefit is a result of synergy derived from a product combination.

Source: Lai, A. W. 1995. Consumer values, product benefits, and customer value: A consumption behavior approach. In F. R. Kardes and M. Sujan, eds. *Advances in Consumer Research*, Vol. 22 (381–388). Provo, UT: Association for Consumer Research.

derive from possession or consumption, going beyond Sheth et al.'s original categorization of product benefits. The typology includes eight generic product benefits: functional, social, affective, epistemic, aesthetic, hedonic, situational, and holistic. The definitions of these terms are discussed in Table 7.2.

Understanding the possible benefits that consumers seek in products can become the fundamental basis for product differentiation or positioning. For instance, to meet the need of consumers seeking the convenience benefit, marketers are inventing time- and effort-saving products. These include delivered pizzas, TV dinners, household cleaning supplies, computer flash drives, and cell phones with Internet and streaming media capabilities.

NECESSITIES VS. INDULGENCES

Just as consumers make a trade-off between benefits and costs of products, they often also make a fundamental trade-off between necessities and indulgences. According to Webster's New World International Dictionary, necessities can be defined as "items that cannot be done without; things that must be had for the preservation and reasonable enjoyment of life." Conversely, indulgence (or items perceived as indulgent) represents "pampering oneself; yielding to the wishes, gratification, or desires of oneself (or another), because of a weak will or an amiable nature." Further, C. J. Berry (1994) characterized necessities as utilitarian objects that relieve an unpleasant state of discomfort, and characterized luxuries as objects of desire that provide pleasure. When consumers spend money, they trade off between what they perceive as necessities (e.g., savings, ordinary food, medical care) and what they perceive as indulgences (e.g., a cruise, gourmet food, an expensive watch).

As such, indulgent products are closely related to hedonic benefits, often involving spending money on items perceived as luxuries relative to one's means (Kivetz and Simonson 2002). In Western society, luxuries and indulgence items are increasingly emphasized by marketers because today's consumers have met their necessities for material needs to a large extent (Mathwick et al. 2002, Sweeney and Soutar 2001).

The consumer efficiency that involves different goals can be observed in the example of eating at a prestigious restaurant versus at a fast food restaurant. On the one hand, there is a utilitarian purpose for food consumption at a fast-food restaurant since the task of eating can be fulfilled in an efficient manner. On the other hand, luxury dining, as in an evening spent at a fancy restaurant, is considered a more hedonic example of indulging.

Consumers can be indulged at P.F. Chang's China Bistro (Figure 7.2).

SHOPPING GOODS, CONVENIENCE GOODS, AND SPECIALTY GOODS

L. P. Bucklin (1962, 50) broadly classifies consumer goods into three categories as follows: *Shopping goods* are consumer goods that customers compare on bases such as suitability, quality, price, and style in the process of selection and purchase. Examples include clothing, shoes, accessories, housewares, small appliances, gifts, sporting goods, small electronics, and home furnishings. *Convenience goods* are the products for which consumers tend to purchase the most accessible items with minimal effort. Examples include groceries and paper products. *Specialty goods* are products for which consumers have a particular attraction and thus are willing to make a special effort. Consumers already know the nature of the merchandise and are thus willing to bypass more readily accessible substitutes to purchase the desired item. Examples include handcrafts and antiques.

Consumers weigh the benefits and costs differently for these three types of goods. For instance, consumers may have a strong determination to reduce costs for convenience goods but a strong willingness to expand shopping costs for specialty goods. In addition, these three categories of products differ in the shopping effort required. For a visual representation, goods can be placed along a continuum with convenience goods at the lowest level of effort and risk and specialty goods at the highest level of effort and risk (Murphy and Enis 1986).

Service Consumption

Service consumption is tied to the act of exchange with the value of the consumption experiences derived from the interaction consumers have with service environments.

7.2 For some, a meal at P. F. Chang's is considered a hedonic indulgence, instead of a basic necessity.

This transition from a product focus to a service focus reflects societal trends such as the participation of women and mothers in the labor force and technological advances that create more communications, information, and entertainment options. Both of these trends have placed added pressure on consumers' time and effort resources. Service consumption efficiency has become more of a function of saving consumers' time and effort than saving them money in buying or using services (Berry, Seiders, and Grewal 2002). The emerging trends of convenient service consumption are reflected in the popularity of wireless phones, computer technology, online bill payment, and delivery services such as FedEx or UPS.

Unlike product consumption, service consumption involves buying intangibles (e.g., convenience, customer service). This requires consumers to make purchase decisions without inspecting a product. For some consumers, this may be of little practical significance; however, others may invest considerable time and effort in selecting non-standardized, labor-intensive services that are personally important to them. An example of such a service might include the advice of financial planners. Consumers have no tangible product but instead trust that their planners will continue to invest income and earnings in ways that maximize their investments. Understanding the differences between product and service consumption helps marketers improve the value of their market offerings (Berry et al. 2002).

Holistic Perspective of Consumption: Beyond Product/Service Boundaries

Product-focused and service-oriented concepts significantly limit how we evaluate the entire consumer shopping activity. If consumption activities are evaluated exclusively within the boundary of product or service acquisitions, then aspects of how one actually carries out a consumption activity or shopping trip are not recognized. Consumers increasingly view the shopping activity itself as consumption, whether it is at a local store, at a shopping mall, from a catalog, or on the Internet. Parallel with this trend, the view of consumer efficiency is broadening to encompass the holistic shopping experience obtained via the shopping setting, its atmosphere, and the entertainment it offers.

BENEFIT AND COST COMPONENTS

Consumer efficiency is made up of benefit and cost components. Benefit components are composed of the outputs (e.g., goods, information, and pleasure) that consumers expect to receive from their shopping activities. Cost components consist of multiple dimensions such as money, time, and energy. More specifically, consumers construct shopping strategies in such a way that the costs of shopping are minimized relative to the benefits received from the act of shopping (Darden and Dorsch 1990).

V. A. Zeithaml (1988) argued that consumers vary in what they want and what they are willing to give or expend to get it. The importance of particular benefits varies by consumer. Some consumers may want prestige while others want low price, convenience, or new information. In a similar way, the importance of cost also varies. Some consumers are primarily concerned with money, while others have more concern about the cost of time or effort.

Suppose two stores carry almost identical products and brands. Consumers who are under time pressures and who value convenience may go to the store that is closer to home. Other consumers may prefer to go to the store that is farther away if it has more prestige, is more attractively laid out, or provides a more pleasant shopping ambience. Both behaviors are consistent with the theory of consumer efficiency as long as the returns they receive outweigh the costs they expend.

There is a trade-off between the benefit and cost components of shopping. For instance, ordering through the Internet may mean better prices; however, adding the shipping and handling costs can reduce or eliminate the monetary savings. For consumers who desire a total shopping experience, saving time is not the primary objective because these consumers see the shopping trip as a social experience. In this respect, traditional brick-and-mortar retailers may have an advantage over catalog and Internet retailers. On the contrary, technology-oriented consumers may derive more pleasure from shopping on the Internet than they would from shopping at a mall. Thus, every type of retailer must consider creating strategies based upon costs and benefits for different consumers that improve their competitive edge over other retailers.

Differences in consumer sensitivity to price and distance can explain some shopping patterns. Homemakers, for example, differ in the way they trade off differences in price, distance, assortment, and quality of stores for their routine shopping. These trade-off differences are related to socio-demographic characteristics, such as family size, income, and availability of a car. Distance-sensitive consumers often have small children or may not have a car available for shopping. These consumers may not be willing to trade off distance for other store characteristics. To these consumers, a convenient location is crucial (Verhallen and Van Raaij 1986). However, discount retailers, many of which are inconveniently located for consumers, appeal to consumers who are willing to trade off travel time with monetary price savings.

Benefits

From a holistic view of consumer efficiency, a benefit can be defined as the desired consequences of some activity (Gutman 1982). A. Downs (1961) identified benefits or outputs as "the goods purchased, information obtained [that] improves the consumers' ability to make future purchases, and pleasure received from the process of shopping itself, such as enjoyment from looking at merchandise not purchased, from making a trip away from home, and from socializing with friends encountered at stores, or feelings of status derived from shopping in quality stores" (9). Other researchers have identified benefits that include low price (Zeithaml 1988), pleasure from shopping (Babin, Darden, and Griffin 1994; Tauber 1972), information (Ingene 1984), "the right goods at the right time in the right place for the right price" (Ingene 1984, 32), and "whatever I want in a product" (Zeithaml 1988, 13). As such, consumers obtain benefits from shopping activities whether they buy something or not.

The benefits gained from shopping reflect utilitarian and hedonic components. Utilitarian benefits can include purchasing the right products or services effortlessly or learning about new trends. Hedonic benefits can include the shopping enjoyment that is derived from browsing merchandise, from making a trip away from home, or from socializing with friends. B. J. Babin et al. (1994) classified shopping benefits into utilitarian and hedonic value (See Table 7.3).

Although shoppers may acquire a specific benefit from performing a shopping activity, they are more likely to receive multiple benefits from a completed

TABLE 7.3 B. J. BABIN ET AL.'S SHOPPING VALUE

SHOPPING VALUE	DESCRIPTION
Utilitarian benefits	• I accomplished just what I wanted to on this shopping trip. • I couldn't buy what I really needed. (−) • While shopping, I found just the item(s) for which I was looking. • I was disappointed because I had to go to another store to complete my shopping. (−)
Hedonic benefits	• This shopping trip was truly a joy. • I continued to shop, not because I had to, but because I wanted to. • This shopping trip truly felt like an escape. • Compared with other things I could have done, the time spent shopping was truly enjoyable. • I enjoyed being immersed in exciting new products. • I enjoyed this shopping trip for its own sake, not just for the items I may have purchased. • I had a good time because I was able to act on the spur of the moment. • During the trip, I felt the excitement of the hunt. • While shopping, I was able to forget my problems. • While shopping, I felt a sense of adventure. • This shopping trip was not a very nice time out. (−)

(−) denotes reversed measuring.
Source: Babin, B. J., W. R. Darden, and M. Griffin. 1994. Work and/or fun: Measuring hedonic and utilitarian shopping value. *Journal of Consumer Research* 20(4):644–656.

activity. These multiple benefits can be hierarchically arranged. When an individual engages in shopping-related activities, these activities take primary and secondary roles. For example, when the primary shopping intention of an individual is to acquire information or purchase merchandise, the acquisition of information and merchandise represents the primary shopping benefit sought by the individual. As a secondary role, shopping-related activities become the vehicle that brings individuals together for the purpose of social interaction. On the contrary, for some consumers whose primary benefit of shopping is social interaction, the acquisition of information or merchandise from a store becomes secondary or tertiary benefits (Darden and Dorsch 1990).

Costs

The basic components of costs have been cited within the contexts of money, time, and effort that need to be expended for consumption (Downs 1961, Kim and Kang 1997). Taking a more general approach, costs can be classified into two categories:

primary costs (price of the goods) and secondary costs (all other costs, including time and psychic costs, exclusive of the item's price) (Bender 1964). Both primary and secondary purchase costs influence consumer choices among competing retailers.

Shopping costs do not have the same level of importance for all consumers, nor do all situations deem the same level of importance for the same consumer. In general, it can be said that consumers regard time as more important than money in relation to buying low-cost standardized items (e.g., chewing gum). However, consumers typically regard money as more important than time concerning the purchase of high-cost items (e.g., automobiles, furniture). Between these two extremes, the importance of each cost depends upon consumer income, specific prices, degree of standardization, and the time pressure under which particular consumers act. Some people who have leisure time but low incomes may be willing to give up time to save money. Others who have high incomes but crowded schedules may be willing to give up money to save time. To general consumers, standardized items require less time when making comparisons and studying product attributes (Downs 1961).

PRIMARY COST

The **primary cost** is the direct price of a product or service. To some consumers, the price of the merchandise is the primary reason for purchasing that particular product. When the choice is based on merchandise price, then the benefit gained from paying a low price for merchandise exceeds the costs expended, resulting in a higher level of satisfaction. Different types of retail formats such as upscale department stores (Neiman Marcus, Nordstrom, Saks Fifth Avenue), mid-range department stores (JCPenney, Dillard's), and discount stores (Wal-Mart, Ross, Marshalls) differ in the price of merchandise they carry. In general, consumers who perceive low price to be more important than convenience or an attractive atmosphere choose to shop at more value-oriented retail centers such as factory outlet malls and discount stores (Lee, Atkins, Kim, and Park 2006).

SECONDARY COST

Consumers weigh costs beyond the direct price of goods. The **secondary costs** include additional monetary and nonmonetary costs. Monetary costs are monetary expenditure other than the direct costs of products or services and include expenditures on transportation and parking. Nonmonetary costs are time and effort expenditures that are associated with purchasing products and services. They include waiting time, waiting for a salesclerk, waiting while payment is arranged, and waiting to receive the merchandise (Bender 1964, Dunne and Kahn 1997). Time and effort are considered opportunity costs that prevent consumers from participating in other activities (Becker 1965, Bivens and Volker 1986).

Secondary costs are viewed in many different ways. P. Kotler and G. Zaltman (1971) stated that "price includes money costs, opportunity costs, energy costs, and psychic costs" (9). S. H. Fine (1981) used social price—made up of time, effort, psyche, and lifestyle—to describe exchange transactions. R. L. Oliver and J. E. Swan (1989) viewed time and effort as contributing relevant and positive inputs to an exchange because, the more time and effort an individual exerts, the more outcome he or she should expect in return.

The shopping cost is expanded to include search cost, which is based on the assumption that shoppers may visit more than one store sequentially until they find a desired good or service (Chun and Sumichrast 2005). Consumers may want to shop in several stores to optimize their costs. Y. H. Chun and R. T. Sumichrast identified three major factors that significantly impact the market share: assortment size of each store, shopper's search cost, and price variation among the stores. Based on these factors, shoppers may determine the optimal search sequence among stores before they begin the search process. Shoppers then make decisions at each store as to whether to visit another store and incur additional search cost, or whether to buy the best product available without continuing the search process.

The importance of secondary costs varies among individuals according to their income, occupation, family composition, and shopping motivation. For example, consumers with lower incomes tend to spend time and energy to save money; consumers with higher incomes spend money to save time and effort (Holman and Wilson 1982). For recreational shoppers who take time to shop carefully because they enjoy shopping for its own satisfaction, the time cost is of little concern (Carsky et al. 1995). Working mothers tend to favor mass merchants who provide easier access to a wide variety of services. Although these consumers are starved for time, they are also more likely to invest considerable energy in secondary shopping expenses such as consulting with their family's doctor regarding product ads and samples, calling toll-free numbers for product information or services, and researching pharmaceutical websites (White-Sax 2004).

The importance placed on the secondary costs may vary even for the same individual according to the purpose and urgency of the trip. Consider the case of the following two shopping situations faced by the same consumer.

One day, she was pressed for time and had a goal of purchasing a particular product item. The retail store she entered was equipped with an attractive interior and décor, pleasant scents, soft lighting, and merchandise that was displayed tastefully with fixtures and props. However, she was not attracted by the ambience but was annoyed when she found difficulty in locating the product she had planned to buy. On a different day, she had plenty of time to shop before buying any items. She reacted differently when she visited the same store. She strolled and browsed leisurely through the store surrounded by its aesthetic ambience.

In both situations, the consumer incurred secondary costs—time and energy. However, in the first shopping situation, this consumer seems to have overspent the secondary cost of time and energy, while in the second situation she has not. In the first situation, the outputs of the shopping trip are the product purchased and the annoyance encountered. In the second situation, the outputs include

personal pleasure with or without buying a product. The consumer optimized consumer efficiency on the second day, while she did not on the first day.

The following discussion examines the three major components of secondary costs—money, time, and energy. Examples of consumers in various situations and retailers who implement strategies to reduce consumers' secondary costs are presented.

Money Transportation expenses, parking fees, and the income forgone by spending time shopping are monetary costs other than the direct costs of products or services. At times, these additional monetary costs can significantly increase the price paid for products and services. For example, purchasing books online is often less expensive than making purchases at retail stores, yet the additional cost of shipping can offset the savings incurred. If the consumer considers the time savings as well as the price savings, then the shipping price may be offset in the total online purchase.

Some consumers are not concerned with additional monetary costs associated with shopping, while others place a higher value on conserving these additional monetary costs. For example, when calculating the enjoyment from outlet center shopping, some shoppers would not mind investing in the $5.00 parking fee, the $10.00 lunch, and the expense of gasoline for the 100-mile round-trip drive to the nearest outlet center. On the contrary, some shoppers purchase products locally. They do not return to stores to take advantage of price adjustment policies. These consumers do want to spend the secondary cost of additional monetary expenses associated with these shopping trips. Since there are both types of consumers in the marketplace, it is important that retail businesses are aware of the additional monetary costs associated with shopping at their stores. One example of a retail business that attempts to offset additional monetary costs is the downtown shopping malls that allow customers to park free with a proof of purchase. This strategy encourages the consumer to shop at the downtown location without having to spend money for parking.

Time Nonmonetary time costs are associated with product and service purchases. Examples include time spent parking, time spent moving from the car (or other mode of transportation) to stores and back, time spent traveling from store to store, searching time (time spent selecting the right merchandise), purchasing time (time spent at counter in purchase transaction such as waiting in line), and post-transaction time (time spent waiting for merchandise delivery). Some customers would rather spend the time looking at sale flyers and cutting coupons to gain monetary savings. Others would rather spend more money on a product than time spent searching for less expensive items. To attract more customers, retailers continually try to reduce the amount of time spent on shopping activities. For example, many drugstores are moving to freestanding buildings that are conveniently located, have adequate parking, drive-through pharmacies, and smaller stores at which it is easy to shop.

The time-pressed consumer is usually willing to pay a higher monetary cost for convenience. Currently, many retail businesses are targeting time-pressed consumers. For example, Portable On Demand Storage (PODS) provides delivery and pickup of large storage containers directly to consumers' homes, thus reducing the amount of time consumers will spend moving or going to a typical storage unit. The consumer may pay a higher price for the PODS containers than for traditional storage units, but the time savings can offset the cost.

Another example of a type of product purchased by time-pressed consumers is prepared foods. Grocery stores such as Kroger, Publix, and Fresh Direct provide precut vegetables, premade salads, and precooked meats for consumers who want to eat fresh meals at home, but do not have time to prepare them. Further, companies such as Papa Murphy's Take 'N' Bake Pizza company offer fresh, high-quality ingredients on their premade pizzas, while allowing consumers to take the pizzas home and bake them when they are ready to eat them. These types of products and services enable consumers to spend less of the nonmonetary cost of time on their purchases.

There is growing support for the view that time is a relevant price or cost in purchasing commercial products. Time is possibly a more important cost for many people contributing to nonprofit groups. For example, donating blood to the American Red Cross or donating old furniture to Goodwill takes time. By minimizing the amount of time and effort that the consumer has to spend giving or donating something to nonprofit organizations, the organizations could encourage or solicit more donations. Examples of minimizing the costs for consumers include the Red Cross using the Blood Mobile for on-site blood collection and Goodwill providing drop-off areas conveniently located throughout most cities. Both of these conveniences provide consumers with the opportunity to give back to the community without requiring an excessive amount of time.

Unlike money, time is a limited and scarce resource. In other words, time is not readily exchangeable; consumers cannot increase their total time resources (Okada and Hoch 2004). From an economic perspective, the value of one's time can be expressed in monetary terms as an opportunity cost (Becker 1965). Further, the value of time may be inferred through the opportunity costs of foregone income or participation in other activities (Jacoby, Szybillo, and Berning 1976). Thus, the term *saving time* actually means reallocating time across activities to achieve greater efficiency (Feldman and Hornik 1981).

Total available time can be categorized into discretionary and nondiscretionary components. Discretionary (free) time is what individuals can use at their own will. Nondiscretionary time is what individuals feel obligated to spend (e.g., on working, sleeping, eating, preparing food, cleaning, and shopping for necessities). Consumers have more control over how they use discretionary time resources than nondiscretionary time resources (Berry 1979). However, they are constantly seeking ways to reduce the amount of time necessary for the nondiscretionary components. This is evident in consumer trends such as working from home to remove commute times, eating out to decrease food preparation time, and using the Internet to make purchases for standardized products such as books, CDs, and movies.

The sense that there is just not enough time has become and will continue to become more pronounced and widespread. Because time-constrained consumers lack adequate discretionary time, it is expected that these consumers are more likely to reduce certain nondiscretionary time expenditures in an effort to increase their discretionary time. One popular way of increasing discretionary time is through shopping efficiencies. In the current environment, demand for time-saving products or services is growing. Examples include convenience foods (e.g., expensive frozen entrees, grab-and-go yogurt), time-saving durables (e.g., impingement oven, one-cup grab-and-go coffeemaker), and paid services (e.g., domestic services, child care). At other times, consumers seek to prolong time expenditures, such as during an enjoyable shopping spree (Jacoby et al. 1976). In this way, consumers decrease their nondiscretionary time expenditures and increase valuable discretionary time simultaneously.

One place where retailers have attempted to save shoppers' time is on the shopping lines. Technology such as U-Scan allows customers to complete the checkout process without waiting in long lines. Especially desirable for customers making small quantity purchases, U-Scan allows for a fast and efficient purchasing process. Another way to save time at shopping lines is through the use of a biometric device that takes a finger scan, as done at Piggly Wiggly supermarkets. Consumers register for the biometric payment system and when their finger is scanned at the checkout counter, money is automatically deducted from their checking accounts.

Many working women struggle with maintaining a successful career and simultaneously running an efficient household. These women may prefer products such as the Swiffer Sweeper and the Swiffer WetJet that contain disposable cloths for cleaning floors. The time savings offered by Swiffer allow women to cut down the time they spend maintaining their households.

The opportunity costs of spending time shopping will be different among individuals and will change as individuals move through their life cycles. Thus, decisions about shopping strategies need to be made with an awareness of total time demands and the net payoff. For example, retired consumers who have low opportunity costs may see time spent shopping at three or four supermarkets as economically and psychologically rewarding. To the contrary, for consumers who are employed full-time, the opportunity costs might dictate shopping at only one familiar supermarket that is geographically convenient.

In addition to actual time expended on shopping per se, shopping time also includes the search and evaluation of alternative products in the decision-making process (Blackwell, Miniard, and Engel 2001). Product rating sources, such as Consumer Reports and consultations with family and friends, are mechanisms used to reduce a consumer's actual shopping time (Murphy and Enis 1986). Product advertisements also help consumers reduce the costs searching for the right product at the right price.

Energy Energy expenditure, or effort, is acknowledged to be a distinct type of nonmonetary cost that, like time, influences the consumer's perceived convenience and satisfaction (Berry et al. 2002). Some shoppers will spend an unlimited amount of energy or effort buying a perfect gift or finding the best buy, while other shoppers spend little effort on making purchasing decisions and buy the first item they see.

A. Downs (1961) reported that energy costs consist of basic energy and extra energy. Basic energy is simply energy needed for a shopping trip, during any normal period, and is directly proportional to the amount of time involved. Extra energy is expended carrying packages, taking care of children while shopping, or in frustration because of traffic, difficulty parking, waiting in lines, and assembling products once purchased. The amount of basic and extra energy a consumer has to spend on a particular shopping trip can differ from task to task and from day to day. In an effort to reduce the amount of energy needed to shop in the retail market, retailers such as Gymboree provide entertainment for children while parents shop. In addition to this strategy, some affluent malls provide valet parking services, package handling services, and even personal shopping services. Some grocery stores reduce basic energy by offering home delivery of orders that customers place using their websites. Each of these measures serves to decrease the amount of energy spent, which in turn raises the level of shopping satisfaction.

Shopping experience costs, which include consumers' time and effort in obtaining products, as well as the psychic cost of shopping (e.g., irritation caused by loud music or crowding), are suggested as potential determinants of merchandise value (Baker, Parasuraman, Grewal, and Voss 2002) and store choice (Bender 1964). Psychic costs include unpleasant aspects of shopping such as inner conflict, frustration, depression, anxiety, tension, and annoyance resulting from human relations, store temperature or humidity, store layout, physical features of a store (Baker et al. 2002, Bender 1964). Further, any of these psychological costs combined with one another can create a particularly volatile mix as they relate to store patronage and purchasing intentions. For example, though a couple visiting their favorite restaurant may enjoy the food and the service received during their meal, a screaming child at a nearby table can cause a psychological disturbance that prevents them from enjoying the experience. Similarly, though a store's atmosphere may be pleasant and inviting, if the merchandise or sales associate is not accessible and easy to find, the consumer may get frustrated. They may leave the restaurant or store unsatisfied and frustrated, and worst of all, they may not return to this restaurant or store again in the future. In both cases, customers with negative experiences repress the positive aspects of the experience and remember only the psychic cost of the negative dining or shopping experience.

Some consumers ignore psychic costs, particularly when the costs are relatively small. Other consumers weigh these psychic costs very heavily and consider them more significant than substantial secondary money costs. One example is the psychic cost of shopping at off-price retailers such as T.J. Maxx and Tuesday Morning. When consumers shop in this environment, they have to expect a certain level of disarray, more crowded aisles than affluent department stores, and less customer service than provided at boutiques. The frequent T.J. Maxx or Tuesday Morning customer knows what to expect and probably considers the costs relatively small in relation to the monetary savings gained.

The design of e-stores (e.g., appearance and layout of home pages) may significantly affect e-shoppers' perceived psychic costs and thus their propensity to shop at those stores because design is the dominant environmental component e-shoppers experience (Baker et al. 2002). The impact of experiences on the Internet such as navigating to find a specific item or address, loading information, catching computer viruses, experiencing broken links and unfamiliar language styles, and waiting for sluggish transmission can increase consumers' psychic costs.

SHOPPING UTILITY

A. Downs (1961) classified shopping costs into two types: fixed costs and variable costs. For any shopping trip, consumers have preconceived fixed costs, such as the minimum amount of money to be expended on purchasing products, time to be spent driving to the store, and energy expected to perform minimum levels of shopping tasks. Variable costs are optional costs such as money, time, and energy that shoppers may expend at their discretion.

D. R. Bell, T-H. Ho, and C. S. Tang (1998) discussed the concepts of fixed and variable costs in the context of the supermarket.

As illustrated in Figure 7.3, a consumer chooses a store based on the perceived utility from that store (i.e., benefits minus costs). A consumer's perceived total utility associated with a shopping trip can be divided into fixed and variable components. Both fixed and variable components contain benefits and costs (Tang, Bell, and Ho 2001). Table 7.4 lists the key drivers of the fixed and variable utility of shopping at a store.

The fixed utility is composed of fixed benefits and fixed costs. Table 7.4 exhibits four fixed benefits. First, the habitual shopping experience provides shopping with ease because of knowledge of the store layout and product shelf location. Second, the value is attached to the service quality from the availability of parking

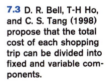

7.3 D. R. Bell, T-H Ho, and C. S. Tang (1998) propose that the total cost of each shopping trip can be divided into fixed and variable components.

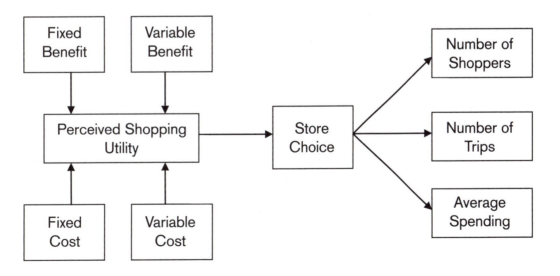

TABLE 7.4 DRIVERS OF SHOPPING UTILITY

PERCEIVED SHOPPING UTILITY COMPONENT	DRIVERS
1. Fixed utility	
(a) Fixed benefits	• Habitual shopping experience (store loyalty, familiarity level with the store layout and product locations) • Service quality (parking space, cleanliness of the store, friendliness of the employees, waiting time at the checkout counter, etc.) • Assortment of products (breadth and depth of assortment, exclusive labels) • Purchase flexibility
(b) Fixed costs	• Store location (distance and time to reach the store)
2. Variable utility	
(a) Variable benefits	• Store-specific price discounts (coupons, loyalty rewards) • Habitual category purchase experience (category-specific store loyalty due to assortment, prices, familiarity)
(b) Variable costs	• Expected price of items on the shopping list

Source: Tang, C. S., D. R. Bell, and T-H. Ho. 2001. Store choice and shopping behavior: How price format works. *California Management Review* 43(2):56–74.

spaces, cleanliness, and employee friendliness. Third, large assortments of products facilitate one-stop shopping and thus reduce a shopper's need to make additional trips to other stores. The last benefit is purchase flexibility that allows a shopper to buy more when the price is low and buy less when the price is high. The fixed costs in the fixed utility involve the time and effort that must be expended in reaching the store (Tang et al. 2001).

The variable utility also consists of variable benefits and variable costs. A variable benefit can be derived from store-specific price discounts such as coupons and customer loyalty rewards. Another variable benefit can come from habitual purchase experience from category-specific stores where a shopper may perceive a lower expected price for a product, even when another store charges the same price for the product. The variable costs are dependent upon the expected prices of items, which are determined by the store's price format (Tang et al. 2001). C. S. Tang et al. concluded that shoppers are likely to visit the store with the lowest total shopping cost that consists of fixed and variable costs. They also explained that an increase in fixed or variable **shopping utility** has a direct impact on the number of customers who visit the store, number of shopping visits, and average expenditure per trip.

WAYS TO ENHANCE CONSUMER EFFICIENCY

In delivering products or services to customers, the benefits must outweigh the costs to provide maximum value for the customers. If the benefit obtained by shopping with a particular retailer is less than the value obtained from purchasing products or services or from the shopping experience, then customers may switch to a different retailer. Thus, maximizing consumer efficiency is an essential task for a retailer. Ways to enhance consumer efficiency include one-stop shopping, cross-shopping, emphasizing important attributes to consumers, increasing fixed utility, increasing variable utility, and multichannel shopping.

One-Stop Shopping

One-stop shopping is provided for customers by retailers who conglomerate multiple products and services into one shopping venue. This has appeal for consumers because the marginal purchase-cost associated with buying another item to a group already selected in a particular store is not much more than the primary purchase-cost of the additional item on a separate trip. Retail supercenters such as Super Wal-Mart, Super Bi-Lo, and Target Supercenter offer one-stop shopping for consumers, by housing at their centers retailers such as hair and nail salons, coffee shops, eye care specialists, and photo shops. This allows customers to save travel time for using these services, while they shop for regularly purchased products. One-stop shopping can also allow the customer a break from the normal shopping routine. At Target, for example, a visit to the Starbucks coffee shop located within the store provides a pleasant break for the customer from the shopping routine.

Cross-Shopping

Cross-shopping happens when consumers patronize multiple types of retail outlets on a single trip. Cross-shopping reduces shopping costs because traveling to another store from the first store on a single trip would not add as much as the primary cost of making a separate trip to the different store. The total cost of shopping is reduced because the variable costs of consumption per unit of quantity of shopping is reduced. In the case of Internet shopping, this additional marginal cost of traveling is eliminated, thus further reducing shopping costs.

To encourage cross-shopping, shopping centers are reshaping the tenant mix (e.g., adding family entertainment centers) and reconsidering the destination attractions (e.g., movie theaters or restaurants instead of traditional department stores). Providing entertainment is thought to increase the positive shopping experience, which in turn makes shoppers stay longer with the possibility of engaging in additional cross-shopping activities. It is expected that this positive experience eventually increases consumers' perceptions of efficient shopping.

The impact of entertainment on mall cross-shopping may not always be positive. For instance, S. Talpade and J. Haynes's (1997) study revealed that a fairly low percentage of shoppers was drawn to malls primarily by an entertainment center and that a significantly lower percentage of this entertainment shopper group visited department stores or other mall shops and spent comparatively less time shopping. Also, J. Baker et al. (2002) indicated that the presence of a cinema in the mall did not increase cross-shopping. In their study, only 14 percent of moviegoers, compared with 28 percent of non-moviegoers, visited department stores on the same trip; 12 percent of moviegoers, compared with 15 percent of non-moviegoers, visited fast food outlets on the same trip. However, going to the movies should be considered as a fixed time cost because it usually takes 90 minutes or more. Thus, time is maximized at the cinema, which does not allow shopping time.

These conflicting issues concerning entertainment in the shopping mall underlie the urgent need to study the utilitarian aspects as well as the hedonic aspects of mall shopping. Offering varying degrees of utilitarian and hedonic benefits to target customers will certainly meet their desire for a satisfactory total shopping experience, which will increase cross-shopping. Experiences gained from cross-shopping will also influence the total shopping experience, both utilitarian and hedonic.

Emphasizing Important Attributes to Consumers

The more benefits received from a given shopping trip, the more costs a consumer is willing to sacrifice (Downs 1961). Thus, if consumers seek certain retail attributes, they are willing to expend a certain amount of cost to receive the desired benefits. For example, time-pressed consumers are willing to pay higher monetary costs for convenience. A pleasant shopping atmosphere can affect both the amount of time and money that customers voluntarily spend in a store. Prestige or attractive ambience can motivate consumers to sacrifice time and effort required to travel to the more distant of two nearby stores, even if the goods in both stores are identical. A retail store providing the environment that matches lifestyles will encourage them to expend the shopping costs because these costs will be equalized by the benefits received from the lifestyle retail outlet.

One current concern in the United States is obesity. This may be a result of individual wealth increase, time pressures, and an increase in the number of meals eaten outside the home, as well as value-size portions. Today, 14 is the most common dress size compared with a size 8 in 1985 (Gardyn 2003). The plus-size clothing niche represents 20 percent of the total apparel market and includes males as well as females (Gardyn 2003). This consumer trend forces the retail marketing function to change accordingly. Product innovations include expandable waist pants and 3-D virtual model based on body measurements. These innovations create value added for the consumer. In addition, many plus-size specialty retailers (e.g., Lane Bryant) as well as mainstream retailers (e.g., JCPenney, Liz Claiborne, Old Navy) are aggressively pursuing this profitable segment by extending the size range of their merchandise or launching new plus-size brands. Further, these retailers are also promoting marketing messages that change the image of plus-size from a sign of moral failure (Pressler 1998) to beauty and acceptance of being a full-figured woman (Clark 2004, Daswani 2004).

Increasing Fixed Utility

As previously mentioned, a consumer chooses a store based upon the perceived utility of that store. Shopping efficiency can be enhanced by increasing a shopper's fixed utility, that is, by maximizing fixed benefits (e.g., service quality, helpful personnel, product assortment, parking) per fixed cost (e.g., time and energy expended to reach to the store). Volume-based stores can focus on increasing the shopper's fixed utility by increasing the breadth of assortment and service.

There are several recent examples of retailers who have implemented strategies to increase fixed utility of shopping. Several specialty stores have relocated to free-standing stores to improve the image of their store locations and parking capacity. Similarly, Wal-Mart's new smaller-format grocery stores called Neighborhood Markets are attempting to provide the convenience of small supermarket style stores with a drive-through pharmacy and half-hour photo service (See Figures 7.4a and b).

Increasing Variable Utility

Consumer efficiency can also be enhanced by increasing a shopper's variable utility, that is, by maximizing variable benefits (e.g., coupons, discounts, loyalty rewards) per variable cost (e.g., merchandise price). There exist notable examples of firms that have moved to aggressively increase unit variable utility. Specialty retailers such as Gap offer incentives to credit card holders for specific dollar amounts that are charged to their store credit cards. Some

7.4a&b Wal-Mart's Neighborhood Market provides the convenience of small, supermarket-style stores.

retailers such as Barnes and Noble, Pottery Barn, and Books-A-Million send out e-mails about online and in-store sales or discounts to encourage shoppers to shop online or at stores. CVS pharmacies print automatic coupons on customers' register receipts, including cash discounts that can be used on further visits. In addition, companies such as Kroger and Albertsons provide weekly discounts to members of their shopper card programs.

Multichannel Shopping

Increases in technology and computer literacy have led consumers to use **multichannel shopping** options, including brick-and-mortar stores, catalogs, and websites to meet their shopping needs. Consumers use multiple channels differently in two stages of the shopper decision process: seeking information and making purchases. Some shoppers use Internet sites before going to the mall to search for information regarding products, sales, stores, services, and events. Other consumers do their preliminary shopping in the mall and use the Web for purchasing. For example, when consumers make big ticket purchasing decisions such as new laptop computers, cell phones, PDAs, or music storing devices, they may first use tools such as the Internet to sort through all the information pertaining to different brands and products and compare product

features. After searching the Internet for a retailer such as Best Buy, Sears, or Wal-Mart, the consumer may ultimately choose to purchase a product at an actual retail store. If the customer chooses Best Buy, for example, the purchase decision can be finalized by asking Best Buy employees about specific product attributes, warranty information, and servicing opportunities. Based on the synergetic relationship between the two retail channels, the Internet is not viewed as a threat but as an opportunity for the brick-and-mortar retail industry.

To meet consumer needs, multichannel retailers need to reduce shopping costs for consumers. Table 7.5 illustrates the compatibility of the three types of retailers (brick-and-mortar stores, catalogs, and the Internet) in cost. In the case of store shopping, shopping costs include money needed for product purchase and transportation; time needed for travel, waiting in checkout lines, and finding products; and energy needed for parking, traffic, and dealing with pushy salespeople. In the case of the Internet, shopping costs include money needed for purchasing and shipping, time needed to locate a specific item or address, and energy spent on broken links.

To meet consumers' expectations toward multichannel retailers, it is critical to determine how, or to what extent, consumers will use the one channel instead of

TABLE 7.5 COST: BRICK-AND-MORTAR STORES VERSUS CATALOGS VERSUS THE INTERNET

COST COMPONENT	BRICKS-AND-MORTAR STORES	CATALOGS	THE INTERNET
Money	Cost of product/service purchase, cost of transportation	Cost of product purchase, shipping cost, return shipping cost	Cost of product/service purchase, shipping cost, Internet connection fee, return shipping cost
Time	Travel time to store, time finding a parking place, time spent in store	Time needed to locate the right product, time spent ordering and waiting for delivery	Time needed to locate an online vendor's address, time it takes to load information, time spent ordering and waiting for delivery
Energy	Energy expended on parking, traffic, pushy salespeople, finding product wanted, waiting on checkout lines	Energy spent finding product wanted, energy expended in returning	Energy spent navigating to find a specific item or address, dealing with website malfunctions (e.g., broken links) and electronic checkout, energy expended in returning

another. To accomplish this goal, it is essential to understand the fundamental differences in consumer experiences that are gained from different channels. After understanding the differences, retailers can implement strategies that will lead to enhanced consumer shopping experiences. For example, the consumer who desires sensory stimulation or entertainment while shopping may find the brick-and-mortar stores and shopping centers more appealing to the five senses of sight, sound, smell, touch, and taste. On the contrary, the Internet may only appeal to the consumer who is seeking satisfaction of two senses (sight and sound) through multimedia presentations and interactive games. To serve these consumers, Internet retailers may focus on reliable and speedy service or on customization of product and service offerings.

RETAIL PRACTICES THAT ENHANCE CONSUMER EFFICIENCY

Consumer efficiency is the basis for making changes in retail mix (product and service offerings, pricing, distribution channels, and promotional strategies) to differentiate retailers from their competitors. Consumer efficiency helps retailers assess which strategies they can use to reevaluate and, as necessary, modify their current retail program to be consistent with their customers' specific needs and expectations. Retail practices that enhance consumer efficiency can be discussed in terms of retail operations and technologies.

Retail Operations

As early as the 1960s, A. Downs (1961) attested that each of the following major postwar retailing trends could be analyzed as a method for reducing net consumer cost. He discussed how retail operations work in a way to enhance consumer efficiency as follows (10):

1. The outlying shopping center minimizes net consumer cost in several key ways: It reduces the cost of parking by providing uncongested parking spaces close to desirable stores without any direct charge to the consumer; it reduces the time of movement between stores by grouping compatible stores adjacent to [one another]; it reduces the cost of movement between home and

stores by placing a wide variety of goods much closer to the consumer than the old downtown area; and it increases the pleasure of shopping by providing a modern, attractive, and aesthetically homogeneous atmosphere.

2. The high-volume unit in convenience goods lines (especially food, drugs, and liquor) lowers prices without lowering total profits by allowing the economies of mass purchasing and mass distribution possible in large firms, and serving a much larger number of customers to compensate for lower markups.

3. The tendency to combine traditionally separate goods lines into one unit (such as drugs in grocery stores and hardware in drugstores) cuts the need for consumers to visit several stores.

4. Self-service reduces prices by allowing distributors to minimize their labor costs per quantity of goods handled.

5. The tendency to stay open evenings and on weekends increases consumer efficiency in four ways: it allows the entire family to shop together, thus achieving maximum shopping per trip; it provides convenient access to stores for working men and women; it allows one-car families to use their automobiles for shopping as well as transportation to work; it allows one parent to babysit while the other shops if children cannot be taken shopping.

Further, A. Downs (1961) predicted that based on the theory of consumer efficiency, some retail strategies and developments would become more prominent in the near future. These included wider use of credit for all types of purchases including food; extension of high-volume, high-quality, discount-type operations into a greater variety of retail lines; joint operations of such discount outlets with food, drug, and other convenience goods facilities, all under one roof and one management; and operation of all types of retail outlets during evenings and for longer periods on weekends. Today's retail operations prove that Down's prediction has come to pass. However, Downs's discussion of retail developments that help consumers increase shopping efficiency was confined to brick-and-mortar retail operations. Current consumer and retail trends in non-store retail formats via catalogs, TV, and the Internet should be discussed in terms of increasing consumer efficiency.

Technologies

As technology changes every day, opportunities to improve consumer efficiency are added. There are costs and benefits, challenges and risks, but as consumers adapt to new technology, these changes can make their lives easier. Identification technologies such as bar or UPC codes were a great jump forward in the 1970s for inventory management that previously was calculated by hand. Physically taking inventory was time-consuming and subject to many human errors. Bar codes saved time and manpower; however, there was a one-to-four second lag for a successful reading. With millions or hundreds of millions of products to scan, those few seconds per item turned into large amounts of time. Radio frequency identification (RFID) significantly reduces the previous amount of scanning time by automating the counting process, which eliminates the stops that occur in most supply chains (Kinsella 2005).

RFID

RFID is a system of integrated transceivers, tags, and a computer system wherein tags are attached to an individual product, a carton, or a pallet of goods. The tag contains information about that product, such as the manufacturer's information or product codes, and can be read by transceivers. The transceiver then converts the information into a digital format and uses it for inventory management. Businesses use these devices to track goods as they go in and out of a warehouse, onto store shelves, or into automatic replenishment systems. Over the next few years, major retailers such as Wal-Mart and Target are requiring their top suppliers to use RFID tags on every carton of goods (Davis and Luehlfing 2004). RFID technology will become more readily available across different industries as major retailers incorporate time-saving systems into their businesses. As a result, consumers should expect to see lower costs and, therefore, increased efficiency.

BENEFITS OF RFID

B. Kinsella (2005) discussed how businesses can benefit from RFID through efficiency, security, and marketing. Efficiency seems to the most important benefit because businesses have wanted to maintain better tracking systems of goods and assets for years. Once the goods are being tracked efficiently, retailers build efficiency gain. Better tracking leads to reduced costs for the manufacturer and the retailer, and ultimately, the consumer. Security benefits are also important for large manufacturers of branded products and pharmaceuticals, as tampering, counterfeiting, and theft have negative impacts on their bottom lines. The pharmaceutical industry was losing more than 30 billion dollars per year, which was the main reason the FDA created a Compliance Policy Guide for employing RFID feasibility studies. The acting FDA commissioner, Dr. Lester Crawford, stated that the FDA had one goal—to increase the safety of drugs that consumers receive by making it possible to track the drugs from the manufacturer all the way to the pharmacy. RFID can also aid in retailers' marketing strategies. Retailers look forward to having the ability to monitor consumers' purchases

and encourage cross-selling. Prada, a higher-end retailer, has shown some early signs of success using RFID for marketing (Kinsella 2005).

RISKS OF RFID

RFID generates some fears among consumers that need to be allayed before RFID is widely accepted. One major concern over the increased use of RFID is that companies will be able to track what businesses and consumers purchase and spend. Though having costs reduced and efficiency increased is good for every manufacturer, retailer, and consumer involved, there is still a risk of misuse that threatens consumer privacy and consumer anonymity (Davis and Luehlfing 2004). There are consumer advocacy groups, including Consumers Against Supermarket Privacy Invasion and Numbering (CASPIAN), who are focused on lowering the risks. These groups are worried that RFID tags can be placed inside a product without the consumer's knowledge; if the tag is not turned off after a consumer purchases the product, the tag can be reread without consumer consent for purposes such as developing consumer profiles of brand and product preferences. Another concern is that since every good has its own number, the good can be associated with a particular person, combining the information on the tag with information gained at the point-of-sale; this potentially makes it possible to track and profile people (Davis and Luehlfing 2004). Reducing these inherent risks seems to be a challenge to manufacturers and retailers to ensure consumer data privacy.

OTHER TECHNOLOGIES

As retailers struggle with differentiating themselves from one another, new technologies give retailers ways to stand apart and provide more efficiency for the consumer.

To provide a more consumer-centric environment, it is important that retailers understand the benefits that can be transferred from using technologies to consumers. IBM conducted a study in 2004 to help determine retail customers' attitudes toward overall shopping experiences and the increasing amounts of in-store technologies (Heckel 2004). The focus groups were conducted in the United States, Britain, Germany, and France. Participants answered questions about their shopping wants and needs, attitudes toward in-store technology, and reactions to new technology concepts. The study found that participants were disappointed with a lack of knowledgeable salespeople, prices not clearly marked, unpleasant employees, long lines, and dirty or crowded stores. The in-store technologies discussed in the focus group interviews included self-checkout, kiosks to gain information or place orders, shopping cart-mounted devices, use of biometrics at checkout, RFID, personalized e-mails, use of loyalty cards, and wireless devices for employees. The participants attested that new in-store technologies must provide tangible benefits such as greater convenience, lower prices, and access to value-added information to encourage consumer adoption. Further, they were more interested in kiosks to gain information and were growing tired of loyalty cards. It clearly demonstrates that consumers are interested in technology adoption and their positive attitudes can be formed from using new technologies.

CHAPTER SUMMARY

Today's consumers are efficient shoppers. They select a retail outlet, with which they can shop most efficiently and satisfactorily. Consumers demand not only money, time, and energy savings, but also pleasure from the shopping experiences. This trend is supported by several changes in the current U.S. consumer market: the expanding number of dual-income, single, and single-parent households; the aging of consumer population; an ever-growing modern-day concern over time poverty; and the revolution of technology.

Consumer efficiency encompasses both benefit and cost components, reaches beyond the boundary of product/service focuses, and engages with both utilitarian and hedonic principles of consumer behavior. Moving away from the focus on product or service acquisition, consumers increasingly view the shopping activity itself as consumption, which leads to evaluation of the entire consumer shopping activity. Benefits consist of utilitarian and hedonic benefits. Utilitarian benefits can include purchasing the right products or service effortlessly or learning about new trends. Hedonic benefits can include shopping enjoyment that is derived from browsing through a variety of merchandise, or from socializing with friends. Costs could be primary costs (price of the good) or secondary costs (all other costs, including time and psychic costs).

The premise of the consumer efficiency theory is that retail trends move in whatever directions increase the shopping efficiency of the average consumer. Therefore, retailers must understand how to develop strategies to help their customers maximize benefits for their investment of money, time, and energy. A. Downs (1961) predicted that the theory of consumer efficiency moves the direction of retail developments (e.g., extending retail hours to evenings and weekends to provide convenience to consumers; carrying high-volume merchandise under one roof and one management). Today's retail operations prove that Downs's prediction has come to pass. Technological advances (e.g., U-Scan,

RFID) provide further opportunities to improve consumer efficiency.

There are several ways to enhance consumer efficiency, including one-stop shopping, cross-shopping, emphasizing important attributes to consumers, increasing fixed utility, increasing variable utility, and offering multichannel shopping. Consumer efficiency is the basis for evaluating and modifying retail mix—product and service offerings, pricing, distribution channels, and promotional strategies—to differentiate retailers from their competitors.

Discussion *Questions*

1. Identify consumer trends influencing consumer efficiency, and describe how each trend impacts consumer efficiency.

2. Describe examples of how brick-and-mortar retailers provide consumer efficiency to their customers.

3. Describe examples of how online retailers provide consumer efficiency to their customers.

4. Describe how shopping centers offer consumer efficiency. Identify the types of strategies used to provide this benefit to shoppers.

5. What would be the relative importance of primary cost versus secondary costs for single parents?

6. In your shopping experience, does catalog shopping or online shopping offer better consumer efficiency than brick-and-mortar store shopping? Support your answer with examples.

7. Why is it important for the Internet to provide both utilitarian and hedonic components to consumer shopping efficiency?

8. What is the difference between fixed and variable costs? Explain how these influence shopping efficiency.

9. Identify strategies that online and catalog retailers can use to enhance shopping utility for their customers.

REFERENCES

Babin, B. J., W. R. Darden, and M. Griffin. 1994. Work and/or fun: Measuring hedonic and utilitarian shopping value. *Journal of Consumer Research* 20(4):644–656.

Baker, J., A. Parasuraman, D. Grewal, and G. B. Voss. 2002. The influence of multiple store environment cues on perceived merchandising value and patronage intentions. *Journal of Marketing* 66(2):120–141.

Becker, G. S. 1965. A theory of the allocation of time. *The Economic Journal* 75: 493–517.

Bell, D. R., T-H. Ho, and C. S. Tang. 1998. Determining where to shop: Fixed and variable costs of shopping. *Journal of Marketing Research* 35(3): 352–369

Bender, W. C. 1964. Consumer purchase-costs: Do retailers recognize them? *Journal of Retailing* 40(1): 1–9.

Berry, L. 1979. The time-buying consumer. *Journal of Retailing* 55(4):58–69.

Berry, C. J. 1994. *The Idea of Luxury: A Conceptual and Historical Investigation*, New York: Cambridge University Press.

Berry, L., K. Seiders, and L. L. Grewal. 2002. Understanding service convenience, *Journal of Marketing* 66(3): 1–17.

Bivens, G. E., and C. B. Volker. 1986. A value-added approach to household production: The special case of meal preparation. *Journal of Consumer Research* 13(2): 272–279.

Blackwell, R. D., P. M. Miniard, and J. F. Engel. 2001. *Consumer behavior*, 9th ed. New York: Harcourt College Publisher.

Bucklin, L. P. 1962. Retail strategy and the classification of consumer goods. *Journal of Marketing* 10:50–55.

———. 1966. Testing propensities to shop. *Journal of Marketing* 30(1): 22–27.

Carsky, M. L., R. Dickinson, and M. F. Smith. 1995. Toward consumer efficiency: A model for improved buymanship. *The Journal of Consumer Affairs* 29(2): 442–459.

Chu, Kathy. 2005. Will that be cash, credit, or finger? *USA Today.* Retrieved August 31, 2006, from www.usatoday.com/tech/news/techinnovations/2005-12-01-cash-credit-finger_x.htm.

Chun, Y. H., and R. T. Sumichrast. 2005. Estimating the market shares of stores based on the shopper's search and purchase behavior. *European Journal of Operational Research* 166:576–592

Clark, E. 2004. Large sizes need focus. *Women's Wear Daily.* October 6, 13.

Community Banker. 2005. Bits & bytes. 14(12):58.

Darden, W. R., and M. J. Dorsch. 1990. An action strategy approach to examining shopping behavior. *Journal of Business Research* 21(3): 289–308

Davis, H., and M. Luehlfing. 2004. Radio frequency identification: The wave of the future. *Journal of Accountancy* 198(5): 43–49.

Daswani, K. 2004. A growing market. *Women's Wear Daily.* October 6, 52S.

Downs, A. 1961. A theory of consumer efficiency. *Journal of Retailing* 6(12): 50–67.

Dunne, P., and R. Kahn. 1997. Retailing in the USA: An interpretation of current trends. *International Journal of Retail and Distribution Management* 25(8): 275–281.

Feldman, L. P., and J. Hornik. 1981. The use of time: An integrated conceptual model. *Journal of Consumer Research* 7:407–419.

Fine, S. H. 1981. Beyond money: The concept of social price in marketing of services. In J. H. Donnelly and W. R. George, eds. *Marketing of Services* (113–116). Chicago: American Marketing Association.

Gardyn, R. 2003. Size matters. *American Demographics* 25(6):29.

Gaski, John F. 1986. The concept of consumer market efficiency: Toward Evaluating the social efficiency of consumer marketing. In R. J. Lutz, ed. *Advances in Consumer Research*, Vol. 13 (88–93). Provo, UT: Association for Consumer Research.

Gutman, J. 1982. A means-end model based on consumer categorization process. *Journal of Marketing* 46:60–72.

Haley, R. I. 1968. Benefit segmentation: A decision-oriented research tool. *Journal of Marketing* 55(4): 20–31.

Heckel, T. 2004. IBM finds that shoppers around the world are increasingly open to new shopping experiences. *European Retail Digest* 44:18–19.

Hirschman, E., and M. Holbrook. 1982. Hedonic consumption: Emerging concepts, methods, and propositions. *Journal of Marketing* 46:92–101.

Holman, R. H., and R. D. Wilson. 1982. Temporal equilibrium as a basis for retail shopping behavior. *Journal of Retailing* 58(1):58–81.

Ingene, C. A. 1984. Productivity and functional shifting in spatial retailing: Private and social perspectives. *Journal of Retailing* 60(3):15–36.

Jacoby, J., G. J. Szybillo, and C. K. Berning. 1976. Time and consumer behavior: An interdisciplinary overview. *Journal of Consumer Research* 2(4):320–339.

Kim, Y-K., and J. K. Kang. 1997. Consumer perception of shopping costs and its relationship with retail trends. *Journal of Shopping Center Research* 4(2):27–62.

Kinsella, B. 2005. Delivering the goods. *Industrial Engineer* 37(3):24–30.

Kivetz, R. and I. Simonson. 2002. Self-control for the righteous: Toward a theory of precommitment to indulgence. *Journal of Consumer Research* 29(2):199–217.

Kotler, P. 1972. A generic concept of marketing. *Journal of Marketing* 36(2):46–54.

———. 1999. *Kotler on marketing: How to create, win, and dominate markets.* New York: Free Press.

Kotler, P. and G. Zaltman. 1971. Social marketing: An approach to planned social change. *Journal of Marketing* 35(3):3–12.

Lai, A. W. 1995. Consumer values, product benefits, and customer value: A consumption behavior approach. In F. R. Kardes and M. Sujan, eds. *Advances in Consumer Research*, Vol. 22 (381–388). Provo, UT: Association for Consumer Research.

Lee, Min-Young, Kelly Atkins, Y-K. Kim, and S. Park 2006. Competitive analyses between regional malls and big-box retailers: A correspondence analyses for segmentation and positioning. *Journal of Shopping Center Research* in press.

Maslow, A. H. 1970. *Motivation and personality*, 2nd ed. New York: Harper and Row.

Mathwick, C., N. Malhotra, and E. Rigdon. 2002. Experiential value: Conceptualization, measurement and application in the catalog and Internet shopping environment. *Journal of Retailing* 77(1):39–56.

Murphy, P. E., and B. M. Enis. 1986. Classifying products strategically. *Journal of Marketing* 50(3):24–42.

Okada, E. M. and S. J. Hoch. 2004. Spending time versus spending money. *Journal of Consumer Research* 31(2):313–323.

Oliver, R. L., and J. E. Swan. 1989. Consumer perception of interpersonal equity and satisfaction in transactions: A field survey approach. *Journal of Marketing* 53(2):21–35.

Pressler, M. W. 1998. Plus consumers get retailers' attention. *The Washington Post.* November 3, A1.

Richins, M. L. 1994. Value things: The public and private meanings of possessions. *Journal of Consumer Research* 21(3):504–521.

Sheth, J. N., B. I. Newman, and B. L. Gross. 1991. When we buy what we buy: A theory of consumption values. *Journal of Business Research* 22:159–170.

Sproles, G. B. 1980. New theoretical and empirical perspectives of consumer efficiency. In J. Olson, ed. *Advances in Consumer Research,* Vol. 7 (178–179). Ann Arbor, MI: Association for Consumer Research.

Sweeny, J. C., and G. N. Soutar. 2001. Consumer perceived value: The development of a multiple item scale. *Journal of Retailing* 77:203–220.

Talpade, S., and J. Haynes. 1997. Consumer shopping behavior in malls with large scale entertainment centers. *Mid-Atlantic Journal of Business* 33(2):153–162.

Tang, C. S., D. R. Bell, and T-H. Ho. 2001. Store choice and shopping behavior: How price format works. *California Management Review* 43(2):56–74.

Tauber, E. M. 1972. Why do people shop? *Journal of Marketing* 36(3):46–59.

Verhallen, Theo. M. M., and Fred van Raaij. 1986. How consumers trade off behavioral costs and benefits. *European Journal of Marketing* 20(3/4):19–34.

Wellman, David. 2005. Grocery trips continue decline. *Frozen Food Age* 53(8):8.

White-Sax, B. 2004. Devotion to home, family makes for frequent shopping. *Drug Store News* 26(8):121–126.

Zeithaml, V. A. 1988. Consumer perceptions of price, quality, and value: A means-end model and synthesis of evidence. *Journal of Marketing* 52(1):2–22.

PART

3

CHAPTER 8

ENTERTAINMENT RETAILING

Revamped FAO Tempers Pedigree with Fun

After shuttering its door for a year, Manhattan toy institution FAO Schwarz reopened its flagship this past Thanksgiving to the delight of both locals and holiday shoppers. While both the assortment and store design reflect much of what consumers loved about the old FAO, new, exclusive merchandise and a number of format changes have given the standby a noticeable facelift. The new store is complementary to the former FAO. We started out with the idea that the merchandise has to be different and the services have to be different. When it was all rolled together, you could really see how the strategy has come alive, said Kim Richmond, director of marketing for FAO Schwarz.

The most noticeable change is in the format of the ground floor of the store, which has been dramatically opened up. Huge columns of merchandise that used to crowd the center of the store have been eliminated and vertical wall displays—including a model of a made-to-order treehouse—take advantage of the multistory ceilings. A decorative lighting array covers the entire ceiling, and the famous window displays have been removed in favor of letting sunlight in and showcasing the store's swank Fifth Avenue surroundings. FAO's traditional plush, from large-as-life tigers and reindeer to affordable smaller models, take up much of the space near the main entrance. There is also a new ice-cream parlor and candy store at FAO Schwartz—featuring extravagances such as the $100 Volcano sundae, filled with a mountain of ice cream and toppings and designed for a group of lucky children to share. FAO used to shut down for parties, but now, with a new party room on the second floor, the store can remain open and ready for business. Sleepovers start at $10,000.

Like the $1,000 stuffed animals lining the first floor, FAO made sure to retain the equity of its reputation for purveying the ultimate in luxury. Upstairs, children and their parents can ooh and aah over a $50,000 Ferrari and other scaled-down vehicles. The difference is, rather than being a toy museum, it is more of a place for kids to have fun, whether watching dancers perform musical numbers on the giant piano keyboard made famous in the movie *Big*, or taking a ride on the $300,000 3-D motion simulator—also available for purchase. "Kids can get a lot more involved; it's incredibly interactive," said Richmond. "There is live entertainment, there are games downstairs, and, when visitors come to see the $50,000 Ferrari, they also will be able to touch it."

While FAO's assortment was always posh, there is a much larger emphasis on exclusives in the new store, items "you can't get anywhere else; unique product is the first merchandising tenet for FAO," noted Richmond. While the old FAO featured showcases filled with collectible Madame Alexander dolls, a new Madame Alexander Doll Factory offers customers the unique chance to design one-of-a-kind dolls, customized with the skin tone and hair and eye color of their choice. FAO has adapted to the personalization trend that has driven toy sales for a number of specialty stores, including American Girl and Build-A-Bear Workshop. Children have the unique chance to adopt a baby from the Lee Middleton nursery, which staffs nurses or doctors on duty, taking customer service to another level. "Customers sit in a rocking chair and actually fill out adoption paperwork. It's a fabulous experience, not just buying a baby doll," said Richmond. Children—and adults—can also design custom Hot Wheels toy cars on seven computer terminals that pump out the result on the spot.

While the Toys "R" Us flagship is a technological marvel, FAO's is still a bastion of tradition, featuring walls of antique toys aimed at adult collectors. The newly redesigned store also features "retailtainment," from air hockey and pinball in a "rec room" on the lower level to the chance to customize toys. While maintaining its blue-chip reputation as a premiere destination for luxe toys, the new average price point of $20 and a playful new attitude have given FAO Schwarz a modern twist.

Source: Scardino, E. 2005. Revamped FAO tempers pedigree with fun. *DSN Retailing Today* 44(3): 22–27.

INTRODUCTION

Entertainment retailing is a concept that has experienced rapid growth since the 1990s. Shoppers have come to expect to be amused when they go to a store. They expect to be entertained, whether it is with music, interactive experiences, or unique scenery. Successful retailers such as FAO Schwarz create an enjoyable experience for shoppers. Consider the consumer experience at FAO. Consumers not only purchase toys, but also are entertained while in the store. Consumers' purchasing experiences extend to complementary entertainment, which may keep them in the store longer and stimulate sales. For example, in addition to buying a doll, consumers have the opportunity to fill out adoption papers for baby dolls purchased in the store's nursery. Their experience is transformed with the addition of entertainment such as dancers performing musical numbers on the giant piano keyboard or a ride on the store's $300,000 3-D motion simulator (Adams 1999).

At Bass Pro Shops, shoppers engage with the Outdoor World superstores that offer about 280,000 square feet of selling space to showcase boats, campers, apparel, and outdoor equipment. Bass Pro's innovative store design features a range of interactive experiences for shoppers, such as archery ranges, fish tanks, restaurants, and video arcades. Upon walking inside a Bass Pro Shop, customers can participate in a variety of activities that enhance their shopping experience. They can try out fly reels at an indoor waterfall, test golfing equipment on a putting green, or practice at an archery range. The massive indoor waterfall can be found inside of a typical Bass Pro Shop store (See Figure 8.1). The store's entertainment elements give it a distinctive identity and set it apart from the competition. Sporting goods retailers REI, Cabela's, and Bass Pro Shops have led the way in making their retail venues an experience. Their stores have emerged as major attractions by offering climbing walls, mountain bike tracks, fishing ponds, archery ranges, putting greens, and a host of other opportunities for customers to test their skills and try out products (*Retail Forward* 2005).

8.1 Massive indoor waterfalls can be found inside a typical Bass Pro Shop.

FACTORS FUELING ENTERTAINMENT RETAILING

Societal trends are changing the way consumers shop and are creating a demand for entertainment in the shopping experience. Several trends such as increases in retailers who employ multichannels, mass customization, technology, *shoppertainment*, and *edutainment* have created more competition in retailing.

Increased Use of Multiple Shopping Channels

Multichannel shopping is contributing to the development of entertainment retailing. **Multiple shopping channels** include brick-and-mortar stores, catalogs, television, direct sales, the Internet, and mobile telephones. According to the Abacus's annual trend report, in 2005 multichannel merchants received 25 percent of direct sales from websites, up from 20 percent in 2004, with an average sale of $166 dollars (Multichannel Merchant 2006). Consumers shopping in more than one retail channel have created more competition for brick-and-mortar stores. Brick-and-mortar stores, therefore, must stand out in the marketplace by creating an experience that consumers will remember. The brick-and-mortar retailer is being transformed into a retail activity theater staffed to offer advice, cooking lessons, beauty makeovers, and fashion shows. These stores are focusing more on experiences that can be gained only by being there (*Retail Forward* 2005).

No matter which channel retailers use to sell merchandise and services, they must be cognizant of the experience the channel creates and try to use the channel to their best advantage. For example, Internet retailers can provide interesting, interactive websites that engage and captivate the consumer and entice the consumer to return for future purchases. Honda is doing a good job at showcasing its automobiles through its website www.honda.com. Shoppers can choose to review specifications or compare the features and benefits of the different models, they can read the latest news articles about Honda vehicles, and they can locate a local Honda dealership.

Mass Customization

Another retail trend that is influencing entertainment retailing is **mass customization**—modifying a basic product or service to meet the needs of a customer. Technological and marketing developments have driven consumers to communicate and shop on the Internet and tailor their own entertainment options from hundreds of offerings. At the same time, many consumers enjoy having products that are different or specially customized to their individual desires. Products such as cars, shoes, and clothing that allow consumers to create products to their own specifications are being offered by many retailers. No longer constrained by time and place, consumers can shop around the clock and around the world from their own homes and on their own terms, while also having direct access to suppliers. Consumers dictate what they want and demand that manufacturers supply it (Roderick 2003). Mass customization is particularly popular with Generation Y consumers because it gives them a chance to express their individuality.

Many companies are implementing mass customization. For example, Marriott's Honored Guest program tracks the preferences of repeat customers. When customers check in, they are assigned a room that best matches their individual preferences, such as smoking versus non-smoking, low floor versus high floor, favorite newspaper, and so on. Levi Strauss lets consumers order a pair of jeans that have a custom-computerized fit.

Consumers can buy personalized storybooks, videos, and dolls for their kids. Hallmark Cards allows buyers to create their own greeting cards by adding personal information to a basic design. Honda also serves as an example of mass customization. Consumers can build and price a car to their personal specifications. The build and price feature allows consumers to choose the make and model of car and the exterior and interior color and accessories. It also provides manufacturer's suggested retail price (MSRP) for every personalized feature. In October 2004, Target introduced Target to a T, online custom jeans for men and women (*Retail Forward* 2005). Each of these retailers is providing unique experiences and opportunities to customize their product to differentiate themselves from the competition.

Technological Advances

The emergence of new technologies also creates an opportunity for retailers to add more entertainment aspects to brick-and-mortar stores. New technology means that intensive entertainment experiences can take place in smaller areas, producing a higher level of performance per square foot than before. Cutting-edge technology also is found on several retailers' websites. For example, Honda's website lets customers get a 360-degree view of any current-year Honda automobile. The Media Player feature enables consumers to look at the car of their choice from every imaginable angle. This experience simulates the experience of being in a Honda showroom looking at an actual vehicle.

Shoppertainment and Edutainment

Shoppertainment unites shopping and entertainment in a single shopping site (Fife 2004). The concept applies in many retail outlets such as malls, town centers, and stores. This strategy is used by brick-and-mortar stores to compete against online shopping and attract customers. Examples of mall shoppertainment include Halloween hunts and puppet shows. Town centers may hire street buskers or artists to entertain customers. Moussa Kouyate is a master kora player from Senegal, West Africa. He plays music outside of the ancient Roman Baths, a tourist destination in the town center of Bath, England. He sells his music to tourists who listen to him as they enter and exit the Roman Baths and to locals. His music also entertains people who are relaxing outside in the area.

In some situations, sales associates use a script to prompt customers to respond. Scripts provide a framework that employees use to describe, analyze, and understand situations (Gioia and Poole 1984). Scripts "guide employee behavior and are written for a category of situations and may provide a basis for an unconscious employee response to a set of circumstances" (Gioia and Poole 1984, 449). As a result, employees who use scripts may consider their behavior to be performances. For example, County National Bank of Pennsylvania provided their tellers with a script that enabled customers to get connected with the people selling their products and services (Adams 2005). Shoppers also act in scripted behavior when they engage in repetitive consumer behavior (Thomas and Garland 2004). Retail grocers' weekly online shopping lists can act as scripts for stimulating grocery sales. Hence, both sales associates and customers are actors in the production of the customer experience.

Similarly, **edutainment** brings together education and entertainment. Retailers use this strategy in a variety of ways. For example, Home Depot offers home-improvement classes so customers can learn how to do it themselves. London's

Selfridges uses demonstrations of kitchen products to educate consumers on how to use new products and stimulate product sales. When Selfridges introduced a new food chopper for sale, they used the store sound system to announce the demonstration location and offered a free gift to customers who watched the new product presentation.

ENTERTAINING SHOPPING EXPERIENCES

Retailers are challenged by consumers who are less excited about shopping than they used to be. In addition, over-storing has produced nearly twice as many retail outlets as needed to support the U.S. population. In this environment, it is no longer enough for a retailer to provide such conventional enticements as broad merchandise selection, everyday low pricing, extended store hours, and liberal return policies to attract consumers (Buss 1997). In fact, the shopping experience itself rather than the procuring of products is becoming more important to consumers. J. M. Carpenter, M. Moore, and A. E. Fairhurst (2005, 43) stated, "As consumers are increasingly demanding enjoyable experiences in their consumption activities, retailers are trying to generate customer excitement through entertainment in stores, shopping centers, and other retail formats." L. Berry (1999) defines customer excitement as "experiencing genuine joy in interacting with the retailer as a result of the freshness and creativity of the store, learning something new from the retailer (such as a new approach to cooking, a cool vacation idea, how to build a deck or put up wallpaper, how to dress better, or how to use the Internet more effectively), solving an important problem (such as fixing a car, fixing a tooth, getting a great wedding dress, finding a stylish pair of glasses, or buying fashionable yet comfortable shoes), and feeling like a smart shopper who is in control and not wasting money or time" (2).

Entertainment retailing is about making an emotional connection with the customer. C. Mathwick, N. K. Malhotra, and E. Rigdon (2002) developed a scale for measuring experiential value based upon playfulness, aesthetics, customer return on investment, and customer service. They identified seven indicators of experiential value: efficiency, economic value, intrinsic enjoyment, escapism, visual appeal, entertainment, and service excellence. Mathwick et al. used these dimensions to examine the differences between catalog and Internet shoppers in terms of their shopping preferences and patronage intent. They found that a customer return on investment influenced Internet shopping preferences; both customer return on investment and aesthetic value influenced catalog shopping preferences. Mathwick et al.'s study shows that the bundle of experiential value dimensions consumers desire varies by shopping channel.

In the example of FAO Schwarz, consumers buying toys also received benefits from the shopping experience, which could have included intrinsic enjoyment, escapism, visual appeal, entertainment, and service excellence. An example of a shopping center that offers entertainment is the Mall of America in Bloomington, Minnesota, which centers its stores, restaurants, a hotel, and other entertainment facilities around The Park at MOA (formerly known as Camp Snoopy), America's largest themed entertainment indoor park (See Figure 8.2). Thus, Mall of America attracts tourists as well as local residents.

M. F. Ibrahim and N. C. Wee (2002) suggested that the entertaining shopping experience is influenced by three factors: retailer factors, customer factors, and transport mode or travel attributes, which is demonstrated in their model as shown

8.2 MOA (formerly Camp Snoopy) adds to the retail experience of Mall of America.

in Figure 8.3. Their model suggests that an entertaining shopping experience begins before the consumer reaches the retail destination. In this model, transportation mode and travel factors such as effort, protection, comfort, enjoyment, and tension, directly influence the entertaining shopping experience. Retailer factors such as atmosphere, shopping center features, and ancillary facilities (e.g., parking, entertainment facilities) also influence the entertaining shopping experience. Lastly, customer factors such as hedonic (emotional) orientation or utilitarian (functional) orientations influence the entertaining shopping experience. Clearly, these three factors—retailer factors, customer factors, and transport mode or travel factors—should be

8.3 This model suggests that the entertaining shopping experience is influenced by retailer factors, customer factors, and transport mode or travel attributes.

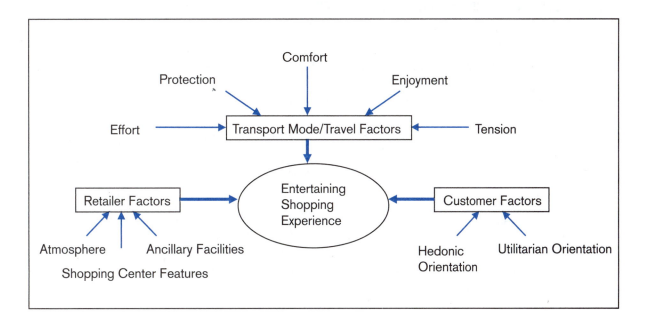

well developed to enhance entertaining shopping experiences, which can eventually boost retail sales.

ENTERTAINMENT-RETAIL CENTERS

Since entertainment and retailing merged, successful retailers have used entertainment in their retail mix. P. Phillips (1995) described five types of entertainment-retail centers: family entertainment centers, high-tech entertainment centers, high-impact film venues, entertainment-driven retail, and nighttime entertainment centers. Characteristics of the different types of retail entertainment centers, including their target markets, retail offers, and key attractions, are shown in Table 8.1.

Rye Playland in New York is an example of a family entertainment center. It is a county-run, 279-acre park located on Long Island Sound that was built in 1928 and is listed as a National Historic Landmark (O'Brien 2003). The admission-free amusement park features some of the original art deco and design, regularly schedules free entertainment such as puppet shows and concerts, and has 52 rides, including 26 for children. Food and souvenirs are sold at the park. Two additional retailers who have embraced family entertainment include Mega Park at Les Galeries de la Capitale in Quebec City and River Fair Family Fun Park at River Falls Mall in Clarksville, Indiana (Barbieri 2005).

An example of a high-tech entertainment center is DisneyQuest located at Downtown Disney in Orlando, Florida. The indoor center is made up of five floors of cutting-edge technology. The complex is made up of entertainment, dining, and shopping. Guests can design their own adventures through Disney's virtual-reality attractions and 3-D experiences. Customers can dine at any of the 15 restaurants depending upon whether they desire special and unique dining, casual dining, or a quick-service restaurant. Moreover, the retail paradise touts "fun environments and unique merchandise" (DisneyQuest 2006).

An example of a high-impact film venue is Metreon—the 375,000-square-foot Sony Entertainment Center in San Fran-

TABLE 8.1 TYPES OF RETAIL ENTERTAINMENT CENTERS

	FAMILY ENTERTAINMENT	HIGH TECH ENTERTAINMENT	HIGH IMPACT FILM VENUES	ENTERTAINMENT-DRIVEN RETAIL	NIGHT-TIME ENTERTAINMENT
Target markets	Families with young children, residents of area	Teenagers	Showcase film destination consumers	Visitors (tourists)	Visitors of theme parks
Retail offers	Limited merchandise	Food, beverages, merchandise	Restaurants, bars, other forms of entertainment, merchandise	Food, beverages, merchandise	Restaurants, nightclubs, entertainment, merchandise
Key attractions	Family entertainment (climbing walls and small-scale rides, etc.)	Sophisticated video games, simulators, and virtual reality	High-definition film theater, 360-degree immersion film, film-based simulator, and/or virtual reality experience	Entertainment, such as casino or Universal Studios	Themed-based entertainment

Source: Phillips, P. 1995. Merging entertainment and retailing. *Economic Development Review* 13(2):13–16.

cisco (Young 2000). This center includes 4 floors of stores, restaurants, interactive edutainment attractions based on children's books, a 15-screen cinema, and a Sony IMAX Theater. Consumers pay a fee to see attractions and theaters, but not to enter the center's public space.

An example of entertainment-driven retail can be found at Universal Studios in Orlando, Florida. It has two theme parks, three hotels, and a shopping and entertainment area called City Walk. Although City Walk does not charge an admission, some venues charge entrance fees. The entertainment experiences created by Universal Studios attract consumers from around the world and help keep them on-site for extended periods of time.

Nighttime entertainment centers offer a combination of restaurants, nightclubs, and live entertainment, augmented by retail. Examples include Church Street Station and Pleasure Island at Disney World in Orlando, Florida. Although they attract consumers primarily during the nighttime, they are also used during the day. This allows the entertainment center to increase its market appeal to attract area workers at lunch, as well as tourists. South Street Seaport, formerly the Fulton Street Fish Market in Manhattan, is a historic area on New York City's East River. It offers historic sailing vessels and a museum as attractions for tourists. The refurbished market area houses restaurants, bars, entertainment, and shopping for tourists and workers from nearby Wall Street.

The success of these centers is often measured by sales per square foot and economic return. Technology and development companies both support investments in entertainment centers because of the symbiotic relationship between the tenants. The entertainment-driven crowds support the retail and food components through sales, which in turn serve these crowds with consumption experiences.

ENTERTAINMENT THROUGH DIFFERENT CHANNELS

Retailers can use entertainment strategies through various shopping channels. These include shopping centers (which includes brick-and-mortar tenants), television home shopping and infomercials, and the Internet.

Shopping Centers

Traditional shopping centers attracted consumers by offering a wide assortment of stores and merchandise at a single location. This assortment has increased to social and entertainment providers and activities (e.g., special events, food courts, cinemas, and video arcades). By broadening the mix of tenants and activities, the mall has repositioned itself from an economic entity to a center for entertainment and cultural events (Bloch, Ridgway, and Dawson 1994). In fact, going to the mall has been called "a culturally ingrained phenomenon" (Cuneo 2000, 38). In 1995, the International Council of Shopping Centers reported that half of all retailers used entertainment to describe their businesses. The concept of entertainment is also broad and diverse, as illustrated in the Typology of Entertainment developed by the International Council of Shopping Centers (1995) (See Table 8.2).

Entertainment offerings in shopping centers tend to encourage consumers to do more cross-shopping, which enables them to shop across multiple types of products or services at multiple tenants. The consequent engagement in cross-shopping activities at shopping centers can produce more enjoyable shopping experiences and a longer duration of shopping trips. This way, consumers are increasing their benefits from shopping compared with their shopping costs, which leads to increased consumer efficiency. These increased shopping time and cross-shopping activities will increase shopping center revenues.

TABLE 8.2 TYPOLOGY OF SHOPPING CENTER ENTERTAINMENT

Owner/ developer driven (entertainment designed by the center owner/ developer)	Permanent (long-term operation)		Carousels, play areas
	Programmatic (temporary operation)		Art exhibits, antique shows, fashion shows, educational/ community-service programs, seasonal promotions, taking pictures with Santa Claus, etc.
Retailer driven (entertainment created by retailers)	Center entertainment (merchandise/services that consumers use at the center)	Food	Food courts, specialty/theme restaurants, locally based upscale restaurants
		Nonfood	Common area (e.g., amusement park retailers)
			In-line (e.g., movie theaters, providers of hardware and software for video games, virtual reality stations, other technology-based entertainment such as Sony, Edison Brothers, or Pocket Change).
	Shopping experience (merchandise/services that consumers use after they leave the center)		Merchandise/service providing entertainment (e.g., bookstores such as Barnes & Noble, computer and electronics stores such as Radio Shack, toy and gadget stores such as FAO Schwarz, sporting goods stores such as Herman's, and music/video stores such as Tower Records)
			Entertainment industry-based merchandise/services (e.g., Sesame Street, Warner Brothers, and Disney)
			Other merchandise/services (e.g., Crate & Barrel, The Museum Store, the Niketown concept store, The Body Shop, and The Nature Company)

Source: International Council of Shopping Centers (ICSC). 1995. Entertainment: The retailer's perspective. *ICSC Research Quarterly* 2(3):15–20.

J. Sit, B. Merrilees, and D. Birch (2003) studied the importance of retail and entertainment attributes to shopping center patrons. They identified six shopper segments, three of which valued entertainment in the retail mix. The first segment, accounting for 22 percent, is labeled entertainment shoppers. This segment is predominantly male, young, single, low income, interested in specialty entertainment, and moderately desire food when shopping. The second segment, about 25 percent, is demanding shoppers. This segment includes middle-aged males and females, married, with low income. They report browsing, meeting with friends and family, and seeking entertainment and food when visiting shopping centers. The third shopper segment, about 16 percent, is service shoppers. This segment is made up of young, married males and females with an average income who shop with family members or friends. They also report entertainment and food are important parts of the retail mix. In particular, they view specialty and special event entertainment vital to the shopping center mix. Managerial implications of Sit et al.'s (2003) findings pointed out the need to identify pro-entertainment and anti-entertainment consumer segments. The pro-entertainment consumer segment could be targeted by using promotions that emphasize innovative video arcades, variety of food outlets, and wide selections of movies. On the contrary, the anti-entertainment consumer segment could be targeted by emphasizing the ease of shopping and accessibility of the center. Informative signs for escalators, elevators, food courts, and restrooms as well as adequate parking and merchandise assortment should be emphasized to meet the needs of this consumer segment (Sit et al. 2003, 93).

Retailers constantly ask themselves why consumers go to shopping malls. One answer is that shopping malls provide products that consumers need as well as a pleasurable diversion from mundane activities and chores. However, many shoppers now consider malls to be repetitive because there is a similar store mix and product assortment in every regional mall (Ibrahim and Wee 2002). This explains the decline that began to take place in early 1990s of many regional malls. Current mall developers and managers explore the benefits that are offered to consumers and how they are responding to these benefits. As they continue to observe the demand for entertainment, developers are building large entertainment centers that provide rides, skating rinks, amusement parks, multiplex movie theaters, museums, and virtual reality centers. I. Kim, T. Christiansen, R. Feinberg, and H. Choi (2005) stated: "As competition between malls increases, enhancing the entertainment value for the consumer appears to be becoming an important way of differentiating the mall product" (487).

Television Home Shopping and Infomercials

Television shopping networks such as QVC, Shop At Home, and Shop NBC, and **infomercials** are two retail venues used to sell merchandise directly to consumers. These two retail venues attempt to develop social relationships with their audiences through warm, friendly, and spontaneous commentators (Burton 2002). One of the most well-known television shopping networks is QVC, which stands for quality,

value, and convenience. Of the 7.2 million people who made a purchase through QVC in 2004, 90 percent of them were women and 93 percent were repeat customers (Esfahani 2005). Television shopping formats have a fun factor, are informational, and give products vitality; viewing these channels is considered a leisure activity.

A QVC success story can be seen in a two-hour show, *Decade of Discoveries*, which showcased Bea Toms and her ham biscuit recipes from a country cookbook that she penned from her 91 years of experience. In three and a half minutes, Mrs. Toms sold her entire inventory of 1,413 books and generated $37,535 in sales (Esfahani 2005). Though an outstanding story, this is not unusual for QVC entrepreneurs.

QVC generates sales through "the combination of soft sell and data-driven rigor" (Esfahani 2005, 94). They adjust camera angles, lighting, and dialogue, and they may use their companion website to maximize sales. QVC blends entertainment and retail into daily programs to build their brand and create loyal customers. Live demonstrations, impromptu chats, and call-in testimonials build trust and relationships with customers and contribute to QVC's brand of entertailment. In 2004, QVC had $5.7 billion in sales revenues, $760 million in operating profit, and a 13 percent operating margin with an average gross margin of 38 percent. These numbers make QVC one of the world's most successful and innovative retailers (Esfahani 2005). In addition, QVC now sells private label products. QVC's business goes beyond the TV dial to include QVC.com, the third largest general merchant on the Internet behind Amazon.com and JCPenney.com. Doug Rose, QVC's vice president of merchandising and brand development, said "we're not in the business of selling items—we're in the business of pleasing customers" (Esfahani 2005, 91).

Internet

Shopping through the Internet is no longer considered something that is different or unique. This is evidenced by the number of people making online purchases. A recent report by Shop.org based on statistics from Forrester Research indicated that e-commerce transactions are expected to reach $316 billion in the year 2010, an 88 percent increase from the year 2005 (U.S. Online Shoppers 2005). As consumers move into online shopping, their shopping habits are changing drastically. Previously, the concept of online shopping was novel and trendy. But as more people have caught onto online shopping, online marketers are facing new challenges.

Today, when consumers shop online, they want their shopping activity to be experiential. Given the choice to purchase from a boring, mundane website versus an interactive website with attractive visuals and audio clips, consumers generally choose the latter. Thus, Internet retailers are spending a significant amount of their resources on improving the quality of their websites. In addition to delivering the right content to the right audience, online retailers must provide tools and resources on their websites to engage, delight, and excite users.

8.4 Paint manufacturer Benjamin Moore has an interactive Web feature called My Scrapbook that allows consumers to customize colors of their home décor.

INTERNET RETAILERS AS ENTERTAINMENT PROVIDERS

Internet retail websites have a unique opportunity to use retail entertainment to attract visitors and convert them into purchasers. Strategies they can use include virtual reality, Web magazines, games, and other interactive formats. American Girl uses both Web magazines and games to keep their customers coming back to visit their website (www.Americangirl.com).

Some apparel catalogs have virtual bodies that are created using customers' actual body measurements. Innovations in technology allow retailers to offer customers a three-dimensional body on their websites. The virtual 3-D body can be made to correspond to the customers' body measurements and type. Customers can try garments on the virtual body and see how garments fit. Thus use of the virtual body creates an experience similar to a brick-and-mortar fitting room experience.

Benjamin Moore, a paint manufacturer, is known for its vivid paint colors that express style and personality. When the company launched its website, the first challenge was to convey that reputation online to its target audience who were primarily home decorators (www.benjaminmoore.com). Research conducted by Benjamin Moore revealed that home decorators constantly search home décor magazines for inspirational decorating ideas, rip out pages, and put them into a file for later use. This led to the idea of creating a personalized feature on their website called My Scrapbook (See Figure 8.4). This interactive feature allows home decorators to experiment with various Benjamin Moore colors and shades within personalized sample rooms that convey unique themes and styles. Users can browse inspirational spaces by mood (e.g., urban, romantic, casual) or by room type (e.g., living room, bathroom, kitchen). Users can then paint their virtual rooms by choosing various colors from a wide range of color choices and save their preferences for later use. Users can modify every item in the room, including lamps, fabrics, and furniture. Users can even e-mail their preferences to friends and families to get opinions or suggestions. The website also contains other features such as painting techniques, home décor advice, a paint calculator to find the amount of paint needed for a particular room, and updates on the latest color trends. The highlight of the project notebook feature is the way it engages the user. With rich and vivid colors, the interactive Benjamin Moore Web page truly creates a memorable experience for the user (Rayson 2004).

Another example of an online entertainment retailer is Jeep (www.jeep.com). Market research conducted by Jeep found that roughly 70 percent of its customers uses the Internet for research six months prior to making a vehicle purchase or lease. They also found that the Jeep customer spent more than five hours online prior to making their purchases. Since the Internet was the place where potential Jeep customers decided whether to pursue their purchase intentions, Jeep decided to invest a considerable amount of resources in making their website attractive and experiential. Jeep created experimental situations, interactive features, and innovative personalized applications on their website that set them apart from other automobile websites. In addition, Jeep created interactive games and gave potential Jeep buyers the ability to configure their own Jeep and get behind the virtual wheel. These interactive experiences have helped the potential Jeep customer make a purchase decision (Rayson 2004).

Internet use has grown and evolved for consumers. At first it was primarily a source of information; then it became a shopping venue. Now, it offers a total consumption experience with entertainment that is marketed to a particular lifestyle. Interactive websites can create unique customer experiences. Online retailers may lose business unless they quickly take steps to incorporate entertainment into their operating strategy.

INTERNET ADVERTISING AND ENTERTAINMENT

Entertainment is a component of Internet advertising. Internet advertising is more aggressive than it was previously. Advertisers strive to be more creative, more targeted, and more effective (Mangalindan, Swisher, Bank, Hamilton, and Clark 2004). It now includes rich media ads with animated objects that move across the consumer's screen and pop-under ads appear on-screen after files are closed.

L. D. Wolin and P. Korgaonkar (2003) compared male and female respondents regarding advertising on the Web, television, radio, and in newspapers and magazines. They identified six advertising dimensions: enjoyable, offensive, informative, deceptive, annoying, and useful. Males found Web advertising more enjoyable than magazine and newspaper advertising, more useful than newspaper and radio advertising, and more informative than newspaper advertising. Females identified Web advertising as more annoying than magazine and newspaper advertising; more offensive than magazine, radio, and television advertising; and more deceptive, but more useful, than television advertising. Males, in comparison with females, had more positive beliefs about Web advertising versus traditional media advertising. While males were more likely to purchase on the Web, females preferred to use the shopping sites for enjoyment and information gathering (versus purchases) and subsequently purchased through more traditional outlets.

Virtual Communities

Increasingly, individuals are connecting to the Internet to interact with others; most of them are participating in virtual communities as a form of social interaction and information exchange (Koh and Kim 2004). The virtual community, born with the advent of online technology, takes part in a new form of communication and represents one of the most interesting developments in the information age (Balasubramanian and Mahajan 2001). A **virtual community** is made up of a specific group of individuals with common goals or interests, interacting together online as a group, and using Internet connectivity as a method to maintain existing relationships (Dholakia, Bagozzi, and Pearo 2004). Some of the most popular types of virtual communities are newsgroups, bulletin boards, Internet forums, chat rooms, e-mail lists, and virtual games. People go to specific bulletin boards on a regular basis to discuss common interests, such as fighting breast cancer, collecting antiques, or improving their children's reading skills.

Differing from traditional communities, virtual communities do not have the limitations of physical location; thus, information in virtual communities can be spread out to millions of consumers instantaneously. In this case, it is important to discover why individuals choose different virtual communities. Identifying motivations of individuals joining virtual communities can be traced back to research in social psychology. Motivations to join regular, off-line communities have been related to the need to belong to a group and be affiliated with others. Groups provide individuals with a source of information, and they help in achieving goals and giving personal rewards (Watson and Johnson 1972). By joining a preexisting social group, an individual forms a social identity (Hogg and Terry 2000). These motivations for joining traditional, face-to-face groups can be extended to understand why people choose to participate in virtual communities. Information exchange, relationships, social support, and entertainment are the four most common motivations for participation in virtual communities.

INFORMATION EXCHANGE

Virtual communities provide a subset of the information available on the Internet. Accessing information is the most frequently cited motivation for using virtual communities (Wellman and Gulia 1999). Unlike other Internet information provided by the site host, most of the content of virtual communities is member-generated and is a self-sustaining process. As more members generate more content, the increased content draws more members (Hegel and Armstrong 1997).

Virtual communities tend to focus on specific topics intended for information exchange among members (Baym 2000). By acquiring opinions and experiences from virtual communities, members can determine and clarify their own preferences and tastes. Yahoo chat rooms (www.chat.yahoo.com) are divided by specific topics such as business, hobbies, games, and regions to organize members' interactions by interest. There are many other chat rooms and forums that are based upon demographic characteristics such as gender and ethnicity.

Through virtual community messages, members tend to provide information, express views and feelings, request information, and suggest solutions (Herring 1996). iVillage (www.ivillage.com) is an Internet community for women who want to share ideas with other women on various topics, including beauty and style, diet and fitness, love, sex, pregnancy, and parenting. iVillage also provides direct electronic links to other Internet resources, including directories of sites relating to various women's magazines such as *Cosmopolitan, Country Living, Good Housekeeping,* and *Marie Claire.*

RELATIONSHIPS

Another possible reason why people join virtual communities is to seek friendships or relationships. The interactivity achieved through chat rooms, instant messaging, and bulletin boards provides ways for individuals to establish friendships. In fact, the structure of the Internet, with its searching capabilities and various virtual community forums, makes it easier to communicate with others in similar situations than it is in real life. People who feel lonely or are going through a crisis in their lives may seek others in virtual communities to exchange opinions and request advice about their problems and also to engage in small-talk with other people.

MySpace.com is a good example of a virtual community whose objective is relationship building. It creates a private community where members can share photos, journals, and interests with their growing network of mutual friends. Within this virtual environment, a small, compact group has developed into a large community with numerous subcommunities, strengthening their relationships.

SOCIAL SUPPORT

A virtual community can also provide support for people who may need to get emotional support, a sense of belonging, or companionship (Wellman and Gulia 1999). Its primary value resides in giving people the chance to come together and share personal experiences. For certain groups of people who may be going through intense life experiences, virtual communities can lead to the formation of deep personal connections.

HealingWell.com provides support for patients, caregivers, and families. It offers health resources, interactive tools, resource link directories, and community support to enable individuals to cope with their illness and start the healing process. Participants talk about how they deal with disorders or chronic illnesses. They have an opportunity to exchange information on topics such as medical research, pain medication, and test results (Armstrong and Hegel 1996). Other virtual communities that specialize in social support for groups include sites for recovering alcohol and drug addicts and those coping with stress from major life changes such as job loss, death of loved ones, infertility, or divorce.

ENTERTAINMENT

Participation in virtual communities may also be motivated by the quest for entertainment and diversion. A good example is Virtual World, a type of virtual community in which users play games with other community members. In Virtual World (www.virtualworld.com), a participant can pretend to be a member in various games. Members exercise their imagination and participate in the creation of an ongoing story in a virtual world. Participants can indulge their need for fantasy by creating their own game groups and game rules, which are then used to compete against teams created by other participants.

A virtual community can also be used as a community of fantasy, where people can create new environments, personalities, or stories. In this kind of community, participants' real identities are not important; rather, interaction with others is the strength of the appeal (Armstrong and Hegel 1996). Neopets is a Virtual Pet site where anyone can create and adopt a virtual pet (www.neopets.com). This site provides games that users can play with other Virtual Pet owners. More than 70 million Virtual Pet owners across the world participate in this community. They enjoy playing games with and taking care of their Virtual Pets, and creating their own stories and experiences (Armstrong and Hegel 1996).

Fort Lee, New Jersey, is a virtual community that provides information about shopping and services, as well as a source for local information. The website (www.fortleeonline.com) lists shops and stores by product category and gives website addresses, locations, and telephone numbers. People shopping in Fort Lee may be able to do so from the comfort of their homes. Some of these community shopping websites charge retailers for listing their information.

Online retailers offer participants the greatest satisfaction when they can address multiple motivations—information exchange, relationships, social support, and entertainment—within the same community. Although this is not always feasible, virtual community organizers should strive to meet as many of these motivational needs as possible to develop newer and stronger relations with participants.

ENTERTAINMENT IN TOURISM

Entertainment retailing venues have become tourist attractions. In fact, nearly 9 out of 10 of overseas travelers reported shopping during their visit to the United States (Knight 1999). Shopping and dining are the most popular activities among tourists. Retailers may receive incremental benefits from tourist shoppers because tourists are on vacation or celebrating special occasions and are thus less price sensitive and more inclined to purchase impulse items (e.g., T-shirts, souvenir items) (Kim 2001).

Entertainment-Oriented Tourist Attractions

In response to consumers' desires for consumption experiences, tourism, recreation, entertainment, and retail have united in a variety of formats. For example, leisure and heritage destination development projects are growing in the United States and are popular because of regional appeal (Field 2005). Examples of such projects include Kansas City's Legends shopping center, with Cavender's Western apparel and experience store, and New York City's the Shops at Atlas Park, with retail, cafés, bistros and restaurants in a mix of new and historically renovated buildings. The Shops at Atlas Park is particularly interesting because it mixes historically renovated buildings with newer ones. These sites mix tourism and leisure activities, while providing an additional opportunity for tourists to shop.

The major entertainment-oriented tourist attractions from which retail developers borrow ideas are Las Vegas and Disney World. Illusion and allusion are used to create environments that foster relationships between individuals and consumption. D. Kooijman (2002) suggested that current consumers want to be efficient, yet appreciate opportunities for recreation. Kooijman illustrated how retailing has evolved from meeting consumers' basic needs by simply supplying goods to a more elaborate recreation experience.

Another example of an entertainment-oriented tourist attraction is the Queen Mary, a floating ship in Long Beach, California. The floating ship is more than 1,000 feet long and is listed on the National Register of Historic Places. The Queen Mary made 1,001 transatlantic trips between 1934 and 1964. During this time she ferried soldiers, statesmen, celebrities, and royal gentry across the ocean. She features 365 hotel staterooms, award-winning restaurants, a wedding chapel, 16 reception salons decorated with art, and a great view of Long Beach. In Long Beach, there are other cultural gems, including the Long Beach Museum of Art, The Pike at Rainbow Harbor, and Shoreline Village (Swartz 2004).

Virgin Entertainment Group, which operates one of the largest media product retail chains in the world, carries a wide range of CDs, DVDs, video games, and books. It designed its Times Square store to include an interactive and emotionally exciting shopping experience. This music-entertainment store offers more than 250,000 CDs, 11,000 DVDs, and 7,000 games and installed 150 new kiosks to help shoppers try out almost any product before they buy it (IBM 2005). Other examples of entertainment-oriented tourist attractions include Forum Shops in Las Vegas, River-walk in San Antonio, Old Post Office in Washington, D.C., South Street Seaport in New York, Pier 39 in San Francisco, and Faneuil Hall Marketplace in Boston. Each of these attractions appeals to tourists through the use of unique restaurants, shopping, and various tourist attractions. These entertainment-oriented sites strengthen tourism and increase visitors' local expenditures (Che 2002).

Tourist Shopping

Shopping is the second largest travel expenditure following accommodation (Turner and Reisinger 2001). Tourist shopping expenditures account for 30 to 36 percent of total travel spending (Littrell, Baizerman, Kean, and Gahring 1994). Shopping opportunities can even be the primary purpose of tourism travel (Turner and Reisinger 2001). The last two decades of the twentieth century produced tourism destinations that are shopping entertainment complexes such as the Mall of America with The Park at MOA, Lego Information Center, Underwater Adventures Aquarium, and West Edmonton Mall with Galaxyland Amusement Park and World Water Park (See Figure 8.5).

Tourism shopping in Las Vegas generates business second only to the gambling entertainment business (Almeida 2004). Much of non-gambling entertainment is

8.5 West Edmonton Mall is Alberta's largest tourist destination.

from the size of the average shopping trip in retail entertainment complexes such as Grand Canal Shops. At Grand Canal Shops, consumers spent an average of $500 to $700 per trip in comparison with $200 to $300 on a typical shopping trip (Smith 2004).

J. Y. Oh, C. K. Cheng, X. Y. Lehto and J. O'Leary (2004) summarized research findings related to tourism shoppers as illustrated in Table 8.3. They also identified seven trip typologies as: people and setting, urban entertainment, intimacy and romance, active outdoor, history and parks, social with friends, and to relax with family groups. They found these groups had distinct motivations for participating in shopping activities. For example, tourists in the group of urban entertainment showed the highest tendency to shop and browse in the books and music category. However, this group had the lowest propensity to socializing with friends. They also found age, gender, and trip typology as predictor variables for tourists' preferences for shopping cate-

TABLE 8.3. TOURISM SHOPPING

STUDY	SUBJECT OR VARIABLES STUDIED	MAIN CONCLUSIONS
Jansen-Verbeke 1987	Gender and age influence on attitude toward shopping	Significant differences exist in gender and between age groups in attitudes toward shopping.
Jansen-Verbeke 1990	Socio-demographic influence on attitude, frequency, and pattern of shopping	Attitudes toward shopping, its frequency, and patterns have been related to consumers' personal characteristics such as gender, age, family status and socio-demographic status.
Littrell 1990	Profile of tourism styles and preference of craft items	Craft item purchases are different across four classified tourism styles: ethnic arts and people oriented; history and parks; active outdoor; and urban entertainment tourists.
Littrell, Anderson, and Brown 1993	Gender and age influence on differences in criteria for authenticity of souvenirs	For both genders, authenticity is derived from uniqueness, workmanship, aesthetics, usage, cultural integrity, craftsperson, shopping experience, and genuineness of souvenirs. There were no gender differences in defining authenticity. Tourists in different stages of travel, career, and ages adopted different criteria for souvenirs.
Anderson and Littrell 1995	Souvenir purchase behavior of women tourists of different age groups	Differences exist in souvenir purchasing behavior and perception of authenticity between early-adulthood women (age 22–45) and middle-adulthood women (age 43–60). Early-adulthood women made most unplanned purchases in malls with their children, while middle-adulthood women made planned purchases in specialty stores and tourist shops with friends or husbands.
US Department of Commerce and The Taubman Company 1999	Correlation between cultural tourism and tourists' expenditure level	Overseas travelers to the USA who visit cultural attractions (i.e., museums, national parks) tend to spend more time and money on shopping during their visit.
Reisinger and Turner 2002	Examination of shopping satisfaction from souvenir product attributes with socio-demographic and trip-type segmentations	Tourists' satisfaction results from the importance of souvenir product attributes of value, display, and uniqueness. It is not likely that different socio-demographic or trip-type segmentation is an important categorization for determining shopping satisfaction from product attributes.
Lehto, Cai, and O'Leary 2004	Examination of socio-demographic characteristics and trip attributes in relation to shopping expenditure and item preference	Travel purpose, travel style, age, and gender were significant factors influencing the amount of money travelers spent on shopping and the items they preferred.

Source: Oh, J.Y., C. K. Cheng, X. Y. Lehto, and J. O'Leary. 2004. Predictors of tourists' shopping behaviour: Examination of socio-demographic characteristics and trip typologies. *Journal of Vacation Marketing* 10(4):308–311.

gories and browsing activities. Tourists 51 to 60 years old were likely to shop or browse in all product categories except clothes, shoes, and jewelry. Young tourism shoppers were least likely to browse and shop, but when they did it was for books, music, clothes, shoes, and jewelry.

G. Moscardo (2004) identified four groups of shoppers based upon a combination of the importance of destination choice and participation in shopping activities. The four groups were serious shoppers, not-so-serious shoppers, arts-and-crafts shoppers, and non-shoppers. Serious shoppers—people wanting opportunities and participating in shopping activities—took in most of the activities available in the region and showed high levels of attendance at many regional commercial tourist attractions. Thus, the serious shopper group can be an important group for developing leisure and heritage or tourism destination projects.

TABLE 8.4. MARKET PROFILE FOR DUBAI FESTIVAL CITY

VARIABLES CONTRIBUTING TO MARKET ATTRACTIVENESS

- A youthful, multicultural population
- High discretionary income
- A rapidly growing tourist segment with 15 million tourists per annum projected by 2010
- The site is central to a trade area
- Market potential of USD 3.94 billion in retail and leisure spending
- Overall market potential is expected to rise to USD 6.93 billion by 2010
- Residents spend approximately 37% of their total income on comparison goods such as apparel and accessories; 47% on convenience goods and 16% on leisure activities
- The youthful profile of local residents indicates a latent demand for aspirational goods
- Government initiatives key to attract both domestic and international shoppers is the annual Dubai Shopping Festival, Dubai Summer Surprises, and the Ramadan Festival

Source: Dubai Festival City. 2005. Website information retrieved October 14, 2005, www.dubaifestivalcity.com

The link between tourism and retail is globally acknowledged. For example, United Arab Emirates (UAE) promotes destination tourism for economic diversification and growth with events such as the Dubai Shopping Festival (*Dubai Festival City* 2005). S. A. Anwar and S. M. Sohail (2004) surveyed 1,200 respondents at different tourist locations in Dubai. They found that shopping festivals attracted the largest number of tourists. Dubai Festival City's Festival Centre complex opened November 2006. It houses traditional mall stores (i.e., Gap and Nike), big-box retailers (i.e., IKEA), and restaurants in its first phase. In the second phase, a three-level, enclosed mall called The Crescent is projected to open with 300 stores. The development uses a street-front known as The Boulevard to link the different complex phases. The market profile for Dubai Festival City is given in Table 8.4.

RETAIL ENTERTAINMENT MIX

R. Harris, K. Harris, and S. Baron (2003) provided a framework for developing a dramatic script for retail and service organizations. The script is used by employees and the organization to reach experiential goals such as positive customer experiences for customers. Techniques from theaters are used in this retail strategy. Stages in Harris et al.'s framework include identifying the type of drama required to satisfy customers, creating the text, exploring the subtext, and setting a goal for the script. Their framework then describes how to select the experience design and experience performers. Elements in experience design are stage management, lighting, sound, costumes, props, and publicity. Development of experience performers requires improvisation, casting, role play, and rehearsal. In the following, the retail entertainment mix that includes music, lighting, celebrities, and sales associates are discussed. These elements help stage the retail experience and can be used to create a positive shopping environment and stimulate sales.

Music

Music contributes to retail marketing at the point-of-purchase and in advertising. It is made up of a complex mix of controllable elements that provide stimuli for moods and emotional reactions. To use music effectively, retail marketers need to understand how it affects consumer behavior.

G. Brunner (1990) reviewed past studies to provide information about music variables that can influence the retail atmosphere. Brunner summarized the review on the music effect based on rhythm, tempo, pitch, volume, and instrument. Firm rhythms project seriousness, smooth rhythms express happiness or playfulness, and uneven rhythms communicate dignity or exaltation. In terms of music tempo, a song in fast tempo is associated with happy or good feelings more often than a song in slow tempo. High pitched music is associated with happiness, and low pitched sounds are linked to sadness. Loud music seems animated while soft sounds express tranquility or delicacy. In terms of timbre, brass instruments produce sounds that are interpreted as triumphant or grotesque; wind instruments, awkward or mournful. Piano melodies sound soothing while strings seem spirited.

C. Lin and S. Wu (2006) examined music effects on consumption emotion and time perception. They found that joyful music stimulates positive consumption emotion, while sad music elicits negative emotions. Joyful music provides positive consumption emotion that contributes to an underestimation of the time perceived in a store. Sad music is associated with negative in-store emotion and contributes to overestimation of time spent in a store. High-volume music in a store is linked to overestimation of time in the store and contributes to negative emotion. Low volume in a store evokes position emotion and leads to shorter time perception.

S. Eroglu, K. A. Machleit, and J. C. Chebat (2005) found an interactive effect of two retail factors—music volume and store density—on shopper response. High-density environments with slow music, compared with high density with fast music, provoked higher hedonic and utilitarian responses. Hedonic responses included statements such as "the trip was truly a joy" and "while shopping, I felt a sense of adventure" (582). Utilitarian responses included statements such as "I accomplished just what I wanted to on this shopping trip" and "while shopping, I found just the item(s) I was looking for" (582). However, in a condition of low density, fast music yielded higher hedonic and utilitarian responses than a slow music environment. The results indicate that shopper response varies under different conditions.

A study by J. C. Sweeney and F. Wyber (2002) suggests that music affects consumers' perceptions of service and merchandise quality in clothing stores. It also is linked to influencing consumers' feelings of arousal and pleasure. In their study, music affected consumers' evaluations of the service quality and shopping pleasure. Consumers who listened to classical music rated service quality as high. When the music was fast, it evoked a sense of pleasure in consumers.

Type of music influences consumption. Stores that play Christmas music report 6 percent higher holiday sales than retailers with Christmas music; "Joy to the World" stimulates sales more often than when the more somber "Silent Night" is played (Hajewski 2000). Country music also plays an important role in increasing the customer traffic to the restaurant. Cracker Barrel, located at highway exits and known for their meals and country store retailing, has a long association with country music. For about 30 years, it has sponsored the Grand Ole Opry, the legendary country music venue (Cebrzynski 2005).

One way retail brands use music in their marketing strategies is to choose a song with lyrics that "drive home a brand promise" (O'Loughlin 2005, 10). UPS recently developed an integrated ad campaign that showed its document and mailbox services along with related products, such as its bubble wrap and shipping cartons. Stevie Wonder's song, "Don't You Worry 'Bout a Thing," was incorporated into the campaign as support for the brand promise made. The goal is for customers to see that the UPS Store can help alleviate some of their daily business worries (O'Loughlin 2005).

As another current practice, retail brands sell music that is appealing to their customers' lifestyles. Starbucks now sells music at its coffee stores. In fact, Starbucks and Concord Records produced and released a CD featuring Ray Charles's last songs. Their *Genius Loves Company* CD sold more than 44,000 copies in its first week (*DSN Retailing Today* 2004). Other retailers sell music CDs related to their image. EMI-Capitol Music produces entertaining themed CDs for Williams-Sonoma and Pottery Barn, owned by Williams-Sonoma, Inc. These CDs complement the product mix of high-end kitchen equipment, housewares, and food ingredients available at Williams-Sonoma and casual home furnishings at Pottery Barn. Bath and Body Works softly plays a remake of a sixties song, "You Beat Me to the Punch" to target older customers. Pottery Barn also plays music from the sixties with a remake of the Mamas and Papas' "Go Where You Want to Go," while Williams-Sonoma plays an older music classic, "Pocketful of Dreams" (Hajewski 2000). Lighthearted classical music is played at Victoria's Secret and is consistent with the lingerie store's original brand image, which includes lacy Victorian undergarments. Other brands such as Trans World Entertainment, Best Buy, and Musicland/Sam Goody use live music venues as part of their marketing mix (Wan 2002).

Music is an important part of the retail mix because it adds emotional meaning to which customers react. Thus, musical offerings should be associated with demographic characteristics, moods, and the product use of the target customers. Retailers should consider whether their customers enjoy the music they selected and its potential influence on their moods.

Lighting

Lighting also plays a role in attracting customers and selling products. When used properly, lighting sets the stage for a positive retail experience and can stimulate sales (*CSNews Online* 2005). R. Heschong, L. Wright, and S. Okura (2002) found that the addition of natural skylights in stores increased sales 40 percent above stores in the same chain without skylights. Aesthetically pleasing lighting designs can attract, direct, and motivate buyers (*Images Retail Bureau* 2004). Types of lighting are associated with specific functions (Levy and Weitz 2001). Incandescent lighting provides warm and cozy illumination. Accent lighting directs attention in merchandise and display areas. Task lighting focuses consumer interest on specific functional areas, while diffused lighting is aesthetically pleasing.

Lighting communicates status level of a retailer (Babin, Hardesty, and Suter 2003). For example, prestigious stores use soft natural lighting, while discounters often use lights that can be harsh on the eye. Whole Foods Market, the Austin-based specialty grocer, has created a theatrical atmosphere for staging their products through the use of lighting design (Moffat 2006). The store uses fiber optics and ceramic metal halide on track, as well as other types of fixtures, as a transition from heavy use of incandescent lights. Whole Foods maintains a 50-foot-candle ambient light level in its stores, which is supplemented by high-bay compact fluorescents, aluminum-reflector pendants, and other light sources.

Celebrities

While consumers see celebrity endorsements as attention-getting, likeable, and influential, they do not find them overly believable (O'Mahony and Meenaghan 1997). G. McCracken (1989) defined a celebrity endorser as "any individual who enjoys public recognition and uses this recognition on behalf of a consumer good by appearing with it in an advertisement" (310). Celebrities endorse through a variety of modes. The explicit mode is "I endorse this product" and the implicit mode is "I use this product." The imperative mode suggests "You should use this product" (O'Mahony and Meenaghan 1997). Celebrity endorsers should have three attributes: credibility, attractiveness, and power to successfully influence a company or product image (Bryne, Whitehead, and Breen 2003).

Celebrity endorsement relies on the symbolic meaning of the endorser, which is supposed to transfer from celebrity to the product and on to the consumer (McCracken 1989). This means that the symbolic meaning of the celebrity should correspond to the symbolic meanings desired in the product by the customers. There is also a significant interaction between the type of spokesperson and the service advertised (Stafford, Stafford, and Day 2002). Credible endorsement sources are associated with favorable evaluations. Celebrities aid the transfer of symbolic meaning from the product to the consumer as part of their concept of self. A study by M. Walker, L. Langmeyer, and D. Langmeyer (1992) showed images of Madonna and Christie Brinkley combined with specific products. Results indicated the celebrities project their images, as well as some of their qualities, onto the product being evaluated by the consumer. However, it is important to note the effectiveness of celebrity endorsements differs by the type of service. Consumers are apt to trust and respect celebrity expertise more for hedonic services than for utilitarian ones (Stafford et al. 2002). The image of celebrities who make endorsements for retailers should match the image of the product or service promoted.

Sales Associates

Sales associates play an important role in providing positive experience to customers. Sales associates contribute to a store's personality by contributing value to consumers' shopping experiences (Roach 1995). Thus, positive experiences with sales associates, such as guidance and good manners, can enhance the value of shopping at a store. Furthermore, salespeople can communicate the vision and mission of the retailer to consumers and contribute to the value of the total retail entertainment experience.

According to G. Warnaby and B. J. Davies (1997), the Servuction (part service, part production) model of service consumption focuses on experiential aspects. The Servuction Model describes the interactive production of services, which involves service personnel as well as the individual consumer and other consumers (See Figure 8.6). Their model includes the visible element, the physical setting, and an invisible element, the social milieu.

Warnaby and Davies's Servuction Model is applicable in entertainment retailing. The quality of interaction (e.g., politeness, responsiveness) among personnel, consumers, and other guests influences the production of the consumer experience. When Disney refurbished its Manhattan operation, hands-on activities for customers and live costumed characters by employees were incorporated in the store in an attempt to attract tourists and local residents (Stanley 2004). Costumed characters greeted customers and posed with them, thus customizing the shopping experience. Disney refers to its employees as cast members and acknowledges their roles in communicating the heritage of their company (Lynch 2001). Disney cast members contribute to service quality and help create positive experience by providing entertainment for customers.

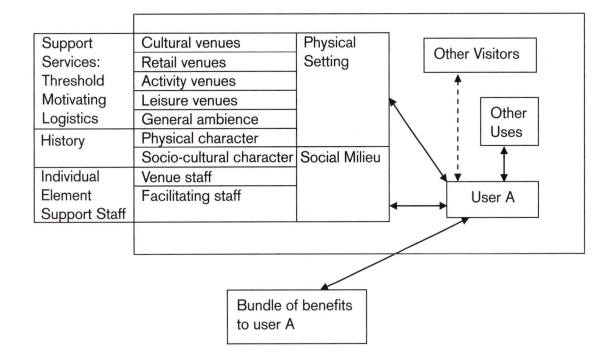

Support Services: Threshold Motivating Logistics	Cultural venues	Physical Setting
	Retail venues	
	Activity venues	
	Leisure venues	
	General ambience	
History	Physical character	
	Socio-cultural character	Social Milieu
Individual Element Support Staff	Venue staff	
	Facilitating staff	

Other Visitors

Other Uses

User A

Bundle of benefits to user A

8.6 G. Warnaby and B. J. Davies's Servuction Model focuses on experiential aspects of service consumption.

CHAPTER SUMMARY

Consumers increasingly desire entertaining shopping experiences. Entertainment helps create a memorable consumer experience. This chapter describes how emerging trends influence retail entertainment strategies. The trends that fuel the growth of entertainment retailing include use of multiple shopping channels, mass customization, technological advances, shoppertainment, and edutainment. The retail mix that lead to entertainment consist of music, lighting, celebrities, and sales associates. Entertainment provides retailers with an opportunity to create differentiation in their store environments and retail offerings. Goals of entertainment retailing include providing more enjoyable shopping experiences, a longer duration of shopping trips, and the potential for cross-shopping activities.

Retailers should align their use of entertainment through various shopping channels such as shopping centers, television home shopping, infomercials, and the Internet as well as traditional channels such as brick-and-mortar stores and catalogs. Virtual communities, a new form of communication, are increasingly used by individuals who want to be connected to the Internet to interact with others for information exchange, relationships, social support, and entertainment.

Entertainment is a critical component in tourism retailing. In fact, shopping is the second largest travel expenditure after accommodation. Also, shopping can be the primary purpose of tourism travel. Retailers in tourist attraction areas can take advantage of this consumer trend.

Although entertainment retailing has been increasingly popular, it provides some challenges. Consumers may encounter the same entertainment mix in different retail venues. For example, they may see similar entertainment tenant mix in shopping malls. Indeed, entertainment retailing has evolved to the point where it should make an emotional connection with customers rather than just providing entertainment. As the retail market in the

United States continues to become saturated, retailers must offer consumer experiences that cannot easily be duplicated.

Discussion *Questions*

1. Discuss why and how entertainment retailing adds value to the consumer experience.
2. Name the five types of entertainment-retail centers and describe how each appeals to their target customer.
3. Identify strategies merchants can use to add entertainment to the retail mix.
4. Describe the Harris et al. (2003) framework for developing a dramatic script for retail and service organizations and explain how it can be applied, using examples from retail that you are familiar with.
5. Explain the benefits of using music in the retail entertainment mix. Give examples of when it adds to the retail experience and when it does not.
6. Give an example of a retailer not mentioned in this chapter that successfully uses retail entertainment strategies. Explain how the retailer uses these strategies and what the outcomes are.
7. Explain how entertainment retailing adds to consumer efficiency.

REFERENCES

Adams, D. 1999. Voices from the street: Both Wall Street and Main Street are looking for excellence. How are you going to define your value to them in 1999? *Progressive Grocer* 78(2):23.

Adams, J. 2005. CNB seeks key leads at the teller window, *US Banker* 115(7):43.

Almeida, C. 2004. Success of luxury stores proves there's more to do in Sin City than gamble. *The Associated Press* retrieved June 9, 2005 from LexisNexis database.

Anwar, S. A., and S. M. Sohail. 2004. Festival tourism in the United Arab Emirates: First-time versus repeat visitor perceptions. *Journal of Vacation Marketing* 10(2):161–170.

Armstrong, A., and J. Hegel. 1996. The real value of on-line communities. *Harvard Business Review* 7(3):134–141.

Babin, B. J., D. M. Hardesty, and T. A. Suter. 2003. Color and shopping intentions: The intervening effect of price fairness and perceived affect. *Journal of Business Research* 56(7):541–551.

Balasubramanian, S., and V. Mahajan. 2001. The economic leverage of the virtual community. *International Journal of Electronic Commerce* 5(3):103–138.

Barbieri, K. 2005. The mall is dropping the ball. *Amusement Business* 118(1):52–53.

Baym, N. K. 2000. *Tune in, log on: Soaps, fandom, and online community.* Thousand Oaks, CA: Sage Publications, Inc.

Benjamin Moore. 2006. www.benjamin-moore.com.

Berry, L. 1999. Creating customer excitement with superior service. *Retailing Issues Letter* 11(6):1–6.

Bloch, P., N. M. Ridgway, and S. A. Dawson. 1994. The shopping mall as consumer habitat. *Journal of Retailing* 70(1):23–42.

Brunner, G. 1990. Music, mood, and marketing. *Journal of Marketing* 54(4):104.

Bryne, A., M. Whitehead, and S. Breen. 2003. The naked truth of celebrity endorsement. *The British Food Journal* 105(4/5):288–297.

Burton, D. 2002. Postmodernism, social relations, and remote shopping.

European Journal of Marketing 36(7/8):792–810.

Buss, D. 1997. Entertailing. *Nations Business* 85(12):12–18.

Carpenter, J. M., M. Moore, and A. E. Fairhurst. 2005. *Journal of Fashion Marketing and Management* 9(1):43–53.

Cebrzynski, G. 2005. Cracker Barrel spins more music into its marketing mix. *Nation's Restaurant News* 39(6):14.

Che, D. 2002. Shopping/entertainment complexes as foundations for regional tourism development: The case of great lakes crossing. *Michigan Academician* 34(1):1.

CSNews Online. 2005. How do shoppers know when a store is both safe and inviting? It's all in the lighting. *CSNews Online* Retrieved through LexisNexis, April 19, 2006.

Cuneo, A. Z. 2000. Malls move to capture sales lost to the Net. *Advertising Age* 71(32):38–46.

Dholakia, U. M., R. P. Bagozzi, and L. K. Pearo. 2004. A social influence model of consumer participation in network- and small-group-based virtual communities. *International Journal of Research in Marketing* 21(3):241–263.

DisneyQuest. Retrieved July 19, 2006 from http://disneyworld.disney.go.com/wdw/entertainment/entertainmentDetail?id=DisneyQuestIndoorInteractiveThemeParkEntertainmentPageandbhcp=1

DSN Retailing Today. 2004. *Entertainment retail brews in new venues* 43(19):32.

Dubai Festival City. 2005. Website information retrieved October 14, 2005, www.dubaifestivalcity.com/content/homepage.asp

Eroglu, S. A., K. A. Machleit, and J-C. Chebat. 2005. The interaction of retail density and music tempo: Effects on shopper responses. *Psychology & Marketing* 22(7):577–589.

Esfahani, E. 2005. A sales channel they can't resist home-shopping giant QVC is becoming one of the most powerful forces in retail. Here's the secret to its surprising success. *Business* 2.0:6(8):90.

Field, K. 2005. Building across America. *Chain Store Age* 81(5):104–106.

Fife, I. 2004. Useful terms. *Financial Mail (South Africa).* April 10, 100, retrieved from LexisNexis August 10, 2006.

Gioia, D., and P. P. Poole. 1984. Scripts in organizational behavior. *The Academy of Management Review* 9(3):449–359.

Hajewski, D. 2000. Retailers increasingly sing for their shoppers: In-store tunes boost sales, set tone for brand. *Milwaukee Journal Sentinel.* April 2, 1D.

Harris, Richard, Kim Harris, and Steve Baron. 2003. *International Journal of Service Industry Management* 14(2):184–199.

Hagel, J., and A. G. Armstrong 1997. Net gain: Expanding markets through virtual communities, *The McKinsey Quarterly* 1:140–153.

Herring, S. C. 1996. Two variants of an electronic message schema. In S. C. Herring, ed., *Computer-mediated communication: Linguistic, social, and cross-cultural perspectives* (81–106). Philadelphia: John Benjamins.

Heschong, R., L. Wright, and S. Okura. 2002. Daylighting impacts on retail sales performance. *Journal of the Illuminating Engineering Society* 31(2):21–25.

Hogg, M. A., and D. J. Terry. 2000. Social identity and self-categorization processes in organizational contexts. *Academy of Management Review* 25(1):121–140.

IBM. 2005. Virgin Megastore Times Square Features 150 New IBM Anyplace Kiosks That Help Create an 'Emotionally Exciting' Shopping Experience. Accessed September 15, 2006 from www-306.ibm.com/software/success/cssdb.nsf/CS/LRYR-6GEW49?OpenDocument&Site=

Ibrahim, M. F., and N. C. Wee. 2002. Determinants of entertaining shopping experiences and their link to consumer behavior: Case studies of shopping centres in Singapore. *Journal of Leisure Property* 2(4):38–58.

Images Retail Bureau. 2004. Light up your sales. [Online], part 1/2 Available: www.imagesfashion.com.

International Council of Shopping Centers (ICSC). 1995. Entertainment: The retailer's perspective. *ICSC Research Quarterly* 2(3):15–20.

Kim, Y-K. 2001. Experiential retailing: An interdisciplinary approach to success in domestic and international retailing. *Journal of Retailing and Consumer Services* 8(5):287–289.

Kim, I., T. Christiansen, R. Feinberg, and H. Choi. 2005. Entertainment and shopping behaviors: A graphical modeling approach. In Alba W. Joseph and J. Wesley Hutchinson, eds. *Advances in Consumer Research,* Vol. 32 (487–492). Provo, UT: Association for Consumer Research.

Knight, M. 1999. America's tourist attractions. *Chain Store Age* 75(3):64–66.

Koh, J., and Y. Kim. 2004. Sense of virtual community: A conceptual framework and empirical validation. *International Journal of Electronic Commerce* 8(2):75–93.

Kooijman, D. 2002. A third revolution in retail? The Dutch approach to leisure and urban entertainment. *Journal of Leisure Property* 2(3):214–230.

Levy, M., and B. Weitz. 2001. *Retailing management.* Boston: McGraw-Hill.

Littrell, M. A., S. Baizerman, R. Kean, and S. Gahring. 1994. Souvenirs and tourism styles. *Journal of Travel Research* 33(1):3–11.

Lin, C-H., and S-C. Wu. 2006. Influence of Audio Effects on Consumption Emotion and Temporal Perception. *Journal of American Academy of Business* 10(1):174–179.

Lynch, L. 2001. Leadership: The 'vision' factor. *Progressive Grocer* 80(6):50.

Mangalindan, M., K. Swisher, D. Bank, D. P. Hamilton, and D. Clark. 2004. Starting to Click: After wave of disappointments, the Web lures back advertisers; new generation of pitches nets data on consumers; not a mass audience; getting drivers to showroom. *The Wall Street Journal,* Eastern edition. February 9, R.3.

Mathwick, C., N. K. Malhotra, and E. Rigdon. 2002. The effect of dynamic retail experiences on experiential perceptions of value: An Internet and catalog comparison. *Journal of Retailing* 78(1):51–60.

McCracken, G. 1989. Who is the celebrity endorser? Cultural foundations of the endorsement process. *Journal of Consumer Research* 16(3):310–321.

Moffat, S. 2006. A holistic experience, Whole Foods showcases efficient food-friendly lighting. *Design and Display Ideas.* Retrieved from LexisNexis September 5, 2006.

Moscardo, G. 2004. Shopping as a destination attraction: An empirical examination of the role of shopping in tourists' destination choice and experience. *Journal of Vacation Marketing* 10(4):294–307.

Multichannel Merchant. 2006. Report: Multichannel retailers saw double-digit growth in 2005, retrieved from http://multichannelmerchant.com/news/abacus-trend-report-08092006/ August 16, 2006.

O'Brien, T. 2003. Playland plans season-long party. *Amusement Business* 115(5):6.

Oh, J. Y., C. K. Cheng, X. Y. Lehto, and J. O'Leary. 2004. Predictors of tourists' shopping behaviour: Examination of socio-demographic characteristics and trip typologies. *Journal of Vacation Marketing* 10(4):308–311.

O'Loughlin, S. 2005. The UPS store sends out new message. *Brandweek* 46(30):10.

O'Mahony, S., and T. Meenaghan. 1997. The impact of celebrity endorsements on consumers. *Irish Marketing Review* 10(2):15–24.

Phillips, P. 1995. Merging entertainment and retailing. *Economic Development Review* 13(2):13–16.

Rayson, E. 2004. Capturing the joy of online experiences. Retrieved May 4, 2006 from www.marketingmag.ca/magazine/current/digital_mkt_rpt/article.jsp?content=20040301_61196_61196

Retail Forward 2005. Retail Innovation: Ten opportunities for 2010. Retrieved July 14, 2006 from www.retailforward.com/freecontent/marketing/soc05doctr.pdf

Roach, L. 1995. The main event. *Discount Merchandiser* 35:66.

Roderick, Edward. 2003. On time, every time. *Manufacturing Engineer* 82(2):20–23.

Scardino, E. 2005. Revamped FAO tempers fun with pedigree. *DSN Retailing Today* 44(3):22–23.

Sit, J., B. Merrilees, and D. Birch. 2003. Entertainment-seeking shopping centre patrons: The missing segments. *International Journal of Retail and Distribution Management* 31(2):80–94.

Smith, R. 2004. New Venetian tower seen as profit booster for Las Vegas Sands. *Las Vegas Review-Journal* Retrieved June 9, 2005, from Lexis-Nexis database.

Stafford, M. R., T. F. Stafford, and E. Day. 2002. A contingency approach: The effects of spokesperson type and service type on service advertising. *The Journal of Advertising* 31(2):17–14.

Stanley, T. L. 2004. Disney repurposes NYC flagship store. *Advertising Age* 75(3):20.

Swartz, N. 2004. The best of Long Beach. *Information Management Journal* 38(5):88–S11.

Sweeney, J. C., and F. Wyber. 2002. The role of cognitions and emotions in the music-approach-avoidance behavior relationship. *The Journal of Service Marketing* 16(1):51–69.

Thomas, A., and R. Garland. 2004. Grocery shopping: list and non-list usage. *Marketing Intelligence and Planning* 22(6/7):623–634.

Turner, L. W., and Y. Reisinger. 2001. Shopping satisfaction for domestic tourists. *Journal of Retailing and Consumer Services* 8(1):15–27.

U.S. Online Shoppers. 2005. Retrieved May 6, 2006 from www.shop.org/learn/stats.asp

Walker, M., L. Langmeyer, and D. Langmeyer. 1992. Commentary-Celebrity endorsers: Do you get what you pay for? *The Journal of Services Marketing* 6(4):35–38.

Wan, A. 2002. Retailers see live music events as mass marketing opportunities: Such chains as FYE target potential customers by tying into events like Ozzfest in order to promote product. *Billboard* 114(30):43.

Warnaby, G., and B. J. Davies. 1997. Commentary: Cities as service factories? Using the servuction system for marketing cities as shopping destinations. *International Journal of Retail and Distribution Management* 25(6):204–210.

Watson, G., and D. Johnson. 1972. *Social psychology: Issues and insights*. Philadelphia: J. B. Lippincott.

Wellman B., and M. Gulia. 1999. The network basis of social support: A network is more than the sum of its ties. In Wellman, ed. B. *Networks in the Global Village: Life in Contemporary Communities* (331–366). Boulder, CO: Westview Press.

Wilson, M. 2001. Redefining retailtainment. *Chain Store Age* 77(3):71–74.

Wolin, L. D., and P. Korgaonkar. 2003. Web advertising: Gender differences in beliefs, attitudes, and behavior. *Internet Research* 13(5):375–385.

Young, R. 2000. Play station. *Building Design and Construction* 41(1):34–37.

THEMATIC RETAILING

Fifth Avenue Will Soon Be Home to a New Bear Market

Build-A-Bear Workshop has been growing rapidly since its launch in 1997. It now has more than 180 stores in America and Canada, as well as locations in England, Japan, Australia, and Denmark. It booked $302 million in revenues in 2004. When the company opened a temporary Rockefeller Center location during the 2004 holiday season, its warm reception confirmed that the city already had a strong customer base.

The process begins with customers picking out unstuffed animals. The selection includes not just bears but also dogs, cats, bunnies, and monkeys, each designed to fit into the same clothes. The dolls range in price from $10 to $25, which includes the shell and the stuffing but not outfits and accessories. After choosing an animal, customers can pick out a sound chip to put inside, with noises ranging from giggles and growls to messages such as "I love you" and songs like "Take Me Out to the Ballgame." There also is an option to record a personalized noise. The animal is then stuffed, and a bar code is placed inside to help locate the animal if it is ever lost. Customers also get to partake in the Heart Ceremony, placing a heart they've picked out inside the animal before it's sewn up and fluffed at the Bear Spa. After the heart is in place and fur fluffed, customers then type up a birth certificate for their new friend before choosing from the many outfits available, including NFL, NBA, NHL, and MLB uniforms, graduation gowns, suits, lacrosse uniforms, and Statue of Liberty outfits.

And the fun doesn't stop there. The New York City store has many other unique features to occupy its young visitors, and probably many of their adult chaperones. At the "T's By Me" station, children can design T-shirts for their animals on paper, and watch as employees transfer their designs onto bear-size shirts. "Designing T-shirts was something kids already liked to do," Ms. Clark said. "We like to adapt ideas that humans like and apply them to bears." Customers also can create their own "United Nations" of bears with the Foreign Friends line. It consists of 41 internationally themed outfits, each with a "passport" full of information about the country.

After making stuffed animals in the Build-A-Bear Workshop, children can go next door to the company's "friends 2B made" store, where they can make, dress, and personalize their own dolls. The Fifth Avenue location will be the third friends 2B made store in the country, and the first on the East Coast.

Source: Richels, H. 2005. Fifth Avenue will soon be home to a new bear market. *The New York Sun* 1.

CHAPTER 9

INTRODUCTION

Thematic retailing plays an important role in the shopping experience. Thematic retailing identifies and develops a story line that promotes a retail identity and brand. Many consumers seek shopping experiences that provide an escape from the mundane and visit stores "to explore, stalk, hunt down, touch, feel, and interact with products that might fit into their lives" (Valas 2004, 26). As such, retail creates a world of fantasy where hope and representations of other cultures in imagined forms can be acquired. Retailers set the stage for consumer experiences using products, services, and entertainment as supporting props in themed retail dramas. For this purpose, retailers ought to consider building stimulating, pleasing designs, appropriate color schemes, and captivating sound systems and signage into their themed retail mix. Because shopping can be thought of as a pleasure-seeking experience, thematic retail environments contribute to this sensory experience.

Previously, thematic retailing was viewed as the domain of entertainment studios such as Disney and Warner Brothers, but it was not a part of traditional retail venues. However, retailers have begun to view it as a strategy for successfully competing in the global market (King 2000). Thematic retailing uses elements of entertainment, education, and the consumers' experience to attract customers (King 2000). It adds hedonic value to otherwise utilitarian shopping and helps differentiate one retail brand from another.

Shopping is a leisure activity that supports a paradigm of visualizing culture, for example, looking at merchandise (Backes 1997). Consumers' affective responses toward a product grouping affect their evaluation of an item when it is juxtaposed with a complementary item (Lama and Mukherjee 2005). Merchandise coordination affects product evaluation when complementary products are put together, so that themed merchandise presentation facilitates the consumer decision-making process. In this sense, thematic retailing makes shopping easier and more efficient. If merchandise is themed, customers save time in selecting products that match or complement other items they are purchasing. Themed merchandise displayed in a themed environment will enhance the consumer's overall shopping experience. Retailers who succeed in creating a differentiated theme connect with consumers who do not mind paying above-market prices for the unique experience (Meyers 2005). Retailers who have successfully used themes include Build-A-Bear, Club Libby Lu, Trader Joe's, and Chuck E. Cheese.

RETAIL THEMES

Retail themes can be used in various ways for different consumption settings. Themes can reflect ethnicity, affluence, craftsmanship, nostalgia, spirituality, holidays, seasonal themes, cultural events, and characters.

Ethnicity

Ethnicity is a theme that attracts customers through differentiated product assortments and appears in different retail formats. One example of a business that used an ethnic theme is Lawrence Memorial Hospital (*FoodService Director* 2006). Director of food and nutrition Debbie Miers began using ethnic cuisines and ethnic-themed days twice a month as a strategy for increasing cafeteria patronage. The food-service department prepares cuisines from countries such as Italy, Africa, China, Russia, Mexico, the Philippines, and the United States. The ethnic themed strategy piques customer interest by holding the events on the same days of each month, by sending out teaser e-mails to hospital staff members, and by not revealing the menu until the actual day of the event. This unique ethnic menu strategy has created added interest in the cafeteria and has helped the meal planners add popular dishes from themed days to the regular menu. For example, enchiladas are such a hit on Mexican day that they are being incorporated into the regular menu. In addition, ethnic days have increased cafeteria employee participation. Cafeteria and hospital staff members have begun bringing ethnic memorabilia from home (i.e., sombreros, posters, photographs) to contribute to the décor of the cafeteria on themed days. Cafeteria sales have increased 41 percent and mealtime participation has increased 24 percent on ethnic-themed days (*FoodService Director* 2006).

Another example is Stanford Dining on the campus of Stanford University that has turned dormitory food-service dining into destination dining (Buchthal 2006). The food-service company has accomplished this by offering fresh organic produce, culinary innovation, and highly trained chefs without subsidy from the university. To date, it serves 5.8 million meals per year to a customer base that includes students, professors and local executives. Stanford Dining's newest plan is called Destination Dining and is made up of ethnic-concept cafeteria stations located in each dorm on campus. These stations include a Middle Eastern themed dining hall; a Mexican *taquería* themed dining hall; and Mediterranean, Italian, and Chinese themed dining halls. Rafi Taherian, executive director of Stanford Dining, wants these stations to be like neighborhood restaurants where students and other locals can dine if they want authentic foods (Buchthal 2006).

Amusement park facilities can also be used to appeal to an ethnic community through ethnic food festivals. These festivals are known to capture the taste, music,

and customs of particular cultures, which creates a new reason to visit or revisit the park. For ethnic food festivals, amusement park managers hire bands and other entertainers, cook ethnic cuisine, adorn staff members in cultural costumes, and decorate at least one section of the park with the country's colors and souvenirs. If the park gets the word out that it is offering something new and different, the event can generate additional traffic and revenue. The park can create ethnic atmosphere by paying attention to details such as authenticity of the food and clothing and by providing good customer service for the festival (Zoltak 2003).

Wal-Mart, the world's largest retailer, has begun stocking Latino-themed apparel to attract Hispanic consumers (Zimmermann 2005). Wal-Mart's circulars

9.1 Wal-Mart's *Viviendo* magazine targets Hispanic consumers

are printed in both Spanish and English, and Wal-Mart along with publisher TFI, developed a Hispanic magazine, *Viviendo*, which profiles Latino leaders and celebrities along with advertisement for Wal-Mart products and services targeted to the Hispanic market (See Figure 9.1). Cincinnati-based Kroger Co. successfully introduced its Hispanic store concept Food4Less in Southern California (Murphy 2002). Nash Finch Co., the Minneapolis-based grocer, opened its first Hispanic-focused store, Avanza, in Denver.

Target also has cross-merchandised thematic table groupings to promote their tabletop mix and attract a deeper, broader customer base (Ziska 2004). One product offering was an Asian-themed grouping with plates, dipping bowls, and accessories. These items were displayed with bamboo mats, chopsticks, and an Asian-inspired color story. Creating themed merchandising venues such as this helps consumers envision products in their own homes.

To stave off competition from a Wal-Mart expansion, Shop 'n Save unveiled a prototype store in the East Liberty section of Pittsburgh, Pennsylvania (Major 2005). This prototype grocery store provides customers with a differentiated shopping experience through the use of open architecture, warehouse lighting, superior service, a wide assortment of specialty store brands, and in-store sets. The specialty store brands include international products and perishable items with identities that go beyond private labels. The objective is to make customers feel as if they are at the Strip District, one of Pittsburgh's renowned food destinations for locals and tourists.

The store's concept was designed in recognition of its increasingly diverse customer base. One theme that Shop 'n Save offers is "Best of Pittsburgh," stocking some of western Pennsylvania's most notable brands such as Wholeys seafood, DeLallo Italian foods, Arbuckles coffees, Mancini's breads, Jenny Lee baked goods, and Sarris chocolates. Each of these brands is an authentic local brand with its own corporate story. DeLallo company history is described in the following:

> In the mid-1940s, George DeLallo began to sell grocery items door-to-door. In 1950, he and his wife Madeline purchased property in Jeannette, Pennsylvania, and established a retail and wholesale Italian grocery store, where they first developed and sold authentic Italian items bearing the DeLallo name. As the years progressed, so did the trade. Today, the original Jeannette location still remains and DeLallo products are proudly distributed throughout North and South America. With such items as olive oil, pasta, vinegars, and tomatoes, retailers and consumers can be assured of authenticity, quality, and the genuine Italian experience that is guaranteed behind every DeLallo product (www.delallo.com/corporate/story.php).

The store has a large selection of international foods divided by geographic regions, which include German, Greek, English, Caribbean, Mexican, Italian, and Asian products. Stop 'n Save also has a wide assortment of fresh and packaged goods, including traditional American, ethnic Kosher, organic, Asian, and deep-fried Southern foods. The store is broken down into distinct districts with each one playing identifiable music that adds to the themed experience. The DeLallo zone plays Italian music; the Sarris Candies area plays carousel music.

A more recent example of retailers targeting the African-American market is Citi

Trends, a family apparel retailer with value pricing that is located in the mid-Atlantic, Southeast, and Texas (www.cititrends.com). This retail chain started in 1946 as Allied Department Stores, a family apparel chain, and became Citi Trends in 1999. The retailer discounts prices of urban apparel and accessories 20 percent to 60 percent less than department stores (Howell 2006). Citi Trends sells branded merchandise, including FUBU, Rocawear, Phat Farm, Baby Phat, Sean Jean, Apple Bottoms, and Dickies. They offer their own private label apparel lines such as Steps, Diva Blue, and Urban Sophistication. There is also a small home department in Citi Trends' store that sells cultural items. Items in this department include African tribal décor and books with African American themes. Citi Trends believes the look is more important than the brands for their customers. In 2005 Citi Trends sales revenues increased 42.5 percent to $289.8 million (Howell 2006). Approximately 70 percent of its customers are African American. Citi Trends' location strategy is to place stores in neighborhoods with a population that matches its target market demographics.

Affluence

One of the influences on thematic retailing is a new upper class made up of 1 of 10 U.S. households that have an annual household income of $100,000 or more (Freeman 2000). U.S. households can afford to buy more than necessary essentials. Affluent consumers try to distinguish themselves as individuals who can afford more than the basic needs and their consumption reflects their goals or status. L. S. Bagwell and B. B. Bernheim (1996) described Veblen effects as a situation where consumers do not want to pay less for products that signal wealth, even if they have the same functional benefits. M. Hickens (1999) argued that increasing

numbers of affluent consumers seek out limited-edition objects or elite experiences. They desire unique, customized experiences in their choices of automobiles, vacations, entertainment, or wine instead of more stuff to fill their homes. These consumers desire life experiences such as trips that are enriching, rewarding, fulfilling, and unique (Freeman 2000).

E. C. Hirschman (1990) suggested that affluence promotes celebrating achievement and wealth, and accumulating possessions to achieve immortality. She suggested that three themes (i.e., entrepreneurial achievement, achievement of celebrity status through consumption, and achievement in artistry and craftsmanship) support the ideology of affluence. Entrepreneurial achievement is based upon the affluent lifestyle that is centered on the acquisition of money, material possessions, and personal achievement. Celebrity status achieved through consumption means acquiring "vast quantities of consumer goods or extremely expensive objects, which in and of themselves possess immortal status (e.g., the Hope diamond)" (Hirschman 1990, 35). Achievement in artistry and craftsmanship is explained by the affluent person's desire to acquire collections of art and craft products. These three themes are exemplified by retailers. Credit card companies are encouraging entrepreneurial spirit and buying with targeted rewards, especially among women. Books on entrepreneurship are flying off the shelves. Mont Blanc commissioned Candace Bushnell to begin writing the Great American Love Story with the world's most expensive, diamond-encrusted pen. An original Pablo Picasso painting can now command more than $40 million.

Several businesses have begun to target the affluent consumer. Magazines such as *Worth*, *SmartMoney*, and *Cigar Aficionado* that concentrate on the concept of wealth have been launched for the affluent consumer (Freeman 2000). Further, there has been an increase in media outlets such as CNN, CNNFN, and CNBC that primarily target affluent consumers. As the number of millionaires and the number of households with net income of more than $100,000 continues to grow in the United States, there is a fast-growing market for luxury products and services. Retailers offering elite luxury products and services that create a unique experience will compete to meet the needs of newly affluent consumers (Freeman 2000).

Craftsmanship

Craft themes used in the retail market can add value to the shopping experience beyond the actual product purchase. The craftsman is depicted as "investing a unique aspect of selfhood into creating products; such products were portrayed as vessels containing the spiritual essence or soul of their creators" (Hirschman 1990, 38). N. Kelly's (2003) study of a woman selling her handmade T-shirts revealed that customers followed her when she started selling at crafts fairs. Customers liked the personal exchange, and they wanted products that reflected their lives and culture rather than the mainstream culture.

Retailer advertisements often include boasts of craftsmanship. For example, Rejuvenation sells period-authentic lighting and hardware in brick-and-mortar stores in Seattle, Washington, and Portland, Oregon, and through catalogs and a website. Rejuvenation describes its medicine cabinets with the following statement: "Rejuvenation's traditional Medicine Cabinets are unmatched in quality of materials, craftsmanship, and period-authentic historical accuracy. They're meticulously detailed and handcrafted from real wood-primed, paint-grade poplar with absolutely no MDF or particleboard" (www.rejuvenation.com).

Bally Shoe Factories Limited, a shoe manufacturer and retailer, focuses on three concepts in promoting its brand: nature, craftsmanship, and heritage with a balance between classic and modern designs (Edelson 2006). Bally, based in Caslano, Switzerland, is an example of a company that demonstrates a commitment to craftsmanship. Marco Franchini, chairman and CEO of Bally Shoe Factories Limited, states that the company's redesigned wingtip shoe is an example of its commitment to craftsmanship in that the shoe takes 250 steps to make (Edelson 2006).

Timberland's store celebrates three pillars of the brand: the outdoors, social responsibility, and craftsmanship. The prototype design has an "outdoorsy" feel and the store's environment provides "visual and tactile stimuli of craftsmanship" (Carlton 2002, 18). The stores are made up of materials such as seeded glass, reclaimed wood, leather, and bamboo flooring, which emphasize the outdoorsy feel. Further, the signature Timberland orange leather, derived from the leather innersole of the classic Timberland boot, is "sprinkled throughout the store on benchtops and in graphics to reiterate craftsmanship in a natural environment" (Carlton 2002, 18).

In the annual Gatlinburg Craftsmen's Fair in Gatlinburg, Tennessee, more than 200 time-honored mountain crafts and traditional art forms are displayed. Craftspeople who are gifted in woodcarving, pottery, broom-making, stained glass, and much more gather at the Gatlinburg Convention Center to create their crafts while people watch and to offer their crafts for sale. In addition, the Fair offers live country and bluegrass entertainment (www.craftsmenfair.com).

Nostalgia

Nostalgia is a longing for and reflecting on times past. It is another theme strategy, as evidenced in the role of the historic town center (Filion, Hoernig, Bunting, and Sands 2004). M. B. Holbrook and R. M. Schindler (2003) identified 10 themes associated with nostalgia and consumption: sensory experience, homeland, rites of passage, friendships and loved ones, gifts of love, security, breaking away, art and entertainment, performance and competence, and creativity (See Table 9.1). Holbrook and Schindler also suggested that object-related experiences are related to past memories. Thus retail marketers should consider how goods are used by consumers during life events and how these goods develop nostalgic sentiment.

Cracker Barrel uses nostalgia as its retail theme. Its guests are mostly families and travelers—people who want to step back in time and enjoy a cultural experience. Cracker Barrel offers a variety of home-cooked country foods with an ambience that is very similar to an old-time country merchant. The product line is remnant of the past, with everything from hand-blown glass to cast-iron cookware. Signage and packaging is reminiscent of what we associate with a Western saloon. Individuals who frequent Cracker Barrel may enjoy nostalgia and items that recall

TABLE 9.1 THEMES ASSOCIATED WITH NOSTALGIA AND CONSUMPTION

THEME	DESCRIPTION
Sensory experience	Simplest, most self-oriented, hedonic level experience, associated treasured objects from the past with various pleasurable sensory experiences from youth, such as the aroma of cookies from Christmas holidays.
Homeland	This represents nostalgic bonding to objects associated with a distant land left to come to the United States. This could be a picture or a treasured gift from home.
Rites of passage	There is a nostalgic bonding to items associated with marked rites of passage or other deeply meaningful transitional moments, such as moving from childhood to teens.
Friendships and loved ones	There is premium placed on family and friends and objects representing close social relationships with friends, family, or other valued loved ones.
Gifts of love	Gifts of love, tangible instantiations of human affection, have nostalgic value. Jewelry stores selling engagement rings, which are gifts of love.
Security	Objects linked with aspects of continuity are valued as tokens of security for troubled familial or other interpersonal relationships. Objects for the lack of a special person in a consumer's life.
Breaking away	There is a fondness for objects linked to freedom and freedom to travel. A touring bike is an example of an object that represents breaking away.
Art and entertainment	A mental or spiritual form of freedom. For example, a consumer regards his first exposure to serious poetry while as a college freshman as a transformational experience tangibly represented by his old textbook.
Performance and competence	Consumers have nostalgic bonds with frequently-used tools that represent how they perfected skills of their own trade. Niketown's photographic collage of ordinary people participating in sports illustrates use of the performance and competition theme.
Creativity	Consumers exhibit fondness for objects from their past that represent artistic creativity and especially musical ability. A musical instrument from elementary school is an example.

Source: Holbrook, M. B., and R. M. Schindler. 2003. Nostalgic bonding: Exploring the role of nostalgia in the consumption experience. *Journal of Consumer Behavior* 3(2):107.

their heritage or reflect their youth (www.crackerbarrel.com).

There is a nostalgic candy market that provides emotional benefits to customers (Fuhrman 2004). These emotions can reflect the innocence of childhood or generate confidence in a shopper. New York City has a whimsically designed, two-level Dylan's Candy Bar that is part café, part store. Its interior was designed for "candy as a lifestyle," with peppermint-shaped barstools, gumdrop-filled tabletops, and giant lollypops. Dylan's café creates a significant number of impulse purchases by attracting adult candy addicts who walk by the store. Its themed environment includes a 10,000-square-foot "candy-plex" with a Tootsie Roll topiary, a Pez dispenser wall, edible Post-its, and 10-pound chocolate bars. Dylan's plays a candy-themed soundtrack and shows old candy ads on TV screens. Dylan's product assortment includes almost 4,000 candy items, presented as a candy museum, and a display of celebrities' favorite candies. Items for sale include Pez shirts and dispensers, board games, key chains, and coffee mugs. Dylan's average transaction is about $18, almost four times more than in other candy stores. Further, its average customer stays in the store for 34 minutes (Salter 2003).

Current consumer trends show that parents want to provide their children with the best of everything and the well-furnished baby nursery has become a symbol of their devotion to their children (Merrick 2002). In response, Pottery Barn opened stores with children's themed merchandise in 2000. They offered themed bedroom vignettes stocked with related accessories such as curtains, cozy quilts, and stuffed animals. These Pottery Barn Kids stores are designed for children who are roaming the store, yet they appeal to the parents who are purchasing for their children. Use of themed bedrooms helps stimulate sales through lifestyle marketing and nostalgia for one's childhood. In this way, Pottery Barn Kids has captured sales revenues in the lucrative infant and youth bedroom furniture market.

Spirituality

Consumers' desire for meaning, purpose, and deep life experiences are often driven by spirituality (Karlgaard 2004). It has dramatic impact on people's lives. The September 11, 2001 terrorist attacks in the United States created massive outpourings of spirituality. Aging baby boomers are transitioning into new life stages where they are becoming more philosophical and spiritually oriented. D. Ball, R. Hampton, A. Chronis, and M. Bunker (2001) defined spirituality as "a connection to the eternal, for its own sake, not for power or status or material gain" (3). Ball et al. interviewed consumers and identified three constructs that influence consumer evaluation. The three constructs of evaluation are benefits to the ego/approval needs, behavior of a religious authority, and behavior relating to the well-being of others. Ball et al. argued that these constructs affect consumer behavior related to product or brand choice, possession and consumption, and advertising response.

Themed retail blends the elements of entertainment, therapeutics, and spiritual growth into a unique harmony to attract customers and establish relationships with them (Kozinets et al. 2002). There is evidence of increasing consumer interest in spirituality shown by box-office blockbuster movies such as *The Passion of the Christ* and successful prime-time television shows such as *Touched by an Angel* (Smith 2003). This interest in spirituality is expected to grow, because baby boomers are focusing more on nonmaterial assets such as family, community, and spirituality, instead of material assets (Smith 2003). Retailers need to offer new promises, benefits, and services to satisfy the spiritual inclinations of customers. Many marketing campaigns are aimed at linking goods and services with spiritual values. An example of a company using spirituality to appeal to consumers is MasterCard. It ran a campaign reminding consumers of the priceless things in life that money cannot buy. It promoted consumers using their MasterCards to purchase objects that make family and friends smile. Another example is Honda's promise for peaceful "simplicity" from the Honda Accord. Consumers seem to approve of marketing efforts that place intangible things on equal footing with tangible goods (Smith 2003).

Holidays

Retailers realize the business opportunities that are connected to holidays. Traditional retail stores take advantage of holiday themes throughout the year and provide consumers with many opportunities for making seasonal purchases. They offer products related to holiday seasons to meet consumer needs and drive store sales. Costume purchases extend into other seasons when consumers buy Santa suits and accessories and products for parties, corporate events, and other themed occasions.

For Valentine's Day, retailers sell chocolates, flowers, and everything in the color red. At Easter, stores are filled with Easter baskets, stuffed bunnies, and pastel colors. During Memorial Day and the Fourth of July, U.S. retailers tout red, white, and blue clothing, home decorations, and party goods. Halloween is rich in symbolic and traditional activity. Across the United States, Halloween parades have become annual events in which whole families participate. A store entirely devoted to Halloween themed products and services can be successful when props, costumes, accessories, collectibles, and novelty items are positioned as playthings (Benitez 2006).

The Christmas holiday is linked to notions of home and family. The home is transformed into a "private utopia" and an idealized place for the holiday (McGreevy 1990). Bronner's Christmas Wonderland, located on 27 acres in Frankenmuth, Michigan, describes itself as the world's largest year-round Christmas store. It is a 320,000-square-foot operation stocked with more than 50,000 Christmas-themed items and 6,000 ornament styles from 70 countries (See Figure 9.2). Bronner's Christmas Wonderland features activities such as Easter Bunny visits and Christmas Sing-a-Longs with owners Wally and Irene Bronner. Bronner's began as a sign painting store in 1945, but quickly added Christmas ornaments (Hickey 2001). It has a half-mile-long Christmas lane decorated with 100,000 lights and contains a replica of the Silent Night Chapel in Oberndorf, Austria. Approximately two million people visit Bronner's Christmas Wonderland annually. This destination location is supported with catalog and online sales, allowing customers to remain connected with the unique destination store and Christmas experience.

9.2 Bronner's Christmas-themed store.

Seasonal Themes

Retailers also use seasonal themes in their retail mix. Burton Snowboards have showcase stores that focus on snowboarding. Their product focus is supported through visual merchandising and sales personnel. Their New York store has a Cold Room (20 degrees Farenheit) decorated with icicles for customers to try on apparel and equipment. Burton stores offer knowledgeable staff, as well as a toll-free rider service number where customers can obtain information on repairs, equipment, and trails for riding. This service helps Burton create a one-on-one relationship with its customer. These stores are owned by Jake Burton who developed his prototype snowboard and has been instrumental in creating interest in this sport (Reingold 2006, 58).

In 1958, Joe Coulombe began Trader Joe's, knows as Pronto Market in the Los Angeles area. The store's format changed in 1967 to include more floor space with upscale domestic and imported wines and gourmet foods offered at "honest everyday low prices." Trader Joe's décor also changed at this time to cedar plank walls and a nautical theme with the store manager dressed as a captain, the assistant manager as a first mate, and staff as crew members in Hawaiian shirts. Trader Joe's built its business on private label grocery products, staff in Hawaiian shirts, and quirky charm (Sarkar 2006a, C1). Trader Joe's is not a traditional supermarket; it operates successfully with its private label products and continuous replenishment with high-quality products (www.trader-joes.com). It offers more than 2,000 exotic private-label products, such as Charles Shaw wine, at 250 stores in 20 states on the East and West Coast (Biesada 2006). Customers travel distances seeking out Trader Joe's for novelty items such as banana crisps, spinach tofu egg rolls, or Mexican red sauce (Sarkar 2006). The number of items sold is limited compared with supermarkets, but sales revenue of $1,300 per square foot is about double the industry average. The store makes customers feel as if they get something out of the ordinary in terms of quality and value; it is worth going out of their way to get it (Leand 2006). By presenting products in an interesting and compelling way and offering quality and value, Trader Joe's builds customer loyalty. Trader Joe's publishes its Fearless Flyer online for customers. The newsletter is entertaining with irreverent product descriptions or stories about their products.

PacSun is another example of a successful retailer that uses a tropical theme. This teen apparel retail chain is found in malls. The store sells surf-inspired apparel, including products with Hawaiian inspired designs and shirts. PacSun's target customers, an average age of 15, mix brands in a single outfit and know what they want to buy. About 35 percent of PacSun's sales is from private-label goods (Kang 2004).

Cultural Events

Selfridges, the U.K.-based retailer, has an exhibition space called Ultra Lounge that hosts themed events to attract customers, which enhances its reputation as a shopping destination, cultural leader, and entertainer. On the ground floor, the Ultra Lounge has street access and uses an under-utilized area that annually houses its Christmas shop. Provided with themed products in an attractive environment such as Ultra Lounge, Selfridges customers expect the best and desire fabulous products and a tremendous experience, as well as cultural events (Wainscoat 2006).

Texas's H. E. Butt (HEB), the small, family-owned retail grocery chain, provides another example of how cultural events can be used successfully to create differentiation. In 1994, this eight-store chain faced competition from the retail giant Wal-Mart; both retailers were frequented by Hispanic customers. At that time HEB had about 57,000 customers, and 40 percent of their shoppers was Hispanic. HEB appeals to Hispanic families and celebrations, as well as Texans' ethnocentricity. HEB has grown to include 21 stores in Northern Mexico (Frazier 2005).

Characters

Besides specific retail formats, characters have been used for thematic retailing. Among well-known characters are Cabbage Patch Kids offered primarily in category killers and Dora the Explorer promoted as animated cartoons.

CABBAGE PATCH KIDS

Cabbage Patch madness swept the United States: Almost 20 years after their introduction, Cabbage Patch Kids, the popular 1980s dolls, grew a Cabbage Patch Kid playhouse in a Toys "R" Us flagship store at Times Square in 2001 (Connell 2002). Christmas of 1983 is forever etched in the minds of parents, who claimed success following a difficult search for a particular doll requested by their children. The rebirth of Cabbage Patch Kids in the Times Square Toys "R" Us store rekindled memories and attracted parents, kids, and collectors. During the late 1970s and early 1980s Cabbage Patch Kids were sold exclusively at BabyLand General Hospital and through authorized retail locations. Two retail outlets were run by the doll's manufacturing operation owner Original Appalachian Artworks Inc. (Geist 1985). Manhattan's BabyLand General Hospital, a Cabbage Patch Kids retail outlet, opened at 475 Fifth Avenue in 1985. The original birthplace of the Kids is in a turn-of-the-

century medical clinic in Cleveland, Georgia, hometown of the Cabbage Patch Kid creator Xavier Roberts. These dolls known as kids, children, or babies were not for sale. Rather, they were adopted by customers who promised to be understanding parents, to provide for the children's needs, to love and nurture them, to train them properly and to cherish their roles as adoptive parents of Cabbage Patch Kids (Figures 9.3a, b).

Retail staffs were trained as Licensed Patch Nurses (LPNs) and doctors at BabyLand General Hospital. The dolls were delivered and appropriately dressed. Cabbage Patch Kids' doctors perform freckle-otomies and dimplectomies— simple, outpatient procedures—and treat crackitis with needle and thread. These services were performed at a nominal cost. Surgery is still available, but only as inpatients. In the beginning, adoption fees for soft-sculpture babies ranged from $60 for a basic doll, to $1,000 for the Grand Edition. Today, babies start at $170 with many Special Limited Editions adopting for almost $400.

The one-of-a-kind focus of the Original Cabbage Patch Kids' collectibles was adapted to fit the mass market. Play Along Inc. is the current Master Licensee. Through the years Coleco Industries, Hasbro Toys, and Mattel Inc., have produced the vinyl-faced babies for the United States market. Many of the original Cabbage Patch Kid adoptive

9.3a, b Cabbage Patch Kids' original selling point was one-of-a-kind collectibles.

parents now have real children of their own. Opening day of Toys "R" Us's Baby-Land General Hospital surpassed sales expectations. As one of the first to offer multiethnic dolls, Cabbage Patch Kids have a wide variety available at www.cabbagepatchkids.com. The story of Cabbage Patch Kids illustrates how this themed environment creates personal value in a consumer experience. Seemingly, nostalgia for these symbols of childhood stimulated opening sales.

DORA THE EXPLORER

Animated cartoons provide insights into how themed entertainment influences retail demand. *Dora the Explorer* is an animated television series for preschool-age children that is broadcast on Nickelodeon in the United States. It is based upon a seven-year-old Latina female character and her friends. The pilot episode for this series aired in 1999 and *Dora the Explorer* became a regular series in 2000. The series airs not only on Nickelodeon, but also on CBS on Saturday mornings and on Noggin, the Nickelodeon-owned channel for preschoolers. The show, created by Chris Gifford, Valerie Walsh, and Eric Weiner, is also broadcasted in selected Latin-American markets. *Dora the Explorer* teaches children (Hispanic and non-Hispanic) basic Spanish words and phrases along with math and music skills and physical coordination. With Dora and a monkey named Boots, children learn how to observe situations and solve problems. Viewers are asked to actively participate—not only by answering questions, but also by getting off the couch and moving their bodies.

Dora the Explorer has been such a success that in 2005 a new show called *Go, Diego, Go!* was launched (Chozick 2005). *Go, Diego, Go!* features Dora's cousin, Diego Marquez, and it also relies on play-along viewing and interaction while introducing kids to Spanish words, encouraging movement, incorporating songs, and teaching kids to overcome challenges. Diego also models important attributes, such as a love of learning, a respect for the environment, and a desire to help others.

Dora has had a big impact on the educational and retailing environments. The Children's Museum of Manhattan (CMOM) and The Rowell Foster Children's Positive Plan featured, through 2005 and 2006, *Dora the Explorer* to benefit families in need. Also, Cheerios offered free *Dora the Explorer* Game CD-ROMs in specially-marked packages as a promotion tool. For Nickelodeon, whose audience is predominantly non-Hispanic, shows such as *Dora* and *Diego* are a way to boost the channel's Hispanic audience share. In 2005, companies wanting to target Hispanic preschool parents sponsored a national mall tour that started in Denver and stopped at 10 U.S. shopping malls in cities with large Hispanic populations. The tour was of a 1,000-square-foot modular house for *Dora the Explorer*. In 2005, *Dora* appeared in the Macy's Thanksgiving Day Parade; she was the first-ever Hispanic character balloon (Jarosz and Laucius 2006). The *Dora the Explorer* TV shows, Internet sites, traveling theatrical shows, and retail merchandise promote themed toys and create consumer demand for the branded merchandise.

THEMATIC RETAILING AT DIFFERENT RETAIL FORMATS

Retailers can enhance the typical retail experience by designing product offerings and environments with themes that resonate with consumers. Restaurants and shopping centers are best known for successfully using themes in their retail mix.

Themed Restaurants

Restaurants can add incremental revenue per visit with theme-related merchandise, especially when establishments focus on tourist customers. The majority of themed restaurants are visited by tourists as opposed to local residents. However, the key to a restaurant's success is repeat business. After the novelty is gone, themed restaurants are doomed for failure unless they harness the basics of any restaurant's success—good food and good service.

Dave and Buster's, which opened in 1982 in Dallas, Texas, markets itself as a place for great food and big fun. It is labeled as an arcade for adults. The idea for the business came from two business owners who happened to be located next to each other, but offered two completely different retail concepts. One of the businesses was a fine dining restaurant and the other was a place for fun. The two business owners began to notice that their patrons were going from one establishment to the next; thus, the idea for Dave and Buster's was born. They developed a business plan that offered both concepts under one roof; a place to get good food and to have fun. In September 2005, Dave and Buster's, Inc. showed second-quarter results as an increase of 23.4 percent or a $21 million increase as compared with the previous year. During the same period, food and beverage revenue increased by 28.4 percent and amusement revenue increased by 17.8 percent (www.daveandbusters.com).

Buca di Beppo describes itself as a family-style southern Italian restaurant. Their table service is different with overflowing platters placed on the table along with three liter bottles of Chianti, reminiscent of restaurants in Italy. "Buca" means basement and "Beppo" is short for Giuseppe, which translates into "Joe." Therefore, Buca di Beppo translates into Joe's basement. The first Buca di Beppo opened in a basement. Patrons sit at the kitchen table, which is actually located in the kitchen and can seat a party of six.

Buca, Inc. reported a 2005 sales increase of 6.9 percent as compared with the 2004 sales increase of 5.1 percent (www.bucadibeppo.com).

Chuck E. Cheese, a family entertainment themed restaurant, owned and operated 453 restaurants and 45 franchises in the United States and Canada as of April 2005. Geared toward children, Chuck E. Cheese offers pizza along with musicals performed by full-size robotic puppets. Children can play a variety of arcade games. Chuck E. Cheese showed an increase in revenue from $454,000 in 2003 to $720,000 in 2004 (www.chuckecheese.com).

Themed Shopping Centers

Thematic retailing also can be developed at a more macro level—shopping centers. Among different types of shopping centers, malls and town centers have been successful in thematic retailing.

MALLS

Malls provide a free, safe, and romanticized shopping environment that keeps in step with today's contemporary world (Lefkowitz 1998). As planned shopping centers evolved, they have become indoor places where merchants display dreams that stimulate consumer desire and fulfill fantasies. Themes such as ethnicity and cultural events help differentiate one mall from another. Southgate Mall in Arizona spent $12 million to reposition a 300,000-square-foot space to attract Hispanic shoppers (Popovec 2006).

An individual who has influenced mall developers is Victor Gruen, a U.S.-born mall architect and designer. Victor Gruen was inspirational through his efforts to reimagine social space in the environment of the mall. He built the world's first fully enclosed, indoor shopping center in 1956 (Lefkowitz 1998). He is known for "The

Gruen Effect," a belief that space should intentionally disorient its inhabitants. Getting lost in an ideal shopping environment is positive for retailers because it provides customers with an exploratory experience conducive to unplanned purchases. This effect transforms task-oriented shopping into a more emotional or blissful wandering.

The objectives for any mall operation are to increase shoppers' length of stay and to inspire them to revisit. Differentiated thematic retail environments can help achieve both of these objectives. Themed retail at a mall can be effective by creating an attractive environment with elements such as music, lighting, architecture, color schemes, and special events (e.g., carnivals), which in turn influence positive consumer experiences at the mall (Martin and Turley 2004).

The Mills Corporation has two separate themes for two property types it owns (Townsend 2005). One theme, "there great shopping lives," is used to promote an entertainment and shopping destination such as the Sawgrass Mills location in Florida. Another theme, "more than you're looking for," is used for their traditional regional mall that sells fashionable and functional items. Another example of

property themes is found in Atlantic City, a destination for conventions and gambling. The city improved its retail offerings to fight competition from gaming in other states (Carstens 2005). Atlantic City's Tropicana Casino and Resort now has a Cuban-themed, three-story, indoor mall.

Entertainment-oriented mall anchors use marketing and promotional activities targeted at the local trade area. This contributes to a constant flow of events that attract shoppers (Feldman 2004). Themed events could include musical performances, sports promotions, radio station broadcasts, and civic and charitable activities. Dolphin Mall is an example of a themed shopping center that was designed to reflect and appeal to Miami's multicultural population (See Figure 9.4). The shopping center has three distinctive zones that patrons can explore. The Ramblas is a square and has entertainment and restaurants. It was inspired by the main thoroughfare that is a Mecca for shoppers in Barcelona, Spain. The Playa reflects South Beach and has apparel, accessories, and home décor stores. The Moda is the fashion boutique district. In keeping with Dolphin Mall's multicultural theme, its website is written in both English and Spanish and restaurants offer a variety of world cuisines and continental favorites.

TOWN CENTERS

Another type of shopping center that provides opportunities for successful thematic retailing is the traditional town center. There are several challenges to town center development, including identification of the right tenant mix for the market area, design of the physical configuration, strategically locating use areas, planning for optimal use of upper floors, positioning convenient and unobtrusive parking, and planning aesthetically appropriate and open public spaces that can be used for social activities (Anziani 2002). Though

9.4 Themed shopping at Dolphin Mall reflects Miami's multicultural population.

there are challenges, these public spaces provide opportunities for themed activities that can attract foot traffic for retailers and provide reasons for shoppers to spend more time in the town center. Properly planned town centers can satisfy consumers' need for lifestyle experiences, such as walking and relaxing. Examples of themed events that attract shoppers to town centers include outdoor concerts, sidewalk sales, parades, carnivals, performances, and children's events.

Spruced-up main streets and historic areas can all be used to attract customers to town shops. The renewed popularity of U.S. downtowns is driven by shoppers' desire to be in an open environment (McCloud 1999). Town centers that are planning to revitalize to attract shoppers should have a clear vision and strategy, be aware of trends, establish a time line for activities, involve local residents, and commit to completing quality work (Loney 2005). Streetscapes, urban furniture, facade improvements, and public art are important components of town centers (Filion et al. 2004).

Each town center should assess its competition to identify opportunities for competitive advantage (Whyatt 2004). For example, people in San Antonio, Texas, would find town center entertainment by a Mariachi band appropriate, whereas those in the rural community of Dubuque, Iowa, might find a community sporting event more authentic. San Antonio offers local residents and tourists a variety of themed shopping opportunities. The San Antonio Riverwalk shown in Figure 9.5 attracts people with its entertainment, shopping opportunities, and restaurants. San Antonio also has many cultural events such as fiestas, the Cinco de Mayo celebration, and the Tejano Conjunto Festival. Dubuque thrived in the 1980s, but faced hardships when U.S. family farms disappeared and its meat-packing and farm-

implement manufacturing failed (Ralfo and Wade 2003). Bill Woodward, a co-owner of the local newspaper, had a vision of developing the community, a Mississippi River education center. This led to the development of a first-class tourism, shopping, and business destination. This includes a river museum, an aquarium, 194-room hotel, a water park, a half-mile-long riverfront walk, and a conference and events center.

Another example of a themed town center is Provincetown, Massachusetts, the oldest artist colony in the United States (Giuliano 1999). This town is where the Mayflower landed in 1620 (Rabin 2003). It later grew into a thriving fishing and whaling town. Provincetown attracted many artists such as Jackson Pollack, Edward Hopper, Jack Kerouac, and Tennessee Williams and became an artist colony. In the past, Provincetown was boarded up for the winter and store signs said "see you next year" (Schorr 2003). Now Provincetown is open most of the year, specialty shops open on weekends during the holiday season, and it is known as romantic getaway.

Town centers attract a critical mass of consumers and offer activities in a distinct environment (Filion et al. 2004). Successful

9.5 The San Antonio Riverwalk attracts tourists with its entertainment.

downtowns may create the illusion of a traditional pre-1950s downtown; thus revitalization should stress the town's historical character and street-level activities, which differentiate downtowns from a mall.

THEMATIC FLAGSHIP STORES

In addition to themes that can be provided by different retail formats, Kozinets et al. (2002) identified three types of thematic flagship stores in the new millennium: flagship brand stores, themed entertainment brand stores, and a hybrid, the themed flagship brand stores.

Flagship Brand Stores

Flagship brand stores sell one (usually identifiable) product brand, which is intended for brand building or reinforcing the image of the brand. Flagship brand stores can be exclusive outlets for the manufacturers' products (e.g., Gap, Limited) or nonexclusive operations (e.g., Ralph Lauren, Niketown, Sony Gallery of Consumer Electronics).

Abercrombie & Fitch is described as thematically exciting and energizing. Store brands are only available at Abercrombie & Fitch, making it an exclusive flagship brand. It is the equivalent of a cool party, one that is very "loud and dark" (Wilson 2006) and "countryclub-meets-surf-bungablow" with a planned store environment that includes the employees (Schlosser 2006). Abercrombie & Fitch markets to college students and pays attention to all aspects of its retail atmosphere, from scent to music, to appeal to their target customers. The differentiated thematic brand experience of Abercrombie & Fitch has transformed a previously lackluster company. In 1977, the company filed for bankruptcy and in 1978 it was sold to Oshmans (now Sports Authority) (*Hoovers Company Records* 2006). Oshmans expanded the firm operations and sold a broad range of unusual products until Abercrombie & Fitch's sale to the Limited in 1992. The Limited focused Abercrombie sales on apparel and launched the *A & F* magazine known for pictures of semi-nude models. This brand has approximately 850 North American stores that are usually located in malls, in addition to company sales via catalogs and online. Abercrombie & Fitch is an example of how thematic retail can successfully differentiate a retail brand experience from the competition.

Themed Entertainment Brand Stores

Themed entertainment brand stores focus on selling services associated with the retail name, rather than products. The idea is for retailers to brand their store experience using entertainment strategies. England's Cadbury World, a theme park owned by the British Cadbury brand, annually attracts 500,000 visitors with its history of chocolate exhibit, factory tour, chocolate-theme rides for children, and free samples. The amount Cadbury World visitors spend in the Cadbury World store is greater than the amount of the park entrance fee (*Brand Strategy* 2003).

Club Libby Lu's brand identity is associated with the brand outlet and unique themed entertainment experience (See Figures 9.6a–c). The entertainment attracts customers as a springboard for building the brand and branded merchandise. The idea is that entertainment at Club Libby Lu is differentiated enough to create loyal customers of tween girls. The company uses thematic retailing with an interactive format and "club" status to differentiate it from competitors such as Limited Too, Rave Girl, and other tween store formats (Wilson 2000). Merchandise is only a part of the attraction; the store also celebrates birthdays and provides an opportunity for

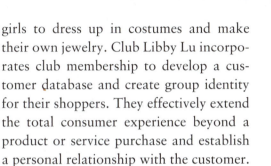

girls to dress up in costumes and make their own jewelry. Club Libby Lu incorporates club membership to develop a customer database and create group identity for their shoppers. They effectively extend the total consumer experience beyond a product or service purchase and establish a personal relationship with the customer.

Themed Flagship Brand Stores

The third thematic type of flagship retail operation is the hybrid themed flagship brand store in which an established brand attracts customers and provides entertainment-oriented services. It is a hybrid because it offers a brand sold through a variety of venues and it is an entertainment destination with sales revenue directly attributed to the sale of entertainment services.

Hershey, home of the Pennsylvania-based chocolate company, is the tourist destination known for the "Town That Chocolate Built" (O'Connell 2002). Hershey extended its brand image using experiential marketing in a Times Square brick-and-mortar advertising project. The Times Square store helps Hershey compete when consumers are apathetic toward traditional campaigns. Hershey's Times Square store appears to tower more than 15 stories over Broadway, with 4,000

lights, 380 feet of neon, four steam machines, and a moving message board. In the Hershey's Times Square store, customers can post personal messages. Also, they can personalize their own giant Hershey's kiss through entertainment-oriented services.

R. V. Kozinets et al. (2002) suggested themed flagship brand stores are created to have mythological appeal through narratives reinforced by their physical and symbolic structure. The Hershey story is propagated through the store environment and atmospherics as well as identifiable symbols such as Hershey's recognizable kiss.

9.6a–c Club Libby Lu is positioned as an experiential retailer.

CHAPTER SUMMARY

This chapter describes how thematic retailing uses a story to promote a retail brand and its identity. The opening vignette about Build-A-Bear Workshop tells a story about a successful themed retail experience that involves the consumer in product production. Thematic retailing addresses consumers' desires for involved, interesting, dynamic shopping experiences. Engaging store environments can enhance the retail experience by appealing to themes that resonate with consumers.

This chapter describes how themes are used in different consumption settings. Themes used in retail include ethnicity, affluence, craftsmanship, nostalgia, spirituality, holidays, seasonal themes, cultural events, and characters. These themes are used by retailers to satisfy customer demand and differentiate the firm's competitive position in the marketplace. Each one of these themes can be used by different types of stores such as department stores, specialty stores, discount stores, category killers, grocery stores, and restaurants. Themed retailing can also be used in the development and revitalization of malls and town centers.

The recent classification of themed flagship brand also is identified. They are flagship brand stores, intended for brand building and reinforcing the brand image (e.g., Abercrombie & Fitch); themed entertainment brand stores, focusing on selling branded services rather than products (e.g., Club Libby Lu); and themed flagship brand stores, selling a brand through a variety of venues to become an entertainment destination (e.g., Hershey in Times Square).

Thematic retailing adds value to shopping trips because it adds a recreational dimension to functional dimensions (e.g., saving time by being able to find merchandise attractively packaged together as a group). When executed correctly, thematic retailing creates a differentiated market position for the retailer, creates an experi-

ence that is not substitutable, attracts customers, stimulates store patronage, and creates customer loyalty. It gives shoppers a reason for staying longer, revisiting the store more often, and receiving hedonic benefits.

Discussion Questions

1. Identify goals of thematic retailing. Give examples of how retailers can successfully attain their goals with thematic retailing.

2. Describe how themes can be used to promote a home furnishings retail brand.

3. Explain how ethnicity-related strategies are used in thematic retailing. Provide current examples.

4. Describe how affluence-related strategies can be used in thematic retailing. Give some examples.

5. Describe how craftsmanship-related strategies are used in thematic retailing. Give current retail examples.

6. Explain how nostalgia-related strategies are used in thematic retailing. Provide current examples.

7. Describe how spirituality can be used in thematic retailing. Give examples, and explain if they are sacred or profane.

8. Discuss whether thematic retail strategies differ by store type (e.g., department store, specialty store, discount store).

9. Explain the roles of fictional characters in thematic retailing.

10. Describe the difference between brick-and-mortar stores and the Internet in the development of thematic retailing. What opportunities and challenges would each retail format have?

11. Discuss how thematic retailing influences consumer efficiency.

REFERENCES

Abercrombie & Fitch 2006. Information retrieved from Abercrombie & Fitch Presentation at the Merrill Lynch Retailing Leaders and Household Products and Cosmetics Conference, March 22, 2005. Retrieved August 30, 2006, from http://library.corporate-ir.net/library/61/617/61701/items/143046/Mar%2022nd%202005%20-%20Merrill%20Lynch.pdf.

Anziani, R. 2002. Town centers: It's all in the mix. *Shopping Center World* 31(5):210,212.

Backes, N. 1997. Reading the shopping mall city. *Journal of Popular Culture* 31(3):1–17.

Bagwell, L. S., and B.D. Bernheim. 1996. Veblen effects in a theory of conspicuous consumption. *The American Economic Review* 86(3):349–373.

Ball, D., R. Hampton, A. Chronis, and M. Bunker. 2001. *American Marketing Association Conference Proceedings* 12(3):305.

Beamon, K. 2002. Edible design. *Hospitality Design* 24(4):15.

Benitez, T. 2006. Scare Tactics; the tricks and treats of selling Halloween year-round. *Playthings* 24.

Biesada, A. 2006. Trader Joe's Company, Inc. *Hoover's Company Records* 47619.

Brand Strategy. 2003. Brand Entertainment: Brands play the world's stage. August 11, 20.

Buchthal, K. 2006. Stanford University. Restaurants and Institutions. 116(9):61–62.

Carlton, R. 2002. Sole seekers. *Display and Design Ideas* 14(12):18–19.

Carstens, K. 2005. Mid-Atlantic States. *Association Meetings* 69.

Chozick, A. 2005. 'Go, Diego, Go!' blazes a new trail; Unique marketing helps Nickelodeon push cartoon aimed at Hispanic viewers. *The Wall Street Journal*. September 8, B6.

Connell, M. 2002. Cabbage Patch Kids sprout up exclusively at Toys "R" Us. *Kidscreen*. January 3, 86.

de Oliver, M. 2004. Marketing Latinos as Development Policy: San Antonio and the Reproduction of Underprivilege. *Latino Studies* 2(3):395–421.

Edelson, S. 2006. A more modern bally debuts on Madison. *Women's Wear Daily* 191(10):14.

Feldman, L. 2004. Successful investment and turnaround strategies for distressed shopping centre properties. *Journal of Retail and Leisure Property* 4(1):32–38.

Filion, P., H. Hoernig, T. Bunting, and G. Sands. 2004. The successful few: Healthy downtowns of small metropolitan regions. *Journal of the American Planning Association* 70(3):328–343.

FoodService Director. 2006. Hospital in heartland embraces ethnic menu. 19(6):1–3.

Frazier, M. 2005. Regional grocer in Texas-size fight with Wal-Mart. *Advertising Age* 76(16):38.

Freeman, L. 2000. Marketing the good life to a new breed of wealth. *Advertising Age,* 71(21):1, 46.

Fuhrman, E. 2004. Unforgettable in a delicious way. *Candy Industry* 169(3):42–43.

Geist, W. E. 1985. About New York: A new cabbage patch arrives on 5th Avenue, The *New York Times*. December 7, Sec 1, 31.

Giuliano, C. 1999. Provincetown: The Lion in Winter. *Art New England* 20(5):106

Hickens, M. 1999. Brand names losing luster for affluent customers. *Management Review* 88(6):9

Hickey, K. 2001. Just for you. *Traffic World* 265(52/53):15–16.

Hirschman, E. C. 1990. Secular immortality and the American ideology of affluence. *Journal of Consumer Research* 17(1):31–32.

Holbrook, M. B., and R. M. Schindler. 2003. Nostalgic bonding: Exploring the role of nostalgia in the consumption experience *Journal of Consumer Behaviour* 3(2):107.

Hoovers Company Records. 2006. Abercrombie and Fitch Co. 53170.

Howell, D. 2006. Citi trends builds success targeting urban fashion. *DSN Retailing Today* 45(4):11.

Jarosz, P., and J. Laucius. 2006. The awesome power of one intrepid little explorer: Elbowing the Senators aside was child's play for Dora, Patricia Jarosz, and Joanne Laucius report. *Ottawa Citizen.* May 2, A1.

Kang, S. 2004. Pacific Sunwear's d.e.m.o. Chain Sells Hip-Hop Lite to Teenagers in Malls. *The Wall Street Journal.* February 20, A11.

Karlgaard, R. 2004. The age of meaning. *Forbes* 173(9):35.

Kelly, M. 2003. Seeking authenticity in the marketplace. *Journal of Popular Culture* 37(2):220–43.

King, J. 2000. All the (Retail) World's a Stage. *Shopping Center World* Retrieved from Lexis Nexis May 15, 2006.

Kozinets, R.V., J. F. Sherry, B. DeBerry-Spence, A. Duhachek, K. Nuttavuthisit, and D. Storm. 2002. Themed flagship brand stores in the new millennium: Theory, practice, prospects. *Journal of Retailing* 78(1):17–29.

Lama, S. Y., and A. Mukherjee. 2005. The effects of merchandise coordination and juxtaposition on consumers' product evaluation and purchase intention in store-based retailing. *Journal of Retailing* 81(3):231–250.

Leand, J. 2006. Not the average Joe. *SGB* 39(4):4.

Lefkowitz, D. 1998. Shopping and the meaning of life: Learning from the Mall of America: The Design of Consumer Culture, Public Life, and the Metropolis at the End of the Century. *New Art Examiner* 25(7):30–33.

Loney, N. 2005. Five secrets of successful schemes. *Regeneration and Renewal.* December 9, 20–22.

Major, M. 2005. Urban renewal. *Progressive Grocer* 84(10):24–31.

Martin, C. A., and L. W. Turley. 2004. Management malls and consumption motivation: An exploratory examination of older Generation Y consumers. *International Journal of Retail and Distribution* 32(10):464–475.

McCloud, J. 1999. U.S. shopping centers thrive as hubs of entertainment. *National Real Estate Investor* 41(6):42–48.

McGreevy, P. 1990. Place in the American Christmas. *Geographical Review* 80(1):32–42.

Merrick, A. 2002. Child's play for furniture retailers? Amid signs of a baby boom, the big chains rush to expand offerings to newborns, kids. *The Wall Street Journal.* September 25, B1.

Meyers, W. 2005. Conscience in a cup of coffee. *U.S. News and World Report* 139(16):48–50.

Murphy, H. L. 2002. Grocers discover Hispanic market. *Crain's Chicago Business* 25(27):4, 46.

O'Connell, V. 2002. You-Are-There Advertising—Fictional Hershey. Factory will send Kisses to Broadway; bricks-and-mortar marketing. *The Wall Street Journal.* August 5, B1.

Popovec, J. 2006. Targeting the ethnic shopper. *National Real Estate Investor.* May 1, 27.

Rabin, D. 2003. Plunky Provincetown; a Cape Cod resort with New England charms and missing norms. *Buffalo News.* May 11, G1.

Ralfo, B. and B. Wade. 2003. Dubuque, Iowa: Revitalization flows from America's River. *American City and County* 118(13):26.

Reingold, J. 2006. Burton Snowboards. *Fast Company* 108:58–59.

Richels, H. 2005. Fifth Avenue will soon be home to a new bear market. *The New York Sun*. July 7, 1

Salter, C. 2003. Mom, look! Cool! *Fast Company* 76, 47.

Sarkar, P. 2006. The tao of Trader Joe's. *The San Francisco Chronicle*. June 6, C1.

Schlosser, J. 2006. Mall star analyst. *Fortune* 153(4):161–165.

Schorr, K. 2003. N.E. travel shopping/ New England: Village shop hops for gifts from funky to top-of-the-line cool weather mean hot deals at the beach. *The Boston Globe*. November 17, M17.

Smith, J. W. 2003. Marketing that's good for the soul. *Marketing Management* 12(1):52.

Townsend, A. 2005. Analysis: Shakedown from the Sheikhdom: Dubai goes empire building in the West; the Emirate is flush with Middle Eastern petrodollars at present. *Independent on Sunday*. November 6, 6–7.

Valas, E. 2004. Creating a retail experience. *Dealerscope* 46(11):26.

Wainscoat, N. 2006. Selfridges is set to take retail spotlight. *Retail Week*. February 3, Retrieved from Lexis Nexis online August 29, 2006.

Whyatt, G. 2004. Town centre management: how theory informs a strategic approach. *International Journal of Retail & Distribution Management* 32(6/7):346

Wilson, M. 2006. The 'pop' factor. *Chain Store Age*. 82(4):78.

Wilson, M. 2000. Girls' club. *Chain Store Age* 76(10):62–64.

Zimmerman, A. 2005. Wal-Mart's Hispanic outreach; retailer does more to woo U.S. fastest-growing minority group. *The Wall Street Journal*. May 31, B9.

Ziska, A. 2004. Aiming for more Target's new fall assortment attempts to address all types of consumer preferences. *HFN*. September 20, 66.

Zoltak, J. 2003. Parks using ethnic food festivals to help entice new, repeat visitors. *Amusement Business* 115(18):13–14.

CHAPTER 10

LIFESTYLE RETAILING

How Pottery Barn Wins with Style

Shortly after Hadley MacLean got married in the fall of 2001, she and her husband, Doug, agreed that their old bed had to go. It was a mattress and box spring on a cheap metal frame. But Hadley never anticipated how tough it would be to find a grown-up bed, one that would be able to accommodate her husband's lanky six-foot-six-inch frame. "We couldn't find anything we liked, even though we were willing to spend the money," says Hadley. The couple finally ended up at Pottery Barn on Boston's upscale Newbury Street, where Doug fell in love with a mahogany sleigh bed that Hadley had spotted in the store's catalog. Not only would the bed go well with the antique dresser that Doug had inherited from his family, but its low footboard also would allow his feet to flop happily over the edge. The couple was so pleased with how great it looked in their Dutch Colonial home that they hurried back to the store for a set of end tables. And then they bought a quilt. And a duvet cover. And a mirror for the living room. And some stools for the dining room. "We got kind of addicted," Hadley confesses. "We like classic pieces that can stand the test of time, and Pottery Barn's stuff is great quality for the money."

The company's smart yet accessible product mix, seductive merchandising, and first-rate customer service have made it the front-runner in a fragmented industry—not just because of the products that it sells, but also because of the connections that it makes with customers. "It has built a furniture brand into a lifestyle brand in a way that nobody else has done," says Carole Nicksin, a senior editor at the home-furnishings trade weekly *HFN*. While sexy seasonal offerings such as espadrille-striped pitchers and pineapple-shaped candleholders keep customers stopping by to see what's new, Pottery Barn executives know that the bread and butter of their business is based on a select group of merchandise. And they aim to keep adding best-of-breed products to that collection of essentials, especially as they grow their bridal-registry business, one of the company's key initiatives for 2003. "We are focused on making sure that the core level of our business is superstrong," says Laura Alber, president of Pottery Barn Brands. "This is what customers think of us for and why they come back."

Celia Tejada, Pottery Barn's senior vice president for design and product development, began developing the company's design studio in 1996. Since then, the company has grown to 160 stores in 37 states and Canada and spawned two offshoots, Pottery Barn Kids and the recently announced catalog PBteen. To pass muster with Tejada and her team, a potential new product at Pottery Barn needs to meet the requirements of a strict five-point test. First, it has to look good, but not be too cutting edge. Second, the product has to feel good. Third, it must be of high quality. Fourth, it has to be durable. The question "Can the kids jump on it?" is a veritable mantra among Pottery Barn staffers, many of whom have children of their own to road test the merchandise. Finally, it must pass the ultimate hurdle: "I ask my designers, 'Will you take it home or give it as a present to your best friend?'" Tejada says. "If they hesitate, I say, 'Throw it in the garbage. Don't even bother.' Emotionally, it has to feel right."

Before launching a new product or line, Tejada and her team must work as much as a year in advance to allow time for sourcing, manufacturing, and shipping. That means that when the summer 2003 line—a Latin theme, complete with paella plates and brightly colored umbrellas, hammocks, and lanterns—appears in the stores, the design team is figuring out what consumers are likely to want in June 2004. It's a process that relies more on gut instinct than on rational science. If you want to create a brand that's inspirational, you can't lead a life that's dreary. The brand's allure is no mystery to Tejada. She likens it to the spirit of her adopted country. "What I love about America," she says, "is that it has its windows totally open. It has influences from everywhere, and it embraces everything. Our brand is also eclectic, an open window. It's a state of mind. And customers can make it their own."

Source: Tischler, L. 2003 How Pottery Barn Wins with Style, *Fast Company* 71:106–113.

INTRODUCTION

Shopping has become a means of self-expression for consumers; they buy products that reflect their personal and social identities. Retailers have created brands with which consumers can identify, brands that reflect their lifestyles, as more people continue to define themselves through product or service purchases. Pottery Barn, owned by Williams-Sonoma, offers versatile home accessories and builds brand equity with its growing assortment of distinctive bed and table textiles, decorative accessories, and furniture. Pottery Barn has carved out its niche by targeting affluent females. As Americans continue to lead more busy and stress-filled lives, Pottery Barn gives its customers the opportunity to create homes that are cozy and stylish, sanctuaries from a troubled world. This enables customers to have emotional ties with the products they bring into their homes.

Lifestyle refers to the way we live or the way we spend our time and money. For some individuals, the very act of shopping is a lifestyle. Recently, the shopping experience, rather than the product per se, has become a major emphasis of those responsible for a substantial portion of consumer goods expenditures (Holbrook 1999). For many consumers, shopping is a leisure activity that is an integral part of their lifestyles (Helman and Chernatony 1999). As more shoppers look for products, brands, or stores that reflect their own lifestyles, retailers continue to create strong images that appeal to consumers. According to G. T. Molitor (2000), as experiences and self-development grow in importance, there are greater opportunities for lifestyle retailing. Retailers using a lifestyle marketing strategy will be successful.

UNDERSTANDING LIFESTYLE

In traditional societies, class, caste, village, or family determined an individual's consumption options. In a postmodern consumer society, however, people are freer to select the set of products, services, and activities that define themselves. In turn, they create a social identity through these selections, which is communicated to others around them. Shopping has become not only the mere acquisition of things but also the purchasing of an identity. Even the consumption of necessities in situations where there are several choices reflects decisions about self, taste, images of the body, and social distinctions (Clammer 2003). One's consumption of goods and services makes a statement about who one is, and about the types of people with whom one desires to identify and even those whom one wishes to avoid (Solomon 2002). As early as 1963, M. Levy argued that the total consumption of goods and services is a mirror image of a person's lifestyle. M. E. Sobel (1981) also conceptualized lifestyle as sets of expressive, observable behaviors that define an individual or a group. In this context, lifestyle manifests both individual and social identity.

The positive economic conditions of the 1980s led to a boom in self-absorbed consumers as well as visible upward mobility. In contrast, in the leaner years of the early 1990s, people were fearful about their futures. As corporations continued to downsize, many consumers faced downward mobility, while others ventured out to start their own businesses. As people became more concerned with the preservation of financial and personal assets, we witnessed a renewed interest in products that allowed people to conserve money to ensure an easier retirement in addition to products that slowed the aging process.

Since late 1900s, globalization has expanded. Companies moved production from developed countries to developing countries because of lower manufacturing costs and higher margins. As a result, people lost their jobs, and most of the manufacturing industries disappeared from the United States. At the same time, population growth in developed countries leveled off, which forced traditional firms to look to other markets for new customers. A growing homogenization of material culture through the export of U.S. television series, films, rock music, and other products is influencing national or cultural identities (Elteren 1996). Today, consumers can buy the same product almost anywhere in the world. You can find Ben & Jerry's ice cream at Victoria Station in London, Talbots anywhere in the United Kingdom, and Nike in Budapest.

Also, advances in technologies and efficiencies are bringing consumers new, improved, and readily available products at competitive prices. G. T. Molitor (2000) predicts that by 2015, technological and organizational advances (e.g., automation and mass production) will reduce time required to accomplish tasks. As a result, there will be an increase in home-based activities, whether for entertainment or work. In addition, people will rely heavily on catalogs, professional shoppers, and home automation. The telecommuting trend will gain popularity, as more people use their personal computers and fax machines to establish offices at home.

Lifestyle as Individual Identity

Lifestyle refers to a consumption pattern associated with how an individual chooses to spend time and money. From an economic perspective, an individual's lifestyle relates to the way he or she allocates his or her income, both in terms of relative allocations to different products and services, and to specific alternatives within these categories (Zablocki and Kanter 1976). However, M. Solomon (2002) argued that lifestyle is not simply about allocating time and money, but rather about embracing the symbolic nuances that differentiate individuals or groups. B. Hawkins, R. Best, and K. Coney (2001) defined lifestyle as a function of inherent individual characteristics that are shaped and formed through social interaction as one evolves through the lifecycle. On Maslow's hierarchy of needs, the upward movement toward self-esteem and self-actualization represents a shift in consumer behavior from meeting needs to satisfying wants (Maslow 1970). As a result of this movement up the hierarchy, lifestyle-oriented shopping experiences have become prevalent.

Lifestyles are not permanent; unlike deep-seated values, people's tastes and preferences evolve over time. Consumption patterns viewed favorably at one point in the past may no longer be preferred. Since consumers' priorities and preferences are constantly evolving, it is essential for marketers to be aware of these changes and, more important, to predict them. Grant McCraken (1991) suggested that new patterns of production, exchange, and demand create change in consumption behavior. The shift in consumption patterns can be seen by observing the business headings in the Yellow Pages. Categories of livestock records, mops, and worms have been dropped from many telephone directories and replaced with new headings such as spa–beauty and day, organ and tissue banks, body piercing, cybercafés, permanent makeup, aromatherapy, and home theaters.

Lifestyle as Social Identity

Individuals use goods as an expression of social identity (Belk 1988), which reflects the need for belonging in Maslow's hierarchy. This leads them to form group identities, whether with fashion leaders, athletes, or hobbyists, and to externalize expressive symbolism in the form of personal attire, automobiles, tattoos, and so on. Self-definitions of group members are derived from the common system to which each group is dedicated. Such self-definitions are described by a variety of terms, including lifestyle, taste, consumer group, symbolic community, and status culture.

Consumption patterns are made up of many common ingredients that are shared among consumers in similar socioeconomic circumstances. However, each consumer may add an ingredient to this consumption pattern that reflects his or her individuality. For example, a teenager might dress much like his or her friends, hang out in the same places, and like the same foods, yet still indulge a passion for rap music or stamp collecting. These lifestyle activities make him or her a unique person. Teen wardrobes, which may at first seem identical to outsiders, are individualized even within specific trends or fads.

For the purposes of marketing, lifestyle describes the behavior of individuals, small groups of interacting people, and large groups of people (e.g., market segments) who act as potential consumers. These categories contribute to lifestyle market segmentation and will be discussed in a later section.

LIFESTYLE TRENDS

General consumption patterns are influenced by internal and external environmental factors such as family life, work experiences, political climate, and world events. Some of the important lifestyle issues currently shaping consumer behavior and retailing are wired or wireless consumers, self-expression, changing family roles, cocooning, connectedness, and casual lifestyle. Trends are dynamic; thus, the accuracy of these trend reports is only as reliable as the consumers' lifestyle environment is constant.

Wired or Wireless Consumers

It has become common to see consumers using cell phones whether they are walking down the street, eating at a restaurant, or shopping at a store. You will find people checking voice mail, reading e-mail, sending text messages, reviewing pictures, communicating with another party, and conducting business on their cellular phones. Now, people can even watch a program on a TV phone. People are constantly in touch with other people.

More consumers are using the Internet to make purchases because they have less time to shop. Consumers are increasingly embracing the Internet, e-kiosks, and wireless technology, anything that enables them to better control their shopping experience (*Retail Forward* 2003). Generations X and Y are the first consumers to be truly online purchasers; however, baby boomers and seniors are becoming less risk averse to buying online.

The Face of the Web, an annual Ipsos Insight survey, revealed that 28 percent of consumers worldwide has used mobile phones to surf the World Wide Web (Halpern 2006). The highest penetration of mobile Internet users is in Japan (40 percent) with Great Britain following at 29 percent, South Korea and the United States at 26 percent, and Canada at 19 percent. Mobile cell phone ownership is highest in Japan, South Korea, and China (90 percent), followed by France at 85 percent, Germany at 83 percent, the United States at 75 percent, and Canada at 61 percent (Halpern 2006). It is projected that global, mobile entertainment revenue will double from $21.3 billion in 2005 to $42.1 billion in 2010 (Carson 2006).

Self-expression

Fashion used to be dictated by a dress-to-impress motivation but has evolved into a dress-to-express philosophy. Looking good, which is closely connected today with how we dress, is driven more by consumers' desires to feel good about themselves than to make a good impression on others. As a result, shopping at prestigious stores simply to signify one's achievement or status is on the decline. In other words, while wearing designer clothing is still important to about half of U.S. consumers, fewer consumers wear designer labels as a symbol of achievement. Teenage clothing is no longer just about conspicuous consumption; it is considered self-expression. Teens are expressing themselves with embroidered jeans,

flashy cell phones, glitter body spray, and graphic T-shirts (Caplan 2005).

Shopping reflects the shopper's individuality and provides an external validation of his or her lifestyle perspective. This shopping mode is ego-intensive and is driven by desires rather than needs. To some consumers, the drive for self-expression is so strong that they perceive other store choice factors (e.g., location, price) almost irrelevant. To these consumers, it is critical for retailers to provide sharply edited merchandise assortments (*Retail Forward* 2003).

Retail providers of accessories for iPods and MP3 players have saturated the market with more than 400 different accessories for portable music; this number doubled in just one year (Kohler 2005). Why did iPod become so popular? M. Kohler (2005) answered this question with the following statement: "The iPod has style—it makes a statement that people are willing to pay for. Thanks to slick design, smart well-designed marketing campaigns, and plenty of advertising, consumers are lusting after an iPod. Accessories to this market are not just about functionality—[they are] about self-expression" (44).

Changing Roles in the Family

The gender roles of men and women are changing due to evolving nontraditional ideas regarding marriages, sexuality, child rearing, and career choices. Many couples in relationships are establishing households together but are not marrying. The result is fewer families having fewer children. As the number of dual income families grows, women are more likely than men to feel stressed at work as they try to juggle the multiple roles of employee, wife, mother, and homemaker.

At the same time, there is a growing number of women who prefers to stay home. This trend is steadily increasing because of women's commitments to their children and their willingness to make financial sacrifices to make it work (Rosenwein 2002). In fact, there is even an e-zine called *Main Street Mom* that positions itself as a publication for "modern mothers with traditional values" (www.mainstreetmom.com). The magazine has lifestyle sections such as family, home, budgeting, crafts, gardening, and just for mom. Magazine advertisements from companies such as Hooked on Phonics and Scholastic target stay-at-home moms and indicate a shift toward their renewed commitment to the family.

Cocooning

Another consumer lifestyle trend is **cocooning**, which is defined as "the act of insulating or hiding oneself from the normal social environment, which may be perceived as distracting, unfriendly, dangerous, or otherwise unwelcome, at least for the present" (www.SearchSecurity. com). The term cocooning was first coined by Faith Popcorn in her book *The Popcorn Report: The Future of Your Company, Your World, Your Life* and became popularized in the 1990s. Popcorn breaks down cocooning into three different types: the socialized cocoon, in which one retreats to the privacy of one's home; the armored cocoon, in which one establishes a barrier to protect oneself from external threats; and the wandering cocoon, in which one travels with a technological barrier that serves to insulate one from the environment (www.SearchSecurity.com).

Socialized cocooning is home-based and supports the trend that people enjoy spending time at home doing activities such as gardening, home decorating, and watching videos or TV shows instead of going to the movies. As a result, home furnishings sales have increased during the

last decade. Americans are also remodeling at record paces. Just look at the crowded parking lots of stores such as Home Depot and Lowe's (See Figure 10.1). Lawn and garden product sales are increasing at phenomenal rates. Because of recent events, cocooning now deals with staying at home out of fear of terrorism, crime, and violence, rather than for fun. This trend is an indication of armored cocooning. Consumers want their cocoons to be cozy and well-equipped, where they can escape from the chaotic and unpredictable outside world. Telephones and the Internet enable people to maintain contact with others, which becomes wandering cocooning. People who exercise or walk around the city wearing earphones retreat into a private world of sound. Today, wandering cocooning is growing rapidly due to wireless technologies such as cell phones and PDAs (www.SearchSecurity.com).

Connectedness

Consumers increasingly want to be connected to the world through media, travel, and electronic networks. To meet this consumer demand, marketers must develop an ongoing, meaningful, two-way dialogue with existing and potential customers. In

10.1 Home Depot sells home improvement products and services to people who are remodeling.

the past, advertising and public relations were dominated by one-way communications originating from the company. Thanks to the Internet, company websites have become the central hub for two-way interconnectedness.

In the last few decades, ATMs and pay-at-the-pump technologies at gas stations have replaced the tasks that traditionally involved human interaction (Rayport and Jaworski 2004). Today, we see new forms of technology that assist frontline employees. Examples include U-Scan checkouts at grocery stores and Easy Check-In at airline terminals where customers can perform entire transactions on their own. As many companies implement these new technologies, customers become more comfortable interacting with machines instead of people. J. Rayport and B. Jaworski (2004) stated, "Machines are proving to be viable alternatives not merely for processing rote transactions but for managing human interactions in sophisticated and unprecedented ways" (48).

However, Rayport and Jaworski (2004) argued that connecting with customers by providing effective customer service is possibly the last frontier of competitive advantage for many retailers. To increase customer satisfaction and loyalty, service interface between a company and a customer must be made. Rayport and Jaworski proposed four dimensions of the service interface: physical presence and appearance, cognition, emotion or attitude, and connectedness. Appearance of the frontline staff members is an example of physical presence and appearance. Employees who remember the names of customers is an example of cognition. The customer-friendly tone of a service representative who is on the phone with an upset customer is an example of emotion or attitude. The efficiency with which a brick-and-mortar retailer can handle a return transaction from the company catalog or website is an example of connectedness. Each of these dimensions can be used by retailers as a strategy to connect with customers and effectively outperform the competition.

Casual Lifestyle

Americans are renewing their interests in living casually, and this informality has extended to many companies that are instituting casual dress policies. In the United States, casual days started on the West Coast, where computer companies encouraged creativity by allowing their employees to dress down (*Training & Development* 2000). Eighty-six percent of U.S. companies allow some form of casual dress. There are also claims that the opportunity to dress casually, as well as dressing-up (depending on the circumstances), makes employees motivated and productive (Muñoz 2001).

The casual lifestyle is reflected in current fashion. Slippers, activewear, boots, camp shirts, and Hawaiian shirts have increased in popularity, while suits, ties, and pantyhose have decreased. The preference for casual apparel significantly affects the retail industry. For example, consumption of cotton whose core business is in casual products has increased, and stain-resistant, wrinkle-free, and easy-care clothing has become a popular choice (Duff 2000).

Although these aforementioned lifestyle trends are what can be witnessed in the United States, they are not applied in the same way to all consumers. Unique consumption patterns are influenced by climate, culture, and resources. Depending on where consumers live, their lifestyles may reflect geographical variations. This variation can be assessed at the level of region, state, and city type.

GEOGRAPHICAL VARIATIONS IN LIFESTYLE

U.S. citizens share a national identity, yet their consumption patterns vary by region. Regional differences create some familiar or different retail names, because brands and stores may not be accessible in all regions. For example, Carvel was an ice-cream brand started by Tom Carvel in 1934, when his ice-cream delivery truck broke down, and he astutely started selling soft ice cream. He developed a machine to dispense soft-serve ice cream and opened his first store in Hartsdale, New York. Carvel grew in popularity within the region until the brand became another word for *ice cream*. Carvel expanded in the Chicago market expecting to satisfy the tastes of transplanted New Yorkers. In this area, it competed with national premium brands as well as regional favorites such as Margie's Candies, which appealed to children and families (Moore 2003).

Regional differences exert a large impact on consumers' lifestyles, since many of our preferences in dress, food, and entertainment are directed by local customs, environment, and the availability of goods and services. For instance, consumers living in the Northeast and West are more likely to purchase mountain-climbing equipment than consumers in the Midwest and South. However, regardless of where consumers live in the United States they can enjoy a rugged mountain-climbing experience on sophisticated rock-climbing walls at stores such as Dick's Sporting Goods.

The type of fashion sought by consumers around the country also differs markedly. More casual clothing is prevalent on the West Coast. People who work in California in occupations such as in the high-tech and entertainment industries do not have to wear formal business attire. People who work in the Northeast and mid-Atlantic, on the contrary, are generally thought of as working in more formal occupations and make greater use of traditional business suits, especially in the financial and political capitals of New York City and Washington, D.C.

As with fashion, musical tastes vary by region. Country-and-western and rock music are popular in the United States. The blues, R & B, and soul are gaining in popularity; however, these preferences are by no means uniform across the country. Country-and-western music is more popular in southern cities and rural areas, while rock is more popular in northern cities. Retailers need to understand the sounds that resonate with their customers, just as radio stations do.

Fishing is another form of entertainment that differs by region based on culture and climate. Bass Pro Shop is more popular in the Southeast, Northeast, and Southwest where fishing is more prevalent. Similarly, some leading food brands sell significantly better in some parts of the country than in others. Pretzels are most popular in the mid-Atlantic area, pork rinds are most likely to be eaten in the South, and multigrain chips tend to be favored in the West. The Mexican influence on the people of the Southwest has determined snacking preferencs—they eat more tortilla chips in that region than elsewhere in the country. Hence, many national marketers regionalize their offerings to appeal to different tastes.

The Lifestyle Market Analyst (2004) conducted a survey with 210 designated market areas (DMAs) and reported associated lifestyle participation statistics, as illustrated in Table 10.1. For instance, San Francisco/Oakland/San Jose, California, ranks first out of 210 DMAs in the rate of attending cultural/arts events, whereas Dallas/Ft. Worth, Texas, ranks 44th. In

TABLE 10.1 LIFESTYLE RANKS OF SELECTED CITIES

	CITY						
LIFESTYLE	ATLANTA, GA	DALLAS AND FT. WORTH, TX	MINNEAPOLIS AND ST. PAUL, MN	NEW YORK, NY	PHOENIX, AZ	SAN FRANCISCO, OAKLAND, AND SAN JOSE, CA	SEATTLE AND TACOMA, WA
Attend cultural/arts events	21[1]	44	51	11	28	1	24
Avid book reading	95	110	73	94	71	78	12
Camping/hiking	170	147	71	208	50	81	33
Collectibles/collections	170	164	146	183	172	208	171
Community/civic activities	44	163	117	196	203	132	126
Cruise ship vacations	16	42	116	14	46	27	74
Fine art/antiques	10	18	62	29	63	5	13
Flower gardening	170	193	80	205	208	181	123
Foreign travel	25	32	39	6	35	1	13
Golf	85	93	1	169	40	120	74
Gourmet cooking/fine foods	37	57	96	4	52	1	8
Health/natural foods	19	68	114	26	30	25	48
Home furnishing/decorating	20	52	148	121	158	200	189
Home video games	113	45	194	132	70	167	85
Home workshop	93	159	68	209	149	206	130
Hunting/shooting	184	161	73	209	162	208	174
Listen to records/tapes/CDs	43	75	128	14	63	36	24
Own a cellular phone	1	5	98	44	28	8	53
Own a vacation home/property	60	150	13	77	26	39	33
Physical fitness/exercise	18	35	46	28	24	8	23
Recreation vehicles	179	169	56	210	62	197	70
Running/jogging	21	25	86	32	64	11	30
Shop by catalog/mail	166	184	191	31	195	104	143
Watching sports on TV	75	80	37	168	58	149	171

Source: *The lifestyle market analyst.* 2004. SRDS. Des Plaines, Illinois.
[1] Atlanta, Georgia ranks 21st out of 210 DMAs in the rate of Attend cultural/arts events.

terms of cruise ship vacations, New York ranks 14th; Minneapolis/St. Paul, Minnesota ranks 116th. As for owning a cellular phone, Atlanta, Georgia, ranks first; Minneapolis/St. Paul, Minnesota, ranks 98th.

LIFESTYLE RESEARCH

Marketers are constantly on the prowl for new clues about consumer lifestyles. They use lifestyle research to identify a consumer segment group that is united by a common lifestyle. A number of marketing research firms predicts social trends or broad changes in people's attitudes and behaviors. The Lifestyle Monitor, now run by the firm Yankelovich Clancy Shulman, interviews 2,500 American adults annually. Their targeted studies include the Yankelovich Youth MONITOR, Yankelovich African American MONITOR, Yankelovich/Cheskin Hispanic MONITOR, and YPandB/Yankelovich Travel and Leisure MONITOR (Yankelovich 2006).

Another research company that conducts lifestyle research is Spatial Insights, Inc., which developed the MOSAIC lifestyle typology based on geodemographic information (*Spatial Insights* 2006). Another is LifeMatrix, run by RoperASW, which segments consumers based on values, lifestyles, and life stages (*Mediamark Research* 2006).

In 2003, My AvantGo surveyed mobile device users in the United States to determine their preferences, buying patterns, and activities (AvantGo 2003). The survey sought to uncover trends among those who regularly carry and use a personal digital assistant (PDA). Of those surveyed, 84 percent was male; 69 percent was between 25 and 50 years of age. Respondents were well educated; more than two thirds had completed a bachelor's, master's, or Ph.D. degree. More than half had an annual household income above $60,000, of which

26 percent made more than $100,000. On any given day more than 80 percent of them participated in outdoor sports, including golfing (19 percent), hiking (17 percent), and cycling (15 percent). Nearly a third in the market purchased a new vehicle in less than a year. They traveled for both business and pleasure. This lifestyle information provides retailers with opportunities to stimulate or orchestrate complementary purchases and strategic alliances between firms.

Faith Popcorn, owner of BrainReserve and author of *The Popcorn Report*, is a globally recognized consumer trend expert and marketing futurist, but somewhat less conservative than other companies that use polls and databases. Since Faith Popcorn founded her company in 1974, she has guided companies in understanding and anticipating consumer behavior and leveraging established brands, new products, and services to meet the needs of future customers. BrainReserve has created strategic trend-based solutions and has provided FutureVisions for many Fortune 500 clients, including Bell Atlantic, BMW, Cigna, GE Capital, IBM, KitchenAid, MetLife, Nabisco, Pepsi/Lipton, and the Queen Mary Hotel (www.faithpopcorn. com). BrainReserve studies consumers in each of these groups to analyze and predict their consumption patterns based upon their individual lifestyles.

Psychographics

Consider a marketer who wishes to target the Generation X consumer. The ideal consumer is identified as a 40-year-old businessperson living in a large metropolitan area who makes between $40,000 and $80,000 a year. You may know many people who fit this description. Do you think they would all be likely to share common interests and buy the same products? Probably not, since their lifestyles are likely to differ considerably. In other words, demographics tell part of the story, but they do not explain the consumers' behavior. Consumers can share the same demographic characteristics and still be very different from one another. For this reason, marketers need to use psychographics as a tool to identify, understand, and target consumer segments that have a similar set of preferences for their products and services. **Psychographics** involves using psychological, sociological, and anthropological factors to determine market segments (Demby 1994, Wells 1968).

Researchers tend to closely relate psychographics to the study of lifestyle. There are three main ways in which psychographics are linked to lifestyle.

- Psychographics refers to the quantitative methods and techniques by which lifestyle profiles are constructed (Wells 1975).
- Psychographics refers to the psychological measures (e.g., attitudes, beliefs, and personality traits), while lifestyles refer to the activities and behaviors (Wells 1974).
- The terms of psychographics and lifestyle are used interchangeably (Gunter and Furnham 1992).

The most widely used approach to psychographic research attempts to group consumers according to some combination of three categories of variables—activities, interests, and opinions—which are known as AIOs (Wells and Tigerts 1971). To group consumers into common AIO categories, respondents are given a long list of statements and are asked to indicate how much they agree with each statement. Using data from large samples, marketers create profiles of customers who resemble one another in these categories. Consumer lifestyles are identified by measuring how people spend their time; what interests they have; what importance they place on their immediate surroundings; and how

they view themselves and the world around them. In addition, basic demographic information contributes to measuring consumer lifestyles. In short, psychographics allow marketers to understand why consumers buy in addition to who buys (Stapes 2000).

Psychographic Research

Many empirical studies have conducted psychographic research to segment a consumer market. Psychographic research must be accurate; otherwise it will be difficult to retain or increase customers. Mainstream magazines such as *Reader's Digest* lost more than three million readers and *People* lost more than two million between 1989 and 1999 (Lach 2000), which might suggest they did not target the right customers. Fashion, home décor, fitness, sports, and culinary arts are among the industries that are catering to markets with specific lifestyles (Solomon 2002). Home and Garden Television (HGTV) found a niche market when it began broadcasting to consumers who are interested in creating homes that reflect their personal tastes and lifestyles. Programs such as *Design on a Dime* help HGTV consumers achieve higher-end lifestyles on a budget price.

A study by N. L. Cassill and M. F. Drake (1987) combined lifestyle segments with evaluative criteria (e.g., attributes associated with desired benefits or incurred costs) for both social and employment apparel. They identified eight lifestyle segments among working women: self-confidence, attractive/fashionable, satisfaction with life, traditional, pro-American/education, price conscious/information seeking, modern traveling/spending, and mobile/impulsive. In terms of the relationship between these lifestyle segments and evaluative criteria, working women who had self-confidence and were concerned with attractiveness and fashion-

TABLE 10.2 TOURIST CONSUMER SEGMENTS

TOURIST SEGMENT	CONSUMER CHARACTERISTICS	MARKETING IMPLICATIONS
Home-loving tourists	They are fundamentally focused on family life, placing special emphasis on having children and taking responsibility for their upbringing. Although they are not materialists, they are cautious in their attitudes toward the future. Quality is always more important than price. They enjoy cultural activities and have a wide range of preferences in reading material.	They enjoy holiday arrangements corresponding to the family needs as a whole. The type of accommodation best suited would give some degree of comfort and quality, but fall within customers' expectations on prices. This is a rather conservative group, whose members in principle would prefer to organize their own trips. Use direct marketing campaigns and regional newspapers, and home and fashion magazines to reach them.
Idealistic tourists	They believe that the attainment of personal success is rooted in a determination to achieve a better world and to fight against injustice. As the most innovative group, they take an active and collaborative part in the enterprises employing them. They enjoy sports, classical music, going to concerts or the theater, and dancing.	Offer a combination of destinations, including interesting villages where they could get in touch with the rural economy. The proposed packages could be aimed at small groups, made up of a family and a few friends. On radio and television, advertising during sports and music programs would be best, while provincial and national newspapers might be the most effective channel.
Autonomous tourists	They see success as linked fundamentally with individual freedom and independence. Enjoying life is one of their fundamental objectives. They try to aspire to upward social mobility in their way of life. They are flexible in politics, religion and social views. Their main interests are frequent cinema visits and going out to enjoy nightlife.	To stress the sensation of independence and freedom characteristic of this grouping, there could be an option for mixing and matching the cities to be visited. The best advertising to use would be either direct marketing or adverts in any media connected with sport. The image to be presented would be a group of people who get on very well together, laughing and enjoying themselves in various situations.
Hedonistic tourists	They accept life as it comes and enjoy it. They have interesting and successful jobs that allow them to fulfill themselves. They are tolerant with regard to discipline, politics, and law and order. They stress personal relationships and tend to travel in the company of friends. They are active and innovative.	Offer a list of cultural events taking place at the destinations. Distribution and marketing to this grouping should be achieved through new technologies such as the Internet as well as via traditional channels. Virtual visits to hotels and information relating to complementary items of any kind should be available, so that bookings and packages could be handled directly from home or from the workplace.
Conservative tourists	This is a home-loving segment, members of which are focused on the well-being of their family and coping with day-to-day life. They are, in general, pessimistic about modern society. They are stricter when it comes to law and order. Their pastimes include enjoying visits to areas of outstanding beauty.	They prefer guaranteed sun and sea for one or two weeks. They often travel together with both family and friends, creating their own organized travel party. Offer accommodation options that are relatively cheap for the group as a whole. The ways of communicating with them would be the mass media, television, and radio, especially through sponsorship of programs such as reality shows, quizzes, or gossip shows.

Source: Gonzalez, A. M., and L. Bello, 2002. The construct lifestyle in market segmentation: The behavior of tourist consumers. *European Journal of Marketing* 36(1/2): 51–85.

ableness evaluated employment apparel based on criteria such as good fit, comfort, and level of appropriateness for the workplace. This result suggests that consumers choose apparel products that fit specific roles in their lifestyles.

A. Gonzalez and L. Bello (2002) used AIOs to segment the tourist market in Spain and predict the behavior of leisure travelers. They identified five lifestyle segments of tourist consumers: home-loving, idealistic, autonomous, hedonistic, and conservative. Marketing implications are provided for each segment, as illustrated in Table 10.2.

Psychographic research also supports online shopping. W. R. Swinyard and Scott Smith (2003) developed an Internet shopper

TABLE 10.3 LIFESTYLE SEGMENTS OF U.S. ONLINE HOUSEHOLDS

SEGMENT	LIFESTYLE DESCRIPTION
Shopping lovers	Are competent computer users who frequently buy online and enjoy doing so.
Internet explorers	Believe Internet shopping is fun and could be considered opinion leaders for online buying.
Suspicious learners	Are not very computer literate and are suspicious of giving out their credit card numbers, but are open-minded to learning new things.
Business users	Do not make personal online purchases often, but mainly use the Internet for business purposes and look at the Internet in terms of what it can do for their professional lives.
Fearful browsers	Are very computer literate and often practice "Internet window-shopping." They usually do not buy since they distrust the security of the Internet, dislike shipping charges, and are reluctant to buy things without seeing them in person.
Shopping avoiders	Are difficult to turn into online shoppers since they do not want to wait for product delivery and want to see things in person before they buy.
Technology muddlers	Do not spend much time online, are somewhat computer illiterate, and are not interested in increasing their computer knowledge. Thus, they may not be an important target market for online retailers.
Fun seekers	Value the entertainment of the Internet, but are afraid of buying online. They have relatively lower education and income levels with not much spending power.

Source: Swinyard, William R., and Scott Smith. 2003. Why people (don't) shop online: A lifestyle study of the Internet consumer. *Psychology & Marketing* 20(7):567–597.

lifestyle measurement that encompasses interests and opinions toward the Internet, as well as Web-specific behaviors. They conducted cluster analysis based on lifestyle factors to identify four shopper and four non-shopper segments among U.S. online households (See Table 10.3). Internet shoppers were segmented into shopping lovers (11.1 percent), Internet explorers (8.9 percent), suspicious learners (9.6 percent), and business users (12.4 percent). Internet non-shoppers were segmented into fearful browsers (10.7 percent), shopping avoiders (15.6 percent), technology muddlers (13.6 percent), and fun seekers (12.1 percent).

M. Brengman et al. (2005) conducted online surveys in the United States and Belgium to cross-culturally validate the Internet shopper lifestyle scale developed by Swinyard and Smith (2003). Their study showed that the Web-usage-related lifestyle had the same basic meaning and structure for U.S. and Belgian consumers. In both samples, six basic dimensions underlie the scale: Internet convenience, perceived self-inefficacy, Internet logistics, Internet distrust, Internet offer, and Internet window-shopping. Although different nations vary in how much and how well they embrace the Internet, consumers who choose home Internet access may respond similarly to online issues.

VALS

The most popular research tool describing lifestyles and psychographics is the Values and Lifestyles System, developed by Stanford Research Institute Consulting Business Intelligence (SRIC-BI) in California. VALS was first introduced in 1978 and focused on activities and interests. In 1989, it was refined with more emphasis on enduring personality traits and less emphasis on social values that changed over time (*SRI Consulting Business Intelligence* 2006). The current VALS system creates an explicit link between personality traits and purchase behavior. VALS uses a battery of

39 psychological and demographic variables to divide U.S. adult consumers into groups, each with distinctive characteristics (www.sric-bi.com). As shown in Figure 10.2, groups are arranged vertically by their resources or degree of innovativeness and horizontally by motivation. Three primary motivations in the VALS system are ideals, achievement, and self-expression. Consumers motivated by ideals guide themselves by a belief system when they make purchases, and they are not concerned with the views of others. People motivated by achievement make decisions based on the perceived opinions of their peers. Individuals motivated by self-expression buy products that have an impact on the world around them. As a result, eight VALS groups emerged: innovators, thinkers, achievers, experiencers, believers, strivers, makers, and survivors. Table 10.4 describes characteristics of each VALS group.

Many businesses use the VALS segments to identify and better understand their targeted consumer groups. For example, a survey of air travelers found that 37 percent were actualizers, while this group represented only 8 percent of the general population. Since actualizers buy merchandise that reflects their high income and status, stores such as The Nature Company and Sharper Image have a greater chance to succeed at airport locations (Levy and Weitz 1998). The original Merrill Lynch advertising campaign, Bullish on America, showing a thundering herd of buffalos, was modified based on a VALS analysis. The market analysis revealed that this ad appealed primarily to belongers rather than the achievers that Merrill Lynch tried to target. The ad message was altered to show a lone bull using the theme A Breed Apart (Levy and Weitz 1998).

Increased globalization of markets requires that marketing strategies include increasing amounts of global planning. If there are discernible lifestyle segments that transcend cultures, marketers can develop cross-cultural strategies that target these segments. Although language and other differences exist, individuals who pursue similar lifestyles in different cultures should respond similarly to product features and communication themes. Suppose you were developing an international strategy for Whirlpool appliances. You would notice that strivers are the largest global segment, although this is not true in all countries. A product line targeted at this group would need to be relatively inexpensive and readily available, would require access to credit, and should have a maximum number of convenience features. The marketing theme would stress convenience, gratification, and value. Promotional efforts would need to be allocated disproportionately to those countries with large concentrations of strivers.

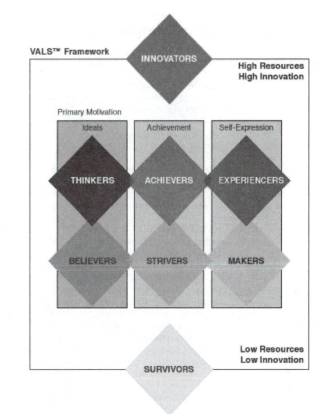

10.2 The VALS system creates a link between personality traits and purchase behavior.

TABLE 10.4 VALS GROUP CHARACTERISTICS

VALS GROUP	INDIVIDUAL PROFILE	CONSUMPTION CHARACTERISTICS
Innovators	Innovators are successful, sophisticated, take-charge people with high self-esteem. Because they have such abundant resources, they exhibit all three primary motivations in varying degrees. They are leaders and are the most receptive to new ideas and technologies.	Innovators' purchases reflect cultivated tastes for upscale, niche products and services. Image is important to them, not as evidence of status or power but as an expression of their tastes, independence, and personality.
Thinkers	Thinkers are mature, satisfied, comfortable, and reflective people who value order, knowledge, and responsibility. They tend to be well educated and actively seek out information in the decision-making process.	Thinkers are conservative, practical consumers; they look for durability, functionality, and value in the products they buy.
Achievers	Motivated by the desire for achievement, Achievers have goal-oriented lifestyles and a deep commitment to career and family. Achievers live conventional lives, are politically conservative, and respect authority and the status quo. They value consensus, predictability, and stability over risk, intimacy, and self-discovery.	Achievers favor established, prestige products and services that demonstrate success to their peers. Because of their busy lives, they are often interested in a variety of time-saving devices.
Experiencers	Experiencers are motivated by self-expression. As young, enthusiastic, and impulsive consumers, they seek variety and excitement, savoring the new, the offbeat, and the risky. Their energy finds an outlet in exercise, sports, outdoor recreation, and social activities.	Experiencers are avid consumers and spend a comparatively high proportion of their income on fashion, entertainment, and socializing. Their purchases reflect the emphasis they place on looking good and having cool stuff.
Believers	Believers are conservative, conventional people following established routines, organized in large part around home, family, community, and social or religious organizations to which they belong.	As consumers, they are predictable; they choose familiar products and established brands. They favor American products and are generally loyal customers.
Strivers	Strivers are concerned about the opinions and approval of others. Money defines success for them, but they do not have enough of it to meet their desires. A lack of skills and focus in their job often prevents them from moving ahead.	Strivers are active consumers because shopping is both a social activity and an opportunity to demonstrate to peers their ability to buy. They are impulsive buyers and favor stylish products that emulate the purchases of people with greater material wealth.
Makers	Makers express themselves and experience the world by working on it—building a house, raising children, fixing a car, or canning vegetables. They are respectful of government authority and organized labor, but resentful of government intrusion on individual rights.	Makers are unimpressed by material possessions other than those with a practical or functional purpose. Because they prefer value to luxury, they buy basic products.
Survivors	Survivors live narrowly focused lives with few resources. They are comfortable with the familiar and are primarily concerned with safety and security. Because they must focus on meeting needs rather than fulfilling desires, they do not show a strong primary motivation.	Survivors are cautious consumers. They represent a very modest market for most products and services. They are loyal to favorite brands, especially if they can purchase them at a discount.

Source: SRI Consulting Business Intelligence. www.sric-bi.com/VALS

LIFESTYLE RETAILING

Lifestyle retailing is defined as retail offers that are tailored to the lifestyles of specific market segments (Blackwell and Talarzyk 1983). Thus, an important part of lifestyle retailing is to identify the set of products and services that seems to be linked to a specific lifestyle. With an emphasis on consumers' lifestyles over demographic and merchandising criteria, retailers must look at how people make choices among a variety of product and service categories to define their lifestyles. They then need to develop appropriate segmentation, positioning, and communication strategies to ensure that their products and services are on target for the respective segment.

Products/Services as a Consumption Constellation

Many products and services (e.g., fast food and Styrofoam containers, or a business suit and PDA) seem to go together or appeal to a certain consumer group because they tend to be selected by the same types of people. Even a relatively unattractive product becomes more appealing when replaced side by side with other like products (Hsee and Leclerc 1998). On the contrary, products do not seem to make sense if they do not complement each other or if products are incongruous in the presence of others (e.g., a professional suit and a nose ring, or a Victorian-style chair in a high-tech office).

A related concept is product complementarities, which occur when the meanings of different products are related to each other. Sets of products are referred to as **consumption constellations**, and they are used by consumers to define, communicate, and perform social roles as the means to self-realization and symbolic activities (Solomon 2002). For example, the U.S. yuppie of the l980s was associated with products such as Rolex watches, Armani suits, BMW automobiles, and Gucci briefcases and shoes. They consumed these products to make a statement about their status and success (Belk 1986).

Indeed, a goal of lifestyle retailing is to allow consumers to pursue consumption activities that provide enjoyment to their lives and express their social identities. Therefore, a key aspect of this strategy is to focus on a consumer's product or service use in a social setting that depicts a certain lifestyle, as illustrated in Figure 10.3. Associating a product with a social situation is a longstanding goal for advertisers, whether the product is included in a round of golf, a family barbecue, or a night at a glamorous club surrounded by jet-setters

(Leiss, Kline, and Jhally 1986). For example, a wealthy, classic, quality-conscious baby boomer may buy high-quality, prestigious designer clothing in an upscale department store; whereas a teenager may go to a record store to hang out with friends surrounded by contemporary displays, merchandise, and music.

Upon identifying product and service sets, a lifestyle retailer can construct retail strategies by selecting the target lifestyle consumer segments, positioning the product and service against its competitors, and developing a communication strategy to reach its market.

Segmentation

Segmentation refers to individuals who sort themselves into groups based upon the things they like to do, how they like to spend their leisure time, and how they choose to spend their disposable income. This allows a population to be viewed as distinct individuals, but addressed in compatible groups or segments. These patterns, in turn, create opportunities for market segmentation strategies that

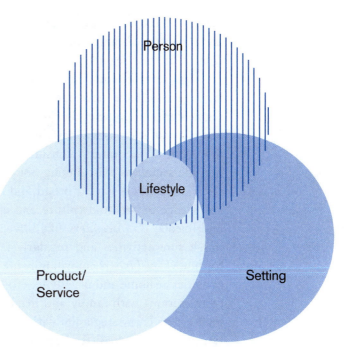

10.3 Product or service use in a social setting depicts a consumer's lifestyle.

determine the types of products offered and the specific brands appealing to a designated lifestyle segment.

Many research companies and advertising agencies have developed their own segmentation typologies. For instance, the Sony Corporation uses a lifestyle approach to segment its target consumers. Six lifestyle segments exist among Sony buyers. *Connoisseurs* have a broad and deep knowledge of arts and culture and enjoy multimedia. *Transcenders* like adventurous leisure activities and regularly travel for fun. *Homelanders* enjoy family life and activities at home and usually like to have conversations with family and neighbors. *Free agents* enjoy single life without marriage, are individualists, heavily participate in social activities, and have a strong sense of entrepreneurship. *Code breakers* avoid traditional values and thinking and tend to seek instant excitement and adventurous activities. *Virtual professionals* have professional jobs and higher social status and seek artificial beauty and entertainment. See www.sonystyle.com for more examples of how this company segments its market.

Porsche Cars North America also uses psychographics to segment its consumers. Porsche thought it sold cars costing between $40,000 and $82,000 to a demographically homogenous group, consisting of 40-something male college graduates who earned more than $200,000 per year. However, Porsche's sales were slipping. They hired a team of anthropologists to figure out the psychographic composition of their consumers. They found that they had been using unsuccessful marketing strategies to target the wrong group of people. Based on the analysis of psychographic information on their consumers, they identified five segments.

1. *Top Guns*: Driven, ambitious; power and control matter; want to be noticed

2. *Elitists*: Old money; a car is just a car, no matter how expensive

3. *Proud*: Ownership is an end in itself earned by hard work; no need to be noticed

4. *Bon vivants*: Worldly jet-setters and thrill seekers; car heightens the excitement in their already passionate lives

5. *Fantasists*: Their car is an escape; uninterested in impressing others; may feel a little guilty about owning a Porsche.

After implementing marketing plans tailored to these specific segments, they ended a 7-year slump and sales rose 48 percent (Taylor 1995).

Another example of a company that successfully used consumer segmentation with psychographics is SK Telecom (SKT) in South Korea. The company has managed its various customer segments on the basis of customer lifestyle and made efforts to provide each segment with services that are well-matched with consumer lifestyles. SKT provides a membership card that has a unique value-added service customized according to the customer's socioeconomic pattern. Box 10.1 is one typical example. SKT identifies new customers from high school students and married women segments, groups traditionally not considered to be wireless customers. Through these marketing opportunities, SKT keeps a lower customer turnover rate than its competitors and is able to increase its profit per customer.

Positioning

Lifestyle segmentation information allows marketers to build company identity through positioning strategies. **Positioning** allows retailers to offer products or services that are closely associated with the lifestyles of specific consumer segments. One example of retail positioning based on customers' lifestyle is Subaru. When this automobile company entered the U.S. market in the early 1970s, it had virtually no name recognition. After linking the brand to the lifestyles of people who enjoy skiing, Subaru became the official car of the U.S. Olympic ski team, and the company obtained the highest market share for imported cars in several Snowbelt states (Swenson 1989).

With the rise in the number of retail brands associated with consumer lifestyles (e.g., Gap, CompUSA, and Home Depot), lifestyle becomes an increasingly important aspect of a retail identity because it sets up the store as a lifestyle merchant. Oftentimes the personality characteristics of a brand's target consumer segment are used to determine the attributes desired by the segment. These personality characteristics reflect hedonic or utilitarian attributes of a brand. A lifestyle retailer should develop and provide special and identifiable attributes so that its customers can have a unique consumption experience.

Communication

Information on the lifestyle characteristics of consumer segments is valuable to firms when planning communication strategies.

How a product is promoted should be guided by the lifestyle characteristics of the target consumer group. For example, Joseph Plummer's (1972) study revealed that heavy beer drinkers tend to be highly masculine, like to take risks, play games of chance such as poker, act impulsively, like sports, and dislike old-fashioned institutions and moral guidelines. It was, therefore, recommended that promotional strategies targeted to beer drinkers must exhibit these lifestyle characteristics.

DuPont agricultural products attempted to hit an emotional chord with farmers by using psychographics to segment consumers by understanding their attitudes, interests, and behaviors. For its Basis corn herbicide campaign, DuPont put family and quality of life center stage. The campaign promised to help farmers reduce herbicide costs and increase profits to provide more for their families and, ultimately, to help them pass down the family farm to their children. The advertisement recognized that farmers use more than just pure reason and logic when deciding which herbicide to use. It helped Basis gain a competitive advantage in an otherwise very cluttered marketplace (Bernick 1996). While other pesticide manufacturers based their advertising on how well their chemicals kill pests, the Basis campaign took agricultural advertising to a new, emotional level.

The lifestyle analysis of a firm's target market also influences media strategy. When promoting a product, a firm must determine the appropriate types of media to use to appeal to its target market. The advertiser should match the lifestyle profile of its target market to that of the viewers of the media that places the advertising. For instance, the readers of *Playboy* and those of *Reader's Digest* tend to exhibit very different lifestyle profiles. Compared with readers of *Reader's Digest*, *Playboy* readers believe that they will make greater achievements in the future and that movies should not be censored. If the heavy users of a product revealed a consumer lifestyle profile similar to the readers of either *Playboy* or *Reader's Digest*, the firm might consider advertising in that periodical (Mowen 1995).

LIFESTYLE RETAILERS

A growing number of retail companies have been successful in using a lifestyle marketing approach. Leading the ranks is Ralph Lauren. Abercrombie & Fitch's Quarterly magalog (magazine plus catalog) offers editorials about campus trends and captures college student lifestyles. With home remodeling and decorating consumer trends, companies such as Pottery Barn, Crate and Barrel, and Restoration Hardware have gained wide popularity and are expanding across the country. Other retail companies such as Apple, IKEA, The Gap, Cornell, Starbucks, Marks and Spencer, Panera Bread, Earth Fare, and Harley-Davidson Motor

Company are using a lifestyle marketing approach to appeal to consumers.

Ralph Lauren, the icon of American style, has successfully used the lifestyle retailing approach. Ralph Lauren stores include not only clothing for men and women, but also furniture and accessories for the home, including wallpaper, sheets, and towels. Moreover, the Ralph Lauren brand has expanded to Home Depot, which sells its designer paint. Ralph Lauren blazed the trail of lifestyle merchandising for discriminating consumers by selling not just merchandise but also his own personal context. Rather than simply putting out new colors or patterns like others in the paint business, Lauren creates products that revolve around themes, such as New England Cottage and English Countryside.

Apple enhances consumers' digital lifestyles through its speed, peripheral acceptance, and rocking software. Apple customers are usually considered to be trendy and youthful. According to Merrill Lynch analyst Steven Milunovich, although the older generation still thinks it is strange to own a Mac, the younger generation considers Apple a core brand for their digital lifestyles (Serwer 2004). Apple has attempted to locate its stores in high-traffic locations such as shopping malls and urban shopping districts, where targeted consumers are typically shopping (Datamonitor 2004). Apple extended the brand by introducing the iPod, a small, portable music player, and the iPhone.

IKEA, an international furniture store based in Sweden, satisfies the lifestyle needs of highly educated young professionals who value style and quality, but not high prices. Its customers are willing to put together their own products. This allows IKEA to ship flat boxes more affordably. This segment of young professionals exists around the world, and IKEA's successful global lifestyle strategy is evident in places such as Milan, Montreal, and New York.

The Gap targets consumers who are looking for casual, classic lifestyle. The Gap family brands are sold at specialty stores—Gap, BabyGap, GapKids, Old Navy, Banana Republic, and GapBody. These family brands are targeted at consumers in different life cycles. Gap products consistently reflect the lifestyle and expected consumption experience.

Cornell Trading Inc, a lifestyle boutique, makes and sells women's and children's apparel in Canada under the April Cornell name. Cornell offers merchandise targeted to consumers who desire all that is whimsical, feminine, and romantic. A backdrop of nature and artistic expressions with flowers, leaves, and birds are the recurring motifs in all elements of their merchandise, from table linens, to apparel, to hand-painted home furnishings (Gentry 2000).

Starbucks Coffee targets people who share interests in coffee, warmth, community, and good companionship (See Figure 10.4). The company establishes emotional ties with its customers through the Starbucks Experience. Starbucks counters are often located in non-competing retail formats with complementary products and lifestyles such as Albertson's and Kroger. They can also be found in international airports.

The British specialty retailer Marks and Spencer, known for soft goods and foods, developed themed worlds or lifestores to group housewares into product assortments (Hall 2004). Lifestores reflect consumer lifestyles with names such as rest, relax, cook, and play and merchandise are displayed in vignettes.

The Container Store is a Dallas-based brand that is the category leader of the storage and organization segment of the housewares industry (see Figure 10.5) (Fox 1996). Founded in 1978, it was among the first to offer multifunctional storage products not generally sold at retail stores (Duff

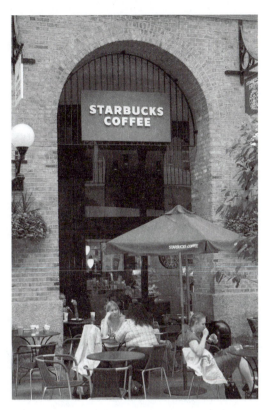

10.4 Starbucks targets people who share interests in coffee, warmth, community, and good companionship.

2004). In 2006, The Container Store launched a new marketing campaign, built its Internet presence, and tied in with a television show. The company partnered with *Real Simple Magazine* for a television

10.5 The Container Store launched a new promotional campaign, "Life's little pleasures. Organized," targeting affluent professional women.

show called *Real Simple TV*, a 26-episode series on PBS that started in January 2006. The show targets affluent professional females with Martha Stewart–type advice on doing things efficiently. A new branding campaign is also being planned around the store's tagline: Life's little pleasures. Organized. Customers are 85 percent female; they are well-educated, well-traveled, and have high household incomes (O'Loughlin 2006).

Harley-Davidson is an iconic motorcycle manufacturer that has built a cult following among consumers who are loyal to the brand (See Figure 10.6). For many owners, the Harley experience is about the enjoyment of being on the open road. The company has worked to establish a close bond with customers and to best fulfill the dreams of a motorcyclist. The Harley-Davidson brand's customers are mostly U.S. baby boomers. But there has been concern that future sales will decline as the company's core customers' age. The median age of new Harley buyers has increased from 45 to 46 and the median income has risen to $80,000 in 2003 up from $72,500 in 1999 (Buss 2004). The company is looking at new markets, potentially targeting baby boomers in Europe and Asia (Pande 2004). Harley also has begun to market to Generation X and female consumers, and launched a range of toys and a children's clothing line to target younger consumers. Harley develops adventure tours, holds rallies, and keeps customers up-to-date through newsletters.

The Panera Bread Company provides fresh baked breads to customers who enjoy the lost culinary delight of homemade, fresh-made bakery items (See Figure 10.7). The company prides itself on its product and believes fresh baked breads intensify the culinary experience. The company has led the nationwide trends of artisan bread and quick casual and specialty foods. In 2003, the company also initiated its bakery cafés with free Wi-Fi (wireless fidelity) access to meet growing consumer demand for high speed Internet access (Boosman 2003). Consumers who frequent Panera Bread are business professionals. People meeting for lunch or starting their day off with a cup of coffee and bagel can be regularly seen at Panera locations (www.panerabread.com).

The Earth Fare supermarket provides products that are fresh, organic, and locally grown in North Carolina, South Carolina, Tennessee, and Georgia. The bakery breads and pastries are produced with unbleached flour and sugar. Meat and poultry sold at Earth Fare is obtained from companies that use naturally grown feed for their animals. Consumers utilizing Earth Fare may be individuals who are not only health-conscious, but also conscious of the environment as well. Earth Fare promotes and promises toxin-free products

10.6 Harley-Davidson has built a cult following by marketing its branded apparel.

as well as humane considerations of all animal products.

The above-mentioned lifestyle retailers illustrate that lifestyle retailing has been viewed at the micro level—product level and store level. However, the concept of lifestyle retailing can be applied at the macro level—shopping center level—because shopping centers can offer a tenant mix and market position that represents a special type of consumer experience and retail environment to suit a particular lifestyle.

LIFESTYLE SHOPPING CENTERS

The significance of consumer lifestyle to retail vitality created the basis for shopping center differentiation (Rabianski 2001). This is particularly attractive because brands and stores already use lifestyle in positioning strategies, and shopping centers can capture this same synergy to create additional sales by grouping lifestyle retailers and products together. Since its widespread development during the 1950s, the planned shopping center industry has continuously reinvented itself through innovation.

Environmental Revolutions

As illustrated in Table 10.5, different types of shopping centers have evolved through environmental factors, including structural and information technology revolutions. However, some shopping centers entered a decline stage because they were no longer relevant to changing consumer lifestyles. The structural revolution refers to the demographic, social, economic, and political factors that determine how markets are formed. The information technology revolution describes the information explosion and new technology development (Helman and Chernatony 1999).

In addition to past structural and information technology revolutions, the environment of the early 2000s reflects an expressive revolution evolving from the emphasis on consumers' lifestyles. The

TABLE 10.5 EVOLUTIONS OF THE SHOPPING CENTER INDUSTRY

DECADE	STAGE OF EVOLUTION	REVOLUTIONARY ENVIRONMENTAL FACTOR	SUCCESS FACTORS	DECLINE FACTORS
1950s	Enclosed shopping mall	**Structural** Highway constructions; rise of suburbs	Diverse retail outlets under one roof with anchor department stores as the main attraction; architecture; ambience; entertainment	Overexpansion; homogeneous look
1970s	Factory outlet mall	**Structural** Adverse economic situations; wide array of middle- and lower-middle-income consumers	Value Assortment	Not located within reasonable distances to consumers
1980s	Power center	**Structural** Increase of dual-income families	Convenience Value Assortment	Challenged by the Internet sales
1990s	Cyber mall	**Structural** Cocooning consumers **Information Technology** Super highway	Convenience Assortment	Not leading to impulse purchasing experiences
2000s	Lifestyle shopping center	**Structural** Affluent consumers; Growing single-person households **Information Technology** Interactive technology; merging bricks and clicks **Expressive** Experiential aspect of shopping; self-actualization; psychographics (reflecting sociocultural changes) more important than demographics for consumer studies	Lifestyle	

Source: Kim, Y-K., P. Sullivan, C. Trotter, and J. Forney. 2003. Lifestyle shopping center: A retail evolution of the twenty-first century. *Journal of Shopping Center Research* 10(2):61–94.

expressive revolution refers to socio-cultural changes (i.e., changes in values, attitudes, beliefs, and behaviors). The following pages outline the three types of environmental revolutions that are driving lifestyle shopping center evolution in the millennium.

STRUCTURAL REVOLUTION

Changes in U.S. families have resulted in an increasing number of affluent consumers and the growth of single-person households. Female career professionals choose to remain single through their 20s and 30s (Gentry 2000). Baby boomers and people in their 40s and 50s are looking for life experiences through vacations, dining, entertainment, and shopping and are thus receptive to experiential retailing that provides unique experiences. All these factors lay the foundation for consumers' interest in lifestyle-oriented shopping experiences.

INFORMATION TECHNOLOGY REVOLUTION

The Internet as a shopping medium has grown tremendously since its opening to commercial traffic in 1994 (Kotkin, 1998).

It is currently influencing retail stores and shopping centers (Rosen and Howard 2000). With the Internet becoming a necessary tool in consumers' busy lives, shopping centers continue to scout innovative ways of merging bricks and clicks to assist in and promote consumer buying. As a result, shopping centers are experimenting with Internet shopping kiosks as a means of expanding customer browsing (Howell 2000). Certainly, integrating interactive technology into shopping center design will align many consumers' shopping experiences with their lifestyles.

EXPRESSIVE REVOLUTION

Consumers are experiencing increased life expectancies and earlier retirement in addition to fewer years devoted to rearing fewer children, less time spent on the job, and less time spent on household chores. Consequently, the percentage of a person's lifetime that is available to pursuing leisure interests has increased. As a result, the traditional exchange of goods for money has been transformed into an exchange of time for the experience of shopping (Helman and Chernatony 1999). This shopping experience focuses upon the symbolic, hedonic, and aesthetic components of consumption.

The twenty-first century appears to have prompted the evolution of the lifestyle shopping center driven by revolutionary environmental forces—structural, information technology, and expressive. These revolutions force the marketing functions to respond accordingly and in doing so create new strategies to optimize sales potential. Consumer experience should be considered as an integral part when retailers develop these strategies.

Characteristics of Lifestyle Centers

A **lifestyle center** is a smaller, village-style operation (Owens 2002). Characteristics of these retail venues are easy access from outside and inside the center, many elevators, and spacious washrooms. These centers are for people who want to park close to storefronts and prefer to achieve their shopping goals quickly (Martin and Turley 2004). Lifestyle shopping centers appeal to middle-aged consumers with higher annual incomes (median of $85,000) than consumers frequenting regional shopping centers (median of $44,500). Consumers' monthly visits to lifestyle centers average 3.8 compared with 2.5 for general malls (Martin and Turley 2004).

Lifestyle shopping centers appeal to consumers who enjoy a community or town center experience that is created by focusing on the surrounding environment (Fiala 2005). This includes the natural landscape, architecture, and surrounding neighborhood design. This creates a sense of an Old World marketplace, but one with modern-day amenities such as retail and entertainment offerings. Lifestyle shopping centers have grown to resemble mini-cities, with urban streets, parks, and mixed-use office, retail (including restaurants), and residential space (Hazel 2005). This format began at about 300,000 square feet, but may now surpass 800,000 square feet in size. Currently, there are about 140 lifestyle centers in the United States and another 15 to 20 are expected to open annually (Lazarus 2006). Lifestyle centers encourage shopper loyalty with sense of place, a space that is special to them, through two main themes: identification and interaction.

Woodbury Commons in Spring Valley has been New York's premium-themed lifestyle outlet mall for more than 20 years (Kuczynski 2005). It has 220 stores in 841,000 square feet of shopping space. Tenants include high-end stores such as Barneys, Celine, Loro Piana, Etro, Versace, and Gucci. It was designed in a cluster model in which stores face inward using linear pedestrian pathways.

The International Council of Shopping Centers (ICSC) conducted consumer intercept surveys at lifestyle shopping centers. Consumer respondents evaluated shopping center attributes for these lifestyle centers and regional centers (Baker 2002). The results reveal that lifestyle shopping centers, compared with regional centers, were rated more positive on several attributes: overall atmosphere and shopping environment, convenience of parking, convenience of location relative to residence, feelings of safety and security, and convenience of getting from store to store (See Table 10.6).

Current Status of Lifestyle Shopping Centers

ICSC initiated a lifestyle center research program in 2000. Prototypes of lifestyle shopping centers were identified. These were the Arboretum at Great Hills, Austin, Texas; Aspen Grove, Littleton, Colorado; The Avenue at East Cobb, Marietta, Georgia; Deer Park Town Center, Deer Park, Illinois; and Huebner Oaks, San Antonio, Texas. Although ICSC identified many lifestyle shopping centers in the nation, these centers tend to be developed based on socio-demographic data, rather than the true lifestyle variables that describe consumers' activities, interests, and opin-

ions. Shopping center management can use lifestyle variables to nurture a loyal customer, which contributes to maintaining a competitive edge in the marketplace.

In an effort to test shopping motivations relative to lifestyle segment and consumers' selection of shopping center design, Kim, Sullivan, Trotter, and Forney (2003) completed a lifestyle shopping center study. They conducted a series of consumer focus group interviews and identified each participant as one of the VALS segments. Each participant was asked to express the ideal lifestyle shopping center design for his or her lifestyle segment, along with the evaluation of existing shopping centers. Based on the result, each prototype shopping center was designed and evaluated by consumers who self-identified with the VALS lifestyle segments. Results showed several differences among segments regarding their desired mall design or environment. Achievers wanted to see a tenant mix with hedonic characteristics, such as spas, salons, and upscale specialty shops. Strivers wanted a format featuring aesthetically pleasing ambience and convenient facilities, such as store zoning (by merchandise category and age group) and people movers. Believers' ideal center was designed around family visits. They wanted family-friendly parking, adequate numbers of family

TABLE 10.6 HOW LIFESTYLE CENTERS COMPARE WITH REGIONAL CENTERS

LIFESTYLE CENTERS COMPARED WITH REGIONAL CENTERS	BETTER	SAME	WORSE
Overall atmosphere and shopping environment	65%	28%	5%
Convenience of parking	65%	25%	9%
Convenience of location relative to residence	58%	19%	22%
Feelings of safety and security	50%	47%	3%
Convenience of getting from store to store	43%	41%	14%
Quality of merchandise	28%	67%	3%
Variety of merchandise in styles you like	26%	45%	27%
Prices for quality offered	19%	68%	11%

Source: Lifestyle Centers—A Defining Moment. 2002. *ICSC Research Quarterly* 9(4):4.

restrooms, and entertainment tenants (e.g., movie theater) along with babysitting services. Experiencers' ideal design was focused on external appearance or architecture, interior décor, and convenient facility locations. Their desired entertainment facilities included restaurants, bars, nightclubs, a center stage, an ice-skating rink, and TVs in sitting areas. Makers requested a centralized arrangement of major department stores and play areas for children.

Clearly, lifestyle shopping centers can differentiate themselves from their competitors through tenant mix, aesthetics, and design that reflect the targeted lifestyles. Given the dynamic conditions in the retail trade, retailers need to employ continuous market research to best identify the lifestyle needs of consumers in their market areas.

CHAPTER SUMMARY

Changes in demographic and economic patterns and in technological advances have given birth to lifestyle retailing. The increases in personal wealth and household incomes during the last half of the twentieth century and the beginning of the new millennium have offered consumers opportunities to buy the things they want to match their personal lifestyle. Furthermore, advances in technologies and efficiencies have reduced time at work and in the home and as a result, more people are looking for goods and services that will reflect their lifestyle and meet their wants versus their basic needs.

Lifestyle is a consumption pattern that reflects both individual identity and social identity. Individuals' upward movement toward self-esteem and self-actualization in Maslow's hierarchy suggests that individuals' consumption patterns reflect their lifestyles. Also, individuals use goods as an expression of social identity, which reflects the need for belonging in Maslow's hierarchy. The current lifestyle trends include wired or wireless consumers; self-expression; changing family roles (i.e., changing gender roles and a growing trend of women who prefer to stay at home); cocooning; connectedness to the world through the media, travel, and electronic networks; and casual lifestyle.

This chapter describes the concept of lifestyle and how it can be applied to specific lifestyle retailing strategies. It is proposed that product and service sets are consumption constellations that consumers use to define their identities as individuals and as part of a group in a society. Based on this concept, the lifestyle retailer needs to conduct psychographic research to develop strategies first by selecting the target consumer segments for certain merchandise or service sets, next by positioning the firm against its competitors, and finally by developing communication strategies for the effective delivery.

A number of retailers has been successful because they associate their brand with a particular lifestyle and market to a niche consumer group to whom that lifestyle is most appealing. Among the successful retailers are Ralph Lauren, Apple, IKEA, The Gap, Cornell Trading Inc, Starbucks, The Container Store, Harley-Davidson Motor Company, The Panera Bread Company, and Earth Fare. However, lifestyle retailing has been extended to the macro level with shopping centers. The evolution of the lifestyle shopping center has been prompted by structural revolution (e.g., an increasing number of affluent consumers and the growth of single-person households looking for life experiences), information technology revolution (e.g., the Internet as a shopping medium), and expressive revolution (e.g., shopping experience focusing on the symbolic, hedonic, and aesthetic components of consumption). Lifestyle shopping centers can differentiate themselves from their competitors through tenant mix, aesthetics, and design that reflect the lifestyles of the target consumer market. Lifestyle retailing, both at micro and macro levels, will lead to building a long-term relationship with customers by offering them more of what they desire.

Discussion *Questions*

1. Describe the widespread social and economic changes that precipitated lifestyle retailing.
2. Many definitions of lifestyle have been articulated. What is the one common characteristic among these definitions?
3. How does individuality, as expressed through Maslow's hierarchy of needs, support lifestyle retailing?
4. Explain how regional differences influence experiential retail strategies. Identify a product that is more popular in your region. Explain how that product reflects the lifestyle of people in your region.
5. What is a consumption constellation? Describe how it helps a lifestyle retailer gain business.
6. Visit two lifestyle retailers. Identify the lifestyle of their target market. Compare their segmentation, positioning, and communication strategies they implement for their target market.
7. Explain how lifestyle shopping centers are influenced by structural, information technology, and expressive revolutions.
8. How can a shopping center maximize its offerings to be aligned with each VALS group? What would the ideal shopping center for each VALS group include in terms of tenant mix and design?
9. Explain if and how lifestyle retailing increases consumer efficiency.

REFERENCES

AvantGo. 2003. Mobile user lifestyle survey available from My AvantGo. Retrieved August 7, 2006 from http://avantgo.com/news/press/press_archive/2003/release02_24_03.html.

Baker, M. 2002. Lifestyle centers—A defining moment. *ICSC Research Quarterly* 8(4):4.

Belk, Russell W. 1986. Yuppies as arbiters of the emerging consumption style. In Richard J. Lutz, ed. *Advances in Consumer Research*, Vol. 13 (514–519). Provo, Utah: Association for Consumer Research.

———. 1988. Possessions and the extended self. *Journal of Consumer Research* 15(2):139–168.

Bernick, K. 1996. Describing the customer psychographics: Hype or hard-hitting strategy? *Agri Marketing* 34:18–20.

Blackwell, R. D., and W. W. Talarzyk. 1983. Lifestyle retailing: Competitive strategies for the 1980s. *Journal of Retailing* 59(4):7–27.

Boosman, F. 2003. The death of pay-as-you-go Wi-Fi. www.boosman.com/blog/2003/10/the_death_of_payasyougo_wifi.html.

Brengman, Malaika, Maggie Geuens, Bert Weijters, Scott M. Smith, and William R. Swinyard. 2005. Segmenting Internet shoppers based on their Web-usage-related lifestyle: a cross-cultural validation. *Journal of Business Research* 58(1):79–88,

Buss, D. 2004. Can Harley Ride the New Wave? *Brandweek*. October 25, 20–22.

Caplan, J. 2005. Gotta Have It. *Time* 166(6):46–47.

Carson, P. 2006. BREW: Alive and well, headed for battle over direct-to-consumer. *RCR Wireless News* 25(22):12–13.

Cassill, N. L., and M. F. Drake. 1987. Apparel selection criteria related to female consumers' lifestyle. *Clothing and Textiles Research Journal* 6(1):20–28.

Clammer, John. 2003. Globalisation, class, consumption and civil society in southeast Asian cities. *Urban Studies* 40(2):403–419.

Datamonitor. 2004. Apple Computer, Inc. company profile. Retrieved on March 20, 2006 from www. datamonitor.com

Demby, Emanuel. 1994. Psychographics revisited: The birth of a technique. *Marketing Research* 6(2):26–29.

Duff, M. 2004. A culture container through customer service. *Chain Store Age*. October, 25–26.

———. 2000. Activewear evolves under casual fashion influence. *Discount Store News* 39(4):20.

Elteren, M. C. M. van 1996. Gatt and beyond: World trade, the arts, and American popular culture in Europe. *Journal of American Culture* 19(3):59–73.

Fiala, M. L. 2005. Building a better mousetrap. *Chain Store Age* 81(11):150.

Fox, B. 1996. Service, not transactions, drives POS. *Chain Store Age* 101–105.

Gentry, C. 2000. Successful strip strategies rejuvenate retail sales. *Chain Store Age* 75(12):208–212.

Gonzalez, Ana, and Laurentino Bello. 2002. The construct "lifestyle" in market segmentation: The behaviour of tourist consumers. *European Journal of Marketing* 36(1/2):51–85.

Gunter, B., and A. Furnham. 1992. *Consumer profiles: An introduction to psychographics*. London: Routledge.

Hall, J. 2004. Marks and Spencer gambles on lifestore. *The Wall Street Journal*. March 3, B.

Halpern, M. 2006. Mobile: the next platform. *Marketing Magazine* 111(18):6.

Hawkins, Dell, Roger Best, and Kenneth Coney. 2001. *Consumer Behavior: Building Marketing Strategy*, 8th ed. Boston: McGraw-Hill.

Hazel, D. 2005. Wide-open spaces. *Chain Store Age* 81(11):120–122.

Helman, D., and L. Chernatony. 1999. Exploring the development of lifestyle retail brands. *The Service Industries Journal* 19(2):49–68.

Holbrook, M. 1999. Introduction to consumer value. In Morris Holbrook, ed. *Consumer Value: A Framework for Analysis and Research* (1–28). New York: Routledge.

Howell, Debbie. 2000. Clicks and bricks to coexist in mall-based kiosks. *DSN Retailing Today* 39(18):6.

Hsee, C. K., and F. Leclerc. 1998. Will products look more attractive when presented separately or together? *Journal of Consumer Research* 25: 175–186.

Kim, Y-K., P. Sullivan, C. Trotter, and J. Forney. 2003. Lifestyle shopping center: A retail evolution of the twenty-first century. *Journal of Shopping Center Research* 10(2):61–94.

Kohler, M. 2005. Booming iPod biz broadens accessories opportunities. *TWICE: This Week in Consumer Electronics* 20(15):44.

Kotkin, J. 1998. The mother of all malls. *Forbes*. April 6, 60–65.

Kuczynski, A. 2005. Mark it down, and they will come. *The New York Times*. May 26, G1.

Lach, J. 2000. The niche's the thing. *American Demographics* 22(2):22.

Lazarus, E. 2006. Main Street malls. *Marketing Magazine* 111(13):11–12.

Leiss, W., S. Kline, and S. Jhally. 1986. *Social communication in advertising*. Toronto: Methuen.

Levy, M., and B. Weitz. 1998. *Retailing management,* 3rd ed. Boston, MA: McGraw-Hill.

The Lifestyle Market Analyst. 2004. SRDS, Des Plaines, Illinois.

Martin, C. A., and L. W. Turley. 2004. Management malls and consumption motivation: An exploratory examination of older Generation Y consumers, *International Journal of Retail and Distribution* 32(10):464–475.

Maslow, A. H. 1970. *Motivation and personality*, 2nd ed. New York: Harper and Row.

McCracken, Grant. 1991. Culture and consumption: A theoretical account of the structure and movement of the cultural meaning of consumer goods. Harold H. Kassarjian and Thomas S. Robbinson, eds., *Perspectives in Consumer Behavior* 581–99. Glenview, IL: Scott, Foresman.

Mediamark Research. What is LifeMatrix? Retrieved August 7, 2006 from www.mediamark.com/memri/quicksheets/LifeMatrix_Quick_Sheet.pdf#search='LifeMatrix'

Molitor, Graham T. 2000. Here Comes 2015. *Vital Speeches of the Day* 66(20):620–627.

Moore, Ann. 2003. NY export with a twist; Carvel tests local ice cream tastes. *Crain's Chicago Business*. August 11. Retrieved August 7, 2006 from http://goliath.ecnext.com/comsite5/bin/pdinventory.pl?pdlanding=1&referid=2750&item_id=0 199–3042208

Mowen, John. 1995. *Consumer Behavior*, 4th ed. Englewood Cliffs, N.J: Prentice-Hall.

Muñoz, Lisa. 2001. The suit is back—or is it? *Fortune* 143(14):202.

O'Loughlin, S. 2006. The Container Store thinks out of the, um, container. *Brandweek*. January 9, 16.

Owens, A. M. 2002. The mall is being turned inside out. *National Post*. October 21, A6.

Pande, B. 2004. Harley's fortunes revived by focus on existing clients. *Media Asia*. January 30, 20.

Plummer, Joseph. 1972. Life style patterns: A new construct for mass communications research. *Journal of Broadcasting* 16(Fall/Winter):79–89.

Rabianski, J. 2001. Shopping center branding: Is it worth the effort? *Retail Estate Review* 29–39.

Rayport, J. and B. Jaworski. 2004. Best face forward. *Harvard Business Review* 82(12):47–58.

Retail Forward. 2003. Twenty Trends for 2010: Retailing in an age of uncertainty. Retrieved July 14, 2006 from www.retailforward.com/retailintel/specialreports/soc03doctr.pdf

Rosen, K., and A. Howard. 2000. E-retail: Gold rush or fool's gold? *California Management Review* 42(3):71–100.

Rosenwein, Rifka. 2002. The baby sabbatical. *American Demographics* 24(2):36–39.

Serwer, A. 2004. The iPod people have invaded Apple's stores. *Fortune*. December 13, 12.

Sobel, M. E. 1981. *Lifestyle and social structure*. New York: Academic Press.

Solomon, M. 2002. *Consumer behavior*, 5th ed. Upper Saddle River, NJ: Prentice Hall.

Spatial Insights. MOSAIC Lifestyle Segmentation. Retrieved August 7, 2006 from www.spatialinsights.com/catalog/product.aspx?product=80.

SRI Consulting Business Intelligence. VALS. Retrieved August 7, 2006 from www.sric-bi.com/VALS/

Stapes, E. 2000. Psychographic target marketing: Buying actions speak louder than words. *Advisor Today* 95(11):86–96.

Swenson, C. 1989. How to sell to a segmented market. *Journal of Business Strategy*. January–February, 9, 18.

Swinyard, William R. and Scott Smith. 2003. Why people (don't) shop online: A lifestyle study of the Internet consumer. *Psychology & Marketing* 20(7):567–597.

Taylor, A. 1995. Porsche slices up its buyers. *Fortune* 131,24.

Tischler, L. 2003. How Pottery Barn wins with style. *Fast Company*. June, 106–113.

Training & Development. 2000. Casual Dress. 54(11):38.

Wells, William D. 1968. Segmentation by attitude types. In Robert L. King, ed. *Marketing and the New Science of Planning*. Chicago: American Marketing Association 124–6.

———. 1975. Psychographics: A critical review. *Journal of Marketing Research* 12(2):196–213.

———. 1974. Life style and psychographics: Definitions, uses, and problems. In W. D. Wells, ed. *Life Style and Psychographics*. Chicago: American Marketing Association 315–63.

Wells, William D., and Douglas J. Tigert. 1971. Activities, interests, and opinions. *Journal of Advertising Research* 11(8):27–35.

Yankelovich. 2006. Yankelovich MONITO® Perspective Series. Retrieved August 7, 2006 from www.yankelovich.com/products/monitor.aspx

Zablocki, Benjamin, and Moss R. Kanter. 1976. The differentiation of lifestyles. *Annual Review of Sociology* 2:269–297.

VALUE RETAILING

CHAPTER 11

Dollar Channel Too Rich for Mass Retailers

Even when [they are] successful, dollar sections pose little threat to the top dollar chains, according to experts. Instead, Dollar General, Family Dollar, Dollar Tree, and 99 Cents Only continue to flourish as destination stores for unbelievable bargains as opposed to the limited assortments and impulse-buy nature of dollar-fare goods sold in other retail channels. "A dollar aisle is going to generate more impulse purchasing, but not make the supermarket a destination like a dollar store is. People still go to dollar stores because they like that treasure-hunt atmosphere," said Nick McCoy, a senior consultant with Retail Forward.

For supermarkets especially, the strategy may help fend off trip losses to dollar chains and add impulse-purchase benefits. Todd Hale, senior vice president of consumer insights at ACNielsen, said the proliferation of dollar sections capitalizes on growing demand for values. "Value retailers are really winning in the marketplace today and consumers are expecting savings," Hale said. For retailers that have added dollar aisles or departments, Hale added, this "demonstrates to their shoppers that they are listening to them and responding." Impact to the major chains appears to be minimal at best from these new competitive responses, again due to the significantly larger assortments at the specialty chains.

Numerous other retailers have made dollar sections a permanent merchandising strategy, including Target, ShopKo, and the Army and Air Force Exchange Service. Target's 1 Spot section was tested in 2004 and was subsequently rolled out chainwide. The impulse section near store entrances offers a small assortment of rotating gift items for $1. "One spot continues to get a strong response, with a sharp lift in sales seen immediately following a reset," noted analyst Patrick McKeever of SunTrust Robinson Humphrey in a report on Target earlier this year.

At ShopKo, dollar aisles were tested back in 2003. All regular ShopKo and ShopKo Express stores now carry this section of about 24 linear feet of branded and private-label goods priced at $1. Items rotate on a regular basis to keep the assortment fresh. "We have seen interest in the dollar merchandise in our store drop off some in the past six months or so, but we find the concept still makes sense to us in its current space allocation," said John Vigeland, a ShopKo spokesperson. "Success for us in the category is driven by newness, value, and brand names. Our customers tell us they check the dollar aisle on a regular basis to see what is new or what has been added."

A similar test took place at stores operated by the Army and Air Force Exchange Service last year. The initiative resulted in a dollar department installed in 120 main stores ranging from 100 square feet to 150 square feet. Goods included housewares, hardware, and stationery. "Customer response to this program has been positive," said Jennifer Johnsen, a public affairs specialist with AAFES. "Refreshing the assortment every 60 to 90 days is paramount to the success of this program. Customers like shopping at the section to see what new bargains await."

Source: Howell, D. 2005. Dollar channel too rich for mass retailers. *DSN Retailing Today* 44(22):11–15.

INTRODUCTION

Sometimes a consumer's experience is the thrill of the hunt. As more consumers demand low prices, some retailers are attracting customers not only with the promise of low prices, but also with the mystery of what items will be in the store at any given time. Excitement can be obtained from various types of value retailers, including close-out stores, whether they primarily target low- or middle-income consumers such as Big Lots or target high-income consumers such as Tuesday Morning.

Big Lots, headquartered in Columbus, Ohio, is one of the largest broadline close-out retailers in the United States. Big Lots operates more than 1,400 stores in the United States and Canada (www.biglots.com). The company sells a broad range of branded products that were overproduced or discounted by manufacturers at prices that are 20 percent to 40 percent below prices of other discounters (Datamonitor 2005). While the store carries a range of never-out items ranging from frozen foods to household appliances, many consumers like to go to Big Lots on a kind of scavenger hunt to see what new and unexpected items will be in the store that day. In this way, Big Lots creates an enjoyable experience for value-oriented shoppers.

Tuesday Morning, based in Dallas, Texas, is a close-out retail chain of more than 700 stores across the United States, specializing in selling deeply discounted, upscale home accessories and gifts. Since inception in 1974, it has implemented concepts and strategies to become a successful and nationally recognized company. Founded on a unique philosophy, "sell first-quality, famous designer, and name-brand merchandise at extraordinarily discounted prices on an event basis," Tuesday Morning appeals to high-income consumers. The stores receive new merchandise shipments that are priced 50 to 80 percent off regular retail prices, 10 times a year (www.tuesdaymorning.com).

VALUE-CONSCIOUS CONSUMERS AND VALUE RETAILERS

The retailing landscape has changed, with the fundamental and ongoing shift of consumer spending toward value retailers. Recession and economic unrest made consumers particularly cautious about how and where they spend their money. Though value-conscious shoppers became mainstream as a result of the recession in the late 1980s and early 1990s, they currently want more value and quality for the price than the consumers of the past (Poloian 2003). Even those consumers who focused on quality now willingly shop in value formats for a significant share of their weekly needs (Frank, Mihas, Narasimhan, and Rauch 2003).

Consumers are on a constant search for low prices and are actively seeking out new formats to get a better price (*Stores Magazine* 2006). To attract this growing population of value-conscious shoppers, retailers strategize ways to offer well-made products at decreased prices. Throughout the last decade, **value retailers** grew faster than any other major retail format, nearly doubling their share of U.S. retail sales

(Back, Haveron, Narasimhan, Rauch, and Sneader 2005). Value retailers continue to flourish, with some manufacturers producing merchandise specifically for these outlets (Frank et al. 2003). This trend toward value retailing is likely to continue into the foreseeable future (*Stores Magazine* 2006).

In addition, value stores are raising their standards to match or outclass their traditional competitors—even on fresh foods. In fact, there has been rapid improvement in customer perception of the quality of fresh categories at value retailers. For example, grocers have historically distinguished themselves by fresh foods. However, consumers now view the value players as having caught up on highest quality fresh foods and good store brands. As a result, value retailers have out-executed their competition and moved beyond price as the sole point of differentiation, offering comparable assortment, convenience, and in-store experience, which make the task of shopping faster and easier (Frank et al. 2003).

While traditional retailers are often susceptible to inflation and unemployment and are pummeled by a poor economy, such is not the case in the value retailing sector. Throughout the recent recession, value retailers reported healthy gains as opposed to actual declines in many other segments of the retailing industry (Back et al. 2005).

Although the concept of value retailing is most popular in the discount store industry, it also is copied by upscale retailers. Recently, consumers have witnessed the unprecedented comingling of what some view as fashion's sacred and profane—luxury and deep discount. From Karl Lagerfeld's signature line at H & M, to Stella McCartney's partnership with Adidas, to Liz Lang's discount maternity wear, the retail world has witnessed the marketing revolution of making luxury items affordable for the masses (Koval 2005).

Robin Koval, president of The Kaplan Thaler Group, discovered that this *mass-clusivity* is changing the rules of luxury marketing. She stated:

> Americans of all stripes who once dreamed of designer wares can now grasp them at bargain basements without emptying their wallets. This marriage of high design and everyday products, what I call the "massclusivity of affordable luxury," reflects a drastic rewriting of the rules of marketing. By democratizing the high life, we are redefining the very idea of luxury and how to sell it. Years ago, luxury products were designed with only the highbrow, design-savvy consumer in mind. It was a product's dreaming "If only I could have that" quality that made it so desirable. But by shooting only for the top, retailers were missing the growing middle class, which earns more disposable income each year and turns out to have a keen appetite for luxury goods (Koval 2005, 1).

As a new group of consumers crave luxury and are willing to pay a little extra for it, luxury is no longer defined as simply an expensive product. Luxury products make consumers feel better and pampered. Owning a designer T-shirt from a value retailer is not about its price point; rather, it is about the emotional attachment and confidence consumers feel (Koval 2005).

In fact, brands that were once available exclusively to the wealthiest have created more affordable product extensions, giving a far broader range of consumers a taste of the good life. Tiffany promotes $50 sterling silver key chains, along with its $100,000 diamond engagement rings. Upscale kitchen appliance company Viking Range Corporation, based in Greenwood, Mississippi, is known for its

Viking range product that costs around $8,000. The company has expanded its product line to include a number of kitchen appliances at more affordable prices, to attract the almost-rich consumers—those who aspire to be rich and desire to live the luxury lifestyle (Gardyn 2002).

Michael J. Silverstein, head of the worldwide consumer and retail group at the Boston Consulting Group in Chicago, labeled the more affordable luxuries as new luxury products. According to Silverstein, "New luxury goods range in price from a $6 Tuscan chicken sandwich at Panera to a $26,000 Mercedes CLK. . . . These new luxury products enable less affluent consumers to trade up to higher levels of quality, taste, and aspiration. These are the luxuries that continue to sell even when the economy is shaky, because they often meet very powerful emotional needs" (Gardyn 2002, 32). The trend that reflects increasing availability of luxury products and services at lower price points and consumers' increasing ability to purchase those products is called the *democratization of luxury* (Garadyn 2002, 31).

THE RISE OF VALUE RETAILING

Types of value retailers include discount department stores, factory outlets, category killers, off-price discounters, warehouse clubs, dollar stores, and value megamalls. The inception and rise of each of these value retailers has been influenced by socioeconomic situations and consumer preferences in the retail market.

Discount Department Stores

Discount department stores are characterized by minimal décor, utilitarian materials, and floor plans crowded with merchandise. Wal-Mart, Kmart, and Target are examples. They are usually located in freestanding buildings or shopping cen-

ters on the outskirts of cities. These large discount stores replaced variety stores, which in turn replaced the Main Street five-and-dime stores in the early 1960s. To buy a wide range of goods at low prices in one location, customers were increasingly willing to get into cars and drive to malls or other non–Main Street locations (*Harvard Business Review* 1993).

Strengths of discount department stores include low price, convenient location, and high consumer demand. Wal-Mart and Target, in particular, have grown successfully due to a strong management and employee development program, an advanced logistics system, and benefits through economies of scale. Although traditional grocery retailers continue to have a strong foothold in core food categories, discount department stores have relentlessly gained share in several grocery categories. Wal-Mart, for example, created Old Roy, now the largest dry dog food brand in the world by volume (Frank et al. 2003).

Factory Outlets

Factory outlets started as an occasional secondary sales channel through which manufacturers could off-load excess, irregular, and dated merchandise. With increased efforts to produce greater manufacturing efficiency and profitability, the need for this type of nontraditional retail outlet grew (Weiss and Lummis 1994). The type of merchandise offered through factory outlets has changed over time and now includes first-quality brand name and designer label goods. Moreover, economic shifts that created overproduction of goods during strong economic times, and traditional retailers reducing, delaying, and canceling orders in recessionary periods have added to the growth of factory outlets (Weiss and Lummis 1994). By combining the status symbol of a designer label with the basic draw of a discount price, factory outlets are well-positioned as shopping destinations throughout the United States (Poloian 2003).

Outlet centers, although they are typically located away from the main streets, are viable during both weak and strong economic times. In a difficult economy, consumers are willing to travel long distances for price savings, while in prosperous economic times, consumers want to enjoy the treasure hunt experience by finding brand-name merchandise at reduced prices.

Category Killers

Category killers are huge, single-focus megastores that specialize in one merchandise category, such as home furnishings, office supplies, consumer electronics, toys, and pet supplies (O'Connor 1999). They sell limited and deep assortments of products with such low prices that competitors cannot compete (Dunne and Lusch 2005). This broad assortment enables customers to comparison shop without having to leave the store. By offering a full selection of nothing but home improvement products, for example, Home Depot is dominating its field. Category killers can capture the consumer's business most effectively by offering products and services that are complementary to the core category and offer solutions to the customer's problem (Berry 1996). For example, PetSmart offers merchandise for pets, but it also offers obedience classes, pet-grooming services, veterinary services, pet-adoption services, and lost-and-found bulletin boards that address the overall needs of pet owners.

Off-price Discounters

Off-price discounters offer brand-name merchandise at lower prices than department or specialty stores. The emergence and proliferation of various kinds of off-price discounters such as T.J. Maxx, Marshalls, and Loehmann's were sparked by the growing stocks of excess inventory in department stores that carried more designer brands and imported goods, largely at the expense of domestic manufacturers' traditional brands during the 1970s. Off-price retailing flourished during the 1980s, when back-to-back recessions eroded consumer confidence and spending. Major department store retailers offset declining sales by cutting back on orders and closing stores (Weiss and Lummis 1994). These economic changes generated an increased consumer demand for off-price retailing. As a result, off-price retailers became important outlets for suppliers who had excess seasonal goods (Weiss and Lummis 1994). The strategy of off-price discounting is "high volume gained through lower markup and faster inventory turnover" (Poloian 2003, 123). These off-price discounters attract many fashion-conscious consumers. For instance, T.J. Maxx customers generally fit the profile of the department store shopper—a savvy consumer who is fashion- and value-conscious (See Figure 11.1).

These off-price discounters have moved into even more value-oriented retailing and have experienced substantial growth from these branches. TJX Cos.

11.1 T.J. Maxx customers are savvy consumers who are fashion- and value-conscious.

(T.J. Maxx/Marshalls) has developed an urban-oriented family apparel concept, A.J. Wright, which offers less costly brands at prices positioned below those of T.J. Maxx/Marshalls. Another powerful off-price retailer, Ross Stores, initiated a new start-up concept, dd's DISCOUNTS, which carries family apparel, footwear, and home fashions that are priced below the Ross Dress for Less presentation, targeting lower-income households (Davidowitz 2004).

Warehouse Clubs

Warehouse clubs are membership club stores that distribute packaged and bulk foods and general merchandise in a no-frills environment and include Sam's Club and Costco. They maintain high volumes, low gross margins, limited assortments, and offer products in bulk quantities to warehouse members only. They have little ambience and offer limited customer service yet sell quality, brand-name merchandise at extremely discounted prices. Minimum staffing levels, low overhead, negligible use of credit cards, minimal advertising, and the small use of credit cards keep prices low. Yet, a sense of shopping excitement is created through the constant turnover of merchandise (Gelbtuch 1990).

Dollar Stores

Dollar stores are another value store type that is gaining popularity in the United States. Dollar stores are characterized by consumable basic products, convenient locations, smaller store formats, and low prices. The dollar store format includes dollar stores, single-price retailers, and close-out chains and is defined as an extreme-value retailer. Small-store formats provide quick and easy access in neighborhoods, which is a key differentiation strategy that enables them to survive in close proximity to big-box discounters such as Wal-Mart. With double-digit sales and earnings growth rates among the top chains and increasing shopper penetration, this new breed of discounter is making waves in the industry. Among the top players are Dollar General, Family Dollar, Big Lots, Dollar Tree, and Fred's. These dollar stores are succeeding because of their operational efficiencies such as narrow and focused merchandising, efficient distribution systems, and effective inventory control (Lisanti 1999). Furthermore, dollar stores have enhanced their images through improvement in product quality by carrying more national brands, in store design by adding architectural elements, and in more appealing merchandising through displays and more spacious aisles (*DSN Retailing Today* 2004).

Consumers, whether affluent or poor, look for deals. Furthermore, dollar stores are typically less susceptible to economic recessions because food and consumables require frequent repeat purchases (Hudson 2005). Dollar stores still function primarily to provide a shopping solution for less affluent consumer groups who are primarily rural, aged over 55, less-educated, and female (*DSN Retailing Today* 2004). However, these stores are gaining shoppers from middle- and upper-income consumer segments. According to the consulting firm Retail Forward, the profile of monthly dollar store shoppers indicates that 29 percent has an income of $50,000 or more (Rivkin 2005). Furthermore, as the largest chains such as Dollar General and Family Dollar expand into more urban locations, their exposure to a broader, higher-income demographic group increases.

Value Megamalls

Value megamalls also are called super off-price centers or super regional specialty malls. They started with the concept that a variety of value retail types may not only

coexist in one center but also thrive there by offering a full-spectrum value draw. They carry a large variety of value-oriented retailers, including off-price retailers, factory outlet stores, department close-out outlets, and large food and entertainment areas. They usually span more than 1.5 million square feet of space, are generally on one level, and in an enclosed mall setting (ICSC 2004). The Mills Corporation, a retail real estate developer, has created a distinctive brand. Starting with the opening of Potomac Mills in Prince William, Virginia, in 1985, the company has built a number of mills, including Colorado Mills, Lakewood, Colorado; Grapevine Mills, Grapevine, Texas; Opry Mills, Nashville, Tennessee; and Katy Mills, Houston, Texas (Ritter 2003) (See Figures 11.2a and b). Mills's existing projects have become well-known tourist attractions and generate millions of dollars in revenues for surrounding cities. They typically draw shoppers from a radius like that of a factory outlet (25 to 75 miles) (Ritter 2003).

TRENDS IMPACTING THE GROWTH OF VALUE RETAILING

The changes that have taken place in the consumer market explain how and why consumers seek value items. Numerous demographic trends, consumer patterns, and retail trends have facilitated the growth of value retailing.

Demographic Trends

Major demographic trends that impact value retailing include slow growth in disposable personal income, income inequality, and the graying of the United States.

SLOW GROWTH IN DISPOSABLE PERSONAL INCOME

Throughout the past few decades, growth in per capita disposable personal income has slowed. The median household income in the United States has declined in the new millennium, while poverty rates rose in four consecutive years from 2000 to 2004 (www.census.gov). Between 1999 and

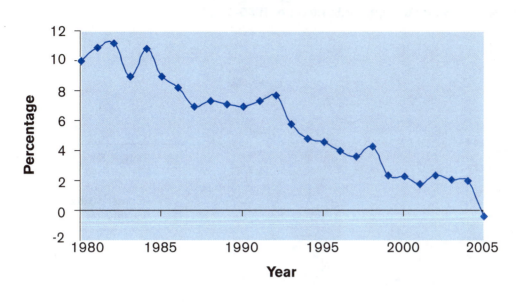

Personal Savings as a Percentage of Disposable Personal Income

2003, median household income dropped slightly from $44,922 to $43,318 (Rivkin 2005). Figure 11.3 depicts personal savings as a percentage of disposable personal income. From the figure, we see that the U.S. personal savings rate dropped to 0 percent in June 2005. Furthermore, consumer debt has grown about twice as fast as personal income throughout the past five years (Pender 2005).

At the same time, consumer purchasing power has been declining. According to a report by Deloitte Research released in 2006, middle- and lower-income consumers experienced declining purchasing power over the previous 24 months. Since early 2004, real wages for nonsupervisory workers have been slipping. This is due, in part, to globalization of the labor force. Some of the drop in purchasing power also can be attributed to the sharp rises in energy prices (Steidtmann 2006). C. Steidtmann (2006) reported, "The share of consumer income going to energy is still higher than at any time in the past 20 years" (4). In addition, many workers are not getting annual raises because companies are trying to save money for the bottom line. As a result, consumer incomes are not keeping up with increasing fuel and health care prices. This makes the sales environment more difficult for retailers, which forces retailers to offer value to their customers.

INCOME INEQUALITY

In the United States, there is currently a fundamental economic movement whereby the rich are getting richer and the poor are getting poorer, as the income gap widens and the middle class—arguably the economic and social backbone of this country—shrinks. From 1979 to 2000, the richest 1 percent of people in the United States tripled with an income rise of $576,000, while the average income of the people in the middle-income scale rose by $5,500 and the poorest fifth of households rose by just $1,100 (*Multinational Monitor* 2003). Figure 11.4 shows trends in the share of aggregate family income for the richest 5 percent of households and the poorest 40 percent. Since 1980, the richest

11.3 The U.S. personal savings average dropped to 0 percent in 2005.

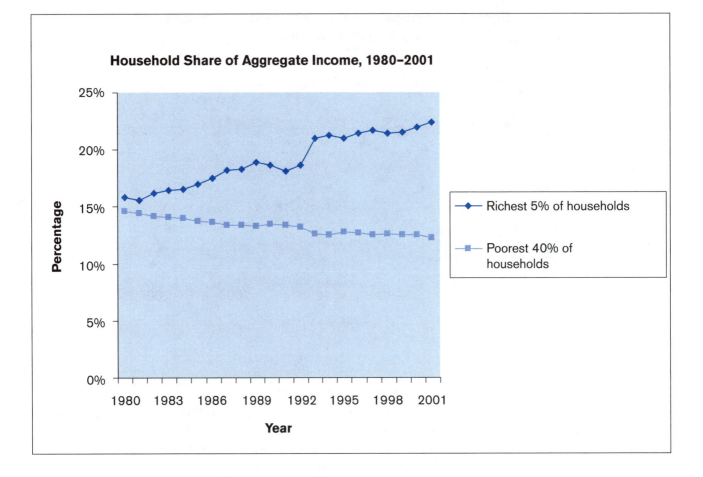

Household Share of Aggregate Income, 1980–2001

- ◆ Richest 5% of households
- ▪ Poorest 40% of households

11.4 The income gap between the rich and the poor widens.

households have seen their share of household income steadily increase (Klass 2002).

This phenomenon of the widening income gap can be explained by several factors. First of all, there was a shift in the U.S. employment structure due to a severe recession in the early 1980s and increased competition from foreign producers. This economic environment led to a massive shift from relatively high-wage, unionized factory jobs to low-wage, nonunion service jobs. A second reason for the widening income gaps is the changes in the tax system in the 1980s and the extremely large tax cuts in 2001 and 2003 (*Multinational Monitor* 2003). Finally, there has been continued influx of immigration. The growing immigrant population in the United States is pushing down the household income rate. For example, the Hispanic population is growing three times faster than the over-

all population, while their overall household income is 35 percent lower (Rivkin 2005). California, which receives the most immigrants, shows the greatest income inequality with an increase of about 710,000 low-income households between 1990 and 2000. Other large increases in poor households are taking place in California, Florida, Texas, and New York. In fact, states with high levels of immigration are experiencing a decline in the middle class at an accelerated rate, while states with lower levels of immigration are less affected (*PR Newswire* 2004).

THE GRAYING OF THE UNITED STATES

As with most countries of the Western world, the United States has an aging population. From 1990 to 2000, the age group 30 to 34 years decreased 6.2 percent and 25 to 29 years decreased 9.1 percent. In con-

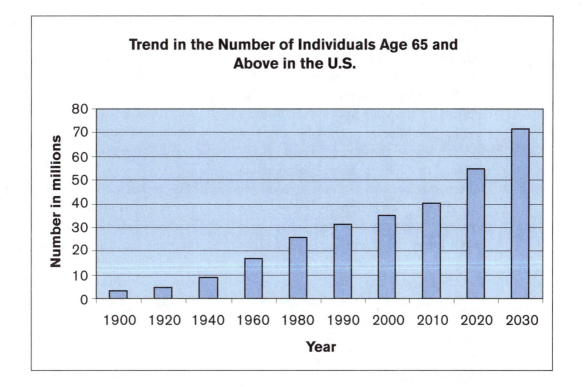

Trend in the Number of Individuals Age 65 and Above in the U.S.

11.5 The older population continues to grow.

trast, in the same period, the age group 50 to 54 years and 55 to 59 years increased 54.9 percent and 27.9 percent, respectively (www.census.gov). The number of people older than 50 make up 39 percent of the U.S. adult population (Johnson 2005). The older population—persons 65 years or older—represent 12.4 percent of the U.S. population, about one in every eight Americans. By 2030, there will be more than twice their number in 2000 (U.S. Department of Health and Human Services Administration on Aging 2006). Figure 11.5 illustrates the growing trend in the number of individuals who are 65 or older from 1900 to 2030.

The aging of baby boomers also affects consumer spending. The 50 and older population is changing its spending priorities. Aging baby boomers are likely to seek out goods and services that provide quality, enhance health and personal growth, and deliver experiences, such as travel, restaurants, cultural events, and sporting events (Seninger 2000). Although the annual household spending on goods and services

by baby boomers is about 10 percent lower than households where the head of household is under age 50, more of the money is spent on fewer people since boomers' kids have moved out (Johnson 2005). In 2000, Seninger reported that the over-50 consumer segment accounted for more than 50 percent of discretionary spending power in the United States.

Consumer Patterns

Consumer patterns that impact value retailing are the shift in the meaning of value, one-stop shopping, comparison shopping, and brand consciousness.

SHIFT IN THE MEANING OF VALUE

There has been a shift in the meaning of the term *value*. The term value used to convey images of bargain hunting, purchases of second merchandise, and even poor or cheap quality. For many, looking for the best value for the dollar was reserved for those who really had to watch their dollars (Mason 1992). However, this perception is changing as the shift to value for consumers cuts across all ages, nearly all income groups and almost all consumer segments (Koch 2005).

Due in part to the influence of value retailing, today's consumers are less resistant toward shopping in value retail stores and bargain hunting has become a way of life for many consumers (Frank et al. 2003). The shift to value phenomenon reflects that consumers desire to look for a good deal. Todd Hale of ACNielsen went so far as to say, "Consumers have found that if you're not saving money these days, something is wrong with you" (*DSN Retailing Today* 2003, 23).

As a matter of a fact, since the 1990s, value shopping increasingly is associated with intelligence and has become a new status symbol (Weiss and Lummis 1994). In addition, the availability of value stores in suburban, urban, and middle-income areas has made them more accessible to consumers who may not have patronized them in the past. Indeed, there is less resistance among consumers toward shopping at discount stores.

ONE-STOP SHOPPING

With the rise in dual-income families, working women, and individuals working two jobs, today's consumers have less time to shop than ever before. As a result, they tend to shop less often and to be more destination-oriented. By choosing stores they know offer the lowest prices, they are able to achieve multiple shopping needs by saving both time and money. Although one-stop shopping was once a trend, it is now commonplace among U.S. shoppers, who tend to be driven by time and monetary pressures and constraints (Weiss and Lummis 1994).

Value retailers are in a unique position to capitalize on this trend since they are able to offer quality goods at low prices on an ongoing basis, thus developing trusting relationships with shoppers who value an efficient, no-frills approach to retailing. Each of these factors—convenience, low prices, and efficiency—offers benefits to consumers who desire one-stop shopping. Elliston (2004) described some of the costs and benefits of one-stop shopping in his series on boomer moms:

Mass merchandisers enjoy a love-hate relationship with boomer moms. The stores are mentioned as favorite shopping locations, but are seen more as inevitable and necessary (not quite evil) than welcome. Consumers like the value and one-stop convenience when they want it, but don't like the large store format when they want to shop for limited purchases. They like mass merchandisers more (and dislike them less) if they are clean and well-lit with wide aisles, and especially love attentive service. Consumers really like "big shopping" (as opposed to big stores), such as department stores and malls, as well as shopping centers that offer the one-stop-shop in a more upscale environment where they shop for things they like to buy—clothing, cosmetics, and shoes—as opposed to "daily chore" shop. Big stores (Target) that come closer to the ambience of those environments— bright, clean, comfortable—are more favored than stores that don't—dark, dirty, rough (convenience stores) (42).

COMPARISON SHOPPING

Comparison shopping involves evaluating the similarities and differences of products to achieve the best value for one's dollar. Comparison shopping can include everything from clothes to hamburgers and involves the evaluations of bottom line figures (Veretto 2002). Consumers do comparison shopping in category killers, in shopping centers, and online. Category killers such as Home Depot and Best Buy offer an extensive amount of merchandise in similar product categories and thus enable consumers to compare prices, features, and styles of different brands. Shopping centers house a number of tenants so shoppers can easily shop at multiple stores on a single trip. Internet shopping guides are a way to enhance comparison shopping online. Leslie Walker, columnist at the *Washington Post*, described Internet shopping guides as hot commodities for companies. Although consumers are not using Internet shopping guides currently to their full potential, it is projected that they will. Companies are paying top dollar for these shopping guide Web locations. For example, E.Z. Scripps Company is buying Shopzilla for $525 million and Lowermybills.com was recently purchased for $330 million. Kamran Pourzanjani, chief executive of Pricegrabbers.com, believes that comparison shopping will continue to grow and become even more popular with consumers by empowering them to make the best choice available (Walker 2005).

BRAND-CONSCIOUSNESS

Traditionally, consumers with high levels of disposable income were more likely to buy brand-name products at full price. It seems that this brand-consciousness continues to drive consumers toward value retailers, which offer famous labels at prices well below those of traditional department stores and specialty stores. Another way to quench consumer desire for brand-name goods is through private labels. Private labels can strengthen consumers' perceptions of value by offering them a premium product that is discounted over national brands (Rivkin 2005). This is frequently seen in the premium private-label food area. Consumers can choose a product that is of higher quality than a generic product, but it is offered at a lower price than a national brand. Value retailers such as Kohl's and Target have increased access to popular brands at value prices and have upgraded the quality of their private label offerings. The Great Atlantic and Pacific Tea Company took one step up by introducing a line of gourmet food products under the label of Master Choice. These products, packaged in an attractive and tantalizing manner, brought outstanding quality to the consumer. Dollar General also has put a renewed emphasis on its private label program, which includes DG Guarantee and Clover Valley brands (Rivkin 2005).

Retail Trends

The growth of value retailing has generated several changes in the retail market. The major changes include growing number of power retailers, increasing retail efficiency, and more competition from traditional retailers.

POWER RETAILERS

Despite more competition and less growth within the retail industry, a number of value retail companies have expanded their customer and sales bases, adopting new technologies and marketing strategies designed to increase their profitability. Often referred to as **power retailers**, these value retailers have expanded into a number of categories, using sophisticated inventory management, merchandise selection, and competitive pricing. This trend is making it more difficult for smaller retailers to compete, due to their lack of efficiency in maximizing profitability and sales volume. The term power retailing was first popularized in citing the competitive advantage of certain large chains where there was a wide and plentiful selection of merchandise (Weiss and Lummis 1994). Value retailers such as Wal-Mart and Dollar General have implemented this strategy successfully.

Although store characteristics and merchandising strategies vary greatly, these successful value retailers share a number of common elements. These elements include high sales per square foot, high inventory turnover, healthy profit margins, and the ability to attract a large customer base with lower prices, good merchandise selection and presentation, and greater convenience (Weiss and Lummis 1994). They quickly identify customer needs, pay constant attention to the marketplace, place orders early and in large quantities, emphasize powerful assortments to dominate competitors, and use modern computer and inventory-control systems. These factors help reduce the inventory and distribution costs, thereby passing on the benefits to the customer (Evans and Berman 2002).

INCREASING RETAIL EFFICIENCY

As retailing becomes more competitive and pricing pressures intensify, retailers are implementing cost-reduction programs and sophisticated inventory management systems designed to cut expenses and provide assortments that consumers prefer. To keep their costs low, value retailers are implementing high-tech retail systems to increase the efficiency of their supply chains, forming closer relationships with supply chain partners, and leveraging the Internet to manage purchases, shipments, and to sell their products. Although most value retailers operate with tight margins, these margins are more than offset by highly efficient ordering and stock control systems, fast merchandise turnover, and in many cases, huge sales volumes. Stores are focusing on core strengths, utilizing third parties to handle noncore func-

tions. Inventory deployment and inventory reduction strategies are being automated and implemented to reduce costs. More retailers, both big and small, are incorporating complex distribution systems into their supply chains (About.com 2004).

One example of the sophistication of the retail supply chain is how Pepsi deals with supplying retailers to reduce out-of-stocks. They instituted a program where warehouse pickers wear bar code scanners on their wrists and headphones. This improves the accuracy of pallet shipments (Terhune 2006). T. P. Stank, P. J. Daugherty, and C. W. Autry (1999) reported that the Collaborative Planning, Forecasting and Replenishment (CPFR) pilot programs benefited retailers with improved in-stock position, significant reductions in inventory levels, increased accuracy of forecasts, increased sales, improved overall channel efficiency through better asset utilization, and reduced risk through co-anticipated benefits. For many value retailers, profit margins are tight, so they seek ways to increase efficiencies in the supply chain. Innovations in supply chain management have added to retailer profitability.

MORE COMPETITION FROM TRADITIONAL RETAILERS

Because value retailers are carrying more popular brands at lower prices and upgrading the quality of their private label offerings, traditional department stores and specialty stores are responding aggressively to compete with these value retailers. Since it is difficult for these traditional retailers to compete with value retailers on a price basis, they are increasingly emphasizing their broader selections, newer styles, more convenient locations, more attractive shopping environments, and superior customer service. Meanwhile, many consumers who expect good quality at low prices from value retailers no longer accept the traditional grocers' premium prices (Frank et al. 2003).

Faced with competition from the fast-growing dollar stores, a number of drug chains, grocery stores, and mass merchandisers have experimented with dollar sections within their stores. Wal-Mart has tested a dollar-store set in some stores called Hey Buck, and Kroger is testing dollar departments in their stores. Food retailer Save-A-Lot completed its acquisition of dollar chain Deal$, and has incorporated dollar-store concept in all of its Save-A-Lot food stores (*DSN Retailing Today* 2003). Target introduced dollar sections at the fronts of their stores, striving to excite the customer with trinkets and gadgets, as well as seasonal items. While retailers introducing dollar sections are not likely to sway dollar-store consumers away from traditional dollar outlets, the sections will increase a sense of excitement among existing consumers (Rivkin 2005).

The steady growth of Wal-Mart Supercenters continues to force traditional supermarket chains to adapt their strategies through expansion of general merchandise and price reductions. Kroger Plus and BI-LO BONUSCARD provide their customers with an opportunity to save money on weekly discounted items. Challenged by the increasing speed with which value retailers reflect the latest fashion trends, traditional apparel retailers try to achieve their distinctiveness by carrying more proprietary brands and merchandise, enhancing the fashion sensibility and quality of their private labels, and re-assorting their stores to drive a better in-store experience for their customer.

PRICE PROMOTION MATRIX

Price and special promotions provide greater value via the discount, which attracts consumers to the store, thus gen-

erating additional traffic. However, retailers cannot depend on price promotions to attract customers on a regular basis. Price discounting may lead to declines in profit margins and more direct price competition between national brands and their own store brands (Seiders and Voss 2004). Additionally, such discounting may undermine consumer perceptions of product quality and may even hurt a store's overall image, lowering the probability of future purchases. These factors have forced some retailers to advocate alternative strategies, such as everyday low-price strategies (EDLPs) that provide a straightforward means of conveying value to consumers and are less likely to undermine product quality (Darke and Chung 2005).

K. Seiders and G. Voss (2004) developed the retail price promotion matrix, a framework that helps retailers make price promotion decisions, as illustrated in Figure 11.6. The matrix shows that the effectiveness of a retailer's price promotion strategy depends on how retail offerings are distinguished based on two fundamental traits: assortment overlap and assortment life span. Assortment overlap is the degree to which a retailer's product assortments are similar to or distinct from another retailer. When a retailer's product assortments are similar to those of another retailer, the retailer has a high level of assortment overlap. Assortment life span is associated with the speed at which a typical assortment loses value or becomes obsolete over time. Assortments that have limited life span can be perishable, as in the case of product categories such as food, fashion, and consumer electronics. For example, a dairy product may have a 7-day life span, a fashion apparel item may have a 3-month life span, and a consumer electronic item, such as a personal computer, may have a 12-month life span.

Seiders and Voss (2004) explained how retailers can be grouped based on whether

Variety promoters
- **Focused specialists (e.g., furniture stores: fast-food restaurants)**
- **Promotional pricing is optimal**
- **Increase traffic and protect share with targeted discounts, couponing, and safe events**

Price point rivals
- Efficient generalists (e.g., home improvement superstores, discount stores, warehouse clubs)
- Everyday low pricing is optimal
- Reinforce low price image with positional price communications

Broadscope promoters
- **Large-scale generalists (e.g., supermarkets, traditional department stores)**
- **Promotional pricing is optimal**
- **Increase traffic and retention with extensive price promotion and loyalty program incentives**

Differentiators
- Innovators (e.g., high-end department stores, specialty boutiques)
- Everyday fair/high pricing is optimal
- Sell select, obsolescent products using targeted discounts, seasonal sales, and retail outlets

Clearout promoters
- **Large-scale generalists (e.g., electronic superstores, automobile dealers)**
- **Promotional pricing is optimal**
- **Increase traffic, attract fringe customers, and sell obsolescent products with frequent discounting**

| Low | Assortment overlap | High |

- **High-gain promoters**   • Low-gain promoters

11.6 The Retail Price Promotion Matrix

they do or do not benefit from price promotion. The low-gain promoters benefit least from price promotions and the high-gain promoters benefit most from price promotions. Each position in Figure 11.6 represents a different approach to retail price promotion. It is recommended that retailers in the low-low position (differentiators) and high-high position (price point rivals) limit the use of price promotion and that retailers on the high-low to low-high diagonal (variety promoters, broadscope promoters, and clearout promoters) follow more intensive price promotion strategies. In the following pages, each of Seiders and Voss's five categories is explained, accompanied by retail examples that fit in each category.

Low-Gain Promoters

Low-gain promoters have either low assortment overlap and low assortment life span or high assortment overlap and high assortment life span. They benefit least from price promotions and are classified as differentiators and price point rivals, respectively.

DIFFERENTIATORS

Where a product's life span and overlap are low, product assortments are relatively perishable and sharply distinctive from those of competitors. For these products, retailers use differentiation strategies that deemphasize the role of price, but continuously offer new products to spur demand and avoid head-to-head competition. This type of retailer includes high-end fashion department stores (e.g., Neiman Marcus and Nordstrom) and specialty stores (e.g., Emporio Armani and Donna Karan) that rely on a high rate of product innovation. These retailers are tied to single designers to maintain the uniqueness of their products and typically use everyday high pricing to reinforce the exclusivity and status of their stores, not dependent upon price promotions. For instance, Coach leather sells its products through catalogs and department store boutiques; and Coach stores avoid promotions, with standard product prices being published and maintained in all channels (Seiders and Voss 2004).

Differentiators often offer alternative price promotions through loyalty programs, outlet stores, and deliberately selected sales. Neiman Marcus has developed an effective loyalty program, InCircle, targeting the most valuable customers who generate the majority of its sales. The InCircle program uses exclusivity that fits with the retailer's status positioning and makes it more compelling for top customers. The richness of rewards, such as exclusive vacations, unique artwork, and rare gifts, increases as spending rises, giving a strong incentive for customers to continue their buying at Neiman Marcus. Bloomingdale's Rewards Plus was created as a way to bring extra value to key customers who use the Bloomingdale's card and shop at Bloomingdale's. Macy's offers four levels of the Star Rewards program (i.e., Red, Gold, Platinum, and Elite) determined by the customer's spending history at Macy's. Chico's also established a program, the Passport Club, which rewards its best customers. The Passport Club offers many exciting benefits, including 5 percent discount on every purchase, free shipping, and discounts on gift certificates. Total Rewards is Harrah's loyalty program that rewards customers. Based on how much

they play and the type of games they play, customers will earn Reward Credits to be used toward meals, popular merchandise, and once-in-a-lifetime experiences. Reward Credits also determine the level of tiered membership (Gold, Platinum, or Diamond).

Faced with pressure to move short-lived products, differentiators also run outlet stores or offer selected annual or semiannual sales to attract value-oriented shoppers. Neiman Marcus operates a successful high-volume outlet store, Last Call, and Saks Fifth Avenue operates its OFF 5TH outlet. Neiman Marcus also publicizes a famous annual clearance sale (also called Last Call). Other fashion department stores such as Barneys and Nordstrom deliberately advertise annual or twice annual sales, and provide the implication that they do not put their products on sale often. When these retailers do offer price promotions, however, they tend to use deep discounts. With higher original margins and infrequent sales events, these retailers can afford to provide deep discounts to generate store traffic and move perishable inventory without damaging the brand and store image.

PRICE POINT RIVALS

Where overlap and life span are both high, retailers implement a mass marketing approach and depend on volume sales. Because both assortment life span and overlap are at high levels, there is limited variation across retailers. In this case, price is the key to differential advantage, and companies rely on economies of scale to lower expenses and support lower prices. The lower gross margins associated with everyday low or fair pricing mandate strong volume increases for these retailers.

Realizing that frequent promotions can be both costly and confusing to consumers, **price point rivals** try to convey a favorable price image by emphasizing EDLP and including a relatively small number of actual price promotions. Key retail sectors that gained a significant market share in the 1990s—home improvement, warehouse clubs, supercenters, manufacturer outlets—promote everyday low or everyday fair pricing.

Power retailers such as Wal-Mart and Target are two retailers that have taken on an EDLP strategy as part of their founding philosophies. These stores further expanded their stores into their supercenter concept—with its combined grocery and discount store assortment. By aggressively pricing their merchandise with everyday low prices, these retailers have gained a loyal consumer base, generated greater volume, and increased their market share.

Differentiation is a challenge in these sectors. For example, an Office Depot store can easily be substituted for an Office Max store or a Staples store, and a Borders store for a bookstop store. Because these retailers are faced with a constant need to defend market share, they invest in high-volume, price-oriented advertising, promoting everyday low prices rather than sales (Seiders and Voss 2004).

High-gain Promoters

The high-gain promoters have either high assortment overlap and low assortment life span or low assortment overlap and high assortment life span. They benefit most from price promotions and consist of clearout promoters, variety promoters, and broadscope promoters.

CLEAROUT PROMOTERS

Clearout promoters are retailers where overlap is high and life span is low, so they offer perishable product assortments that are relatively undifferentiated across competitors. These sectors include automobile dealerships and consumer electronics

retailers such as CompUSA and RadioShack. The assortments in the stores have limited life spans due to the frequent introduction of stylistic or technical changes. Therefore, retailers are compelled to deepen product assortments with many modifications of basic products. By offering price promotions on products that may become obsolete, retailers accelerate sales of these products and increase store traffic. For instance, automobile dealers use promotions and generous financing terms to attract customers who may have low loyalty to the manufacturer. Because assortment overlap is high, some automobile dealers in this sector seek differentiation by selling exclusive models from branded manufacturers or by offering superior service and selection. To provide superior service, The Tweeter Home Entertainment Group, an electronics retailer, focuses on personal selling in its stores and offers an automatic price protection policy. However, these retailers generally operate in markets where it is difficult for consumers to evaluate products. Thus, price promotion serves as a strong motivator of consumers' purchasing decisions (Seiders and Voss 2004).

VARIETY PROMOTERS

Variety promoters are retailers where overlap is low and life span is high, so they offer product assortments that have distinctive attributes. These retailers include furniture stores and fast-food companies. Customers of these retailers seek variety among alternatives. Those who are looking for a classic furniture style for the dining room can go to Bombay Company or Ethan Allen. Someone who is looking for a quick lunch might choose to go to Pizza Hut, KFC, or McDonald's. Because consumer inertia can be an obstacle for variety promoters, it is important to offer promotions that encourage trial and protect market share. Retailers can increase store traffic with promotions that target fringe customers who seek variety or are undecided as to their shopping destination. Fast-food companies frequently use weekly coupons, often featuring new menu items or value meals to target these fringe customers (Seiders and Voss 2004).

BROADSCOPE PROMOTERS

Broadscope promoters are retailers that provide broad product assortments, which are both low and high in life span and overlap. These sectors, which include traditional department stores and supermarkets, offer many product categories that vary in life span and overlap. For example, supermarkets offer national-brand packaged goods (high life span, high overlap), store-brand packaged goods (high life span, low overlap), and perishable items such as deli, seafood, and bakery products (low life span, low overlap). Similarly, traditional department stores offer basic, commodity-type soft goods (high life span, high overlap), store-brand apparel (high life span, low overlap), and designer apparel items that follow fashion seasons (low life span, low overlap).

Because their assortments include many product categories that are not easily differentiated, broadscope promoters face intense competition both within and across retail sectors. Furthermore, the perishable product assortments generate substantial product loss pressures. Therefore, price promotions can help these retailers to attract customers, control a large and diverse store inventory, and encourage frequent shopping. To do this, most supermarkets and department stores use weekly circulars and in-store deals, as well as more targeted initiatives (delivered at checkout, through mail, or online) based on their own store credit card or loyalty card data (Seiders and Voss, 2004).

VALUE RETAILERS' PRACTICES IN EXPERIENTIAL RETAILING

Although value-oriented outlets have paid more attention to the tangible utilitarian benefits (e.g., price, assortment, and convenience), these retailers also have demonstrated the ability to draw consumers based upon intangible benefits (e.g., enjoyable shopping experience and emotional connection). This suggests that value retailers not only provide economic value by lowering the consumer expenditure to receive the same product benefit but also provide the perceived merits of the deal that goes beyond the economic outcome (Darke and Chung 2005).

A bargain, in particular, can be explained from two perspectives. From an economic standpoint, a bargain leads to the objective monetary benefits. From a psychological standpoint, getting a discount may also satisfy ego-expressive goals. In other words, consumers who receive a bargain are likely to attribute it to internal causes such as their own skill and effort and should thereby feel more rewarded due to the pride and accomplishment involved. Or consumers may like a bargain simply because it makes them feel very lucky. Getting a bargain from pure luck might also increase purchase satisfaction simply because it is a pleasant surprise (Darke and Dahl 2003). For instance, Dollar Tree customers can discover new treasures in the store every week. Excitement also is derived from finding famous brand names at low prices and making price comparisons with full price stores (*DSN Retailing Today* 2004, Young 2004). Because of this treasure hunt shopping experience, middle- and upper-class consumers have become loyal to many value-oriented outlets (Rivkin 2005).

In a study done by A. Cox, D. Cox, and R. D. Anderson (2005) of 1,369 women, the most enjoyed shopping experience was searching for and finding bargains (nearly 75 percent). The appeal of bargain hunting was quite universal in that it cut across all incomes, ages, and child-rearing categories of the respondents. In addition, even very affluent consumers whose household incomes were more than $110,000 reported enjoying bargain hunting more than any other aspect of shopping. Cox et al. (2005) concluded, "Above all, consumers enjoy hunting for bargains" (257). Indeed, most consumers shop in value retail outlets not just for the savings, but also for the fun of it. With their frequently turned and unusual assortments of merchandise, value retailers can engender a feeling of excitement among shoppers looking for bargains.

Costco's success in targeting higher-income consumers with ample discretionary income—both via its merchandise assortment and the location of its stores—contributes significantly to the stores' sales volume. The merchandise assortment provides some clues into the affluence of the Costco customer. For example, it is not unusual to find a display of Dom Perignon champagne for sale at Costco (www.costco.com).

In the United Kingdom, Tesco developed the Clubcard program that uses two well-defined tiers to reach two customer segments. The first tier has a points structure, through which club members get one point for each pound spent at Tesco. This way, points enhance the overall value proposition with easily attainable rewards to a broad customer base. The second tier aims at Tesco's frequent, high-spending customers. This program seeks to change the behavior of heavy spenders by using aspirational rewards such as giving discounts on top leisure attractions, theater tickets, sporting events, and hotel stays. This program attracts top segments to spend more frequently at Tesco (www.tesco.com).

IKEA, an international home décor and furniture retailer, organizes its store so its customers can walk through a fully decorated built home. If customers wish to purchase a piece of furniture, placed in an actual room setting, all they need to do is to write down the model number on a piece of paper provided. An IKEA employee then will retrieve the item upon customer checkout. Customers also can pick up and carry smaller items to the checkout area (www.ikea.com).

The Payless Shoe Source chain of discount shoes used to focus on function and price, reflecting more of a utilitarian shoe store. In 2002 Payless began a repositioning focused on fashion and featuring talk-show host and shoe diva Star Jones in television spots (Cuneo 2003). The company now focuses on the more hedonic aspects of shoe shopping, giving customers the latest fashion trends at affordable prices, and is expanding in its designer shoe collection.

Isaac Mizrahi's strategy is just the opposite of Payless's. Mizrahi is a famous designer whose collections are featured in high-end retailers such as Bergdorf Goodman. Although he is well-known by affluent shoppers, he has taken a bold step to create a line for discount retailer Target. Mizrahi described what he called bipolar shopping disorder as the reason consumers want both luxury and discount goods. He stated there has been a conceptual shift in the shopping patterns of affluent customers who have the compulsion to buy $9.99 cotton tanks along with $20,000 ball gown skirts (Foley and Wilson 2004). Mizrahi was criticized for the Target collection because critics thought it would drag down the image of his designer brand. However, both the upscale and Target Mizrahi collections are gaining sales (Karimzadeh 2005).

Target Corporation is recognized for creating energetic, trendy, organized, and enjoyable shopping experiences (Target Corporation 2004). While Target focuses on providing competitively priced merchandise, it is also known for in-stock reliability, fast and friendly service, and increasing speed and efficiency within the stores. At the other end of the spectrum, Target is reputed for its community enrichment programs that provide indirect emotional benefits to consumers through donations to schools and community projects. Every time customers participate in these programs, they are emotionally connected with Target for helping the community.

In honor of its landmark opening in Joliet, Illinois, Family Dollar made a $6,000 donation to the school library at Pershing Elementary, which is located less than 2 miles from the store (www.family-dollar.com). The company also commemorated the milestone by presenting a matching donation to the Classroom Central program of the Charlotte-Mecklenburg school system, which provides much-needed school supplies for local low-income students. The opening of the new Joliet store represented a significant milestone for Family Dollar through its involvement in the community.

Dollar General initiated the Learn to Read Program as a community investment program, recognizing that the individuals who shop at their stores are more than just customers; they are their neighbors and friends (See Figure 11.7). Dollar General believes in strengthening communities by investing in programs that contribute to the advancement of literacy and basic education, which are necessary to achieve personal and professional success. Dollar General launched a grass-roots literacy referral program in 1987, which offers free referral information services to their customers and employees regarding local learn-to-read, GED, and English as a second language programs. At the checkout

counters of any Dollar General store, customers can find brochures that tell the story of Dollar General's founder, J. L. Turner, who was functionally illiterate. Since its inception, the Dollar General referral program has provided more than 50,000 referrals to literacy programs across Dollar General's market area (www.dollargeneral.com).

11.7 Dollar General strengthens communities by investing in the Learn-to-Read Program that contributes to the advancement of literacy and basic education.

ONLINE AUCTIONS

Most consumers like to talk about their purchases and generally speak highly of their choices. One consumer might say, "I bought a Mercedes." Another might say, "How much do you think I paid for this? Ten dollars. Can you believe it? Just ten dollars." A third consumer might say, "I found a rare piece of antique furniture at a yard sale." Consumers like to speak of their purchases—how good a product they purchased, how cheap they got it, or how rare their purchase is. Online auctions enable consumers to combine all of these factors, which has created exciting and fast-growing Internet auctions. In Internet auctions, it is possible to find quality products, cheap prices, novelty items, and quick transactions.

The auction-based electronic market represents a change of commerce from Business-to-Consumer (B2C) to Consumer-to-Consumer (C2C). One of the pioneers of online auction is eBay. eBay was started when its founder, Pierre Omidyar, came up with the idea of an online flea market where anybody could sell anything at bargain prices. eBay's popularity among the public has been growing steadily in the recent years. From 1998 to 2004, eBay grew to more than 135 million registered users, a 43 percent increase over the 94.9 million users reported in 2003. At any specific time, more than 25 million items can be found on eBay with an additional 3.5 million items being added each day. In 2004, eBay reported annual gross merchandise sales (GMS) of $34.2 billion, an increase from $23.8 billion in 2003. This translates into more than $1,000 GMS per second (Oliva 2004). About 30 percent of all U.S. households participated in an eBay online auction in 2004 (Wang, Jank, and Shmueli 2005).

Participating in online auctions offers a variety of hedonic benefits. Some of these benefits are variety, explorational search process, and fun in the bidding process (Standifird, Roelofs, and Durham 2004). First of all, a buyer interested in purchasing a product via an eBay auction is presented with a smorgasbord of 25 million products arranged in 21 major categories. While the variety can seem daunting, it is an important component of hedonic shopping. Next, the potential buyer engages in the search process for a specific product and gets to experience the thrill of perusing a multitude of available products. The potential buyer considers the items for purchase while categorizing the many variations in each individual auction. This part of the search process is explorational, one of the hedonic shopping benefits. Finally, the potential buyer decides on an item for purchase and starts the active bidding process whereby the highest bidder wins the auction. This process of bidding can be considered hedonic because it is a process of active play and fun (Standifird et al. 2004).

eBay and other similar online auctions have created a new business culture that will change consumer behavior in the future. As people begin to find the best deals at online auctions, they may move away from middle-market vendors and retailers. They experience the feeling that is very similar to going to a yard sale or flea market—not knowing what one would find and finding some unexpected items. The thrill in bidding and out bidding other sellers gives many people the feeling of gambling. A successful transaction often gives the seller or buyer a feeling of satisfaction and boosts his own ego about his competence in taking risks and making decisions (Standifird et al. 2004).

O. Lin and D. Joyce (2004) identified five benefits of online auctions for buyers and sellers. First, online auctions offer a huge selection of merchandise. Second, online auction sites charge a nominal fee to the seller for setting up and running auctions. Third, they have lower entry barriers for auctioneers, suppliers, and customers. First-time users would find it convenient to buy and sell products on online auction because they are usually familiar with Internet access. Fourth, buyers may benefit from the competitive market because more suppliers are using online auctions to sell their products. To achieve competitive advantage, suppliers lower the cost of the merchandise or strive to provide better quality products, which ultimately leads to the buyer's advantage. Finally, buying from and selling on online auctions can be done from home and offers advantages to people who are forced to work from home such as stay-at-home mothers or retired people (Lin and Joyce 2004).

As such, online auctions offer a rich environment enabling both the buyer and seller to emerge as winners. Online auctions can be considered a new form of value retailing where customers can purchase new, old, used, or out-of-stock merchandise at substantially lower prices.

CHAPTER SUMMARY

Consumers are cautious about how and where they spend their money. Even consumers who are considered middle class or affluent are looking for bargains. The increasing demand for lower-priced goods has given new life to retailers who serve value-oriented consumers. Many value retailers focus on offering low prices to customers, but they also provide hedonic benefits to meet their customers' needs. Consumers may receive hedonic benefits from exploration, never knowing what items they will find at such low prices, or from emotional connections companies are making through community enrichment programs and aspirational rewards. On the contrary, upscale retailers also have copied the concept of value retailing. Famous designers have developed less expensive product lines to reach more price-conscious consumers and have partnered with mid- or low-end stores to make luxury items available to the masses.

Types of value retailers include discount department stores (Wal-Mart, Target), factory outlets, category killers (Home Depot, PetSmart), off-price discounters (Marshalls, Ross), warehouse clubs (Sam's, Costco), dollar stores (Family Dollar, Dollar General), and value megamalls (Grapevine Mills, Texas, and Opry Mills, Nashville, Tennessee). Most recently, online auctions have become proper market places for value retailing. Through finding quality products or novelty items at low prices, and making quick online transactions, consumers are experiencing the thrill in bidding and outbidding other sellers. These value retailers have been growing faster than any major retail format in the United States.

Consumer preferences toward value retailers have been impacted by numerous demographic trends, consumer patterns, and retail trends. Demographic trends include slow growth in disposable personal income, widening income gaps, and the graying of the United States. Consumer patterns include less resistance toward value shopping due to the shift to value phenomenon, one-stop shopping, comparison shopping, and brand-consciousness. Retail trends include increasing power retailers, increasing retail efficiency, and more competition from traditional retailers.

In this chapter, Seiders and Voss's (2004) price promotion matrix is introduced. The matrix explains that effectiveness of a retailer's price promotion strategy depends on how retail offerings are distinguished based on assortment overlap (i.e., the degree to which a retailer's product assortments are similar to or distinct from another retailer's) and assortment life span (i.e., the speed at which a typical assortment loses value or becomes obsolete over time). The low-gain promoters benefit least from price promotions, and the high-gain promoters benefit most from price promotions. It is suggested that retailers in the low-low position (differentiators) and high-high position (price point rivals) should limit the use of price promotion; retailers on the high-low to low-high diagonal—variety promoters, broadscope promoters, and clearout promoters—should follow more intensive price promotion strategies.

While traditional retailers are often susceptible to inflation and unemployment and are pummeled by a poor economy, the value retailing sector seems to thrive in both good and bad times. Throughout the recent recession, value retailers have shown healthy gains in sales as opposed to actual declines in many other segments of the retailing industry. Retailers—whether they are at low end or at high end—must understand that consumers are on a constant search for low prices and are actively seeking out new formats to receive a more positive experience.

Discussion Questions

1. Discuss demographic trends that affect the growth of value retailing.

2. Discuss consumer trend patterns that affect the growth of value retailing.

3. Discuss retail trends that affect the growth of value retailing and give specific retail examples.

4. Explain how high-end department stores can provide utilitarian benefits to their customers.

5. Explain how value retailers can provide hedonic benefits to their customers.

6. According to the text, consumers have recently witnessed the unprecedented commingling of what some view as fashion's sacred and profane—luxury and deep discount. Link this statement to the consumer trends.

7. Apply the statement in question 6 to current retail practices.

8. Discuss the conditions that affect the success or failure of value retailers.

9. Discuss what value retailing contributes to a total consumer experience.

10. Discuss what value retailing contributes to experiential retailing.

References

About.com. 2004. Retailers to increase spending on technology. Retrieved April 16, 2006 from http://retail industry.about.com/cs/technology/a/bl_nrf011304.html

Back, Tekla, Kelly Haveron, Laxman Narasimhan, Stacey Rauch, and Kevin Sneader. 2005. Winning in a Value-Driven World. McKinsey & Company, retrieved February 21, 2006 from http://retail.mckinsey.com

Berry, L. 1996. Retailers with a future. *Marketing Management* 5(1):9–38.

Cox, A., D. Cox, and R. D. Anderson. 2005. Reassessing the pleasures of store shopping. *Journal of Business Research* 58(3):250–259.

Cuneo, A. 2003. Wal-Mart gains on Payless turf. *Advertising Age*. July 28, 4.

Darke, P. R., and C. M. Chung. 2005. Effects of pricing and promotion on consumer perceptions: It depends on how you frame it. *Journal of Retailing* 81(1):35–47.

Darke, P. R., and D. W. Dahl. 2003. Fairness and discounts: The subjective value of a bargain. *Journal of Consumer Psychology* 13(3):3280338.

Datamonitor. 2005. Big Lots, Inc. company profile. Retrieved on August 15, 2006 from www.datamonitor.com

Davidowitz, H. L. 2004. Opportunity knocks. *Chain Store Age* 80(10):48.

DSN Retailing Today. 2003. Low prices, treasure hunts build dollar empire. 42(22):23–24.

DSN Retailing Today. 2004. Core demographics expand beyond traditional blue collar shopper. 43(21):20–21.

Dunne, P., and R. Lusch. 2005. *Retailing,* 5th edition. United States of America: Thomson South-Western.

Elliston, M. 2004. Voice of the customer. *Retail Merchandiser* 44(1):42.

Evans, J. R., and B. Berman. 2002. Retrieved April 16, 2006 from http://retailindustry.about.com/library/uc/be/uc_be_power.html

Foley, B. and E. Wilson. 2004. The two faces of Isaac. *Women's Wear Daily.* June 16, 8.

Frank, R., E. Mihas, L. Narasimhan, and S. Rauch. 2003. Competing in a value-driven world. Retrieved March 30, 2006 from www.mckinsey.com/practices/retail/knowledge/articles/competinginavaluedrivenworld.pdf

Gardyn, R. 2002. Oh, the good life. *American Demographics* 24(10):30–35.

Gelbtuch, H. C. 1990. The warehouse club industry. *Appraisal Journal* 58(2):153–159.

Harvard Business Review. 1993. The evolution of Wal-Mart: Savvy expansion and leadership. 82–83.

Howell, D. 2005. Dollar channel too rich for mass retailers. *DSN Retailing Today* 44(22):11–15.

Hudson, K. 2005. Making sense of dollar stores. The *Wall Street Journal,* Eastern Edition. 246(58):C1–C4.

International Council of Shopping Centers (ICSC). Shopping center definitions (2004). Retrieved January 25, 2006 from www.icsc.org/srch/lib/SCDefinitions.pdf

Johnson, Bradley. 2005. Older buyers will drive vehicle sales into next decade. *Automotive News* 80(6173), 30P.

Karimzadeh, M. 2005. Mizrahi's new moves. *Women's Wear Daily.* November 13, 13.

Klass, G. 2002. Presenting data: Tabular and graphic display of social indicators. Retrieved April 16, 2006 from http://lilt.ilstu.edu/gmklass/pos138/datadisplay/sections/poverty.htm

Koch, D. 2005. The rising dollar. *Retail Traffic* 34(5):72–75.

Koval, Robin. 2005. Living the high life. *Adweek* 46(45):1.

Lin, O., and D. Joyce. 2004. Critical success factors for online auction websites. Retrieved May 5, 2006 from www.naccq.ac.nz/conference05/proceedings_04/lin_auction.pdf

Lisanti, T. 1999. Extreme segment, extreme growth. *Discount Store News* 38(14):13.

Mason, J. C. 1992. Value: The new marketing mania? *Management Review.* May, 16–21.

Multinational Monitor. 2003. Ever-widening income gaps. Retrieved March 30, 2006, from www.allbusiness.com/periodicals/article/686846-1.html

O'Connor, P. C. 1999. Which retail properties are getting market share? *The Appraisal Journal* 67(1):37–40.

Oliva, R. 2004. B2B for sale. *Marketing Management* 13(5):48–49.

Pender, K. 2005. Personal savings rate drops to zero percent. Retrieved April 16, 2006 from www.sfgate.com/cgi-bin/article.cgi?f=/c/a/2005/08/07/BUG5JE423K1.DTL

Poloian, L. 2003. *Retailing principles.* New York: Fairchild Publications.

PR Newswire. 2004. American middle class shrinks as mass immigration expands. April 19, 1.

Ritter, Ian. March. Mills shifts focus to traditional malls. *Shopping Centers Today.* Retrieved August 15, 2006 from www.icsc.org/srch/sct/sct0303/page1c.php?region

Rivkin, J. 2005. On the radar: Dollar store growth forces other retail formats to take notice. *Private Label Buyer.* Retrieved March 30, 2006, from www.allbusiness.com/periodicals/article/585664-1.html

Seiders, K., and G. Voss. 2004. From price to purchase. *Marketing Management.* November/December, 38–43.

Seninger, S. 2000. Winnebagos, funeral homes, and cruise ships: The graying of baby boomers in the new millennium. *Montana Business Quarterly* *38*(1):2–5.

Standifird, S., M. Roelofs, and Y. Durham. 2004. The impact of eBay's buy-it-now function on bidder behavior. *International Journal of Electronic Commerce 9*(2):167–176.

Stank, T. P., P. J. Daugherty, and C. W. Autry. 1999. Collaborative planning: supporting automatic replenishment programs. *Supply Chain Management* 4,2,75–85.

Steidtmann, C. 2006. The consumer takes a breather. *Progressive Grocer 85*(4):93.

Stores Magazine. 2006. 2006 Global Powers of Retailing. 88(1):G1–G52.

Target Corporation Annual Report. 2004. Retrieved October 3, 2005, from www.targetcorp.com/targetcorp_group/investor-relations/annual_report.jhtml

Terhune, C. 2006. Business technology: Supply-chain fix for Pepsi; bottler's move to modernize delivery yields efficiency benefits. The *Wall Street Journal.* June 6, B3.

U.S. Department of Health and Human Services. Administration on Aging.

Profile of older Americans: 2005. Last updated May 24, 2006. Retrieved August 15, 2006 from www.aoa.gov/PROF/Statistics/profile/2005/2005profile.doc

Veretto, P. 2002. Comparison shopping pays very well. *Frugal Living Newsletter.* Retrieved April 7, 2006 from http://frugalliving.about.com/library/weekly/aa020502a.html

Walker, L. 2005. Comparison Shopping Online. *Washington Post.* Retrieved April 7, 2006, from http://findarticles.com/p/articles/mi_0NTQ/is_2005_June_9/ai_n13807145

Wang, S., W. Jank, and G. Shmueli. 2005. Forecasting eBay's online auction prices using functional data analysis. Retrieved May 4, 2006 from www.smith.umd.edu/ceme/statistics/Predicting percent20Online percent20Auction.pdf.

Weiss, D. A., and D. M. Lummis, 1994. *Value retailing in the 1990s.* New York: John Wiley and Sons, Inc.

Young, V. 2004. Dollar stores gain momentum. *Women's Wear Daily 187*(37):22.

CHAPTER 12

Why the Harley Brand's So Hot

Most products and services masquerade as brands. They have logos and positive associations to which they can lay claim, but most lack that deep, visceral connection and unshakable loyalty that characterizes true brands from fungible products and services. When competing products drop their price or add a new feature or benefit, you've often got a turncoat customer on your hands. The reason is simple: The depth of connection is weak. The marketer failed to create sufficient rational and emotional "switching costs" for the consumer.

Marketers that understand the power of building deep connections to customers are the true builders of real brands. They benefit from long and dependable life cycles that serve as annuity revenue streams and withstand competitive attacks. What separates them from others? A core belief is that the consumer owns the brand, not the company. When viewed in this way, consumers become individuals with whom you need to build relationships. The rational side of any purchase decision is important; it's the emotional side that keeps them coming back.

Harley-Davidson over its 100 years has been very smart in its approach. It established its reputation based on producing tough, high quality, and reliable motorcycles. Word of the durable bikes spread rapidly, and they became the motorcycle of choice for police departments across the country. During World Wars I and II, most of Harley-Davidson's production was devoted to supplying U.S. and allied troops with motorcycles—an action that further strengthened its linkage to American culture, values, and imagery. Following World War II, returning troops had a strong affinity for Harley's tough and reliable motorcycles, creating significant demand for the company. During the entire period, Harley-Davidson motorcycles retained their distinctive styling, creating a sense of nostalgia and continuity that has been carried forward to this day.

What Harley-Davidson clearly understands is that the people who buy Harleys want to be part of an extended family—a community of free-spirited adventure seekers. To build and reinforce this strong sense of community, Harley-Davidson creatively leverages all its customer touch points: It gives plant tours, conducts special events and races, and holds bike rallies. It launched a line of durable, branded motorcycle clothing and accessories. It selectively licenses the Harley brand on products (there's even a Barbie biker doll and a chrome Visa credit card). And there's the H.O.G.—the Harley Owners Group. H.O.G. [is made up of] 650,000 members worldwide and provides an organized way for Harley riders to share their passion and show their pride. At the celebration of the company's 100th anniversary last year on August 30, more than 250,000 people from around the world descended on Milwaukee to celebrate the event. How many of your customers would attend a celebration of any one of your brands?

Source: Speros, J. 2004. Why the Harley brand's so hot. *Advertising Age* 75(11): 26–26. Reprinted with permission from the March 15, 2004 issue of *Advertising Age*.

INTRODUCTION

In the mature U.S. marketplace, consumers face a multitude of spending opportunities and marketers are forced to creatively implement various differentiation strategies. Product quality and pricing strategies have proven to be less effective as the number of alternative products and brands increases. Thus, thriving in today's market is not simply a matter of enticing the masses to purchase a company's product or service and then relinquishing their attention to another supplier; rather, it is a matter of developing a relationship with a customer who will eventually purchase more frequently, require a lower quantity of service, be less price-elastic, and serve as a spokesperson for the brand (Boone and Kurtz 1998).

In this consumer-driven market, the most successful retailers are associating their brand with a particular lifestyle and marketing to a specific niche of consumers to whom that lifestyle is most appealing. The opening article shows how a company's name, brand, and its related visual symbols precisely con-

vey a complex message to its existing and potential new customers. However, branding is something that cannot be achieved overnight. If Harley-Davidson is a popular brand today, it is because of the time, energy, and money wisely invested by Harley-Davidson from its inception (See Figures 12.1a and b).

InterContinental Hotel Group launched a completely new concept in the hotel industry, Hotel Indigo, aimed at the mid-market traveler who would be willing to pay more for a higher style than would typically be found in a cookie-cutter hotel room (See Figure 12.2). Hotel Indigo first opened in Atlanta and Chicago in 2005. Targeting both the business and leisure traveler seeking an out-of-the-ordinary experience, Hotel Indigo offers a tranquil and harmonious environment to enjoy; a product beyond the neutral-colored, boxy décor of most hotel rooms. Following the trends in retail outlets, they update and alter interior details to keep the experience fresh for their customers (Clark 2004). Steve Porter, president for the Americas, stated, "For the first time in the hotel industry, we're defining customers by mindset rather than a price point." He further stated that the company caters to "middle-market consumers who are

12.1a & b Harley-Davidson's popularity is unchallenged.

trading up to higher levels of quality and taste, but still seeking value" (*Lodging Hospitality* 2004, 14).

As U.S. consumers are more brand-oriented than ever, branding can be used as a retailer's unique strength that their competitors cannot easily copy. Developing a well-positioned brand secures a competitive retail niche and provides consumers with a shopping experience that is different, unique, special, and identifiable (Caylor 1999). Effective branding presents a marketable image that provides specific retail advantages, such as customer attraction from farther distances, increased retail patronage, and more targeted customers for retailers and developers.

THE CONCEPT OF BRANDING

In the past, branding was thought to be a strategy developed to publicize the name of a product. Branding was more about the packaging, logo design, and font. This concept of branding does not suffice today, when there are so many media channels and so many competitors in all product categories. Brands are the primary means through which a cumulative image of a product or service crops up in people's minds when they think about a particular brand. Brands need to strike the right chords and connect to the customer on an emotional level. This can only be achieved when one understands the true concept of branding.

Use of Brands

A consumer may choose a particular brand not only because the branded product provides the functional or performance benefits expected, but also because it can express the consumer's personality, social status, or affiliation, or fulfill his or her internal psychological needs. With the vast amount of products and services in each category, often the only way a company or

product stands out is because of its brand name. However, a brand is not just a name, a striking logo, or a catchy slogan. It is a distinctive identity that differentiates a relevant, enduring, and credible promise of value associated with a product (Briggs 2001). Although a single, generally accepted definition of a brand does not exist, there is a consensus that a brand is a name, term, sign, symbol, or design that differentiates the products or services of a seller from those of competitors by consistently delivering a specific set of features, benefits, and services to buyers (Kotler and Armstrong 1996).

An entertainment or thematic mix is now a standard element in new retail outlets. This, however, presents a marketing dilemma for retailers. Shoppers may initially exhibit a high level of interest in the ever-more-stimulating activities of entertainment retail outlets, but the novelty may wear off in time. One solution to this dilemma is for a retailer to create a brand that differentiates it from all other retailers, thus continuing to attract customers. T.G.I. Friday's offers a casual, relaxed Friday afternoon atmosphere (See Figure 12.3). Red Lobster offers an atmosphere where seafood lovers get together with

12.3 T.G.I. Friday's offers a casual relaxed atmosphere.

four years. Based on the survey with chief marketing officers and consumers, brands that were both growing fast and innovative were identified. Apple reached the top spot with an increase in its brand value by 38 percent in the last four years due to the popularity of its portable music device, the iPod. Blackberry, the handheld e-mail and phone device, and Google, the Internet search engine, both tied for the second spot, earning a 36 percent growth in brand value. Internet portals Amazon and Yahoo! ranked fourth and fifth place, respectively (Badenhausen and Rodney 2005).

family and friends. Cheesecake Factory offers a high-energy, high-gloss environment with a huge selection of menu options—not just cheesecake. These retailers have built more than a name; they have built a brand (Lozito 2004).

The top 10 brands of 2005 are given in Table 12.1. These brands were those whose values increased the most within their respective industries during the past

TABLE 12.1. TOP 10 BRANDS

BRAND NAME	BRAND VALUE INCREASE
Apple	38%
Blackberry	36%
Google	36%
Amazon	35%
Yahoo!	33%
eBay	31%
Red Bull	31%
Starbucks	24%
Pixar	23%
Coach	22%

Source: Badenhausen, K., and M. Rodney. 2005. Next generation. *Forbes Global* 8(11): 36–37.

Goals of Branding

The essence of **branding** is to create an emotional connection with the customer. One large consumer segment with which retailers strive to create emotional connections is baby boomers. Baby boomers are currently enjoying the rewards of being at the apex of their income potential. The average baby boomer is looking for products that appeal to them emotionally and provide a sense of self-gratification and fulfillment. Always sentimental about their past, baby boomers search for products and services that are reminiscent of the rebellious youth movement of their generation. Examples of retailers who are attempting to capture the interests of baby boomers are Apple/MacIntosh and Volkswagen. Both have recently used retro 1960s music and color schemes to elicit emotional product associations, attempting to invoke sentimentality and create a customer connection (Mahajan and Wind 2002).

The most important goals of branding are creating and maintaining brand equity. **Brand equity** can be defined as an intangible asset of added value or goodwill that results from the favorable image, impressions of differentiation, and the strength of consumer attachment to a retailer name, brand name, or trademark (Aaker 1991). Increasingly, brands are positioned on the basis of their intangibles and attributes and benefits that transcend product or service performance. Accordingly, brand equity considerations are one of the most important drivers of contemporary retailing practices. Brand equity allows a brand to earn greater sales volume and higher margins than it could without the name, providing the retailer with competitive advantages (Cobb-Walgren, Ruble, and Donthu 1995). The strong equity position a retailer or its brand enjoys is often reinforced through marketing. Harley-Davidson motorcycles command a premium price because of their high quality as well as the strong brand equity they have developed through marketing activities.

Positioning brands has become more difficult because of mature and saturated retail markets. In addition, product quality is a universal expectation and unique product features are easy for competitors to copy. As a result, brands are seeking to create distinct brand images that separate them from the competition (Aaker 1997).

EVOLUTION OF BRANDING

The concept of branding has evolved from products, to service, to retailers (e.g., brick-and-mortar stores, the Internet), and to shopping centers. At each level, retailers have used different approaches to enhance consumer perceptions of their brand image.

Product Branding

The concept of **product branding** is discussed primarily in the context of a product having a set of characteristics that clearly differentiate it from all other products; examples are Levi's, Nike, and Coke. At this lead, branding is mainly applicable to tangible purchases rather than services

(Davies 1992). In the case of packaged goods, the physical product is the primary brand, and branding is achieved from the experience with the product. Through packaging, labeling, and displaying, marketers enhance the visual appeal of the brand.

PRODUCT BRANDING APPROACH

Marketers consider various branding approaches when launching a new brand. Some of the approaches to product branding are individual product branding, family branding, private branding, and co-branding.

Individual Product Branding Individual **product branding** is an approach whereby new products are assigned different names with no connection to other existing brands offered by the parent company. Under this approach, the parent company must aim to create a unique identity for a new brand. The advantage of this approach is that it facilitates brands standing on their own. Also, if another brand from the same company receives negative publicity, the new brand will remain unaffected because consumers will probably be unaware that both brands come from the same parent company. Under this branding approach, each brand builds its own separate equity, which allows the company to sell off individual brands without impacting other brands owned by the company. The most famous organization following the product branding strategy is Procter & Gamble, which has introduced several new brands without any association to other company brands or to the company name. Currently, there are many well-recognized Procter & Gamble brands that are unique and do not depend on the company name to be successful. For example, Olay and Pringles are Procter & Gamble brands, but Procter & Gamble does not make an effort to identify either of these brands with the parent company (Kotler and Armstrong 2006). Thus, they are both identified as individual product brands rather than as Procter & Gamble brands.

Family Branding Family branding is the strategy whereby new products are placed under the same umbrella as the existing company brands. The major advantage of this approach is that it enables the company to build market awareness and reputation with ease since the brand is already established and known to the consumer. D. Boush et al. (1987) described family branding: "When an existing brand name is applied to a new product, previously formed evaluations about the existing brand may also influence consumers' affective impressions about the new product" (226). One example of successful family branding is the Hershey brand that offers a range of products, such as Hershey's Kisses, Hershey's Milk Chocolate, and Hershey's Syrup bearing the parent company name.

Boush et al. (1987) explored whether consumers' prior associations with the brand would extend to the new product when the similarity between a brand's new product and previous products is not immediately evident. They found that "product similarity (between the new and existing product) strongly influences the effects of brand evaluation transfers [and] the greater the similarity of the new product to the existing product, the greater the transfer of positive or negative affect to that new product" (Boush et al. 1987, 234). Therefore, managers of family brands need to be careful to keep new products inside the realm of similar products.

Private Branding Private brands are brands that are owned by a particular retailer. They are called many names, including: distributor brands, retail brands, private labels, store brands, own labels, and own brands (Herstein and Gamliel 2006). They are often perceived to be less expensive than national brands because, in the case of private brands, the retailer also acts as the manufacturer (Halstead and Ward 1995). As a result, the typical retail markup is not included and hence the cost is reduced. Examples of private or store brands include Arizona Jeans by JC Penney, Kenmore by Sears, Great Value by Wal-Mart, and Private Selection by Kroger.

Private brands are also prominent in grocery retailing where they are usually called store brands. Store brands' sales have grown significantly in the United States over the last decade (Wellman 1997). They were originally limited to large foodstore chains (Burt 2000), but in the 1970s, they began to be used for a wider range of retailers (Herstein and Gamliel 2006). Previously, private labels offered consumers a value-priced alternative to national brands, but at an inferior quality. However, many retailers have now moved upscale with high quality private labels, which directly compete with national brands. The majority of traditional retailers have now introduced private labels in their brand strategy. Grocery retailers' expanding into private labels appears to be driven by factors such as increased retailer concentration, retailers' aim for higher profits, and retailers' greater proficiency at managing private brands as part of their retail format (Choi and Coughlan 2006). Other examples of retailers who use private labels include restaurants that sell mineral water or wine under their own brand name; hair salons that offer hair care products featuring the name of the salons as the brand name; automobile garages that sell parts, oils, batteries, and so on under their service brand name; and airlines that provide drinks, meals, headphones, and other accessories that carry the company name and logo (Herstein and Gamliel 2006).

Co-Branding Co-branding, sometimes called strategic alliance, occurs when two existing brands join to create a synergy that is expected to be stronger than a single brand would otherwise be. It is used to establish positive associations between brands in the eyes of the customer (Jevons, Gabbott, and de Chernatony 2005). R. Grossman (1997) described this strategy succinctly: "This technique has been used to pair new brands with existing brands that have powerful images attached to them in the hope of associating those positive images with the new products" (198).

Major credit card companies, such as Visa and MasterCard, offer co-branding. Besides tapping into awareness for multiple brands, the co-branding strategy also is designed to appeal to a larger target market. Co-branding becomes especially effective if each brand, when viewed separately, does not have extensive overlapping target markets with the other brand. Thus, co-branding allows both firms to tap into market segments where they did not previously have a strong position. An example of this strategy would be the co-branding of Slim-Fast and Godiva that resulted in the Slim-Fast Godiva chocolate cake mix.

Researchers have found conflicting information regarding co-branding. Grossman (1997) reported that co-branded retailers experienced erosion of brand profitability. This resulted from the value of a high-equity brand being leveraged in an attempt to cause increased sales for other brands that the store carries. S. Samu, H. S. Krishnan, and R. E. Smith (1999) showed that advertising alliances' successes depended on the complementarity of the products or brands. J. H. Washburn, B. D. Till, and R. Priluck (2000) found that using co-branding in pairing two or more branded products improved consumers' perceptions of brand equity, whether the co-branding partner was with a high or a low equity brand. In summarizing the previous research, C. Jevons et al. (2005) concluded that there is "comprehensive evidence that co-branding works, in the sense that the alliance causes a different effect to that which would be caused by unassociated brands" (303).

Service Branding

Branding is just as important to services as it is to products. However, with services, the company becomes its own brand. Strong **service brands** increase customers' trust of the invisible purchase by reducing perceived monetary, social, or safety risk in buying services (Berry 2000).

For the pre-purchase evaluation of physical goods such as computers, clothing, sporting goods, and food products, it may be easy for the consumer to determine the attributes of the product before actual purchase because these items can be easily seen, touched, and in some cases, tasted prior to making the purchase. However, the pre-purchase evaluation of service offerings is more difficult (Grace and O'Cass 2004). This is because service attributes can only be discerned after purchase or during consumption or may be impossible to evaluate even after purchase and consumption (Comm and LaBay 1996). For instance, an entertainment or transportation service cannot be packaged and displayed in the same way that Kodak packages and displays film. People may make stock investments through financial services; however, financial services cannot be evaluated within a short period of time. Customers might lose their money in a short-term investment, or they may earn money in a long-term investment. Therefore, service companies must understand that the attributes they present at the outset and during consumption have the greatest potential to impact the consumers' service experience (Grace and O'Cass 2004).

Strong service branded companies strive for excellence, uniqueness, and consistency to be distinctive from competitors in performing and communicating the service (Berry 2000). When customers patronize Starbucks, they purchase the company brand. Starbucks's founder Howard Schultz alluded to the source of the service brand experience in his statement, "Our competitive advantage over the big coffee brands turned out to be our people. Supermarket sales are nonverbal and impersonal, with no personal interaction. But in a Starbucks store, you encounter real people who are informed and excited about the coffee, and enthusiastic about the brand" (Schultz 1997, 247). Another example of a company that is known for its branded service is the Ritz Carlton. The hotel chain is known for exquisite accommodations, exemplary service, and unique experience. The company motto says it all: "We are ladies and gentlemen serving ladies and gentlemen" (www.ritzcarlton.com).

BUILDING A SERVICE BRAND

Although services are typically based upon intangible dimensions, businesses can create strong service brand image to differentiate themselves from the competition. L. L. Berry (2000) suggested two important ways in which service companies build strong brands: develop an identity and make an emotional connection.

Develop an Identity Companies can build a service brand by developing a distinctive identity. Companies such as Toni & Guy, Chick-fil-A, and Dial-A-Mattress all craft a separate, integrated identity, via facilities, service provider appearance, and advertising. Toni & Guy, started by brothers Toni, Guy, Anthony, and Bruno Mascolo, built its brand through identity (Anderson 2006). Toni & Guy has at least 400 hair salons around the world, either

franchised or partially company owned (Fifield 2004). Toni & Guy are known their multilayering, double-cut technique and became popular in the 1960s (Anderson 2006). This differentiates Toni & Guy from the competition, such as Aveda. Toni & Guy position themselves as the most powerful world hairdressing brand with a dynamic and modern image, an innovative company, an educator of hairstylists, with excellent hair care products. Their website mission statement states that Toni & Guy expand the boundaries of hairdressing by delivering creativity, quality, and consistency to every client (Toni & Guy Hairdressing 2006). Mascolo Ltd, Toni & Guy's parent company, operates a dozen Toni & Guy hairdressing schools in Asia, Australia, Europe, and North America, as well as sells branded products in retail stores, such as Boots, the British drugstore.

Quick-service restaurant chain Chick-fil-A tries to establish a distinct brand personality with its dare to be different principle. Competing against large national television advertisers such as McDonald's, Burger King, and Wendy's, Chick-fil-A's brand strategy is to command shopper attention, encourage product trials, and stimulate unplanned purchases. Using cows that urge consumers to eat more chicken, Chick-fil-A reminds consumers that they don't have to eat a hamburger today and presents Chick-fil-A as the alternative. By providing humorous, fun, and different experiences to customers, Chick-fil-A cows give a quick service restaurant chain a more distinct and personable identity (Berry 2000).

Dial-A-Mattress is another company that has developed its own identity. Dial-A-Mattress sells its products 24 hours a day, 7 days a week, and delivers orders as soon as customers want them. Customers also can send the mattress back with the driver if they are not fully satisfied. In addition, the company will remove the customer's old mattress at no additional cost. Napoleon Barragan, founder and president, explained: "Buying a mattress is not a pleasurable experience; it's a chore. If you can make it easy for consumers, if you give them what they want, the way they want it, and when they want it, you can do business" (Berry 2000, 132).

Make an Emotional Connection Strong brands also make an emotional connection with the targeted audience. They transcend specific product features and economic benefits to penetrate consumers' feelings of closeness, affection, and trust (Webber 1997). Aveda, another hair salon, makes an emotional connection with customers through their efforts in corporate social responsibility (Aveda 2006). Contrast Aveda's service position with that of Toni & Guy. Aveda service brand is positioned as an environmentally responsible company offering a holistic salon and store experience (Sacks 2004). Aveda is interested in environmental sustainability and source ingredients from worldwide tradi-tional communities. Aveda's mission seeks to care for the world through the products they make and give back to society to demonstrate an environmental leadership around the world.

St. Paul Saints, a baseball team in St. Paul, Minnesota, one of the best known minor-league baseball teams in the United States, is well known as a brand that makes a strong emotional connection with its fans (See Box 12.1). By being more than just a professional baseball team, the Saints presents its core brand value as "Fun is good" (Berry 2000).

Hallmark Cards, Inc. is a company that creates an emotional connection with customers through its heartfelt television advertising, perfect-for-the-occasion greeting cards, and tear-jerker movies on the Hallmark Channel. With advertising taglines such as, "They'll never forget you remembered" or "Cards work," the company focuses on customers' building relationships with other customers, which always translates into making an emotional connection.

BOX 12.1. ST. PAUL SAINTS

The St. Paul Saints, a minor-league baseball team in St. Paul, Minnesota, sells out every home game and has a long list of people on the season-ticket waiting list. The St. Paul Saints illustrate the emotional content of a strong brand. To most of its fans, the Saints are far more than just a professional baseball team. The Saints are part of the town's culture; a spirited community citizen; a maverick organization with a heart; an organization whose top management greets fans as they enter the ballpark; a team with a blind radio announcer; a team that in 1997 signed the first female pitcher, Ila Borders, ever to pitch on a regular basis for a professional men's baseball team.

The core of the Saints's presented brand is its basic value: "Fun is good." From sumo wrestling to fans racing around the bases in a contest, mini events occur during breaks in the game action. The Saints not only have a pig as the team mascot, [but also] hold an annual contest for elementary school children to name the pig. One thousand schoolchildren participated in the 1998 name-the-pig contest; the winning entry was "The Great Hambino." The Saints hold a "Dead of Winter Tailgate Party Recipe Contest" in their parking lot to raise funds for a nonprofit community organization. An RBI (Reading Books Is Fun) Club attracted 1,000 fourth- and fifth-grade students in 1998 to participate in a reading program. Children plant flowers in the "Reading Tree" area of the stadium, and children and players paint murals on the stadium fence. The team holds a charity golf tournament. The Saints care, and the community knows it; caring is integral to its brand. The St. Paul Saints connect emotionally with their fans and the fans with each other. "Going to a Saints game is like going to your high school reunion," explains General Manager Bill Fanning. "You may not know the people sitting next to you when the game begins, but they are old friends by the time it ends." The St. Paul Saints epitomize every branding principle discussed thus far: The company dares to be different, clearly defines its reason for being, and connects emotionally. For these and other reasons, the St. Paul Saints may be the best known minor-league baseball team in America.

Source: Berry, L. L. 2000. Cultivating service brand equity. *Journal of the Academy of Marketing Science* 28(1): 128–137.

Retailer Branding

Retailer brands are distributed primarily through specialty retailers and catalog companies (Gertner and Stillman 2001). In this sense, the concept is the store as the brand, meaning that both the store and brand communicate the same identity. Examples of these retailer brands are: Abercrombie & Fitch, Ann Taylor, Apple, and Gap.

The company Abercrombie & Fitch controls the operations of four popular casual clothing brands that are each designed to appeal to different market segments. Abercrombie & Fitch appeals to the college-age male and female consumer, while Abercrombie is made more for the 7- to 14-year-old boys and girls crowd. Hollister targets the high school aged consumers, and Ruehl 925's merchandise targets the post-college customers who desire business casual and trendy fashion merchandise. Even though each division of Abercrombie & Fitch is geared toward a specific segment of the market, each Abercrombie & Fitch division sells its clothing and accessories in the single-brand store format. As soon as you walk into any one of these stores, you will hear loud music that is popular among the target age group.

The music and lighting levels are used to give the store a social party atmosphere. To appeal to the customers who are tired or just want to hang out, Abercrombie & Fitch places benches and chairs throughout their stores where customers can sit down and scan through their company magazines. The music, light, associates, seating, and cologne all contribute to the Abercrombie & Fitch consumers' brand image.

Ann Taylor, designer of fine female business and business casual apparel, operates stores under the Mono Brand format with the emphasis on the customer's hedonic experience. Instead of the hip party scene found at the Abercrombie & Fitch stores, Ann Taylor plays up the classy and sophisticated style of female business apparel. The music is calm and soothing, while the lighting in an Ann Taylor store is bright. The sales associates partner up with customers and walk them through the store, while suggesting particular outfits in which they might be interested. This experience becomes the retailer brand.

Another example of a retailer brand store is The Apple Store. The Apple Store brings the meaning of hedonic shopping to a new and exciting level. Each store is well-lit and its format is the same as the Apple products—sleek and modern. The greatest part of The Apple Store experience is that customers have a chance to play with and try out every Apple product before they decide to make a purchase (See Figure 12.4). Each store has numerous iPods, iPhones, iBooks, PowerBooks, eMacs, and accessories displayed on big, broad tables throughout the store (See Figure 12.5). The music heard in the stores is generated by the iPod boom boxes on display at the back of the store, so any customer has the ability to change the songs played throughout the store, giving the illusion that The Apple Store is run by the customers.

12.4 Customers can test out the latest Apple products at a local Apple store.

Since it was founded in 1969, Gap has established itself as a leading specialty retailer, both inside the United States and abroad. Although this apparel retailer has faced numerous financial challenges in the past years, it is still a U.S. leader in apparel retailer branding. Challenges to their success have included varying supply and demand trends and several misinterpretations of fashion trends (Hoover's Company Records 2006). The company has realized that it must refocus on its traditional, conservative apparel. Despite the short-term financial mistakes, Gap Inc. has succeeded in several ways. They have adapted to accommodate customer needs and established themselves as a household brand name for apparel. In addition, Gap Inc. has added a social dimension to its business by joining forces with Product RED, a global business initiative supported by Bono and Bobby Shriver to help people inflicted with AIDS, tuberculosis, and malaria in Africa. A portion of revenues from products produced in Africa go directly to the fund. As of spring 2006, Gap sold 100 percent African-made, men's and women's vintage-style T-shirts in red and a range of other colors. While this collection is based on classic Gap items, it incorporates special details inspired by RED (*Canada Newswire* 2006). Through this line, Gap demonstrates corporate social responsibility.

Although some department stores such as Neiman Marcus and Macy's carry different brands of merchandise, they are labeled as retailer brands because their branded merchandise reflects their identifiable image. Recently, Federated, Macy's parent company, completed its purchases of competing retail firms, such as May Department Stores. With these purchases, Federated has positioned Macy's as a national department brand (Byron 2006). Macy's seeks to strengthen customer relationships by enhancing the store experience and enacting service strategies to support their brand image. Long-time traditions such as the Macy's Thanksgiving parade continue to reinforce the Macy's brand as part of U.S. consumers' life (See Figure 12.6).

Retailer brands thrive on providing the customer with a more hedonic than utilitarian shopping experience. Retailer brands are typically more multisensory in nature than product brands and can rely on rich consumer experiences to impact their identities. With the strategic use of music, lighting, furniture, smell, salespeople, and sometimes beverages, stores such as Abercrombie & Fitch, Ann Taylor, Apple, Gap, and Macy's use the customer experience to create loyalty and repeat patronage.

Shopping Center Branding

In addition to branded products, services, and retailers, consumers increasingly view malls as brands (Caylor 1999, Davies 1992). In this way, the mall becomes the product, and consumption of the product can be linked directly to the shopping experience in the mall itself—its atmosphere, the entertainment it offers, and its

12.5 Apple's iPod is one of the best-selling music players.

12.6 Macy's Thanksgiving Day Parade has become a way of life.

addition to tenant mix, landscaping, architectural style, interior design, music, and special events are all important to creating a positive branded experience. A unique shopping center brand image will result in increased consumer trips.

The Mills Corporation has been very successful in its shopping center branding efforts. Mills has used name branding to denote a certain shopping experience at its huge venues. Each Mills center has 200 or more stores in an average 1.5 million square feet of space and often includes five or six times as many anchor stores as most regional malls. Coupling the Mills name with the location of the Mills project (e.g., Grapevine Mills, Sawgrass Mills, Potomac Mills) has led to destination shopping and these projects have grown into tourist attractions (Gambill 2000). Other examples of branded malls are the Galleria in Dallas and Houston, Forum Shops in Las Vegas, Mall of America in Minneapolis, and West Edmonton Mall in Canada.

BRAND COMMUNITY

A community tends to be identified on the basis of commonality or relationships among its members, whether it refers to a neighborhood, an occupation, a leisure pursuit, or a devotion to a brand. Through a community, members share cognitive, emotional, or material resources that are instrumental to their well-being (McAlexander, Schouten, and Koenig 2002). Based upon this concept, a **brand community** is referred to as "a specialized, non-geographically bound community, based on a structured set of social relationships among admirers of a brand" (Muñiz and O'Guinn 1996, 412). The idea of brand communities was introduced and sparked by ethnographic research on the extremely loyal customers of Harley-Davidson motorcycles (Schouten and McAlexander

range of goods and services. The lack of an established, recognizable brand is causing regional shopping centers to decline in popularity.

The assortment of preferred anchor and nonanchor tenants and the existence of stores that target customers contributes to branding of that shopping center. Also, to create a distinctive and successful shopping center brand, the tenant mix must have a relatively high degree of uniqueness in the market area, without containing the same anchor tenants and the similar array of nonanchor tenants (Rabianski 2001). In

1995) and the television series Star Trek (Kozinets 1997).

Marketplace communities can be traced back to what D. J. Boorstin (1974) called "consumption communities." Boorstin described consumption communities as "invisible new communities . . . created and preserved by how and what men consumed" (89). He supported this statement with his observation of the shifting sense of community. He further argues that in the emerging consumer culture that followed the industrial revolution, the sense of community shifted away from the geographically bound interpersonal bonds to the common but tenuous bonds of brand use and affiliation. Thus, brand communities are groups of people held together by the bond of a shared consumable. Through events and activities to promote the brand, the company physically brings together its community of customers to share experiences, lifestyles, and collective culture (Muñiz and O'Guinn 1996).

Brand community members spread the brand message, as well as enthusiasm for it into the market. Also, brand community members receive information about the brand from others and provide market feedback to retailers or manufacturers. Numerous brand communities have websites or Web pages maintained by the members. On these websites, members can share their recent experiences with products, gossip about brand rumors via forums and other member postings, as well as read recent media publications about the company. A good example of a website run by community members is www.lexusownersclub.com. The main page of the Lexus Owners Club is dedicated to informing members about current events and future plans having to do with Toyota/Lexus Motor Company. After signing in, members can select one of four regional chapters, or branches, to interact with: the United Kingdom branch, the USA branch, the New Zealand branch, or the Euro branch. In this way, the Lexus brand community has a worldwide presence.

Brand communities can also be experienced by visiting a H.O.G. (Harley-Davidson) rally or Jeep Jamboree (See Figures 12.7), participating in a Saturn homecoming, or going to a DeWalt contractors' night at the local lumberyard. In these settings, invisible consumption communities are converted into visible ones (McAlexander, Schouten, and Koenig 2002). These communities often orchestrate group gatherings where community members get the opportunity to meet and greet one another. These gatherings often evolve into a major social event. In addition to seasonal Harley-Davidson bike rallies, the Jeep Freaks routinely meet in the mountains and trails around the nation and hold Jeep Jamborees. The Jeep Jamborees consist of hundreds of proud Jeep owners meeting to show off their automotive works of art. From factory stock models to extremely modified Jeeps, big and small, they hit the trails for some good old-fashioned off-road fun. On www.jeepjamboreeusa.com, Jeep enthusiasts can sign up to enter Jeep Jamborees, rate and review

12.7 Harley-Davidson has a brand community called H.O.G.

off-road trails, and even buy Jeep Jamboree apparel (See Figure 12.8). Truck manufacturers such as Ford and Chevrolet also have communities like the Jeep community.

More recently, the Apple iPod was introduced to the Apple Computer community and has been attracting new members unlike any community ever before. One of the newest brand communities on the rise is the Starbucks community. Ever since the rapid worldwide expansion of the luxury coffee shop, extremely loyal brand community consumers have described Starbucks coffee as addictive.

As such, brand communities tend to be a tight-knit group of people who are brought together through the same level of enthusiasm and loyalty for a particular brand or product. Brand community members insist on staying in touch with one another via websites on the Internet; community members love meeting up with one another a few times a year at social events.

12.8 Jeep Jamborees from around the world are forming a brand community.

BRAND EXPERIENCE

Branding is an experience rather than a collective mass of individual properties. Branding "starts first and foremost with the experience. If the shop or the customer can have a very particular type of experience that is different, that is unique, that is special, that is identifiable, then you are on your way to branding. It is an overall experience rather than a multiple number of properties" (Caylor 1999, 74). To understand branding, a consumer-oriented approach is needed for addressing the experiences of consumers in retail settings. This entails investigating how brand attributes are related to aspects of the consumption experience, which is the foundation for understanding the total experience.

Brand Attributes

As early as 1955, S. J. Levy suggested that consumers buy products or brands not only because of their attributes and functional consequences, but also for the symbolic meanings associated with them. After Levy, several researchers have proposed brand attribute typologies. They include objective and subjective (Alpert 1971), utilitarian and value expressive (Katz 1960), utilitarian and symbolic (Levy 1959), and utilitarian and experiential/hedonic (Holbrook and Hirschman 1982). These typologies lead to the consensus that branding can be viewed as a total experience encompassing both utilitarian aspects and hedonic aspects. Utilitarian attributes correspond to a cognitive and rational evaluation of the brand based on its objective characteristics and the performance of its physical attributes. On the contrary, hedonic attributes have been associated with the emotional aspect of the brand, which is based upon more subjective and expressive aspects, such as the sensations associated with the brand and the lifestyles associated with the typical user of the brand (Vázquez, Del Río, and Iglesias 2002).

Utilitarian and hedonic aspects of brands are linked to the fact that consumers often imbue brands with human personality traits. G. Fullerton (2005) argued that a consumer's interaction with the brand personality contributes to a continuation of buying the retail brand. This is the type of association successful retailers must create among the product, service, brand, and experience. Both utilitarian and hedonic attributes were exemplified by B. Mittal, B. Ratchford, and P. Prabhakar (1990) who listed possible brand attributes of perfume as follows:

- Functional (utilitarian): lasts long, is strong, is mild, is convenient to apply, does not irritate the skin, masks body odor, adjusts to different skin types, combines more than one fragrance
- Expressive (hedonic): appears prestigious, has attractive bottle shape, will impress people, is for fanciful people, is masculine, is feminine, shows sophistication, is for people who show off, is effective in attracting others

Using the same concept, retail attributes of a shopping center can be illustrated as follows:

- Utilitarian: well-located, convenient, inexpensive, informative, functional, courteous, safe, educational, family-friendly
- Hedonic: modern, pleasant, relaxing, adventurous, casual, fashionable, sophisticated, exciting, classic, attractive, unique

D. A. Aaker (1996) linked several human personality types to specific brands, as illustrated in Table 12.2. Two elements affect an individual's relationship with a brand. The first element is the relationship between the brand-as-person and the customer. This is similar to the relationship between two people. The second

TABLE 12.2 BRAND AND PERSONALITY

PERSONALITY	BRANDS
Down-to-earth, family oriented, genuine, old-fashioned (sincerity)	This might describe brands such as Hallmark, Kodak, and even Coca-Cola. The relationship might be similar to one that exists with a well-liked and respected member of the family.
Spirited, young, up-to-date, outgoing (excitement)	In the soft-drink category, Pepsi fits this mold more than Coca-Cola. Especially on weekends, it might be enjoyable to spend time with a friend who has these personality characteristics.
Accomplished, influential, competent (competence)	Perhaps Hewlett-Packard and the *Wall Street Journal* might fit this profile. Think of a relationship with a person whom you respect for their accomplishments, such as a teacher, minister, or business leader.
Pretentious, wealthy, condescending (sophistication)	For some, this would be BMW, Mercedes, or Lexus (with gold trim), as opposed to the Mazda Miata or the VW Golf. The relationship could be similar to one with a powerful boss or rich relative.
Athletic and outdoorsy (ruggedness)	Nike (versus L. A. Gear) and Wells Fargo (versus Bank of America) are examples. When planning an outing, a friend with outdoorsy interests would be welcome.

Source: Aaker, D. A. 1996. *Building strong brands.* New York: The Free Press.

element is the brand personality that reflects the type of person the brand represents. The formation of the brand-customer relationship is not limited to functional benefits, just as two people can have a strictly business relationship. The relationship can be further developed by the depth of feelings the customer has toward the brand.

Total Brand Experience

Experiential retailing aims to provide consumers with compelling and memorable experiences each time they buy a brand. According to John V. Bum, partner of Brand XP and former marketing director of Heijieken NV in Latin America and the Caribbean, "experiential clues are more than just the physical, rational delivery of the benefits of your key brand. They are also the summation of all rational and emotional touching points you have with the consumer. This connection leaves an impression that is evident and provides sufficient impact to become an experience" (Cortes 2004, 41). John Bum elaborated his brand experiences with the following statements:

> Recently, I was boarding a British Airways flight to London for a business meeting. While waiting for the plane to take off, all I could think about was the fact that for the past two weeks I have been away from home traveling and now was taking off again for a seven-day trip, away from my wife and daughters. While all this was playing in my head, the plane took off. . . . Then, when dinner was served, I noticed a small folded card on the corner of my tray that read, "We know how you are feeling, and inside is a number that can help you." When I opened the card, there was a message from

AT&T long distance with a list of numbers to help "stay in touch with your loved ones" from practically anywhere in the world. The mix of brand messages in this situation—the cost of the card, one cent, with an emotional connection—was priceless! (Cortes 2004, 41).

Emphasizing emotional attributes leads customers to enhance the brand experience, to make quicker purchasing decisions, and to develop stronger loyalty to a brand. Thus, strong emotions seem to be integral to brand experiences, consumer decisions, and customer loyalty. The emotional bond between companies and customers is difficult to break, while rational benefits can be easily copied by competition. Hence, strong emotion can build a strong barrier for competitors to surmount (Crosby and Johnson 2002). However, companies compete best when they combine both utilitarian and hedonic benefits into their offerings. Retail strategies that deliver total customer experiences consistently create superior customer value, making it very difficult for competitors to copy them (Haeckel, Carbone, and Berry 2003).

Sony Corp. opened its concept store in Malaysia to provide a "One Sony Experience" and create wider exposure for its expanding product range. With features such as a children's playroom, nursing room for mothers, and concierge service with a lime-green and orange color scheme for shoppers, the store offers a friendly shopping environment where families can explore products and communicate with staff members at the store before making purchases. Masaki Nakayama, manager of the Sony direct stores, stated, "It is a lifestyle concept brand that integrates with the Sony website, emerging as an exciting retail outlet offering a total One Sony Experience" (White 2005, 11).

In sum, branding can be successfully built by understanding consumers' total shopping experience derived from fulfilling utilitarian functions and enjoying the pleasure achieved through consumption. Retailers should differentiate themselves through branding that represents a specific type of experience in the retail environment. They should make concerted efforts to create an overall brand image from all individual products and services underneath the retail brand.

CHAPTER SUMMARY

In the mature U.S. marketplace where a multitude of products and brands are available, product quality and pricing strategies are no longer effective to entice the masses to purchase a company's offering. As consumers are more brand-oriented than ever, branding can be used to a retailer's competitive advantage. Branding is an overall experience that is different, unique, special, and identifiable. The survival of a retailer depends upon delivering a brand experience to consumers that includes both utilitarian and hedonic benefits. The retail mix should be shaped based on the degrees of utilitarian and hedonic experiences their target consumers desire.

The concept of branding has evolved from products, to service, to retailers (e.g., brick-and-mortar stores, the Internet), and to shopping centers. The concept of product branding has been discussed primarily in terms of tangible attributes that differentiate a brand from all other products. Examples of successful product branding are Levi's, Nike, and Coca-Cola. Approaches to product branding include individual product branding (i.e., an approach whereby new products are assigned different names with no connection to other existing brands offered by the parent company), family branding (i.e., the

strategy whereby new products are placed under the same umbrella as the existing company brand), private branding (i.e., developing brands that are owned by a particular retailer), and co-branding (i.e., joining two existing brands to create a synergy). With service branding, the company becomes its own brand by increasing customers' trust of the invisible purchase by reducing perceived monetary, social, or safety risk in buying services.

Retailer branding is developed by specialty stores or catalog companies that exclusively develop and distribute their own brands, such as Gap, Apple, and Abercrombie & Fitch. Department stores such as Neiman Marcus and Macy's have become retailer brands because the merchandise they carry reflect the brand image of the store. Most recently, the branding concept has been extended to shopping centers, prompted by the lack of established, recognizable branding of regional shopping centers. Successful branded shopping centers include Galleria, Mall of America, and Forum Shops.

People who show enthusiasm and loyalty toward a particular brand become a brand community. Brand community members, therefore, share experiences and collective culture through events, activities, and communicating via websites. Well-known brand communities are Jeep Jamboree and H.O.G. (Harley-Davidson).

In sum, branding can be successfully built by understanding consumers' total shopping experience derived from fulfilling utilitarian functions and enjoying the pleasure achieved through consumption. As such, retailers should differentiate themselves through branding that represents a specific type of experience in the retail environment. The growth of experiential retailing is not exemplified by a single transaction, but rather is sustainable because it is founded on a long-term customer relationship.

Discussion Questions

1. Why is branding becoming increasingly important in retailing?
2. Describe the benefits consumers receive from purchasing branded products. Explain their value and support your arguments with examples.
3. Are Wal-Mart and Target perceived as brands? Provide the justification for each.
4. How is product branding different from service branding?
5. How is retailer branding different from product branding?
6. Identify some successful retailers who are providing total consumer experience. Explain how they implement strategies to provide total consumer experience.
7. Discuss the situations in which a retailer benefits from having private brands, and explain how private branding should be implemented.
8. Identify two branded shopping centers, and explain why they have been successful.
9. How are brand communities developed, and how do they support the brand? Provide specific retailer examples in your explanation.

References

Aaker, D. A. 1991. *Managing brand equity: Capitalizing on the value of a brand name.* New York: The Free Press.

———. 1996. *Building strong brands.* New York: The Free Press.

Aaker, Jennifer L. 1997. Dimensions of brand personality. *Journal of Marketing Research* 34(3):347–356.

Alpert, M. 1971. Identification of determinant attributes: A comparison of methods. *Journal of Marketing Research* 8:184–191.

Anderson, S. 2006. Mascolo Ltd., *Hoovers* 101734.

Aveda. 2006. Information retrieved from Aveda website, August 25, 2006.

Badenhausen, K., and M. Rodney, 2005. Next generation. *Forbes Global* 8(11):36–37.

Berry, L. L. 2000. Cultivating service brand equity. *Journal of the Academy of Marketing Science* 28(1):128–137.

Boone, L. E., and D. L. Kurtz. 1998. *Contemporary marketing.* New York: The Dryden Press.

Boorstin, D. J. 1974. *The Americans: The democratic experience.* New York: Vintage.

Boush, D., S. Shipp, B. Loken, E. Gencturk, S. Crockett, E. Kennedy, B. Minshall, D. Misurell, L. Rochford, and J. Strobel. 1987. Affect Generalization to Similar and Dissimilar Brand Extensions. *Psychology and Marketing* 4(3):225–237.

Briggs, W. 2001. Global branding. *Communication World* 18(2):29–31.

Burt, S. 2000. The strategic role of retail brands in British grocery retailing *European Journal of Marketing* 34(8):875–90.

Byron, E. 2006. Macy's Markets National Brand and Changes Face of Shopping. *Wall Street Journal.* March 22, B3C.

Canada Newswire. 2006. Gap joins product RED, a global effort supporting Africa. January 26. Retrieved May 9, 2006 from LexisNexis.

Caylor, P. 1999. Branding: What's in a name! *National Real Estate Investor* 41(6):72–75.

Choi, Chan S. and Anne T. Coughlan. 2006. Private label positioning: Quality versus feature differentiation from the national brand. *Journal of Retailing* 82(2):79–93.

Clark, J. 2004. Atlanta's hotel Indigo: High style, nice price. Retrieved May

19, 2006 from www.usatoday.com/travel/hotels/2004-07-22-style-price_x.htm.

Cobb-Walgren, C. J., C. A. Ruble, and N. Donthu. 1995. Brand equity, brand preference, and purchase intent. *Journal of Advertising* 24(3):25–40.

Comm, C. L., and D. G. LaBay. 1996. Repositioning colleges using changing student quality perceptions: an exploratory analysis. *Journal of Marketing for Higher Education* 7(4):21–34.

Cortes, R. 2004. Create emotional connections with consumer. *Caribbean Business* 32(41):41.

Crosby, L. A., and S. L. Johnson. 2002. Managing the future. *Marketing Management* 11(6):10–11.

Davies, G. 1992. The two ways in which retailers can be brands. *International Journal of Retail and Distribution Management* 20(2):24–34.

Fifield, A. 2004. Brit-hair rules, OK?: Anna Fifield considers the rise and rise of the UK's star hairdressers and tries to find the secret ingredients in the conditioner. *Financial Times*. May 1, 10.

Fullerton, G. 2005. The Impact of Brand Commitment on Loyalty to Retail Service Brands. *Canadian Journal of Administrative Sciences* 22(2):97–110.

Gambill, M. 2000. Shopping center branding: Does it make sense? *Real Estate Issues* 25(1):13–27.

Gertner, R. H., and Robert S. Stillman. 2001. Vertical integration and internet strategies in the apparel industry. *Journal of Industrial Economics* 49(4):417–441.

Grace, Debra, and Aron. O'Cass. 2004. Examining service experiences and postconsumption evaluations. *Journal of Services Marketing* 18(6):450–461.

Grossman, Randi Priluck. 1997. Co-branding in advertising: developing effective associations. *Journal of Prod-*

uct and Brand Management 6(3):191–201.

Haeckel, S. H., L. P. Carbone, and L. L Berry. 2003. How to Lead the Customer Experience. *Marketing Management* 12(1):18–23.

Halstead, D., and C. B. Ward. 1995. Assessing the vulnerability of private label brands. *Journal of Product and Brand Management* 4(3):38–48.

Herstein, R., and E. Gamliel. 2006. The role of private branding in improving service quality. *Managing Service Quality* 16(3):306–319.

Holbrook, M., and E. Hirschman. 1982. The experiential aspects of consumption: Consumer fantasies, feelings, and fun. *Journal of Consumer Research* 9:132–140.

Hoover's Company Records. 2006. Gap Inc, retrieved May 9, 2006 from Pro-Quest.

Jevons, C., M. Gabbott, and L. de Chernatony. 2005. Customer and brand manager perspectives on brand relationships: a conceptual framework. *Journal of Product and Brand Management* 14(5):300–309.

Katz, D. 1960. The functional approach to the study of attitudes. *Public Opinion quarterly* 24:163–204.

Kotler, P., and G. Armstrong. 1996. *Principles of marketing*. Upper Saddle River, NJ: Prentice Hall.

Kozinets, R. 1997. I want to believe: A netography of the X-Philes subculture of consumption. In M. Brucks and D. MacInnis, eds. *Advances in Consumer Research,* Vol. 24 (475). Provo, UT: Association for Consumer Research.

Levy, S. J. 1959. Symbols for sale. *Harvard Business Review* 37:117–119.

Lodging Hospitality. 2004. IHG goes retail with Indigo. 60(9):14.

Lozito, W. 2004. Brands: More than a name. *Restaurant Hospitality* 88(9):56–60.

Mahajan, V., and Y. Wind. 2002. Got emotional product positioning? *Marketing Management* 11(3):36–41.

McAlexander, J. H., J. W. Schouten, and H. F. Koenig. 2002. Building brand community. *Journal of Marketing* 66(1):38–54.

Mittal, B., B. Ratchford, and P. Prabhakar. 1990. Functional and expressive attributes as determinants of brand-attitude. *Research in Marketing* 10:135–155.

Muniz, A., and T. O'Guinn. 1996. Brand community and the sociology of brands. In K. P. Corfman and J. G. Lynch, eds., *Advances in Consumer Research*, Vol. 23 (265–266). Provo, UT: Association for Consumer Research.

Principles of Marketing. 2006. Approaches to branding . Retrieved May 6, 2006 from www.knowthis. com/tutorials/principles_of_marketing/managing_products/4.htm

Rabianski, J. 2001. Shopping center branding: Is it worth the effort? *Retail Estate Review*. Winter, 29–39.

Sacks, D. 2004. It's easy being green. *Fast Company* 85:50–51.

Samu, S., H. S. Krishnan, and R. E. Smith. 1999. Using advertising alliances for new product introduction: Interactions between product complementarity and promotional strategies. *Journal of Marketing* 63(1):57–74.

Schouten, J. W., and J. H. McAlexander. 1995. Subcultures of consumption: An ethnography of the new bikers. *Journal of Consumer Research* 22(1):43–61.

Schultz, H. 1997. *Pour your heart into it*. New York: Hyperion.

Speros, J. 2004. Why the Harley's brand is so hot. *Advertising Age* 75(11):26–26

Toni & Guy Hairdressing. 2006. Accessed August 29, 2006, from www.toniguy.com/home/index.html.

Vázquez, R., A. B. Del Río, and V. Iglesias. 2002. Consumer-based brand equity: Development and validation of a measurement instrument. *Journal of Marketing Management* 18(1/2):27–48.

Washburn, J. H., B. D. Till, and R. Priluck. 2000. Co-branding: Brand equity and trial effects. *Journal of Consumer Marketing* 17(7):591–604.

Webber, S. P. 1997. Some stores are so unique, they double as attractions. *Travel Agent* 286(6):12–12.

Wellman, D. 1997. Souping up private label. *Supermarket Business* 52(10):13–20.

White, A. 2005. Sony woos Malaysia with Style roll-outs. *Media Asia*. August, 11.

BRAND EXTENSION

Soft Drink Makers Seek New Forms of Refreshment

Coca-Cola's decision to launch a lime-flavored version of its flagship beverage is hardly revolutionary. But the innovation marked the start of a crucial year for the soft drinks industry, with a series of product launches and brand extensions planned to reinvigorate sales in 2005. Soft drink makers have been hit by a consumer shift away from sugary carbonated beverages such as Coke and Pepsi toward healthier beverages, such as bottled water and juices.

Sales of carbonated soft drinks (CSD) in North American supermarkets fell 3.5 percent in November [2005] and 3.9 percent in December [2005], signaling an acceleration of the trend as people become more concerned about rising levels of obesity. "Health and obesity is the most serious issue this industry has faced," said Mike Weinstein, former chief executive of Snapple Beverage Group, at a recent conference. "Our industry is built on image and the image has been seriously damaged."

Coca-Cola, PepsiCo, and their smaller rivals have responded by diversifying from their core cola brands into water, juices, teas, and energy drinks. However, while Coke and Pepsi dominate the soda market, they face greater competition and weaker brand loyalty in noncarbonated segments. Against this backdrop, soft drink companies are seeking ways to stem the exodus of consumers from sodas while at the same time strengthening their noncarbonated brands. In addition to the launch of Coca-Cola with Lime, the company also is believed to be developing a new low-calorie cola. Both innovations are part of Coca-Cola chairman Neville Isdell's promise to restore growth momentum to the flagship brand. Coca-Cola is poised to launch a new energy drink, called Full Throttle, to compete with Red Bull, the privately owned Austrian brand that has secured more than half its segment. Meanwhile, both Coca-Cola and PepsiCo are introducing fruit-flavored bottled water sold at a premium to regular water.

The companies—which sell water under the Dasani and Aquafina brands, respectively—hope the innovation will increase brand loyalty and provide relief from the fierce price war raging in the water market. However, William Pecoriello, analyst at Morgan Stanley, is sceptical. "It's a long shot that the new products announced thus far will be enough to offset continued weakness in the CSD category," he said in a recent report. Mr. Pecoriello doubts that low-calorie sodas will protect beverage companies from the obesity backlash because many health-conscious consumers are suspicious of the artificial sweeteners used in diet drinks. Morgan Stanley research found that only 14 percent of consumers consider diet sodas healthy.

In addition to health concerns, the soft drink market also is suffering from price inflation caused by the rising cost of raw materials and packaging. This is encouraging more consumers to opt for retailers' cheaper own-brand sodas, which command 11 percent of the U.S. market. Analysts credit PepsiCo with handling the industry's challenges better than Coca-Cola, diversifying into snack food through its Frito-Lay division and acquiring strong noncarbonated drink brands, such as Gatorade and Tropicana. Coca-Cola, by contrast, with 119 years of history behind its flagship brand, has been more cautious about branching out. Analysts say the company's focus on Coke makes it ill-equipped to develop and nurture new products, pointing to last year's disappointing launch of C2, a reduced-calorie cola. "Pepsi has an engine of growth in Frito-Lay that gives it the confidence and cash to innovate and take risks on the beverage side. Coke lacks that confidence," says Nick Hahn, former global director of marketing for Coca-Cola and now managing director of Vivaldi Partners, a marketing strategy firm. "Rather than relying on brand extensions such as Coke's addition of lime," says Mr. Pecoriello, "soft drink companies must develop new beverages that break the existing product paradigms."

Source: Ward, Andrew. 2005. *Financial Times*. January 10, 27.

INTRODUCTION

Brand extension, through which firms introduce their brands into new product lines, involves the application of an established core brand name to new products. A **core brand** name is associated with a particular set of attributes based upon a consumer's association with that brand. As a new brand extension is introduced, it will have its own set of attributes that may either be consistent with, or inconsistent with, the core brand's image (Riel, Lemmink, and Ouwersloot 2001). The image that consumers hold regarding a particular core brand is composed of two distinct types of brand concepts: function-oriented and prestige-oriented concepts. A function-oriented brand concept emphasizes the product performance such as reliability or durability, as in the case of Timex or Tupperware. A prestige-oriented brand concept is associated with images related to luxury and status as in the case of Rolex or Rolls Royce.

Well-known brands can expand within the same product category and beyond the product category where the firm originally built its reputation (Riel et al. 2001). Steve and Barry's University Sportswear, which operates more than 130 stores across the United States, has recently expanded its list of lifestyle brands by generating contracts with General Mills, Coors Brewing Company, and Yamaha Motor Corporation. These deals revolve around a mix of merchandise for men, women, and children based upon the three companies' brand names such as Betty Crocker, Cheerios, Yamaha Rhino 660 side-by-side vehicles, Coors, and Killian's (Wilensky 2006).

Other recent extensions can be observed in retail categories such as home furnishings, jewelry, and coffee. Pulaski Furniture Corporation is assisting Build-A-Bear Workshop in designing a line of furniture and home décor items for and by kids (Wilensky 2006). Jewelry Brands Group has produced a collection of baby-Gund fine jewelry, gifts, and tabletop merchandise that includes tennis bracelets, necklaces, charms, rattles, cups, spoons, and ornaments made of fine gems and metals (Wilensky 2005). Starbucks launched a ready-to-drink coffee drink that is milky and sweet with light and regular varieties. It is sold nationally at convenience stores and is targeted to appeal to Starbucks coffee lovers (*National Petroleum News* 2006). Each of these extensions has the potential for success because they build upon a strong brand name and image.

BENEFITS AND RISKS OF BRAND EXTENSION

Companies with a strong brand name and image, such as Coke, Apple, and Procter & Gamble, are in good positions to extend their product lines to increase profits and build brand awareness (Taylor and Bearden 2002). Apple's entrance into the portable media player category with iPod resulted in 24.8 million digital music players sold at retail price in 2005, representing a 250 percent growth from unit sales in 2004 (Heller 2006).

While many companies are successful with brand extensions, some brand extensions are mistakes. According to IRI Research, the success rate of a new product is reduced by half if consumers are not already aware of part of the product's name (Bashford 2004). As a result, there are many brand extension failures. Failure stories include a Harley-Davidson cake-decorating kit, a padded bra filled with Evian water, Budweiser's "B to the power of e" energy beer, the Everlast fragrance and grooming line, Sylvester Stallone high-protein pudding, and Lycra hair spray (Kenneth 2005). Laura Ries, president of marketing consultancy Ries and Ries, Atlanta, recently stated, "Line extensions are damaging. The more things you put your name on, the weaker the brand becomes" (Kenneth 2005, 8).

Richard Branson's company Virgin is a prime example of brand extension gone too far. Branson successfully extended Virgin music labels to Virgin Airlines, but his attempts to break into other markets with Virgin Vodka, Virgin Mobile, and Virgin Cosmetics failed (Roberto and Roberto 2005). Virgin cola products have had the same bad fate. S. Bashford (2004) believed that Branson got carried away with extending product lines. David Taylor, author of *Brand Stretch*, said Virgin went wrong when it forgot why it was famous.

Virgin is known as being irreverent, fun, and challenging and its new products failed to reflect Virgin's values (Bashford 2004).

Benefits of Brand Extension

Brand extensions can be very beneficial to a company's bottom line. Major benefits of brand extension strategies include building a strong brand position, increasing the probability of trial, reducing entry barriers, and reducing advertising costs.

BUILD STRONG BRAND POSITIONING

The systematic extension of a brand can strengthen its position in the consumer market for different reasons. First, the value of a brand in signaling quality can be elevated as the number of products associated with the brand increases (Wernerfelt 1988). Second, preference toward a brand increases with increased exposure or as a brand is used on multiple products. Finally, successful extensions lead to positive consumer evaluations of the core brand (Keller and Aaker 1992).

Robert Passikoff, president of Brand Keys, Inc., a research firm that specializes in customer loyalty, said "Bebe has been [so] successful in translating the sexy image to resonate with women that its brand means more than just clothing . . . It stands for something—people are buying meaning. They're not just buying a pair of pants. On a relative basis, they have a stronger emotional bond with their customers than the other boutiques we look at" (Owen 2006). Bebe draws on the strength of its brand with new Bebe brands that expand its category offerings. The brand extension BEBE SPORT was launched in 2003 inside their existing stores and on the Internet. Several more BEBE SPORT stand-alone stores have already opened and more are planned for the future (Owen 2006).

INCREASE THE PROBABILITY OF TRIAL

Brand extension is more effective with stronger brands than with weaker ones. Brand extension research reveals that brand attitude can be defined more precisely in terms of consumer perceptions of quality associated with a brand (Aaker and Keller 1990). D. Aaker and K. Keller stated: "If a brand is associated with high quality, the extension should benefit; if it is associated with inferior quality, the extension should be harmed" (29). As a related concept, consumers often rely upon a recognizable brand as a means of decreasing perceived risk (Roselius 1973). Even if consumers do not have personal experience in buying and consuming an extension of a well-known brand, the brand name can still serve as a vehicle for reducing risk (Wernerfelt 1988). In short, the strength of a brand is linked to its ability to reduce perceived risk. Brands of higher quality should provide greater risk relief, which can encourage trial with less investment than brands of lower quality.

Pottery Barn, a lifestyle specialty store, used a brand extension strategy to enter the children's market. They began to sell products that appealed to children in their Pottery Barn Kids stores. They also developed a line for the teenage consumer called PBteen that is available through its own catalog and on the Internet at www.pbteen.com. PBteen offers teenagers creative accessories for their rooms. The strength of Pottery Barn's reputation appeals to parents who are spending money on their children. The success of Pottery Barn's brand extension contributed to a 22.7 percent increase in children's sales between 2003 and 2004 (French 2005).

REDUCE ENTRY BARRIERS

While brands can be a barrier to entry into new categories, they also can be the means of entry. If existing brand names are well-known, they can serve as a way for a company to enter a new category that would otherwise be impossible to enter. In extending an established brand name to a new product, the company can use the brand name as a signal of the quality of the product (Wernerfelt 1988). For instance, Reese's, a division of The Hershey Company, identified peanut butter as a logical brand extension. Thus, the Reese's brand could easily enter the peanut butter category with the Hershey name (Tauber 2004). In effect, brand extensions allow a company to capitalize on the already-established recognition, reputation, and brand equity of an existing brand. Further, positive brand equity can be enhanced at a lower cost than is required to introduce a completely new product. When this extension is done effectively, it reinforces the image of the existing parent product through synergy. Thus, sales of a parent product can sometimes rise after the launch of a successful brand extension (Tauber 2004).

Sean Combs, also known as P. Diddy, was first known for his Grammy-award-winning music. He extended his personal brand by launching an apparel line. His first collection in 1999 was jeans, T-shirts, and baseball caps (Agins 2004). His reputation contributed to the rapid success of his full line of menswear with urban apparel appeal. Combs's products have luxury appeal and his personal image contributes to his brand equity (Betts, Larenaudie, Morton, and Mustafa 2004).

REDUCE ADVERTISING COSTS

Brand extensions provide the opportunity for consumers to have increased exposure to a brand in multiple product contexts. This increased exposure also should reduce the amount of additional information consumers need to evaluate the extended product. This, in turn, generates a greater level of sales from a given advertising investment. In addition, a company can attain its sales objectives with less investment in advertising than would be necessary to develop consumer awareness of and consumer trust in a new brand.

Companies that extend their brands can capitalize on spill-over effects from advertising for other products affiliated with the brand. In other words, by reinforcing consumers' impressions of the existing brand, advertising may indirectly stimulate demand for the extensions. Victoria's Secret has established brand equity in its customers' minds. This allows The Limited Company to spend less on promoting and advertising their products because the existing brand has a reputation on which Victoria's Secret can stand.

Risks of Brand Extensions

Brand extensions always have an element of uncertainty associated with them. It is estimated that about 80 percent of brand extensions in fast-moving consumer good (FMCG) product categories fail (Sattler and Volckner 2006). Therefore, parent brands should seriously consider the risks associated with this popular branding strategy.

An extension can dilute the brand equity because it could create confusion or negative connotations in consumers' minds. In addition, an extension could cannibalize the company's other products if the extended product is not adequately distanced from the original product (Grime, Diamantopoulos, and Smith 2002). It is particularly important to avoid careless brand extensions that can damage the brand and potentially create permanent negative effects on the parent company (*Journal of Consumer Marketing* 1997).

New products or services extended from core products or services must address a specific consumer need. Unless a new product or service is developed based upon consumer demand, it will fail because it does not attract a significant consumer group. A parent brand's position should be able to connect to the market position of the new product or service. This requires conducting market research to determine how to best make a connection. It should define what aspect of the brand can be brought into this new position. Finally, the company must deliver on the new message from an extended brand.

TYPES OF BRAND EXTENSION

There are two types of brand extension: horizontal and vertical extension. Horizontal brand extension occurs when an existing brand name is applied to a new product or service. Vertical brand extension occurs when companies introduce new product lines under the same brand name.

Horizontal Brand Extension

A **horizontal brand extension** is used when an existing brand name is extended to a new product or service, either in a similar product or service class or in a category completely new to the firm. Introducing horizontal brand extension is a useful strategy because the equity that has built up within the core brand is projected upon the new product or service (Kim, Lavack, and Smith 2001).

In the case of a horizontal brand extension into a similar product or service category, the extension exhibits the similar level of prestige, status, or quality as the core brand. An example of horizontal brand extension is illustrated by several lifestyle retail brands—Next and Next for Men, Next Boys and Girls, Next Interiors, and Next Directory (Riel et al. 2001).

Extending brands to similar categories can also be exemplified with a number of apparel designers who have extended their brands into home furnishings. This type of brand extension is a result of taking advantage of the growth in the home furnishings industry, which is mainly derived from more affluent consumers and the cocooning effect. Because the aging population has the money and inclination to invest in soft goods, apparel designers and retailers are moving into the home furnishings category. As a result, home furnishings sales are likely to outpace the growth in the apparel market for years to come. Spiegel has experienced stronger growth in home furnishings than in apparel; Saks Fifth Avenue, which phased out its home-and-gift departments in stores, has introduced a catalog to fill the void; and some stores, such as Iverson, are reallocating their floor space to include home furnishings products.

The trend of fashion crossover between clothing and home furnishings forces designers and manufacturers to cross-brand between clothing and home furnishings products. Thus, home fashions mirror clothing fashions as can be seen in the work of designers such as Calvin Klein, Donna Karan, Liz Clairborne, Versace, and Guess. This phenomenon actually exists in many areas in the retail market. Ready-to-wear fashions in apparel have proven to be an inspiration for patterns and hues in everything from sheets to decorative pillows and casual slipcovers. Retailers are increasingly combining home furnishing soft good products with ready-to-wear clothing in a single store environment for shoppers to cross-shop between clothing and home furnishings products. This type of experience offers customers a total look and a unique shopping experi-

ence. J. C. Forney, E. J. Park, and L. Brandon (2005) found image, quality, color/style, and design/beauty were important criteria used to purchase extended brands of casual apparel and home furnishings. Image of fashion products was the strongest predictor when apparel brands were extended to home furnishings brands. This finding suggests that retailers need to focus on brand or store image when they extend an apparel brand to home furnishings.

Horizontal brand extensions are not necessarily limited to a similar product category. Marketers often try to capitalize on previously acquired brand equity by extending brands to dissimilar categories or by introducing extensions containing attributes that are inconsistent with those of the core brand (Taylor and Bearden 2002). Chicago-based Sara Lee Corporation has a diverse line of product brands. It manufactures and markets many key brands in the food and beverage, household and body, and branded apparel industries (www.saralee.com). The brands in the food business include Ball Park, Earth Grains, Ironkids, Jimmy Dean, Maison du Café, and Sara Lee. The household and body care brands include AmbiPur, Kiwi, and Sanex. The branded apparel brands include Bali, Champion, Hanes, Just My Size, and Playtex. Brand differentiation has been successful in the past for Sara Lee because the brand names are well-associated with the products they represent. Ball Park is synonymous with hot dogs, Champion with athletic wear, Jimmy Dean with sausage, and Hanes with hosiery and underwear. Sara Lee Corporation has kept the brand names separate, which has helped them succeed.

Other examples of horizontal extension exist. Harley-Davidson has extended its brand into other product categories such as apparel, leather accessories, and toiletries. This has given the company an additional revenue stream and has heightened visibility for the brand (Pande 2004). The company has hundreds of licensed items that boast the Harley-Davidson logo. Products range from leather pants, to Harley brand beer, to Harley-themed Barbie dolls. Land Rover has successfully launched a baby push-chair or stroller and has now added a line of bicycles using the names of the Land Rover automobiles. The Land Rover Defender, Freelander, and Discovery are now also available in two wheels, and the bikes are designed to imitate the attributes of the cars. Buxton Foods introduced Peter Rabbit Organics baby food, which contains no added salt or refined sugar, and is made of fruit, vegetables, and grains. The line also carries wheat-free, gluten-free, and dairy-free options while relying on the brand's wholesome and trusted image. Another company that has grown its business by expanding into other product categories is Crayola. The brand has been extended into apparel, cake-decorating kits, home furnishings, toys, and electronic games (O'Loughlin 2004) (See Figure 13.1).

Vertical Brand Extension

A **vertical brand extension** involves introducing a similar brand in the same product category, but usually at a different price point or level of quality or for a different lifecycle. With vertical extensions, companies seek to capture new target markets to increase profits. In the apparel and jewelry industry, many designers are utilizing vertical brand extensions. Among the examples are Donna Karan and DKNY, and Zale and Gordon. In the automobile market, the variety of models reflect different price and quality levels. The Toyota company offers Tercel, Corolla, Camry, and Lexus models with

13.1 Crayola extended its product line to apparel, cake decorating kits, home furnishings, toys, and electronic games.

increasing price and quality, respectively (Riel et al. 2001).

Kraft, after purchasing the frozen pizza brand Tombstone in the late 1980s, acquired frozen pizza products through Jack's, DiGiorno, and California Pizza Kitchen. These products fit into a pyramid structure of product positioning and pricing that met the needs of different consumers with the four different product concepts (Jones 2006). M. C. Jones (2006) quoted Sarah Delea, spokeswoman for Kraft International, as she outlined the segmentation:

California Pizza Kitchen is our super premium line, using gourmet recipes and unusual ingredients, it's the closest to the restaurant experience at home. DiGiorno is aimed at an adult audience and also tries to replicate the delivery-style pizza. Tombstone focuses on traditional values and appeals largely to teens and families, while Jack's has a milder flavor and is aimed at families with children (27).

Sales growth was rekindled as a result of this pyramid strategy. In the first year, DiGiorno's boosted sales by 20 percent.

Kraft's four differentiated brands create a balance in their portfolio that positions the brand effectively in the frozen pizza market (Jones 2006).

Unilever Ice Cream in Green Bay, Wisconsin, is a leader in the frozen novelty ice-cream category that includes well-known brands such as Popsicle, Klondike, and Breyers. Of these, Popsicle is the number one brand of frozen novelties; Klondike brand is the number one ice-cream novelty; and Unilever commands 12 of the top 14 best-selling frozen novelties (Terreri 2006). The company has achieved its success with constant innovation and brand extensions. Such strategies have recently included Double Churned Light ice-cream bars and sandwiches, the four best-selling carb products under Breyers CarbSmart, Klondike Bars with Reese's Peanut Butter Cups, and ice pops with real fruit juice. In addition, Unilever has expanded its Popsicle brand through licenses with companies such as Nickelodeon. The parent company uses national TV, print advertising, and POS materials to market to consumers in addition to in-store and offsite product sampling opportunities.

Specialty retailer, Gap, founded in 1969, originally sold clothes to teenagers and featured Levi's jeans as a staple item. Gap grew quickly and expanded the number of store locations while developing its image and broadening its product offerings. In 1983, the company created private label Gap Brand, which eliminated many nationally branded products from their stores. In 1985, the brand extension Gap-Kids was introduced, accompanied by the BabyGap line in 1990. By 1991, Levi's jeans were no longer sold by Gap, making everything in the stores private label. In 1993, Gap, Inc. purchased the safari clothing company Banana Republic (Besida 2006). This company complemented the Gap's existing product assortment by appealing to a slightly older and more affluent target market. Eventually, Banana Republic dropped their safari wear and started selling higher-end leather goods and quality apparel items. When the Gap's earnings fell due to low margins by 1993, the company responded by opening Old Navy Clothing Co., a family-focused, budget-conscious store. In 1998, Gap introduced complementary products through a brand extension, GapBody, which sells intimate and athletic product lines. In 2005, Gap introduced another new retail brand, Forth and Towne, which sells women's clothing targeted at the 35 and older crowd (Hoover's Company Records 2006). As a result of these brand extensions, Gap now attracts customers from several age brackets and price ranges than their original retail position commanded (See Figure 13.2 on page 355).

DISTANCING

Distancing techniques are used to increase or decrease the perceived separation between a core brand and a vertical brand extension. The relationships between the core brand and the extended brand are expressed in the way in which they are tied together linguistically (e.g., name) or graphically (e.g., logo) (Kim et al. 2001).

Greater distancing of a brand extension using graphical or linguistic methods can reduce the likelihood of diluting the core brand. Therefore, if a significant difference in price and quality between a core brand and a vertical brand extension does not exist, then the company needs to create a larger distance between the core brand and the brand extension by using graphical or linguistic distancing methods (Kim et al. 2001). However, this strategy should be used based upon the type of vertical brand extension (step-up or step-down) and the type of brand concept (prestige-oriented or function-oriented), as illustrated in the following sections.

TYPES OF VERTICAL BRAND EXTENSION

The direction of a vertical brand extension may be characterized as being either a step-up or a step-down from the core brand.

Step-up Extension The **step-up brand extension** refers to distancing upward from the core brand. The step-up brand extension can become more favorable if it is perceptually more distant from the core brand's image because it avoids being associated with the core brand's lower level of quality. In this way, the step-up brand extension can stand on its own and establish its own clear identity and brand personality without being mixed up with the lesser quality of its core brand (Kim et al. 2001).

Step-up extensions have limitations in prestige-oriented core brands. A prestige-oriented brand has little room for introducing a step-up brand extension because it is already at the highest levels of price and quality, creating a ceiling effect (Riel et al. 2001). On the contrary, a function-oriented brand has more room to move upward on the vertical continuum to improve its image and emotional attributes. Therefore, step-up extensions may be more successful for function-oriented brands.

Bashas', the 153-unit supermarket chain based in Chandler, Arizona, used a step-up extension strategy when it started selling a new line of private label refrigerated soups. This private label product line targeted consumers desiring a special take-home product for quick meal consumption. The take-home soup line, called Bashas' Kitchen Fresh Soups, comes in eight varieties (e.g., chicken noodle, tomato basil, crab and corn chowder, chicken tortilla) (Gatty 2005).

13.2 Gap Inc. has a vertical brand extension with brands such as Banana Republic and Old Navy.

Step-down Extension The **step-down extension** refers to distancing downward from the core brand. If the core brand and extension are closely linked, the positive quality implied in the core brand name will be transferred to the step-down extension. However, if the step-down vertical extension is introduced at much lower price and quality levels, the core brand could suffer from dilution of its image. In other words, the step-down extension will be more successful when it is not distanced too far from the core brand name (Kim et al. 2001).

When a prestige-oriented brand has a step-down extension, there is plenty of room for the extension to move downscale and be introduced at reduced price and quality levels because the core brand is upscale. On the contrary, a function-oriented brand may not readily accommodate a step-down extension because there is less room to move downscale on the

13.3 The Courtyard downplays the Marriott name with graphical distancing by having the Marriott name in small type in the logo.

vertical continuum, possibly resulting in a floor effect (Riel et al. 2001).

An example of a step-down brand extension is The Courtyard Inn by Marriott. The Marriott Hotel used distancing techniques when they introduced a step-down extension called the Courtyard Inn, targeting a less upscale consumer audience. The word Courtyard provides a new distinct identity and the word Inn implies a less expensive, less luxurious type of accommodation as compared with hotel. This is an example of linguistic distancing. Further, the Courtyard downplays the Marriott name with graphical distancing by having the Marriott name in small type in the logo (Kim et al. 2001) (See Figure 13.3).

FACTORS AFFECTING BRAND EXTENSION EFFECTIVENESS

Although brand extensions represent one of the most often used branding strategies, the success of brand extensions is uncertain. Consequently, understanding the factors that affect the outcome of a brand extension is of considerable importance. Unsuccessful extensions may weaken or jeopardize the core brand as a result of the undesirable associations with the extended brand. The success of brand extension can be determined by several factors such as brand strength, brand image, fit, type of goods, and number of competitors.

BRAND STRENGTH

Extensions of major brands tend to work better than those of minor brands (Reddy, Holak, and Bhat 1994). Major brands signal better quality and create positive brand associations from consumer predispositions toward the brand more easily (Wernerfelt 1988). Also, brands that consumers perceive as having a higher quality reduce the consumers' risk of a new trial, as opposed to brands of lower quality.

Many leading brands have held their market position for quite a few years due to their well-established family name. Sir Adrian Cadbury, for example, uses his family name on new products, such as Cadbury's Time Out bar (See Figure 13.4). In fact, many corporate brands, including Nestlé chocolate or Kellogg's corn flakes, are associated with the reputation of the parent brand. These leading firms use parent brand names that are deeply embedded in the company's past. For these firms, brand trust and consistency are maintained through tradition and core values for the brand and its extensions.

BRAND IMAGE

A **brand image** is the perception consumers have about a particular brand. High-image brands are easier to extend than low-image brands because prestigious brands signal more manufacturer competence and trust than their low-end counterparts (Park, Milberg, and Lawson 1991). E. Nijssen and C. Augustin's 2005 study found that managers prefer extensions when a parent brand has an excellent or good image versus a moderate image. Louis Vuitton and Cartier are examples of **parent brands** that have successfully extended their names into categories adjacent to their core products. Cartier extended its brand name from jewelry to watches, perfumes, and accessories. Louis Vuitton extended its name from handbags to clothing, jewelry, perfumes, and accessories.

When firms extend their brands in non-adjacent categories, they should consider whether the brands have appropriate symbolic power to cross categories and whether the symbolism can be consistently promoted in the new categories (Reddy and Terblanche 2005). It is unthinkable that Hanes could extend its name into salad dressing or that Levi's could extend its name into wine. One example of a brand that did not effectively introduce a new product is Harley-Davidson's venture into fragrances. Customers did not link the new fragrances with the Harley characteristics of ruggedness and masculinity (Haig 2003).

Many companies choose to extend their brands through licensing agreements. In this situation, the parent company does not retain control of the product. Therefore the brand can be misrepresented; in some situations, the extensive licensing agreements cause overexposure of brands (Brumback 2006). The luxury brand Salvatore Ferragamo extended its brand into the watch product category because it fits the company's overall strategy and remains close to the core product categories of shoes, handbags, accessories, and apparel. However, it has chosen not to extend a new line of watches through licensing agreements in fear of damaging its brand image (Brumback 2006).

While corporate image may be improved through a brand extension strategy, there are exceptions. The negative effects of brand extension include the dilution of the extended brand's image and sales cannibalization between products from the same corporation (*The Economist* 1990). For example, A. Ries and J. Trout (1993) observed that IBM, which represented big computers, did not maintain a clear image and lost considerable

revenue due to its intensive extension policy since 1991. Another negative effect can be demonstrated by the cannibalization effects that have occurred in the beer market due to line extensions. Light beers rose in popularity in the early part of the millennium due to the Atkins movement that spurred consumer interest in low-carbohydrate products. However, its increase in popularity has cannibalized or taken away sales from regular domestic premium beers (Phillips 2004).

FIT BETWEEN PARENT BRAND AND EXTENSION PRODUCT

Fit between the parent brand and extension product is a central part of new product development (Smith and Andrews 1995). Brands and product categories that fit together perform better when transferring from an existing product category into a new product category (Aaker and Keller 1990, Keller and Sood 2003). In other words, if a brand extension lacks fit, it is likely to fail.

When too many non-fitting brand extensions are launched, the damage will be traumatic to the parent brand. Brand names such as Betty Crocker, General Electric, and Kraft have experienced profuse brand extension. Although they have not lost consumer awareness as household brands, the strong associations they once had with specific products such as cake mix, light bulbs, and cheese, may be weakened. This risk is even greater when a brand is used synonymously with a specific product, such as Kleenex, Scotch (tape), and Band-Aid. This example is contrasted by the success story of Healthy Choice, which offered the common thread of low fat or low carbs in all of their products (Tauber 2004).

In Nijssen and Augustin's (2005) study, most brand managers mentioned that the target audience's perception of the fit between a parent brand and an extension was a requirement for the success of brand extension. The managers expressed concerns that poor fit would result not only in a lack of acceptance of the new product, but also could damage the parent brand's image and sales (Nijssen and Augustin 2005).

Pierre Cardin's early extensions into perfumes and cosmetics in the 1960s were so successful that the company sold licenses indiscriminately afterward. By 1988, it had granted more than 800 licenses in 94 countries, generating $1 billion annual revenue. However, when the Pierre Cardin name began to appear on nonadjacent products such as baseball caps and cigarettes, margins started to collapse (Reddy and Terblanche 2005).

Johnson & Johnson is a brand name synonymous with baby care products. Johnson & Johnson experimented with the idea of extending their product line into the baby food category, following the logic that mothers would trust both baby care products and baby food of the same company. Before launching, Johnson & Johnson tested the concept first by gaining mothers' opinions about the extension. They discovered that while mothers did trust the company with products such as powder, shampoo, soap, and lotion, these products

were for external use. Since moms reinforced the idea that Johnson & Johnson is considered the expert and category owner for external baby care products, the company stopped the search to extend into the other categories and maintained their expert and category owner status in external baby care products (Roberto and Roberto 2005).

TYPES OF GOODS

The effectiveness of a brand extension may be determined by the type of goods; whether it is experience goods or search goods. **Experience goods** are intangible products (e.g., services, entertainment) that cannot be evaluated on visual inspection and therefore must be assessed through actual trials. **Search goods** contain attributes that can be evaluated through visual inspection as in the case of the more tangible consumer goods (Smith and Park 1992). Since consumers can obtain useful information about quality through visual inspections of search goods, the importance of the reputation of the brand name is reduced for search goods.

Conversely, in the case of intangible services or entertainment, consumers tend to rely heavily on cues such as known brand names, because they do not have actual experience with them based on concrete attributes before purchase (Smith and Park 1992). This characteristic of experience goods presents more challenges than those faced in search goods. For example, because consumers perceive minimal differences between competing service brands, they may have more difficulty choosing between service brands. However, well-established corporate branding of service brands can enhance the perceived differentiation of the brand, which may lead to a greater propensity of trial (Piña, Martinez, Chernatony, and Drury 2006).

Furthermore, the complementarity of the service delivery process helps consumers expect similar performances in different usage situations, as can be seen from the cases of a car rental service and an accommodation service, or an Internet provider and a cable operator. Direct Line, a U.K. car insurance company, has built a strong brand by selling car insurance directly over the telephone to provide convenience and lower premiums to customers. Direct Line uses brand extensions in two areas: car-related services, such as breakdown coverage, and financial services, such as house insurance and loans (Witzel 2004). Another example is EasyGroup, which began as a budget airline. EasyGroup is building the market in each of its many sectors, including car rentals and cinemas, by attracting customers to its no-frills, low-cost services, rather than trying to win market share from rivals (Witzel 2004). On the contrary, in the context of consuming tangible search products, complementarity of the product categories (e.g., coffee and rolls, or laundry detergent and fabric softener) may not influence consumer evaluation of the extension as much.

In conclusion, the advantages of the extension strategy are more beneficial to experience goods than to search goods. Thus, the brand extension strategy may be a successful risk-diminishing alternative for introducing new services or entertainment venues.

NUMBER OF ESTABLISHED COMPETITORS

In a market where there are few established competitors, the difficulty of gaining consumer trial for a new brand is reduced (Smith and Park 1992). On the contrary, the presence of many well-established competing brands in a market makes it difficult to gain trial of a completely new brand, and thus requires greater investment to launch a new brand.

Nestlé Waters plans to combat their weak performance in the traditional water market with a series of brand extensions (Clark 2006). They are doing this by increasing their presence in the added-value beverage market with products that have active benefits beyond hydration. Health benefits include energy-boosting qualities. The company plans to develop water products in the following four categories: "water (still and sparkling); water+ (flavored water, with an indulgence positioning); nutrition and health products; and wellness drinks, which will be promoted to meet consumers' moods, as well as addressing traditional health problems" (Clark 2006, 6).

Coolbrands International, a frozen snacks company, is competing in the ultra-premium ice-cream category with its 10 flavors of Godiva Ice Cream. This line of ice cream is sold in pint-size containers that feature elegant packaging in the distinctive gold and black Godiva colors. Coolbrands has built upon Godiva's brand equity with the best ingredients, upscale packaging, and decadent flavors such as Belgian Dark Chocolate with Mint and Cappuccino with Chocolate Hearts (*Frozen Food Age* 2006). This company has chosen a small segment of the ice-cream market—superpremium ice cream—instead of competing against many other well-established brands within the overall ice-cream category.

CHAPTER SUMMARY

Brand extension involves the application of an established core brand name to new products. Attributes of a newly extended brand may be consistent with or inconsistent with the core brand's image. Brand extension is important for experiential retailing because this strategy extends the retail brand's product and service offerings and allows the retailer to capture a consumer's purchase through complementary product and service purchases. One of the most successful extensions is Apple's entrance into the portable media player category with iPod.

Brand extensions can be beneficial as well as risky to a company. Companies with a strong brand name and image are in a good position to extend their product lines to increase profits and build brand awareness. Successful brand extension provides several benefits such as building strong brand position, increasing the probability of trial, reducing entry barrier, and reducing advertising costs. Brand extension also can be risky when the extended products dilute the company's core image or do not address a specific consumer need. Some of Richard Branson's Virgin companies are examples of brand extension failure. Branson successfully extended Virgin music labels to Virgin Airlines, but his attempts to break into Virgin Vodka, Virgin Mobile, and Virgin Cosmetics have failed because these new products failed to reflect the Virgin values—irreverent, fun, and challenging.

There are two types of brand extension: horizontal and vertical. Horizontal brand extension occurs when an existing brand name is applied to a new product or service. Examples include many clothing designers' extending into home furnishing products such as Calvin Klein, Donna Karan, and Polo. Vertical brand extension occurs when companies introduce new product lines under the same brand name, usually having a different price point or quality level, or targeting different lifecycles. Examples include: Gap, Old Navy, Banana Republic, babyGap, and GapKids; and Toyota's models such as Tercel, Corolla, Camry, and Lexus.

As a concept related to vertical brand extension, distancing technique is used to increase or decrease the perceived separation between a core brand and a vertical brand extension. The relationship between the core brand and the extended brand is determined whether they are tied together linguistically (e.g., name) or graphically (e.g., logo). Greater distancing of a brand extension using graphical or linguistic methods can reduce the likelihood of diluting the core brand. The direction of a vertical brand extension may be characterized as being either a step-up or a step-down from the core brand. Step-up extensions tend to work better with function-oriented brands than with prestige-oriented brands, because a prestige-oriented brand has little room for introducing a step-up brand extension, creating a ceiling effect. On the contrary, step-down extensions tend to work better with prestige-oriented brands than with function-oriented brands, because there is less room for function-oriented brands to move downscale on the vertical continuum, resulting in a floor effect.

The success of brand extensions is affected by brand strength, brand image, fit between parent brand and extension product, type of goods (e.g., experience goods, search goods, service), and number of established competitors. Brand extension allows the established brand name to provide information about the new product's quality by extension. Thus, a new product can be launched at a lower cost by using informational leverage provided by an established brand name. Also, firms using brand extension tend to spend less on advertising expenditures than firms with comparable new name products for a given level of sales. In addition, brand extension tends to be more effective with experience goods and fewer competitors.

Discussion Questions

1. Identify the benefits of brand extension. Describe situations when it is advantageous to use a brand extension.
2. Identify the risks of brand extension. Explain situations when brand

extension is risky. Take examples of specific product or service categories.

3. Discuss the conditions under which a retailer can benefit from a horizontal brand extension.

4. What is *ceiling effect*? Apply it to vertical brand extension.

5. What is *floor effect*? Apply it to vertical brand extension.

6. Take an example of a retailer who has been recently successful in extending its brand. Discuss the factors that explain the success of this brand extension.

7. Identify two retailers—one retailer who has done horizontal extension and the other retailer who has done vertical extension (step-up or step-down). Discuss why each retailer has been successful or not successful.

References

Aaker, D., and K. Keller. 1990. Consumer evaluations of brand extensions. *Journal of Marketing* 54:27–41.

Agins, T. 2004. Style and substance: Mainstreaming hip-hop; Combs's Sean John sets move into women's high fashion with big stake in Zac Posen. *The New York Times*. April 20, B1.

Bashford, S. 2004. Path to extension. *Marketing* 35–36. Retrieved April 1, 2006 from LexisNexis database.

Besida, A. 2006. Banana Republic, Hoovers Company Information. Retrieved May 9, 2006 from ProQuest.

Betts, K., S. R. Larenaudie, C. Morton, and N. Mustafa. 2004. The new luxury leaders. *Time* 58–61.

Brumback, N. 2006. Taking measured steps to bolster luxury brands. *Women's Wear Daily* 191(98):20.

Clark, N. 2006. Nestlé water chief outlines plans for expansion. *Marketing (UK)* 6.

The Economist. 1990. Brand-stretching can be fun—and dangerous. 5:77–80.

Forney, J. C., E. J. Park, and L. Brandon. 2005. Effects of evaluative criteria on fashion brand extension. *Journal of Fashion Marketing and Management* 9(2):156–165.

French, D. 2005. Little change in Top 20 kids retailers. *Kids Today*. July 1, 6.

Frozen Food Age. 2006. Coolbrands brings Yoplait Yogurt, Godiva Chocolate, and Total Breakfast Cereal to the ice-cream freezer case. 54(6):7.

Gatty, B. 2005. Preferred stock. *Progressive Grocer* 84(13):64–67.

Grime, I., A. Diamantopoulos, and G. Smith. 2002. Consumer evaluations of extensions and their effects on the core brand: Key issues and research propositions. *European Journal of Marketing* 36(1/12):1415–1438.

Haig, Matt. 2003. Big brand balls-ups. *Brand Strategy* 171:34

Heller, L. 2006. Opportunities open up for iPod's cheaper cousin. *DSN Retailing Today* 45(7):20.

Hoover's Company Records. 2006. Gap Inc. Retrieved May 9, 2006 from ProQuest. www.proquest.com.

Jones, M. C. 2006. Case study: Kraft. Brand *Strategy* 203:26–27.

Journal of Consumer Marketing. 1997. Careless brand extension can damage your business. 14(4/5):389–390.

Keller, K., and D. Aaker. 1992. The effects of sequential introduction of brand extensions. *Journal of Marketing Research* 29(1):35–50.

Keller, K. L., and S. Sood. 2003. Brand equity dilution. *MIT Sloan Management Review* 45(1):12–14.

Kenneth, H. 2005. Brand extensions can go too far. *Adweek* 46(47):8

Kim, C., A. Lavack, and M. Smith. 2001. Consumer evaluation of vertical brand extensions and core brands. *Journal of Business Research* 52:211–232.

National Petroleum News. 2006. Starbucks extends ready-to-drink offerings. *98*(4):44.

Nijssen, E., and C. Augustin. 2005. Brand extensions: A manager's perspective. *Journal of Brand Management* 13(1):33–49.

O'Loughlin, S. 2004. Crayola Plans to Think Out of the (Crayon) Box. *Brandweek* 45(23):12.

Owen, E. 2006. Bebe hopes sales will blossom in Spring. *Wall Street Journal*. February 22, B3C.

Pande, B. 2004. Harley's fortunes revived by focus on existing clients. *Media Asia*. January 20, 20.

Park, C., S. Milberg, and R. Lawson. 1991. Evaluation of brand extensions: The role of product feature similarity and brand concept consistency. *Journal of Consumer Research* 18:185–193.

Phillips, B. 2004. Drinking better. *Convenience Store News* 40(5):73–74.

Pina, J., E. Martinez, L. Chernatony, and S. Drury. 2006. The effect of service brand extensions on corporate image. *European Journal of Marketing* 40(1/2):174–197.

Reddy, S., S. Holak, and S. Bhat. 1994. To extend or not to extend: Success determinants of line extensions. *Journal of Marketing Research* 31:243–262.

Reddy, M., and N. Terblanche. 2005. How not to extend your luxury brand. *Harvard Business Review* 83(12):20–24

Riel, A., J. Lemmink, and H. Ouwersloot. 2001. Consumer evaluations of service brand extensions. *Journal of Service Research* 3(3):220–231.

Ries, A., and J. Trout. 1993. *The 22 Immutable Laws of Marketing*. New York: McGraw-Hill.

Roberto, N., and A. Roberto. 2005. The brand extension temptation. *Financial Times* [London], np. Retrieved April 1, 2006 from LexisNexis database.

Roselius, T. 1973. Consumer rankings of risk reduction methods. In Harold H. Kassarjian and Thomas S. Robertson, eds. *Perspectives in Consumer Behavior*. Glenview, IL: Scott, Foresman.

Sattler, Henrik, and Franziska Volckner. 2006. Dominant design arises based on product traits; success factors. *Marketing News*. April 1, 45.

Smith, D. C., and J. Andrews. 1995. Rethinking the effect of perceived fit on customers' evaluations of new products. *Journal of the Academy of Marketing Science* 23(1):4–14.

Smith, D., and W. Park. 1992. The effects of brand extensions on market share and advertising efficiency. *Journal of Marketing Research* 24:296–313.

Tauber, E. M. 2004. Benefits of brand extensions. *Brand Extension Research* Accessed May 31, 2006 www.brandextensionresearch.com/benefits.html

Taylor, W., and W. Bearden. 2002. The effects of price on brand extension evaluations: The moderating role of extension similarity. *Journal of the Academy of Marketing Science* 30(2):131–140.

Terreri, A. 2006. Unilever Finds Success Through New Ice Cream Flavor Experiences. *Frozen Food Age May 2006 Supplement* 40.

Ward, A. 2005. *Financial Times*. January 10, 27.

Wernerfelt, B. 1988. Umbrella branding as a signal of new product quality: An example of signaling by posting a bond. *Brand Journal of Economics* 19:458–466.

Wilensky, D. 2005. Family jewels. *License!* 8(6):64.

———. 2006. Retail extensions. *License!* 9(5):26.

Witzel, M. 2004. The value of a perception: The corporate life cycle brand extension. *Financial Times* (London, England). August 10, 13.

STRATEGIC ALLIANCE

History Afield

There's the prototypical tour guide, either bored stiff or cheerleader enthusiastic, chattering into a raspy microphone in a bumpy bus on the way to an overcrowded tourist mecca. There's shuffling along single-file, trying to get a glimpse of a famous painting or a natural wonder to the accompaniment of cheesy canned comments, recycled textbook history uttered every day of the week. This may be the perception, and in some cases the reality, of guided tour vacations. But this is not what The History Channel had in mind when it launched its own branded tours last year. Armed with research that said vacationers in general and baby boomers in particular are looking for trips with an educational underpinning, the cable network struck up some alliances with established tour operators and licensed its well ingrained name for history-based trips throughout the United States. Since then, scores of people have cruised the Mississippi, spent Christmas in Charleston, South Carolina, and retraced the steps of George Custer through several of his epic Civil War battles.

Because of the response, the cable network has taken the next step in its brand extension plan, expanding the tours internationally, and, via partner IST Cultural Tours, has started booking trips to France, Italy, Greece, Turkey, Israel, and China. As do the domestic tours, each has an exploration theme, such as The Great Composers tour of central Europe. "It's not about following the guy with the flag around the Vatican," said Tom Heymann, vice president of A&E Television Networks Enterprises. "It's not your father's tour."

Demographically, the tours have skewed toward history buff boomers and empty nesters who have the time and disposable income for leisurely trips. But network executives think the addition of international vacations, with their focus on adventure, could bring in a younger traveler, potentially aging-down the channel's audience and seeding brand loyalty in Gen X and Y consumers. Sort of "Xtreme" versions of the tour business, the trips, such as the Treasures of the Nile cruise through Egypt, are designed for people who would rather go on an archaeological dig than laze at the beach. "These trips are more experience-driven than destination-driven," said Jonathan Paisner, manager of consumer product development, AETN Enterprises.

A few other entertainment companies have responded to the current passion for mind-expanding vacations. The Disney Institute in Orlando, Florida, for example, opened several years ago with animation, culinary arts, and sports clinics. But The History Channel is the first television network to do so. While the concept of a cable network sponsoring guided vacations may seem far afield, History Channel executives saw the concept as springing naturally from the channel's own tagline: Where the past comes alive. "It is a bit unexpected, but I don't know if there is such a thing as a typical brand extension anymore," Heymann said.

CHAPTER 14

"We felt this was a natural because our brand is about bringing history to life. What better way to do that than have people live with us for two weeks."

The network, through its licensing and merchandising arm, struck deals with History America Tours and Mayflower Tours for themed trips in 1998 that included Castles of the Northeast, a seven-day trek around the homes of John D. Rockefeller, the Astors, and Franklin Roosevelt; Lincoln at Gettysburg, with reenactments of Lincoln's famous address; and Fredericksburgh Battlefields, where visitors traveled along Stonewall Jackson's march to the Battle of Chancellorsville. The channel now works exclusively with History America on domestic trips, and the offerings have expanded this year to include Historic Hawaii, a trip to Florida for spring training called Take Me Out to the Ballgame, and several Delta Queen cruises on the Mississippi. "We're not a travel company, and we don't intend to be," Paisner said. "The challenge is delivering an experience with our partners that is consistent with our brand image."

Source: Stanley, T. L. 1999. *Brandweek* 40(10):18–20.

INTRODUCTION

Suppose your favorite clothing store brand teamed up with a television network with which you are not familiar. Would you be more likely to watch the network? Or what if you frequently watched the network, but did not shop at the store? Would the alliance make you more likely to shop there? Wal-Mart and television network BET hope consumers answer yes to these questions. In 2005, Wal-Mart created an alliance with BET to target African American consumers. BET provides Wal-Mart with DVDs and CDs that contain exclusive programming and content related to urban-oriented music and movie releases (*DSN Retailing Today* 2005). The products are branded as BET Official and sold in specially designated sections and displays located in Wal-Mart stores and Sam's Clubs. The alliance has two potential opportunities: to make Wal-Mart more relevant to urban consumers and to make BET more mainstream.

Entering new markets is becoming more expensive and financially risky for many retail firms. This is because media costs are rising, established firms are using more extensive and aggressive promotions, and acceptable distribution levels are more costly to obtain. Therefore, many firms are using established brand names to enter new markets. Alliance formation is one way in which firms attempt to survive in the changing marketplace, maintain relationships with the customers, and expand the customer base. M. Ritson (2006) reported that "the marketing world is changing: Many marketers now perceive other brands not simply as rivals, but as potential partners in mutually beneficial projects" (21). When companies form alliances, there is cooperation that produces better results for all parties involved; 1000ventures.com is a clearinghouse of informative and inspirational articles for businesses and individuals considering strategic alliances. Articles cover everything from maximizing your own potential to maximizing the power of human resources.

GOALS OF STRATEGIC ALLIANCE

Strategic alliance, a term used interchangeably with co-branding, brand alliance, co-marketing, and joint branding, uses two or more brands on one product (or service) or set of products (or services) to promote sales. The reasoning behind it is that multiple brands can promote additional customer awareness of single brands when they are used together. With more brand extensions in the market, strategic alliances are becoming a popular strategy to introduce new products. Two brand names on a product bring two different markets together to purchase the same product or service, therefore generating customers, increasing the likelihood of sales, and increasing the chances of a return purchase. The revenue generated by the partnership can outweigh the expense of forming the alliance; as a result, budgeted expenditures can be concentrated in other areas (Yip 2005).

Strategic alliance is beneficial for both partners regardless of whether the original brands are perceived by consumers as having high or low brand equity (Washburn, Till, and Priluck 2000). Strategic alliance often occurs through brand licensing of one or more products. Licensing agreements allow one organization to use another company's brand name for a specified fee. Marketers are using brand alliances more frequently as they try to capitalize on the complementary features of different brands (Abratt and Motlana 2002).

BENEFITS AND CHALLENGES OF STRATEGIC ALLIANCE

Strategic alliances between organizations are created through successful partnership relationships. However, the linkage created by a strategic alliance can either enhance or detract from consumers' perceptions of each individual brand. Hence partners must understand that strategic alliances offer several benefits and challenges as well.

Benefits of Strategic Alliance

Benefits of strategic alliance include delivering a better attribute profile, producing synergies, providing access to new, untapped markets, reducing barriers to market entry, providing strategic benefits, and providing operational benefits.

DELIVER A BETTER ATTRIBUTE PROFILE

Strategic alliances recombine subsets of attributes from each of the two parent brands to create new product (Kumar 2005). As such, strategic alliances strengthen the attributes of both partnering brands and thus improve customer attitude toward the brands (Park, Jun, and Shocker 1996; Simonin and Ruth 1998). Smucker's Dove ice-cream topping is a product co-branded by Smucker's, a fruit preserves brand, and Dove, a chocolate brand (Kumar 2005). The strengths of the attributes of the two brands, Smucker's and Dove, are combined to create a new product and to strengthen the two brands. In 2005, Procter & Gamble reported three consecutive years of double-digit growth in a mature industry. Its success can be attributed to many brand success stories that include examples of strategic alliance. Tide with a Touch of Downy introduced in 2004 added 8 percent market share and helped Tide climb to record sales. In addition, this was accomplished without significantly hurting Downy or other products in their fabric softener category (*Advertising Age* 2005). This strategic alliance transfers a subset of attributes from each of the two parent brands (i.e., Tide and Downy), which were then recombined into a coherent composite concept of a new product (i.e., Tide with a Touch of Downy).

A strategic alliance strategy also was used successfully for Schwan's Bakery brand, Mrs. Smith's, which focuses primarily on fruit pies. A strategic alliance with Cinnabon to create the Cinnabon Apple Crumb Pie is one example. Mrs. Smith's Apple and Mixed Berry Pie Slices sweetened with Splenda is another example. These pie lines have been a huge success for this category of Schwan's desserts (Terreri 2006). Another example of a recent unique partnership is a Valentine's Day promotion for Ralph Lauren perfume, Romance, and Lindt's chocolates, Petites Merveilles. This promotion ran for almost a month before February 14, 2006 in fragrance and department stores in the United Kingdom. To ensure there was a consistent, unified presentation in stores that positively represented both brands, the companies worked together on marketing and presentation. Romance was one of the top 5 perfumes in the stores running the promotion and this alliance was considered a success by both companies (Ritson 2006).

PRODUCE SYNERGIES

Strategic alliances produce synergy without diluting each brand's visibility and power in the marketplace. For partnering retailers, strategic alliances enable them to increase profit without a proportionate increase in investments. Synergies are illustrated from combined brands such as Nike/iPod, and 7-Eleven/Citgo. As these examples illustrate, a retail co-brand has the potential to provide synergy by combining offerings that are targeted to more or less the same purchase occasion, but offer mutually exclusive products as in the case of Nike/iPod. The co-brand also might combine offerings that are targeted to different purchase occasions but can be consolidated in a single visit as in the case of 7-Eleven/Citgo (Leuthesser, Kohli, and Suri 2003).

Another example of the power of strategic alliances to produce synergies can be found in the publication of a U.S. cookbook. Wayne Gisslen, a leading chef in the United States, wrote a cookbook, *Professional Cooking*, published by John Wiley & Sons. In an effort to improve sales of the fourth edition, the publisher co-branded the new cookbook with the highly respected Le Cordon Bleu culinary academy. The strategic alliance of this fourth volume increased sales dramatically (Boad 1999).

PROVIDE ACCESS TO NEW UNTAPPED MARKETS

Strategic alliances enable a particular brand to be associated with a partner's core values and tap into the partner's market. This can reinforce the image of a product or service brand by enabling the brand to acquire some of the values it may have aspired to, but previously lacked.

One such example is the partnership between Adidas, a global brand, and the New Zealand All Blacks, the leading brand of the New Zealand Rugby Union (NZRU). Adidas aimed to sell more of its rugby attire by expanding into new markets. To do this, the company first needed to increase the targeted sports market around the world. Partnering with the renowned All Blacks rugby team met this need by increasing TV exposure that promoted the brand association between Adidas and rugby. Likewise, one goal of the NZRU was to introduce the All Blacks brand in countries where rugby is not a popular sport. Through a strategic alliance with Adidas, the NZRU did not have to invest in developing strategic or marketing expertise. It could merely take advantage of its new partner's established brand equity and global distribution channels (*Strategic Direction* 2004).

Intel Corporation was preparing to launch its wireless processor Centrino in 2003 when it realized it needed a Wi-Fi service provider whose network infrastructure worked with the Centrino platform. Intel approached T-Mobile to set up hot spots around the world, targeting the market of mobile professionals. In establishing a strategic alliance partnership with T-Mobile USA Inc., they placed advertisements in airports for hot spots in terminals that told users how they could use the Centrino laptops and T-Mobile service. In addition, Intel created strategic alliance relationships with hotel chains in several key U.S. cities by providing W-Fi wireless services that targeted business professionals. Again, signs advertising Intel and T-Mobile services were put in the hotels and logos were placed on hotel room keys to remind customers of the benefits available at this particular hotel. The partnership was also beneficial for hotels because they were able to create a reputation for service among the business travelers with the addition of T-Mobile and Wi-Fi wireless services (Vence 2005).

REDUCE BARRIERS TO MARKET ENTRY

For a brand that enters a new market, an alliance with a relatively well-known brand can be a good strategy, especially when the brand cannot effectively signal its own high quality (Rao, Qu, and Ruekert 1999). In fact, dual branding plays a key role in enhancing the perception that the two products have a similar quality. For instance, two brands may be co-branded and the target brand may not be as well known as the partnering brand. In this case, the image of the target brand could converge with the better-known partner brand, adopting its brand value in the eyes of consumers.

Even major brands often use a strategic alliance strategy to increase their odds of success when entering new markets. One example is the Weight Watchers from Heinz reduced-calorie products. Weight Watchers brand had considered entering the highly competitive market of prepared foods and Heinz had considered the possibility of producing a line of diet products, but neither brand was strong enough in the other category. The combination of Weight Watchers' recognition and credibility within the target audience and Heinz's experience with canned and bottled foods produced an attractive strategic alliance strategy for both brands. This partnership reduced barriers to entry for both brands and enabled them to compete in the rapidly growing diet food product category (Boad 1999).

PROVIDE STRATEGIC BENEFITS

Strategic alliance agreements between two companies may be strategically made to create competitive advantage within the market (Spekman, Isabella, MacAvoy, and Forbes 1996). An example of a strategic benefit can be illustrated by the strategic alliance of Kellogg and Walt Disney. Kellogg has exclusive rights to co-brand its breakfast cereals with Disney. Displaying famous Disney characters on packages of cereals gives Kellogg a differential advantage over other cereal companies. As a result, characters such as Mickey Mouse and Winnie the Pooh add appeal for the child consumer and further improve the brand awareness of the cereal (Prince and Davies 2002).

Strategic alliance, especially in the hospitality industry, can be difficult and complicated. For example, hotel management teams have to be sure that strategic partnering with a branded food and beverage outlet will not result in direct competition with the hotel's existing in-house food and beverage services; rather, the alliance should complement the hotel's established amenities (Yip 2005). However, there are a number of examples of successful firms within the hospitality and travel industry. Starbucks coffee is being served on United Airlines flights and in various nationally branded hotels. Denny's restaurants are operating in Holiday Inn properties. Renaissance Hotels feature only toiletries by Bath and Body Works. Choice Hotels International's EconoLodge brand chose to exclusively use Mr. Clean products to clean its hotels; the use of special marketing efforts to promote this partnership was used to inform their customers about their serious focus on cleanliness (Yip 2005).

PROVIDE OPERATIONAL BENEFITS

Strategic alliance also may provide operational benefits, when partnering companies share one retail site. As an example, related brands can form a partnership to increase operational benefits by sharing customer space, parking lots, and rest areas. In the case of Dunkin' Donuts and Baskin-Robbins, both partners enjoy lower operational costs and more customer traffic. In the same store, Dunkin' Donuts are sold primarily in the early morning and ice cream is sold primarily in the afternoon or evening; therefore, customer traffic flow is not negatively impacted by their sharing of the site (Prince and Davies 2002).

Vermont Living magazine has a website at www.vtliving.com that has a heading category called products. When viewers click on products, they are guided to an Internet listing of made-in-Vermont products with links and information about how to research the company. This website provides operational benefits to companies that make Vermont products. Therefore, these companies benefit from synergy created by their association as the Vermont name. These companies share an Internet page that enables them to expand their market and attract sales from new customers.

Challenges of Strategic Alliance

Although strategic alliances provide a number of benefits, they face several challenges. According to M. Lindstrom (2005), more than 90 percent of strategic alliance ventures fail. Issues faced in strategic alliance include unobservable product quality, consumer confusion, and transitory nature.

UNOBSERVABLE PRODUCT QUALITY

Danger exists that one brand might get lost in another due to unobservable product quality, as can be found in the story of NutraSweet. When NutraSweet first appeared in the market, it faced two challenges: assuring consumers that it did not have an aftertaste, and that it was safe. NutraSweet accomplished the first challenge by mailing large quantities of chewing gum containing NutraSweet to consumers for a risk-free trial. The customers were able to sample the NutraSweet in the gum to determine for themselves if it had an aftertaste. The second challenge was more difficult to overcome because the claim that NutraSweet was noncarcinogenic and harmless if properly used could be confirmed only after prolonged use. If the claim turned out to be false, little could be done to correct the problem. Their claim of being a safe sugar substitute did not gain credibility until Coca-Cola and Pepsi backed the claim by offering products that contained NutraSweet (Rao and Ruekert 1994). In effect, these firms communicated to the marketplace as follows:

> Should the product turn out to be injurious to consumers' health, then Coca-Cola (and Minute Maid and other Coca-Cola products), Pepsi (and KFC, Taco Bell, and other PepsiCo products), and other firms allied with NutraSweet would all suffer from adverse publicity or potential consumer boycott. Given the monetary value of one market share point in these markets, any potential consumer boycott was a threat with teeth. Certainly, consumers do not generally penalize companies involved in a brand alliance every time a jointly branded product does not perform, yet the fear of adverse publicity and the potential monetary consequences if a competitor leverages any embarrassment are generally enough

to make companies very careful when trading their brand names (Rao and Ruekert 1994, 91).

CONSUMER CONFUSION

Sometimes, brands are not recognized as similar in attributes or purposes; thus, positioning these brands together may create confusion for the consumer. For instance, an alliance between Kemper Securities and Pillsbury cookie dough mix might not be a particularly successful strategic alliance because consumers do not think about buying insurance and baking cookies at the same time. Retailers involved in strategic alliances must have a clear understanding of the purpose of the alliance and of who the targeted consumers will be. If confusion occurs, then consumers will not purchase the products, and the negative effects could flow to other products or services under the same name brands.

Successful examples of strategic alliance include the Coach leather edition of Lexus and the Orvis edition of the Jeep Cherokee. Coach leather and Lexus both appeal to a luxury-oriented consumer base, but it is likely that people who appreciate a fine automobile also appreciate a well-respected leather goods company. The combination only increases the positive association of both companies.

There are also unsuccessful examples. Nestlé and L'Oreal announced a partnership to produce healthy products. However, consumers did not know what these two brands had in common; therefore the strategic alliance partnership has not been a success (Lindstrom 2005). Fisher-Price and McDonald's entered into an alliance to produce a line of play food and appliances for children. However, the brand alliance failed. Allying with McDonald's did not provide any incremental benefit for Fisher-Price although both brands target the same children's market segment. For the product category of toys, the addition of attributes that enhanced the product's performance quality was relatively more important than a guarantee that the product would not fail through the well-established brand name of McDonald's. What Fisher-Price needed were products with new features or higher levels of existing attributes. A strategic alliance with Nintendo, offering a new line of video-driven toys, may have resulted in a more appropriate alliance (Rao and Ruekert 1994).

TRANSITORY NATURE

Some partnerships are functional until they meet their goals. Consider Konica using US Air (a national carrier) and Kemper Securities (a conservative financial corporation) to endorse the quality of its copiers. This alliance is probably temporary because the experience of airlines, financial planning, and copiers may change with technology and income gains. Therefore, what may be profitable in the short term may not be sustainable in the long term. Another example of a transitory strategic alliance is Lindt, the Swiss Chocolatier, Valentine's Day promotions with the grocery chain Tesco, lingerie group La Senza, and luxury cosmetics company Molton Brown. Lindt sought to attract more of a younger female market that enjoy occasional indulgence. They used a two-week sampling campaign that focused on the experience of pampering and indulgence (O'Reilly 2006).

FACTORS AFFECTING THE SUCCESS OF STRATEGIC ALLIANCES

The success of strategic alliances is influenced by both product fit and brand fit. **Product fit** refers to the closeness or complementarities of the product categories regardless of the individual brands, as in the case of ice cream with maple syrup.

Brand fit refers to the level of consistency between perceptions of each brand based on logical and expected associations. When the fit is considered poor at either level, there will be a negative spillover effect on how the co-branded offering is perceived (Prince and Davies 2002).

Product Fit

A relatively high degree of product fit is important for consumers to form positive attitudes toward a strategic alliance. Product fit in strategic alliances refers to the relatedness of the product categories implied by the strategic alliance (e.g., ice cream with chocolate fudge), regardless of the brands. Sun Microsystems created a strategic alliance arrangement with Specialized Bikes. This arrangement was based on the joint ambitions of technological advancement in designing cutting edge products for their respective target markets. This strategic alliance concept extended to offering distribution and promotional efforts. For example, Sun offers online connections to Specialized Bikes dealers to provide consumers greater choices, more accessibility to product information, and better convenience than what can be obtained through traditional distribution channels. Specialized Bikes puts Designed by Sun logos on all its bikes and helmet

packaging, creating greater awareness for both Sun and Specialized Bikes (Prince and Davies 2002). These products fit together in terms of use and lifestyle.

Another example of product fit is the promotion of Frito-Lay chips with KC Masterpiece barbecue sauce, which represents an efficient alternative to traditional brand-extension strategies (Rao and Ruekert 1994). Giro, a bicycling, snowboarding, and action sport helmet manufacturer, is entering the footwear industry through a strategic partnership with TRG Group Inc. Giro's Footwear brand will be in three product categories: After-sport, Active Lifestyle (that includes road bike-influenced and mountain bike-influenced offerings), and Indie/Skate. Design influences follow Giro helmet's lead in color and vamp styling, such as venting curves on the Atmos helmet. Their Roc Loc helmet retention system will appear in footwear closure systems. Product line design, operations, sales, marketing, and global distribution will be done by TRG Group Inc. (Leland 2006).

Brand Fit

Brands must complement each other. Consumers should perceive the brands as providing equal or complementary value, status, and experience. With brand fit, companies with two distinct brands can be marketed together to form a unique composite offering that adds value for the consumer.

Two brands that joined together and formed a strategic alliance are Coca-Cola and Disney (See Figure 14.1). Disney allowed Mickey Mouse, one of their famous characters, to appear on packaging labels for Coca-Cola products (Campbell 1999). The two well-known brands gave strength to the product they represented. Samsung and Microsoft also are partnering to produce a product that will enhance the consumer experience in

14.1 Coca-Cola and Disney joined together to form a strategic alliance.

relation to video games. Microsoft makes the Next Generation Xbox video game system. Samsung is a well-respected electronics producer. The two companies claim that the combination of their expertise will allow the most advanced and realistic experiences for the gaming consumer, worldwide (*Electronic News* 2005).

Another profitable example is the partnership between British Air and Hertz. Each company promotes the other to its customers, thereby increasing mutual exposure, brand equity, and profit. Target market segments of the two companies are compatible because frequent flyers are likely to rent cars. Thus, customer targeting is made easier for these two companies through sharing of their customer databases. Also, benefits to British Air include the added convenience of providing a smooth transfer of their customers from air to road (Prince and Davies 2002). This level of customer service is consistent with British Air's market position.

For more than 20 years, Ford Motor Company and Eddie Bauer have been joined together to create the line of Eddie Bauer Explorers and Expeditions. The line represents an inventive sports utility vehicle with distinctive style, superior performance, and many features exclusive to the line. The Explorer claims to be as quiet as a luxury car with gold exterior accents, leather-trimmed bucket seats, dual-zone temperature control, and a 280-watt sound system (www.eddiebauer.com). The 2006 Expedition adds class with the Eddie Bauer name (See Figure 14.2). Avon and Mattel have developed an alliance to benefit both parties. The joint initiative produced new Barbie dolls and other Mattel products as well as Barbie doll clothing and other Barbie registered trademark cosmetics to be sold through Avon (See Figure 14.3). Mattel developed a series of Barbies for Avon by blending Mattel's high-quality products with Avon's sales expertise. Through this

strategic alliance effort, Avon benefited from Mattel's brand equity; Mattel has benefited from Avon's direct sales force (Chonko 1999).

14.2 Ford Motor Company and Eddie Bauer have joined together to create the line of Eddie Bauer Explorers and Expeditions.

14.3 Mattel has developed a series of Barbie dolls for Avon.

The American Marketing Association conducted a study on strategic alliances, in which 80 percent of respondents said they would purchase a digital-imaging product if it were co-branded by both Sony and Eastman Kodak (Lindstrom 2005). However, only 20 percent said they would buy the product if it were branded by Sony or Kodak alone. AT&T and British Telecom's alliance Concert was launched in 1998, backed by $10 billion and the names of two of the world's most well-known telecommunication companies (Lindstrom 2005). Concert did not last more than two years, and left doubt in the minds of marketers that strategic alliance was a good idea. In this case, strategic alliance failed due to the lack of brand fit.

STRATEGIC ALLIANCE AT DIFFERENT LEVELS OF RETAIL DEVELOPMENT

When strategic alliances are effectively used among partners who have the same values and goals, this leads to a win-win situation for all partners involved. Strategic alliances can be formed at three different levels of retail development: products and services, brick-and-mortar stores, and community planning and development.

Product/Service Level

Strategic alliances can be created at the product or service levels. Product or serv-ice co-marketing alliances span diverse contexts such as ingredient strategic alliance involving physical product integration, experiential goods with celebrity performers, same company strategic alliance, and multisponsor strategic alliance. A discussion of each type of product brand partnering follows.

INGREDIENT STRATEGIC ALLIANCE INVOLVING PHYSICAL PRODUCT INTEGRATION

Strategic alliances can be formed for brands in which one product cannot be used or consumed without the other. The objective of this situation is reaching the current target market with the core product complementarity. Through core complementarity, each brand makes a significant contribution to the co-brand's core benefits. Examples include Reese's Peanut Butter Cups with Hershey's chocolate, Dell computers with Intel inside, and Audi and Mercedes-Benz automobiles using Goodyear tires (Leuthsser et al. 2002).

There also are instances where high-quality or high-image brands are paired with brands of lesser status. Associating a nationally branded ingredient with a lesser known product (e.g., Heartland Raisin Bran with SunMaid raisins) usually does not adversely affect the national brand. A. Rao et al. (1999) found that high-quality brands can convey a sense of higher quality to partner brands. For example, in 2005, Coca-Cola endorsed Splenda by using it in Diet Coke (See Figure 14.4). Similarly, low-equity brands gain more in a strategic alliance situation than high-equity brands; however, they do not damage the high-equity brands with which they partner. Well-respected, powerful brands have little to lose in strategic alliance ventures, even when the partner brand is a weak one (Washburn et al. 2000). The DuPont company supplies Silverstone, Kevlar, StainMaster, and other brands to

14.4 Coca-Cola endorsed Splenda by using it in Diet Coke.

manufacturers, from ones offering high-profile, high-equity primary brands to ones with marginal, low equity marks; nearly all of those instances have involved strategic alliance. DuPont has had success and achieved market dominance and near monopoly status in some instances (Leuthesser et al. 2003).

Many food categories use strategic alliance. Betty Crocker baking products advertise Hershey's chocolate in cake mixes and brownies, and Sunkist brand lemon flavoring in their lemon-flavored desserts. Braun and Oral-B came together to create a plaque remover. G4, a video game network, and Hasbro, a worldwide leader in entertainment products, are creating entertainment for the G4 audience featuring many products manufactured by Hasbro.

EXPERIENTIAL GOODS WITH CELEBRITY PERFORMERS

Broadcast network shows have partnered with print magazines to form alliances. CNN launched new magazines based on Time Inc., titled as the *CNN Newsstand* brand in June 1998. *CNN Newsstand/Time* appeared on Sunday nights; *CNN Newsstand/Fortune-Money* appeared on Wednesdays; and *CNN Newsstand/Entertainment Weekly* appeared on Thursdays. (Lafayette 1998).

Other examples of products endorsed by celebrities include Martha Stewart's signature paint made by Sherwin Williams; Visa International's celebrity branded credit card featuring Chinese Olympic Champion Liu Xiang; and Elizabeth Taylor's White Diamonds perfume by Elizabeth Arden. Coty is noted as having the largest number of celebrity licenses among all fragrance companies. The licenses that Coty holds have helped the 101-year-old company grow to $2.1 billion in June 2005 up from $1.4 billion in 2001 (Boorstin 2005).

SAME COMPANY STRATEGIC ALLIANCE

In the same company strategic alliance strategy, brands are partnered with the objective of achieving greater market share in the company's current target market (Leuthesser et al. 2003). Oscar Mayer explored strategic alliance opportunities with fellow members of the Kraft Foods family, such as Taco Bell meals and DiGiorno pasta, to help boost sales of Deli Select offerings (*National Provisioner* 1999). Another example is Nestlé's Kit-Kat chocolate bar where Nestlé is the family brand and Kit-Kat is the mono brand name.

MULTISPONSOR STRATEGIC ALLIANCE

Multiple organizations or firms can be involved in forming strategic alliances. This type of strategic alliance exists between Georgia Pacific, the paper towel and toilet paper manufacturer, and Walt Disney Co. (*The Atlanta Journal-Constitution* 2005). Georgia Pacific brands include Brawny and Sparkle paper towels, Quilted Northern and Angel Soft toilet paper, and Dixie cups. Walt Disney Co. owns Disney World, the ABC and ESPN TV networks, movie studios, and licensed toys. In 2005, Georgia Pacific's brand Brawny paper towels sponsored Lights, Motors, Action! Extreme Stunt Show at Disney's MGM Studios in Florida (*Paper and Pulp* 2005). This sponsorship agreement promotes the Brawny name in Disney markets.

Reach/awareness strategic alliance is associated with cooperation where a partner increases awareness by quickly gaining access to the other partner's customer base (Blackett and Boad 1997). Credit card companies commonly use reach/awareness strategic alliance. An example is American Express's Optima card with Delta Airlines' SkyMiles program.

An increasing number of credit cards issued worldwide are co-branded. Co-branded credit cards, specifically affinity and rewards cards, connect credit card issuers with market segments served by the linked (secondary) brand. Affinity cards, which can be linked to universities and charities, designate a portion of the transaction fees to the linked organizations. Users of these cards know that each time they make a purchase it benefits an organization with which they have a strong sense of commitment (Punch 2001). Rewards cards encourage continued patronage from the customer and provide benefits to the customer such as discounts or points. Examples of rewards cards include car, airline, lodging, and retail credit cards. An important benefit to the credit card issuer is gaining access to the customer list of its strategic alliance partner. This list can be used to solicit new customers for its other products and services (Leuthesser et al. 2003).

Brick-and-Mortar Level

The second area that can benefit from strategic alliances is at the brick-and-mortar level. Brick-and-mortar alliances can be from store to store, from store to Internet, or from store to product. These alliances are created to improve the overall shopping experience.

STORE-TO-STORE

Store-to-store alliances can be observed in Bass Pro Shops and Big Buck Brewery and Steakhouses. They offer freestanding utopias for individuals wanting a unique shopping experience. The marriage of Bass Pro Shops and Big Buck Brewery and Steakhouse in Grapevine, Texas, was pursued based upon the outdoor themes of both venues. Big Buck offers steaks, chicken, seafood, and pasta dishes in a casual family dining atmosphere along with award-winning handcrafted beer (www.bigbuck.com).

Another example of a store-to-store alliance includes convenience stores and fast-food restaurants. Convenience stores and fast-food restaurants both serve a niche of goal-oriented consumers who shop for specific items. The popularity of purchasing meals on the run in one stop can be proven through positive sales figures. Taco Bell, for example, put 75 percent more of its Taco Bell express units into convenience stores (Silver 2001). By having a fast food location at their stores, convenience stores are removing the negative food reputation that once plagued them (Kramer 1995). A convenience store that has partnered with fast food stores is BreadBox. The BreadBox Convenience store, based in Fayetteville, North Carolina, offers their patrons the latest features and services of convenience stores. There are also fast food venues, such as KFC, Taco Bell, Subway, and Godfather's Pizza, attached to several of the BreadBox convenience stores. They strive to provide an inviting store as well as convenience for customers (www.breadbox.biz).

STORE-TO-INTERNET

Brick-and-mortar stores partnering with Internet sites have become a necessity. Consumers do not always use the same criteria for shopping; therefore, different retail channels can improve value for consumers who shop in different shopping venues (Mathwick, Malhotra, and Rigdon 2002).

Kroger is an example of a brick-and-mortar store that has paired up with an Internet retailer Priceline. The Kroger Company signed up its 106 Michigan stores to Priceline's network. Office Depot has formed a marketing alliance with an Internet company—America Online, Inc. (*Chain Store Age* 2000). There is some controversy as to whether an allegiance between brick-and-mortar and Internet companies can benefit the consumer instead of just benefiting the allied companies. Take, for example, Toys "R" Us and

Amazon.com during the Christmas season of 1999. Toys "R" Us overpromised and under delivered; 53 percent of online shoppers did not receive their products on time for gift giving (Davis 2000). The focus needs to be on the customer, not just on the benefits to the companies involved.

STORE-TO-PRODUCT

Stores can benefit from having exclusive agreements with certain product brands. Benefits are obtained by creating consumer loyalty, attracting shoppers to the brand, and improving the store image (Lisanti 2001). Examples of well-known brands partnering up with brick-and-mortar locations include Kmart with Disney, Sesame Street, Jaclyn Smith, Kathy Ireland, and Martha Stewart; Target with Eddie Bauer, Martex, Mossimo, Nikki Taylor by Liz Claiborne, and Michael Graves; and Wal-Mart with George, Stanley tools, Olsen Twins, and Kathie-Lee Gifford. By partnering with well-known product brands, brick-and-mortar stores can add to their own store equity, leading to competitive advantage (Mentzer, Min, and Zacharia 2000).

Community Planning and Development

At the community planning and development stage, city officials, owners, and developers work together to pique consumer interest in community development. At this stage, there are two main areas to be considered: new development and redevelopment.

NEW DEVELOPMENT

Retailers must create different ways to entice consumers who are looking for new and stimulating shopping experiences. Shopping center owners and developers are eager to zero in on a winning retail formula (Porter and Tindall 2002). A winning retail formula does not consider retailing as a separate entity but as a partner with an overall development concept. One current winning retail formula is a pedestrian lifestyle village that encompasses a total retail experience. The overall concept of such a village is attractive as a destination; it is a shopping resource; and it provides entertainment venues for consumers. The village itself is defined as a special consumer experience. A big part of the village charm is its vibrant, people-friendly environment that is designed to hold park benches, fountains, and other amenities conducive to socializing and casual browsing. The atmosphere includes a variety of community-oriented entertainment possibilities. Retail tenants of this type of village are expected to offer creative and exciting stores. The restaurants usually have outside seating available and are adjacent to gathering areas in the village.

This type of strategy requires a careful planning at the community level. Each location of the preplanned village is researched and customer demographic characteristics are taken into consideration to provide a complementary retail design for that location. Examples include Flatiron Crossings located in Broomfield, Colorado, and Mall of Georgia located in Buford, Georgia (See Figure 14.5). Flatiron Crossing is an architectural representation of the mountain canyons, high country trails, and prairies that are located not too far away from the village. Flatiron Crossing is strategically located between Denver and Boulder just at the foot of the Rocky Mountains (Porter and Tindall 2002). The Mall of Georgia is set apart by the development design that is reminiscent of an old-fashioned town square (Sicard 1999).

Retailers must work together with developers, other retailers, business owners, and city officials to maintain the village feel and ambiance. The guidelines for most of the planned villages have to remain flexible to grow with changing customer

14.5 Shopping development Mall of Georgia creates a strategic alliance at the community level.

demographics and to ensure the customers' desires are met as much as possible (Springer 2002). This could require adding or changing retail tenants or changing locations of retail tenants to better suit consumer needs and expectations.

Another good example of strategic alliances at the community level is Triangle Town Center in Raleigh, North Carolina. Development companies, design firms, city officials, and retailers have worked together to present a total experience for the consumer with this village. The center opened in August 2002 and houses shops and restaurants in an inviting open-air, pedestrian-friendly environment. The shopping experience is enhanced by unique landscape design fea-

tures such as decorative river rock, textured pavers, walking bridges, and a river flowing through the common area, all culminating at a multitiered water fountain (www.carolinanewswire.com). Mark Carter, a senior vice president at TVS and Associates, stated that each side of the center has its own personality and expresses the uniqueness of the Raleigh area (Springer 2002).

REDEVELOPMENT

Certain downtown districts are redeveloped through strategic alliances. Downtown Chicago has areas where up to 250,000 people in a three-mile radius are underserved (Chicago Roundtable 1999). Recognizing that different kinds of experiences can enhance consumer shopping, the city tries to meet the needs of locals who enjoy reading, learning, and participating in meaningful experiences, as well as tourists who are looking for entertainment. City Park at Lincolnshire is one redevelopment project that hopes to bring in a cooking school for consumers to participate in and enjoy. The addition of an ice-skating rink to North Center was developed for consumers and their families to experience while they were downtown shopping. City officials work with retailers in the downtown locations to offer these unique opportunities for consumers to enlighten and educate retailers by showing local sites and by providing them with information on sales and demographics of the downtown area (Chicago Roundtable 1999).

The city of Rockville, Maryland, used eminent domain to help start a redevelopment project in response to residents' request for a revitalized town center. A master plan for redevelopment incorporated a mixed-use design with spaces for public, commercial, residential, retail, cultural, restaurant, and entertainment in the town center. Rockville partnered with private developers in creating a town center that would be a focal point for civic, social, and business activity (Rothenberg 2005).

GLOBAL STRATEGIC ALLIANCES

Strategic alliances are valuable opportunities for brand development in foreign countries. Honda Motor Company and Hong Kong Disneyland formed a strategic business alliance when Honda was named the official sponsor of the Autotopia attraction at the new park. Autotopia is a driving attraction where the visitor experiences outer space on the cosmic highways of tomorrow at Disneyland by driving innovative electric cars created specifically for the attraction. Honda also supports the park's educational and entertaining Wild About Safety Campaign, which promotes guest safety and comfort while visiting the park. Honda received exclusive rights to feature images of Hong Kong Disneyland in its promotion of Honda automobiles, motorcycles, and selected power equipment (*JCN Newswire* 2006).

Eraman, Malaysia's largest airport retailer organization, formed strategic partnerships with 40 retail outlets appealing to their target customers who are seasoned and discerning travelers with refined tastes and a desire for exclusive goods. Eraman partnered with suppliers of international brands, like Bally, Burberry, Tie Rack, Royal Selangor Pewter, and Lanvin. These partnerships give credibility and add strength to Eraman's position in the industry. Eraman is using brand-building strategies in advertising and promotional activities. These activities focus on celebrations, such as Mother's Day, Father's Day contests, Merdeka, Ramadan, and the Miss Tourism International Pageant. In addition, Eraman also is involved with a joint television program with Sistem Televisyen Malaysia Bhd (TV3). The program *Enak Berselera di KLIA* highlights various food and beverage outlets available at the airport (*Malaysian Business* 2004).

CHAPTER SUMMARY

Strategic alliances use two or more brands on one product (or service) or set of products (or services). Two brand names on a product or service brings two different markets together to purchase the same goods, therefore generating customers, increasing the likelihood of sales, and increasing the chances of a return purchase. With strategic alliance, several brands can create synergy and power through customer awareness, which in turn yields more traffic than a single brand-name operation. Thus, strategic alliance can be a win-win strategy for both partners.

Benefits of strategic alliances include: delivering a better attribute profile, producing synergies, providing access to new untapped markets, reducing barriers to market entry, providing strategic benefits, and providing operational benefits. However, strategic alliances face several challenges such as unobservable product quality, customer confusion, and transitory nature. The success of strategic alliances is influenced by both product fit and brand fit. Product fit refers to the closeness or complementarities of the product categories, as in the case of Sun Microsystems and Specialized Bikes. Brand fit refers to the level of consistency between perceptions of two or more brands, as in the case of British Air and Hertz.

Strategic alliances to benefit the retail experience can be found at three different levels of retail development: products/ services, brick-and-mortar stores, and community planning and development. Product/service strategic alliances span diverse contexts, such as ingredient strategic alliance involving physical product integration (e.g., Reese's Peanut Butter Cups with Hershey's chocolate), experiential goods with celebrity performers (e.g., Martha Stewart's signature paint made by Sherwin Williams), same company strategic alliances (e.g., Nestlé's Kit-Kat chocolate bar), and multisponsor strategic alliances (e.g., American Express and Delta Airlines' SkyMiles program). Brick-and-mortar alliances could be from store to store (e.g., Bass Pro Shops and Big Buck), from store to Internet (e.g., Kroger with Priceline), or from store to product (e.g., Target with Mossimo). At the community planning and development stage, city officials, owners, and developers work as a team for new development (e.g., Mall of Georgia, Buford, Georgia) or redevelopment (e.g., downtown Chicago).

Discussion Questions

1. Discuss similarities and differences between brand extension and strategic alliance. Explain when one strategy is preferred over another in retailing.

2. Explain why strategic alliance is becoming more popular. Identify the benefits of a strategic alliance, and give retail examples.

3. Explain the difference between product fit and brand fit. Give retail examples (other than the examples provided in the text) of both.

4. Pick an example of a recent strategic alliance case. Explain its short-term benefits to both companies. Discuss whether this alliance will be successful in the long term and, if so, why.

5. Find an example of a past strategic alliance failure (other than examples in the text). Explain why this alliance was a failure.

6. You have just moved to a small historic town that attracts tourists with its historic sites and autumn foliage. You own a small bed and breakfast inn, with no hotels located in town but several other bed and breakfast inns. All bed and breakfast inns face high occupancy rates in the fall, which pose a threat to developing long-term repeat customers. How can you become engaged in strategic alliance in the community to stabilize annual sales?

References

Abratt, R., and P. Motlana. 2002. Managing strategic alliance strategies: Global brands into local markets. *Business Horizons* 45(5):42–50.

Advertising Age. 2005. Five barnburners 76(50):S2.

The Atlanta Journal-Constitution. 2005. Georgia blue chips. January 14, 2F.

Blackett, T., and B. Boad. 1997. *Co-branding: The science of alliance.* New York: St. Martin's Press.

Boad, B. 1999. Strategic alliance comes of age. *Managing Intellectual Property* 94:20–26.

Boorstin, Julia. 2005. The scent of celebrity. *Fortune* 152(10):67–70.

Campbell, Lisa. 1999. Coca-Cola and Disney link in dual promotion. *Marketing.* April 22, 5.

Chain Store Age. 2000. Electronic retailing news 76(7):1–2.

Chicago Roundtable. 1999. Shopping center world staff. Retrieved May 3, 2006, from www.retailtrafficmag.com/mag/retail_chicago_roundtable/index.html.

Chonko, L. 1999. Case study: Alliance formation with direct selling companies: Avon and Mattel. *Journal of Personal Selling and Sales Management* 19(1):51–62.

Davis, S. 2000. Will the mes have it this holiday season? *Brandweek* 41(48):28.

DSN Retailing Today. 2005. BET alliance targets urban consumer 44(17):26.

Electronic News. 2005. Samsung, Microsoft Ink HDTV Alliance for Next-Gen Xbox Console 51(18):1.

JCN Newswire. 2006. Honda and Hong Kong Disneyland form strategic alliance. *Japan Corporate News Network* (Tokyo). July 12, 1.

Kramer, L. 1995. A marriage of convenience: C-stores hitch their future to fast feeders. *Nation Restaurant News* 29(26):33.

Kumar, P. 2005. The impact of co-branding on customer evaluation of brand counterextensions. *Journal of Marketing* 69(3):1–18.

Lafayette, J. 1998. Despite drops, more magazines. *Electronic Media* 17(49):81–82.

Leland, J. 2006. Giro moves from heads to toes *SGB* 39(8):12.

Leuthesser, L., C. Kohli, and R. Suri. 2003. Academic papers 2 + 2 = 5? A framework focusing strategic alliance to leverage a brand. *Journal of Brand Management* 11(1):35–47.

Lindstrom, M. 2005. Brand plus brand doesn't always equal success. *Media Asia.* April 8, 21.

Lisanti, T. 2001. Retailers continue to chase exclusivity for good reasons. *DSN Retailing Today* 40(4):11.

Malaysian Business. 2004. Shopping paradise. *Malaysian Business.* May 1, 16.

Mathwick, C., N. Malhotra, and E. Rigdon. 2002. The effect of dynamic retail experiences on experiential perceptions of value: On Internet and catalog comparison. *Journal of Retailing* 78:51–60.

Mentzer, J., S. Min, and Z. Zacharia. 2000. The nature of interfirm partnering in supply chain management. *Journal of Retailing* 76(4):549–569.

National Provisioner. 1999. Lunchmeat manufacturers on the attack to regain market slippage. *213*(8):80–81.

O'Reilly, G. 2006. Lindt trials chocs in luxury living rooms. *Promotions & Incentives.* February, 5.

Paper and Pulp. 2005. Disney G-P seal cooperative deal 79(2):12.

Park, C. W., S. Y. Jun, and A. D. Shocker. 1996. Composite branding alliances: An investigation of extension and feedback effects. *Journal of Marketing Research* 33(4):453–466.

Porter, T., and R. Tindall. 2002. What works on retail villages. Retrieved May 1, 2006, from www.retailmag.com/mag/retail_works_retail_villages/index.html.

Prince, M., and M. Davies. 2002. Strategic alliance partners: What do they see in each other? *Business Horizons* 45(5):51–55.

Punch, L. 2001. Loyalty theater: Co-branding 10 years after. *Credit Card Management* 14:42–50.

Rao, A., and R. Ruekert. 1994. Brand alliances as signals of product quality. *Sloan Management Review* 36(1):87–97.

Rao, A., L. Qu, and R. Ruekert. 1999. Signaling unobservable product quality through a brand alley. *Journal of Marketing Research* 36(2):258–268.

Ritson, M. 2006. Sleeping with the enemy can pay off. *Marketing (UK)* 21.

Rothenberg, P. V. 2005. Pondering public use. *Journal of Property Management* 70(6):12.

Sicard, A., 1999. Mall of Georgia debuts. Retrieved May 2, 2006, from www.retailtrafficmag.com/mag/retail_mal_georgia_debuts/index.html

Silver, Deborah. 2001. A matter of convenience. Restaurants *and Institutions* 111(20):36–41.

Simonin, B., and J. Ruth. 1998. Is a company known by the company it keeps?

Assessing the spillover effects of brand alliances on consumer brand attitudes. *Journal of Marketing Research* 35(1):30–83.

Spekman, R., L. Isabella, T. MacAvoy, and T. Forbes III. 1996. Creating strategic alliances which endure. *Long Range Planning* 29(3):346–357.

Springer, J. 2002. Raleigh mall's design mingles local history and progress. *Shopping Centers Today*. Retrieved May 3, 2006 from www.icsc.org/srch/sct/sct0103/page37.html

Stanley, T. L. 1999. History afield. *Brandweek* 40(10):18–20.

Strategic Direction. 2004. Adidas and All Blacks build winning partnership: The benefits of corporate strategic alliance. 20(1):7–9.

Terreri, A. 2006. Schwan's Bakery: Success is easy as pie. *Frozen Food Age* 54(10):28.

Vence, D. L. 2005. Product enhancement. *Marketing News* 39(8):19–25.

Washburn, J. H., B. D. Till, and R. Priluck. 2000. Strategic alliance: Brand equity and trial effects. *The Journal of Consumer Marketing* 17(7):591–604.

Yip, P. 2005. Basic concepts of strategic alliance, with examples from the hospitality industry, could strategic alliance improve your bottomline? *Hotel Online*. Retrieved July 28, 2006 from www.hotel-online.com/News/PR2005_3rd/Sep05_CoBranding.html

GLOBAL EXPERIENTIAL RETAILING

CHAPTER 15

An Octopus in the Shopping Trolly

Tesco made a strategic decision when it entered the local South Korean market and recruited Samsung, the country's largest conglomerate and most powerful brand, as a local partner. Holding a 19 percent stake in the business, a Samsung executive was appointed chief executive and Samsung was put first in the joint-venture title of Samsung-Tesco.

When the Samsung-Tesco new store in Youngdeungpo, southwest Seoul, opened in December 2001 it had little resemblance to any of the U.K. company's domestic supermarkets. Shoppers at a Tesco in the United Kingdom would not be able to buy a pet iguana, pick an octopus from a tank of live seafood, visit the dentist, or take ballet lessons. The seven-story hypermarket makes its U.K. counterparts look as drab and limited as corner shops in comparison.

"This is Korean culture," said Eric Bowen, chief operating offer of Tesco's 14 South Korean outlets, gesturing to the vibrant market atmosphere of the Seoul store's fish counter, where assistants in traditional Korean dress bow to each arriving customer. "It would have been totally wrong to import the sterile shopping environment of a Tesco in Skipton, Bridgend, or Watford," he said.

Tesco's strategy to incorporate community services and the lively and colorful local shopping culture into its South Korean stores was to neutralize opposition that has faced the entrance of Western retailers into some Asian markets. In South Korea there was concern about the impact of hypermarkets on small family-owned shops known as mom-and-pop stores, which still dominate the retail industry.

Tesco has localized its service better than its Western rivals Wal-Mart and Carrefour, [which] appear to be less capable of responding to local consumers' tastes [and] makes them less competitive. Local tastes include a demand for much more fresh food than shoppers would see in a U.K. Tesco. The sprawling fish counter at the Youngdeungpo Tesco offers more varieties of seafood than the average British consumer would think possible. Besides octopuses, live specimens include squid, lobsters, and fish that are plucked live from the tank and chopped up alive in traditional sushi style. The hypermarket offers 70 checkout lanes.

Beyond the food hall, there are clothes, home appliances, and other household goods, toys, books, a golf shop, fast-food bars, coffee shops, and good restaurants. Cars can be serviced while their owners shop. Pedestrians can reach the store by public transport via a dedicated subway stop. Toddlers can be left in a play area, while older children and adults can visit the store's art gallery or attend one of the classes held in the community center or cookery demonstration kitchen.

Korean consumer behavior has shifted from the conspicuous consumption of the 1990s to a more value-oriented consumption. This benefits the discount store industry as time-strapped and efficiency-minded consumers look for low prices, varied merchandise, and convenient shopping environments.

Korean customers want the human touch and customer-friendliness. Samsung—Tesco has combined the best of Tesco and the Western way and the best of Samsung and the Eastern way. Tesco brought professionalism and logistical strength while Samsung retained Korean qualities.

Source: Ward, A. 2002. An octopus in the shopping trolly. *Financial Times* [London, UK]. January 11, 12.

INTRODUCTION

Globalization is influencing retailing and hospitality service industries as companies seek to expand operations in ways that will retain and attract new customers. These industries face daily challenges to improve the effectiveness of their marketing efforts within this complex and competitive global market environment (Daouas 2001, Riege and Perry 2000). The Internet presents further challenges and opportunities to retailers since it offers a virtual shopping environment where consumers can access products and services from all over the world (See Figure 15.1).

To stay competitive, retailers must differentiate themselves not only at local, regional, and national levels but also globally. Retailers who are on the cutting edge will be differentiated by the product, brand, and retail environment experiences that they offer consumers. This chapter examines globalization and dimensions of consumer cultures, international retailing, global e-tailing, outshopping, and opportunities and challenges for global experiential retailing.

GLOBALIZATION AND DIMENSIONS OF CONSUMER CULTURE

Consumers are distinguished by socio-demographic characteristics and culturally unique consumption patterns. They can be organized into cohesive segments that are based on shared characteristics, ideas, and behaviors. Retailers who use strategic segmentation can offer products, services, media, and social environments that support the cultural identities of the consumers that they seek to engage. Segmentation also helps the retailer support and foster consumption of the cultural artifacts that are important to these targeted consumers (Peñaloza and Gilly 1999). Globalization affects three dimensions of consumer culture: local, foreign, and global (Alden, Steenkamp, and Batra 1999).

Local Consumer Culture

A **local consumer culture** reflects the cultural meanings associated with indigenous

15.1 Consumers have worldwide access to goods and services via online shopping using computers.

(native to an area) norms, values, and identities. Local tastes and traditions are evident in the local retail environment and in the products that are sold there. Local people consume branded products that are produced locally for their consumption.

Local consumer culture in Japan is reflected in a very distinct retail environment. Department stores remain an important retail segment and social institution in spite of the existence of specialty retailers and Internet shopping. Japan lacks competitive supermarkets and gourmet shops. A big draw for department stores are the extensive food halls that offer groceries and prepared foods. Customer service is integrated into every aspect of shopping. Takashimaya, Japan's largest chain of department stores, maintains a 400-member staff of experts certified by various professions (e.g., architects, art curators, sommeliers, interior designers) who provide shoppers with specific services. In the flagship Nihombashi store, there are 38 specialists to assist customers with etiquette and purchases such as kimonos, tuxedos, and gifts (Olmsted 2006) (See Figure 15.2).

A concern in many countries is the loss of local culture as foreign and global cultures expand. Budget airlines and growing discretionary income for travel have made Barcelona, Spain, accessible to a global pool of tourists. This boom was stimulated by the 1992 Olympics, which generated international awareness of the cultural attractions in the city. Alien forms of retail sprung up, which do not portray the cultural uniqueness of the city. The Maremagnum shopping center on the waterfront includes an IMAX theater, a multiplex, an aquarium, shops, and a fast food court that includes a proliferation of foreign restaurants such as Texas Steak Company. Hard Rock Cafe, Foot Locker, and Dunkin' Donuts are in the Gothic center of the city. Significant changes in retail

15.2 Customer services retain the local Japanese culture.

and entertainment venues that resulted from increased tourism have led some to wonder if the culture people come to experience will be watered down beyond recognition, and Barcelona will become the same as everywhere else (Turner 2006).

China, with more than one billion people, has the single largest consumer market in the world. Although growing affluence, mobility, and access to media have led to more importance being assigned to self-fulfillment, individual values, and internationalism, consumers retain distinct, traditional Chinese core values (e.g., proper living, social consciousness, moderation, and moral self-control) that are associated with a collective-oriented culture (Gong 2003). In examining cross-cultural issues and decision making of Chinese consumers, W. Gong (2003) concluded that retailers who want to do business in China need to perfect cultural adaptation in the country. For example, retailers may need to rethink promotional strategies such as coupon

redemption, which can be perceived as a sign of cheapness or a poor product quality among Chinese consumers.

Foreign Consumer Culture

Foreign consumer culture includes the consumer perceptions, attitudes, and behaviors that are exhibited toward products, brands, and companies that are not indigenous. For example, in many developing countries, such as China and Vietnam, foreign retail brands are equated with modern, clean, and air-conditioned shopping experiences (Birchall 2005) (See Figure 15.3). Country image, country-of-origin image, and consumer ethnocentrism are aspects of foreign consumer culture that international retailers need to consider when they expand into foreign markets.

COUNTRY IMAGE

Country image refers to the broad notions that consumers hold about the products associated with that country. It is generated by the mental impression and reputation that consumers and businesspeople assign to a particular country (Nagashima 1970). Country image also includes "stereotypes held about a country's economic and political environment, while ethnic image refers to a country's cultural environment; country image and ethnic image together can be viewed as dimensions of national stereotypes" (Ahmed, Johnson, Ling, Fang, and Hui 2002, 282).

Country image is influenced by cognitive, affective, and conative consumer responses to products and people of a specific country (Roth and Romeo 1992, Parameswaran and Pisharodi 1994). Country image is created through products, national characteristics, economic and political backgrounds, a historical past, and traditions (Nagashima 1970). D. B. Holt, J. A. Quelch, and E. L. Taylor (2004) concluded that "consumers still prefer brands that hail from countries that are considered to have particular expertise" (75). For example, heritage and class are associated with England (See Figure 15.4). France is linked to quality living and chic lifestyle. Italy is associated with style and fashion. Quality and reliability are part of the German brand image. Switzerland is associated with methodical precision and trustworthiness. Miniaturization and advanced functionality are linked to Japanese brands. Brand-neutral countries such as Belgium, Portugal, Austria, Chile, and Canada have produced very few brand leaders in international markets (Anholt 2000, Holt et al. 2004, 282).

Country image can cause a nation or a region within a nation to be considered a brand. The nation becomes an indicator of product quality and a definer of image and target market. When a country image is integrated into brand image, the qualities that characterize a country are key attributes for successful global brands. It is difficult to identify global brands that are not associated with strongly branded countries. Only a few, mostly European, countries have clear, consistent, and universally understood national brand images (Anholt 2000). France is a brand that is associated worldwide with the culture of food. It is a formidable competitor in the food categories of wine and cheese (Miller 2006). The strength of France as a brand was recognized by the French government, which launched a blue-ribbon commission in 2006 to consider how to enhance the concept of France, the country, as a brand (Musnik 2006).

The country image of the United States represents freedom, tolerance, and democracy (Tomkins 2004). Nike is a global U.S. brand that has built its success in part on the fact that it is American (See Figure 15.5). Conversely, country image can sometimes detrimentally affect consumer choice. For U.S. companies, this is important because 62 of the world's most valuable global brands are American (Holt et al. 2004). R. Tomkins (2004) suggests that negative perceptions associated with the U.S. involvement in the Iraq War, unilateralism on treaty negotiations, and corporate scandals may have contributed to declining consumer support for U.S. brands in countries outside North America in the early twenty-first century. However, recent anti-American sentiment may not be enough to interrupt the underlying equity of U.S. brands.

COUNTRY-OF-ORIGIN IMAGE

When the perspective of a country image is applied to the evaluation of products, it is a **country-of-origin image** (Pereira, Hsu, and Kundu 2005). A brand's country-of-origin image influences consumer brand perception. Harrod's of London is a fine example. Chinese consumers are responsive to country-of-origin (Zhang 1996) and they perceive imported products as more

prestigious and higher class than domestic products because of their long-time association of low quality with domestic products (Tai 1998). Z. U. Ahmed et al. (2002)

15.4 Trolleys in front of Harrod's in London

15.5 Nike is a global brand that reflects a U.S. country image. This Nike store is in Malaysia.

known Spanish specialty retailers include Zara, Mango, and Cortefiel. El Corte Inglés (literally *The English Cut*) is the most important and successful local retailer in Spain (See Figure 15.6). Its success can be attributed to a number of factors, including a clear understanding of department store format, customer expectations, retention of operational control, consistent and clear positioning and brand identification, a focus during periods of growth on the core business, and an emphasis on customer service and quality (Gold and Woodliffe 2000).

For much of the twentieth century, most global brands originated from European and U.S. companies. Country image was a powerful base for promoting products. For example, Gucci positioned itself in the United States as offering prestigious and fashionable Italian products. As consumers become wealthier, better informed, and able to exercise more purchasing power, their desire to buy brands based on country of origin may not prevail as in the past. In examining key characteristics that consumers associate with global brands, D. B. Holt et al. (2004) found that U.S. values did not have much importance to consumers when deciding to purchase a branded product.

found Singaporean consumers were more likely to use country-of-origin cues in making purchase decisions when compared with foreign consumers.

A consumer's national loyalty is related to country image, and it can explain why consumers make some product choices (Ahmed et al. 2002). K. Hyllegard, M. Eckman, A. M. Descals, and A. G. Borja (2005) found Spanish consumers held strong commitments and preferences for national and regional retailers and brands. Moreover, they perceived Spanish retailers offered better merchandise, customer service, payment options, and store characteristics when compared with U.S. retailers. Well-

CONSUMER ETHNOCENTRISM

The universal inclination of consumers to hold beliefs about the appropriateness, morality, and purchasing of foreign-made products is referred to as **consumer ethnocentrism.** Ethnocentric consumers feel it is wrong to purchase foreign products because it hurts the local or national economy, causes job loss, and is unpatriotic (See Figure 15.7). They view products from other countries as objects of disapproval. Conversely, non-ethnocentric consumers evaluate foreign products on the merit of their attributes, not on country of origin. In some cases the fact that they are foreign-made gives them a more favorable evaluation. Many ethnocentric consumers associate their purchasing domestic products with a sense of identity, feelings of belongingness, and an attitude that doing so is acceptable behavior (Shimp and Sharma 1987).

T. A. Shimp and S. Sharma (1987) developed a 17-item CETSCALE to measure consumer ethnocentric tendencies toward purchasing foreign-made versus U.S.-made products. The scale prompts people to pick from the following statements: "Only those products that are unavailable in the United States should be imported," "It is not right to purchase foreign products because it puts Americans out of jobs," and "A real American should always buy American-made products." In testing the CETSCALE with U.S. consumers, they found that consumers who felt the most threatened by foreign competition had the highest scores on the statements associated with "loss of job" and "lower quality of life," which indicated the most ethnocentric attitude. They suggested the CETSCALE would be useful for gaining an understanding of regional differences in consumer ethnocentrism.

Retailers need to align communication programs in regional magazines, local newspapers, and spot broadcast advertising with local customer sentiment and preferences. They also recommended that retailers use the CETSCALE when making decisions on store locations where the targeted market segment exhibits consumer ethnocentrism. In this situation, a store that imports most of its merchandise (e.g., Pier 1, The Bombay Company, World Bazaar) might not fare as well as a store that features domestic products.

Global Consumer Cultures

Globalization has produced **global consumer cultures,** which are not characterized by the similar attitudes, preferences, and behaviors that were predicted by many businesses, governments, and consumers; rather, they are composed of well-defined consumer clusters that cross national boundaries, especially in Western and newly industrialized nations (Holt et al. 2004). D. B. Holt et al. (2004) described these consumer clusters as global citizens, global dreamers, antiglobal, and global agnostics (See Table 15.1).

TABLE 15.1 GLOBAL CONSUMER CLUSTERS

CLUSTER	GLOBAL PERSPECTIVES	REPRESENTATION
Global citizen	Companies that have achieved global success are also of high quality and innovation. Companies should behave responsibly on issues of consumer health, environment, and workers' rights.	**55% of overall population** High representation: Brazil, China, Indonesia Low representation: United States, United Kingdom
Global dreamers	Global brands are quality products. We are not concerned with a company's social responsibility, but rather their market image value.	**23% of overall population** High representation: Egypt, Turkey Low representation: South Africa, India, Brazil
Antiglobals	Global brands rarely deliver higher quality. Companies are not to be trusted to behave responsibly. Companies should not preach American values.	**13% of overall population** High representation: United Kingdom, China Low representation: Egypt, South America
Global agnostics	All brands, local and global, should be evaluated using the same criteria. Global image should not have an effect on purchasing decisions.	**8% of overall population** High representation: United States, South Africa Low representation: Japan, Indonesia, China, Turkey

Source: Holt, D. B., J. A. Quelch, and E. L. Taylor, 2004. How global brands compete. *Harvard Business Review* 82(9):68–75.

Global consumer cultures share demographic and sociocultural characteristics such as being better educated and having greater affluence as well as similar needs, motivations, and behaviors. A convergence across national boundaries has resulted from growth in consumer income, increasing availability of satellite television, movies, the Internet, and growth in the travel industry. This convergence has exposed many more consumers to different cultures and experiences and reshaped consumer cultural traits and shopping patterns. These clusters of global consumers are expressing more similar needs, tastes, and lifestyles (Douglas and Craig 1997; Ramarapu, Timmerman, and Ramarapu 1999) that are not limited by geographic location (Globerman, Roel, and Standiford 2001).

Globalization, however, does not mean that the world has become a single culture with unified global tastes. Rather, global consumer cultures are experiencing a greater range of available choices (Tomkins 2004) that include an immense assortment of local, regional, and global products and brands. Consumers can purchase products and services from all over the world through local retailers who offer global brands, international retailers who have opened stores in foreign nations, and e-tailing.

Identifying subsets of similar consumers in foreign as well as domestic markets facilitates retail marketing decisions, particularly in the early stages of globalization (Ganesh, Kumar, and Subramaniam 1997). Focusing on specific target markets helps retailers anticipate and react to market changes more effectively and efficiently and facilitates a higher level of customer loyalty (Samiee and Roth 1992).

Each generation has a characteristic global culture. This culture generally is shaped by Western themes and values that are promoted through the mass media and are sold as lifestyle products and services (Wee 1999). The emergence of global consumer cultures has made it easier to identify similar consumer segments across retail markets in different countries. These cross-border segments tend to be university educated, younger, richer, and more urban than the rest of the national populations they represent (Quelch 1999). These young adults are considered the first true global consumers because of their extended exposure to instantaneous communication via the Internet (Alden et al. 1999) during their developmental teen years and young adulthood. This exposure has created a consumer population with a broader knowledge of products, events, and international fashion than previous generations at the same life stage. While these teens and adults experienced local and national social and cultural differences, their experiences also included globally shared historical events (i.e., the collapse of the World Trade Center in 2001, the 2005 Pacific rim tsunami) that have shaped their lives, even though they were not directly involved (Wee 1999). Thus, the similarities among these younger consumers across nations are greater than in the past. Furthermore, these global consumers are more prone to purchasing certain brands to reinforce their membership in this segment (Hannerz 1990). Retailers have a unique and profitable opportunity to target these younger populations as a transnational, homogenized global consumer segment.

The evolution of global teens has intensified with technological innovation. Teens gain global experiences through cross-border media such as satellite TV and radio. They engage in a multitude of Internet-based activities that include conversing by e-mail and in chat rooms, using hot-links from their cellular telephones, and bonding together through Web-based video gaming (See Figure 15.8). Their cell phones allow them to send text messages and photographs. Despite membership in different cultures, middle-class youths around the world seem to live their lives as if they were in a parallel universe. Even teen dress is reflecting more universal behavior as teens are seen around the world wearing Levi's, Nikes (de Mooij and Hofstede 2002), and other global brands. FUBU (For Us By Us), a U.S. urban outfitter and hip-hop brand, is sold in the United Kingdom and appeals to the youth market there. Retailers are commercializing the notion that teenagers possess similar values and lifestyles, regardless of their country of origin.

Brands that attract and satisfy young consumers, especially those ages 18 to 24, may engender their ongoing loyalty when they achieve increasing disposable income and begin setting up households both as singles and as young families (Ritchie 1995). Increasingly, young consumers are determining the styles and brands that trickle up to the rest of the population. Therefore, it is critical that businesses endeavor to understand this group of global consumers and predict what they will buy. In examining apparel preferences of Spanish consumers, K. Hyllegard et al. (2005) found younger Spanish males demonstrated higher acceptance of U.S. apparel brands when compared with other age groups and females. They concluded that this young male consumer group offered a viable market for U.S. specialty retailers such as Abercrombie & Fitch and Nautica.

Brands that target teens often relate to images of rebellion, individuality, freedom, confidence, sexiness, and Americanness. T. T. T. Wee (1999) cautioned against using these traditional youth themes when promoting brands across global teen markets because the images they communicate are not valued universally. In examining Singapore teens, Wee concluded that tra-

ditional mores and parental influence remain strong. He also suggested that in countries where teens have less understanding of branding and advertising, upfront effort is needed to build brand awareness and equity.

Individualist and Collectivist Consumer Cultures

G. Hofstede (1991) identified five dimensions that characterize variations in consumer cultures: individualism-collectivism (I-C), power distance, uncertainty-avoidance, masculinity-femininity, and Confucian-dynamism. **Individualism-collectivism** describes the relationship between an individual and how close or tight the social groups that distinguishes between in-groups and out-groups in the culture is. Power distance refers to how individuals deal with unequal members of society. Uncertainty-avoidance explains how a society deals with an unknown future. Confucian-dynamism explains the emphasis on long-term values (Confucian) versus short-term values (dynamism). His work is a standard on which cultural differences among consumer cultures are validated (Triandis 2004). I-C is particularly

15.8 Teens are the largest up-and-coming purchasers of personal technology. Young consumers, ages 18 to 24, are considered the first true global consumer group. These young people are determining the styles and brands that trickle up to the rest of the population.

15.9 Consumerism starts at a very young age.

eties are more self-centered and self-enhanced. In relationship to the goals, norms, interests, integrity, and consequences of their in-groups, they are less willing to sacrifice, less loyal, and less emotionally attached (Hofstede 1980, Kagitcibasi 1997). However, a significant number of the world's populations live in societies where the collective group takes precedence over the individual (Naumov and Puffer 2000).

H. C. Triandis (1995) distinguished I-C on dimensions that are vertical and horizontal. Horizontal I-C places an emphasis on equality while vertical I-C emphasizes hierarchy. Table 15.2 describes these tendencies toward idiocentrism (i.e., equality) and allocentrism (i.e., hierarchy). Characteristics that define both individualistic (idiocentric) and collectivist (allocentric) cultures can be found in consumers who live in countries that are considered collectivist (Ho and Chiu 1994, Sinha and Tripathi 1994).

Some researchers have argued that I-C generates descriptive labels of cultures and societies that are not representative of complex cultures (Voronov and Singer 2002), and it is a default explanation of cultural differences in human behavior (Kagitcibase 1994). M. Voronov and J. A. Singer (2002) suggested that ecological variables might be influential in the developmental process that is exhibited by societies as either individualistic or collectivist behaviors. In this case, the ecological variable describes open and limited access to markets and the element of trust that is associated with these markets.

important in global experiential retailing as Western retailers (i.e., from individualistic nations) expand into Asian nations that have strong collectivism cultures.

The fundamental cultural difference involved in I-C is the relationship between the individual and the group to which he or she belongs (Hawkins, Best, and Coney 2001). G. Hofstede (1980) identified this dichotomy as one of the most significant ways in which cultures vary and it offers a means of explaining cross-cultural differences in consumer behavior. According to Hofstede (1991), "individualism stands for a society in which the ties between individuals are loose; everyone is expected to look after himself or herself and his or her immediate family only. . . . Collectivism stands for a society in which people from birth onward are integrated into strong, cohesive in-groups, which throughout people's lifetime continue to protect them in exchange for unquestioning loyalty" (260–261) (See Figure 15.9). Hofstede (1980) stated that individualism represents an emotional independence for "groups, organizations, and other collectivities" (221). Consumers in individualistic soci-

RETAIL INTERNATIONALIZATION

Retail internationalization is a process of expanding into nondomestic markets. It includes exporting retail operations and private brand products (Burt, Davies, McAuley, and Sparks 2005). The top

TABLE 15.2. TENDENCIES TOWARD IDIOCENTRISM AND ALLOCENTRISM IN INDIVIDUALISM AND COLLECTIVISM CULTURES

INDIVIDUALISM AND COLLECTIVISM CULTURES BY CHARACTERISTICS OF INDIVIDUALS	TYPE OF INDIVIDUAL BY PERCENT OF POPULATION HAVING CULTURAL CHARACTERISTICS	
	IDIOCENTRIC	ALLOCENTRIC
INDIVIDUALISM	**35–100%**	**0–35%**
Characteristics of individuals in individualism cultures	• Highly expressive • Dominant • Initiate action • Aggressive • Argue logically • Regulate flow of communication • Use eye contact • Strong opinions	• Accommodating • Avoid arguments • Shift opinions easier
COLLECTIVISM	**0–35%**	**30–100%**
Characteristics of individuals in collectivism cultures	• Affluence • Leadership roles • Much education • International travel • Exposure to Western mass media • Acculturated for years in Western Culture	• Financially dependent on some ingroup • Low social class • Limited education • Little travel experience • Socialized in a unilateral family • Traditional religion • Acculturated to a collectivist culture

Source: Triandis, H. C. 2004. The many dimensions of culture. *Academy of Management Executive* 18(1):88–93.

global retailers are Wal-Mart (United States), Carrefour (France), The Home Depot (United States), and Metro (Germany)—all large big-box retailers. Among the top 50 global retailers, 21 are U.S. retailers (McIntosh and Valerio 2005). Table 15.3 lists the 50 largest retailers in the world by sales in U.S. dollars and by country.

A fundamental aspect of international retail expansion is operating networks of physical stores (Picot-Coupey 2006). A retailer's operation mode is the "institutional arrangement that makes possible the development of a company's products, technology, and managerial or human resources into a foreign country" (Picot-Coupey 2006, 216). Picot-Coupey developed a conceptual framework that integrates core aspects of operational mode choice for international retailers (See Figure 15.10 on page 394). Three explanatory variables—the marketing policy of the company, the retail company profile, and the foreign market's characteristics—affect the moderating variables of motives for internationalization and relationship networks. Collectively, the explanatory variables and moderating variables affect the underlying dimensions of dissemination risk, control, flexibility, and resource commitment. Finally, all of these variables influence which operational mode the retailer selects: shop-in-shop, franchised store, company-owned store, plural form, and composite form. From case studies of French specialty retailers that identified key determinants of operation mode choice, Picot-Coupey concluded that retail organizational structures are not static and they reflect ongoing change. "Multi-brand retailers and/or in-store boutiques are used to test the market or to expand in markets with limited potential. The development process is then organized by combining different modes: shop-in-shops with

TABLE 15.3. 50 LARGEST RETAILERS IN THE WORLD (RANKED BY SALES)

RANK	COMPANY	SALES USD (IN MILLIONS)	HEADQUARTER COUNTRY
1	Wal-Mart Stores Inc.	$285,222	United States
2	Carrefour SA	90,297	France
3	Home Depot Inc.	73,094	United States
4	Metro AG	70,093	Germany
5	Royal Ahold NV	64,615	The Netherlands
6	Tesco PLC	62,284	United Kingdom
7	Kroger Co.	56,434	United States
8	Sears Holding Corp.	55,800	United States
9	REWE Handelsgruppe	50,698	Germany
10	Costco Wholesale Corp.	48,107	United States
11	ITM Enterprise SA	47,218	France
12	Target Corp.	45,682	United States
13	Groupe Casino	45,155	France
14	Aldi Einkauf GmbH & Co OHG	42,981	Germany
15	Schwarz Group (Lidl & Schwarz)	42,571	Germany
16	Albertson's Inc.	39,897	United States
17	Edeka Gruppe	39,227	Germany
18	Walgreen Co.	37,508	United States
19	Groupe Auchan SA	37,335	France
20	Lowe's Cos. Inc.	36,464	United States
21	Safeway Inc.	35,823	United States
22	Aeon Col Ltd.	35,307	Japan
23	Ito-Yokado Co. Ltd.	33,547	Japan
24	E.Leclerc SA	32,060	France
25	Tengelmann	31,715	Germany
26	CVS Corp.	30,594	United States
27	Pinault Printemps Redoute SA	30,086	France
28	J Sainsbury PLC	28,034	United Kingdom
29	Best Buy Co. Inc.	27,433	United States
30	Coles Myer Ltd.	23,112	Australia
31	Delhaize Group	22,331	Belgium
32	Wm. Morrison Supermarkets PLC	22,245	United Kingdom

(continued)

TABLE 15.3. 50 LARGEST RETAILERS IN THE WORLD (RANKED BY SALES) *(continued)*

RANK	COMPANY	SALES USD (IN MILLIONS)	HEADQUARTER COUNTRY
33	Loblaw Cos. Limited	20,140	Canada
34	Woolworth Ltd.	19,866	Australia
35	SUPERVALU Inc.	19,543	United States
36	Publix Super Markets Inc.	18,554	United States
37	JC Penney Co. Inc.	18,424	United States
38	Systeme U Centrale Nationale	18,241	France
39	Otto GmbH & Co KG	17,951	Germany
40	El Corte Ingles, S.A.	17,006	Spain
41	Rite Aid Corp.	16,816	United States
42	Karstadt Quelle AG	16,709	Germany
43	Gap Inc.	16,267	United States
44	Federated Department Stores Inc.	15,630	United States
45	IKEA Ab, a subsidiary of INGKA Holding B.V.	15,460	Sweden
46	TJX Cos. Inc.	14,913	United States
47	Dalei Inc.	14,745	Japan
48	Staples Inc.	14,448	United States
49	May Department Stores Co.	14,441	United States
50	GUS PLC	14,360	United Kingdom

*Sales are estimated.
Source: McIntosh, J., and D. Valerio. 2005. Spanning the globe. *Chain Store Age 81*(12):58–66.

company stores, franchised stores and/or stores dedicated to the brand. Company stores are mainly used as flagship stores to create an identity and to legitimize the brand and the positioning of the store concept. The company store is a medium to establish the brand and to develop a distinctive image toward various stakeholders in the foreign market (i.e. consumers, journalists, department store managers, or competitors). . . . In-store boutiques and franchised shops are used to achieve geographic presence and help multiple the number of points of sale" (225).

International retail expansion was prompted by push-pull factors in the 1970s (Alexander 1990). By the 1990s, push factors included saturated domestic markets and increasing government regulations. This was the situation for specialty retailers who entered international operations as reactive measures to robust competition in strong mature markets. Pull factors were driven by the characteristics that make a foreign country appealing for international expansion.

Specialty retailers are now expanding to international markets based on proactive

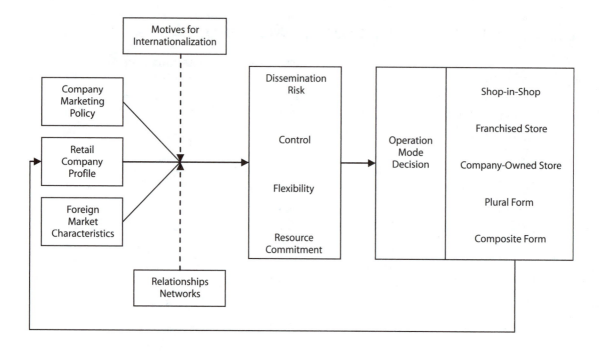

15.10 Conceptual model of the determining factors of retail store networks' operation mode choice in a foreign market

pull motives (Gripsrud and Benito 2005, Hyllegard et al. 2005). There are still opportunities for international retail expansion in mature markets. German-based Aldi, which is considered a world leader in extreme value food retailing, opened its 700th store in the United States in 2004 (Craig 2005). In 1999, Wal-Mart completed one of the most successful international expansions into a developed consumer market when it acquired Asda in the United Kingdom. Asda was an established retailer similar to the U.S. discount superstore (Birchall 2005).

The fastest growth of the top U.S. retail companies is in their international divisions (Craig 2005) with fashion and category killer retailers dominating international retailing expansion (Fernie, Hahn, Gerhard, Pioch, and Arnold 2006). Their growth has come from expanding retail operations as well as from selling private brand products. Alternatively, some retailers have shifted from exporting retail operations to focus on the internationalization of private brands. This is the case for Boots, a U.K. pharmacy-led retailer that sells health and beauty products and

lifestyle products that have strong private brand recognition. Boots executed an implant strategy where its branded products are offered in small outlets that are imbedded in larger non-Boots retail stores (Burt et al. 2005).

Companies are classified as international, multinational, and transnational based on their level of international penetration and how the company is managed. International retailing can take many forms and retailers can be grouped by organizational structure, market entry strategy, and operation mode. In addition, operational structures include exporting, direct foreign investment, licensing agreements, franchising agreements, management contracts, and turnkey operations (Asheghian and Ebrahimi 1990). Market entry strategies are the methods used to gain presence in a country and include business arrangements such as joint-venture and franchising. Operation mode is the institutional plan that supports how a company's products, technology, and managerial or human resources are integrated into a foreign country (Picot-Coupey 2006).

International, Multinational, and Transnational Companies

When a company crosses national borders to conduct its business, it is considered an **international company**. The business may be trade, manufacturing, or a service that includes retailing, hospitality, tourism, wholesaling, transportation, information technology, construction, advertising, and mass communications. Virtually all of these service industries contribute in some way to the expansion and execution of an international business.

When the production and marketing of products occurs in multiple countries then the company is considered a **multinational company.** A multinational company has three objectives. First, the company selects the type of operation that will result in the best overall results. Second, company resources are allocated in ways that can improve efficiency. Third, the company seeks to retain the largest percent of profit feasible (Asheghian and Ebrahimi 1990). Many specialty retailers are multinational such as Gap, Nike, and Sally Beauty Supply from the United States. and Zara from Spain. In general, global fashion brand companies do not challenge the national retail structures in the countries that they enter (Fernie et al. 2006) (See Figure 15.11).

Transnational corporations, sometimes referred to as TNC, have their ownership and management divided uniformly between the nations in which they operate. Big-box retailers such as Wal-Mart, Carrefour, Ahold, Tesco, and Metro are competitive transnational corporations. Big-box retailers can significantly upset the structure of any large foreign market that they enter. Many of these big-box companies are primarily grocery retailers. They are stimulating retail internationalization. Until the 1990s, food retailers were perceived as having limited international potential because they tended to be more culturally defined than other retail categories. The Institute of Grocery Distribution (IGD) (www.igd.com) located in the United Kingdom developed a Global Retail Index (GRI) that gauges leaders in global development. The GRI includes measures for turnover, number of countries of operation, clarity of global strategy, and level of global learning and sharing (Fernie et al. 2006).

Joint-venture Arrangements

When a multinational corporation partners with either a private business or a government entity in a host country, they create a **joint-venture arrangement.** A number of interchangeable names are used to describe retail joint-ventures: cooperative arrangements, contractual joint ventures, cross-shareholdings links, collaboration, cooperative linkages, equity joint ventures, franchise joint ventures, interfirm linkages, conglomerchant joint ventures, business partners, and interfirm alliances (Palmer and Owens 2006).

The advantage of a joint-venture is that it reduces host government controls

15.11 Gap, a specialty retailer, is a global fashion brand company.

15.12 Versace is blending its signature fashion sold in retail stores into new designer hotel concepts. This Versace store is in Singapore.

value-oriented shopping experience. Wal-Mart's Sam's Club is an example of this concept. For this concept to work, the retailer must be able to gain cost efficiencies in sourcing goods. Daiei, one of Japan's largest retail groups, unsuccessfully launched wholesale clubs. It had to close stores due to high costs. Joint-venture agreements are one way that international retailers are moving this concept into foreign markets. Germany's largest retailer, Metro, and Marubeni, a Japanese trading house, agreed to form a joint-venture where Metro's expertise in supply-chain management would be aimed at direct purchases of goods from local producers and manufacturers (Benoit and Nakamoto 2001).

A merging of service industries is occurring through joint ventures of fashion and hotel brands that cater to consumers' desires for luxury experiences (Foroohar 2005). For example, Versace plans to open a resort in Dubai (Barrskog 2005). At the Versace Palazzo on Australia's Gold Coast, the hotel has become a platform for Versace retail stores that promote a signature lifestyle (Ings-Chambers 2004) (See Figure 15.12). See Table 15.4 for a summary of information on designer hotels.

Sandro Alfano, general manager of the Lungarno Alberghi hotel chain owned by the Ferragamo fashion brand, stated that "fashion is an experience now. People don't buy shoes because they need to walk but because they make them feel a certain way. That's not so different from hotels. People no longer go to hotels just to sleep—they want to stay somewhere that gives them the best experience" (Focus—Italy 2005, 12). Alfano suggested that the Ferragamo hotel experience is equated with living the Ferragamo fashion brand (Focus—Italy 2005).

Bulgari, an Italian luxury jewelry brand, began exploring ways to diversify beyond the standard beauty and accessory

against business operations by the multinational corporation. Secondly, it involves local partners in the company's operations and ownership. This allows the multinational corporation to be more effective in addressing the cultural elements that are unique to the host country. The advantages to host countries include involvement in company decisions and profit sharing (Asheghian and Ebrahimi 1990). In a joint venture, it is possible to use several overlapping entry modes to internationalize a company (Palmer and Owens 2006).

An international joint-venture operates day to day in three strategic areas: business policies, decision-making processes and governance systems, and knowledge management. These three areas include repetitive and disruptive change processes. Repetitive processes are adaptive to small changes or modifications in existing methods. Disruptive changes come when an adjustment is necessary for existing retail functional areas (Palmer and Owens 2006) such as buying, merchandising, promotion, and service.

Bulk stores and wholesale clubs are growing retail formats that provide a

TABLE 15.4. DESIGNER HOTELS

DESIGNER	COUNTRY ORIGIN	OWNERSHIP	HOTEL	HOTEL LOCATION(S)
Armani	Italy	Joint-venture Giorgio Armani Spa and Emmar Properties	Dubai Armani Hotel	Dubai (2008)
Bulgari	Italy	Joint-venture Marriott-Ritz Carlton and Bulgari Group	Bulgari Hotel	Milan, Italy
Diesel	Italy	Owner	The Pelican	Miami, Florida
Ferragamo	Italy	Owner	Lungarno Alberghi Hotel Chain	Florence, Italy
Versace	Italy	Joint-venture	Palazzo Versace	Australia Gold Coast

Source: Focus—Italy. 2005. A Fashionable move to the hotel industry. *Brand Strategy*. April 5, 12.

products in the mid 1990s. Francesco Trapani, chief executive of Bulgari, states "We had noted this great success that tourism was having. There's no question that in the last 15 years interest in travel has exploded. We could see it in our travel retail experience, in the notable investment in the shopping areas of airports, and the duty-free services on airplanes. That is materially interesting for a company like ours" (Houlder 2004, 12). Bulgari diversified into the hospitality industry by opening a joint-venture luxury hotel in Milan in 2004 with the Marriott International's Ritz Carlton brand. Guests at the Bulgari Hotel can view a Bulgari catalog in their rooms and salespeople are available to bring over jewels that guests would like to see (Brinkley and Galloni 2004).

Giorgio Armani, who has built a 30-year fashion brand empire, has extended the Giorgio Armani Spa brand to luxury hotels in a joint-venture arrangement with Dubai's Emaar Hotels and Resorts (EMAAR Properties PJSC). EMAAR committed more than $1 billion to building, managing, and maintaining the hotels. Armani is responsible for hotel style and design. At least 10 hotels and 4 resorts are planned for Dubai, London, Paris, New York, Tokyo, Shanghai, and Milan with the first hotel being built in Dubai. The hotels and resorts showcase Armani merchandise, including home wear, furniture from the Armani Casa range, and fashion and beauty products. Armani expects to sell furniture, staff wardrobes, and guest amenities to the hotels (Armani supports 2006, Focus—Italy 2005, Garrahan 2005).

Market Entry Strategies

Retailers are motivated to enter international markets by consumer demand factors, while manufacturers enter for advantageous production costs and resource access. In traditional retail formats, the focus is on the local customer with the attractiveness of a specific market closely linked to customer number and wealth (Gripsrud and Benito 2005). International retailing is characterized by four strategies that are used for global market entry: penetration, diversification, product development, and brand development.

PENETRATION

Penetration strategy is used to enter a market with a new product where there is an existing brand in an existing product category. In this situation, the retailer is building on the high brand awareness of an existing product category that is held by consumers in the targeted market. Penetration offers the lowest-risk option because it builds on the consumers' existing perceptions rather than developing new perceptions toward the brand or product.

When Starbucks extended its product line into the ice-cream category this represented a penetration strategy in the U.S. grocery channel. Starbucks already possessed high brand awareness in the coffee sector, and it leveraged its brand equity in an existing product category. Another example is T.G.I. Friday's, which moved its branded appetizers into the frozen food section of grocery stores. This strategy is often deemed a halo effect, which is the transfer of goodwill from one brand across product categories.

Walt Disney penetrated the Chinese online gaming market by partnering with Shanda Interactive Entertainment, a local Internet company. China has a tightly regulated media market that bars foreign companies from directly operating online games. This made it almost impossible for Disney to raise its online profile. Shanda Interactive Entertainment will develop and distribute casual online games using Disney's core content (Dickie 2006).

DIVERSIFICATION

Diversification strategy describes the entry of a new brand in a new product category. This strategic option is associated with risk because the challenge of brand development is made more difficult by uncertainties associated with the market environment. However, successful diversification strategies can yield long-term brand development success.

"Lodging is in the midst of a profound, multidimensional business transformation that will affect virtually every part of the industry. . . . Lodging is changing from a product-focused, physical asset–intensive industry to a more customer-focused, brand-intensive one. . . . In the future, the focus will be on developing and marketing a more holistic product wrapped within specific brands and based upon a deeper understanding of the wants and needs of a more precisely targeted set of customers. Product and brand will be designed to provide customizable guest experiences that connect with each customer on an emotional level. The goal is building customer loyalty that is durable, tangible, and extendable across a broader array of products and services" (Dickinson 2006, 60).

The Waldorf Astoria in New York City, a Hilton Hotel, has diversified into new product lines. The Waldorf Collection, which can be purchased online or through a catalog, includes select, extravagant treasures that reflect the hotel's reputation of exemplary service and sophisticated style. The website (www. waldorfcollection-hotelsathome.com/home.html) states: "The Waldorf Collection is composed of signature, handpicked personal accessories, collectibles, and gifts that define The Waldorf Experience. Each item reflects extraordinary craftsmanship and attention to detail. Together they are the vanguard of refinement—the ultimate expression of life's greatest pleasures." The diverse product categories offered include Bed and Bedding, the Chef's Kitchen, Waldorf Pooch, Distinctly Waldorf, and Waldorf Gallery.

PRODUCT DEVELOPMENT

Product development strategy involves the leveraging of an existing brand name in a new product category. Scents can be used to extend branded products into new product categories. Riviera Concepts Inc., a fragrance producer, was approached by a licensing agent for General Motors with the idea of a Hummer scent. Riviera launched the Hummer Fragrance for Men in a signature Hummer yellow packaging in 2004. It was expected to reach $36 million worldwide in sales in its first year. The Hummer fragrance, which targets 25- to 45-year-old men, was built on the brand awareness of Hummer vehicles. Adrian Ellis, president of Riviera, stated, "It's got credibility with men. Everyone seems to know about Hummer; the awareness is high. What other brand for men would make more sense?" (Evans 2004, 14). A benefit to Riviera in launching the Hummer fragrance was to increase the company's presence in travel retail, which was limited to shops on the border between the United States and Canada. Because European markets are aware of the Hummer brand, it was expected that the Hummer fragrance would appeal to business travelers and enhance Riviera's entry into European markets (Evans 2004).

Sony Corporation is partnering with adult-targeted retailers to drive shoppers to see its movies. When the studio launched its movie *Memoirs of a Geisha* in 2005, it had already worked with Gap, Banana Republic, Limited Brand's Bath and Body Works, and Fresh, a high-end beauty products subsidiary company of Paris-based LVMH Moët Hennessy–Louis Vuitton. "The screen-to-store approach, though still novel, is not exactly new. For the launch of the 2001 movie musical *Moulin Rouge!* News Corp's Twentieth Century Fox engaged Federated Department Stores's Bloomingdale's unit to create a line of apparel with a turn-of-the-century Parisian theme. Stores carried special items by Christian Dior cosmetics and lingerie and cocktail dresses from the likes of Anna Sui and Max Azria. In Manhattan, *Moulin Rouge!*–themed windows were personally unveiled by the movie star Nicole Kidman" (Kelly and Kang 2005, B1).

BRAND DEVELOPMENT

Brand development strategy is the introduction of a new brand in an existing product category. Limited Brands is using brand development to extend its lines. The Pink brand was created by Victoria's Secret to develop lingerie and pajamas for younger consumers. Tutti Dolci, which is Italian for *all sweets* was developed for Bath and Body Works. Beauty products in this line had fragrances such as lemon meringue, angel-food cake, and chocolate fondue (Merrick 2005).

The Unilever Ice Cream division had difficulty selling ice cream in Asia and Africa. The annual per capital consumption of ice cream is less than 1 liter per person in Asia compared with more than 22 liters per person in the United States. To grow the market in Malaysia, Unilever launched transparent take-home tubs and two new brands in its existing ice-cream product category: Wall's Twister and Wall's Mini. Wall's Mini reflected product innovation by using smaller portion sizes to satisfy consumers who felt guilty about eating large portions of ice cream (Sudhaman 2006).

Brand development grows out of defining the experience that the consumer will receive. Hotel Indigo is an example of how a brand was developed by first defining the experience. Bart Mills, principal of Back Lot Productions, a brand development and retail design firm, worked with Inter-Continental Hotels Group to create Hotel Indigo. Mills said, "Retailers strive to differentiate their brands from the competition and create a built-environment that evokes an emotional connection. Contrary to that, in the hotel industry there's so much sameness, and a mentality to keep up with the Joneses" (Gunter 2006, 26). New brands must define customers before defining a brand print. The brand print helps create a story about the brand that is uniformly carried out. Mills further stated that "everything that touches customers and employees speaks back to that brand print—from the language to the uniforms, to the architecture, to the attitude. That's when brands become successful" (Gunter 2006, 26). Hotel Indigo developed its story around art work, the built environment, continuously changing elements of color, and employee knowledge (Gunter 2006).

Branding Strategies

A challenge to global retail expansion is the ability to retain uniqueness in a market. Most brands attract interest and even excitement when they enter a new marketplace. However, retaining consumer interest can be difficult. This is especially true when the brand's uniqueness is shared by competitor brands as well. This is the case at the Teeside Park shopping center in Middlesbrough, England, which has numerous U.S. branded restaurants (e.g., KFC, T.G.I. Friday's, Frankie & Benny's New York Italian Restaurant and Bar, and McDonald's). The novelty of being a U.S. brand is lost when so many share that same draw (O'Keefe 2001).

Brands that have a large disparity in how consumers think about their image are not as likely to achieve standardized global positioning and become a global brand (Alden et al. 1999). For these brands each market must be addressed individually by the retailer (Gray 2000). In international retailing, brand name can be a critical component of a product's success since the name of the brand creates culturally specific images in the consumer's mind. Some characteristics of brands that need to be considered by global retailers include brand image, brand-product interface, and brand awareness.

BRAND IMAGE

The power and value of a brand is enhanced by building a global image (Shocker, Srivastava, and Ruekert 1994). This global image reflects the positive and negative attributes that a brand possesses. A global image can significantly contribute to increased sales (Buzzell 1968). However, J. Birchall (2005) suggested that "the greatest cultural resistance to global brands seems to come not in the developing world but in fully developed consumer markets. Not only are 'modern' local shopping habits already established but there is often regulation in place to protect the status quo, and fierce competition from the locals" (13).

Many large national brands continue to use strategies based on massive global brand uniformity, a strategy that does not recognize regional attitudes and preferences (Vazdauskas 2006). Successful multinational retailers secure brand loyalty from culturally diverse consumers by tailoring the brand's image to reflect individual national cultures (Alden et al. 1999).

When Chinese consumers purchase items for holidays and special occasions, the brand name can take on special meaning since it sends a message to the gift recipient. Companies need to consider culture, norms, values, traditions, and history when they consider translating a brand name into Chinese. English names often do not translate well into Chinese. One contributing factor to the success of Coca-Cola is that its translation into Chinese means "tastes good and makes you happy" (Dong and Helms 2001).

BRAND-PRODUCT INTERFACE

An overarching decision that retailers must address in international market entry and expansion strategies is the interface between brand positioning and product availability within the market environment. The **brand-product interface strategy** may be viewed as a cross-classification of existing and new brand identities and product availability.

Marks and Spencer Group P.L.C. (M & S), the U.K.–based mid-priced apparel and home products company, sells most of its merchandise under its "very

British" St. Michael brand. It failed in Canada because its private label merchandise did not compete effectively against more recognizable brands. Also, its apparel and food product assortments were uncommon in Canada. To retain its 400 M & S stores in the United Kingdom, M & S sold its ownership in 220 Brooks Brothers apparel stores in the United States and Asia and 17 M & S stores in France. It retained M & S stores in Ireland and Hong Kong and franchises in 30 countries. Falling sales were attributed to stores in the United Kingdom that had outmoded pricing, product mix, lack of segmentation, weak visual displays, poor store locations, and mediocre store environments (Biesada 2006, Voyle 2004). The M & S example demonstrates how important it is for international retailers to retain both local and global appeal to retain viability.

BRAND AWARENESS

Consumer awareness of brand identity, from food and beverage to apparel and athletic shoes, has increased worldwide since the 1970s (Sternquist 1997). **Brand awareness** is the extent to which consumers know about a brand and recognize the attributes associated with that brand. Global brand identity has taken on importance since consumers are buying what they know (Hirsch 1997). U.S. brand concepts are interpreted very well in many global markets (Groeber 2002). Many U.S. retailers are viewed as unique brands. U.S. global retailers (e.g., Gap, The Disney Store) (See Figure 15.13) and restaurants (e.g., Planet Hollywood, T.G.I. Friday's, Outback Steakhouse) (See Figure 15.14) are successful partly because consumers in other countries recognize their brands as unique.

Younger consumer segments in many parts of the world are attracted to specific brands such as Calvin Klein, Old Navy, Bennigan's, and Hooters. There is a unique

and profitable opportunity to target these younger populations as a transnational homogenized segment using brand extension (e.g., Coca-Cola Apparel) or co-branding in the retail store (Day 1999). Retailers who target young consumers through brand affinity need to understand the similarities and differences that may exist across cultures (Ritchie 1995).

Many retailers are exploring international expansion where there is significant

15.13 Many U.S. retailers, such as The Disney Store, offer brands that are unique to that retailer. This store is in Stonebriar Mall, Frisco, Texas.

15.14 Hard Rock Cafe is widely recognized by consumers worldwide as a unique brand associated with U.S. music. This restaurant is in Bangkok, Thailand.

growth in youth and young adult markets (Cohen and Carey 2000). Japanese youths, world leaders in hip youth culture, were successfully targeted by U.S. retailer The Athlete's Foot as part of its aggressive international expansion (Groeber 2002). Fossil is a U.S. brand that is gaining recognition among younger consumers. It has expanded its branded stores to Australia, Canada, Germany, Greece, Hong Kong, The Philippines, Taiwan, Malaysia, The Netherlands, United Kingdom, Singapore, and South Africa (www.fossil.com). It offers a wide assortment of watches, apparel, and fashion accessories (See Figure 15.15).

One way to understand local cultural and social practices of communities as they relate to brands and retail businesses is to use ethnography. Ethnographic research generates textual and visual social and cultural descriptions through participation and observation. This methodology can be very useful in determining how changing social and cultural contexts directly or indirectly affect brand. Brands increasingly have become commodities of cultural change and exchange. The importance of a brand's cultural context includes how consumers interact with brands and communicate about brands to other consumers. Consumers are taking ownership of brands in such as way that the rules of change and exchange have become bottom-up, that is, from the practices of individual consumers, rather than top-down from the company (*Brand Papers* 2003).

Retail Strategies

Retailers who expand into foreign markets need to choose and employ well-organized programs that result in lower costs and higher margins. Achieving these goals requires retailers to tailor their strategies to the countries they enter. Global retail strategies that are discussed in this section include standardization, localization, customization, cultural swapping, clustering, and spatial segmentation.

Standardization and localization are contrasting approaches to entering and serving foreign markets. If these two approaches were viewed as a continuum, complete standardization would execute uniform product, brand, and retail operations across all global markets. At the opposing end of the continuum, complete localization would implement unique product, brand, and retail operations in each locale. Customization and clustering are retail strategies that make localization more efficient. Spatial segmentation combines characteristics of both standardization and localization by using a multi-attribute approach to segmentation.

STANDARDIZATION

When consumer segments are similar and homogeneous across nations, companies involved in international expansion may rely on **standardization** to appeal to a market niche (Ramarapu et al. 1999). This strategy is used by many global brands to gain instant brand recognition across multiple consumer groups. It is worth noting that 69 percent of 3-year-old children in the United Kingdom recognize McDonald's golden arches (Hill 2003).

Few markets, however, are exactly alike. This makes it inevitable that global retailers need to localize some aspects of a retailing concept or marketing mix for each target market, instead of employing a single approach. What elements to localize and to what extent needs to be determined through cross-national analyses of demographic characteristics, geographic characteristics, economic factors, technological factors, sociocultural factors, and political and legal factors (Czinkota and Ronkainen 1996).

Often companies in global markets do not take into account the influence of local culture. After centralizing operations and marketing, many companies find centralized efficiency resulted in reduced profitability, a phenomenon that may be attributed to a neglect of the centralized control to local sensitivities (de Mooij and Hofstede 2002). When the clothing retailer C & A decided to standardize its buying operations in 1997, it took substantial losses because British and Irish tastes differed from the tastes of consumers in continental Europe. The losses resulted in C & A closing all 109 of its stores in Great Britain and Ireland (de Mooij and Hofstede 2002).

When a single European market was created in 1992, predictions were made that consumers soon would become very similar. Large differences in traditional consumers' value systems still remain for many consumers who continue to be very resistant to change. However, for many Europeans, there is a convergence of consumer behavior in their consumption, ownership, and use of numerous products and services (de Mooij and Hofstede 2002).

IKEA, the world's largest furniture retail company, was founded in 1942 by Ingvar Kamprad. It is owned by the private Stichting INGKA Foundation. IKEA opened its first store outside of Scandinavia in Zurich, Switzerland, in 1973, fol-

lowed the next year by a store in Germany. IKEA now operates 224 stores in 33 countries and employs more than 84,000 workers (See Figure 15.16). All but four of the stores belong to the IKEA Group; the remainder are owned and run as franchise arrangements (Jonsson and Elg 2006).

Germany is IKEA's top selling country, followed by the United Kingdom, the United States, France, and Sweden. IKEA furniture is manufactured by the industrial group Swedwood. IKEA of Sweden is responsible for the design and development of about 10,000 IKEA products. In each country where IKEA is located, there is a service office that is responsible for the local IKEA stores. The IKEA corporate service office is located in Helsingborg, Sweden (Jonsson and Elg 2006).

IKEA uses a standardized retail concept that offers customers products and shopping experiences that are associated with the strong IKEA brand. Upon entering the store, customers pass by a play area where children can stay while their parents shop. Upon entering the retail floor, the shopping experience becomes an adventure as customers wind their way through the store and push their carts. Products are displayed in open floor bins and along the

15.16 IKEA is the world's largest furniture retail company. It uses a standardized retail brand concept that creates a strong association with the IKEA brand worldwide. This IKEA store is located in Frisco, Texas.

wall so customers can see, touch, and smell. Customers walk through multiple vignettes representing different room arrangements and apartment sizes. This helps customers visualize how IKEA furniture can be used to create totally furnished living spaces. Signage is prominently displayed in both the local language and Swedish. The IKEA restaurant is a Swedish food market and bistro where customers can eat in a café-type setting. They can order traditional Swedish foods such as Swedish meatballs, lingonberries, and cream sauce and potatoes. When customers have finished shopping, they walk through a large warehouse space where larger pieces of furniture and household items are retrieved and moved on rolling dollies. The customer pay at a multi-station checkout lane and exits the store.

LOCALIZATION

Complete **localization** of a retailing program is based on the development of distinctive customized products, pricing, promotion, and distribution policies that have no standardized elements (Jain 1989).

15.17 Heinz, which is a global cultural icon that symbolizes quality, convenience, and great taste, is the most global U. S. food company. It offers standardized products in 140 countries as well as localized products to meet the needs of specific markets.

When Unilever and Procter & Gamble entered China and other emerging markets, they redeveloped their products to gain local appeal. This redevelopment included the use of smaller and more economical packaging sizes and cheaper product formulations (Halliday 2005). Heinz, the most global U.S. food company, offers both standardized and localized products. According to its website (www.heinz.com/About.aspx), Heinz is a global cultural icon that symbolizes quality, convenience, and great taste. It generates $2.5 billion in annual sales. Heinz sells standardized ketchup in 140 countries, but it also sells localized condiments in specific markets. For example, it sells salad cream in the United Kingdom, an Orlando range of condiments in Spain, the Banquette line in Costa Rica, banana ketchup in the Philippines, and ABC soy sauce in Indonesia (See Figure 15.17).

The concept of localization applies within national borders as well. National markets constitute local components of the global marketplace. The concept of a monolithic global brand that is consistently sought by all consumers does not describe most markets. Consumers continue to organize their lives around where they live, not the products they want. A national study by UCLA and the University of Chicago found that "for a typical national brand, the geographic variation in market shares, perceived quality levels, and local dominance is so large that it places in question the concept and relevance of a 'national brand'"(Vazdauskas 2006, 34).

D. K. Rigby and V. Vishwanath (2006) suggested there is a quiet revolution in the consumer marketplace toward localization, and it is leading to the end of standardization. Future success of retailers and manufacturers pivots on their ability to localize while retaining efficiencies of scale. Consumer markets that increasingly reflect diversity in ethnicity, wealth, lifestyle, and values, are dictating the need for local uniqueness. This uniqueness can be expressed through local architectural styles, favored brands, different kinds of stores and product lines, and variations in pricing, marketing, staffing, and customer service.

Local competitive advantage can be gained by applying localization and standardization as dual strategies. One strategy is to introduce an international brand along with creating strong local brands to meet indigenous tastes and preferences. In its competitive entry into mainland China, Nestlé's introduced Drumstick, an international brand, along with specially designed ice creams, including Snow Moji, a vanilla ice cream filled rice pastry that looks like dim sum, and Frosti, an ice milk product offered in locally preferred flavors such as red bean and green tea. At the same time Nestlé launched 29 new low- to mid-priced ice-cream brands that were positioned as value products. The new products were accompanied by a media blitz, which used a Blue Ice Cream Genie as its brand icon (Halliday 2005).

The long-time strategy of McDonald Corporation was to use local independent advertising for each country. This changed in 2004 when the company unified its international markets under the theme of "I'm Lovin' It." This advertising slogan was created to appeal to a universal human insight that could go beyond nationalities and borders. Although it was a standardized campaign, McDonald's was still able to apply a localized strategy. McDonald's used "I'm Lovin' It" along with the 2005 Lunar New Year, an event that transcends Asian cultures, to launch the spicy Prosperity Burger in nine Asian countries. The challenge of this strategy was to create a single ad campaign that could overcome cultural variations in language and tastes as well as differences in consumers' physical appear-

ance (Fowler 2005). "The ad featured a boy who needs better luck fishing. His brother passes him a beef Prosperity Burger—which looks like a variation on the restaurant's McRib sandwich—and his fortunes change, culminating in the arrival of a computer-generated whale" (Fowler 2005, 1).

Three emerging trends are influencing the localization of store formats and products. First, purchase occasion in addition to consumer segment are influencing consumer purchasing patterns. This trend is reflected in cross-shopping where consumers may buy a product at a big-box store and then buy accessories or peripherals at a local store. Second, chain stores are selling the same item in multiple formats (i.e., brick-and-mortar, catalog, online). Technology now offers retailers the ability to localize to customer demand. By using customer loyalty cards to track what, where, and when customers buy, Tesco is able to offer specialized food formats for each of its five store types in the United Kingdom: Tesco Superstore (traditional supermarket), Tesco Extra (one-stop hypermart), Tesco Metro (smaller urban supermarket), Tesco Express (neighborhood convenience store), and Tesco.com (Web retailer). The third trend is the growth in customer purchases through multiple retail formats. It is producing increased profits as well as a meaningful understanding of consumer behavior. As customers shop across the many retail formats in brick-and-mortar (e.g., neighborhood store, big-box, or mall) to virtual formats, the opportunity to retain customer loyalty increases (Rigby and Vishwanath 2006).

While IKEA uses a standardized shopping experience, it does localize many of its products through its New Product Development organization. When IKEA entered Russia, IKEA products were adapted and new IKEA products created to meet the unique needs of the Russian market. Product localization was initiated in part due to tariffs and high import duties. IKEA gained local market knowledge by working closely with customs officials, local suppliers, and locally recruited employees (Jonsson and Elg 2006).

CUSTOMIZATION

Customization is a strategy for shifting from standardization to localization. The benefits of customization include promoting local experimentation, making it difficult for competitors to replicate and track, and providing a long-lasting competitive advantage. Conversely, standardization discourages experimentation, making it is easy for competitors to duplicate. Standardization by large chains has left many with limited opportunities for expansion due to saturation of existing markets.

Many communities are resisting standardized cookie-cutter retailers and are passing ordinances that prescribe the size and architecture of buildings. Another

problem with standardization is that it creates similar products and services that move all the way through the pipeline (Rigby and Vishwanath 2006). According to D. K. Rigby and V. Vishwanath (2006), standardization leads to commoditization, which results in reductions in growth and profit. They suggest that there are many elements of a company that can be customized when the what, where, and when of consumer markets are understood. The what includes characteristics of retail offerings associated with store attributes, merchandise, and vendor-retailer interactions. The where are the drivers of retail location that include consumer attributes, geopolitics, unique demand drivers, and market environment. The when addresses elements of time. Figure 15.18 shows the variables that influence retail localization and customization.

Advances in technology offer retailers opportunities to meet local needs by customizing their stores, products, and services with high accuracy. This can be done

15.18 Variables influencing retail localization and customization

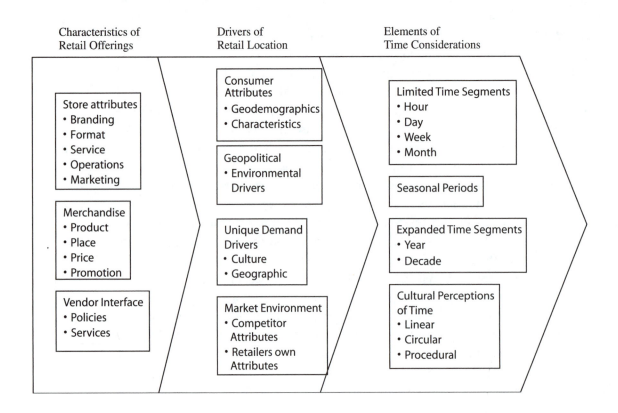

by using checkout scanners, data-mining software, and radio frequency identification (RFID) to track local consumer preferences and purchasing behavior. The key to successful localization is balancing the key business elements that need to be considered so the brand is not damaged and costs do not escalate. Product customization can be costly if it is done for every locale; however, strategic packaging and promotional efforts may create a local effect at a lower cost (Rigby and Vishwanath 2006).

CULTURAL SWAPPING

Cultural swapping occurs when multicultural businesses and ethnically diverse consumers coexist. It is a form of cultural diffusion that creates a multicultural marketplace through the interactions between multicultural marketers and consumers (Peñaloza and Gilly 1999). Multicultural marketplaces meet the experiential needs of consumers who are no longer individually or collectively identifying with a specific ethnic category. A benefit of cultural swapping is that it generates greater tolerance and acceptance of diverse cultures and consumer lifestyles (Jamal 2003).

Cultural swapping also happens when multinational retailers and consumers interact and adapt to each other. The diffusion of cultures can produce operational strategies. Wal-Mart offers an example of adaptation of operational strategies through cultural swapping. After visiting a Carrefour hypermart in France, Sam Walton reinvented the hypermart concept as a Wal-Mart Supercenter in the United States (Birchall 2005).

Retailers can use cultural swapping to extend the breadth and depth of their merchandise mix, attract customers into their stores, and create new products. Cultural swapping occurs when consumers try new and foreign foods and flavors. An increasing availability of ethnic foods in Western food markets offers alternatives to local foods. In the restaurant industry, cultural swapping is used to generate creative new products. Wolfgang Puck Cafés have sushi bars that combine elements of traditional sushi with nontraditional ingredients and flavors such as barbecued shrimp and salmon sushi and hosion-glazed rib sushi. Roy's, a joint-venture partnership with Outback Steakhouse, offers a Euro-Asia or Hawaii Regional cuisine that appeals to U.S. consumers who have more adventurous tastes (Boorstin 2001).

Consumers engage in culture swapping when they seek out the tastes, sounds, and experiences of different cultures. In a study of the perceptions of ethnically diverse consumers regarding the food and service in Indian restaurants in the United States., B. M. Josiam and P. A. Monteiro (2004) found that eating in an Indian restaurant was perceived as a cultural experience by consumers who were not South Asian. Conversely, South Asian consumers associated the experience with a cultural familiarity of the food, service, and atmosphere of the restaurant. They concluded that Indian restaurants in the United States serve two distinct ethnic market segments composed of white Americans and South Asians. However, they also determined that there were universal likes and dislikes with the most important restaurant attributes being quality of food, taste of food, hygiene, and cleanliness. Ethnic foods can become mainstream food. This is evident in the United Kingdom where there are more than 10,000 Indian restaurants (Bromage 2002).

CLUSTERING

Clustering offers retailers a more precise and simpler way to localize by focusing on the actual small number of attributes that drive the majority of consumer purchases. Companies can do this by analyzing local purchasing behavior to identify where there are similarities in consumer demand.

This method allows retailers to customize for a group of locations that have similar consumer preferences. Product assortments and promotions are developed for clusters of locations, rather than for specific stores. Efficiencies of standardization along with the benefit of customization are gained by sorting locations into similar clusters. An example of this strategy in the United States is Best Buy, which is using clustering to create customer-centric store formats that appeal to local consumers (Rigby and Vishwanath 2006).

A tool that can be used to generate clusters is CHAID, which stands for chi-squared automatic interaction detection. It is a statistical classification method that can sort items into statistically unique clusters that meet a specified outcome. For example, a retailer might like to know which clusters (e.g., customer income level, competitor stores, and product assortments) are associated with store profitability. CHAID allows the retailer to examine attributes in combination, rather than independent of one another (Rigby and Vishwanath 2006).

SPATIAL SEGMENTATION

Spatial segmentation is a way to target consumers and gain cost efficiency. In traditional international retailing spatial retail segmentation is defined by national or political borders (Hofstede, Wedel, and Steenkamp 2002). The assumption is made that countries are defined by socioeconomic, cultural, and other national characteristics that create distinct spatially-connected areas (Helsen, Jedidi, and DeSarbo 1993). This strategy creates a countries-as-segments that may account for within-country consumer homogeneity and the similarities of consumers across different countries. Cross-national consumer segmentation is used to group consumers in different countries based on their similar needs. Expansion efforts of international retailers now rely on targeting geographic market segments (Hosfstede et al. 2002).

The Geographical Information System (GIS) is a useful tool for understanding spatial segments. GIS uses geographical data to create a detailed picture of retail performance. It helps retailers determine the variance in market share that occurs from one market to another. Of importance in global retailing is the opportunity to examine zone boundary data that creates small geographic areas by dividing a territory (e.g., region, country, or aggregated countries) so consumer product demand can be analyzed in these specific zones (Thompson and Walker 2005). Table 15.5 provides examples of the use of GIS in retail network strategies.

TABLE 15.5. USE OF GIS IN RETAIL NETWORK STRATEGIES

MARKET	EXAMPLE OF USES
Retail	New store sales forecasts Impact analysis Store performance analysis
Leisure	Loyalty card/customer database analysis Demand elasticity Local marketing Site development Support for licensing
Finance	Local market channel strategy Optimal networks Service planning Merger impact analysis Optimal ATM networks
Property	Feasibility studies Catchment analysis Planning research
Fast moving consumer goods	Supply chain logistics POS/channel management Marketing campaign support

Source: Thompson, A., and J. Walker. 2005. Retail network planning—achieving competitive advantage through geographic analysis. *Journal of Targeting, Measurement, and Analysis for Marketing 13*(3):250–257.

Competitive and Comparative Advantages

The relationship between the competitive advantage of a company and the comparative advantage of the country that is entered underlies successful international expansion strategies (Kogut 1985). **Competitive advantage** is the unique advantage that a company would have if it should enter a foreign country. This advantage is a proprietary attribute of the company, either in product or process, which is not easily copied by its competitors without acquiring noncompetitive investment costs. Brand name would be an example of competitive advantage. **Comparative advantage** is a location-specific advantage associated with sourcing and markets. Wages, materials, and capital charges are macroeconomic factor costs that can create or eliminate comparative advantage (Frear, Alguire, and Metcalf 1995; Kogut 1985).

Competitive and comparative advantages are found in three types of international competition. The first relates to the distribution of comparative advantage across multiple countries. Comparative advantage occurs when commodities are exported from countries with similar factor costs. Interindustry trade occurs when the cross flow of commodities is dissimilar and competitive advantage is lost (Kogut 1985).

When factor costs are similar across nations, then international competition can be driven by differences in the competitive advantages of companies. This second type of international competition, referred to as intraindustry and horizontal, generates a cross flow of trade where similar goods and foreign direct investment are used for market penetration (Kogut 1985).

In the third type of international competition, there is an interaction between competitive and comparative advantage that is related to the value-added chain. In international companies, this combination produces a more complex diffusion of activities. The company's competitive in-house strength includes its ownership of specialized production processes, technologies, and quality control measures that are not easily replicated in the marketplace. These international companies are able to compete based on the relative exclusive overseas arrangement of sourcing locations, competitive advantages, and decisions regarding products and markets (Kogut 1985).

Successful global retail strategies require a market position that reinvents competitive advantage in new markets (Barth, Karch, McLaughlin, and Shi 1996). Companies need to recognize that "success in a world of homogenized demand requires a search for sales opportunities in similar segments across the globe in order to achieve the economies of scale necessary to compete" (Levitt 1983, 94). The success of global expansion is largely dependent on the market environment and the competitive intensity within that market setting. Often, retailers have trouble with international expansion because they failed to critically identify the brands, skills, and productivity that were required in specific global markets. Galleries Layette, the high fashion Parisian retailer, failed to be successful in New York. Although the retailer was identified as high fashion, its product offering was not considered exclusive in the New York market (Barth et al. 1996).

To survive stiff competition, U.S. retailers need to employ unique concepts or techniques that differentiate them from domestic and international competitors (Good and Granovsky 1995). Retailers may garner a competitive advantage in foreign markets by leveraging brand loyalty and developing long-term customer relationships (Pelton 2000). Some U.S. retailers are recognized globally for their private (e.g., Gap) or national brands (e.g., Levi's) and the quality and value that consumers attribute to these brands. The value associated with U.S. retail brands likely enhances the appeal of these retailers to international consumers. However, in some markets the attractiveness of particular country brands is not enough to entice consumers. K. Hyllegard et al. (2005) concluded that changing the perceptions of the products and services offered by U.S. apparel retailers was one of the biggest challenges in entering the Spanish market.

Competitive advantage also depends on the purchasing power of consumers in different countries. In 1986, *The Economist*, a business newspaper, introduced an annual Big Mac Index that is computed for 120 countries. Based on the theory of purchasing power parity (PPP), it argued that if an identical shopping basket of goods and services in any two countries are compared, the currency exchange rates should gravitate to equal levels. The Big Mac Index is useful in comparing exchange rates across countries and most useful when comparing countries that have similar per capita incomes. Pricing in each country is influenced by non-tradable goods and services such as the cost of rent and localized factors such as trade barriers, transportation costs, taxation differences, and labor costs (*Fast Food and Strong Currencies* 2005, *Food for Thought* 2004, *McCurrencies* 2006).

Big Mac prices can be compared in local currency, dollars, and implied PPP. For example, if a Big Mac costs $3.10 in the United States, then the implied PPP means that for every $1.00 in the United States it takes $1.60 in Britain to have the same currency purchasing power. If the U.S. Big Mac Price baseline is $3.10, the Big Mac would cost the least in China ($1.31) and the most in Denmark ($4.77). Using this same baseline, the dollar would have the greatest purchasing power in

Indonesia, Venezuela, and South Korea (*McCurrencies* 2006).

Even though purchasing power parity differs across countries, consumer demand for a particular good or service can place that item in a premium category. McDonald's opened its first restaurant in Moscow in 1990 as a joint-venture with Mosobshepit, which is the food service division of the Moscow City government (Palmer and Ownes 2006). At the grand opening, militiamen were called in to prevent a riot and customers waited for hours for their turn to eat a dvoini gamburger (double hamburger) and kartofel-free (French fries). The restaurant was considered high class compared with local standards. Opening day shattered McDonald's opening day record of 14,000 in Hong Kong by serving 30,000 Moscow customers. At that time, Moscow workers had to work for two and a half hours to purchase a Big Mac sandwich compared with only 20 minutes in the United States (Debbs 1990).

GLOBAL E-TAILING

E-tailing was the first e-commerce industry to proliferate with the growth of the Internet (Zhao and Levary 2002). **E-commerce** uses fixed tools (e.g., computers and user-friendly browsers) for commercial transactions (Dholakia and Doholakia 2004). E-tailing has extended the consumer marketplace from local to global (George 2003) by offering an international shopping experience to everyone who logs on to the Internet.

M-commerce is the next generation of e-commerce, and has eliminated time and distance as factors in consumer shopping interaction equations. M-commerce uses mobile, wireless terminals such as PDAs, mobile phones, and other electronic devices (e.g., watches, pens, music players). These mobile hand-helds are portable to anywhere in the world and allow global shopping through instantaneous communication links (Dholakia and Doholakia 2004).

Whether the transaction base is e-commerce or m-commerce, e-tailing is a global phenomenon that has created a new form of consumption directly linked to lifestyle. S. Bellman, G. L. Lohse, and E. J. Johnson (1999), in their study of more than 10,000 participants from the United States, Europe, and Asia, found that the most important attribute for online shopping was a wired lifestyle (measured by months and/or years of Internet experience, what was being bought, and why). E-tailers need to view themselves as globally competitive because their competition can come from any segment of the world (Singh, Furrer, and Ostinelli 2004).

While e-commerce and m-commerce have allowed companies to expand geographically, it is important that they understand and acknowledge the diversity in cultures, political systems, economies, and technologies that are represented by the consumers who shop their website. Cultural differences exist in how consumers use a website. For example, how the Web is navigated can differ by country. Technical limitations in many countries (e.g., broadband is not available) slows Internet connections. This influences the types of images and animation that can be used (Bannon 2006, Gray 2000). Localization of websites needs to take into account what is available to consumers logging onto the local URL. This section examines the influence of search engines and browsers and localization on the success of e-tailers.

In 2005, the French and German governments announced a plan to fund the development of a Eurocentric search engine code-named Project Quaero (Latin for *I am searching*). The capabilities of Quaero will include audio, video, text, and still images. Although a French search engine is offered by Google (www.Google. fr), Quaero is envisioned as a competitor for Google. There is a belief in France that the underlying software and structure of a search engine in the English language is Anglocentric and creates a distorted view of the French culture (*Special Report–Online* 2005 *Marketing Week*).

Localization

Localization of websites needs to address four areas: translation, local interpretation, local look and feel, and local value creation. Also, localized merchandising processes need to take into account regional differences in consumer attitudes and preferences. In examining communication content on websites in five countries (Italy, India, The Netherlands, Switzerland, and Spain), N. Singh, O. Furrer, and M. Ostinelli (2004) concluded that consumers prefer localized, adapted Web content.

TRANSLATION

Variations in languages, multiple languages, and multiple dialects influence how consumers react to a website. Localization of a website needs to acknowledge slang, language composition, customs, and social mores and their impact on text and images (Bannon 2006). Customers need to be able to communicate in a language that they understand. Online language translation services offer customers the ability to understand information in their native tongues (e.g., babel.altavista.com). These tools can translate Web pages into Chinese, English, French, German, Italian, Japanese, Korean, Portuguese, and Russian (George 2003).

As the Internet becomes a global mass market medium, there is a need for businesses to meet country-specific language requirements (Gray 2000). In many countries, multiple languages are needed to conduct business. In Canada everything must be offered in English and French. In Belgium, people speak Dutch, French, and English. In India, English is the common language of business, but when selling products to consumers, it is important to offer the website in Hindi or in some of the other 15 languages spoken there (Bolen 2006).

The majority of websites are in English. This dominance is changing with the growth of Asian language websites. More than 4 billion people speak a language other than English and for many consumers their preference is to use a website in their native tongues (Singh, Furrer, and Ostinelli 2004). The research firm Computer Economics predicted that by 2005 non-English speakers would account for 60 percent of all Internet users. Ipsos-Reid, another research company, found that 90 percent of Internet users preferred to receive local information in their native language in every global region where English is not the main language spoken. Forrester Research found that sales completion and order inquiries were three times more likely when consumers were offered the content in their own language versus English (Stewart 2001). Hotels.com has found that most consumers who use their website prefer to use their native language, with a few exceptions such as the Finns's preference to search for international hotels in English rather than Finnish (*Special Report–Online* 2005 *Marketing Week*).

LOCAL INTERPRETATION

Connecting with international consumers requires an understanding of how to attract them and to make a sale. Thus, how a company interprets consumer needs in each market is important. A significant component of the online shopping experience is completing the sale. Even though the trend is to standardize the purchasing process of online consumers, there remains a need for localized consumer interfaces that give local interpretations of the sales transaction. Customers need to know their actual costs when completing transactions and making payments. Currency translators help customers understand the true costs of a purchase. For example, the currency translator (www.xe.com) lists a wide range of currencies and it updates every minute. E-tailers need to provide information regarding shipping costs, taxes, and in the case of international sales, any duties (value-added tax or VAT), that must be paid upon receipt of the purchase.

Another consideration at point-of-sale is the form of payment and the format for data collection. Consumers differ in their use of credit cards for online purchases. For example, Germans prefer not to use credit cards (Gray 2000). Furthermore, all online data forms need to be adjusted for the country where the order is being placed. While in the United States consumers would know the meaning of a zip code, in the United Kingdom this is referred to as the postal code. The manner in which addresses and dates are written differs from country to country as well (George 2003). In the United States the standard practice is to write month, day, and year (e.g., 9-1-06 would be read September 1, 2006). In the United Kingdom, the date is written day, month, and year (e.g., 9-1-06 would be read January 9, 2006). These subtle differences can cause confusion and create frustrating shopping experiences where misunderstandings deter consumers from shopping at a website again.

Local interpretations vary by the intrinsic differences in languages. In the Asian languages, ideographic characters are used where each character stands for one word or syllable. In China, people speak Mandarin, Cantonese, and/or a vast number of dialects, and they use different character sets. In mainland China, a simplified character set is used, while in Hong Kong and Taiwan, the traditional Chinese character set is used. In general, Chinese consumers can read the simplified characters (Stewart 2001). Consumers attach visual symbolism to words. In examining Japanese packaging, J. F. Sherry and E. G. Camargo (1987) found Chinese ideograms (*kanji*) represented tradition and formality; simplified one or two stroke characters (*hiragana*) represented femininity and softness; and characters used to communicate foreign words (*katakana*) denoted newness, foreignness, and directness. Another consideration for websites is the language used to register domain names. Using Asian characters for registration offers access to larger markets compared with registrations with domain names using Western alphabets (Stewart 2001).

LOCAL LOOK AND FEEL

The Web is not a culturally neutral medium. Localized characteristics need to be built into each page of a website. In comparing 80 U.S. and Chinese websites, N. Singh, H. Zhao, and X. Hu (2003) found the sites to be full of cultural markers that produced a look and feel unique to the local culture. Cultural preferences, which are exhibited by consumer reactions to color, aesthetics, spatial orientations, positioning of words, and word meanings, influence the user-friendliness of the consumer interface (Chau et al. 2002).

Cultural differences influence how consumers interpret the look and feel of a website. For example, cultural meanings of colors may deter consumers from visiting or using a company website when the colors are used incorrectly. In the United Kingdom and United States, yellow is associated with cowardice and caution, while in Japan it is linked to grace and nobility. Red signifies danger in many Western countries while it means happiness in China (Stewart 2001).

Cultural sensitivity is also critical when determining which products to sell on a website. In some countries, there is a prohibition on selling certain products. For example, it is illegal to sell alcohol in Muslim countries (Bannon 2006) and Nazi memorabilia in Germany. These types of restrictions pose problems to online auction sites such as Yahoo! and eBay when sellers post these items, which are available to buyers, regardless of country (George 2003).

Culture is also evident in the subtle differences that exist in consumer online behavior and how they interact with technology. P. Y. K. Chau et al. (2002) examined five impressions (i.e., relevance, confusion, entertainment, information content, and transformation content) of U.S. and Hong Kong consumers for four uses of global automobile manufacturers' websites (i.e., social communication, e-commerce, hobby, and information search). Relevance referred to how meaningful the website was to the consumer. Confusion was evaluated based on how much the website confused the consumer. Entertainment measured the entertainment value of the website. Information content determined how well the website provided factual, relevant product information in a clear and logical format for the consumer to develop confidence in judging the advantages of buying the product. Transformation content assessed how well the website connected using the product with specific psychological attributes such as enjoyment and self-image. See Table 15.6 for a summary of the positive and significant differences in their impressions.

Chau et al. (2002) concluded that improvements in the quality and quantity of information provided on a website may positively affect consumer attitudes and behaviors during use and make the consumer feel at home. When consumers used the Internet as a social communication

TABLE 15.6. SIGNIFICANT POSITIVE CULTURAL DIFFERENCES (X) IN THE PURPOSE OF USE OF A WEB SITE BY IMPRESSIONS OF THE WEBSITE BY U.S. AND HONG KONG CONSUMERS

PURPOSE OF USE OF WEBSITE	IMPRESSION OF WEBSITE				
	RELEVANCE	CONFUSION	ENTERTAIN	INFORMATION CONTENT	TRANSFORMATION CONTENT
U.S. Consumers					
Social communication					
E-commerce		X			
Hobby					
Information search	X		X	X	X
Hong Kong Consumers					
Social communication	X	X		X	X
E-commerce			X		
Hobby					
Information search					

Source: Chau, P. Y. K., M. Cole, A. P. Massey, M. Montoya-Weiss, and R. M. O'Keefe. 2002. Cultural differences in the online behavior of consumers. *Communications of the ACM* 45(10):138–143.

device, such as the Hong Kong consumers, or for information search, as was the case for the U.S. consumers, they were likely to be transformed in their view of a product and would use the site's information for improved decision making. Chau et al. recommended that website designers focus on features of information search for U.S. consumers and the social communications features for Hong Kong consumers.

LOCAL VALUE CREATION

Between 25 percent and 60 percent of all online searches are reported to be local (Vazduskas 2006). The Internet makes it simpler to target messages, products, and content to specific customers in specific locations at specific times. Technology solutions such as ShopLo-cal, Local Thunder, and ReachLocal offer e-retailers a platform for responding to local queries and creating local relevance on the Internet (Vazduskas 2006). In addition, the extent to which cultural adaptation is manifested on the website influences consumer perception of its effectiveness.

K. Bolen (2006) suggested it is appropriate to host a site for each country of operation, even if there is similar content on every site. ChateauOnline (www. chateauonline.com), a wine specialty e-tailer, offers wines from all over the world. It delivers wine to France, United Kingdom, Germany, Belgium, The Netherlands, Switzerland, Italy, Luxembourg, and Denmark. Each country site is tailored to the country and information is in the local language. This e-tailer has developed a core business that revolves around wine, but uses an electronic platform that allows for flexibility in accommodating consumer preferences and attitudes in multiple countries (Gray 2000).

Greater development of international businesses that rely on Internet search marketing requires more localized strategies.

Also, with increased use of the Internet in foreign markets it will become imperative to create a localized website to drive traffic. If a website offers driving directions, contact information, pricing, and services, then these should reflect the country where they are offered. In addition, tariffs and taxes are country- and location-specific. Localization of a search engine requires three components: search technology, local support on directories, and local mapping. Launching a localized search service requires sensitivity to local points of view and culture.

OUTSHOPPING

Outshopping is a retail phenomenon where consumers move from one retail trade area to another to seek better shopping options and deals (Varshney 2005). Piron (2001) characterized it as a universal consumer behavior. Consumer movements can be from rural to urban, rural to rural (i.e., to larger rural markets or weekly markets), urban to urban (i.e., small town to larger city), downtown to regional shopping centers in suburbs or close towns, international, online/catalog, and specialized services (Varshney and Goyal 2005). Outshopping is a form of retail leakage that can produce detrimental effects for local retailers and positive effects for external retailers who attract outshoppers.

Cross-border shopping (Lucas 2004) and round-tripping (Macklem 2003) describe international outshopping that occurs when consumers are motivated to travel outside their home country for the purpose of shopping (Tansuhaj, Ong, and McCullough 1989). Despite cross-national similarities of consumers, effective retailing requires an understanding of the differences among consumers across borders (de Mooij and Hofstede 2002). International outshopping can create lucrative markets for inbound countries while it drains revenues and taxes from the outbound countries. This section examines retail environments, Internet, destination shopping, consumer motivations, and consumer ethnocentrism as they influence outshopping.

Retail Environments

The environment of a retail service area influences outshopping. Consumers might choose to outshop when specific services and amenities are missing in the local area, when they are more mobile, and when the secondary costs of shopping do not discourage outshopping (Piron 2001). India has a high prevalence of outshopping, mainly because retail centers and department stores are not highly developed in either rural or urban areas. It is not uncommon for rural and urban Indian consumers to travel great distances to find a greater variety of options when they shop. The repercussion of this outshopping is the lack of development of local rural and urban retail centers (Varshney and Goyal 2005).

Outshopping can also generate retail development. This was the case for the 15.5 km long Øresund Bridge, which opened on July 1, 2000 and directly connected Copenhagen, Denmark, and Malmö, Sweden, by road and rail. The bridge can be crossed at any time by auto and approximately three trains run every hour. Planners and politicians expected outshopping to increase substantially to take advantage of products, shopping times, and tax rates that were unique to each country. The Swedes began constructing a new shopping mall close to the bridge before the bridge was completed. The Danes approved construction for a large shopping mall near their end of the bridge even though the country had a ban on new malls and large-scale stores (Bygvrå and Westlund 2004).

Distance and situational mobility influence outshopping. Location, long-distance travel, and transportation needs and costs affect distance mobility. Situational mobility is a function of convenience (Piron 2001). The Channel Tunnel or Chunnel, which opened in 1994 to connect Folkestone, England, to Calais, France, is an example of how distance and situational mobility affected outshopping. The Chunnel was envisioned as an attractive transportation option to travelers since it reduced the travel distance to a quick 35-minute trip compared with several hours for ferry passage. It was expected that as consumers traveled back and forth between France and England they would outshop. However, opportunities to spend money during the channel crossing were lost on the Chunnel. What was not considered was that the ferry crossing offered time to indulge in duty-free alcohol and on-board shopping with the average passenger spending $18 on merchandise (Levine 1994). This travel and shopping experience was eliminated on the Chunnel where passengers stayed in their cars.

Internet

The Internet provides a virtual outshopping experience by effectively transporting the consumer to any retailer who has a presence on the World Wide Web. E-consumers travel the Internet to shop. They have nonmonetary and psychological costs that are similar to outshoppers who patronize brick-and-mortar retailers. Foreign retailers benefit from e-consumer outshopping (Piron 2002).

Canadian shoppers are frequent outshoppers on U.S. websites and account for about 40 percent of all Canadian online purchases. Cross-border shopping in a virtual store is not hassle free. Canadian consumers experience higher shipping costs, lengthy delivery times, and the problems associated with returning items and being reimbursed for duties and taxes. The Canada Post and Toronto-based Border-

free developed a partnership that offers Canadian catalog and Internet shoppers wider product selection and greater convenience in their cross-border shopping experience. Borderfree technology (www.borderfree.com) provides a total cost calculator that includes payment and return processing that converts to the buyer's local currency as well as tools for management of cross-border data and customer service. This technology gives U.S. e-tailers the ability to confirm the total cost (product, taxes, duties, and shipping) of Canadian orders in the local currency and provide an approximate delivery date. Using this method, purchases are delivered to a U.S. consolidation site where they are validated by a customs broker and made ready for importation. Two U.S. e-tailers making use of this new technology are Crate and Barrel and Brookstone (Lester 2003).

Destination Shopping

Global consumers have become more mobile and travel both for pleasure and business (Douglas and Craig 1997). When travel decisions are based in part or entirely on travel to a specific destination to shop, then this is considered **destination shopping**. Destination shopping can occur within short distances, such as travel from rural areas to urban regional malls, within a country, or across national borders. Consumers who engage in destination shopping often do so to experience a shopping environment that is different from that at home.

Tourist shopping is a form of destination shopping. It occurs during times of vacation travel and differs from purchasing behaviors at home, which tend to be rational and ordinary. During vacation time, tourists are not as thrifty and tend to break from normal routines. Tourist shoppers seek excitement and pleasure in their shopping experiences. In international tourism settings, retailers need to consider differences in attitudes, values, perceptions, and practices of consumers who come from different countries and cultures (Oh, Cheng, Lehto, and O'Leary 2004).

Destination shopping offers opportunities for international retail expansion. As consumers travel they have increased exposure to brands, products, and lifestyles from other countries. For U.S. retailers, producers, and manufacturers, this means greater opportunities to profitably promote U.S. products and brands.

Numerous strategies are used to encourage destination shopping. In 1996, Air India initiated a ladies' fare program that offered female passengers a 33 percent discount to travel between India and shopping destinations of Dubai, Hong Kong, and Singapore (Brady 1996). When U.S. retailers, mall managers, and Chambers of Commerce started offering Canadians all-in-one packages that included discounted prices, post-shopping dinner reservations, hotel accommodations, and organized bus trips, U.S. border towns became shopping destinations for Canadian outshopping (Macklem 2003).

Hong Kong is a famous shopping destination (See Figure 15.19). More than half of its total visitor expenditures is generated by shopping. Its place as a shopping desti-

nation is being challenged by Singapore, Thailand, and South Korea (Yeung, Wong, and Ko 2004). In a comparative study of international visitors perceptions of tourism shopping in Hong Kong and Singapore, S. Yeung et al. (2004) examined shopping expectations and shopping experiences in the two countries. They found six shopping attributes were perceived significantly more favorable in Hong Kong: price for product, accessibility of shop, value for money, variety of product selection, opening hours of shop, and availability of product. Eight attributes were perceived as significantly more favorable in Singapore: language ability of sales staff, attitude of sales staff, window display, neatness and cleanliness, lighting and physical setting, choice of payment methods, product reliability, and efficiency of sales staff. Availability of sales label was the only attribute that performed the same in Hong Kong and Singapore. They concluded that workforce-related attributes (e.g., language, attitude, and efficiency) placed Singapore ahead of Hong Kong. This supports the need for hiring and training a quality workforce. Since perceptions were similar on the availability of sales labels, this suggests that retailers may need to differentiate themselves on aspects of the shopping experience.

15.19 Hong Kong is a famous shopping destination. More than half of its total visitor expenditures are generated by shopping.

Consumer Motivations

Economic benefits are strong motivators for outshopping. Price can drive consumers to cross borders to purchase goods. Price considerations need to include secondary and hidden costs such as transportation and time costs, and taxes and duties (Piron 2002). Retailers combating retail leakages from outshopping might emphasize the true cost of outshopping to retain local customers.

International outshopping may be driven by price and selection from foreign retailers, not dissatisfaction with local retailers (Tansuhaj et al. 1989). Bygvrå and Westlund (2004) compared the purchasing behaviors of outshoppers who used the Øresund Bridge that links Sweden and Denmark with consumers who traveled across the Danish-German land border to outshop. They found a greater variety of products in the Øresund shopping baskets but less quantity when compared with land-border outshopping. Several factors influenced consumer cross-border outshopping. Øresund was more expensive in time and money while the price differences were greater between Denmark and Germany. However, S. Bygvrå and H. Westlund suggested that when incentives are sufficient enough, people will cross a border to make purchases. This was evident for Swedish consumers who crossed the Øresund specifically to purchase alcoholic beverages at a lower cost in Demark. Similarly, F. Piron (2001) found that economic reasons were the greatest motivator for Singaporean consumers who outshopped. Although Singapore is considered a modern, well-developed city-state that offers excellent shopping, local consumers perceived they received better value for their money when shopping in Malaysia, even for day-to-day needs. The Singapore example illustrates the importance of devising competitive retail strategies that are convincing enough to get consumers to shop locally, especially for daily necessities.

Noneconomic benefits drive outshopping as well. Hedonic motivators create joy and fun when shopping. For some consumers, there is satisfaction in paying lower taxes that might be available by shopping in another country. Also, the discovery of unique products and experiences that are not available at home can create a pleasurable consumer experience (Piron 2002). Outshopping is encouraged by the stimulation that comes from experiencing environmental attributes in a new marketplace, by engaging in new and different social interactions, and by learning about new trends and innovations (Varshney and Goyal 2005). Canadian outshopping to the United States is driven by the greater variety of shops and choices offered there and the recreational aspect of shopping where cross-border shopping is perceived as fun (Macklem 2003).

Outshopping is associated frequently with bargain hunting. In Singapore, a unique national phenomenon called the *kiasu* spirit drives Singaporean outshoppers. *Kiasu* refers to a disposition to ignore commonly accepted standards of behavior to take advantage of bargains. The *kiasu* spirit eliminates feelings of guilt that might be associated with foreign shopping, rather than at home (Piron 2002). Outshopping provides the excitement of the hunt. So even though bargains are sought, the thrill of finding the bargain may be the motivator.

Consumer Ethnocentrism

Retail shopping ethnocentrism is the tendency to purchase locally instead of outshopping (Piron 2002). An ethnocentric consumer might choose not to outshop because of ethnocentric beliefs. Beliefs that outshopping created a loss of jobs and demonstrated a lack of national pride made outshopping a political issue in Singapore. Government interventions were considered to prevent almost 900,000 Singaporean consumers a month from traveling across the Causeway to Johor Baru, Malaysia for shopping, food, and recreation. Consumers were not just recreational shopping, they were outshopping for daily necessities (Lucas 2004, Piron 2002). In examining ethnocentrism of Singaporeans who outshopped in Malayisa, Piron (2002) found that consumers who outshopped for economic reasons did not feel they had a lack of national pride or low consumer ethnocentrism.

Governments become involved in outshopping due to potentially lucrative taxation for inbound shoppers. Conversely, consumers often outshop to avoid taxes that they would have to pay when purchasing similar merchandise in their home country (Lucas 2004).

OPPORTUNITIES AND CHALLENGES FOR GLOBAL EXPERIENTIAL RETAILING

Global experiential retailing has developed into a successful format for all types of retailers, restaurateurs, and hoteliers. It entices customers to enter, to stay, to browse, to shop, to experience the environment and products, and to make a purchase. As a result, delineations between retailing and hospitality experiences are blurring as each industry merges aspects of the other into its product, service, and experience offerings.

The following section highlights some opportunities associated with growth in regional consumption, demand for luxury goods, shopping malls, and *shoppertainment*. In addition, challenges related to regulatory, geopolitical, and cultural differences facing the expansion of global experiential retailing are discussed as well.

Opportunities

Opportunities to apply the concepts and strategies associated with experiential retailing are growing at a phenomenal rate. New markets are opening around the world where consumers seek to have more satisfying experiences when they shop. Mature marketplaces are changing into more exciting places to be. Differentiation, more than ever before, is based on creating consumer experiences that are unique, exciting, stimulating, and memorable.

GROWTH IN REGIONAL CONSUMPTION

European markets offer exceptional opportunities for retail growth, especially for U.S. retailers who are looking for international expansion. Sweden ranks highest, with 190 square feet of retail space per person, which is about one tenth of the amount in the United States, followed by The Netherlands, United Kingdom, France, Austria, Ireland, and Spain, which average between 100 and 150 square feet per person. The gross-domestic product of Europe as a whole is expected to increase 8 percent between 2002 and 2006, with some markets increasing by more than twice that amount. Retail growth for malls is expected to increase as well. There are very few malls in Europe that have more than 1 million square feet. Those malls that do have more than 1 million square feet average sales that are 2.5 times higher than in the United States (i.e., Bluewater in the United Kingdom at 1.6 million square feet, Colombo in Portugal at 1.3 million square feet, and Oberhausen in Germany at 1.1 million square feet) (Siegel 2003).

In Eastern Europe, there are three different retail opportunities. Russia is large enough to stand on its own. Traditional Eastern European countries such as Hungary and Romania are open for retail development. Also, new Eastern European countries such as the Ukraine, Slovenia, and Latvia are opportunities for retail development (India tops 2005). In addition, Poland, Hungary, and the Czech Republic offer growth opportunities for international retailers; these countries need everything, so the opportunities cross all product categories. In Russia, brand image supports consumer purchasing from retailers with strong global brand images. Lifestyle purchases have become more apparent among consumers in many foreign countries. Starbucks, which sells a lifestyle as much as a product, has gained popularity in Russia and China (McLinden 2004).

The Far East represents a growth region for U.S. and European retailers. With relaxation of trade regulations in 2004, China has become a prime location for expansion. Tesco, Metro, Carrefour, and Wal-Mart, four of the world's largest retailers, are expanding into China (Craig 2005). "While the US and Europe have taken more than 100 years to develop their retail markets from small local stores to department stores, national chains, hypermarkets, and shopping centers, China is well on its way to making the same transformation in just 10 years of development" (Hawkey 2006, 8). Other new targets for international retail are being identified in Africa, India, and Russia (Craig 2005).

According to a study by A. T. Kearney, which publishes the Global Retail Development Index (GRDI), India offers one of the most compelling opportunities for international retail expansion of mass merchants and food retailers. Accounting for over $300 billion in retail sales, the India retail market is vastly underserved. It is experiencing a 10 percent average annual growth. Foreign retailers have incentive to relocate to India with the relaxation of direct ownership restrictions by the Indian government. The retail market in India is one of the most fragmented in the world with the top five retailers in India holding less than 2 percent of the market. Pantaloon, Westside, and Big Bazaar are leading Indian retailers (India tops annual list 2005).

DEMAND FOR LUXURY GOODS

Consumers worldwide are demanding access to more luxury goods. "Traditional luxury items and brands, once accessible to those in upper-income brackets, have become more available to more consumers. Manufacturers and retailers alike have recognized that consumers, particularly those in the mass affluent income category ($50,000 plus), are attracted to entry-level luxury items and will trade-up to more substantial purchases as their income/wealth increases" (McIntosh and Valerio 2005, 59).

In 2004, there were 8.3 million households worldwide that had assets of at least $1 million. This was up 7 percent from the year before. The newly wealthy affirm their wealth by seeking the luxury products that the already wealthy consume. Conspicuous consumption is driving demand for luxury goods. In addition, many consumers are trading up to luxury goods in some categories and trading down to lower-priced merchandise in other categories. This selective extravagance is evident also in the growth of fractional ownership of luxury goods and services such as NetJets private jets. From Bags to Riches is a retail venture that rents designer handbags to consumers who can not or choose not to pay the full price for ownership (Inconspicuous consumption 2005).

Luxury brands are no longer the domain of a few retailers. A growing variety of retailers are offering luxury goods at a wide range of price points. In September 2005, Wal-Mart launched a two-year advertising campaign in *Vogue*. The campaign includes 112 advertising pages that focus on Wal-Mart as a source for dressing fashionably (McIntosh and Valerio 2005).

The demand for luxury has increased the global presence of many luxury companies. TAG Heuer is a Swiss watch manufacturer whose retail stores are appearing in major cities throughout the world. On its website (www.tagheuer.com), the company identifies its brand with prestige, performance, avant-garde technology, and absolute reliability. Because TAG Heuer shares similar values of pushing one's limits and the quest for perfection and absolute precision, it partners with some of the world's most well-known sports icons. Tiger Woods is one such preferred partner (See Figure 15.20).

Japan remains one of the most important luxury markets in the world. Coach is a U.S. luxury brand that offers fine quality leather merchandise, with handbags being the most notable (See Figure 15.21). Coach has become the number two brand in Japan through aggressive retail expansion and "by redefining its products as 'affordable luxury'" (Sanchanta 2006, 3).

The luxury good market in China is growing by as much as 60 percent per year. As Chinese people become richer, they have become very interested in luxury brands. Chinese customers make up about 5 percent of the worldwide sales of luxury goods. This represents about 2 percent from mainland China and 3 percent from Hong Kong (Ong and Forden 2005).

Many global luxury brands are entering and expanding in China. Bulgari, the Italian jeweler, has 17 outlets in the greater region. Prada has 22 outlets with a flagship store in Shanghai. Valentino opened its first store in 2005. Giorgio Armani is opening 22 outlets by 2006. Prada and Bulgari do not produce their luxury goods in China because many Chinese consumers perceive locally produced goods as being low-cost and low-quality (Ong and Forden 2005).

15.20 TAG Heuer is a luxury Swiss watch brand that has retail stores in major cities throughout the world. This store is in Kuala Lumpur, Malaysia. Tiger Woods, the noted championship golfer, is a preferred partner for this brand.

India is an emerging luxury market whose growth is outpaced only by the United States, Japan, and China (See Figure 15.22). The consumer population represents a youth market where 54 percent of the population is under the age of 25. India has over 209 million households; 6 million households are considered wealthy, spending $28 billion annually,

15.21 Coach has become the number two brand in Japan where the brand is defined as affordable luxury.

who are trendy, fashion conscious, and love branded and lifestyle products. Younger Indians from wealthier families are bypassing the purchasing power of their counterparts in Europe and the United States, and they are spending their disposable income on luxury products. In 2005, this consumer segment accounted for about 1.6 million Indian households, which averaged $9,000 a year on luxury goods purchases. Sought out brands that are sold in boutiques include Jimmy Choo, Gucci, Louis Vuitton, Hermes, Cartier, Piaget, Tiffany, Moschino, and Christian Dior (See Figure 15.23). In October 2005, the Chanel brand was launched at an exhibit and haute couture extravaganza at the luxury Imperial Hotel in New Delhi. In the same month, Swatch Group introduced its Breguet watches, which averaged $30,000 apiece. High-end watchmaker TAG Heuer has averaged a 40 percent growth each year from 2002 (Narayan and Carsen 2006).

15.22 India is emerging a one of the fastest-growing luxury markets in the world. It has 6 million wealthy households that spend $28 billion annually and one million households with household purchasing power of U.S.$200,000 each.

and 1 million households are considered very wealthy, with household purchasing power of U.S. $200,000 each. These wealthy households are generating a high demand for luxury goods, urban fashions, and international brands (Biswas 2006). India's youthful consumer segment has generated a "shift from price consideration to design and quality along with a willingness to experiment with mainstream fashion as greater emphasis is placed on looking and feeling good" (Biswas 2006, 2).

The booming economy in India has created a critical mass of affluent consumers

SHOPPING MALLS

The U.S. shopping culture, characterized by shopping malls, is a unique American symbol of convenience and excess. Shopping malls have become a dominant U.S. export (Margolis 2005). Maturation of the U.S. shopping industry has led developers to partner with local affiliates to expand in Europe and Asia (McLinden 2004) with the most immediate promise for retail expansion being Eastern and Western Europe (Groeber 2002). Compared with U.S. shopping malls, international shopping centers are generally smaller with only two to four anchor tenants (McLinden 2004) (See Figure 15.24).

International shopping center development reaches across nations and continents, which is making mall shopping available to the global masses. Malls are creating economic and real-estate booms. For example, megamalls have created an

15.23 Luxury goods are a high growth area in Singapore. Christian Dior is one of the many luxury brands experiencing high demand there.

economic explosion in the Philippines. In developing countries, malls have become vehicles for economic growth by attracting a wide range of service-oriented businesses. Banks, art galleries, museums, car-rental agencies, and government services are not unusual. In San Salvador, El Salvador, people would likely consider a Roman Catholic Church that holds mass twice a day to be the anchor store in the Galerías shopping arcade (Margolis 2005).

In 2005, Simon Property Group, a major U.S. mall developer, created a partnership with Morgan Stanley and a government-owned Chinese company to open up to a dozen major retail centers in China. The Arab Emirate of Dubai, referred to as the Oz of malls, had 88.5 million mall visitors in 2004. In Brazil, almost 180 million shoppers visit shopping arcades each month, nearly the same number as in the United States (Margolis 2005).

Malls developed outside the United States are being created as regionalized retail centers that reflect local tastes and preferences. The three-story Kingdom Center in Riyadh, Saudi Arabia, created a shopping experience for Saudi women that accommodated culturally specific shopping needs. Strict *sharia* law (religious law) in Saudi Arabia forbids Saudi women from appearing in public without a veil. This makes it difficult for women to try on clothing and accessories. Women's Kingdom, which occupies the entire third floor of the Kingdom Center, is dedicated solely to female customers. This floor is the most profitable floor for the whole center (Margolis 2005). M. Margolis (2005) suggested the success of this mall is an example of the global desire for consumer culture as well as the importance of the right to shop in fostering democratization and development (See Figure 15.25).

In planning strategies for overseas growth, retailers need to employ unique

concepts or techniques that differentiate them from their competitors. Outlet shopping was a foreign concept to Japan until the New Jersey–based developer Chelsea Property Group, in a joint partnership with Mitsubishi Estate Company and Nissho Iwai Corporation, built its first outlet mall in Japan in 1999. Chelsea, which brought its proprietary knowledge about outlet shopping to the Japanese marketplace to fill a very specific retail niche, has expanded to four outlets (McLinden 2004).

The first mega mall with international draw was the West Edmonton Mall in Edmonton, Alberta, Canada. It offered visitors 20,000 parking spaces, an ice-skating rink, a miniature-golf course, an indoor amusement park, and a water park. It was the largest mall in the world until 2005 when it was overtaken by the $1.3 billion Golden Resources Shopping Center, which employs 20,000 people, in northwest

15.24 Shopping malls have become a U.S. export industry where partnerships are being formed with local affiliates in Europe and Asia. This is a modern shopping center in Kuala Lumpur, Malaysia.

stronger infrastructures, affluent urban youth populations, and consumers with greater disposable incomes. Indian real estate developers are hiring international mall developers and building stronger ties with retailers and consumer brands that will be located in their malls (Biswas 2006).

Shopping malls that include entertainment are becoming major global attractions. European consumers have negative reactions to retail and malls, but they are interested in malls when entertainment is the focus with retailing being ancillary (Foster 2003). Groeber (2002) suggested one opportunity for international retail development was the combination of a food merchant that offers lower everyday pricing on staples along with an entertainment component.

SHOPPERTAINMENT

The Mills Corporation has led the way in the multi-leisure concept known as **shoppertainment,** which it has incorporated into nearly 40 shopping malls and leisure projects. A key concept of shoppertainment is the integration of entertainment into the shopping experience. This transforms a shopping center into a leisure destination. Because consumers spend about 52 percent of their leisure time shopping, the shoppertainment concept has the potential to draw in consumers who want a broader experience during their shopping time (Foster 2003, Levitt 2003, Pickard 2005).

Mills Corporation exported the shoppertainment concept to Europe when it opened Xanadu Madrid in 2003, its first European venture. Most recently it purchased the St. Enoch Centre in Glasgow, Scotland, for further expansion. Xanadu Madrid is the first large shopping/ entertainment center in Europe. Xanadu Madrid is located about 15 miles from Madrid, Spain (Groeber 2002, Levitt 2003,

15.25 Women in Saudi Arabia have culturally specific shopping needs that arise from *sharia* law, which requires women to wear a veil when they are in public. The Women's Center, which occupies the third floor of the Kingdom Center in Riyadh, is a women's-only floor. This allows women to shop without veils.

Beijing. South China Mall in Dongguan, China opened in 2005. It is the largest mall in the world. By 2010 China is expected to have 10 of the world's largest malls. Dubai is developing two malls that contain man-made, five-run ski slopes and are expected to be even larger than malls in China (Margolis 2005).

Malls are leading the $330 billion retailing industry in India (Margolis 2005). In 2001 there were three shopping malls in India. By 2005 that number increased to 100 and it is expected to grow to 345 by 2007 (Zakaria 2006) and to 600 by 2010 (Biswas 2006). In 2006 there were 220 mall projects underway, 125 of them were located in the large metropolitan areas of Mumbai, Delhi, Chenai, Kolkata, Bangalore, and Hyderabad. These cities have commercial land for development,

McLinden 2004, Pickard 2005). Xanadu Madrid is a 1.2-million-square-feet shopping complex developed through a joint venture between Mills Corporation and Parcelatoria de Gonzao Chacón (PGS). It features the first of its kind Snow Dome, an indoor Alpine-style winter sports complex that offers snowboarding, skiing, sledding, and other Alpine recreational activities. Also, visitors can race go-karts, go bowling, play billiards, see a movie, dine in one of 20 restaurants, dance, and shop at more than 220 stores. Retailers include Spain's largest department store El Corte Inglés and specialty store Zara. The retail mix includes about 10 percent U.S.–based retailers such as Nike and other foreign retailers such as H & M from Sweden. Unlike other retail operations in the area, it is open 365 days a year. Xanadu Madrid was expected to attract between 25 and 30 million visitors in its first year of operation (Foster 2003, Groeber 2002, Levitt 2003, McLinden 2004). This suggests that shoppertainment is a major up-and-coming wave of experiential retailing.

Challenges

International retail expansion is not without its challenges. Many retailers fail because of poor planning, poor product development, and lack of cultural understanding. Highly restrictive zoning laws, geopolitics, high taxes, and complex bureaucracies can be difficult roadblocks to overcome. Companies who decide on global market entry and expansion need to put into place management teams with specialized managerial skills and training (Strutton and Pelton 1997). Most important, the success of retailers and retail developers who expand their operations and products into foreign markets hinges on understanding the unique characteristics of the consumers they target and the often complex cultural needs of the countries they enter.

REGULATORY

As international retailers expand operations into foreign countries they face many regulatory challenges such as trade regulations. For example, until China joined the World Trade Organization in 2001, it had severe restrictions on foreign investment in the retail sector. Before 2005, foreign-owned retailers could only operate in designated cities such as the capital city of each province and in China's five Special Economic Zones. Only joint-venture retailing companies, not 100 percent foreign-owned retail companies, were allowed. Joint-venture companies were subject to approval by the State Committee of Economy and Trade that dictated minimum annual sales and total assets for both the foreign investor and the Chinese partner. Also, it dictated the percentage of the company's annual revenue that could be dispersed to foreign shareholders, and the time limit (i.e., 10 years) after which payments could not be made (Ni 2004). Table 15.7 compares old and new retail and distribution laws in China.

Before January 2006, India did not allow foreign companies to own controlling interest in joint ventures. Now, single brand stores can own up to 51 percent. This new regulation is stimulating the growth of fashion brands that are sold in exclusive outlets such as Nike and Cartier. However, multinational chains like Tesco and Wal-Mart remain barred from India (Narayan and Carsen 2006). J. Groeber (2002) suggested that when an effort is made to understand local consumer demands and needs it is possible to gain approval for retail expansion.

Operational regulations impact how retailers do business in foreign countries. In France, shopping centers operate like a

TABLE 15.7. RETAIL AND DISTRIBUTION LAWS IN CHINA: COMPARISON OF OLD AND NEW RULES

	OLD RULES	NEW RULES (JUNE 2004)
Retailers	Joint ventures	Sole proprietorship available
Store locations	Provincial capitals and big cities	Anywhere
Store openings	Require central-government approval	Require provincial-government approval; *except* 9,900+ square feet set up by largest chains
Distribution	Only foreign companies that manufacture in China and the largest retailers	Any foreign company
Import/export	Only selected Chinese companies	Any foreign wholesaler or retailer

(created table from text)
Source: Chang, L. 2004. China opens retail to foreign investors. *Wall Street Journal* [Eastern edition]. June, A2.

condominium. Anchor tenants own their retail space and participate in decisions regarding other tenants (McLinden 2004). In Germany, the government enforces strict regulations that protect small retailers from large competitors (Groeber 2002). In the Madrid area of Spain, department stores and shopping malls are allowed to stay open only 21 Sundays or holidays per year (Levitt 2003).

GEOPOLITICAL

Geopolitics influence consumers' perceptions of international retailers. Common U.S. brands often are interpreted as American symbols and as such can draw unwanted attention. In 2001, thousands of Pakistani protesters filled the streets in response to American warplanes bombing Afghanistan. They attacked a locally owned KFC franchise that had its red, white, and blue KFC logo prominently displayed (O'Keefe 2001).

Starbucks is a global company that operates almost 3,000 coffeehouses in 37 countries. It opened its first store in 1971 in Seattle, Washington and its first international coffeehouse in Tokyo in 1999. As with many global brands, it draws politically charged attention. The Starbucks website (www.starbucks.com) has a dedicated link under the About Us section labeled rumor response to combat inaccurate rumors, where political points of contention are raised and addressed. The website has numerous pages devoted to Corporate Social Responsibility.

CULTURAL

Cultural differences, not legal concerns, are the greatest challenges to international retail expansion. Cultural differences delineate how people live, the types of space they have, and their product preferences. When Costco entered the U.K. market with its bulk-commodities model, the retailer failed to take into account the lack of freezer and storage space in the average household. It had to repackage its products for sale in the United Kingdom (McLinden 2004). For retailers, the influence of culture on employee work ethic is a major consideration to international expansion. In Europe, employees generally work fewer hours per week and take a compulsory four-week vacation (McLinden 2004), a work pattern that is unusual in U.S. retail.

A misconception held by many retailers is that the brand needs to present one face to the world (Mazur 2002). It is important that retailers have an ongoing process for identifying the right combination of products, pricing, brand image, and service levels that meet the wants of targeted consumers. While Starbucks appears to offer its brand the same worldwide, it uses a subtle approach to meeting local cultural needs. Starbucks hires staff who can execute the company's consistent service model along with a local understanding of how to create an atmosphere that is right for each market (Mazur 2002).

In some foreign markets, the challenge of a new product or experience is that it is not understood. This is the case for Disney as it focuses on generating new international growth in emerging markets. While Disney as a brand has global recognition, the concept and products do not always translate in foreign markets. To create a better understanding of Disney characters and to build relationships with retailers, Disney signed a licensing agreement with Eastern Media Holdings to sell toys, apparel, and other consumer products in Vietnam, Cambodia, and Laos (Chaffin 2006).

A lack of cultural understanding of the Disney experience led to numerous problems when Hong Kong Disneyland opened in 2005 (See Figure 15.26). Many Chinese visitors did not understand the park, how to enjoy it, or even why it would be considered enjoyable. Disney had to create a one-day trip guide in addition to the standard park guides to explain in clear terms how to enjoy Disneyland (Fowler and Marr 2006). The problems outside of the park included advertising campaigns that featured a nuclear family composed of two parents and two children that were directed to families in a society where parents are encouraged to have only one child. When Hong Kong Disney employees studied Chinese visitors, they found that it took the Chinese an average of 10 minutes longer to eat when compared with Americans. Disney accommodated the additional dining time by adding 700 additional seats to dining areas. Although for some experiences, Disney used separate queues for Mandarin, Cantonese, and English speakers so riders could hear the narration in their native tongue, Chinese visitors did not understand waiting-line protocol and would hop lines. Adding Mandarin subtitles to shows helped visitors understand what was going on and when to respond by clapping and laughing. Many Chinese tourists purchase their travel from tour operators whose profit is dependent upon commissions from pre-arranged meals. When Disney realized that tour operators were not booking the park because group dinners were not being offered, it had to consider new strategies such as dining with Disney and meals with Disney characters (Marr and Fowler 2006). Many Chinese families prefer to visit Ocean Park in Hong Kong over Disneyland because it offers traditional family-oriented activities (e.g., Pandas, an aquarium, and a Sky Tram) that are better understood and enjoyed.

15.26 Hong Kong Disneyland faced a number of problems when it opened due to lack of cultural understanding of how the Chinese consumer would interpret the Disney experience. Chinese visitors did not know the Disney characters, did not understand the park, did not know how to enjoy the park, or even why it would be considered enjoyable.

CHAPTER SUMMARY

Globalization is influencing retailing and hospitality service industries as companies seek to expand operations in ways that will retain and attract new customers. Globalization is influencing three dimensions of consumer culture: local, foreign, and global. Local consumer culture reflects the cultural meanings associated with local norms, values, and identities. Foreign consumer culture includes consumer perceptions, attitudes, and behaviors that are exhibited toward products, brands, and companies that are not indigenous. Country image, country-of-origin image, and consumer ethnocentrism are important considerations associated with foreign consumer culture.

Global consumer cultures are composed of well-defined consumer clusters that cross national boundaries. They have similar needs, tastes, and lifestyles that often are shaped by Western themes and values, promoted through the mass media, and sold as lifestyle products and services. Young adults are considered the first true global consumers because of their extended exposure to instantaneous communication via the Internet. These younger consumers have an increased proneness to purchase certain brands that reinforce membership in a consumer segment. Retailers have a unique and profitable opportunity to target these younger populations as a transnational, homogenized global consumer segment.

When targeting global consumers, retailers need to consider the relationship between the individual and the group to which he or she belongs. Individualism-collectivism (I-C) is particularly important in global experiential retailing as Western retailers (i.e., from individualistic nations) expand into Asian cultures which have strong collectivism cultures.

Retail internationalization is a process of expanding into nondomestic markets by exporting retail operations and private brand products. Push factors, such as mature and saturated domestic markets and increasing government regulations, and pull factors, which are those characteristics that make a foreign country appealing for international expansion have driven international retail expansion. Fashion and category killer retailers are dominating current international retail expansion efforts.

International retailing takes many forms. Retailers are grouped by organizational structure, market entry strategy, and operation mode. Companies are classified as international, multinational, and transnational based on their level of international penetration and how the company is managed. Strategies for global market entry include penetration, diversification, product development, and brand development. Operational mode is based on how the company's products, technology, and managerial or human resources are integrated into a foreign country.

A challenge to global retail expansion is the ability to retain uniqueness in a market. This uniqueness can be created through branding strategies that are associated with brand image, brand-product interface, and brand awareness. The power and value of a brand is enhanced by building a global image where global consumers assign consistent attributes to a particular brand. Brand-product interface is the cross-classification of existing and new brand identities and product availability. Brand awareness is the extent to which consumers know about a brand and recognize the attributes associated with that brand. Brands are becoming commodities of cultural change and exchange.

Global retail strategies include standardization, localization, customization, cultural swapping, clustering, and spatial segmentation. Standardization and localization are contrasting approaches to entering and serving foreign markets. Complete standardization would execute product, brand, and retail operations uniformly across all global markets. Complete localization would implement unique product, brand, and retail operations that are specific to the locale. Customization and clustering are retail strategies that make localization more efficient. Spatial segmentation combines characteristics of both standardization and localization by using a multi-attribute approach to segmentation.

One of the first e-commerce industries to proliferate with the growth of the Internet was e-tailing. E-tailing has extended the consumer market from local to global. International retailers need to understand and acknowledge diversity in the cultures, political systems, economies, and available technologies that are represented by the consumers who shop at their websites. Search engines and browsers are integrated components of e-tailing. E-tailers need to understand how to best use these technologies to improve bottom-line results. Localization, an important aspect of e-tailing, includes aspects of translation, local interpretation, local look and feel, and local value creation on the website.

Outshopping occurs when consumers move from one retail trade area to another to shop. One form of outshopping is destination shopping that is generally associated with tourists who target a specific place to visit based on its shopping opportunities. Economic and hedonic benefits are important drivers of outshopping. Other drivers include mobility and search for specific services and amenities that are missing in the local area. The Internet provides a virtual outshopping experience by effectively transporting the consumer to any retailer who has a presence on the World Wide Web. In some situations, con-

sumer ethnocentrism motivates consumers to purchase locally instead of outshopping.

Global experiential retailing has developed into a successful format for all types of retailers, restaurateurs, and hoteliers. It entices customers to enter, to stay, to browse, to shop, and to experience the environment and products, and to make a purchase. Opportunities for global experiential retailing are associated with growth in regional consumption, demand for luxury goods, shopping malls, and shoppertainment. Retailers who seek to expand experiential retailing concepts into international markets need to be prepared for regulatory, geopolitical, and cultural challenges that can deter or defeat expansion strategies. Probably the most important challenge is to understand the unique characteristics of the consumers they target and the often complex cultural needs of the countries they enter.

Discussion Questions

1. How does collectivism or individualism affect the consumption patterns of a culture? Use a particular culture to explain each distinction and its consumer outcomes.

2. Starbucks is very successful in entering foreign markets. What were the difficulties encountered when Starbucks decided to pursue the English market?

3. What types of products have established the following country images: Switzerland for precision and trustworthiness, Japan for miniaturization and advanced technology, and Germany for quality and reliability. Explain.

4. Why is country-of-origin becoming less of a consideration for many consumers? Describe at least two countries where country-of-origin

remains a significant influence on consumer purchasing behavior.

5. Hypermarkets have a significant global presence in retailing. Explain the causes and implications of this retailing trend.

6. Relate the concepts of standardization and localization to IKEA. How does this company accomplish both?

7. Why do global fashion brand companies refrain from challenging the national retail structure in the foreign countries they enter?

8. Describe the U.S. brand concept and why other countries perceive it as being unique? What factors might reduce the effectiveness of this image?

9. Identify at least two ethnic foods in the United States, besides tortillas, that have become or are in the process of becoming mainstream foods. Provide explanations of why this is happening.

10. Coca-Cola is a global brand image and has been successful in developing websites with cultural appeal. By visiting this company's various websites, identify the attributes that have made its strategy successful.

11. Have you or someone you know experienced an unsuccessful outshopping experience? How could it have been avoided? Otherwise, provide an example of a positive outshopping experience.

12. What factors are driving the rapid growth of shopping malls in India? Why is India one of the most compelling countries for retail development?

REFERENCES

Alexander, N. 1990. Retailers and international markets: Motives for expansion. *International Marketing Review* 7(4):75–85.

Ahmed, Z. U., J. P. Johnson, C. P. Ling, T. W. Fang, and A. K. Hui. 2002. Country-of-origin and brand effects on consumers' evaluation of cruiselines. *International Marketing Review* 19(3):279–302.

Alden, D. L., J. E. Steenkamp, and R. Batra. 1999. Brand positioning through advertising in Asia, North America, and Europe: The role ofglobal consumer culture. *Journal of Marketing* 63:75–87.

Anholt, S. 2000. The nation as brand. *Across the Board*. November/December, 22–27.

Armani supports its hotels online. 2006. *Marketing*. March 16, 3.

Asheghian, P., and B. Ebrahimi. 1990. *International business: Economics, environment, and strategies*. New York: Harper & Row.

Bannon, K. J. 2006. Lost in translation. *B to B* 91(7):21–22.

Barrskog, H. 2005. New Palazzo Versace to open in Dubai. *Fashiongates.com* Retrieved September 5, 2006 from http://www.fashiongates.com/magazine/New-Palazzo-Versace-in-Dubai-25-05-05-78011.html

Barth, K., N. J. Karch, K. McLaughlin, and C. S. Shi. 1996. Global retailing: Tempting trouble? *The McKinsey Quarterly*. Winter, 117–126.

Bellman, S., G. L. Lohse, and E. J. Johnson. 1999. Predictors of online buying behavior. *Communication of the ACM* 42(12):32–28.

Benoit, B., and M. Nakamoto. 2001. Metro in Japan link with Marubeni Retailing German company to open bulk stores as part of cash-and-carry expansion in Asia. *Financial Times* [London]. April 16, 23.

Biesada, A. 2006. Marks and Spencer Group p.l.c. Retrieved at: http://

premium.hoovers.com/global/cobrands/proquest/factsheet.xhtml?COID=41199

Birchall, J. 2005. The cultural maelstrom of international retailing. *Financial Times* [London]. June 4, 13.

Biswas, R. 2006. India's changing consumers. *Retail News*. Spring, 2–4.

Bolen, K. 2006. Let Web visitors choose how to explore your site. *B to B* 91(7):21.

Boorstin, S. 2001. Eastern evolution. *Restaurant Hospitality* 85(1):32–40.

Brady, D. 1996. Airlines in Asia offer personalized prices by age, race, gender—Air India has its ladies fare to shopping destinations; Chinese fliers are wooed. *Wall Street Journal* [Eastern edition]. September 30, A14.

Brand papers: In the eye of the beholder. 2003. *Brand Strategy*. September, 32.

Brinkley, C., and A. Galloni. 2004. Style & substance: A bitter suite mix; Ritz-Carlton's Bulgari venture aimed to elevate hotel brand; now, divas duel for spotlight. *Wall Street Journal* [Eastern edition]. October 8, B1.

Bromage, N. 2002. Captain Spice. *Supply Management* 7(7):26–28.

Burt, S., K. Davies, A. McAuley, and L. Sparks 2005. Retail internationalization: From formats to implants. *European Management Journal* 23(2):195–202.

Buzzell, R. D. 1968. Can you standardize multinational marketing? *Harvard Business Review* 55:102–113.

Bygvrå, S., and H. Westlund. 2004. Shopping behaviour in the Øresund region before and after the establishment of the fixed link between Denmark and Sweden. *GeoJournal* 61:41–52.

Chaffin, J. 2006. Disney targets Vietnam in drive for growth Media. *Financial Times* [London]. May 2, 23.

Chang, L. 2004. China opens retail to foreign investors. *Wall Street Journal* [Eastern edition]. June, A2.

Chau, P. Y. K., M. Cole, A. P. Massey, M. Montoya-Weiss, and R. M. O'Keefe. 2002. Cultural differences in the online behavior of consumers. *Communications of the ACM* 45(10):138–43.

Cohen, I., and E. Carey. 2000. Moving into the 21st century at Internet speed. *Stores* G3–G4.

Craig, T. 2005. Most growth potential beyond U.S. borders. *DSN Retailing Today* 44(11):48.

Czinkota, M. R., and I. A. Ronkainen. 1996. *Global Marketing*. New York: Dryden Press.

Day, J. 1999. Coke plans global clothing brands. *Marketing Week* 21(45):5.

Daouas, M. 2001. African faces challenges of globalization. *Finance & Development* 38(4):4–5.

Debbs, M. 1990. Big line greets Moscow's Beeg Mac. *San Francisco Chronicle*. February 1, A1.

de Mooij, M., and G. Hofstede. 2002. Convergence and divergence in consumer behavior: Implications for international retailing. *Journal of Retailing* 78:61–69.

Dholakia, R. R., and N. Dholakai. 2004. Mobility and markets: Emerging outlines of m-commerce. *Journal of Business Research* 57:1391–1396.

Dickie, M. 2006. FT.com site: Disney to tap China's online game market. *FT.com* [London]. May 24, 1.

Dickenson, C. B. 2006. Transformation in the lodging industry. *Lodging Hospitality* 62(8):60–63.

Douglas, S. P., and C. S. Craig. 1997. The changing dynamic of consumer behavior: Implications for cross-cultural research. *International Journal of Research in Marketing* 14:379–395.

Dong, L. C., and M. M. Helms. 2001. Brand name translation model: A case analysis of US brands in China. *Brand Management* 9(2):99–115.

Evans, M. W. 2004. Riviera looks to drive sales with Hummer scent. *Women's Wear Daily* 188(37):14.

Fast food and strong currencies; *The Economist*'s Big Mac index. (June 11, 2005). *The Economist* [U.S. Edition]. Retrieved July 21, 2006 at http://web.lexisnexis.com/universe/document?_m=e62f82c5dbb02868b1d37755a2a651e8.

Fernie, J., B. Hahn, U. Gerhard, E. Pioch, and S. J. Arnold. 2006. The impact of Wal-Mart's entry into the German and U.K. Grocery Markets. *Agribusiness* 22(2):247–266.

Focus—Italy: A fashionable move to the hotel industry. (April 5, 2005). *Brand Strategy* 12.

Food for thought; The Big Mac Index. 2004. *The Economist* [U. S. Edition]. May 29. Retrieved July 21, 2002 at http://web.lexis-nexis.com/universe/document?_m=e62f82c5dbb02868b1d37755a2a651e8

Foroohar, R. 2005. Maximum luxury; as luxury brands move into the mass market, they need a new way to make the superrich feel special. Welcome to the experience economy. *Newsweek.* July 25, 44.

Foster, L. 2003. Shoppertainment heads to Europe: A pioneering U.S. developer has overseas ambitions. *Financial Times* [London]. March 11, 24.

Fowler, G. A. 2005. McDonald's Asian marketing takes on a regional approach. *Wall Street Journal* [Eastern edition]. January 26, 1.

Fowler, G. A., and M. Marr. 2006. Disney and the Great Wall; Hong Kong's Magic Kingdom struggles to attract Chinese who don't understand park. *Wall Street Journal* [Eastern edition]. February 9, B1.

Frear, C. R., M. S. Alguire, and L. E. Metcalf. 1995. Country segmentation on the basis of international purchasing patterns. *The Journal of Business & Industrial Marketing* 10(2):59–68.

Ganesh, J., V. Kumar, and V. Subramaniam. 1997. Learning effect in multinational diffusion of consumer durables: An exploratory investigation. *Journal of the Academy of Marketing Science* 25(3):214–228.

Garrahan, M. 2005. Armani to develop range of hotels. *Financial Times.* June 1, 28.

George, T. 2003. International appeal: How to make your website sing in any language. *Black Enterprise* 33(8):54.

Globerman, S., T. W. Roel, and S. Standiford. 2001. Globalization and electronic commerce, *Journal of International Business Studies* 32(4):749–769.

Good, A. J., and S. Granovsky. 1995. Retail goes abroad. *The Canadian Business Review* 22(2):31–33.

Gong, W. 2003. Chinese consumer behavior: A cultural framework and implications. *Journal of American Academy of Business* 3(1/2):373–380.

Gold, P., and L. H. Woodliffe. 2000. Department stores in Spain: Why El Corte Inglés succeeded where Galerías Preciados failed. *International Journal of Retail & Distribution* 28(8):333–340.

Gray, R. 2000. Make the most of local differences. *Marketing.* April 13, 27–28.

Gripsrud, G., and G. R. G. Benito. 2005. Internationalization in retailing: Modeling the pattern of foreign market entry. *Journal of Business Research* 58:1672–1680.

Groeber, J. 2002. A new frontier: Looking to raise revenues, developers and retailers turn their focus to international expansion. *National Real Estate Investor* 44(11):27–31

Gunter, H. 2006. Indigo takes branding cue from retailers. *Hotel and Motel Management* 221(6):26.

Halliday, J. 2005. Nestlé's hits mainland with cheap ice cream. *Advertising Age*. March 7, 12.

Hannerz, U. 1990. Cosmopolitans and locals in world culture. In M. Featherstone, *Global Culture: Nationalism, Globalization, and Modernity* (295–310). Thousand Oaks, CA: Sage.

Hawkey, J. 2006. Developers need retail therapy shopping space has proliferated but imaginative solutions to create an enticing, long-lasting environment are also required. *Financial Times* [Asia Edition]. May 31, 8.

Hawkins, D. I., R. J. Best, and K. A. Coney. 2003. *Consumer Behavior: Building Marketing Strategy*, 9th ed. Boston, MA: BPI/Irwin.

Helsen, K., K. Jedidi, and W. S. DeSarbo. 1993. A new approach to country segmentation utilizing multinational diffusion patterns. *Journal of Marketing* 57(4):60–71.

Hill, D. 2003. The kids aren't alright, *The Guardian*. November 11. http://www.guardian.co.uk/g2/story/0, 3604,1082152,00.html.

Hirsch, P. 1997. Global industries must foster brand identity. *Marketing News* 31(13):6.

Ho, D. Y. F. and C. Y. Chiu. 1994. Component ideas of individualism, collectivism, and social organization: An application in the study of Chinese culture. In U. Kim, H. C. Triandis, C. Kagitbasi, G. Choi, & G. Yoon (Eds.), *Individualism and Collectivism: Theory, Method and Applications* (137–156). Thousand Oaks, CA: Sage Publications.

Hofstede, G. 1980. *Culture's Consequences: International Differences in Work-Related Values*. Beverly Hills, CA: Sage.

———.1991. *Cultures and Organizations: Software of the Mind*. London: McGraw-Hill.

Hofstede, F. T., M., Wedel, and J-B. E. M. Steenkamp. 2002. Identifying spatial segments in international markets. *Marketing Science* 21(2):160–177.

Holt, D. B., J. A. Quelch, and E. L. Taylor. 2004. How global brands compete. *Harvard Business Review* 82(9):68–75.

Houlder, V. 2004. Rise of the haute couture hotels: Travel now carries as much cachet as fashion and jewelry. How are luxury goods companies responding? *Financial Times*. May 20, 12.

Hyllegard, K., M. Eckman, A. M. Descals, and A. G. Borja. 2005. Spanish consumers' perceptions of U.S. apparel specialty retailers' products and services. *Journal of Consumer Behaviour* 4(5):345–362.

Inconspicuous consumption; Luxury. 2005. *The Economist* [London]. December 24, 71.

India tops annual list of most attractive countries for international retail expansion. 2005. *Business Credit* 107(7):72.

Ings-Chambers, E. 2004. From good shoes to good hotels: What do they have in common? *Financial Times* [Weekend — Travel]. June 12, 16.

Jain, S. C. 1989. Standardization of international marketing strategy: Some research hypotheses. *Journal of Marketing* 53:70–79.

Jamal, A. 2003. Marketing in a multicultural world: The interplay of marketing, ethnicity and consumption. *European Journal of Marketing* 37(11/12):1599–1622.

Jonsson, A., and U. Elg. 2006. Knowledge and knowledge sharing in retail internationalization: IKEA's entry into

Russia. *International Review of Retail, Distribution, and Consumer Research* 16(2):239–256.

Josiam, B. M., and P. A. Monteiro. 2004. Tandoori tastes: Perceptions of Indian restaurants in America. *International Journal of contemporary Hospitality Management* 16(1):18–26.

Kagitcibasi, C. 1994. A critical appraisal of individualism and collectivism: Toward a new formulation. In U. Kim, H. C. Triandis, C. Kagitcibasi, S. C., Choi, and G. Yoon, eds. *Individualism and Collectivism: Theory, Method, and Applications* (137–156). Thousand Oaks, CA: Sage Publications.

———.1997. Individualism and collectivism. In J. W. Berry, M. H. Segall, and C. Kagitcibasi, eds. *Handbook of Cross-Cultural Psychology*, 2nd ed., 1–50. Boston: Allyn & Bacon.

Kelly, K., and S. Kang. 2005. The selling of a Geisha; To promote its film, Sony turns to big retail partners; Mr. Golden's makeup lesson. *Wall Street Journal* [Eastern edition]. October 31, B1.

Kogut, B. 1985. Designing global strategies: Comparative and competitive value-added chains. *Sloan Management Review* 26(4):15–28.

Lester, L. Y. 2003. Canada: Cross-border shopping made easier. *Target Marketing* 26(4):18.

Levine, J. 1994. Chunnel vision. *Forbes* 153(4):146.

Levitt, J. 2003. Spaniards may shop through siesta. *Financial Times* [London]. May 23, 31.

Levitt, T. 1983. The globalization of markets. *Harvard Business Review* 61:92–102.

Lucas, V. 2004. Cross-border shopping in a federal economy. *Regional Science and Urban Economics* 34:365–385.

Macklem, K. 2003. Roundtripping. *Maclean's* 116(50):30.

Margolis, M. 2005. It's a mall world after all. *Newsweek International*. December 5. Retrieved September 5, 2006 from http://www.msnbc.msn.com/id/10217695/site/newsweek/

Marr, M., and G. A. Fowler. 2006. Chinese lessons for Disney; At Hong Kong Disneyland, park officials learn a lot from their past mistakes. *Wall Street Journal* [Eastern edition]. June 12, B1.

Mazur, L. 2002. Global retailing can trip up even the best brands. *Marketing* [London]. February 21, 18.

McCurrencies; Economic Focus. 2006. *The Economist*. May 25. Retrieved from http://www.economist.com/markets/bigmac/displayStory.cfm?story_id=6972477 on July 21, 2006.

McIntosh, J., and D. Valerio. 2005. Spanning the globe: Discounters lead the top 100 global retailers, while several large chains struggle. *Chain Store Age* 81(12):58–66.

McLinden, S. 2004, Retailing roster grows overseas. *National Real Estate Investor* 46(2):22–24

Merrick, A. 2005. Inside out: For Limited Brands, clothes become the accessories; specialty retailer stresses lingerie, beauty products; seeing P&G as role model; Victoria's Secret Hair Care. *Wall Street Journal* [Eastern edition]. March 8, A1.

Miller, S. 2006. Food fight: French resistance to trade accord has cultural roots; WTO talks promise benefits but farmers retain hold on the nation's stomach; 'Politicians are frightened.' *Wall Street Journal* [Eastern edition]. May 16, A1.

Morrison, K., T. Tassell, G. Tett, and W. Wallis. 2006. Markets shaken as Israel steps up Lebanon attacks. *Financial Times [London, 3rd edition]. July 14, 1.

Musnik, I. 2006. Levy to lead study of France, the brand. *Advertising Age.* April 10, 6.

Nagashima, A. 1970. A comparison of Japanese and U.S. attitudes toward foreign products. *Journal of Marketing* 34(1):68–74.

Narayan, S. and J. Carsen. 2006. India's lust for Luxe India's nouveaux riches are spending like never before, and high-end retailers from Hermes to Tiffany are eager to oblige. *Times International* [Asia edition] 167(14):36.

Naumov, A. and S. Puffer. 2000. Measuring Russian culture using Hofstede's dimensions. *Applied Psychology: An International Review* 49(4):709–718.

Ni, P. 2004. Taxation and regulations in China. *Chain Store Age* 80(5):A 6–7.

Oh, J. Y-K., C-K. Cheng, X. Y. Lehto, and J. T. O'Leary. 2004. Predictors of tourists' shopping behaviour: Examination of socio-demographic characteristics and trip typologies. *Journal of Vacation Marketing* 10(4):308–319.

O'Keefe, B. 2001. Global brands. *Fortune* 144(11):102–109.

Olmsted, L. 2006. One-stop shopping in Japan. *American Way.* February 15, 34–38.

Ong, J., and S. G. Forden. 2005. Luxury brands upbeat on Chinese market. *International Herald Tribune.* May 23. Retrieved from: http://www.iht.com/bin/print_ipub.php?file=articles/2005/05/22/bloomberg/sxlux.php

Palmer, M., and M. Owens. 2006. New directions for international retail joint venture research. *International Review of Retail Distribution and Consumer Research* 16(2):159–179.

Parameswaran, R. and M. Pisharodi. 1994. Facets of country of origin image: An empirical assessment. *Journal of Advertising* 23(1):43–56.

Pelton, L. 2000. Death of the supply chain: The fallacy of fit. *Journal of Business and Industrial Marketing* 14(5/6):349–52.

Peñaloza, L., and M. C. Gilly. 1999. Marketer acculturation: The changer and the changed. *Journal of Marketing* 63(3):84–104.

Pereira, A., C-C. Hsu, and S. K. Kundu. 2005. Country-of-origin image: Measurement and cross-national testing. *Journal of Business Research* 58:103–106.

Pickard, J. 2005. Few doubt the strength of the U.S. industry REITS: It is not only U.S. corporations that are expanding in Europe, says Jim Pickard. Australians are lurking in the waters, too. *Financial Times* [London]. March 9, 10.

Picot-Coupey, K. 2006. Determinants of international retail operation mode choice: Toward a conceptual framework based on evidence from French specialised retail chains. *International Review of Retail, Distribution and Consumer Research* 16(2):215–237.

Piron, F. 2001. International retail leakages: Singaporeans outshopping in Malaysia. *Singapore Management Review* 23(1):35–58.

———. 2002. International outshopping and ethnocentrism. *European Journal of Marketing,* 36(1/2):189–210.

Quelch, J. A. 1999. Global brands: Taking stock. *Business Strategy Review* 19(1):1–14.

Ramarapu, S., J. E. Timmerman, and N. Ramarapu. 1999. Choosing between globalization and localization as a strategic thrust for your international marketing effort. *Journal of Marketing Theory and Practice* 7(2):97–105.

Riege, M. A., and C. Perry. 2000. National marketing strategies in international travel and tourism. *European Journal of Marketing* 34(11/12):1290–1305.

Rigby, D. K., and V. Vishwanath. 2006. Localization: The revolution in consumer markets. *Harvard Business Review* 82–92.

Ritchie. K. 1995. Marketing to generation X. *American Demographics* 17(4) 34–40.

Roth, M. S. and J. B. Romeo. (1992). Matching product category and country image perceptions: A framework for managing country of origin effects. *Journal of International Business Studies* 23i(3):477–497.

Samiee, S., and K. Roth. 1992. The influence of global marketing standardization on performance. *Journal of Marketing* 56:1–17.

Sanchanta, M. 2006. Youngsters display a yen for exclusive stuff in Japan: Mariko Sanchanta explains why the market is changing dramatically. *Financial Times* [London]. June 5, 3.

Siegel, L. C. 2003. Retailers, start your engines. *Chain Store Age* 79(9):122.

Sherry, J. F., Jr., and E. G. Camargo. 1987. "May your life be marvelous:" English language labeling and the semiotics of Japanese promotion. *Journal of Consumer Research* 14:174–188.

Shimp, T. A., and S. Sharma. 1987. Consumer ethnocentrism: Construction and validation of the CETSCALE. *Journal of Marketing Research* 24:280–289.

Shocker, A., R. Srivastava, and R. Ruekert. 1994. Challenges and opportunities facing brand management: An introduction to the special issue. *Journal of Marketing Research* 31:149–158.

Singh, N., O. Furrer, and M. Ostinelli. 2004. To localize or to standardize on the Web: Empirical evidence from Italy, India, Netherlands, Spain, and Switzerland. *Multinational Business Review* 12(1):69–87.

Singh, N., H. Zhao, and X. Hu. 2003. Cultural adaptation on the Web: A study of American companies' domestic and Chinese Websites. *Journal of Global Information Management* 11(3):63–80.

Sinha, D., and R. C. Tripathi. 1994. Individualism in a collective culture: A case of coexistence of opposites. In U. Kim, H. C. Triandis, C. Kagitcibasi, S. Choi, and G. Yoon, eds. *Individualism and Collectivism: Theory, Method, and Applications* (137-156). Thousand Oaks, CA: Sage Publications.

Special Report—Online: Non, je ne Google pas! 2005. *Marketing Week.* October 13, 45.

Sternquist, B. 1997. International expansion of U.S. retailers. *International Journal of Retail & Distribution Management* 25(8):262–268.

Steward, A. 2001. Increasing demand for multilingual websites. *Financial Times.* August 8, 5.

Strutton, D., and L. Pelton. 1997. Scaling the great wall: The yin and yang of negotiating resolutions to business conflicts in China. *Business Horizons* 34(5):22–34.

Sudhaman, A. 2006. Warming Asians to ice cream. *Media.* February 24, 19.

Tai, S. H. C. 1998. Factors affecting advertising approach in Asia. *Journal of Current Issues and Research in Advertising* 20(1):33–45.

Tansuhaj, P. W., W. C. Ong, and J. McCullough. 1989. International outshoppers: What are they like. *Singapore Marketing Reivew* 4:93–97.

Tomkins, R., 2004. A deeper reason why Europe is rejecting U.S. brands. *Business Life* [London, 1st edition]. November 5, 13.

Tompson, A., and J. Walker. 2005. Retail network planning—achieving competitive advantage through geographic analysis. *Journal of Targeting, Measurement and Analysis for Marketing* 13(3):250–257.

Triandis, H. C. 2004. The many dimensions of culture. *Academy of Management Executive* 18(1):88–93.

Turner, L. 2006. When tourist reinvention spins out of control Barcelona's success in turning itself from a little-known industrial port to an international mecca is beginning to backfire. *Financial Times* [London]. April 29, 13.

Varshney, S. 2005. A review and extension of the outshopping paradigm to the Indian context. *Asia Pacific Journal of Marketing and Logistics* 17(4):30–62.

Varshney, S., and A. Goyal. 2005. A review and extension of the outshopping paradigm to the Indian context. *Asia Pacific Journal of Marketing and Logistics* 17(4):30–62.

Vazdauskas, D. 2006. To stay relevant, large brands must embrace localization on Internet. *Advertising Age*. April 10, 34.

Voronov, M., and J. A. Singer. 2002. The Myth of Individualism-Collectivism: A critical Review. *The Journal of Social Psychology* 142(4):461–480.

Voyle, S. 2004. Rebuilding Marks and Spencer: Can the former high street favourite stay in touch with retailing's new trends? *Financial Times* [London]. May 15, 9.

Ward, A. 2002. An octopus in the shopping trolley. *Financial Times*. January 11, 12

Wee, T. T. T. 1999. An exploration of a global teenage lifestyle in Asian societies. *Journal of Consumer Marketing* 16(4):365–275.

Yeung, S., J. Wong, and E. Ko. 2004. Preferred shopping destination: Hong Kong versus Singapore. *The International Journal of Tourism Research* 6(2):85–96.

Zakaria, F. 2006. Indian rising. *Newsweek*. March 6, 32–43.

Zhang, Y. 1996. Chinese consumers' evaluation of foreign products: The influence of culture, product types, and product presentation format. *European Journal of Marketing* 30(12):50–61.

Zhao, H., and R. R. Levary. 2002. Evaluation of country attractiveness for foreign direct investment in the e-retail industry. *Multinational Business Review* 10(1):1–10.

GLOSSARY

Acculturation:
A form of cultural diffusion that occurs when two or more cultural groups come into extended direct contact with each other and the cultural patterns of one or both groups change as a result of the contact.

Affect:
A mental state of subjective feeling that is knowingly experienced along with emotion, mood, preference, and attitude.

Ambient scent:
Odor that is present in an environment but that does not emanate from a specific object in that environment.

Atmospherics:
The controllable physical and nonphysical components of a store that are able to change customer and employee behaviors.

Balanced consumption experience:
A consumption situation that includes both utilitarian and hedonic experiences.

Bicultural or multicultural subcultures:
Individuals who switch between two or among more cultural meaning systems based on the cultural cues they encounter in their environments. They may demonstrate strong ethnic identities and belonging to a new culture.

Biometric technology:
A finger-touch technology where consumers have their fingers scanned on a pad that properly identifies them and processes payment.

Brand awareness:
The extent to which consumers know about a brand and recognize the attributes associated with it.

Brand community:
A specific community that is not bound by geographic boundaries and is based on an assigned group of social relationships among consumers who admire a particular brand. Members of a brand community share an awareness of one another and display moral

responsibility, practice rituals, and have traditions.

Brand development strategy:
A strategy that is used to introduce a new brand in an existing product category.

Brand equity:
The improved beliefs about greater value or goodwill that consumers assign to a brand name as the result of the favorable image, differentiation, and degree of attachment that are assigned to a brand name.

Brand extension:
The application of an established core brand name to a new product or service with the extended brand either being consistent or inconsistent with the core brand's image.

Brand fit:
Refers to how consistent the consumer perception is of each brand in a strategic alliance, based on logical and expected associations with the brands.

Brand image:
The perceptions held by a consumer regarding a particular brand.

Branding:
The cumulative image of a product or service that consumers quickly associate with a particular brand. It offers an overall experience that is unique, different, special, and identifiable.

Brand-product interface strategy:
Cross-classifying existing and new brand identities and product availability to determine the alignment of brand position and product availability within a market environment.

Brick-and-mortar retailer:
Retailers who offer goods for sale in store environments.

Broadscope promoters:
Retailers who offer broad product assortments that have both low and high life span and overlap and thus are not easily differentiated from their competition.

Browsers:
Software packages that help Internet users navigate the Web and access text, graphics, hyperlinks, audio, video, and other multimedia.

Category killers:
Very large super retail stores that focus on a single merchandise category, such as home furnishings, office supplies, pet supplies, toys, and consumer electronics.

Ceremonies:
A series of interdependent rituals executed at a particular time.

Clearout promoters:
Retailers who have high assortment of overlap of perishable products that are mostly undifferentiated from other retailers.

Clustering:
A focus on a small number of product or service attributes that drive the majority of consumer purchases.

Co-branding:
When two existing brands join to create a synergy that is stronger than each brand independently.

Cocooning:
Retreating to the privacy of the home to be insulated from a social environment

associated with external chaos and external threats.

Comparative advantage:
The location-specific advantage associated with sourcing and markets that is held by a country.

Competitive advantage:
The unique advantage that is attributed to a company should it enter a foreign country to do business. The advantage is associated with product and/or process proprietary attributes of the company that are not easily copied by competitors.

Consumer acculturation:
Using modeling, reinforcement, and social interactions to learn how to buy and consume goods and the associated values, meanings, and behavior assigned to consumption of those goods. It can describe how consumers in one culture learn to consume products from another culture.

Consumer culture theory:
An explanation of the way the marketplace mediates social arrangements between a lived culture and its social resources. It examines the context, symbolism, and experiences that consumers have in the processes of acquisition, consumption and possession, and disposition of goods and services.

Consumer efficiency:
The degree to which a consumer trades fixed resources of time, energy, and money to receive the highest benefit of utility or satisfaction from consumption activities.

Consumer ethnocentrism:
The universal inclination of consumers to hold specific beliefs about the appropriateness, morality, and acquisition of foreign-made products.

Consumption:
The exchange of energy for objects or services that satisfy a human need and improve the quality of life.

Consumption communities:
People gain a feeling of social belonging by purchasing specific products and obtain emotional benefits and satisfaction by being with others who share similar involvement with that product category.

Consumption constellations:
The sets of complementary products that are used by consumers to define, communicate, and perform social roles.

Consumption experience:
A holistic experience that results from interactions among the consumer, product, distribution channel, organization, and environment.

Consumption subculture:
A commitment to a particular brand, product class, or consumption activity by a unique, self-selected subgroup of consumers.

Core brand:
A brand associated with a specific set of attributes that are the result of a consumer's involvement with the brand.

Country image:
The mental impression and reputation consumers have regarding the products associated with a particular country.

Country-of-origin image:
The evaluation of a product based in whole or in part on a country image.

Cross-border shopping:
International outshopping, where consumers travel outside their national boundaries for the purpose of shopping. It is sometimes referred to as round-tripping.

Cross-shopping:
The act of patronizing multiple types of retail outlets on a single shopping trip.

Cultural diffusion:
The exposure to new cultural elements when diverse societies come into direct or indirect contact with one another; the new elements may be accepted or rejected depending on how well they fit into the cultural patterns of the receiving culture.

Cultural patterns:
Shared intrinsic (i.e., vital aspects of cultural heritage) and extrinsic (i.e., products of adjustment to a local culture) characteristics within a cultural group.

Cultural swapping:
The result of coexistence and interaction between multicultural businesses and ethnically diverse consumers; it is a form of cultural diffusion.

Cultural time:
The way in which people anticipate, live through, and reflect upon their experiences; it is classified as either linear, circular, or procedural time.

Cultural values:
Characteristics of a culture that differentiate it from other cultures; these characteristics are learned, guide behavior through acceptable standards in daily life, are permanent and dynamic, and are widely accepted within a society.

Culture:
The commonly held values, beliefs, mores, and symbols that affect behaviors and consumption within a specific group of people.

Customization:
Meeting local market needs by offering products and services that are designed specifically to meet those unique needs.

Destination shopping:
When the decision to travel is based in whole or in part on going to a particular destination for the purpose of shopping.

Diderot effect:
When consumers purchase an assortment of goods and services that are consistent with their lifestyles.

Diderot unities:
The assortment of goods and services that are consistently purchased by a particular consumer group.

Differentiators:
Retailers who offer products with low assortment overlap with other retailers, are relatively perishable, and are quite distinctive from their competitors. They de-emphasize price and use uniqueness for differential advantage.

Discount department stores:
Retailers who are characterized by minimal décor, utilitarian materials, large volumes of merchandise on the sales floor, and offer low prices and a convenient location to meet high consumer demand.

Distancing:
A technique used to increase or decrease the perceived division between a core brand and a vertical brand extension.

Diversification strategy:
This strategy is used by a company to enter a market with a new brand in a new product category.

Dollar stores:
Extreme-value retailers who operate in small store formats, have quick and easy access, and offer consumable basic products at very low prices.

E-commerce:
Using fixed tools such as computers and user-friendly browsers to complete business transactions.

Edutainment:
The strategy of blending education and entertainment to stimulate sales.

Entertainment retailing:
The act of using entertainment in the retail environment to amuse customers while they shop.

E-tailing:
An international shopping experience that is available by logging on to the Internet and visiting sites created for retail business.

Ethnic identity:
The self-identity that defines any particular ethnic group.

Ethnic subculture:
A group of people who are set apart from other groups based on specific combinations of cultural traits, national origin, race, religion, wealth, social status, political power, and segregated neighborhoods.

Experience economy:
An environment where consumption is used by consumers to express who they are and define what their important relationships are by using products to engage and connect in personal and special ways.

Experience goods:
Intangible products (e.g., services, entertainment) that cannot be evaluated through visual inspection; rather, they are evaluated through actual use.

Experiential retailing:
A retail strategy that transforms products and services into a total consumption experience. It satisfies emotional or expressive (hedonic) desires as well as rational or functional (utilitarian) needs of the consumer. The sum of the product or service purchased is greater than either the performance or the emotional experience.

Factory outlets:
Retailers that offer discounted prices on well-known brands and designer-label goods.

Family branding:
New products are assigned names that are under the same umbrella as the existing company brands.

Feng shui:
The art of placement within a physical space. It brings balance between the five elements that flow through life (water, earth, fire, wood, and metals), yin and yang (acceptance of opposites or polarities), and chi (energy flow and the essence of life).

Flow:
Using a physical space to communicate with the consumer so that the consumer is immersed in a pleasurable state where time seems to pass by.

Foreign consumer culture:
Consumer perceptions, attitudes, and behaviors that are exhibited toward products, services, brands, and companies that are not local.

Global consumer culture:
Well-defined consumer clusters that cross national boundaries and share similar demographic and sociocultural characteristics and have similar needs, motivations, and behaviors.

Hedonic benefit:
Receiving shopping enjoyment derived from browsing through merchandise, socializing with others, and having experiences.

Hedonic consumption:
The consumer focus is on the interaction between the consumer and the product.

Hedonic consumption experience:
The evaluation of a consumption experience based on gratifying wants or needs derived from emotional needs.

Horizontal brand extension:
The application of an existing brand name to a new product or service with the horizontal brand either being in a similar product or service class or in a new category.

Human constructed environment:
The production, consumption, and sociocultural systems that define a society.

Icon:
A sign that resembles a product in some way.

Index:
A sign that is connected to a product because they share a similar property.

Individual product branding:
New products are assigned names that have no association with other brand names offered by the parent company.

Individualism-collectivism:
A dimension of consumer culture that describes the relationship between an individual and how close or tight that individual is with the in-groups and out-groups within that culture. Individualism represents a society where there are loose ties between the individual and society. Collectivism represents a society where from birth its members are assimilated into strong, cohesive in-groups.

Infomercials:
A commercial television program designed to sell a specific product.

International company:
A company that crosses national borders to conduct business.

Joint-venture arrangement:
A business arrangement created between a multinational corporate partner and either a private business or government entity in a host country.

Lifestyle:
The way in which consumers choose to live and spend their time and money, which creates individual and social identities.

Lifestyle center:
An open-air retail shopping center that groups lifestyle retailers and products together.

Local consumer culture:
Culturally-based consumption activities in a local marketplace where the cultural meanings of goods and services are associated with local norms, values, and identities.

Localization:
Using distinctive products, pricing, promotion, and distribution policies that are unique to a particular retailing program.

Logo:
A material symbol that communicates the identity of a company or an organization.

Mass customization:
A process by which manufacturers and merchants provide individualized (i.e., customized) products to their customers. A basic product of service is modified to meet the needs of a customer.

M-commerce:
The use of mobile, wireless terminals and electronic devices that allow users to instantaneously communicate with anyone anywhere in the world.

Millennial generation:
Another name for Generation Y consumers. It includes individuals who were born between the years of 1977 and 1993.

Mnemonics:
Using cues such as rhymes, key words, music, imagery, and storytelling to improve one's memory.

Multichannel shopping:
When people shop at brick-and-mortar stores, catalogs, and websites to meet their needs.

Multinational company:
A company that is a producer and marketer of goods and services in multiple countries.

Multiple shopping channels:
These include brick-and mortar stores, catalogs, television, direct sales, the Internet, and m-commerce devices.

Multisensory experience:
A consumer experience that combines sight, sound, scent, touch, and taste stimuli in a retail environment.

Natural environment:
The natural resources, climate, space and time, and geography that make up the environment.

Neuromarketing:
Understanding consumer cognitive activity by using magnetic resonance imaging (MRI) to map how specific stimuli activate different areas of the brain.

Off-price discounter:
A retail store that offers brand-name merchandise at lower price points than specialty or department stores.

Outshopping:
The movement of consumers from one retail trade area to another to obtain a perceived or an actual benefit that is not offered in the local trade area.

PAD:
A consumer's approach or avoidance behavior toward an environment such as a retail store is determined by the intermingling of the three emotional states of pleasure (P), arousal (A), and dominance (D).

Parent brand:
The original or major brand assigned to goods or services associated with a particular company.

Penetration strategy:
This strategy is used by a company to enter a market with a new product where there is an existing brand in an existing product category.

Personalization:
When retailers offer products, services, lifestyles, and information that meet their consumers' own unique needs and preferences. Sometimes it is referred to as customization.

Pilgrimage:
A consumption activity where people travel to a site to experience something sacred.

Positioning:
A retail strategy where products and/or services are offered that are closely aligned with the lifestyles of specific consumer segments.

Postmodernism:
A consumer movement that focuses on nostalgia. It blurs the line between authenticity and fantasy.

Power retailers:
A category of value retailers that has expanded into multiple categories and uses sophisticated inventory management, effective merchandising, and competitive pricing to offer customers lower prices, broader merchandise selection and presentation, and greater convenience.

Price point rivals:
Retailers who offer products that have high assortment overlap with other retailers, have a high life span, and are similar to other retailers. They use price for differential advantage.

Primary cost:
The monetary price paid in dollars for a product or service.

Private brands:
Brand names that are owned by a specific retailer; also called distributor brands, retail brands, private labels, store brands, own labels, and own brands.

Product branding:
The characteristics that quickly and easily differentiate a product from all other products.

Product categorization:
Measuring the presence or absence of particular attributes associated with categories of products.

Product development strategy:
This strategy involves the leveraging of an existing brand name in a new product category.

Product fit:
Refers to how close or complementary the product categories are in a strategic alliance, regardless of the individual brands.

Profane:
A form of consumption by a social or consumer group that is considered an ordinary part of everyday life.

Psychographics:
The use of psychological measures for attitudes, beliefs, and personality traits to construct consumer lifestyle profiles.

Quintessential:
The treatment of ordinary, everyday objects as extraordinary.

Radio frequency identification (RFID):
A system of integrated transceivers, tags, and computer system that tracks individual products, cartons, or pallets of goods from the manufacturer to consumer purchase.

Retail internationalization:
The process used to expand retail operations and private brand products into non-domestic markets.

Retailer branding:
The identity of the retail store is communicated as the brand.

Rites of intensification:
The ceremonies that mark events and transitions within a society as a whole; they may be seasonal and can mark changes in weather and activities.

Rites of passage:
The ceremonies that mark important transitions in life such as birth, naming, puberty, marriage, and death.

Rituals:
The sacred or profane customary, formalized, and ceremonial acts or rites that are embedded in culture.

Sacred:
A type of consumption that is set apart from ordinary consumption and is considered a transcendent experience by a particular social or consumer group.

Search engine:
A tool that is used for information search and sharing on the Internet. The search engine is triggered by keywords or tags that route consumers to a particular site or groups of sites.

Search goods:
Tangible products (e.g., consumer products) evaluated by the visual inspection of unique product attributes.

Secondary cost:
The additional costs paid for a product or service that can include monetary costs expended to buy a product or service and non-monetary costs such as time, effort, and psychic costs.

Segmentation:
Sorting consumers into similar groups based on preferences related to activities, leisure time, and spending disposable income.

Semiotics:
Refers to the examination of the correspondence between signs and symbols and how they create meaning in verbal and nonverbal language in a culture at a particular time.

Sensory channels:
They are the five senses of sight, sound, scent, touch, and taste.

Sensory memory stores:
A combination of memory (long-term sensory memory stores) and sensation (extremely short-term sensory memory stores).

Service branding:
Service companies are their own brand; they build their brand on trust related to reducing the risk associated with the economic, social, or safety risks associated with buying the service.

Shoppertainment:
The integration of entertainment into the consumer shopping experience, it can transform a shopping center into a leisure destination.

Shopping utility:
Combining fixed and variable costs that are spent by consumers on shopping tasks.

Sign:
A unique representation of a specific object.

Situational ethnicity:
When an individual demonstrates a greater visibility of ethnic identity in some situations but not in other situations.

Spatial segmentation:
The use of geographic data to create retail segmentations based on consumer product demand.

Standardization:
The use of a common marketing plan in each country of operation; it is used by international companies.

Step-down extension:
A strategy that creates a more favorable brand extension by distancing it downward from the core brand while at the same time transferring the positive quality associated with a core brand to the brand extension.

Step-up extension:
A strategy that creates a more favorable brand extension by distancing it upward from the core brand; perceptions of the brand extension are associated with higher quality than the core brand.

Strategic alliance:
The use of two or more brands on one product (or service) or sets of products (or services) to promote sales. The term is used interchangeably with co-branding, brand alliance, co-marketing, and joint branding.

Symbol:
A sign that is related to a product through either conventional or agreed-upon association.

Subculture:
A group of people or consumer segment whose homogeneous values and customs make them distinctly different from society as a whole.

Symbolic interaction:
The interaction between human beings and their continuous adjustment to behavior as they interpret the meaning of one another's actions rather than just reacting to one another's actions.

Thematic retailing:
Using a story line delivered through entertainment, education, and experiences to promote a retail identity or brand to consumers.

Tinies:
A marketing term for newborns and toddlers who are targeted for branded consumer products.

Total consumption experience:
The result of both utilitarian and hedonic experiences derived from multiple attributes of objects and the environment in which consumption occurs.

Touchpoints:
Emotional associations and beliefs about a brand are created when consumers interact with a brand and remember, savor, and communicate to others their brand experience.

Trademark:
A word, symbol, or design that is used by a company to distinguish that company's goods from all others.

Tradition:
The practice of customs in relationship to one another so that they become habitual cultural patterns that are transmitted across generations and societies.

Transnational corporations:
Also referred to as TNC, these corporations have their ownership and management divided uniformly among the nations in which they have operations.

Tweens:
A marketing term for pre- and early adolescents, usually ages 8 to 14, who exhibit radical gender differences in entertainment and consumer product preferences and vary in age group by product category.

Twixters:
A marketing term for young adults ages 18 to 25 who are in an intermediate transition stage between adolescence and adulthood. Often referred to as youthhood, adultescence, kidults, boomerang kids, and threshholders.

Universals:
Similar cultural patterns regardless of cultural and social background that reflect social, political, technological, economic, and ideological cultural phenomenon.

Utilitarian benefit:
Purchasing the right product or service expended from the least amount of time, effort, and cost to gain the maximum benefit.

Utilitarian consumption:
The consumer focus is on a product's physical or technical performance.

Utilitarian consumption experience:
The evaluation of a consumption experience based on achieving a particular consumption goal related to necessity.

Value megamalls:
Also called super off-price centers or super regional specialty malls, the tenants in these malls include off-price retailers, factory outlet stores, department closeout outlets, and large food and entertainment venues.

Value orientations:
Commonly held values that underlie consumer behavior in a given society or culture.

Value retailing:
Retailers who offer low prices plus additional benefits such as quality and novelty that meet the needs of value-oriented consumers. Types of value retailers include discount department stores, factory outlets, category killers, off-price discounters, warehouse clubs, dollar stores, and value megamalls.

Variety promoters:
Retailers who offer product assortments with distinct attributes that differentiate them from competitors. They often use promotions to maintain or gain market share.

Vertical brand extension:
The introduction of new product or service lines under an existing brand name but at different price points, quality levels, or targeting different life cycles. It uses a distancing technique that either increases or decreases the perceived departure between the core brand name and the vertical brand extension.

Virtual community:
A community formed through the Internet where people can interact socially and exchange information.

Warehouse clubs:
Large membership-only retail stores that sell packaged and bulk food and general merchandise in warehouse-type environments.

CREDITS

Chapter 1

Figure 1.1 – *Photograph © Stew Leonard's*
Figure 1.3 – *Photograph courtesy of Hard Rock Café International (USA), Inc. All rights reserved*
Figure 1.4 – *Photograph courtesy of Algerian Coffee Stores Ltd.*
Figures 1.7a–c – *Photographs courtesy of Kokon To-zai*
Figure 1.8a – *Photograph © Picture Contact/Alamy*
Figure 1.8b – *Photograph © Marc Romanelli/Alamy*
Figure 1.9 – *Photograph courtesy of the Bluewater Mall*
Figure 1.10 – *Photograph © La Maison Simons*

Chapter 2

Figure 2.1 – *Illustration © Steve and Ghy Sampson*
Figure 2.2 – *Photograph credit: Elizabeth Jordan. Model credit: Hannah Jordan*

Chapter 3

Figure 3.3 – *Photograph courtesy of Mall of America®/Tony Nelson*
Figure 3.6a – *Photograph courtesy of Fairchild Publications, Inc.*
Figure 3.6b – *Image: © Envision/Corbis*
Figure 3.6c – *Photograph courtesy of Fairchild Publications, Inc.*
Figure 3.6d – *Photograph courtesy of Fairchild Publications, Inc.*

Chapter 4

Figure 4.1 – *Photograph © Dennis Hallinan/Alamy*
Figure 4.2 – *Photograph © Frank Micelotta/Getty Images*
Figure 4.3 – *Photograph © Alamy*

Chapter 5

Figure 5.1 – *Photograph by Judith Cardona Forney*
Figure 5.2 – *Photograph by Joronda Crow*
Figure 5.3 – *Photograph by Judith Cardona Forney*
Figure 5.4 – *Photograph by Jerry Dickenson*
Figure 5.5 – *Photograph by Judith Cardona Forney*
Figure 5.6 – *Photograph by Joronda Crow*
Figure 5.7 – *Photograph by Joronda Crow*
Figure 5.9 – *Photograph © Robert Mitra/Fairchild Publications*

Figure 5.10 – *White, H. and Kokotasaki, K. (2004). Indian food in the UK: Personal values and changing patterns of consumption.* International Journal of Consumer Studies, 28(3), 284–294.

Figure 5.11 – *Phinney, J. S. (1990). Ethnic identity in adolescents and adults: Review of research.* Psychological Bulletin, 108(3), 499–514.

Figure 5.12 – *Stayman, D. M. and Deshpande, R. (1989). Situational ethnicity and consumer behavior.* Journal of Consumer Research, 16, 361–371.

Figure 5.13 – *Photograph by Joronda Crow*

Figure 5.14 – *Image © Reuters/Corbis*

Figure 5.15 – *Penaloza, L. (1994). Atranesando Fronteras/Border Crossings: A critical ethnographic exploration of the consumer acculturation of Mexican immigrants.* Journal of Consumer Research, 21, 32–54.

Figure 5.16 – *Photograph by Sua Jeon*

Figure 5.17 – *Photograph by Bharath Josiam*

Figure 5.18 – *Photograph by Bharath Josiam*

Figure 5.19 – *Photograph © Stewart Cohen/Getty Images*

Figure 5.20 – *Photograph © Comstock Images/Alamy*

Figure 5.21 – *Photograph by Judith Cardona Forney*

Figure 5.22 – *Koki Iino/Getty Images*

Chapter 6

Figure 6.1 – *Photograph © FAN travelstock/Alamy*

Figure 6.2 – *Photograph by Thao-Vi Thi Dotter*

Figure 6.3 – *Photograph © Jack Hollingsworth /Getty Images*

Figure 6.4 – *Photograph by Pauline Sullivan.*

Figure 6.5 – *Photograph by Thao-Vi Thi Dotter.*

Figure 6.6 – *Photograph by Thao-Vi Thi Dotter*

Figure 6.7 – *Turley, L. W. and Chebat, J. C. (2002). Linking retail strategy, atmospheric design and shopping behavior.* Journal of Marketing Management, 18(1/2), 125–144.

Figure 6.8 – *Photograph Courtesy of Fairchild Publications, Inc.*

Figure 6.9 – *Photograph by Thao-Vi Thi Dotter*

Figure 6.10 – *Photograph by Thao-Vi Thi Dotter*

Figure 6.11 – *Photograph by Mr. K. N. Vinod c/o Indique Heights, Chevy Chase, Maryland*

Figure 6.12 – *Photograph by Amber Geisler*

Figure 6.13 – *Photograph © Dennis Flaherty/Getty Images*

Figure 6.14 – *Photograph by Judith Cardona Forney*

Figure 6.15 – *Photograph courtesy of Fairchild Publications, Inc.*

Figure 6.16 – *Photograph by Thao-Vi Thi Dotter*

Figure 6.17 – *Photograph by Shawn McClure*

Figure 6.18 – *Photograph © Plush Studios/Getty Images*

Figure 6.19 – *Photograph by Mr. K. N. Vinod c/o Indique Heights, Chevy Chase, Maryland*

Chapter 7

Figure 7.1 – *Photograph © Brand X Pictures/Alamy*

Figure 7.2 – *Photograph courtesy of P.F. Chang's China Bistro, Inc.*

Figure 7.4a – *Photograph Courtesy of © 2004 Walmarfacts.com, All Rights Reserved*

Figure 7.4b – *Photograph courtesy of © 2004 Walmarfacts.com, All Rights Reserved*

Chapter 8

Figure 8.1 – *Photograph © Bass Pro Shops®*

Figure 8.2 – *Photograph © Mall of America®/Tony Nelson*

Figure 8.4 – *Photograph courtesy of Benjamin Moore & Co.*

Figure 8.6 – *Photograph © West Edmonton Mall Property Inc.*

Chapter 9

Figure 9.1 – *Photograph courtesy of TryFoods International*
Figure 9.2 – *Photograph © Bronnerís Christmas Wonderland*
Figures 9.3a–9.3b – *Photographs courtesy of Original Appalachian Artworks, Inc. and www.cabbagepatchkids.com*
Figure 9.4 – *Photograph courtesy of Dolphin Mall*
Figure 9.5 – *Photograph © Corbis*
Figures 9.6a–c – *Photographs © Saks Incorporated*

Chapter 10

Figure 10.1 – *Photograph © Home Depot Inc.*
Figure 10.2 – *Courtesy, 2003 by SRI Consulting business intelligence*
Figure 10.3 – *Adapted from Michael R. Solomon,* Consumer Behavior, *5th ed., (2002), p. 175. Upper Saddle River, New Jersey: Prentice Hall.*
Figure 10.4 – *© Exotic eye/Alamy*
Figure 10.5 – *Photo compliments of The Container Store*
Figure 10.6 – *Photograph © Piotr & Irena Kolasa/Alamy*
Figure 10.7 – *Photograph © Rough Guides/Alamy*

Chapter 11

Figure 11.1 – *Photograph © Jeff Greenberg/Alamy*
Figure 11.2a – *Photograph courtesy of the Mills*
Figure 11.2b – *Photograph courtesy of the Mills*
Figure 11.7 – *Photograph courtesy of Dollar General*

Chapter 12

Figure 12.1a – *Photograph © Digital Vision/Getty Images*
Figure 12.1b – *Photograph © Photodisc/Getty Images*
Figure 12.2 – *Photograph © Image and HOTEL INDIGO® appear courtesy of InterContinental Hotels Group*
Figure 12.3 – *Photograph © Stephen Roberts/Alamy*
Figure 12.4 – *Photograph courtesy of Apple*
Figure 12.5 – *Photograph courtesy of Apple*
Figure 12.6 – *Photograph © Photofina (New York)/Alamy*
Figure 12.7 – *Photograph © Devinder Sangha/Alamy*
Figure 12.8 – *Photograph © James Cheadle/Alamy*

Chapter 13

Figure 13.1 – *Photograph © Andre Jenny/Alamy*
Figure 13.2 – *Photograph © Andrew Holt/Alamy*
Figure 13.3 – *Photograph courtesy of Marriott International, Inc.*
Figure 13.4 – *Photograph © dirimage/Alamy*

Chapter 14

Figure 14.1 – *Photograph © China Photos/Getty Images*
Figure 14.2 – *Photograph © Transtock Inc./Alamy*
Figure 14.3 – *Photograph © bobo/Alamy*
Figure 14.4 – *Photograph © Richard Levine/Alamy*
Figure 14.5 – *Photograph © Robert W. Ginn/Alamy*

Chapter 15

Figure 15.1 – *Photograph © Blend Images/Alamy*
Figure 15.2 – *Photograph © Dave & Les Jacobs/Getty Images*

Figure 15.3 – *Photograph © Skip Nall/Getty Images*
Figure 15.4 – *Photograph © Royalty-Free/Corbis*
Figure 15.5 – *Photograph © Shawn McClure*
Figure 15.6 – *Photograph © Kevin Foy/Alamy*
Figure 15.7 – *Photograph © Visions of America, LLC/Alamy*
Figure 15.8 – *Photograph © Dynamic Graphics Group/IT Stock Free/Alamy*
Figure 15.9 – *Photograph © Noel Hendrickson/Getty Images*
Figure 15.10 – *Figure adapted from Picot-Coupey, K. (2006). Determinants of international retail operation mode choice: Towards a conceptual framework based on evidence from French specialized retail chains.* International Review of Retail, Distribution, and Consumer Research, *16(2), p. 215–237.*
Figure 15.11 – *Photograph by Thao-Vi Thi Dotter*
Figure 15.12 – *Photograph by Amber Geisler*
Figure 15.13 – *Photograph by Thao-Vi Thi Dotter*
Figure 15.14 – *Photograph by Amber Geisler*
Figure 15.15 – *Photograph © Ian Dagnall/Alamy*
Figure 15.16 – *Photograph by Thao-Vi Thi Dotter*
Figure 15.17 – *Photograph by Amber Geisler*
Figure 15.19 – *Photograph © Stockbyte/Getty Images*
Figure 15.20 – *Photograph by Amber Geisler*
Figure 15.21 – *Photograph by Thao-Vi Thi Dotter*
Figure 15.22 – *Photograph © Photosindia/Getty Images*
Figure 15.23 – *Photograph by Amber Geisler*
Figure 15.24 – *Photograph by Amber Geisler*
Figure 15.25 – *Photograph © Subin Shroff/Getty Images*
Figure 15.26 – *Photograph by Christy Crutsinger*

INDEX